>EMOTION AND MOTIVATION

FOURTH EDITION

AUTHORS

Michelle N. Shiota
ARIZONA STATE UNIVERSITY

Sarah Rose Cavanagh
SIMMONS UNIVERSITY

OXFORD
UNIVERSITY PRESS

OXFORD
UNIVERSITY PRESS

Oxford University Press is a department of the University of Oxford.
It furthers the University's objective of excellence in research, scholarship,
and education by publishing worldwide. Oxford is a registered trade mark
of Oxford University Press in the UK and in certain other countries.

Published in the United States of America by Oxford University Press
198 Madison Avenue, New York, NY 10016, United States of America.

For titles covered by Section 112 of the US Higher Education Opportunity
Act, please visit www.oup.com/us/he for the latest information about
pricing and alternate formats.

Library of Congress Cataloging-in-Publication Data

Names: Shiota, Michelle N., author. | Cavanagh, Sarah Rose, author. |
   Kalat, James W. Emotion.
Title: Emotion and motivation / Michelle N. Shiota, Sarah Rose Cavanagh.
Description: Fourth edition. | New York, NY : Oxford University Press,
   [2023] | Previously pulished as Emotion by Jim Kalat and Michelle "Lani"
   Shiota. | Includes bibliographical references and index. | Summary:
   "Comprehensive and integrated survey of the field of affective science.
   The text covers the major theories of emotion in detail and reviews both
   classic and cutting-edge research on emotional processes from various
   subdisciplines. The authors' thoughtful engagement with ongoing
   controversies, contradictory findings, methodological limitations, and
   replication failures encourages critical thinking. While highly
   rigorous, the text is also student-friendly, with a light, humorous
   tone, real-world stories, and an intuitive structure. Emotion, Third
   Edition, addresses the questions undergraduates are most likely to ask:
   Why do we have emotions? How do they affect our lives? and How can we
   improve emotional well-being?"—Provided by publisher.
Identifiers: LCCN 2022045724 (print) | LCCN 2022045725 (ebook) | ISBN
   9780197586877 (paperback) | ISBN 9780197604335 (epub) | ISBN
   9780197664674 (ebook) | ISBN 9780197664681
Subjects: LCSH: Emotions.
Classification: LCC BF531 .K35 2023 (print) | LCC BF531 (ebook) | DDC
   152.4—dc23/eng/20220930
LC record available at https://lccn.loc.gov/2022045724
LC ebook record available at https://lccn.loc.gov/2022045725

Printed by Integrated Books International, United States of America

BRIEF TABLE OF CONTENTS

TABLE OF CONTENTS

PREFACE

Can you imagine life without emotion? Give it a try. What would happen to your experience of the world if you had no capacity for emotion? How might your beliefs, judgments, and decisions change? What about your actions? What would your relationships with other people be like if emotions were not involved? Consider your experience of music, literature, film, dance, art, architecture, and the natural world without emotion. It's difficult to imagine, right? Emotion is fundamental to being human, woven into every aspect of our lives.

Imagining life without motivation is more baffling still. One might even argue that life without motivation is impossible—at least within the animal kingdom. Perhaps a houseplant does not have motivation (or does it? SRC regularly rotates the plants in her windows because they gradually, but surely, grow toward the sun). Even bacteria and worms move toward nutrition. Insects move away from danger. Move up the animal kingdom in complexity, and the motivated behaviors by which creatures strive toward good outcomes and avoid bad ones become increasingly sophisticated. Of course, human motivation is even more complicated. Worms and flies do not care whether other worms/flies love or respect them, nor do they invest many years in education in pursuit of a bigger salary and a more fulfilling career. Humans do.

Among students of psychology, many of the most pressing questions about human experience involve emotion and/or motivation in some way. For those interested in clinical psychology, difficulties with emotion (too much, too little, inappropriate for the situation) are among the most common and disabling symptoms of mental health struggles. Among educational and industrial/organizational psychologists, motivation is a topic of enormous relevance. Emotions and motivation also play important roles in information processing, social interaction, and human development. Motivation and emotion are key mechanisms of methods for improving physical, mental, social, ecological, and economic health and well-being across society. Anyone trying to understand why people do what they do is, by definition, interested in motivation and emotion.

Given the ubiquity of emotion and motivation in human experience, you may find some features of the research on these topics surprising. First, the field of affective science—the scientific study of emotion—is still very young compared to other branches of psychology. During the mid-twentieth century, when behaviorism dominated experimental psychology, research on emotions was sparse. When laboratory research did occur, it was mostly limited to the *conditioned emotional response*, which researchers used to study how classical conditioning worked rather than focusing on emotion itself. The same goes for motivation; researchers studied the effects of reward and punishment on behavior, but staunchly refused to speculate about what went on in the "black box" of the mind. Behaviorists considered emotion and motivation private, subjective, unobservable, and therefore unfit for serious empirical study. Rigorous scientific research on emotion, in particular, did not really begin until the 1970s and 1980s.

A further oddity of the research on motivation and emotion is that for decades, there was little overlap in these fields. As affective science began to emerge during the late twentieth century, most emotion researchers were trained in social or developmental psychology. In the 1990s, as functional neuroimaging methods became increasingly available for basic behavioral science, researchers with interests in emotion began to take advantage of that new technology as well. In contrast, motivation researchers tended to be in the fields of industrial/organizational and educational psychology. As a result, despite a growing number of college courses and even an academic journal called *Motivation and Emotion*, research in these fields did not cross-pollinate very often. If you think about it, though, motivation and emotion have a lot in common, and are not easy to disentangle—points we emphasize repeatedly throughout this text.

In the 20 years since Jim Kalat and Michelle "Lani" Shiota began writing the first edition of this textbook, research on emotion and motivation has increased dramatically—in quantity, quality, and connection. Affective science is a far more prominent branch of psychology than it was in the early years of the twenty-first century. Several peer-reviewed journals are devoted to emotion theory and research; a growing number of psychology departments have graduate programs in affective science; and emotion is the focus of multiple research societies and conferences. Both Lani and Sarah use this textbook in their own undergraduate courses on emotion (and in Sarah's case, motivation)—now two of many throughout the world. A 2021 editorial in one of the premier journals in science (*Nature Human Behavior*) declared a rise of "affectivism," proposing that emotion may be *the* predominant theme in our contemporary understanding of human experience (Dukes et al., 2021).

Moreover, the interrelations of emotion and motivation are appreciated to a much greater extent than was true 20 years ago. Once shoved into a single course in part because neither seemed sufficient to fill a semester's syllabus alone, emotion and motivation are increasingly recognized as fundamentally intertwined. While this textbook is still heavy on emotion, reflecting its origin as a pure emotion text, we have sought to acknowledge these deep connections in the current edition. We are delighted to present the fourth edition of this text, which has evolved along with the field itself. We hope you enjoy reading it as much as we have enjoyed writing it.

THE GOALS OF THIS TEXT

Our goal in preparing this textbook is to provide a comprehensive survey of theory and research on emotion, infused with modern motivation science, across the traditional subdisciplines of clinical, biological, social, personality, developmental, and cognitive psychology. Although the emphasis is largely on theory and research within psychology, we also address relevant content in philosophy, anthropology, and sociology, among other disciplines. We aimed this text at undergraduate students who have had an introductory psychology course and who remember the essentials about research design, classical conditioning, what a neuron is, and so forth. However, we assume no additional background, and we believe the text should be suitable for a course that enrolls undergraduate sophomores, juniors, seniors, and even students in terminal master's programs.

Although we discuss major theories of emotion and motivation extensively in the first few chapters, and return to these theories throughout the text, we also strongly emphasize the value of a rigorous scientific approach. Without downplaying extremely important contributions of the arts and humanities to our understanding of what motivates human action, what emotions are, why we have them, and how they shape our behavior, we have sought to highlight the distinct role of empirical research in addressing these questions. The behaviorists of the mid-twentieth century were not entirely wrong—emotion and motivation are fundamentally internal and difficult to measure—and you will find us making that point repeatedly throughout this text. Despite these challenges, however, researchers have devised new and clever ways to elicit and measure emotion and motivation, both in the laboratory and in the real world.

We also strongly encourage students to think critically about the theories and research they encounter in this textbook. Many important questions remain partly answered, at best. No scientific study is perfect, and we hope readers will consider the limitations as well as the strengths of each study we discuss. You will find studies that seem to contradict each other, previously accepted findings that are suddenly called into question, and basic principles that are still hotly debated. Across psychology, the "replicability crisis" has challenged the validity of many canonical findings; affective science and, to a lesser extent, motivation science have been impacted by this crisis as well. Rather than presenting the science of emotion and motivation as a complete and tidy field, we've chosen to address its gaps and complexities honestly, trusting that you will carefully evaluate the evidence and develop your own conclusions.

Finally, Kalat and Shiota made a conscious decision when writing the first edition to keep the tone informal, accessible, and fun, and we've maintained that style through to the current edition. We play with language and ideas, we use a lot of humor, and we invite you into our lives with personal examples. We encourage you to apply the concepts and principles you learn here to your own lives. The study of emotion and motivation has the potential to enrich students' lives in many ways. In reading this textbook we hope that you find not only academic knowledge, but also techniques and wisdom for enhancing your own and others' well-being.

PEDAGOGICAL FEATURES

This textbook includes several pedagogical features designed to facilitate active engagement with the material, critical thinking, and application to students' own lives. These include the following:

- Presentation of major theoretical issues in initial chapters, which are then revisited regularly throughout the text as they are addressed by empirical research findings.
- Frequent detailed discussion of study methods, as well as results and conclusions, emphasizing the scientific study of emotion and motivation, and inviting readers to critique the relationship between method and interpretation.
- Each major headed section begins with clearly stated learning objectives, targeting varying levels of Bloom's taxonomy.
- Readers are often invited to engage in active learning—applying course material to their own lives, developing their own hypotheses, recalling relevant content from prior chapters, and thinking through questions for themselves before the text offers an answer.
- Extensive use of relatable, real-life examples, illustrating abstract concepts and processes in an engaging way.
- Each chapter includes a link to a brief video conversation with the authors, introducing the topic and highlighting major questions.
- Each chapter includes a series of thought/discussion questions, intended to facilitate critical thinking about and application of the material. These may be used as individual study aids, as group discussion topics, or even as essay questions for assessment.
- Each chapter also offers several suggestions for further reading. These include key empirical articles, academic literature reviews written to be accessible to an undergraduate audience, and popular-press books by prominent emotion researchers, all encouraging further exploration of major issues.

New Material in the Fourth Edition

Readers familiar with prior editions of this text will note one major change from the third edition. Previously titled just *Emotion*, the text is now *Emotion and Motivation*, and its content reflects the new title. In agreeing to join the team for this new edition, Sarah Rose Cavanagh—who has long used this book in her own classes—proposed adding core content on motivation. Shiota agreed, recognizing the blurriness of the emotion-motivation distinction in research on elicitors of emotional and motivational states, nonverbal expression, functional neuroscience, cognitive processing, clinical psychology, and more. To those teaching or taking a course exclusively on emotion, as does Shiota, never fear! This new edition still contains all major topic areas from the last, and it is still mostly an emotion text. To those teaching and taking courses that include motivation as well, the textbook now includes major sections on motivation theory in Chapter 1, a dedicated chapter on goal setting and pursuit, and motivation science content throughout. For all adopters, we hope this new approach will meet your needs and spark new ways of thinking about both topics.

Beyond this major update, several hundred new cites of cutting-edge research have been added across all original topics, and we have updated the real-life examples, historical touch-points, and pop culture references as well (although *Star Trek*'s Spock is still on point!). We have sought to expand inclusiveness, in the language throughout the text, in our treatment of gender and sexuality, and of research beyond the mainstream cultures of North America and Europe. Where the latter is lacking—sadly still too common in these fields—we repeatedly acknowledge this problem and call for research on more diverse populations.

At a finer-grained level, the fourth edition also features the following:

• New material on physiological drives and needs, as well as fundamental psychological motivations, in Chapter 2;
• New sections on ideal affect and socioecological determinants of culture in Chapter 3;
• Discussion of the complex interrelation of elicitors of drives, instincts, and emotions in Chapter 4;
• Restructuring of Chapter 6 ("Emotion, Motivation, and the Central Nervous System") to emphasize neural circuits rather than brain structures, and richly represent motivational neuroscience;
• Expanded sections on emotional development across adolescence and adulthood in Chapter 8;
• A new section on interactions of motivation and cognition in Chapter 10;
• Substantial revision of content in Chapter 11 ("The Value of Negative Emotions") reflecting new developments in basic theory and research as well as cutting-edge work applying this knowledge to real-world problems;
• New topics in Chapter 12 ("Happiness and the Positive Emotions"), including research on positivity resonance, psychosocial effects of awe, and possible roles for positive emotion in behavior change;
• Reframing throughout Chapter 13 ("Emotion in Clinical Psychology") to reflect evolving terminology and an appreciation of human individual differences;
• A brand-new chapter on goal setting and striving in Chapter 14; and
• Expanded material on emotion regulation and health and emotion regulation flexibility in Chapter 15.

ACKNOWLEDGMENTS

Before going any further, we must convey our tremendous respect for and appreciation of James Kalat, whom our "regulars" will recognize as the initial lead author of this text. In the fall of 2001, this highly accomplished textbook author contemplated how interesting and challenging it might be to write a text on emotion . . . but only with a coauthor with deep expertise in that field. He connected with a recent, anonymous reviewer of his introductory psychology text—a strong writer who mentioned being a specialist in emotion. That reviewer was Lani Shiota, then a graduate student at the University of California, Berkeley. A rich collaboration soon developed, and the first edition of *Emotion* was the result. Over the years, Jim has been extremely generous with his mentorship, support, and training in the fine art of communicating science to undergraduates in a vivid and accessible way. He's incredibly knowledgeable, and one of the nicest guys you will ever meet. In preparing the third edition of *Emotion* Jim let Lani know it would be his last. Yet his writing, ideas, humor, and emphasis on critical thinking are still richly infused throughout the fourth edition. We cannot express our gratitude strongly enough!

Our heartiest thanks go to Oxford University Press, particularly our editors, Joan Kalkut, Jessica Fiorillo, and Elizabeth (Lizzy) Bell, and editorial assistants Mal Labriola and Megan Mentuck. We're extremely grateful for your expertise, encouragement, support, and especially your patience throughout the preparation of this new edition, which took place entirely during the stress and upheaval of the coronavirus pandemic. In addition, we are most grateful for the insightful comments and helpful suggestions offered by Yulia Chentsova-Dutton and Eric Nook, as well as reviewers who examined drafts of chapters in this textbook.

We also extend many thanks to students, mentors, family, and friends who have supported us throughout our efforts on this text. Lani Shiota sends affection and gratitude to current and former graduate students who have worked with her in the trenches of affective science for the past fifteen years. Each has helped build her knowledge and shape her interests, and made the work fun! She extends deep thanks to her graduate advisor, Dacher Keltner—a rock star in psychology who first introduced her to the rich and complex world of affective science. To Lani's husband, Bob Levenson, words can never fully capture how much you are valued. Thank you for all the knowledge and rigorous training you shared; for engaging richly over many years in conversations about ideas that have made their way into this textbook; and for all of your patience and support through the last, overwhelming couple of years. She also sends gratitude and love to those who have shaped her own rich emotional life, and help keep her whole: mother Mary Gorman and late father Norman Shiota; siblings Michie, Janine, Bob, Mimsie, Lynsie, and Greg; Paula, sweet Mila, Derende, and Kirstin; and back-in-the-day mentors Davida Wills and Paul Archer. Last, but definitely not least, Lani is deeply thankful for new coconspirator Sarah, who is completely charming to work with as well as bringing much knowledge, skill, and a fresh perspective to this new edition.

Sarah Rose Cavanagh is grateful first to Lani, who took a huge risk on inviting her to the project (MNS: It really wasn't!), and who put up with so many textbook-writing "newbie" questions and mistakes with grace and patience (MNS: Awww!). She also owes deep thanks to her predoctoral and postdoctoral mentors Lisa Shin and Heather Urry, who opened doors, provided guidance, and ushered in a world of possibility. Sarah's early years in affective science were more fun than seems fair, and she owes this fact to Heather Urry along with her Emotion, Brain, and Behavior Laboratory partners-in-crime Jennifer DiCorcia, Philipp Optiz, and Jeff Birk. Sarah has always been more of a teacher than a researcher, and to her many students who shaped and enlivened her thinking over the years—thank you. And to her dear spouse, child, parents, and (as you will learn in Chapter 1) smelly brothers—thank you for all the motivation.

Finally, we both extend our gratitude to the professors who have selected this textbook for their own courses on emotion. We welcome comments from our readers, students and faculty alike. We'll update this text again in a few years, and your suggestions are greatly valued. Our email addresses are lani.shiota@asu.edu and sarah.rose.cavanagh@gmail.com. We hope you enjoy the book!

—M. N. Shiota and S. R. Cavanagh

PART I

What Are Emotions and Motivations, and Why Do We Have Them?

CHAPTER 1

The Nature of Emotion and Motivation

Many textbooks begin with an explanation of why you should care about the subject. Do you need to be convinced that emotions and motivation are important? Probably not. We seek out information on emotion and motivation all the time. We routinely ask one another, "How are you feeling?" We care about other people's emotions, and we want them to understand our own (Figure 1.1). We ask what moves people to behave the way they do, why they make the choices they make. We spend endless hours puzzling over the motivations of our romantic partners, our bosses, and our family. We seek opportunities to experience emotions through stories told in film, literature, music, and art, as well as in our own lives. We commonly explain our own and other people's behavior in terms of emotion and motivation, and emotions guide our decisions in a variety of ways. Emotions are woven into our understanding of the world around us, and how it works. As Antonio Damasio (1999, p. 55) has written, "Inevitably, emotions are inseparable from the idea of good and evil."

From a scientific standpoint, emotion and motivation are central to the field of psychology. Clinical psychologists often want to help people control their harmful or dysfunctional emotions, and try to motivate people to behave in healthier ways. Cognitive psychologists consider how emotions influence people's thought processes and decisions, finding that even seemingly objective phenomena such as perception and reasoning are biased by our motivations. Social psychologists study our needs for belongingness, relatedness, and affiliation, and consider how emotions impact our relationships with other people. Personality psychologists study systematic differences between people in terms of their emotions, and what types of motivations drive their behavior.

Although the importance of emotion and motivation is intuitively obvious, these are difficult subjects for scientific research. We hope you are starting this book with healthy skepticism about whether the scientific study of emotion is even possible. For decades, experimental psychologists virtually ignored emotion because it is so subjective, and even today, some researchers have misgivings about scientific research into private, internal

FIGURE 1.1.   Emotions are intuitively interesting, and play a compelling role in many aspects of our lives.

experiences. Scientific progress depends on good measurement, and as we shall emphasize repeatedly throughout this book, it is challenging to accurately measure emotions. Studying motivation scientifically also presents complications. It is much easier to study variations in objective behavior than it is to study the underlying forces and mechanisms driving that behavior, which we cannot observe directly, and of which many people may not even be aware.

We begin this chapter with attempts to define motivation and emotion. We consider the history of ideas on each topic, first describing some classic approaches. We will also take a deep dive into three modern theories of emotion, each offering an account of how major *aspects of emotion*, such as subjective emotional feelings, physiological responses, and observable behaviors, relate to each other. We then ask, what is the relationship between motivation and emotion, and how will we approach this issue moving forward through the text? Finally, we begin our discussion of methods used to study motivation and emotion scientifically—though of course, we'll continue to introduce and discuss new techniques throughout the book.

WHAT IS MOTIVATION?

Learning Objectives
- Define motivation, highlighting the two key aspects of its influence on behavior.
- Differentiate intrinsic and extrinsic motivation and summarize the process by which behaviors can change from extrinsically to intrinsically motivated.
- List the three psychological needs emphasized in self-determination theory.
- Differentiate promotion goals from prevention goals, recognizing examples of each and giving examples from your own life.

Let's start with motivation. In common speech we use the word "motivation" in several different yet related ways. You might observe your friend making what seems to you a terrible decision, and ask yourself, "What could possibly be their motivation?" You might wish to be more physically fit by next summer, and wonder how you can motivate yourself on a regular basis to get up early to work out or go to the gym after a long day. You might have to figure out how to motivate your partners in a group project to do their share of the work—and do it well. You might imagine the great vacation you will take after graduation as motivation for working hard in classes now (and saving money for the trip!). Your school might invite a motivational speaker to campus, who will speak vigorously and excitedly about your future and how you can go about pursuing your dreams.

These uses of the word "motivation" all have a few things in common. The examples above each involve summoning some sort of *energy* to fuel behavior, and pointing that energy in a particular *direction* (Bargh, Gollwitzer, & Oettingen, 2010)—toward some kind of goal. The energy manifests in activation (getting mobilized), intensity (how hard you work), and persistence (how long you keep at it) of whatever behavior(s) will help you achieve the goal (Locke & Latham, 2013). The direction captures the purpose and aim of expending that energy. In sum, we can define **motivation** in terms of energy that is directed toward achieving some goal. This includes why someone might pursue one goal rather than another, but also why they pursue their goal with greater or lesser intensity and persistence (if at all).

To begin working with these concepts, let's use you as a test case. Take out a spare sheet of paper or fire up a spreadsheet. Using Table 1.1 as a model, consider a typical day in your current life and note all the behaviors and actions that take up your time. We have populated a few rows with examples (which your authors find relatable) to give you some inspiration. Once you have the list, consider how much effort and time you invest in that behavior—how much energy goes into that behavior? Then identify the goal of each behavior—the direction in which the energy is expended. *Why* are you spending time and energy (even a little) on that behavior, when you could be doing something else?

Now glance through your own table. Do you see any patterns emerging, ways that you could cluster some of your behaviors and the reasons why you spend time and energy on them? In the next two sections we will consider two categories of motivations that have proved especially important in research.

Intrinsic and Extrinsic Motivation

If you are like most people, some of your motives spring naturally from internal forces, whereas other motives reflect external pressures. These motivational gears have been dubbed **intrinsic** and **extrinsic motivation**, respectively. Hopefully you engage in many of the activities on your list because you enjoy them, because they feel good, and/or because they are inherently fulfilling or meaningful. This is intrinsic motivation. Your morning run, reading your favorite author, hanging out with friends, and spending time on a hobby

TABLE 1.1 **Daily behaviors and engagement**

What are your daily behaviors, how much energy goes into them, and why do you engage in them? Using this table as a model, create your own list.

Behavior	Energy	Direction/Goal
Brush teeth	Low	Avoid future cavities
Grade papers	Medium	Prevent being fired
Go for a walk at lunch	Medium	Physical, mental health
Work on textbook chapter	High	Impact on field
Cook dinner	High	Enjoy cooking, eating
Snuggle with the dog	Low	Comfort, affection
Read novel before bed	Medium	Enjoyment, relaxation

might all fall under this category. (Well, SRC's motivation to run is intrinsic; MNS's definitely is not). These activities are thought to be inherently rewarding because they fulfill basic human psychological needs for **autonomy** (choosing your own path and behaviors), **competence** (succeeding at existing tasks and mastering new skills), and **relatedness** (connecting with social others). The overall idea that human beings are intrinsically motivated by autonomy, competence, and relatedness is called **self-determination theory** (Ryan & Deci, 2000; Ryan & Deci, 2020); we'll discuss this theory further in Chapter 2, when we consider innate psychological needs.

You likely also listed other behaviors, such as brushing your teeth or shifts at your job stocking shelves at the grocery store, that are not inherently enjoyable or meaningful. We do not engage in these behaviors because they seem like fun, or because they fulfill some burning psychological need. Rather, we do them because they have a downstream effect that we want, such as avoiding cavities or continuing to get paid. These are extrinsic motivations.

Go back through your list and see if this intrinsic/extrinsic motivation dichotomy works well for your daily behaviors. See Table 1.2 for our examples, now with a new column added.

You may have noted that some of your behaviors do not fit neatly into the intrinsic versus extrinsic distinction. Perhaps you listed "do homework," and you do homework partly because you want a good grade and course credit and a degree, but also because you are interested in the content of your courses and enjoy seeing your skills improve from semester to semester. We are writing this textbook in part to make a little extra money (not a lot, let's be honest), but also because we care about the students reading this book—how its content might shape the lives they lead—and about the future of affective science as a field. Also, writing the book is moderately amusing.

Rather than thinking of intrinsic versus extrinsic motivation as a dichotomy, researchers Richard Ryan and Edward Deci suggest that they are really a continuum (Ryan & Deci, 2020; see Figure 1.2, which we've adapted from Ryan and Deci's article). You might engage in certain behaviors because you know the social norms of your ingroup and you want to avoid shame and guilt based on your internalization of these rules (called **introjected regulation**), or because when first learning this behavior you were rewarded for it but now you consciously value it (called **identified regulation**), or because it now feels like a natural part of your identity (called **integrated regulation**).

TABLE 1.2   Daily behaviors and motivation

Now list whether these "why" explanations fit better with a model of intrinsic or extrinsic motivation.

Behavior	Energy	Direction/Goal	Intrinsic/Extrinsic
Brush teeth	Low	Avoid future cavities	Extrinsic
Grade papers	Medium	Prevent being fired	Extrinsic
Go for a walk at lunch	Medium	Physical, mental health	Intrinsic
Work on textbook chapter	High	Impact students, field	Both
Cook dinner	High	Enjoy cooking, eating	Intrinsic
Snuggle with the dog	Low	Comfort, affection	Intrinsic
Read novel before bed	Medium	Enjoyment, relaxation	Intrinsic

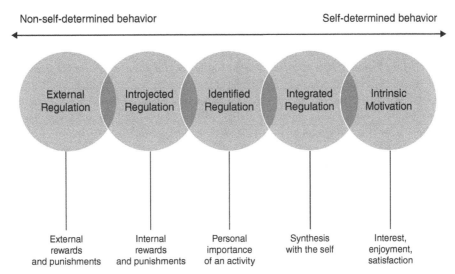

Non-self-determined behavior   Self-determined behavior

External Regulation	Introjected Regulation	Identified Regulation	Integrated Regulation	Intrinsic Motivation
External rewards and punishments	Internal rewards and punishments	Personal importance of an activity	Synthesis with the self	Interest, enjoyment, satisfaction

FIGURE 1.2. Extrinsic and intrinsic motivation is not a dichotomy but a continuum, and often behaviors start as controlled and move to autonomous. Adapted from Ryan & Deci (2020).

For instance, you might start exercising as a child or adolescent because your parents forced you off your phone and onto the soccer field with ice cream bribes and lectures (extrinsic). But as you grew up and became more independent, you continued exercising at first because you felt guilty when you didn't (introjected), and then because you began consciously valuing physical activity and considering it an important part of your goal of being physically healthy (identified), and then because you became someone whose self-concept involved physical fitness and health (integrated).

Which kind of motivation do you think leads to greater initiation, intensity, and persistence of behavior—intrinsic or extrinsic? Take the perspective of someone who has the job of motivating other human beings—an employer, a teacher, or a tennis coach. To coax harder work and better performance from your team or class, should you offer **incentives** and threats of punishment, or should you try to design activities that tap into people's innate desires for autonomy, competence, and relatedness? Take your time . . .

If your answer was "well, it depends," then you're on the right track (and also thinking like a psychologist). Some research has asked an interesting question—does extrinsic motivation alter intrinsic motivation? Presumably a team of college extramural tennis players is intrinsically motivated to pursue the sport—they love the challenge of keeping the ball in play, the thrill of competition, and the pride of winning a game. What if you start offering them prizes for who performs best during practice? Quite a lot of research indicates that this would be a terrible mistake (e.g., Deci, 1971; Deci, Koestner & Ryan, 1999; Wiechman & Gurland, 2009). Extrinsically rewarding behaviors people already enjoyed appears to *decrease* the original intrinsic motivation, almost as if the mind says, "well, I mustn't have liked that very much, if I did it to earn a reward."

What if the person you're trying to motivate has no intrinsic motivation at all? In that case, by all means use external rewards, but use them strategically. One principle is that unexpected rewards are more likely to promote increased future target behavior than expected rewards—those the person intentionally worked for. For example, if you toss an empty soda can in the recycling bin one day, and it suddenly lights up and spits out a coupon for a discount at the student store, your brain's reward circuitry lights up and says "hey, maybe I should do that more often!" Ideally, rewards come often at first and then decrease over time, still a bit unpredictably; this reinforcement schedule helps to build new habits (Miller, Shenhav, & Ludvig, 2019). Also, social rewards do not seem to undermine intrinsic motivation as much as material or financial rewards (Spinrad & Gal, 2018). In one clever study, researchers gave teenagers the opportunity to donate tokens to a public good, rather than keeping them for themselves, in an online game with several trials. Participants who got thumbs-up signs from supposed peers after making donations (these were actually manipulated by the experimenters) made increasing donations over the course of the study, whereas no such effect was seen for those who got thumbs-down signs, or no feedback at all (Van Hoorn et al., 2016). These effects show that rather than being stuck at one point on the extrinsic-intrinsic continuum, behaviors can shift along that continuum based on experience.

Approach and Avoidance Motivation

In addition to the extrinsic to intrinsic continuum, another core principle in motivation science is that human beings (along with many of the other creatures with whom we share this planet) are generally motivated to *approach* pleasure and reward and to *avoid* punishment and pain. Try your hand at your table again, this time adding a column that considers whether these motivated behaviors of yours involve more approach or avoidance motivation (Table 1.3).

One influential theory of approach and avoidance motivation is called **regulatory focus theory** and was proposed by E. Tory Higgins. He argues that in addition to understanding how human beings approach and avoid certain situations and outcomes, we would do well to also consider whether these motivations are focused on achieving gains or avoiding losses. For instance, some of our motivated behaviors work to *promote* a desired end state (something we want to happen) while others work to *prevent* an undesired end state (something we don't want to happen; Higgins, 1998). Your motivation to find a romantic partner to snuggle with before the winter is a promotion focus; your motivation to pay your bills on time to duck a bad credit score is a prevention focus.

TABLE 1.3   Daily behaviors: approach and avoidance

Add a column to your table indicating whether each goal is more approach or avoidance focused.

Behavior	Energy	Direction/Goal	Intrinsic/Extrinsic	Approach/Avoidance
Brush teeth	Low	Avoid future cavities	Extrinsic	Avoidance
Grade papers	Medium	Prevent being fired	Extrinsic	Avoidance
Go for a walk at lunch	Medium	Physical, mental health	Intrinsic	Approach
Work on textbook chapter	High	Impact students, field	Both	Approach
Cook dinner	High	Enjoy cooking, eating	Intrinsic	Approach
Snuggle with the dog	Low	Comfort, affection	Intrinsic	Approach
Read novel before bed	Medium	Enjoyment, relaxation	Intrinsic	Approach

These variations in goal orientation matter because promotion versus prevention goals influence numerous aspects of motivated behavior, such as how much effort you will put into pursuing your goal, whether you will involve others in the process, and which emotions you feel along the way. Let's consider an example relevant to your own concerns: that of grades. Consider one scenario in which a student is focused on the promotion goal of getting a good grade, and another in which a student is focused the prevention goal of avoiding a failing grade. Which student would you expect to work harder, persist more when stress arises, and think creatively about how to accomplish their goal? Much research confirms that the student pursuing the A would work harder and better than the student avoiding the F, leading some to characterize promotion-focused approach motivation as "thriving" and prevention-focused avoidance motivation as "surviving" (Elliot & Gable, 2019). That said, other researchers have pointed out that promotion and prevention goals may not be mutually exclusive (you might really want that A *and* want to avoid an F on your transcript), with each conferring benefits of different kinds and/or in different contexts, such that flexibility during goal pursuit might be most adaptive (Cornwell, Sholer, & Higgins, 2019).

This emphasis on approach and avoidance provides our first bridge between motivation and emotion. One of the principal ways we are motivated to approach or avoid situations is through the experience of emotions. We generally feel positive about situations we want to approach, and may approach them in order to experience pleasant feelings; we generally feel negative about situations we want to avoid, and may withdraw from them in order to avoid unpleasant feelings. Generally speaking, we approach situations associated with joy, contentment, and interest; we avoid situations associated with fear, disgust, and frustration.

In this vein, there is evidence from the study of simple motor tasks that the act of approach is instinctively linked to the evaluation of stimuli as positive, and the act of avoidance is correspondingly linked to the evaluation of stimuli as negative. For example, a team of researchers used a computer-based task to determine whether participants found it more or less natural to associate movement in different directions with positive and negative concepts (Krieglmeyer et al., 2010). In each trial of this task, participants viewed a word on a screen with a little manikin (a small person-shaped icon) above or below it. In half of the trials, participants were instructed to press a key that would move the manikin up if it was a positive-valence word and a key that would move the manikin down if it was a negative-valence word; in the remaining trials, the keys moved the manikins in the opposite directions (down for positive, up for negative). Because the manikin sometimes first appeared above the word and sometimes below, the up and down directions might move the manikin toward or away from the target word (Figure 1.3). The important finding was that participants responded more quickly when the correct key moved the manikin toward positive words and away from negative ones, regardless of whether the direction was up or down. This suggests that the impulse to approach positive things (and avoid negative things) is automatic, difficult to override, and stronger than associations of positive valence with movement up (e.g., "feeling on top of the world," "rising to the occasion," etc.).

The idea that approach and avoidance are more consequential for behavior than pleasantness/unpleasantness is further supported by work by Eddie Harmon-Jones, who has conducted

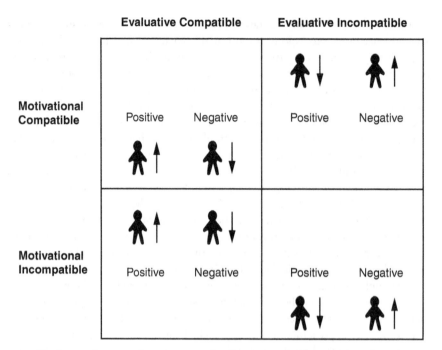

FIGURE 1.3. The four trial types in Krieglmeyer and colleagues' study of approach and avoidance motivation (Krieglmeyer, Deutsch, De Houwer, & De Raedt, 2010). In half of the trials participants were instructed to move the manikin up in response to positive words and down in response to negative words; in the other trials, these directions were reversed. Because the manikin sometimes first appeared above the word and sometimes below, the up and down directions might move the manikin toward or away from the target word. Participants responded more quickly when the correct key moved the manikin toward positive words and away from negative ones, regardless of whether the direction was up or down.

an extensive body of research linking anger to approach motivation, despite its subjectively negative valence (e.g., Carver & Harmon-Jones, 2009; Harmon-Jones & Harmon-Jones, 2016). For example, when people are angry, they show greater activation in the left frontal cortex of the brain than in the right—a pattern seen in many positive emotions but not in most negative emotions (Harmon-Jones & Allen, 1998). Studies using questionnaires to ask people about how often they feel anger, and tend to use physical aggression, find that scores on these measures are more linked with behavioral approach than avoidance (Harmon-Jones, 2003). Studies also suggest that low-approach-motivation positive emotions, such as contentment after receiving a reward, have different kinds of cognitive effects than high-approach positive emotions (Gable & Harmon-Jones, 2010).

This consideration of approach and avoidance has provided our first bridge between motivation and emotion. We will discuss the intersection of motivation and emotion further in a few pages. Now that we have a solid handle on the definition of motivation and some of the core concepts in its study, let's turn to a brief consideration of how motivation researchers have approached the topic through the ages.

Motivation Theory: A Historical Overview

The first appearances of motivation in the written record include the Roman scholar Marcus Tullius Cicero in 45 B.C. talking about *motus animi,* or the stirring of the soul; and Arthur Schopenhauer (1813) discussing motivation as a way of understanding the causes of human behavior in his doctoral dissertation. Though well in the past and millennia apart, these treatments each capture the essence of contemporary motivation science—a consideration of the animating energy underlying changes in behavior.

Some of the earliest philosophers argued that **hedonism**—the approach of pleasure and avoidance of pain—is one of the driving forces underlying human behavior (Figure 1.4). Other philosophers, from Plato to Aquinas to Hobbes, have debated the tensions among emotion, motivation, and cognition (usually called "reason") through the ages. Their thinking diverged as to whether emotions are a destructive or constructive force in driving behavior; how human beings manage and control their bodily appetites and their passions; and the roles of emotion versus reason in determining moral behavior. We'll see these questions come to fruition when we consider goal setting and goal striving in Chapter 14—how can we best harness the energy and direction of motivation to bring ourselves closer to a healthier, happier ideal self?

So far we've discussed how early philosophers thought about motivation rather than how psychologists did, because back in those days psychology wasn't invented yet! As a discipline, psychology grew out of philosophy as a method of examining many of the same questions about human nature, but with a more empirical, scientifically grounded approach. One of the first treatments of motivation in the psychological literature investigated what was called **will**—the ability of an organism to freely make choices. At the dawn of the twentieth century, psychologists such as Wilhelm Wundt and William James wrote about the contribution of will to human behavior. We can see the modern versions

FIGURE 1.4.   While in common speech the word "hedonism" calls up ideas of debauchery, the philosophical definition simply means the motivation to approach pleasure and avoid pain.

of these ideas in considerations of willpower or self-control. We'll take a close look at modern research on self-control in Chapter 14.

The rise of evolutionary theory and the thinking of scholars including Charles Darwin greatly influenced the ongoing study of human motivation. Psychologists began discussing the roles of instincts, drives, and physiological needs in our understanding of what motivates human beings. We'll address this work in much greater length in Chapter 2, which covers evolutionary perspectives on both emotion and motivation.

In the mid-twentieth century, the behaviorist movement argued that psychology should only concern itself with behaviors that can be objectively recorded, a revolution in perspective that affected motivation science as well. Researchers stopped worrying about all that messy, mushy stuff that goes on inside people's minds, focusing instead on the effects of rewards and punishments on observable behavior. But then the rise of cognitive psychology in the 1960s flipped the attention of motivation researchers back toward interest in the inner workings of the human mind—specifically, what people expect, and what they value. Human beings were again presumed to play an active role in choosing their own behaviors, and research on goal setting and goal striving was born. In the last few decades social psychology and affective science have jumped into the mix, adding a thorough consideration of the social and emotional needs that fuel much of goal-directed behavior.

While the predominant and most influential theories of motivation varied over the years in the ways that we have depicted here—starting with a strong philosophical approach, then moving to biological, then to behaviorist, then to cognitive, then to social and affective—contemporary motivation researchers appreciate the importance of all these approaches in studying human motivation. Clearly some of our motivations are rooted in our biology (just try skipping a few meals and see how motivated you are to approach a donut!). We are definitely influenced by rewards and punishments, or else parents would never bother to offer treats or threaten time-outs to change their children's behavior. There is clearly a strong role for thinking and feeling in the energy and direction underlying our choices. Considering the contributions of all these approaches gives us the best vantage point to understanding the enormous complexity of human motivation.

Next we'll take the same approach to considering theories of human emotion, first considering history, and then a step-by-step review of competing modern theories. As in the section above, a wide-angle view recognizing the contributions of each of these theories will serve us best.

WHAT IS EMOTION?

Learning Objectives

- Summarize William James's theory of emotion, and explain how it differs from the common-sense view.
- Summarize the definition of "emotion" offered by Plutchik, emphasizing four main aspects of emotional responding.
- Define "core affect," identifying the aspect of emotion emphasized and the two dimensions in Russell's circumplex model.
- Explain the three differences between emotion and mood, as these terms are used by researchers.

In 1884, William James, the founder of American psychology, wrote an influential article titled "What Is an Emotion?" More than a century later, psychologists continue to ask that same question. According to Joseph LeDoux (1996, p. 23), "one of the most significant things ever said about emotion may be that everyone knows what it is until they are asked to define it." Even people studying emotion often disagree about how to define it, and some doubt it refers to any natural category at all. James Russell (2003) has suggested that the concept of emotion is just a convenient label for experiences that seem to share common ground but are really different, much as the categories *art* and *music* include many dissimilar items. Some languages do not have a word for emotion at all (Hupka, Lenton, & Hutchison, 1999), and in those that do, these words do not map to exactly the same meaning (Niedenthal et al., 2004). However, to study some phenomenon scientifically, we need at least a tentative definition to guide our theories and methods.

Imagine you have accepted a job in your nation's space program. They send you as a psychologist/astronaut to a newly discovered planet. Previous astronauts have learned much about the animals on this planet. Their evolutionary history is separate from ours and their body chemistry is entirely different, but their behavior resembles ours. They see, hear, and smell. They eat, drink, and reproduce. They can learn to approach one color and not another to get food, so evidently they have color vision, motivation, and learning. Now it's your job to determine whether they have emotions. What will you do? Try to answer before you read further.

We find that our students' most common answer is to put the animals in a situation that we consider *emotional* and then watch their behavior. For example, you might swing a weapon threateningly at the animals and see whether they scamper away. Or you might try to steal their food and see whether they attack you. Suppose they do. Could you then conclude that they have emotions?

You don't have to leave Earth to face this problem. If you wave your arm at a housefly, it flies away. Do you conclude that the housefly feels fear? We don't know what a housefly feels, if anything. If you damage a beehive, the bees come at you to sting you, and they sure seem mad. But are they angry? Again, you could reasonably answer either "no" or "I don't know."

Do you have a pet? What kind? Does it love you? How do you know? Does it greet you at the door when you come home? Does it seek out opportunities to snuggle with you? Does it run to you when startled, or stay close to you when you're upset or ill? Do any of these behaviors necessarily mean the pet feels love? (Figure 1.5) One of us (MNS) often has this debate with people because her pet is a cat, and many people insist that cats are incapable of loving anyone.

Let's say these animals (alien or earthly) were able to learn our language, so you could just ask them whether they have emotions. Sorry, that won't work either. How are you going to teach them the meaning of the word "emotion," or the meanings of *fear, anger,* and other specific emotional states? You could explain, "*Fear* is what you feel when you are in danger," but that's not fair. You can't tell them they feel fear unless you already know that they feel fear, and we are trying to discover whether they feel fear! The animals may feel *something* when they are in danger, but neither of you knows whether the animal's feeling in that situation is the same as your own would be.

FIGURE 1.5. Dog lovers got mad when a *Psychology Today* post went viral that claimed that dogs hate being hugged, based on coding nonverbal cues of pets in pictures. Good news for dog huggers though—this was just an informal report on a blog post, not a peer-reviewed research study.

How did you learn the meaning of words like *frightened, angry, happy,* and *sad*? At some point in your childhood you saw something scary, like a barking dog or a creepy-looking clown, and you started crying. Your parents or someone else said, "Did that scare you? Are you afraid? It won't hurt you, it's okay!" At another time, you were crying because you'd lost a beloved stuffed animal, and someone told you that you were sad. In each case, whoever gave your emotion a name inferred your feelings from the situation and from your reaction to it. Other people learned the meaning of emotion words the same way. As a result, you have the same problem in understanding other people's emotions as you do with babies and nonhuman animals—there's no way to know whether their feeling in some situation is the same as yours would be, even if you use the same word.

If you were paying close attention to the last several paragraphs, you may have noted that we went back and forth between the terms "emotion" and "feeling." When talking about emotions in casual speech, we tend to use these words interchangeably. By emotion we often refer to internal feelings as well as observable behaviors, and we even assume that feelings are valid explanations for behavior ("Don't mind her, she's just cranky today"). We may also refer to physical sensations such as the feeling of icy hands and a pounding heart, or to thoughts about the person or situation at which the emotion is directed ("That guy is such a jerk!"). In casual conversation, this complexity in what we mean by emotion is not a problem, because at least among English-language speakers, we share a concept that is close enough.

In science, however, this ambiguity in the colloquial meaning of emotion becomes a big concern. Feeling is totally subjective and difficult to compare across people—not ideal for scientific measurement. The observable aspects of emotion—eliciting situations, behaviors, physiological changes—are far from perfectly correlated with each other, and with people's reports of their feelings. Which aspect of emotion is most important? Which should be the gold standard? To return to our question about the aliens (or your pet), does it matter whether they *feel* anything, or can we just agree that their observable response to some situation fits a certain prototype well enough to call it an emotion? Different researchers have different answers to this question, and very different ideas about whether and why the various aspects of emotion hang together at all. Let's consider the earliest attempt to define emotion within psychology, and the associated theory.

William James's Definition

The founder of North American psychology, William James (Figure 1.6), offered the first major theory of emotions, indeed one of the first general theories in all of psychology. The Danish psychologist Carl Lange ([1885] 1922) proposed a similar idea at about the same time. Although the theories differ in several ways and William James's version has been far more influential, they share enough similarities that this general approach is often referred to as the **James–Lange theory**.

According to this theory, emotional feelings are based on body's instinctive reaction to certain kinds of situations (James, 1884, 1894). In James's words, "The bodily changes follow directly the perception of the exciting fact [the situation], and . . . our feeling of the same changes as they occur IS the emotion" (James, 1884, p. 190). James used the example of fear of a bear: he said that you don't run away because you are afraid of the bear; rather, the sight of the bear itself causes you to run away, and you feel fear because you run away. That idea contradicts the common-sense view that you feel angry and therefore you attack, or you feel frightened and therefore you try to escape. The James–Lange theory reverses the direction of cause and effect: You notice yourself attacking and therefore you feel angry. You notice yourself trying to escape and therefore you feel frightened. (See Figure 1.7 for how these two approaches contrast.)

FIGURE 1.6. William James, founder of psychology in the United States. He theorized that emotional feelings are based on sensations from the muscles and internal organs, reflecting the body's automatic reaction to certain kinds of situations.

More specifically, according to James–Lange theory, sensation from the muscles and/or the internal organs is necessary for the full experience of emotion. Any decrease in this sensation decreases the emotion. One example Carl Lange ([1885] 1922) offered in support of this theory was the common observation that drinking wine decreases anxiety. The wine decreases your body's response to a stressor, and as you feel your body become calmer, you feel less negative emotion.

In addition, James (1884) proposed that every "shade of emotion" might be associated with a unique profile of changes throughout the body (p. 15), although he was not always consistent on this point. Thus, the difference between one emotion and another (e.g., fear versus sadness) reflects real differences in your body's instinctive responses to the eliciting situations (e.g., danger versus loss). We will return to this possibility in Chapter 2.

James's theory is easily misunderstood, partly because he did not at first state it clearly enough (Ellsworth, 1994). Critics pointed out that his assumption about our response to a bear is obviously wrong: You do not automatically run away from a bear. You would not run away from a caged bear, a trained bear in a circus, or a sleeping bear. True, James (1894) conceded: the cause of your running away is not really the bear itself, but your perception and interpretation of the situation (e.g., a dangerous animal coming toward you). Still, he argued, when you assess that situation as one calling for escape, your body prepares for escape and starts to run, and your perception of these physiological changes and behavior is your fear. This idea—that how we *interpret* a situation is what determines an emotional response—has become profoundly important for our understanding of emotion.

Let's fast-forward in time to consider some modern approaches to defining the term "emotion," and see where they lead.

A Common Definition of Emotion

As a starting point for discussion, let's consider one proposed definition. It was a relatively early attempt within the modern era, but it has had a great deal of influence, and it includes elements shared with several more recent and widely recognized definitions (e.g., Ekman, 1992; Frijda, 1986; Izard, 1992; Keltner & Shiota, 2003; Lazarus, 1991; Levenson, 1999; Tooby & Cosmides, 2008). It is a little long-winded, but bear with us:

> [Emotion is] an inferred complex sequence of reactions to a stimulus [including] cognitive evaluations, subjective changes, autonomic and neural arousal, impulses to action, and behavior designed to have an effect upon the stimulus that initiated the complex sequence. (Plutchik, 1982, p. 551)

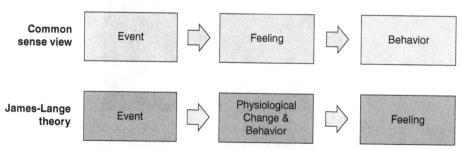

FIGURE 1.7. Common sense view of emotions contrasted with the James–Lange theory, which argues that conscious feeling is a result rather than a cause of physiological changes and behavior.

Yeah, that's a mouthful. Let's highlight some key elements, implications, and complexities of this definition.

1. The definition proposes that emotions are *functional* in the sense that they are geared toward having an effect on the world around us. That is, emotions are useful. Many philosophers, including Immanuel Kant and the Buddha, considered emotions disruptive or dangerous. Extremely emotional behaviors—panic, for example—are undeniably disruptive. However, under many circumstances, emotions guide us to quick, effective action. For example, when we feel fear, we try to escape. When someone commits an injustice against us, we protest and/or retaliate. When people take care of us, we stay close to them. We shall address this point in more detail in Chapter 2.

2. According to this definition, every emotion is a reaction to a stimulus—a specific event that takes place. Ordinarily, our experiences support this idea: we are happy *about* something, we are angry *at* someone, or we are afraid *of* something out there in the world. This aspect of the definition distinguishes emotions from purely internal **drives** such as hunger and thirst. However, this aspect of the definition is controversial, and will be addressed further in Chapter 4.

3. This definition, like many others, proposes that emotion includes four aspects: cognitive evaluation, or **appraisal** of what the stimulus means for our goals, concerns, and well-being; feelings ("subjective changes"); physiological changes ("autonomic and neural arousal"); and behavior. Note that "appraisal" is basically what William James meant by your interpretation of the emotion-eliciting situation, e.g., a *dangerous* bear, being the thing that elicits emotion.

So there we have it—a definition of emotion. Of sorts. A complex sequence of reactions to an internal or external stimulus that involves changes in thinking or cognition, physiological arousal and brain activity, subjective feeling, and motivated behavior, all geared toward affecting the initial stimulus. Whew!

This definition has become highly controversial, however. One important implication is that emotion is like a square: a "real" emotion has all four aspects, just as a real square has all four sides (see Figure 1.8 on page 18). If someone has three aspects of emotion but the fourth is missing, it's not an emotion. Is that true? Not necessarily (Russell, 2003). Imagine your heart suddenly starts pounding for no apparent reason, as it does in a panic attack. You can't explain this physiological change—that is, it's not based on your cognitive appraisal of your situation—but you feel frightened, you are sweating and trembling, and you want to run away. Do we say this is not an emotion because no cognition led to it? Or do we count "I'm panicking" as the cognition? If so, it's not much of a cognition. What if you see a funny meme on social media, think "that is *hilarious*!" and smile a little, but there is no change in your heart rate, and you remain firmly planted on the couch? Is that an emotional response? There are important theoretical reasons for assuming that cognitive appraisals, feelings, physiological changes, and behaviors hang together in emotions, but the evidence is scant and a bit hard to interpret. We will discuss this topic throughout the text. For now, let's consider one prominent alternative approach.

An Alternative: Core Affect

Instead of defining emotion as a required combination of cognitions/appraisals, feelings, physiological responses, and behaviors, some researchers have proposed that we select one

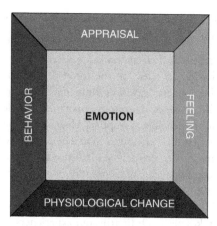

FIGURE 1.8. Four major aspects of emotional responding.

aspect of emotion as primary, and then ask how strongly and why that aspect relates to other aspects (e.g., Barrett, 2006; Russell, 2003). Researchers taking this approach have typically focused on the feeling aspect of emotion. Their findings suggest that discrete categories (e.g., fear, disgust, anger) are not the only way to describe feelings, and may not be their most meaningful characteristic.

An alternative is to arrange feelings along dimensions. We can describe many things in terms of dimensions. For example, if you were displaying diamonds at a store, you might arrange them in columns from largest to smallest and in rows from most to least sparkling. Similarly, we can describe emotional feelings as positions along continuous dimensions (e.g., Cacioppo, Gardner, & Berntson, 1997; Russell, 1980, 2003; Watson & Tellegen, 1985). To determine what these dimensions are, researchers have shown people various feeling words and asked them to rate the similarity for each pair of words, or asked people to report how strong their emotions are at various moments and note which emotions tend to co-occur. These data can be analyzed with a method called multidimensional scaling that allows us to see what dimensions emerge statistically from peoples' ratings of their experience.

Using this method, James Russell (1980) reported the arrangement of emotional feeling terms shown in Figure 1.9. Studies using other languages have produced similar outcomes (Yik & Russell, 2003). Based on these results, Russell (2003) has proposed the **circumplex model**, in which emotional feelings form a circle defined by the dimensions of pleasantness and arousal. Using this model, we can describe excitement as a combination of pleasure and high arousal, contentment as a combination of pleasure and low arousal, and so forth. Keep in mind that this model includes an emphasis on the feeling aspect of emotion, not cognitive, physiological, or behavioral aspects. For example, anger and fear are close to each other on this graph, although we associate anger and fear with different cognitions and behaviors. The feeling aspect of emotion in terms of pleasantness and arousal is called **core affect** (Russell, 2003).

Other researchers, starting from a different theoretical basis and emphasizing the evaluation of external stimuli rather than the valence of subjective feelings, have proposed a different pair of dimensions. According to the circumplex model of emotion, an

FIGURE 1.9. Feeling terms people rated as more similar to each other appear close together, whereas terms rated as dissimilar appear far apart. The resulting two-dimensional core affect space is defined by pleasantness and arousal. From Russell (1980).

emotional feeling is good or bad or somewhere in between, so it should not be possible to feel strong positive emotion and strong negative emotion at the same time. According to the **evaluative space model** (Cacioppo, Gardner, & Berntson, 1997), our evaluations of some target's goodness and badness are independent of each other, such that something can be good and bad at the same time. As a result, positive and negative affect should be independent dimensions of feeling, rather than opposite ends of a single dimension.

Consider the model shown in Figure 1.10. This model, proposed by David Watson and Auke Tellegen (1985), includes the possibility that positive and negative feelings are independent and can co-occur. Rather than dimensions of valence and arousal, the two dimensions are for positive and negative affect. Each dimension includes a built-in arousal or activation scale, so that being high on either positive or negative affect is very activated, and being low on both positive and negative affect means low activation. Unlike the circumplex model, however, being low on positive activation is not the same as being low on negative activation. As a result, *calm* is distant from *sleepy*.

Which set of dimensions is right? In part because of differing measurement and data analysis choices, some researchers find positive and negative affect to be nearly independent of each other (Tellegen, Watson, & Clark, 1999; Watson, Clark, & Tellegen, 1984, 1988), whereas others find that positive and negative affect are polar opposites—you can feel one or the other at a time, but not both (Remington, Fabrigar, & Visser, 2000; Russell, 1980). According to the results of one study, positive and negative affect are opposites in most situations, but in a few bittersweet situations people do feel both

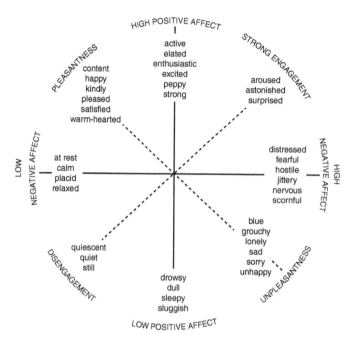

FIGURE 1.10. In this alternative model of feeling space, the main dimensions are positive activation and negative activation, rather than pleasantness and arousal. From Watson & Tellegen, (1985).

(Larsen, McGraw, & Cacioppo, 2001). Mixed emotions often occur when a meaningful experience in one's life is coming to an end, and they are increasingly common as people age (Ersner-Hershfield et al., 2008; Schneider & Stone, 2015). Also, researchers do not always measure emotion on the same time scale. The relationship between positive and negative affect may differ depending on whether you ask people how they feel overall in their lives (e.g., Watson, Clark, & Tellegen, 1988), versus how much positive and negative affect they are feeling right at this moment (e.g., Barrett & Fossum, 2001).

Let's not get too embroiled in this controversy. You might have noted that Figures 1.9 and 1.10 look more similar than different. If you flip Figure 1.9 right to left, and then rotate it clockwise 45 degrees, it will look a whole lot like Figure 1.10 (just before writing this, MNS explained the options for rotating a new four-seat circular dining table to her emotion-researcher husband as "Watson and Tellegen, or Russell?"). For our purposes, there are a few key points of agreement among the various dimensional models: (1) they emphasize the feeling aspect of emotions, rather than cognitive or behavioral aspects; (2) they agree that emotional feelings are best described in terms of continuous dimensions, rather than discrete categories; and (3) they emphasize that feelings are mainly defined in terms of valence (positive and negative) and degree of arousal or activation. Throughout this text, we'll often refer to emotional feelings, defined in terms of dimensions, as core affect.

There is one more dimension along which aspects of emotions and feelings vary that we need to consider in defining key terms, and that dimension relates primarily to time.

Emotions Versus Moods

Are you having a good day or a bad day today, emotionally speaking? Some of what constitutes a good versus bad day might reflect specific emotion-eliciting experiences and activities—whether you have something fun planned, how many red lights you hit on the way to work, whether some long-awaited news was positive or negative. Sometimes the cause is more diffuse, but still identifiable—you've been sleeping poorly, have too many assignments to complete, or are coming down with a nasty cold. Sometimes it's a complete mystery. You are just in a good or bad **mood**, for no reason that you can discern (Figure 1.11).

Emotions and moods are clearly related, but the distinction is useful for research (Fox et al., 2018). Although researchers are not always explicit about which they are studying, and (as we have already seen) there is much debate about what emotions really are, there is at least some consensus on the ways in which the concepts of emotion and mood differ. The first difference is time. Emotions tend to be short-lived phenomena, measured in minutes, whereas moods can linger over hours, days, or even multiple days. Second, emotions and moods differ in terms of their causes. As discussed earlier, emotions are linked to an easily identified internal or external trigger—they are reactions to some stimulus or event. We sometimes can come up with a plausible account of our mood, but there may be multiple, diffuse reasons for it, and sometimes it's difficult to identify any explanation at all.

Third, whereas emotions are tied to specific behaviors (at least in theory), moods are less obviously connected with specific actions. If you're angry (an emotion), presumably you are angry *at* someone and *about* something, and you want to do something to resolve

FIGURE 1.11. Sometimes you just wake up in a grumpy mood, for no obvious reason. Researchers differentiate moods from emotions as lasting longer, having less clear-cut causes, and being less associated with specific action tendencies.

whatever situation is provoking your anger. If you're just in a grumpy mood, what can you do? Sulk? Complain a lot? Glare at your professors? If it's not clear what you're upset about, the actions needed to improve your mood may be less apparent, or at least less closely linked to the cause of your mood. Stronger evidence suggests that moods may be tied to how you process information (Forgas, 2013) and the amount of effort you are willing to invest in a given task (Richter, Gendolla, & Wright, 2016)—topics we'll address in Chapters 10 and 14.

So much controversy about the meaning of one word! But maybe we can move forward without agreeing on a single definition of emotion. Some concepts can be defined precisely, others cannot. For example, we can precisely define *equilateral triangle*: it is a figure with three sides of equal length. Given any object, we can say for certain whether it is or isn't an equilateral triangle. In contrast, try to define *disco music*. You might do best to provide a few good examples and say, "music like that." Not every song is or isn't disco. Something can be a borderline case, not exactly a member or a nonmember of the category. People may even disagree about what songs do or do not count as disco. It's still useful to talk about disco when explaining what kind of music you favor for a night out dancing. Perhaps the same is true for emotion. Moreover, in some cases the question "Is X or is it not an emotion?" may be less important than how X works, and what effects X has on our bodies, minds, and behavior.

While we might not need a single definition to move forward, we do need to clearly state in any discussion or research study what definition we are using, and why, to both avoid confusion and be aware of the implications of choosing that definition. Throughout this text, we will continue to discuss different ways of defining emotion, as well as implications of the definitions used by various researchers. For now, let's examine the different theories of emotion that reflect the definitional conundrum.

THEORIES OF EMOTION

Learning Objectives
- Summarize the three main propositions of basic/discrete emotion theory.
- Explain how the structure of appraisal differs between basic/discrete emotion theory and the component process model, and apply to an example specific emotion.
- Describe the construction of emotion concepts as a psychological process.
- Differentiate the major tenets of the three modern theories of emotion, and correctly identify examples of each.

Like William James's early theory, modern theories of emotion address how the cognitive/ appraisal, feeling, physiological, and behavioral aspects of emotion relate to each other. Each major theoretical perspective offers a proposal about the psychological mechanisms that produce emotional experience, and implications for the structure of emotion space. Are emotions such as fear, anger, love, and pride evolved, universal, categorically distinct "packages" of responses to ancient threats and opportunities? Alternatively, are they real, complex, and finely tuned responses to a multidimensional appraisal of the current situation? Or are they mainly constructs of the mind, stories learned from the people around us about the interconnections of our inner feelings, situations, bodies, and actions?

FIGURE 1.12. The categories anger, disgust, joy, fear, and sadness, as illustrated in the movie *Inside Out*, are examples of basic/discrete emotions.

For now, we will briefly introduce these theories. We will describe them, compare them, and emphasize their relationships with the definitions discussed earlier—but we shall also return to them repeatedly throughout the text. For as you will see, these theories have played important roles in driving the past few decades of emotion research.

Basic/Discrete Emotions

After publishing his initial book introducing the theory of evolution, *On the Origin of Species* (Darwin, [1859] 1991), Charles Darwin spent many years considering emotion. Although his research methods lacked rigor in many ways (more on this in Chapter 5), his efforts to study nonverbal expression of emotions systematically and through an evolutionary lens were innovative, and very influential. In *The Expression of the Emotions in Man and Animals*, published in 1872, Charles Darwin ([1872] 1998) described the similarity throughout the world of people's facial expressions of happiness, sadness, fear, anger, and several other emotions. In doing so, he suggested two things: (1) that we should think of emotions in terms of distinct categories (see Figure 1.12); and (2) that emotional responses reflect our evolutionary heritage and are thus part of universal human nature.

Consistent with this proposal, many psychologists have proposed lists of *basic* or *discrete* emotions (the two terms are not interchangeable but have a similar enough meaning for our purposes). For example, the best-known list of basic emotions—happiness, sadness, anger, fear, disgust, and surprise—is based on Paul Ekman and colleagues' (Ekman, 1972; Ekman et al., 1987) extensive research on facial expressions of emotion; we'll discuss this work in detail in Chapter 5. Other researchers have proposed additional candidates, such as contempt, shame, guilt, interest, hope, gratitude, pride, love, awe, amusement/play, boredom, jealousy, regret, and embarrassment (e.g., Cowen et al., 2019; Izard, 2007; Panksepp, 1998; Shiota et al., 2017).

Basic/discrete emotions are defined as complex psychobiological reactions that evolved in response to prototypical threats and challenges in the environment of our early human ancestors (Tooby & Cosmides, 2008). The basic/discrete emotions model entails three main propositions. First, each emotion is thought to serve a distinct adaptive function. For example, fear presumably evolved to help us escape the threat of predators and similar sources of immediate physical danger (Öhman & Mineka, 2003). Prototypical disgust is thought to be an evolved emotional response to threats of contamination, such as rotting food, disease-carrying parasites, and obviously ill people (Rozin & Fallon, 1987). For this reason, the basic/discrete emotion model conceptualizes emotions in terms of distinct categories, such as those used to classify stone, flowers, and different species of animals.

Second, basic emotions serve to coordinate the individual aspects of emotion—appraisals and other cognitions, physiological changes, subjective feelings, and behaviors—producing a coherent package of responses that should help you respond effectively to the situation at hand (Levenson, 1999). For example, a fear response includes heightened visual acuity, attention compelled toward nearby threats, increased fight–flight sympathetic nervous activation preparing the body for physical activity, increased tension in the large skeletal muscles, and an impulse to freeze or run, as well as subjective feelings associated with danger (Tooby & Cosmides, 2008). In another situation, each of these might occur separately, but fear pulls them together so you have the best chance of escaping with life and limb intact.

The third proposition is that some of the conceptual categories people have for their emotions—fear, anger, sadness, and so forth—reflect distinctions among real, naturally occurring categories of human psychological experience, at least to some extent. Although basic/discrete emotion theory acknowledges that people from different cultures may interpret these natural categories in somewhat different ways, and even create culture-specific emotion concepts, some categories should be inherent in human nature.

Because the basic/discrete emotions model describes emotions primarily as instinctive, adaptive physiological and behavioral responses to stimuli in the environment, placing less emphasis on subjective feelings, it is closely aligned with the James–Lange classic theory of emotion. James (1884) also suggested the possibility that different emotional feelings might correspond to distinct physiological profiles. However, James was somewhat skeptical about whether emotions could be divided into neat categories, so the James–Lange and basic/discrete emotions perspectives are not identical. We will discuss the tenets of basic/discrete emotion theory further in Chapter 2. For now, let's introduce another theory.

The Component Process Model

Like the basic/discrete emotions model, our next theory proposes that emotions are responses to events in the environment, that they reflect our evolutionary heritage, and that they include multiple aspects that tend to hang together in similar ways across cultures. Like the core affect model we considered earlier, however, it indicates that emotion space is better described in terms of dimensions than in terms of categories. How does this work?

In basic/discrete emotion theory, observable aspects of emotion such as physiological changes, facial expressions, and other behaviors are considered the most important aspects of emotion because they reflect evolved, functional responses to important kinds of eliciting events. According to the **component process model**, the cognitive appraisal aspect of emotion is particularly important. Following William James, basic/discrete emotion theorists also acknowledge that appraisal is needed for an emotional response to occur, and determines which emotion is activated. These appraisals are thought to be categorical; for example, to be disgusted by a cockroach in your kitchen, you must appraise it as a source of contamination that is likely to make you sick.

In contrast, appraisals in the component process model are dimensional, with the same set of dimensions used to evaluate the significance of every event we experience. The primary proponent of the model, Klaus Scherer (2009), has argued that novelty, pleasantness, expectedness, certainty, goal conduciveness, need for change, and controllability are among the key appraisal dimensions, although the list varies somewhat across publications. In the component process model your appraisal of the cockroach would be that it is moderately novel (presumably you've seen cockroaches before, but not often), unpleasant, highly unexpected (in your kitchen), certain (if you are sure that it is really a cockroach), and in conflict with your goals (we hope you do not want a cockroach in your kitchen). Importantly, people may reasonably differ as to whether they appraise the cockroach as controllable, and this would influence their emotion. Some people would go get a can of bug spray, or a sturdy broom and a bag, returning ready for battle; others would run screaming from the house.

In the component process model our physiological and behavioral responses to emotional events are real, and predictable, but determined by the combined effects of each individual appraisal dimension rather than a preset package corresponding to a basic emotion category. Imagine that emotion theories are restaurants. In the basic/discrete emotion theory restaurant you have only a few price-fixed menus from which to choose, each with an appetizer, salad, main course, and dessert; your meal comes as a set package, and you cannot swap out individual dishes. In the component process model restaurant, you order the four courses separately, and that combination is your full meal. In both cases your choice corresponds to the appraisal, and the appraisal determines the emotional response, but the component process model has more flexibility in what your order can look like.

Let's see how this difference plays out in facial expressions of emotion, as an example. Consider the expression of anger shown in the bottom right corner of Figure 1.13. Instead of calling this a single pre-packaged expression, we could describe it as the result of four appraisals (Ortony & Turner, 1990; Scherer, 1992). First, the widened eyes indicate that the stimulus is unexpected. This part of the anger expression is also a component of surprise and fear.

A second element is turning down the corners of the mouth. According to component process theory, this movement indicates displeasure, which also occurs in sadness and disgust. Third, the furrowed brows indicate a desire to change the situation. People often furrow their brows when they are frustrated or concentrating, as well as when they're angry. Fourth, the tightened lips indicate a sense of control. That movement is characteristic of anger, but also contributes to the expression of pride—another emotion that involves feelings of power and control (Campos et al., 2013).

This example is about facial expression, but the same could be true of other aspects of emotion. The key point is that what we call anger (a category) could actually reflect the intersection of appraisals along several dimensions, each pertaining to a different aspect of the situation. A given situation might require just a few of these dimensions. Even when a situation does involve appraisal along several dimensions, these take place in sequence, not all at once (Grandjean & Scherer, 2008).

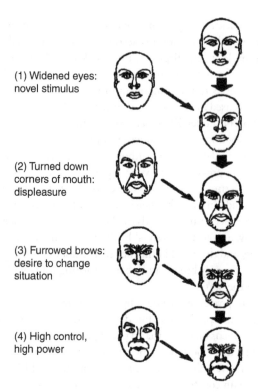

(1) Widened eyes:
novel stimulus

(2) Turned down
corners of mouth:
displeasure

(3) Furrowed brows:
desire to change
situation

(4) High control,
high power

FIGURE 1.13. According to the component process model, the expression we call anger is really a compound of muscle movements reflecting four different appraisal elements.

Scherer (2009) has noted that the component process model allows for *modal* or most-common emotion states that look a lot like basic/discrete emotions, and agrees that these modal emotions probably reflect prototypical threats and opportunities humans faced throughout evolution. In some cases, the basic emotion and component process models may make similar predictions. However, there are important differences. First, in the component process model, various instances of the same general emotion will look different if the underlying appraisals are not quite the same. For example, when all appraisals associated with anger occur, we recognize a clear example of anger, but parts of anger can arise without the full profile. Second, appraisal dimensions can combine in a variety of ways, producing emotional responses that do not fit cleanly into a distinct emotion category. This allows for a variety of quirky, uncommon, but real emotional experiences.

Psychological Construction

Let's play a game you may have played in your childhood—which of these things does not belong with the others? Your choices are *cow, salmon,* and *lungfish* (see Figure 1.14).

If you are like most people, you probably want to toss the cow. Two of these creatures are fish, and the other is not. Two swim and have scales, one walks and has hair. It seems to be common sense.

Fun fact: lungfish and cows both have lung-like organs that allow for breathing; a small flap of skin covering the windpipe, called an epiglottis; and more similarly structured hearts than do lungfish and salmon. Does this change your mind?

FIGURE 1.14. Which of these things is least like the others? From Scherer (1992).

What if we tell you that fish don't exist?

In *Why Fish Don't Exist: A Story of Loss, Love, and the Hidden Order of Life* writer Lulu Miller (2020) argues that "fish" probably don't exist—that this is not a biologically valid or meaningful category. The evidence? Scientists who specialize in the categorization of species began to use complicated statistical and computer science techniques in an effort to classify living beings based on their similarities with each other, and the degree to which they shared "evolutionary novelties"—strong markers of a shared heritage. They were startled to discover that the word "fish" as commonly used didn't map to a meaningful category in these analyses (even after removing sea-dwelling mammals, such as dolphins and whales).

What does this have to do with emotion? Well, some researchers have argued that in equating concepts such as "fear" and "pride" with categories appropriate for scientific study, we're committing a similar error as lumping all sea-dwelling animals with fins and scales in a class called "fish." Thinking of emotions as categories feels intuitive, and is consistent with folk wisdom and personal experience, but it might be inconsistent with the actual psychology and biology of affective states. The same concern has been raised regarding "emotion" (Russell, 2003), and as we have seen, researchers fail to agree on a definition that clearly differentiates emotions from nonemotions. If "fear," "anger," "pride," "love," and so forth do not map to the kinds of innate categories proposed by basic/discrete emotion researchers, why do we tend to think of emotions in this way, and where did the categories come from?

An alternative is that cognitions—specifically our learned emotion concepts—play an even stronger role in determining how we experience and label our emotional feelings than the prior two theories proposed. In an early demonstration of the effects of appraisals and expectations on how we label our emotional feelings, Stanley Schachter and Jerome Singer (1962) conducted a widely known and rather diabolical study. Imagine you are a participant. At the start of the study protocol, all participants received a shot of something they were told contained vitamins. Based on random assignment to condition, one group of participants actually received an injection of epinephrine (also known as adrenaline), a hormone that increases physiological arousal. Of those receiving the epinephrine injection, half were informed that the injection would increase their heart rate, make them sweat, and so forth. The other half were not warned about these effects, so they had no idea what was happening to them (please note that this practice would never be allowed by a human subjects review board today). The remaining participants received a placebo injection—that is, one with no pharmacological effects.

At that point, some participants were put into a "euphoria" situation and the others into an "anger" situation. In the euphoria situation participants waited with a young man

FIGURE 1.15.   Sarah's brother, Andrew.

who was supposedly also a participant, but who was in fact a confederate paid to play the role of a happy, playful person. He flipped wads of paper into a trash can, sailed paper airplanes, built a tower with manila folders, played with a hula hoop, and tried to get the other participant to join in his play. In the anger situation, participants had to fill out a lengthy questionnaire, full of personal, insulting, and downright rude questions (e.g., "which member of your immediate family does not bathe or wash regularly?" (*Note*: SRC is surprised that this question would anger people, because the answer is obviously her brother Andrew; see Figure 1.15). Each participant in this condition was also paired with a confederate. In this case, he muttered in annoyance at the questions and ultimately ripped up the questionnaire and stormed out of the room.

Having been exposed to the situation and the confederate's actions for a while, all participants were asked to rate how happy and how angry they felt. What would you predict: How did the emotion ratings of participants in the epinephrine-unwarned condition (whose hearts were pounding for no apparent reason) differ from those in the epinephrine-warned condition, who had an easy explanation for their body's antics, and from those in the placebo condition?

Rather than reporting separate data for happiness and anger ratings, the researchers reported happy-angry rating differences; this is not a great practice and makes the results harder to interpret, but let's review the findings anyway. First, participants in all conditions reported being more happy than angry; hence, all of the values in Table 1.4 are positive. Participants given the placebo were not affected much by the situation—they reported about the same ratio of happiness to anger whether they were in the euphoria or

TABLE 1.4 Physical arousal and emotional feelings

Results of Schachter & Singer's (1962) study of the effects of physical arousal in different situations on emotional feelings. Cell entries are mean "happy" minus "angry" rating differences for individuals in that experimental condition.

	Placebo	Epinephrine Warned	Epinephrine Not Warned
Fun Situation	1.61	0.98	1.78
Annoying Situation	1.63	1.91	1.39

the anger condition. Those who were given epinephrine without knowing what to expect differed in the hypothesized way. People in the epinephrine–euphoria condition reported being more happy than angry, and sometimes joined in the play! Their ratings were about the same as that of people in the placebo–euphoria condition, however, so the epinephrine seems not to have affected them at all. Of those in the epinephrine–anger condition, people did not report being more angry than happy, but the two ratings were closer, and some muttered angry comments or refused to complete the questionnaire. The implication is that participants in this condition might have interpreted their body's arousal as anger (to a greater extent than those injected with the placebo), simply because they were in a situation that would justify anger.

The overall picture is a bit confusing because of the results for the people who were told what to expect from the epinephrine. Those in the euphoria situation reported *less* happiness (relative to anger) than in any other condition, suggesting that the epinephrine made them relatively upset, although they knew what sensations to expect. Those in the anger situation reported the greatest bias toward *happy* feelings relative to angry ones. The main findings from the study seem to be as follows: (1) people's interpretation of their arousal in terms of specific feelings is slightly, but not strongly, influenced by the situation; and (2) telling people to expect arousal can help detach people's emotional feelings from the situation.

Can you see the connection with the proposal by William James, discussed earlier in this chapter? One of James's suggestions was that the body produces qualitatively distinct bodily patterns, which can be experienced as distinct emotions. Schachter and Singer disagreed, arguing that the physiological arousal that often accompanies emotion is essential for determining how strong the emotional feeling will be, but does not differ among different emotions. Instead, you identify which emotion you feel based on all the information you have about your situation. In other words, the main difference between one emotion and another is in the cognitive appraisal aspect, not the physiological aspect.

As it turns out, some of the assumptions Schachter and Singer made about the autonomic nervous system are wrong—it actually produces more diverse profiles of "arousal" than they believed (Folkow, 2000; Jänig & Häbler, 2000). Also, the results of this particular study are perplexing at best. Subsequent studies suggested that people may generally tend to interpret unexplained physiological arousal in terms of negative affect, regardless of the situation (Maslach, 1979). Nonetheless, the idea behind the study—that the words and concepts we use to describe our emotions are largely learned and based on what we think we are supposed to feel at the time, rather than reflecting objectively real, categorically distinct physiological states—has proved highly influential.

Modern accounts of the importance of appraisals and expectations in driving emotional feelings have been proposed by James Russell (1991) and Lisa Feldman Barrett (2006; 2017). They argue that categories of emotional experience such as fear, anger, and so forth are created not by evolved human nature, but rather through **psychological construction**—the formation of mental concepts that people use to organize their experience of the world. Earlier we discussed "fish" as one possible example. For another, consider the concept of *pet*. Pets are animals that people own and care for, not for practical purposes such as agriculture or protection, but out of affection. The most common pets are dogs, cats, hamsters, and the like, but it's not the species that defines a pet, it's the relationship with a human owner. In nature, there is no naturally occurring, objectively real category of "pet." People in different cultural contexts have different ideas of what a pet is, and some cultures have no concept of pets at all. The definition can vary from person to person as well. Can a tarantula be a pet? You be the judge. (MNS: Absolutely not, nope, definitely no!)

Researchers emphasizing psychological construction argue that emotions such as "anger" are concepts like "pet"—learned through experience and varying across individuals and cultures, rather than elements of human nature. This is a clear point of disagreement with basic/discrete emotion theory. Researchers working from the psychological construction perspective propose that the experience and two-dimensional structure of core affect (the feeling aspect of emotion) are universal among humans. However, the categorical emotion concepts (such as anger) we use to combine core affect with specific eliciting situations (being insulted), appraisals (perceiving disrespect), physiological changes (face turning red), and behaviors (yelling at the offender) are stories we tell to classify and make sense of human feelings, not categories that are part of human nature (Barrett, 2006; Barrett, 2017; Neimeyer, 1995; Russell, 1991). Returning to our emotion-theory restaurant analogy, psychological construction theory is a buffet—there are all kinds of dishes to choose from, and each person puts whatever the heck they want on their plate.

How do emotion concepts form? According to Barrett (2006; 2017), the process starts when we first learn a particular emotion word from a parent or other caregiver. In our mind, we associate the word with that experience, and add in every subsequent encounter with that word, whether it's in our own life, a friend's, or a fictional context, such as a book or a movie. Over time we link the word to a rich network of specific experiences, and an emotion concept emerges. Although each individual develops unique emotion concepts, reflecting a unique set of associations with a given word, people who share a language and a culture will have similar-enough concepts to be able to talk about emotions effectively. However, as we will discuss in Chapter 3, people from different languages and cultures may have very different emotion concepts.

Which Modern Emotion Theory Is Right?

So many theories! At this point you may be asking yourself, Which of these is right? Surely researchers have figured this out by now!

Sorry, but no. As you'll see throughout this text, much research on emotion takes one of these theories as its starting point, but few studies explicitly pit two or more theories against each other. Looking across studies, there are some that seem to support one theory and some that support another. We hope that rather than trying to decide too quickly which theory is right, you approach the following material with an open mind, asking how the evidence speaks to each theory and which new studies could be done to answer more and better questions about the nature of emotion. You may even wonder whether these theories are mutually exclusive, in the sense that only one can be correct. A growing number of researchers are asking this same question. Perhaps each theory holds a piece of the puzzle, and we need to better differentiate the multiple layers of experience to fully understand the emotional lives of human beings.

THE RELATIONSHIP BETWEEN EMOTION AND MOTIVATION

Learning Objective

• Analyze the similarities and differences between motivation and emotion.

Now that you have learned the basics of how psychologists think about motivation and emotion, consider their similarities and differences. While some psychology programs split the topics into separate courses, many lump them into a single course. There's even an academic journal called *Motivation and Emotion*, in which psychological scientists publish some of their research. Take a moment and think for yourself—what is the relationship between emotion and motivation (Figure 1.16)?

Consider the examples of motivation earlier in this chapter—surely the motivational speaker influences your actions in part through the emotions you feel during their speech? Isn't the idea of saving for a vacation energizing because you anticipate the emotions (fun, pleasure, enjoyment) the trip will bring about? You may have noticed that part of our proposed definition of emotion included the phrase "impulses to action" and its resulting effect on behavior, which sounded a lot like motivation. Indeed, the words "emotion" and "motivation" both stem from the Latin root "motus," which means "to move." Approach and avoidance, reward and punishment, energy and direction are critical underpinnings of both concepts. A historical analysis of the concept of emotions (Dixon, 2012) finds it to be "a keyword in crisis" and notes that over the long history of emotion and motivation scholarship, philosophy and psychology have combined and separated and combined again terms such as passions (which seem to largely refer to motivational drives) and feelings (milder states consistent with many of the basic emotions).

FIGURE 1.16. What is the relationship between motivation and emotion?

In other words, these concepts overlap quite a bit, and they share a deep history. That said, there are differences between these topics, and they have traditionally been studied by distinct groups of scientists. For one thing, emotions, core affect, and moods all focus on the present moment. In contrast, much of motivation research concerns itself with longer-range and across-situation behaviors, such as goal setting, budgeting, and academic achievement. One will certainly feel emotions at various times while pursuing these broader and more long-reaching goals, but there are multiple psychological processes other than emotion at work. For this reason, we see emotions as subsumed under the concept of motivation.

Emotions also intersect with motivation in two specific ways. First, emotions are often critically involved in providing that critical energy component of the "energy + direction" formulation of motivation. In the next chapter we'll consider an evolutionary perspective on emotions, and discuss further how emotions serve as predispositions to action (in other words, motivation), summoning the energy necessary to respond to threats or opportunities in the environment. Second, emotions provide feedback on how well we are or are not fulfilling our goals or other motivational needs; a signal to the organism that things are going well (how pleasant!) or poorly (how unpleasant!). As we'll see when we dig into goal setting and pursuit in Chapter 14, monitoring progress and getting feedback is critical to successful motivated behavior.

The division between emotion and motivation science may grow ever more blurry over the years, as we gather knowledge and conduct research. We may well find ourselves back where we began, understanding emotion and motivation from a singular perspective. Going forward, we will consider research and experiments from both fields in an interleaved fashion, without always clearly demarcating which relate to motivation versus emotion. We'll be honest and note that as emotion researchers, we'll lean more heavily on the emotion side of the equation, while also appreciating the broader perspective that motivation science gives us.

RESEARCH METHODS: HOW DO WE STUDY EMOTION AND MOTIVATION?

Learning Objectives

- Analyze the advantages and drawbacks of various methods for inducing emotion and activating motivation in experimental research.
- Differentiate reliability from validity in measures of emotion and motivation, and identify/generate examples of face, content, convergent, and predictive validity.
- Compare and contrast self-report, biological, and behavioral measures of emotion, and analyze the appropriateness of each for a given research question.

We now turn away from theory and toward a more practical problem—how do we study emotions and motivation scientifically? This is tricky business. First, we must get research participants into a motivated or emotional state, or catch these occurrences in real life. Then, because both emotion and motivation may involve so many different aspects, measuring them can be complex. Let's see how researchers have dealt with this challenge.

Inducing Emotion and Activating Motivation

Suppose you want to study the effects emotions have on people's behavior, their relationships, or some other outcome. How would you start? You might begin by finding people who are already happy, frightened, or angry and see whether they differ from people not feeling that emotion on your outcome of interest. However, that would not be convincing research. Maybe the people who tend to be happy are different from not-happy people in some other way causing your outcome, and happiness has nothing to do with the effect. Happy people tend to be healthier than unhappy people, for example, and the differences in your outcome may be caused by differences in health, rather than differences in happiness. As with any other research, the only way we can be confident of a cause-and-effect relationship is to experimentally manipulate the variable we think is the cause, while holding other factors constant, and then see whether the outcome changes in predictable ways.

Emotion researchers use several methods to induce emotion. For example, researchers may ask participants to think of a time in their life when they experienced an emotion very strongly, to remember that experience vividly, and then to talk or write about the experience (e.g., Bless et al., 1996; Ekman, Levenson, & Friesen, 1983; Tsai et al., 2002). This procedure works better for some participants than others, depending on the recency and intensity of their experience. Alternatively, researchers may ask participants to read and vividly imagine themselves in a story designed to evoke a strong emotion, such as fear or pride (e.g., Griskevicius, Shiota, & Neufeld, 2010; Keltner, Ellsworth, & Edwards, 1993). Still others evoke emotions by showing photographs (e.g., Bradley et al., 1992) or short film clips (e.g., Gross & Levenson, 1995; Maner et al., 2005; Papousek, Schulter, & Lang, 2009) with emotional content.

These methods are used most often by researchers to elicit emotions in the laboratory. One advantage of all of these methods is that they are *face valid*—researchers typically use stories or images (such as a story about receiving a high grade on an exam or a photograph of a spider) with emotional meaning on which most people can agree. Another advantage is that these methods can be used to target specific emotion states, such as fear, pride, and disgust.

However, these methods have limitations as well. They generally serve to evoke emotion through a memory or imagined situation, rather than a real event happening in the present moment. In some studies researchers have evoked emotions by putting participants directly into emotional situations, such as giving them small gifts (e.g., Isen, Daubman, & Nowicki, 1987), complimenting them on their "creativity" on a preliminary task, or asking them to give a speech to a cold and unresponsive audience (e.g., Taylor et al., 2010). Although such strategies are *ecologically valid*, resembling the real-life situations in which people feel emotions, the emotions may not be specific, and people may respond in different ways. In the end, the best researchers try to evoke emotions using a number of methods in different studies to see whether the effects of emotions are the same regardless of which method is used to elicit them.

A serious problem in emotion research is that emotions elicited in laboratory settings are at best weaker than those people can experience in the real world, and may even be qualitatively distinct. Consider this—if you watch a movie clip in which a character you care about dies, how is that similar to, or different from, actually having someone you love die (or move far away, or end the relationship in some other way)? It is difficult to elicit powerful, personal emotions without violating important ethical principles for research (e.g., we can't lie and say a participant's best friend has just been hit by a bus). Researchers must remember that the states studied in the lab may be only a pale reflection of emotions people experience in their real lives.

Experimentally manipulating motivation also introduces complexity. Much motivation research focuses on the setting and achievement of personal goals. Goals themselves do not lend themselves easily to experimentation; if you can figure out how to randomize people (e.g., school-aged children) to heightened intrinsic motivation to do well in school, please let the authors know without delay. However, researchers can **prime** existing motivations and goals by making them especially salient in the moment, using short stories or other techniques similar to those for eliciting emotions (e.g., Li et al., 2012; Sawada, Augur, & Lydon, 2018). Specific strategies for achieving goals are more amenable to experimentation, and these research programs tend to study participants over long periods of time as they pursue their goals.

Over the past decade or so, a growing number of researchers have dealt with the challenge of studying ecologically valid motivation and emotions through a technique called **experience sampling**. The researcher gives each participant a device of some kind, like a smartphone or tablet, that buzzes at unpredictable times throughout the day. When the buzz happens, the participant is supposed to answer questions about his or her situation, feelings, activities, and so forth right away. Researchers can also "scrape" data about emotion from text, images, and emojis in people's social media posts and other online content. The advantage of these approaches is that they examine people in real life (Figure 1.17). Drawbacks include the fact that people aren't experiencing intense emotional or motivational states most of the time; these are not experimental designs and so you cannot assess

FIGURE 1.17. Emotion and motivation researchers have taken advantage of modern technological innovations, such as smartphones, to collect data from participants as they go about their daily lives.

cause/effect relationships; and the measures you can collect are usually limited to simple, quick, self-report items. Whether these are problems depends on the question the study is designed to answer. Let's look more closely at the issue of measurement.

Measuring Emotion and Motivation

Scientific research on emotion and motivation requires some kind of measurement, but this also presents challenges. Both motivation and emotion occur inside the "black box" of people's minds, and thus cannot be measured directly; they can only be inferred based on responses researchers *can* measure objectively. If we have trouble defining emotions clearly, as seen earlier in this chapter, we will have trouble agreeing on a measure. We noted that the definition of emotion typically includes four aspects: cognitions, feelings, physiological changes, and behaviors. Each of these can be measured, but if they fail to converge, researchers disagree as to which is the gold standard.

Motivation is problematic as well. People don't always have the best insight into why they do what they do. Their stated motivations often correlate poorly with their behavior, and in many cases people's actions are predicted much better by subtle features of the social and physical environment of which they were totally unaware (Harmon-Jones & Harmon-Jones, 2019). For instance, we tend to mimic other people's facial expressions, mannerisms, and even grammar, something that has been dubbed "the chameleon effect" (Chartrand & Bargh, 1999). When we set goals that involve resisting temptation, we often underestimate how enticing the temptation will be in the future ("that ice cream cone doesn't really sounds so delicious"; Fishbach & Trope, 2008). People could generally not tell you about either of these influences (because they are likely unaware of them), but it doesn't mean they aren't impacting motivation and behavior.

Nonetheless, researchers must measure *something* that captures emotion and motivation as well as possible, given the questions addressed by the study and available resources. Psychologists rely mainly on these kinds of methods:

- **Self-reports** are participants' descriptions of their own feelings, thoughts, beliefs, goals, and other aspects of emotion and motivation. Self-reports can be used to measure physiological sensations and behavior as well, but the accuracy of such reports is always in question.
- **Biological measurements** include measures of heart rate, blood pressure, sweating, and other variables that fluctuate during emotional arousal, as well as brain activity and hormones.
- **Behaviors** are actions we can observe, such as facial and vocal expressions, speech, task performance, and real-world action. Although participants may report their own behavior, it's best if some objective observer assesses it.

For any kind of measurement, researchers want to know whether it is reliable and valid before they trust research using that measure. The **reliability** of a measure reflects the consistency or repeatability of its scores, and is typically measured on a scale from 0 to 1. If the reliability is high (close to 1), then people who are tested repeatedly under the same conditions get nearly the same score each time. If the reliability is close to 0, scores fluctuate randomly from one test administration to another. If reliability is low, then the test is not measuring anything. For example, a questionnaire might have low reliability if the items are worded in a confusing way, because participants give a different answer to the same question each time it's asked. Similarly, if a physiological sensor is not attached correctly, then an estimate of heart rate will contain a lot of random noise.

Validity is an assessment of whether scores on some measure represent what the researcher claims they represent. In a highly valid measure, the intended **construct** (typically a psychological process, ability, or event) is the only or primary determinant of people's scores. A questionnaire could be invalid if many people answer it untruthfully, or if it is influenced by characteristics other than the one intended. For instance, one scale of self-esteem includes this true/false item: *There are lots of things about myself I'd change if I could.* If you say yes, does that answer indicate low self-esteem, or high ambition? As another example, sweat gland activity is sometimes used in law enforcement as a measure of lying. The problem is that sweating is not a measure of lying per se; it is a measure of activity in one branch of the sympathetic nervous system. That activity tends to increase when people are nervous (among other emotional states), and people are often nervous when they are lying. But not everyone is nervous when they lie (sociopaths aren't); people may be nervous about a key question even if they're not lying; and not everybody sweats when they are nervous. As a result, sweat gland activity is not a very valid measure of lying, and most courts do not accept it as evidence (Honts & Perry, 1992).

There are several kinds of validity (see Figure 1.18), and researchers ideally try to ensure a new measure is valid in all of these ways (Joint Committee on Standards, 1999):

- The content of the measure should match the intended construct in a reasonably obvious way (face validity).
- If a measure is supposed to capture some construct, it needs to cover the whole of that construct without being influenced by a bunch of stuff beyond the intended construct (content validity).
- Different measures of the same general thing should correlate positively with one another (convergent validity). For example, separate items on a questionnaire should correlate strongly with each other, as should different measures of a person's heart rate in a physiological index.
- Most important, scores on the measure should accurately predict some theoretically relevant outcome (predictive validity).

Because emotion and motivation are complex, internal, multifaceted processes, the question of validity is both important and tricky. As you read about the studies presented in this textbook, we encourage you to question the validity of measures in each study, to note when and why you think validity is low, and to think about whether there are alternative interpretations of the results from the interpretations the researchers claim. Here are the main types of measures in emotion and motivation research.

Self-Reports

Self-reports are easy to collect, though not necessarily to interpret. For instance, participants might rate their nervousness, happiness, or level of some other emotion on a scale such as this:

Not at all nervous		*Somewhat nervous*		*Very nervous*	
1	2	3	4	5	6	7

Face Validity
- Content of the measure matches intended construct
- e.g., Depression scale measures clinically relevant sadness and fatigue

Content Validity
- Captures whole construct without including unrelated constructs
- e.g., Self-esteem scale doesn't also cover satisfaction with life outcomes

Convergent Validity
- Different measures of the same construct correlate positively
- e.g., High scores on your nostalgia scale are correlated with other nostalgia scales

Predictive Validity
- The measure should accurately predict some theoretically relevant outcome
- e.g., Measure of academic motivation predicts higher gpa

FIGURE 1.18. Types of validity, with examples.

Self-reports cannot be exact because each person's standard differs from everyone else's. Centuries ago, people measured distances in cubits and spans. A cubit is the distance from the elbow to the tip of the middle finger; a span is the distance from the end of the thumb to the end of the little finger when extended. The problem is that your cubit or span is different from someone else's. Self-reports of emotions have the same problem; if you rate your nervousness as a 5, your 5 may differ from someone else's 5, or even from your own 5 at some other time.

Self-reports sometimes conflict with other, more objective measures of emotion. Suppose you ask someone who is yelling, "Why are you angry?" and the person replies, "I'm not angry! I'm completely calm!" Do you believe that self-report? (Figure 1.19). It probably depends on whether you have other reasons to believe the person might be angry, and whether there is a reasonable alternative explanation for the yelling (e.g., a jackhammer working in the street outside their house means they are yelling to be heard). However, when behavior and self-report conflict, we are justified in questioning the validity of the latter.

A further limitation of self-reports, especially in emotion research, is that it can be difficult to compare people who speak different languages or dialects. Emotion words can be translated, but important meaning is often lost in translation, and we may incorrectly assume that all the nuances of meaning for corresponding words in two languages are the same (more on this in Chapter 3). Also, researchers sometimes want to study emotions in beings who do not speak at all—for instance, infants, people with certain types of brain injuries, or nonhuman animals.

Despite these problems, self-reports are useful for many purposes. For example, if you rated your nervousness 5 yesterday and 2 today, the change probably means your nervousness has decreased, even if your 5 means something different from someone else's. Also, there is really no other way to measure the feeling aspect of emotion except through self-reports.

FIGURE 1.19. Sometimes people's outward expression contradicts their self-report. If this person told you they weren't angry, would you believe them?

Biological Measures

Consider the statement 17 + 33 = 50. When you contemplate that thought, do you feel anything physical? Do you get any bodily sensations at all? Probably not. However, our emotional experiences often do include a physical component—your heart beats faster, your stomach tightens up, and your hands start to sweat. Increased activation of the **sympathetic nervous system** is important for producing this arousal, readying the body for fight-or-flight emergency action. In general, the physiological changes prompted by the sympathetic nervous system increase the flow of blood and oxygen to your muscles, so you're prepared for hard physical work. In contrast, the **parasympathetic nervous system** relaxes the body, facilitates growth, and increases maintenance functions that conserve energy for later use.

Like self-reports, physiological measures of emotion have some limitations. Think of it this way—is emotion the only time your heart beats faster? How about when you're walking up the stairs? Your heart rate definitely speeds up then—if not, you're going to feel awful by the time you reach the top. But are you feeling an emotion? Not necessarily. When you are cold, the blood vessels in your hands constrict just like they do when you are afraid. Does that mean you're scared? Again, not necessarily. One of the authors of this book (MNS) has to remove data from her study every time a research participant sneezes, because that messes up her physiological measures. Researchers using physiological measures must ask whether the changes they're seeing are caused by emotion, movement, or something else unrelated to emotion.

Also, like self-reports, physiological measures of emotion differ widely from person to person. If you were to measure your own heart rate right now, that of your best friend, that of your romantic partner, and so on, you would get different numbers. Some of this variation would arise because you're all engaged in different activities, but even in the same activity, people's bodies are different. For these reasons, researchers usually look at the effects of some emotion in terms of change in physiology from an unemotional (or at least less emotional) baseline period, usually in response to some instruction or stimulus.

Physiological measures offer some strong advantages over self-reports. If someone says their nervousness went from 2 to 5, we're not sure what that means, except that it's higher now than it was before. If someone's heart rate increased from 75 beats per minute to 80 beats per minute, however, that is more specific. Also, the definition of heart rate is unambiguous, whereas we're never sure whether someone else's definition of nervousness is the same as ours.

In addition to the sympathetic and parasympathetic nervous systems, **hormones** can also produce changes in the body that characterize strong emotion. Hormones are molecules that carry instructions from one part of the body to another by way of the blood. For example, the hormone cortisol is released into the bloodstream when a stressor has gone on for a while, and increases can be detected in saliva about 20 minutes after the stressful experience begins. Collecting hormone data is a bit messy (participants must spit into a small vial), and it's not free (you have to pay a lab to analyze the contents), but for some hormones it's not difficult.

Researchers also examine brain activity in research on emotion and motivation. One technique is **electroencephalography (EEG)**, in which the researcher attaches electrodes to the participant's scalp to measure momentary changes in electrical activity of the brain. An EEG is relatively inexpensive, and yields millisecond-by-millisecond information about the activity of cells in the brain area closest to each electrode. However, EEG is best for recording activity from neurons nearest the electrodes on the scalp. As we shall see in Chapter 6, much of the neural activity in emotion occurs much deeper in the brain. Another limitation is that each electrode summates activity over a large area, so EEG supplies precise information about the timing of brain activity, but not its location.

Functional magnetic resonance imaging (fMRI) measures neural activity based on changes in oxygen uptake by cells in the brain (Detre & Floyd, 2001). A brain area that increases its activity uses more oxygen, so the hemoglobin molecules in the nearby blood vessels release their oxygen. Hemoglobin molecules with oxygen respond differently to a magnetic field than do hemoglobin molecules without oxygen, and an fMRI scanner surrounding the head detects this difference. An fMRI image taps into changes in brain activity within around a second after it happens—not on the order of milliseconds as with an EEG, but still good enough for many purposes. It also indicates the location of these changes to within 1 to 3 millimeters, even deep in the brain—far greater spatial accuracy than an EEG (Figure 1.20). The procedure is generally regarded as safe.

An fMRI does have important practical disadvantages. The person must lie motionless in a very noisy device that surrounds the head. Many young children are unable or unwilling to do so, as are people with claustrophobia (fear of closed-in places). Also, fMRI technology is extremely expensive, and few researchers outside hospitals or major research centers have access to it. Furthermore, the procedures restrict the kinds of experiences an investigator can test. Most of our everyday emotional experiences occur while we are walking around and interacting with other people, not while lying motionless in a noisy

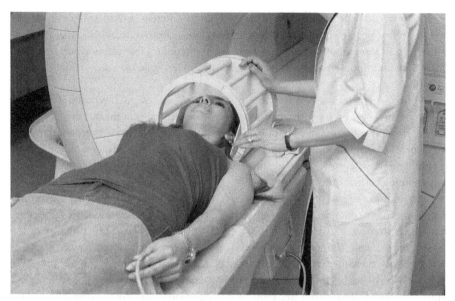

FIGURE 1.20. A functional magnetic resonance imaging scan detects the uptake of oxygen from the blood in brain areas with recent neural activity. The participant must remain motionless in a small, noisy space, which may itself affect emotional experience.

machine, looking at pictures and instructions on a small monitor. As with so many areas of research, we sometimes decide whether to trade the **ecological validity** of a study—the extent to which what happens in the study reflects what really happens in everyday life—for more precise measurement.

Behavioral Observations

When people jump and scream at the sight of a spider, we infer that they are afraid. When they make a fist and shout, we infer anger. Researchers necessarily rely on behavioral observations like these when dealing with nonhuman animals or with human infants too young to talk, but they are often useful with adults as well. For example, researchers often assess nonverbal expressions of emotion such as facial muscle contractions, changes in posture, and tone of voice. If your roommate suddenly grins broadly and begins laughing, you might reasonably infer that that they are amused by something and ask "what's so funny?" (Figure 1.21). Using the Facial Action Coding System (FACS; Ekman & Friesen, 1984), researchers can record which facial muscles contract and for how long and how intensely.

As with the other measures of emotion, coded nonverbal expressions have their limitations. First, people can try to fake or conceal their emotions, with varying degrees of success (Ekman, 2001). Second, coding facial expressions is extremely time intensive. The muscle movements can be subtle, and it takes much training and patience to distinguish all the movements correctly. Also, a typical emotional expression lasts only 1 or 2 seconds, so to catch every instance, you must watch videotapes of a person's behavior many times,

FIGURE 1.21. Researchers may measure facial expressions, such as this expression of amusement, to assess the emotions people feel during a study.

slowing down to catch the exact start and stop of each movement, and then decide which specific muscle movements, called *action units*, are present: Do the inner eyebrows raise? The outer brows? Did the brows contract in the middle? Do the eyes widen? and so forth. It can take 30 to 60 minutes to code a single minute of videotape!

Teams of scientists and engineers have been working to develop computerized FACS coding technology, but the reliability and validity of these programs are not yet fully established. In time, automated FACS coding may be widely accepted, but so far, few researchers are publishing research using these programs (and you should think critically about advertisements for webcams or software programs that claim to do this work automatically).

Which of these measures is best? To some researchers, feelings are the most important aspect of emotion, so self-reports are the gold standard. Others consider feelings too subjective to trust as the ultimate criterion for emotion; these researchers tend to emphasize physiological and/or behavioral measures. Many motivation researchers lean toward experience sampling as a method of accurately capturing motivation in the moment, but these reports still have all the subjectiveness problems of self-reports, so others prioritize studying behavioral choices in the laboratory. As with so many things we can study, the more kinds of evidence we have, the better. For example, if we include behaviors, self-report measures, and physiological measures in a study (often called the "trifecta" of measuring emotion), we can note areas of agreement or disagreement. When measures disagree, we have a problem, because we must decide which measure we're going to trust most. However, that situation can itself lead to interesting new research ideas. In any case, the strength of any conclusion is no better than the quality of measurements that led to it.

SUMMARY

What have we learned so far? Emotion and motivation are complex, elusive, and hard-to-define concepts. Motivation science emphasizes goal-directed behaviors that vary in their energy and direction. Key predictors of this variability include extrinsic versus intrinsic underlying motivational forces, as well as the distinction between goals toward which we strive (approach goals) and outcomes we hope to avoid. We noted that the experience of emotion is one major form motivation can take.

Many psychologists define emotion in terms of the convergence of cognitions/appraisals, feelings, physiological responses, and behaviors, all in response to an eliciting situation. Although such definitions presume these four aspects of emotion hang together much of the time, this is not always the case. As a result, controversy persists about which aspects of emotion are most important, how they are connected to each other, and whether the relationships among different aspects are most consistent with a few universal basic/discrete emotion categories, culturally variable psychological concepts, or a single complex, multidimensional space defined by several appraisal dimensions.

We raised several big questions in this chapter, and didn't give many answers. Welcome to emotion and motivation research! Affective science is an exciting field—many of the big questions are still being addressed, and researchers are actively debating all these issues. The different perspectives are important because they encourage us to ask different kinds of research questions, all of which help us understand these phenomena better. We hope that you will try to keep an open mind about these issues as you work your way through this text, and consider all of the evidence. Perhaps you'll think of a way to integrate perspectives that have been treated as distinct or opposing in the past. At the end of the text, we hope you'll be able to answer the questions "What is emotion? What is motivation?" in a way that satisfies you, while appreciating the complexity of the question.

KEY TERMS

appraisal: cognitive evaluation of what a stimulus or situation means for one's goals, concerns, and well-being (p. 17)

autonomy: core motive to self-direct one's own behavior and feel in control of one's life (p. 6)

basic/discrete emotions: categories of emotional experience, such as fear, anger, and sadness, thought to have evolved in response to specific kinds of threats and opportunities faced by human ancestors. (p. 24)

circumplex model: a model in which emotional feelings form a circle; emotions close to each other on the circle are similar or likely to be experienced at the same time (p. 18)

competence: core motive to apply one's skills to have an impact on the world, to feel capable of handling the demands of the world (p. 6)

component process model: the idea that emotions reflect the intersection of several appraisal dimensions that can be combined in different ways (p. 24)

construct: the underlying psychological phenomenon (process, ability, event) a researcher is aiming to measure. (p. 36)

core affect: a model for describing the feeling aspect of emotion, emphasizing dimensions of pleasantness and arousal (p. 43)

drive: a motivational force that arises when a human biological need (e.g., hunger, thirst) is deprived (p. 17)

ecological validity: extent to which what happens in a study reflects what really happens in everyday life (p. 40)

electroencephalography (EEG): method in which a researcher attaches electrodes to someone's scalp and measures momentary changes in the electrical activity under each electrode (p. 39)

evaluative space model: a model of attitudes, proposing that evaluations of some target's goodness and badness are independent rather than opposites (p. 19)

experience sampling: research method in which participants are asked to report on their experience at random intervals throughout the day (p. 34)

extrinsic motivation: motivation sourced from external incentives and threat of punishment rather than internal forces (p. 5)

functional magnetic resonance imaging (fMRI): research method that measures brain activity based on changes in oxygen uptake from the blood (p. 39)

hedonism: the tendency of human beings (and other organisms) to approach pleasure/reward and avoid pain/punishment (p. 11)

hormones: molecules that carry instructions from the brain to other bodily organs by way of the blood supply (p. 39)

incentives: stimuli in the environment that motivate one to engage in a behavior (p. 7)

intrinsic motivation: motivation that springs from internal needs, forces, and desires rather than incentives or threat of punishment (p. 5)

identified regulation: motivation based on behavior feeling like it is part of one's identity (p. 6)

integrated regulation: motivation that began with rewards and punishments but is transitioning to a more internalized appreciation of this behavior (p. 6)

introjected regulation: motivation based on awareness of societal norms regarding this behavior and wish to avoid internal feelings of shame or embarrassment that might arise if you didn't behave in concordance with these norms (p. 6)

James–Lange theory: view that emotions (especially the feeling aspects of emotions) are the labels we give to the way the body reacts to certain situations (p. 15)

mood: a diffuse, longer-lasting affective state of being not tied to a particular stimulus (p. 21)

motivation: the energy and direction underpinning human behavior and choice (p. 5)

parasympathetic nervous system: branch of the nervous system that conserves energy for later use and facilitating digestion, growth, and reproduction (p. 38)

priming: experimental technique in which mental representations are called to mind (p. 34)

psychological construction: process by which people develop mental concepts linking different aspects of emotion to each other and to eliciting situations; an alternate explanation for the emotion categories used in basic/discrete emotion theory (p. 30)

regulatory focus theory: view that it is important to consider whether a motivation is focused on promoting a desired end state or preventing an undesired end state (p. 8)

relatedness: core motive to be meaningfully socially engaged with other humans (p. 6)

reliability: the repeatability of the results of some measurement, expressed as a correlation between one score and another (p. 35)

self-determination theory: view that human beings are intrinsically motivated to determine their own lives, shaped by the core needs of autonomy, competence, and relatedness (p. 6)

sympathetic nervous system: the fight–flight branch of the autonomic nervous system that readies the body for intense physical activity (p. 38)

validity: whether a test measures what it claims to measure (p. 36)

will: the ability to freely make decisions and choices (p. 11)

THOUGHT/DISCUSSION QUESTIONS

In each chapter we will suggest several thought/discussion questions for you to contemplate. These can be considered on your own or used as a basis for discussion in a study group or in class. In some cases, we do not believe the evidence to date offers a "right" answer. For all questions, however, thinking through your answer requires organizing and analyzing the information from the chapter in a way that will add depth to your studying. We hope you will consider not only what would be good answers to these questions, but also what research would help improve our ability to answer each one.

1. Do you think that emotion is a naturally occurring category, with objective criteria and clear boundaries? What makes some psychological states an emotion? What properties differentiate a state that is an emotion from states that are not emotions? What about motivation? Are boredom, curiosity, relief, fatigue, and sexual excitement more emotional states or motivational ones? Does the concept of emotion help psychology researchers conduct their science, even if the boundaries of this category are not clear-cut?

2. The plots of several movies have revolved around the question of whether robots or computers could someday be capable of experiencing emotion (e.g., *Blade Runner*; *Her*; *Ex Machina*). Assuming infinite possible programming ability, do you think this is possible? What capabilities would the robot or computer need to have to have emotion? How do you think the various emotion theorists we discussed in this chapter would answer this question?

3. Researchers often use film clips, photographs, relived personal experiences, and guided imagery to evoke participants' emotions and prime motivational states in the lab. In what ways might the psychological states elicited by these methods differ from emotions and motivations experienced in real life?

4. Which measure(s) of emotion would you expect to be prioritized by researchers representing each of the major modern theoretical perspectives (basic/discrete emotions, core affect/psychological construction, component process model)? Which measure of emotion, if any, do you think should be the gold standard, and why?

5. Choose an instance from your life in which you made a pivotal decision or pursued an important goal. Are the motivational terms and concepts we covered in this chapter consistent with your experiences? Which are and which are not? What do you think is missing from our account of motivation thus far?

SUGGESTIONS FOR FURTHER READING

Fishback, A. (2022). *Get it done: Surprising lessons from the science of motivation*. Little, Brown.

Fox, A. S., Lapate, R. C., Shackman, A. J., & Davidson, R. J. (2018). *The nature of emotion: Fundamental questions* (2nd ed.). Oxford University Press. Major emotion researchers offer their answers to core theoretical questions about emotion.

James, W. (1884). What is an emotion? *Mind, 9,* 188–205. William James's original article introducing his theory of emotion.

CHAPTER 2

The Evolution of Emotion and Motivation

In Chapter 1, we asked whether a housefly has emotions. Although we don't know how you answered, you could reasonably have said no, and most emotion researchers would agree with you. But let's move up the food chain. Does a snake have emotions? How about a pigeon? A mouse? A housecat? A dog? A chimpanzee?

Your answers to these questions depend on how you define *emotion*. Since we couldn't give you an agreed-on definition in Chapter 1, you won't be surprised to learn that researchers disagree about whether any nonhuman animals experience emotions in the way that humans do and, if so, which do and which do not. But if you said there is no way a snake has emotions, and then you were more inclined to say yes as the animals above got smarter and furrier, your response would be typical. If you said it depends on the emotion (snakes might show some behaviors consistent with fear, but not with nostalgia), your response would also be typical.

A similar story applies to motivation. Houseflies probably don't set conscious goals, and dogs are unlikely to diet. But surely the way that lions get thirsty, and go to great lengths to seek out water, bears some similarity to your willingness to pay seven dollars for a bottle of water at an amusement park in August. You might also note similarities between your cat's love of curling up in front of the fire for a comforting, toasty-warm nap and your own pleasure-seeking behavior on a cold winter afternoon.

Researchers adopting an evolutionary perspective on emotion and motivation believe that evolution has shaped our affective experience of the world, and that by understanding how and why certain emotions and motivations evolved, we can better understand these phenomena in contemporary life. Last chapter we began to consider the many ways that emotion and motivation intersect and overlap. We'll continue that discussion in this chapter, as an evolutionary perspective blends the two phenomena quite a bit.

Soon after developing his theory of evolution, Charles Darwin ([1872] 1998) noted that the expressions of many animals and small children in emotional situations are similar to those of adult humans, and he proposed that emotional expressions are part of our evolutionary heritage (see Figure 2.1). Since Darwin's time, psychologists have debated the role of evolutionary processes in producing the emotions experienced by modern humans. Darwin also speculated that many behaviors of both humans and nonhuman animals operate as evolved **instincts**, innate patterns of behavior that occur automatically, without the need for learning (Darwin, [1859] 1991, [1872] 1998). William James was influenced by Darwin's theory of instincts when he formulated the James–Lange classic theory of emotions. Recall from last chapter that according to this theory, you run away from a bear before you even feel afraid. To James, running away from a scary wild animal was an instinct that unfolded automatically, and made you more likely to survive the encounter and reproduce.

For many psychologists, thinking of affective experiences as products of evolution has strong implications for the kinds of research questions that they ask. They presume that emotions are functional in the evolutionary sense—that at some time far in the past individuals with emotions were more likely to pass their genes on to future generations than were individuals without emotions, so over time genes that enable emotions spread through the population. If we think of emotions in terms of their adaptive functions, we can generate specific predictions about the effects of those emotions in several domains. As we will see, arguments for the adaptive functions of emotions assume that emotions are adaptive because they energize us and point our behavior in certain directions—and as you'll recall from last chapter, motivation is all about the energy and direction underlying behavioral choices.

In this chapter we introduce the broad principles of an evolutionary approach, and we'll consider implications of this approach for how we define and study emotion and motivation. We'll first return to historical approaches to motivation, considering theories about instincts and drives as evolved forces in the push-and-pull of motivated behavior. We will then explain what it means to posit that emotions are functional in the evolutionary sense, and we will contrast two ways in which emotions can be adaptive—by helping the individual survive and thrive, and by facilitating the relationships on which humans (and many other species) depend. We will also consider the different ways modern theories of emotion incorporate an evolutionary perspective. Later, in Chapters 11 and 12, we will consider the possible adaptive functions of several specific emotions, and we'll examine research emerging from these functional accounts.

WHAT IS AN EVOLUTIONARY PERSPECTIVE?

When we talk about an *evolutionary perspective*, what does that mean? Although scientists consider the evidence supporting evolutionary theory overwhelming, the basic tenets and implications of this theory are commonly misunderstood. Let's clear up some basics and then turn to implications for emotion and motivation.

Learning Objectives
- Define the term "adaptation" as it applies to evolutionary theory.
- Summarize the process of natural selection, including the role of genetic mutation.
- List three criteria for calling a gene-based characteristic "functional" in the evolutionary sense, and apply these criteria to evaluating the functionality of a given characteristic.
- Define the term "environment of evolutionary adaptedness (EEA)."

FIGURE 2.1. In developing his theory of evolution, Charles Darwin noted similarities in emotional expressions across several species, including humans. He went on to propose that emotional expressions are part of human nature, rather than being culturally learned.

Our story starts with genes. Genes are lengths of DNA—deoxyribonucleic acid—that each person inherits from both parents (Figure 2.2a). Each gene is like a recipe, describing the ingredients and cooking instructions for a particular protein used by your body. You can think of your whole genome as a cookbook describing how your body should be put together or, if you're more mechanically inclined, as an instruction manual for do-it-yourself furniture. DNA also includes many stretches that do not code for any protein, but that control the speed or timing of action by other parts of the DNA molecule.

Here is an interesting point: when Darwin developed the theory of evolution, he didn't know about genes. Darwin knew there must be some way that traits were passed down from parents to their offspring, but he didn't know how it took place. It wasn't until the 1920s and 1930s that biologists combined Darwin's idea of natural selection with Gregor Mendel's research on the inheritance of traits and started looking for a physical substance that would explain both. The chemical structure of DNA and its role in heredity were not understood until the 1950s. The subsequent research on DNA allowed for Darwin and Mendel's theories to be combined into modern evolutionary theory.

Chromosomes—long strands of DNA containing many genes—come in pairs. In sexual reproduction new chromosomes are copied from parents' chromosomes in a process called replication (Figure 2.2b) and then recombined so that each offspring receives a half-copy of the mother's genes and a half-copy of the father's genes. Genes often come

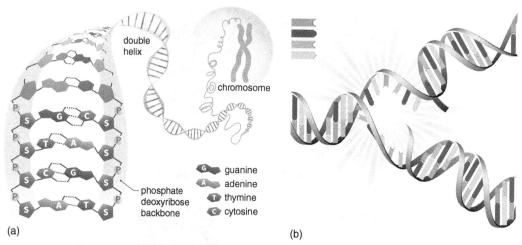

FIGURE 2.2.   Genes are strands of deoxyribonucleic acid, or DNA, that provide recipes for making the proteins that are the building blocks of your body. (a) The double-helix structure of DNA was discovered by James Watson, Francis Crick, Rosalind Franklin, and Raymond Gosling in 1953. (b) In reproduction, strands of the parents' DNA are copied via a process called replication. When a copying error occurs during replication, the result is a mutation.

in multiple different versions, called *alleles*, that occur on the same location of the chromosome and provide recipes for proteins serving the same function, but have slightly different effects (imagine using milk chocolate vs. dark chocolate chips in a cookie recipe). For each gene, because you receive one copy from each parent, you could end up with two copies of the same version, or two different versions.

A traditional example of a genetic effect is eye color. Someone with two genes for blue eyes will have blue eyes, and someone with two genes for brown eyes will have brown eyes. Someone with one of each type will have brown eyes. We say therefore that the gene for brown eyes is dominant. This is a simple example, but a bit misleading, because most of the characteristics that psychologists care about—such as personality, intelligence, or a predisposition to mental illness—depend on many genes as well as many environmental influences. Even eye color reflects contributions by several genes. Also, each gene has multiple effects, not just the one that is easiest to notice or measure. Furthermore, many aspects of the environment—such as exposure to stressful experiences or prolonged inhaling of cigarette smoke—can alter the activation of genes, turning some on and others off (Launay et al., 2009; Tsankova et al., 2007). Even the feeling of being socially isolated alters the activity of many genes (Slavich & Cole, 2013). Genetics is a far more complex field than we once thought.

Sometimes the gene-copying process goes awry, and the copy is off, just by chance. This is called a mutation. Some mutations are a real problem—they disrupt an important process and prevent survival or reproduction. To continue with our cooking analogy, if a cook forgets to put baking soda into a recipe for chocolate chip cookies, the cookies won't rise, and they will hardly be edible. Other mutations don't make much difference. If walnuts are left of out a chocolate chip cookie recipe, for example, the cookies will taste different, but still good.

Occasionally a mutation leads to an improvement, just as accidentally adding a bit more vanilla to the cookies might make them taste better. Maybe a mutation makes the muscles more efficient, so there's a better chance of survival when facing a predator. Maybe the mutation makes neurons communicate with each other more efficiently, so this person is a little quicker to respond to emergencies than everyone else and thus catches more food, attracts better mates, and so on. When this happens, there's a good chance that the person will have more offspring than average, so this version of the gene (when passed on to the children) becomes more common in the next generation. If this keeps up, that mutation ends up in more and more people, until sometime down the road, almost everyone has it.

That's it. To recap, **natural selection** is the process by which random genetic mutations that happen to be problematic are removed from the population (because they cause the individuals who have them to die or underreproduce), whereas mutations that happen to be beneficial spread through the population (because they cause the individuals who have them to have more offspring or to take better care of their relatives, who share their genes). Beneficial characteristics that spread as a result of natural selection are called **adaptations**. Once the genes for an adaptation spread throughout the population, that adaptation tends to persist. Evolution is conservative—only a new mutation that happens to improve on the previous version will replace what's already there, and even that will spread through the population very, very slowly in most cases. If the environment changes so that an adaptation later becomes harmful, natural selection will start to remove the allele for it.

As we noted in Chapter 1, many psychologists' definitions of emotion emphasize that emotions are functional, and certainly quite a lot of our understanding of motivation relates to biological drives that keep us alive and reproducing. From an evolutionary perspective, the term "functional" has a specific meaning. A gene-based characteristic (either a physical feature or a behavior) is functional if it meets one or more of the following criteria:

1. The characteristic increases the probability that you will survive long enough to reproduce.
2. The characteristic increases the probability that you will have more offspring than your neighbor who lacks the characteristic, and these offspring survive and reproduce.
3. The characteristic increases the probability that your relatives will survive and have more offspring. For example, if your genes prompt you to take better care of your relatives, you help them pass on their genes, which are mostly the same as your own. By helping them survive and reproduce, you indirectly spread your own genes.

This is a strict definition of the term "functional." A characteristic is not functional because it makes you happy, because it makes you feel good about yourself, or because it makes you a better person. These effects are great, of course, but from an evolutionary perspective a characteristic is functional only if it leads to increased representation of your genes in future generations.

This has been the source of much confusion. When scientists propose that some characteristic is functional, they are not necessarily arguing that it is desirable or morally right. A gene that made you happy, rich, famous, and sterile would be extremely disadvantageous from an evolutionary standpoint. On the other hand, a gene that helped you produce many children (who were healthy enough to survive) would be adaptive in the evolutionary sense, even if it somehow made you feel unhappy, lonely, and underappreciated. In such cases, it is helpful to explore the mechanism by which some characteristic is adaptive. Understanding the adaptive function of an otherwise undesirable characteristic can even help researchers study ways to alter its expression, so that it doesn't interfere with other goals that are important to people.

Also, if we propose that some characteristic is an adaptation, it doesn't necessarily mean that characteristic is functional now. The characteristic would have been functional in its **environment of evolutionary adaptedness (EEA)**, the time and place in the past when that characteristic spread throughout the population as a result of natural selection. Functionality during a characteristic's EEA is enough to explain why it would have spread through the population, even if its effects seem neutral or harmful now.

For example, humans really, really like fatty, sugary foods (mmm, donut!). We know this affinity has a genetic basis, and it's an important adaptation. Throughout most of the history of life, calorie-rich food has been scarce. A person never knew when he or she would go hungry for a while, so storing energy in the form of fat was a good plan. In that environment, fatty and sugary foods—which contain many calories per unit of volume— were precious resources, to consume whenever possible. It's only in recent years, with these foods readily available in every convenience store, café, snack bar, and fast-food restaurant, that our love of them has become a health problem. Liking the taste of fats and sugars was adaptive in the EEA in which this characteristic evolved, but it may be harmful in modern, resource-rich societies.

This is the end of the detour into the basics of evolutionary theory. Now we can see how it applies to emotion and motivation.

AN EVOLUTIONARY PERSPECTIVE ON MOTIVATION

Learning Objectives
- Distinguish between instincts and drives and explain how drives relate to the concept of homeostasis.
- Critique drive theories of human motivation. Discuss their limitations.
- Summarize Abraham Maslow's hierarchy of needs and articulate how Douglas Kenrick and colleagues expanded upon this theory.
- Describe self-determination theory (SDT) and explain the three psychological needs that lead to self-determination.

Since an evolutionary account of motivation is pretty straightforward and will inform our consideration of the evolutionary nature of emotion, we'll tackle motivation first. In the last chapter we noted that after an early focus on an animating power of will, motivation theorists began to focus more on biology—considering the nature of human instincts, drives, and needs.

To what extent are human beings motivated by basic biological needs to survive and reproduce? Might even complicated patterns of human behavior have instinctual influences at their core (Figure 2.3)? It might seem as though human motivation and behavior

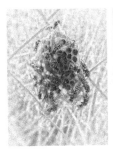

FIGURE 2.3. Innate instincts can govern very complex behaviors in nonhuman animals. Might they also govern complex behavior in human beings?

are too complex to be influenced by evolutionary pressures. But even among nonhuman animals instincts can govern complex behaviors, such as nest-building in birds and hive-building in honeybees. Some theorists, including psychologist William McDougall (1908, 1919), have argued that human beings are *mostly* driven by instincts—that without them we would never engage in volitional behavior. McDougall's list of instincts included not just obviously biological motivations such as hunger and sex, but also behaviors such as laughter, maternal care, gregariousness, and comfort-seeking. He believed that environmental cues trigger these instincts, which elicit emotions, which then pushes the organism toward a certain behavior. For instance, your infant's cry (cue) triggers a parenting instinct (motivation), that elicits feelings of care, concern, and craving (emotions), which lead you to pick up your infant and soothe it (behavior).

The study of instincts dominated motivation research for quite some time. As with many historical theories in psychology, however, the popularity of instinct theory rose and then fell, in part because other scholars began critiquing instinct-focused explanations of behavior as circular and untestable. Instinct theorists tended to observe a behavior and then speculate that since the behavior was observed, human beings must possess an instinct to exhibit that behavior. What does it mean to say that human beings have a social instinct, because they tend to gather in groups? Or that they have an aggressive instinct because they fight? Underscoring this criticism, the list of proposed human instincts expanded to a ridiculous degree, at one point including as many as 6,000 proposed instincts (Bernard, 1924; Dunlap, 1919). When your list includes nearly every human behavior you can think of, and you label each one an instinct rather than a motivated behavior of other sorts, your theory loses its precision and explanatory power.

Instinct theory thus fell out of fashion. However, it was not yet time for biological explanations of behavior reflecting an evolutionary perspective to exit the stage. Instead, drive theory arose to replace instinct theory.

Physiological Needs and Drives

In the *Nightmare on Elm Street* horror movie series, the blade-fingered villain Freddy Krueger visits you in your dreams. In reality, dreams are phantasms that disappear upon awakening and have no real-world effects. In the fictional universe of the *Elm Street* films, however, if Freddy kills you in your dreams, you die in real life too. Pretty early on in

FIGURE 2.4.   Your brain and body have complicated systems for alerting you when you need food, water, or rest. These biological systems are often called drives.

each film, the main characters figure out that they are safe so long as they stay awake, and they spend the rest of the movie unsuccessfully trying to not fall asleep.

Unsuccessfully, because doing so is an impossible task. Stay awake long enough and your body has mechanisms that will drop you into sleep wherever you are—whether you're at the dinner table, swimming in a pool, or driving a car. This is because you have an innate physiological need for sleep, and your body possesses sophisticated levers and mechanisms for detecting when this need is deprived and for driving you toward fulfilling it. This need, and the associated mechanisms for monitoring and fulfilling that need, offer one example of a **drive** (Figure 2.4).

When our drives are satiated, the systems for detecting and fulfilling them are quiescent and do not greatly motivate behavior. When these needs are not met, however, the organism is strongly driven to change its behavior to satiate the need. This process of detecting a biological deficiency and activating motivated behavior to re-establish a stable internal state is known as **homeostasis**. Homeostasis involves complex interacting systems of neurochemicals, hormones, and feedback from our internal organs.

Consider the example of hunger. After you have binged on Friday night pizza (plus ice cream for dessert), your brain detects your fullness, and you are much more likely to camp out on the couch in front of Netflix than you are to engage in further food-seeking behavior. If you instead sleep late on a Sunday and then skip lunch, your brain will register your hunger, and Sunday evening will likely involve cooking or seeing what is available at the dining hall. We can create similar scenarios for thirst, for relief of pain, and (with some additional layers of complexity and many individual differences) for sex.

Thinking about sex as a drive may bring to mind one of the most famous figures in psychology: Sigmund Freud. Actually, Freud was a medical doctor and a physiologist—training that shaped his heavily biological theories of human motivation. Freud was one of the scholars who pushed the field to consider the motivated nature of human behavior, and specifically the biological underpinnings of these drives (Freud, 1957). He argued that drives such as hunger, aggression, and sex were constantly fluctuating between need and satiety. When deficits in fulfilling these needs built up, they led to an uncomfortable excess of energy in the nervous system that was experienced by the individual as anxiety, or some other discomforting mental health symptom. The desire to reduce anxiety then motivated the person to satiate the drive, thereby releasing the energy and bringing relief. This theorizing was the basis for Freud's widely known (though now largely discredited) belief that much anxiety and other psychological distress is rooted in unfulfilled, even unacknowledged, need for sex.

Freud's thoughts on drives were certainly influential, but they were based largely on his own speculations and observation of individual patients under his care. They were *not* based on good science—on systematically collected data or controlled experiments. In contrast, psychologist Clark Hull (1943, 1952) formulated a drive theory of motivation that paved the way for experimental investigation. He saw all bodily needs as summing to a sort of pooled energy, which he called drive, and which he thought related to the energy component of motivation. When needs were unfulfilled, the organism would become energized to satiate the need. This accounts for the energy aspect of motivation, but what about the direction aspect? Hull theorized that the direction of energized behavior reflects habitual, well-learned actions that previously been rewarded, in the individual's experience, by drive satiation. He even got a little mathematical about it, speculating that Behavior = Drive x Habit. The stronger the drive, and the more entrenched the learning that a specific behavior will satiate the drive, the more intense or frequent that behavior will be.

Let's say you take a little mouse, and deprive it of lunch, so it is hungry. You then put that mouse in a maze with food at the end. Because it is hungry, the mouse will be energized to run the maze quickly to get to the food (Figure 2.5). Once the mouse has run the maze a few times and been rewarded (by the hunger-satiating food) for finding its way to the end, learning will build up toward an automatic habit. The key implications of this proposed process are that (1) a hungry mouse should run the maze faster than a full one; and (2) having received rewards for running the maze a few times, the mouse should complete it even faster in the future.

This mouse example is working double time for us here—it demonstrates both Hull's theory and why it was testable. His theory allowed motivation researchers to experimentally manipulate drive and observe its effects on both learning (habit) and behavior. This opened up what some have characterized as a golden age of experimental research on motivation. However, not all the key concepts in Hull's theory are supported by research. For instance,

FIGURE 2.5. Hungry mice run mazes to earn a cheese reward faster than full mice, supporting the drive theory of emotion.

a study by Rosenberg and colleagues (Rosenberg et al., 2021) found that water-deprived mice did *not* solve a maze with water at the end significantly faster than nondeprived mice, as Hull's theory would have predicted. In addition, Hull's theory does not account for all the ways that intrinsic motivation can spur behavior, nor for the fact that human beings often intentionally deprive themselves of biological needs to pursue other goals (for instance, have you ever deprived yourself of sleep in order to fit in more studying or socializing?).

You might also be thinking that drive theory works well for the basic physiological needs that human share with other creatures, but that you also possess more complex needs than hunger, thirst, sleep, pain reduction, and sex. If so, you would be right! Human beings have also evolved to be ultrasocial, to explore, and to manipulate the environment, behavioral tendencies linked to more complex needs. In other words, we also have evolved *psychological* needs.

Psychological Needs

Psychologist Henry Murray (1938) described psychological needs as "predispositions to act" in certain ways, given certain circumstances. As we shall soon see, this description is relevant to emotion as well. Murray included the physiological needs described above as well as needs linked to intrinsic psychological experiences, such as independence, power, and ambition. Theorist Abraham Maslow (1943) further argued that these needs are not equal in terms of importance and priority, but are organized in a hierarchical structure. Physiological needs and need for safety are fundamental, followed by needs for social belongingness and self-esteem, with a state of achievement and transcendence called "self-actualization" beyond that.

The implication of Maslow's theory is that more fundamental needs must be fulfilled before you can really be concerned about the ones further up the hierarchy. For example, you aren't likely to worry about whether your job fulfills your dreams if you're not even sure where your next meal is coming from. Although Maslow did not actually represent his hierarchy of needs as the pyramid that often appears in textbooks (intrepid scholars recently traced the pyramid's origin to a consulting psychologist's article in the management journal *Business Horizons;* Bridgman, Cummings, & Ballard, 2019), the pyramid does illustrate the point that some needs take priority over others, and fulfilling these needs provides a foundation that can then support attention to "higher" needs.

While Maslow's hierarchy of needs is among the most familiar theories to people outside psychology, it has its critics within the field. First, Maslow's theory may have been strongly influenced by his time working with indigenous people of the Blackfoot Nation, although the hierarchy of needs he proposed had a more Western, individualistic spin (the indigenous version prioritized community to a much higher degree; Brown, 2014). Second, despite its lay appeal Maslow's hierarchy has not generated much in the way of empirical research.

Douglas Kenrick and colleagues (Kenrick et al., 2010) have revitalized the proposal for a hierarchy of human needs, however, based on a synthesis of contemporary behavioral science data and evolutionary theory. Think back to the definition of "function" from an evolutionary standpoint, offered earlier in this chapter. What are the elemental needs involved in survival, reproduction, and ensuring your genes are well-represented in future generations? Kenrick and colleagues propose that these elements correspond to the fundamental motives behind much of human behavior (see Figure 2.6). Like Maslow, Kenrick

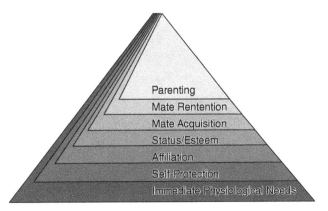

FIGURE 2.6. The renovated pyramid of fundamental motives by Kenrick, Griskevicius, Neuberg, & Schaller, 2010.

and colleagues acknowledge that simply staying alive is crucial for evolutionary fitness; fulfilling basic physiological needs and protecting oneself from harm are at the bottom of the pyramid. The next two levels—affiliation and status—also correspond to levels of Maslow's hierarchy and recognize the crucial role that relationships with groups and communities play in human life. We'll consider this issue more deeply later in the chapter.

One striking feature of the new pyramid is its inclusion of relationships involved in reproduction—namely, mating and parenting. This makes sense, if you think about how we direct our energies and efforts across the lifespan. One of your textbook authors (SRC) always begins her course on motivation and emotion by asking her students: What motivates you? Far and away the most common response, over fifteen years of teaching, is "family." Of course, mating and parenting are crucial for evolutionary fitness, so we should expect to have evolved psychological mechanisms promoting those endeavors. In an update, Kenrick and colleagues now include kin care as an additional fundamental motive (Ko et al., 2020), rounding out the buffet of ways to get your genes into the future.

Perhaps you're wondering, "If mating and parenting are such fundamental motives, why do so many people choose not to have children?" It's a great question! First, most people do have children; even in the United States, where rates are lower than in many other parts of the world, about 85% of women eventually have at least one child (for the record, author MNS is an exception). More important, the theory is that humans should have evolved psychological mechanisms that facilitated having offspring *in the human ancestral environment*. To the extent that the modern environment is different, those mechanisms may not have the same effects. One crucial feature of modern, industrial societies is the widespread availability of birth control, allowing many people to place a barrier between wanting to have sex and having a child. There are ways of fulfilling parenting/kin care motives beyond having children as well, mainly through close involvement with family members' and other loved ones' children (Kenkel, Perkeybile, & Carter, 2017; see Figure 2.7).

Beyond common sense and anecdotes, Kenrick and colleagues review of decades of evidence from evolutionary biology, anthropology, and psychology supporting their argument for mating, parenting, and kin care as some of our ultimate motivations.

FIGURE 2.7. The fundamental motives of parenting and kin care can be fulfilled through close involvement with other people's children, as well as one's own.

Moreover, this taxonomy of needs has generated a rich and growing body of research on the consequences of activating different motives for social cognition and behavior; on the developmental changes in emphasis on these motives across the lifespan; and on ways in which environmental threats and opportunities dynamically interact with fundamental psychological needs (e.g., Cook, Krems, & Kenrick, 2021; Neel et al., 2016; Schaller et al., 2017).

Another theory of psychological needs, with both lasting power and supportive empirical evidence, grew out of some research discussed in the last chapter. This work revealed that extrinsic motivational forces could not explain all behavior; instead, intrinsic motivation for learning, for self-direction, for mastery, and for affiliation drives much human behavior, and even that of simpler species. **Self-determination theory**, proposed by Richard Ryan and Edward Deci, argues that human beings possess innate psychological needs for autonomy, competence, and relatedness (Ryan & Deci, 2000; Ryan & Deci, 2020). While the adaptive function of these needs is less glaringly obvious than it is for biological needs such as hunger and thirst, Ryan and Deci propose that human beings evolved to be motivated to seek out psychosocial experiences that are necessary for mental health and well-being, and thereby reflect core human motivations (Ryan et al., 2021). While these needs do not have *direct* impact on one's survival or reproduction, these theorists argue that human ancestors who were able to choose their own behaviors freely, who were competent in their environment, and who were socially connected would have had advantages in the living-and-mating game. You might be able to imagine a number of ways in which someone who was happier and more fulfilled might also be more successful in procuring resources and attracting mates. Let's consider each of these briefly in turn.

The concept of autonomy is baked right into the name of this theory: human beings desire to determine their own path, to feel in control of their lives. Behavior is autonomous when it is freely chosen and in line with what one perceives to be one's own motivations and values (Ryan & Deci, 2017). Greater levels of perceived autonomy in one's life are robustly associated with psychological well-being (Fischer & Boer, 2011), and teacher practices that emphasize student autonomy are associated with better educational outcomes (Ryan & Deci, 2020; Pekrun, 2006).

Competence refers to the feeling that one is an instrument of change in the world, applying one's skills to good effect, and that these skills are increasing over time (Figure 2.8). Thus, competence encompasses both self-efficacy and mastery (Ryan & Deci, 2017). When people feel like their skills are an exact match to the challenge before them—when they have to apply every bit of focus and skill to the task at hand—they tend to report a cluster of positive feelings. Time seems to stop; self-concerns and worries disappear; and they become "one with" the activity. This feeling, dubbed **flow** by researcher Mihaly Csikszentmihalyi (pronounced "chick-sent-me-HAI-ee"), has been studied extensively in the context of intrinsic motivation across activities from athletics to art to surgery (Csikszentmihalyi, 2020; Nakamura & Csikszentmihalyi, 2009). People report experiencing flow to be so pleasurable that they regularly seek it out, though the data are still unclear as to whether flow results in better performance in addition to greater enjoyment of the activity. (e.g., Admiraal et al., 2011; Guo et al., 2007).

FIGURE 2.8. Human beings share a psychological need for competence, feeling both effective in the present and like their skills are getting better over time.

Need for relatedness (or belongingness) completes the self-determination theory triad. Humans rely on each other for the most basic survival needs. Somewhat like ants and bees, humans are *ultrasocial*, conducting almost all the business of life in highly cooperative groups (Campbell, 1983). Paleoanthropological evidence, as well as studies of modern hunter-gatherers, shows that until recently the human way of life included acquiring food, raising and educating children, and protecting against predators and other threats using carefully coordinated teamwork among dozens of people or more (Eibl-Eibesfeldt, 1989; Wilson & Sober, 1998). Even now, in big, industrialized cities where one can go days at a time without talking to anyone, it would be impossible to survive without relying on hundreds of other peoples' efforts. Humans simply are not built to survive alone; social ostracism (Williams, 2007) and loneliness (Hawkley & Cacioppo, 2010) are negatively associated with both mental well-being and physical health.

Hopefully you have already noticed all the intersections of emotion and motivation that emerge when we adopt an evolutionary perspective. From Darwin's thoughts on instincts informing James's theory of emotions, to McDougall's *environmental trigger → motivational instinct → emotion → behavior* model, to the degree to which pleasantness and unpleasantness define so much of what motivates us, emotions and motivation are deeply intertwined (Beall & Tracy, 2017). Fully informed by an evolutionary perspective on motivation and how this perspective melds emotion and motivation, let's now turn to research on emotion specifically.

AN EVOLUTIONARY PERSPECTIVE ON EMOTION: EMOTIONS AS ADAPTATIONS

Learning Objectives

- Articulate what it means to assume emotions are adaptations, and identify some common misperceptions surrounding emotions and evolutionary theory.
- Compare and contrast some intrapersonal (within a person) and interpersonal (social) functions of emotions.

What does it mean to say that emotions evolved? When researchers say this, they are proposing that emotions are adaptations. Thus:

- Genes provide our capacity to experience emotions;
- The genes needed for emotions began as random mutations long ago;
- On average, individuals with emotions had more offspring than individuals without emotions, and/or took better care of their genetic relatives in such a way that their relatives had more offspring; and
- Because of this process of natural selection, the genes supporting emotions spread through later generations to become typical of the human species.

The proposal that emotions are adaptations has important implications for how we define and study them. One implication would be that emotions are part of human nature—that people everywhere share at least some aspects of emotion. It is possible for a characteristic to be an adaptation without being a human universal. For example, people in many tropical areas of Africa and Asia evolved genes for sickle-shaped blood cells because these cells are malaria resistant. Unfortunately, sickle-shaped blood cells also break easily, so if malaria isn't a problem where you live, the gene is harmful. Even in malaria-infested areas, having one gene for sickle cells is helpful, but having two is fatal. Thus, sickle-cell anemia is an adaptation only seen in a small proportion of humans. However, researchers taking an evolutionary perspective generally propose functions that are relevant for all humans to some degree, and these aspects of emotions are expected to be universal.

If emotions are the product of natural selection, then we must consider the possibility that other animals have them as well. We share many features with other animals because of shared evolutionary history. Like all female mammals, humans capable of pregnancy produce milk to feed their infants. Like most other primates, people have opposable thumbs that allow us to pick up objects easily. The functions proposed for some emotions are relevant to other animals as well as humans, and these emotions could have ancient roots. If the function of fear is to help you escape from predators (Öhman & Mineka, 2003), then fear would be adaptive for any animal that could become some other animal's lunch—in other words, almost any animal species. If the function of pride is to claim high status within one's group (Shariff & Tracy, 2009), then we should see pride in group-living species with a social hierarchy, but not necessarily in solitary species. If we inherited the same mechanisms for emotion as did some other animals, this means that animals are fair game (so to speak) for research. As we shall see, this has resulted in much interesting work.

This is not to say that human and nonhuman animal emotions are likely to be identical. Recall our discussion last chapter about an emotion's many aspects. The argument above applies to some aspects better than others. While you may be able to observe physiological changes and behavior consistent with fear in a cat or a mouse, we have no idea what (if anything) the animal is feeling inside. It is highly unlikely that that the creature consciously labels what it's experiencing ("oh gosh, I'm so scared!"), or engages in sophisticated appraisal of *why* it feels that way ("I wonder why I'm so jumpy right now?"). Comparative psychologist Eliza Bliss-Moreau (2017) has argued that rather than looking for "fear" in nonhuman species, we should seek to identify the neurobiological and physiological mechanisms by which an animal withdraws from threat. Neuroscientist Joseph LeDoux (2015) refers to this as a "defensive circuit" of brain and behavior. We should also remain open to the possibility that nonhuman animals may have evolved different emotional response patterns, in response to different adaptive problems than humans faced. In applying an overly human lens to our study of affect in animals, we risk missing some very interesting phenomena (Bliss-Moreau, 2017).

In proposing that emotions are adaptations, it's also helpful to be clear on what that does *not* mean. This proposal does not assume that every episode of emotion will lead to desirable outcomes, especially in the modern world. You may be asking yourself, if emotions are adaptive, why do people do such stupid things when they're angry? This is a good question. Theorists have proposed that the adaptive function of anger is to communicate that we are not receiving the level of respect and consideration we deserve, and assert our expectation of better treatment (Sell et al., 2017). In intense anger we may feel an impulse to yell at or physically intimidate the person who has offended us. In the modern world, the offense in question is often trivial, yet we possess tools that can inflict damage way out of proportion to that offense (e.g., guns, fast-moving cars). In the escalating conflict we may get hurt ourselves, or end up in prison. Neither of these outcomes is good for fitness. However, anger presumably evolved in an environment where offenses such as stealing food or disrespecting someone's place in society could threaten survival and chances of reproducing. In this situation, on average, communicating anger might have helped protect your possessions and reputation, so that others would know not to bother you again. In the next chapter we will consider how the adaptive function of anger might interact with features of the physical and cultural environment, amplifying or diminishing people's tendency toward violence when they are insulted (Cohen et al., 1996).

Saying that emotions are adaptations also doesn't mean that emotions are identical everywhere. It is possible for an adaptation to be universal, and yet to manifest differently in various cultures. For example, although humans evolved to like high-fat foods, different cultures satisfy this craving in different ways depending on what's available. In some cultures, such as the United States, red meat supplies much fat. In other cultures, dairy products meet this need, and in yet other cultures it's met by high-fat vegetables such as avocadoes, olives, and nuts. Dietary preferences vary so much from culture to culture that you might easily think humans hadn't evolved any food preferences at all, despite underlying consistency in the chemical structure of fats and how people respond to them. The evidence for cultural differences in emotion is just as rich as the evidence for cross-cultural similarities, so something similar is probably happening.

Also, some aspects of our emotions could be universal without actually being adaptive. A single mutation typically has several different effects. Some of those effects may be beneficial, some harmful, and some neutral. A characteristic that is itself neutral, but caused by a mutation that also causes some beneficial trait, will be carried along into the population as though it were adaptive. For an obvious but trivial example, the genes that cause your liver to produce useful activities also cause it to be brown. The color of an internal organ is neither beneficial nor harmful. Such characteristics are referred to as **byproducts** of natural selection (Buss et al., 1998).

For example, infants of all mammalian species share certain physical features—big heads, stubby limbs, big cheeks, and tiny noses—that adult mammals respond to with tenderness and nurturing (Figure 2.9; Lorenz, 1971). The technical term for this set of features is *cuteness*—we're not making this up. Mammals are thought to have evolved emotional responses to cuteness because those responses facilitate taking care of one's own offspring (Hildebrandt & Fitzgerald, 1979). Among humans, these caregiving responses are also easily elicited by the cuteness of other species. Our emotional responses to kittens, puppies, and the like prompt the sale of millions of calendars and posters every year, not to mention a huge industry in products for pets, and are responsible for

FIGURE 2.9. Although many people have a strong emotional reaction to these baby animals, that reaction is likely a byproduct of natural selection rather than an adaptation.

pet-sharing social media accounts being some of the most-followed on the internet. This doesn't mean that humans have a kitten-loving gene, or that loving kittens is adaptive in the evolutionary sense. These emotional responses are more likely to be byproducts of responses that prompt caring for our offspring and young kin, who share the features of cuteness with kittens. In discussing any aspect of emotion from an evolutionary perspective, the possibility that it is a byproduct, rather than an adaptation, should always be considered.

Functions of Emotion

If emotions are adaptations, what kinds of functions might emotions serve? In this section we distinguish between two major categories—intrapersonal functions of emotion and interpersonal or social functions of emotion.

Intrapersonal Functions of Emotion

In many theories adopting an evolutionary perspective, psychologists have emphasized the **intrapersonal functions of emotion**. The term "intrapersonal" means "within person," so an intrapersonal function is one that directly benefits the individual experiencing the emotion. In the example we gave earlier, fear is functional because it helps save the life of the frightened person, facilitating that person's escape from a predator or some other physical threat. Fear does this by changing things within the person, including cognitive biases, physiological conditions, and behavioral responses (Figure 2.10).

When the function of an emotion is intrapersonal, then the situation eliciting the emotion poses a problem for the individual's fitness, and the effects of the emotion within that individual increase the chance that he or she will behave in a way that solves the problem. The problem might be a roommate who steals your food. If you get angry and

FIGURE 2.10.   Fear promotes physiological, cognitive, and behavioral changes that facilitate escaping from physical danger. Because escape directly promotes the frightened individual's adaptive fitness, this is an example of an intrapersonal or within-person function of emotion.

reclaim the food, that solves the problem. Or perhaps the food has begun to rot and would make you sick if you ate it. If you feel disgust when you smell the food and don't eat it, the problem is solved. The process is more complicated than that, of course. Between detecting the problem and resolving it lie dozens of more specific processes, including perceptual shifts, activation of relevant memories, biases in cognitive processing, and physiological changes, all of which facilitate an appropriate behavioral response (Levenson, 1999). But the idea is that the behavioral response facilitated by the emotion directly resolves the problem, or at least has a good chance of doing so.

Many negative emotions are explained well in terms of intrapersonal functions. The most widely accepted explanation of disgust also involves intrapersonal functions, just as for fear. However, intrapersonal functions fail to account for many other emotions, including positive emotions such as love and pride and desire, and self-conscious emotions such as embarrassment and shame. This observation prompted researchers to consider another kind of function.

Social Functions of Emotion

We considered how very social human beings are above, when we discussed our psychological need for belongingness. In other ultrasocial species, cooperative groups generally consist of closely related individuals. For example, in a bee colony all bees are the offspring of the same queen. They are so closely related that from a genetic standpoint, they have more to gain by working together than by trying to fend for themselves. Among humans, however, typical groups include individuals who are not as closely related. Moreover, throughout most of human history, people spent their entire lives in a tribe of, say, a hundred people. The need to cooperate with many unrelated individuals over long periods of time poses interesting challenges. Several researchers have suggested that emotions help solve these problems. The **social functions of emotion** support the committed, interdependent, and complex relationships among people that in turn, help us to survive and pass on our genes (Keltner & Haidt, 1999; Keltner, Haidt, & Shiota, 2006; Sznycer, 2019).

Consider love. Humans feel strong emotions toward the people they depend on and who depend on them—families, romantic partners, children, and close friends. What is the function of love? This question had emotion theorists stumped for a long time. It feels nice some of the time, but as we said earlier, feeling nice isn't a valid function from an evolutionary point of view. In a series of studies, Beverly Fehr and Jim Russell (1991) asked research participants to identify the kinds of people toward whom they felt love, and to describe what love meant to them in that context. Fehr and Russell found that when people talk about loving someone, they typically mean that they are committed to that person's well-being. We might say that the function of love is to help build a sense of commitment in our important relationships, so that we're prepared to help each other out the next time a group effort is needed. It is comparably easy to understand how the motivational and emotional properties of sexual desire, mate selection, and mate competition benefit reproduction, though these been the focus of less research in emotion science than negative emotions (Al-Shawaf et al., 2016).

Even negative emotions may serve important social functions. Think about the last time you felt embarrassed. What function could embarrassment have, other than making you feel miserable? We don't know what happened to make you feel embarrassed, but you probably violated a social convention or norm (Figure 2.11). Maybe you slipped and fell in front of a bunch of people. Maybe you accidentally knocked something over. Maybe you burped loudly in public. Your display of embarrassment lets people know that you realize you made a mistake, you didn't do it on purpose, and you feel bad about what happened (Keltner & Buswell, 1997). This display makes people more inclined to like and trust you, ensuring that you won't be ostracized by the group for whatever weird thing you did.

In these examples, love and embarrassment have something in common. Both emotions help establish and stabilize relationships with other people. These emotions do not arise because our lives are in imminent physical danger (although a well-timed display of embarrassment after accidentally offending someone might protect you against a confrontation), nor do they lead directly to material resources such as food and shelter. Sometime in the future, however, your survival may depend on the relationships that these emotional displays supported, and emotional commitment to mates and offspring helps increase the chance that our genes will make it successfully into future generations.

We have distinguished social functions from intrapersonal functions conceptually, but an emotion can be functional in both ways. Earlier we described an intrapersonal function of anger—protecting your own resources against theft or vandalism. However, anger may have a relationship-building function as well. Not every episode of anger leads to a violent attack. Suppose someone close to you does something hurtful or offensive,

FIGURE 2.11. Embarrassment feels awful, but sends an important message to other people that we value their opinion and realize we've done something silly (such as stumbling and falling while walking to accept a major award).

making you angry. If you show that person your anger, they will realize what has happened. If the person values the relationship, they may apologize or find a way to repair the damage. At the least, they can avoid repeating the mistake. These constructive expressions of anger can be good for relationships (Tafrate, Kassinove, & Dundin, 2002).

In summary, emotions can be functional (in the evolutionary sense) in many ways. They can benefit individuals directly, by promoting behavior that will solve a problem. Emotions can also benefit individuals indirectly, by supporting relationships with other people. Both types of function stand in stark contrast to the image of emotions as irrational, destructive forces, and explain why they play such important roles in our lives.

ROLE OF EVOLUTION IN MODERN THEORIES OF EMOTION

There is one point on which all modern theories of emotion agree—that at least some aspects of emotion are functional adaptations, part of human nature. Thus, all theories include an evolutionary perspective. The disagreement (which is intense) revolves around which aspects of emotion are the product of our evolutionary heritage and how those aspects are adaptive.

In this section we discuss several ways in which emotions might enhance human fitness, as articulated in different theories of emotion. Remember that these may not be mutually exclusive. Each explanation emphasizes a different aspect of emotional responding, and just as in Chapter 1, these explanations are not incompatible. We'll discuss the evidence relevant to each approach and let you evaluate the claims.

Learning Objectives

- Describe the affect infusion model. Give an example from everyday life that illustrates its arguments.
- Explain what is meant by the term "superordinate neural program" and relate it to basic emotion theory.
- Evaluate the evidence for and against emotional response coherence.
- Explain the phylogeny of emotions.

The Signal Value of Emotional Feelings

When you're in a cheerful mood, how do you feel about your situation? Would you evaluate the same situation differently if you were in a bad mood? According to the **affect infusion model** (Forgas, 1995), emotional feelings influence our judgments and decisions in a variety of important ways. This explanation of emotions' function emphasizes the valence aspect of emotional feelings, and their value as a signal to the individual about what is going on in the environment. A positive, happy mood tells us that we are safe, things are going well, and we should be on the lookout for opportunities. A negative, distressed mood tells us something has gone wrong; we need to slow down, find the problem that is making us feel bad, and either avoid it or take steps to correct it. In each case, emotional feelings prompt us to ask why we are feeling that way (Russell, 2003). This draws our attention toward features of the environment that are congruent with our mood, and evokes mood-congruent thoughts and memories (Forgas, 1995). Once a plausible cause of the mood is identified, we can act appropriately toward it.

The evidence for this process is strong. Many studies have found that when people are in a good mood, they tend to wear rose-colored glasses in evaluating people and things around them (Pham, 2007). When in a bad mood, people tend to see the world in a more negative light. This is true even when the objective reason for the mood has nothing to do with the target being evaluated. For example, participants in one product evaluation study liked a set of stereo speakers more if they listened to happy, cheerful music through it than if they heard music inducing a bad mood (Gorn, Goldberg, & Basu, 1993). In another study, participants who had just written for several minutes about a negative personal experience perceived the slant of a real hill (the study was done outdoors, on a college campus) as steeper than did those who had written about a positive experience (Figure 2.12; Riener et al., 2011).

Most work on affect infusion has examined people's responses to material objects, abstract arguments, or people presented in media or in hypothetical situations. One compelling recent study asked whether the same phenomena can be detected in real-life social interactions. Megan Goldring and Niall Bolger (2021) asked 311 married or cohabitating heterosexual couples to complete daily mood and relationship quality diaries during the weeks before and after one partner took the bar exam—an experience most people find stressful (Figure 2.13).

The results of this study supported the affect infusion model in several ways. First, each participant's own mood predicted their rating of their relationship quality that day, consistent with the basic affect infusion process (better moods linked to better evaluations of the relationship). Second, each participant's relationship quality ratings were also impacted by *their partner's* mood on a given day; the researchers called this phenomenon "affect diffusion." Intriguingly, yet consistent with previous research on individual-level affect infusion effects, the impact of mood on relationship judgments diminished when

FIGURE 2.12. Two studies by Riener and colleagues (2011) demonstrated that people perceive a hill like this as steeper, and therefore more difficult to climb, when they are in a negative mood compared to when they are in a positive mood.

FIGURE 2.13.   Taking the bar exam is a stressful time for aspiring lawyers. One study took advantage of this naturally occurring stressor to study emotions.

there was a clear explanation for the mood. Specifically, as the bar exam approached and the exam-taking partner grew increasingly stressed, moods impacted relationship ratings much less. The authors propose a modified affect infusion model they call the dyadic affect infusion/diffusion (DAID) model. Mood not only influences your own judgments, but the moods of people close to you can diffuse (spread) and affect your judgments as well.

Affect valence influences not only the direction of evaluation, but also how people process information from the world around them more generally (Forgas, 1995). When they are in a good mood people tend to be on cognitive autopilot, often relying on effort-saving shortcuts such as stereotypes (Bodenhausen, Kramer, & Süsser, 1994), event scripts (Bless et al., 1996), and similar kinds of heuristics. A positive mood promotes reliance on the current "default setting" for cognition, though recent studies suggest that under certain circumstances, a different "default setting" for cognition can be primed than the person would normally use (Ray & Huntsinger, 2017). When people are in a bad mood, they tend to process information more cautiously and critically. For example, studies consistently indicate that people in an experimentally elicited sad mood evaluate persuasive messages more carefully, convinced by strong arguments but not weak ones, whereas people in a happy mood are equally convinced by strong and weak arguments (e.g., Bless et al., 1990).

In sum, this perspective on the adaptive function of emotions holds that feelings are important because they provide an overall evaluation of the environment as good, bad, or somewhere in between; they guide our attention to features of the current situation that might explain our mood; and they promote retrieval of mood-congruent memories and ideas that will help us respond appropriately to the situation. Notably, these effects may not stay within the individual, also spreading to one's social interaction partners. An emphasis on emotional feelings links this perspective to core affect/psychological construction theories of emotion. The emphasis on searching in the environment for an explanation of one's current mood also connects this perspective to the classic Schachter–Singer research.

Emotions as Superordinate Neural Programs

Another major explanation of emotions' adaptive function weights all the aspects of emotion equally, rather than focusing on feelings. This explanation is strongly influenced by modern thinking in evolutionary psychology (Tooby & Cosmides, 2008), while also descended from a long line of theories of the adaptive functions of basic or discrete emotions (e.g., Levenson, 1999; Tomkins, 1963). This perspective emphasizes the information-processing aspect of the brain, an organ that is specialized to take in information from the outside world, process that information, and decide what to do about it. In this way, the brain has much in common with a computer. Like a computer, the brain exists to gather data and manipulate those data according to some established principles to provide output. In our case, that output is behavior. This is just a fancy way of saying that our brains exist to help us understand the situation we're in and decide how to act. This point is not particularly controversial.

The question of where the specific information-processing principles come from is more controversial, however. According to evolutionary psychologists, many of these principles (although by no means all of them) are part of human nature—they are encoded into our genes in such a way that almost everyone develops them. In this proposal, the brain is packed with many little information-processing programs, each serving a specific purpose. We seem to have such a program for detecting faces (Kanwisher, 2000), another for noticing when we've made a mistake (Hajcak & Foti, 2008), another for risk evaluation (Tooby & Cosmides, 2006), and one for figuring out what other people are thinking (Baron-Cohen, 1995), for example.

In certain kinds of situations, it is important to coordinate all these little programs to accomplish some overarching goal quickly and efficiently, and according to this perspective, emotions serve this purpose. Researchers John Tooby and Leda Cosmides (2008) define emotions as **superordinate neural programs** activated in certain kinds of situations with serious implications for fitness. The job of these superordinate programs is to activate any little programs (we'll call them subroutines) that will help resolve the situation, and to inhibit any subroutines that would interfere with resolving the situation.

This is where the computer analogy becomes helpful. Let's say that you're on your computer, writing a term paper. You're probably using a word-processing program. Given that the function of word-processing programs is to help people write documents such as letters, essays, or textbooks, it is useful for those programs to make sure you spell words correctly. When you open the software, it activates a spell-checker that is in your operating system (this depends on your computer—just go with us here). The spell-checker is activated by other programs as well, such as web browsers and presentation software. However, the spell-checker is unnecessary in accounting software, since you're probably working with numbers. In this analogy, the spell-checker is the subroutine, which is activated by the word-processing program, but is not activated by the accounting software.

What are some possible subroutines the human mind might contain? Some of these might be calculate route to home; calculate route to place where you found your last meal; prioritize self-protection goal; prioritize caregiving goal; kin-detection algorithm; animal-detection algorithm; distance measurement algorithm; mating preference algorithm; eye-contact detector; physiological arousal mechanisms (which supply energy to your muscles); and physiological calming mechanisms. We could continue, but you get the idea.

Let's consider a situation with powerful implications for survival and reproduction. You're walking through the forest alone, and you hear padding footsteps behind you (Figure 2.14). First you need to find out whether you're really in danger. An animal-detection algorithm would be helpful. You might be more biased toward interpreting some subtle image as a threat than you would if you felt safe and secure (Maner et al., 2005). If you see a predator, you need to know how far away it is, so the distance measurement algorithm should be activated immediately. In contrast, the algorithm for mating preferences is not currently useful and should be inhibited. Your favorite celebrity crush could flash a smile at you, but unless that person is carrying a handy weapon, you probably won't pay much attention.

Certain memories should be activated, and others should be inhibited. You may suddenly find yourself thinking about home and how to get there, or about people who have taken care of you in the past (Mikulincer, Gillath, & Shaver, 2002). You're probably not thinking about where you last had lunch—that is not a helpful memory right now. Your self-protection goal will become salient. Your kin-detection algorithms may kick in

FIGURE 2.14. Walking through the woods alone when you hear footsteps coming up behind you might introduce a host of reactions that would help you escape the situation should it prove threatening.

to help you decide which relatives you should try to assist, and who can fend for themselves (Burnstein, Crandall, & Kitayama, 1994).

If you are in the presence of a predator, what should you do? Your options are to stay hidden and hope it doesn't see you; to run away; to fight it out; and to play dead. Which of these is your best bet depends on the situation, and a useful program should help you determine what to do. An eye-contact detector might kick in to help determine whether the predator sees you (Carter et al., 2008). If not, then staying very still is a good plan, and you may feel as though you were frozen in place. If the predator sees you and is moving in your direction (there's that distance detector), you should try to escape. In this case, physiological arousal mechanisms will activate to deliver extra sugar and oxygen to your muscles (Sapolsky, 1998). If the predator sees you and you are cornered, you should prepare to fight, and you may feel a powerful urge to attack. If the animal is a mother bear defending her young, you could play dead and hope she won't attack someone who is no longer perceived as a threat. According to Cosmides and Tooby, the activity of all these subroutines is coordinated by a superordinate neural program called *fear*.

A few interesting points emerge from this way of thinking about emotion. First, note that to explain what we meant by *superordinate neural program*, we had to focus on a specific emotion—fear. In this model there is no such thing as emotion, generally speaking; there are only separate superordinate emotion programs, each of which has its own properties. This links the model closely to basic/discrete emotion theories.

Another implication of the superordinate program model is that no one aspect of emotion is the gold standard for measurement. According to Tooby and Cosmides (2008), emotion is not reducible to one single aspect, such as feeling, physiology, or behavior. Instead, emotions are defined as the entire package of effects elicited by certain kinds of situations and serving an adaptive function in those situations. More modern theories focus more on how emotions *coordinate* existing functions like attention, perception, memory, and energy allocation (Al-Shawaf et al., 2016) rather than assuming that the subroutines themselves are equivalent to an emotion.

Finally, again consistent with basic/discrete emotion theory, the superordinate program model emphasizes specific adaptive function as a key part of each emotion's definition. Identifying the likely function of some emotion allows researchers to predict the situations in which that emotion should emerge, as well as its effects in many different domains (as we did above for fear).

If such emotions do exist, how do we know which ones they are? Several criteria have been proposed by basic/discrete emotion theorists. We focus here on those that have led to the most research. One criterion is that these emotions should be universal among humans and may be present in other species as well. If an emotion is an evolved part of human nature, then except for people with brain injuries, genetic mutations, or other anomalies, everyone should have the capacity to experience it. The alternative is that only people in certain cultures, and not others, show any signs of experiencing that emotion. Finding evidence of an emotion in all societies is no guarantee of evolutionary origin, but if it only appears in a few societies that would suggest it is socially constructed rather than a built-in aspect of human nature.

A second criterion is that people should have a distinct, built-in way of expressing the emotion, such as facial expression, tone of voice, and other behaviors. In accordance with the first criterion (similarity across cultures), it is important to demonstrate that people across many cultures express the emotion, and interpret these expressions, in the same or at least a similar way. We shall consider this topic in detail in Chapter 5.

A third criterion is that the emotion should be evident early in life. For example, we would not consider nostalgia or patriotism basic emotions because they typically emerge in adulthood, if at all. How early must an emotion occur to qualify? This is a matter of controversy. Newborns show generic distress and pleasure, but not much else. They do not smile or laugh, although they do respond to a parent's happy tone of voice by opening their eyes more widely (Mastropieri & Turkewitz, 1999). Perhaps they feel happiness, perhaps not. Smiling and frowning begin to emerge within two or three months (Izard, 1994). Fear expressions become distinct from distress expressions by age six months, but anger expressions emerge gradually over a much longer time. How early is early enough for something to qualify as an emotion by this standard?

Potentially the most important criterion is that each emotion should be physiologically distinct. This could involve a particular profile of effects in the body and/or activation of a unique network within the brain. As we will see in Chapter 6, the notion that each basic/discrete emotion can be linked to activation in a particular chunk of brain tissue has been discredited. Nevertheless, the question of whether basic emotions are characterized by distinct patterns of activity in the brain and/or body remains an open, and difficult, question.

Do Different Aspects of Emotion Hang Together?

A repeated question has arisen regarding the extent to which the various aspects of emotion (appraisals, behavior/physiology, expression, and feeling) "hang together." Recall that different theories of emotion offer different predictions about this, with basic/discrete emotions theory betting on stronger correlations and the core affect/psychological construction approach betting on weaker ones.

Initial studies of **emotional response coherence**, or the extent to which self-reports of emotion predict physiological changes and simple behaviors like facial expressions, offered only weak evidence for this claim (Bradley & Lang, 2000). In these studies, researchers measured people's sympathetic nervous system arousal while they performed a task, like watching an emotional film, and then asked them to rate how strong their emotional feelings were during the task. They would then study whether the people who had the strongest sympathetic nervous system reactions were the same people who reported feeling the strongest emotion. Many researchers found little relationship—self-reports of emotion and sympathetic arousal only weakly predicted each other, and sometimes they were inversely related.

Think about this for a minute, however. Let's say that Iris, for example, reported very strong feelings while watching an emotional film, relative to all the other participants, but she showed relatively weak increases in physiological arousal. Is that the same as saying that her arousal did not go up at the same time that her own self-report of emotion increased? Not at all. Here we run into one of the big problems in emotion research—self-reports are one of the gold standards we use for other measures, but we know they are subjective. Iris's idea of strong feelings may be different from other participants', but as long as her own self-reports of emotion and her arousal seem to hang together over time, the coherence hypothesis is in good shape.

Researchers in one study have carefully tested this *within-subject* approach to emotional response coherence (Mauss et al., 2005). A within-subject approach is helpful because it avoids comparing each participant's self-rating to everyone else's; instead, each participant's self-rating at one time is compared to their own self-ratings at other times (the same is true for physiological arousal). In the study, participants watched a five-minute film clip that went from funny to sad and back to funny again, three times. Each time, participants' cardiovascular activation (a composite of several measures) and skin conductance level (a measure of sympathetic nervous system activation) were measured throughout the film. Once they just watched the film; another time they used a handheld rating dial to indicate, continuously, how amused they felt throughout the film; another time they used the same dial to indicate, again continuously, how sad they felt throughout the film. Facial expressions of amusement and sadness were coded during the first viewing of the film as well.

Afterward, the researchers asked whether people's self-reports of emotion, facial expressions, and physiological responses tended to travel consistently together over the course of the film. The results are illustrated in Figure 2.15. Self-reported amusement experience correlated strongly with amusement expression over time (average within-subject $r = .73$), as did sadness experience and expression ($r = .74$). Self-reported amusement showed a small positive correlation with cardiovascular arousal ($r = .22$) and a moderate positive correlation with skin conductance ($r = .51$), suggesting participants' amusement was consistently accompanied by sympathetic activation. Self-reported sadness was unrelated to cardiovascular activation over the course of the film, but it was negatively related to skin conductance ($r = -.39$), suggesting that sadness was associated with decreased sympathetic activation. Correlations of facial expressions with the physiological measures followed a pattern similar to that for self-reports and physiology.

This study yielded much better evidence of coherence than had been found before. But is it strong enough to declare victory for the basic emotion perspective? Many of the correlations are statistically significant, but they vary widely in size. Notably, the average within-subject correlations of facial expression and subjective experience—the amusement- and sadness-specific measures—were higher than the correlations of either with physiology. In psychology researchers rarely expect perfect correlations or anything close. In this case, however, the results are ambiguous, and you could be either impressed or unimpressed with the correlations.

In a follow-up study (fifteen years later), some of these same researchers conducted a similar study, this time using different films (Brown et al., 2020). The findings were similar; moreover, coherence was greatest during more emotionally intense films. In addition, the researchers asked whether participants who showed a greater degree of emotional coherence fared better than people with lower coherence. They theorized that an individual who perceives an emotional challenge, and quickly mobilizes their body, behavior, and feelings to act in a coordinated fashion, might be better off than someone who does not. In the study, participants also completed self-report questionnaires that measured their life satisfaction and emotion regulation strategies. The results indicated that indeed, people with greater emotional coherence reported greater well-being. As we noted earlier, psychological well-being is not the same as adaptive fitness; this study did not demonstrate that people with higher emotional coherence have more children, for

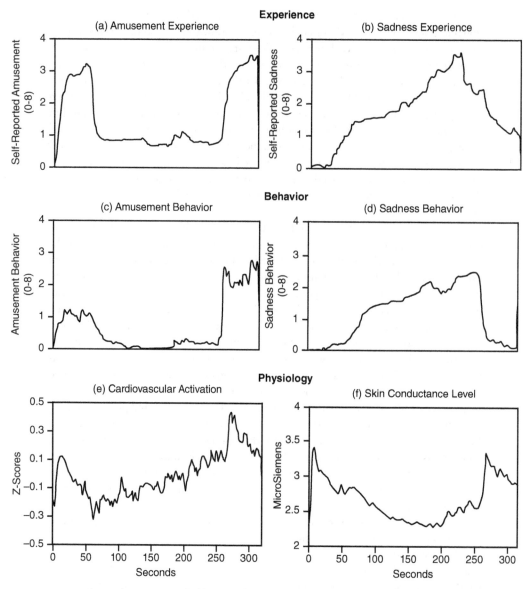

FIGURE 2.15. Average trajectories of self-reported amusement and sadness, facial expressions of amusement and sadness, cardiovascular activation, and skin conductance level over the course of a five-minute film clip. From Mauss et al. (2005).

example. However, it does suggest that relatively high emotional coherence characterizes people who feel their lives are going well, on the whole.

These studies illustrate both the sophistication and the complexity of modern emotion research, as well as the difficulty of drawing clear conclusions about the competing theoretical models. Over the course of this book we will see many more examples. Keep in mind that good science often prompts us to ask new questions in a different way, rather than revealing a clear-cut answer. However, we will also encounter solid evidence for many important emotional processes and effects, with clear theoretical and practical implications.

A Phylogeny of Emotions

The final explanation we consider is also informed by modern evolutionary theory and acknowledges the likelihood of independent information-processing modules, but offers a different account of how these modules combine to create emotional experience. Researchers Randolph Nesse and Phoebe Ellsworth (2009) have proposed that we should think of emotions not only as evolved responses to our ancestors' environments, but also as having a **phylogeny** or evolutionary tree of their own, in which newer emotions evolved from more archaic ones in response to new selection pressures.

Look at the tree in Figure 2.16, which illustrates this idea. According to this perspective, the phylogenetically oldest emotions (those in our most distant ancestors, shared with fish and reptiles) responded only to the most basic opportunities, such as food, and basic threats such as predators. These animals had primitive nervous systems that dealt with a few crucial features of the environment—the distinction between good (go get it!) and bad (run away!).

Our more recent ancestors developed abilities to process and respond to the environment in more nuanced ways. As a result, the primordial emotions of excitement and apprehension would have differentiated into responses to distinct kinds of opportunities and threats. This differentiation would have accelerated further in birds and mammals, whose reproductive processes and social environments introduced new opportunities

FIGURE 2.16. A "family tree" depicting the idea that modern human emotions might have descended from more primordial states over the course of our ancestors' evolution. This approach emphasizes areas of overlap among emotions more strongly than basic emotions theory does, but preserves the idea of emotion prototypes (Nesse & Ellsworth, 2009).

(attractive mating partners, potential allies) and threats (death of kin, rejection by other animals in your community, other animals stealing your food). You still want to approach all opportunities, but in different ways; the same goes for the threats. The clusters of leaves at the end of each branch represent different emotions in modern humans, resulting from this process.

You may have noted that this approach has elements of all of the explanations discussed previously. It accounts for a basic distinction between positive and negative stimuli and between approach and avoidance responses, but also allows that more specific positive and negative emotions might have evolved in response to specific kinds of opportunities and threats. What is crucial about this perspective is that the differentiation among emotions of the same valence is only partial; negative emotions have much in common, reflecting their shared evolutionary origins, just as rats and humans share many aspects of physiology and psychology. Nesse and Ellsworth (2009) have proposed that rather than reflecting superordinate neural programs that evolved to deal with distinct categories of problems in the environment, human emotions reflect progressive fine-tuning of ancient emotional responses based on new abilities to appraise multiple aspects of the environment at once. In this way, the phylogeny of emotions approach is most closely aligned with the component process model discussed in Chapter 1.

AN EXAMPLE: ARE PHYSIOLOGICAL ASPECTS OF EMOTION UNIVERSAL?

Learning Objective
- Describe and critique limitations of the study by Levenson et al. (1992).

What does research on emotion from an evolutionary perspective look like?

Here is a prominent example of research on emotion from an evolutionary perspective: if emotions are adaptations, and their physiological aspects evolved to prepare our bodies for the challenges presented by emotion-eliciting situations, we should expect that the way emotions affect our bodies will be universal. Do people around the world show similar physiological responses during the same emotional experiences? This is a difficult question to answer, but a few researchers have tried. Let's take a really close look at one such study—we will pick up the topic of physiological aspects of emotion and whether they are universally experienced in Chapter 7.

In this study, Robert Levenson, Paul Ekman, Karl Heider, and Wallace Friesen (1992) asked whether participants from an indigenous community in Indonesia showed physiological responses in emotional situations similar to the responses of young adults in the United States. This was a major study in the field, and so we consider it at length below. Since it was conducted thirty years ago, however, it necessarily has some limitations in terms of methodology. This is a great study to use to practice your research critique skills. In your notebook, as you read through the methods, note your critiques and then compare them to the ones we point out.

The researchers traveled to Indonesia to work with the Minangkabau, a community on the island of Sumatra. Traditional Minangkabau culture differs greatly from that of the United States. Residents live in the mountains, and their economy is based largely on community agriculture. The primary religion is Islam, and gender roles are strictly observed. However, the Minangkabau are also the largest matrilineal society in the world, meaning that property is traditionally controlled by and passed down through women. Although at the time of the study the Minangkabau had been visited several times by Western researchers (including Heider, who had learned the local language), they were still isolated from the Western world. Despite heavy rains, power outages, and other problems, the researchers were able to study 46 Minangkabau men (cultural rules prohibited women from working with the male researchers) and to compare their physiological responses with those of 62 people in the United States.

In both samples, the researchers elicited emotion in an unusual way. Remember from Chapter 1 that it is possible to generate an emotion by moving your facial muscles in a way that mimics a certain emotional expression. In this study, a researcher instructed all participants to make facial expressions of anger, fear, sadness, disgust, and happiness while recording their physiological responses. Importantly, researchers did not use the actual emotion words in the instructions. Instead, they gave people instructions such as "wrinkle your nose" and "stick your tongue out a little bit" (these instructions were translated into the local language). Although many people in both the United States and Sumatra did not have enough control over their facial muscles to produce the right expressions, the people included in the analyses were able to do so.

The results of the study are shown in Figure 2.17. The top row shows the average physiological changes that occurred while the Minangkabau participants posed each emotional expression; the bottom row shows data from the US participants. The important thing to note is the overall similarity between responses in the two samples. For example, in both groups, heart rate increased significantly while participants posed expressions of anger, fear, and sadness, but not while they posed disgust or happiness. In both groups, finger temperature increased most while posing anger. A statistical analysis called multivariate analysis of variance, which allows researchers to compare two or more groups on several different outcome variables, did not detect a difference in the two groups' patterns of physiological responding across the five emotions and three physiological variables.

However, there were some cultural differences. Note that the bars in the top row of Figure 2.17 are generally smaller than those in the bottom row. Statistical tests suggested that the magnitude of physiological responses was smaller among the Minangkabau than among the Americans. What might explain this difference? It could be that the Minangkabau have smaller physiological responses during emotion. It could also be that the facial expression task was less effective at eliciting emotion in this group. A third possibility is that the American participants were better able to discern the purpose of the experimenters, and had a stronger response based on experimental demand. There's no way to know which interpretation is correct.

Another interesting difference emerged when the researchers asked the participants to describe how they felt while making each expression. Americans reported feeling the target emotion more strongly than any other emotion on about a third of the trials—more often than could be attributed to chance. Minangkabau participants reported feeling the target emotion most strongly on only 15% of trials, less than half as often. The researchers concluded that physical sensations and facial expressions may be sufficient for American participants to conclude that they are experiencing a particular emotion, but

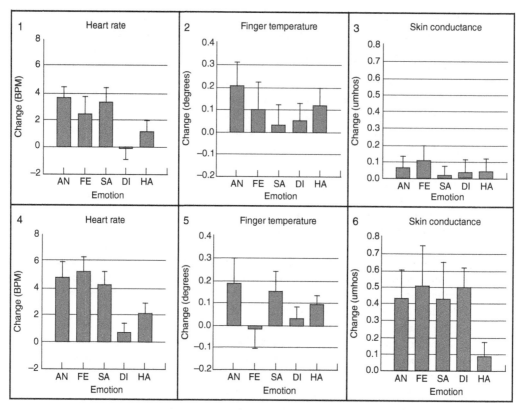

FIGURE 2.17. Physiological reactivity among Minangkabau (top) and US participants (bottom) while posing expressions of anger, fear, sadness, disgust, and happiness. From Levenson et al. (1992).

Minangkabau participants are less likely to interpret their feelings this way in the absence of a reasonable emotion-eliciting situation.

In addition to the limitations we have noted already, researchers had to translate their instructions, which can pose problems. Also, the Minangkabau participants had more trouble following the instructions than the American participants did, and reported that the task was more difficult. Most important, asking people to move their facial muscles is an unusual way to elicit emotions. These researchers tried using more traditional ways of eliciting emotions, such as asking people to relive emotional experiences or watch emotional film clips, but the cultural and language barriers proved problematic. Thus, these results are promising, but far from definitive. In Chapter 3 we will consider cultural variations in emotional experience and expression in much greater depth.

In science, the value of theories is to guide empirical research. A good theory should define the constructs of interest, offer guidance on how to manipulate and measure important variables, and support generation of specific, falsifiable hypotheses. An evolutionary perspective on emotions leads to specific categories of research questions and makes certain methods appropriate, but it also has some limitations. Let's review these methodological considerations.

METHODOLOGICAL CONSIDERATIONS
Learning Objective
- Clarify several critiques of an evolutionary perspective on emotions.

There's one major problem with the evolutionary perspective on emotion: it's hard to test. Let's say a researcher proposes that an emotional response is an adaptation with a specific function. How do they go about providing evidence for that claim? The researcher can't go back in time and experimentally manipulate the conditions that supposedly led to the evolution of fear. They can't just show that fear involves the predicted package of effects, because college students (the typical participants in psychology research) might have learned a cultural definition of fear starting in early childhood (Russell, 1991).

One line of support for evolutionary models is any evidence that some aspect of emotion is *universal*—that it plays out in a similar way throughout the world. Just as Darwin invoked similarities among species of finches on different islands as evidence that they must have shared a common ancestor, finding a common psychological process in people throughout the world suggests that the process is part of human nature. Over the course of this text, we will discuss several studies that examine the question of whether some aspect of emotional responding is similar around the world or highly culture-specific.

The process does not need to play out in the same way everywhere. Evolutionary and learned mechanisms of emotion may often interact with each other, producing important differences between cultures. If an aspect of emotion is part of human nature, however, researchers should be able to explain and predict how the same universal mechanism should manifest one way in some cultures and another way in others. This often means trying to tease out the aspect of emotion that is cross-culturally common amid a host of salient cultural differences, just as researchers interested in explaining food preferences determined that people around the world like the taste of fat molecules in food, although the specific sources of fat vary greatly from region to region. Unfortunately, few researchers have the resources or the connections to collect data from more than one cultural group, much less from dozens of countries around the globe (although such studies are extremely valuable).

Similarly, if some aspect of emotional responding is part of our evolutionary heritage, it might be shared with at least some of our nonhuman animal relatives. After all, tasty food items, mates, babies, predators, bullies, and other prototypical emotion stimuli go way back in our phylogenetic history; they didn't suddenly become issues for humans when we split off from the other primates. This opens the door to doing animal research to understand human emotion better. Such studies are generally limited to the neurological and behavioral aspects of emotion, rather than the cognitive or feeling aspects. For example, researchers are permitted to do experiments with animals that they cannot do with humans, especially studies using neurosurgery and administration of mind-altering drugs. Aside from the complex ethical issues involved in this kind of research, there are also practical issues. How do you know what emotion a rat is feeling or how similar the rat's experience of emotion is to a human's? Because the rat can't talk with us, we have no way of probing its subjective experience; we can only watch its behavior, which is far less sophisticated (especially in labs) than our own. We must rely on inference even when making assumptions about other peoples' emotions, and this problem is far greater with nonhuman animals.

Many researchers adopting an evolutionary perspective have taken a different approach, using theory about the adaptive function of some emotion or aspect of emotion to predict effects in humans that would be hard to explain in terms of cultural learning. In this case, a study may indicate compelling support for an evolutionary approach even if the research participants are only from one cultural background. For example, if the adaptive function of disgust is to help people avoid disease, then when people experience disgust, they should show biological signs of preparation to fight off pathogens. Consistent with this hypothesis, a team of researchers found that participants exposed to particularly disgusting stimuli showed increases in core body temperature and immune system activity not seen under control conditions (Stevenson et al., 2012). It's unlikely that learned scripts for disgust (people thinking, "Oh no, there is a moldy piece of pizza, I must be about to get sick!") trigger involuntary biological responses, so the evolutionary explanation seems more plausible.

In using this strategy, however, we should base our hypotheses on careful, logical analyses of the evolutionary problem the emotion is thought to solve and what a good solution should look like (Lewis et al., 2017). For example, if disgust evolved as a response to the threat of disease, what features should disgust have (in terms of physiology, cognition, behavior, and so forth)? What kinds of stimuli should or should not elicit disgust? To what extent might these stimuli vary from society to society while still showing a common theme? Can we explain the variations, as well as the commonalities? Should people in some societies be more disgust-prone than others? Thoughtful selection of control conditions is important, separating the effects specific to disgust from those pertaining to anger, fear, and sadness.

It is important in this approach to minimize **post hoc theorizing**—coming up with an explanation for phenomena after already observing them. Ideally, one should generate a novel hypothesis and then collect data to test the hypothesis. The whole point of science is to use theory to predict the outcome of some study if your theory is correct, as well as the likely outcome if your theory is wrong. If you already know the outcome and are simply making up an evolutionary explanation for it, then it may be a good, coherent story but it's not good science. You haven't given the theory a fair chance to fail in predicting study outcomes, which is what good science is all about. (For analogy, economists' explanations of why the stock market went up or down yesterday are not impressive if they cannot predict what the stock market will do today or tomorrow).

Evolutionary psychologists are often accused of post hoc theorizing, sometimes with good reason. For example, if a researcher were to propose that anger is an evolved response to being insulted and then went on to collect data demonstrating that people who were insulted by a confederate reliably became angry, the study would not be taken seriously. We already know that people become angry when insulted, so claiming the researcher predicted it sounds fishy. Let's say the researcher predicted that people become angry at insults from some people but not from others, or at insults about some topics but not about others, or in some contexts but not in others, based on a novel theory of the specific threat to adaptive fitness posed by having someone insult you. That study would be more impressive, and would be a stronger application of the evolutionary approach.

SUMMARY

Emotion and motivation are complex, personal phenomena, and yet some aspects of these experiences seem familiar to everyone. If you have ever traveled to a different society, or read a book or seen a reasonably authentic movie about people from a different culture, you may have been struck by vast differences in what people think and how they behave. Yet sometimes our emotional and motivational responses show us how much we have in common, with reactions to situations such as danger, loss, disrespect, reunion with a loved one, and the smile of a child highlighting what it means to be human.

To researchers interested in the evolutionary origins of emotion, the aspects of emotion that we share with people around the world, and even with some other animals, are extremely important. Emotional universals likely reflect ways in which emotions helped our ancestors survive and thrive over time. Understanding these functions allows researchers to predict and understand specific effects of emotions that might not be apparent without an evolutionary perspective. An evolutionary perspective also suggests that in studying the emotions of other animals, we can learn a lot about ourselves.

In this chapter, we saw that evolution occurs through a process of random genetic mutations, some of which improve survival and reproduction and through the process of natural selection spread through a population. Positive emotions may have evolved to signal the adaptive value of approaching new opportunities, and negative emotions may have evolved to signal caution and withdrawal in circumstances of uncertainty and threat.

Proposing that emotions have functions in the evolutionary sense does not mean that emotions are always good, that they are pleasant, that they invariably make us do the right thing, or that we should not seek to limit their effects in some situations. It also does not mean that people's emotions are the same throughout the world. As we shall see in the next chapter, culture has tremendous implications for how emotion is experienced and expressed. However, an evolutionary perspective has helped researchers organize large amounts of information about emotions into useful, consistent principles, and these principles have generated a great deal of important research.

KEY TERMS

adaptation: a beneficial, genetically based characteristic that has become species-typical as a result of natural selection (p. 49)

affect infusion model: a theoretical model explaining several ways in which affective valence influences judgment and decision-making (p. 64)

byproduct: a genetically based characteristic that is neutral, but is the result of a mutation that also causes some beneficial trait and becomes species-typical as that mutation spreads through the population (p. 60)

drive: mechanisms underlying the motivating force of biological needs such as hunger and thirst; when these needs are deprived, the organism experiences a state of arousal (energy) to satiate the need (direction) (p. 52)

emotional response coherence: the extent to which self-reports of emotion predict physiological changes and simple behaviors like facial expressions (p. 70)

environment of evolutionary adaptedness (EEA): the time and place in the past when an adaptation spread through the population as a result of natural selection (p. 50)

flow: a psychological state encompassing positive emotions, attentional focus, and a sense of being one with the activity that seems to occur when someone is applying all of their skills to the challenge at hand (p. 57)

homeostasis: the body's tendency to maintain a stable internal equilibrium (p. 52)

intrapersonal functions of emotion: ways in which emotions directly benefit the reproductive fitness of the individual experiencing the emotion (p. 61)

instincts: innate patterns of approach or avoidance behavior (p. 46)

natural selection: the process by which problematic genetic mutations are removed from the population, whereas beneficial mutations spread through the population, because of the mutation's effect on reproduction (p. 49)

phylogeny: description of relationships among different species (or in this case, emotions) in terms of shared evolutionary history and branching from a common ancestor (p. 73)

post hoc theorizing: generating a theoretical explanation for information that is already known, rather than using the theory to generate a new hypothesis in advance (p. 78)

self-determination theory: theory that human beings are motivated to determine themselves, primarily by satisfying needs for autonomy, competence, and relatedness (p. 56)

social functions of emotion: ways in which emotions support committed, interdependent, and complex relationships among people that in turn help us to survive and pass on our genes (p. 62)

superordinate neural program: a hypothesized neural "program" that coordinates the activities of many smaller programs, activating those that will be useful for the function of the program and inhibiting those that will interfere (p. 67)

THOUGHT/DISCUSSION QUESTIONS

1. What aspects of emotion do you think are most likely to be universal? What aspects should be more strongly influenced by culture?

2. We mentioned that the human predilection for high-fat, high-sugar foods is likely an adaptation to our ancestors' environment, but is now maladaptive in the modern world, where such foods are easily accessible. What other universal human characteristics may now be maladaptive or undesirable? What is it about the modern environment that causes the mismatch?

3. Self-determination theory argues that our core psychological needs are autonomy, competence, and belonging. Do you think other psychological needs are also important—what about desire for achievement? Power? Can you imagine that the importance of these needs might vary by culture? If so, how?

4. We have offered a few examples of social functions of emotions. Can you think of additional ways in which emotional responses help strengthen our relationships with other people?

5. Can you think of a kind or aspect of emotional experience that is probably a by-product of evolution, rather than an adaptation? To what adaptation do you think that by-product might be linked?

SUGGESTIONS FOR FURTHER READING

Beall, A. T., & Tracy, J. L. (2017). Emotivational psychology: How distinct emotions facilitate fundamental motives. *Social and Personality Psychology Compass, 11*(2), e12303. https://doi.org/10.1111/spc3.12303

Carroll, S. B. (2005). *Endless forms most beautiful: The new science of Evo Devo and the making of the animal kingdom.* Norton.

Panksepp, J., & Biven, L. (2012). *The archaeology of mind: Neuroevolutionary origins of human emotions.* Norton.

Sapolsky, R. M. (2017). *Behave: The biology of humans at our best and worst.* Penguin.

Schaller, M., Kenrick, D. T., Neel, R., & Neuberg, S. L. (2017). Evolution and human motivation: A fundamental motives framework. *Social and Personality Psychology Compass, 11*(6), e12319. https://doi.org/10.1111/spc3.12319

CHAPTER 3

Culture and Emotion

In Chapter 2 we proposed that modern humans have emotions at least in part because ancient emotional responses helped our ancestors deal effectively with important problems—those impacting survival and reproduction—thereby increasing the representation of their genes in future generations. Mechanisms of emotion that evolved in this way should be part of human nature. As a result, researchers who emphasize an evolutionary perspective typically ask questions about ways in which emotion are similar, or operate in similar ways, among humans everywhere—perhaps among other animals as well.

However, there is also enormous evidence that people around the world differ in how they experience, express, and talk about emotion. These differences have led other researchers to emphasize the **social construction of emotion**, processes by which cultures construct and communicate emotional concepts in ways that shape individual emotional experience (Averill, 2012; Boiger & Mesquita, 2012). Researchers emphasizing a social construction perspective investigate aspects of human emotion that are culturally defined, rather than innate and universal. From this perspective, emotions can be thought of as stories our culture uses to make sense of our experience; other cultures may have other stories, and therefore experience emotions in different ways. If this description reminds you of the psychological construction account of emotion covered in Chapter 1, that's a good sign. Here we address ways in which the psychological construction of emotion is shaped by the cultures in which you have lived.

The evolutionary and social construction perspectives might appear to be opposites, such that only one or the other can be true. There is a way to resolve the conflict, however: perhaps some *aspects* and/or *mechanisms* of emotion are evolved, innate, and universal, whereas others are constructed in different ways by different cultures, and different individuals within those cultures. Even if some of the underlying mechanisms of emotion are the same across cultures, the ways those mechanisms are expressed can differ dramatically. Remember the analogy to human food preferences—people throughout the world like the taste of fat molecules, but different cultures emphasize different sources of fats and different ways of combining the fats with other foods, so different cultures have different cuisines.

In this chapter we discuss what it means to talk about culture at all, we ask how culture can have such a powerful influence on our understanding of the world, and we consider the implications of all these considerations for human emotion.

WHAT IS CULTURE?

If you look up the term "culture" in a dictionary, you may find five to ten different meanings. Clifford Geertz (1973) complained that one article offered 11 definitions of human culture within 27 pages! To be fair, those 11 definitions had several common themes. Still, it helps to focus on a single definition, so let's discuss one particularly suited to our purpose.

Learning Objectives
- Analyze the concept of culture, as defined by Shweder, in terms of three key points contained in his definition.
- Explain how words relate to conceptual categories, and how concepts recognized within a language's vocabulary can reflect both a culture-specific worldview and objective features of the world.

Here is a well-known definition of culture, offered by the anthropologist Richard Shweder (1993, p. 417): **culture** consists of "meanings, conceptions, and interpretive schemes that are activated, constructed, or brought 'on-line' through participation in normative social institutions and practices (including linguistic practices) ... giving shape to the psychological processes in individuals in a society." That's a mouthful! But the idea is not as complicated as it sounds. Let's break it down and highlight some key points.

First, cultures are *systems of meaning*—ways of interpreting, understanding, and explaining what is going on in the world around us. Units of meaning are often represented in words—the labels we use to symbolize certain categories of experience. In some ways, words can be shaped by real categories in the natural world, and we would expect most, if not all, cultures to reflect some categories in language. For example, the English term "human" refers to members of the species *Homo sapiens*, and most languages have a word differentiating humans from not-humans. However, the categories captured through these words are not identical, and they have connotations that reflect the worldview of those who use them. Whereas the English-language word "human" derives from the Latin *homo*, which in turn derives from the Indo-European word for "earth," the Arabic word *insan* alludes to mortality, and the Japanese word *ningen* refers to human society.

Language is so complex that the same concept can also appear via multiple words, with subtly different meanings. For example, the English term "person" differs from "human" in connoting sentience and possession of inherent individual rights that have ethical status ("personhood"), but the corresponding terms in other languages may only emphasize membership in a particular in-group (e.g., words referring to a particular cultural community or tribe as literally "the people," leaving everyone else out; Shweder & Bourne, 1982). Words in every language reflect some combination of references to observable phenomena in the world, associations with other concepts, and category boundaries that are meaningful in the context of that specific culture, but may differ from boundaries recognized by other cultures.

FIGURE 3.1. What do these images mean to you? Depending on the culture(s) in which you were raised, each image may have very rich meaning, or little or no meaning at all. The exact meaning will vary somewhat from person to person, but meanings are similar across people within the same culture, reflecting a shared worldview.

Language distinctions are only one example of how a culture expresses meaning. Think also about religious rituals, holidays, graduations, and marriage ceremonies. Consider several objects: your national flag, an autograph by a celebrity, or a monument commemorating a historical event (see Figure 3.1). In each case, something has a certain meaning or significance in the context of a culture's history and social structure.

The second point contained in Shweder's definition is that culture activates or constructs meaning through social participation. For example, in one class you might sit quietly throughout the lecture, whereas in another you discuss your ideas and argue with others. How did you know to behave differently in the two classes? You might sit quietly during a symphony, but not sit at all during a rock concert. Again, why? In each case, you learn largely by imitation. You watch what other people do, and you do the same. But according to Shweder (1993), the behaviors also express how we are expected to *think* about these events, why we are there and who we are supposed to be in each context.

Shweder's third point is that shared cultural systems of meaning influence psychological processes in individuals. By this, Shweder (1993) means that how we think about and behave in the world depends on the concepts we have learned, and how those concepts relate to each other. For example, people in the Western world think of animals such as dogs, cats, hamsters, and some other small mammals as "pets." Many less-wealthy cultures have no such concept. They think of animals as food, workers, or a source of danger, but not as friends or members of the family. They would be baffled by the idea of cat food. At best, it would make no sense; at worst, it would seem immoral to buy special food for a cat instead of for a needy person. On the other hand, some ancient cultures have classified cats as holy beings, worshipped them, and offered them the choicest food and shelter. To many in Western countries this would seem wasteful, or even sacrilegious. In short, differences in concepts and meanings can translate into substantial differences in behavior.

Defined in this way, culture is much more complicated and richer than the set of rituals and symbols you happened to grow up with, although these are all interconnected. Next let's consider the implications of culture, as defined above, for emotional experience across the globe.

CULTURAL DIFFERENCES IN CONCEPTS OF EMOTION
Learning Objectives
- Compare and contrast the English-language concept of sadness with the Tahitian concept *pe'a pe'a*.
- Describe the Japanese concept of *amae*, and analyze ways in which *amae* experience may reflect human nature, as well as ways in which it is culture-specific.
- Define colexification, and explain what Jackson and colleagues' (2019) study of English emotion word colexification suggests regarding the universality versus culture-specificity of emotion concepts around the world.
- Define the Sapir–Whorf hypothesis, evaluate the evidence regarding this hypothesis, and summarize alternative descriptions of the relationship between emotion vocabulary and capacity to experience a particular emotion.

Cultural differences in the ways people think about, classify, and find meaning in emotion can be dramatic. If you and your classmates try to define "emotion" or list typical emotional experiences, you will probably find that you agree, for the most part, on what the term means. If we ask the same question of people from other cultures, however, they may have a different answer. You may not even be able to ask the question in some cultures, because some languages do not even have a word corresponding to emotion (e.g., Tahitian, Samoan, the language of the Gidjingali of Australia; Russell, 1991).

Even when a language does have a word that translates as emotion, it might not refer to the same set of concepts that the English term does. For example, the Japanese term *jodo* includes angry, happy, sad, and ashamed, which are states that most American psychologists readily identify as emotions (Matsuyama et al., 1978). However, it also includes states that translate as considerate, motivated, and lucky, which would not classify as emotions in English. Keep in mind that these English terms are inexact translations as well. What the Japanese mean by lucky may not be what Americans mean by lucky, so it is not obvious whether lucky in Japanese would count as an emotion in English.

Other languages have words that seem to correspond to the English word "emotion," or to a particular emotion, except that they refer to the *situation* rather than to the internal *feeling* that the situation produces. For example, among the Fula people in Africa, the word *semteende* denotes a social situation in which an American would probably feel embarrassment or shame. The term is often translated as "embarrassment," but it refers to the situation and not how the person feels (Riesman, 1977). A better translation might be "embarrassing." The Ifaluk of the South Pacific also tend to emphasize social situations over internal states in their emotion lexicon (Lutz, 1982).

Here's another example. You walk into a friend's house because no one has seen him in a couple of days, and you wonder how he's doing. He seems droopy and lethargic, sighs frequently, and lowers his eyes. He says he doesn't really feel like doing anything. He also tells you that his girlfriend recently left town for a long trip, and he won't see her again for a while. In one word, how would you describe him?

An anthropologist studying life in Tahiti found himself in a similar situation (allowing for a bit of literary license) and drew the conclusion most Americans would draw—the man was sad because he missed his partner (Levy, 1973). The man himself, however, did not describe his state as an emotion, and in fact Tahitians don't have a word for what we call *sadness*. Instead, he described himself as *pe'a pe'a*, a Tahitian term that means sick, fatigued,

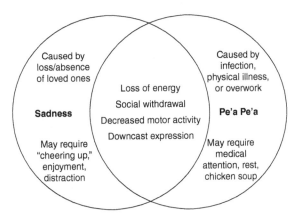

FIGURE 3.2. The conceptual territory of sadness in English overlaps somewhat, although not exactly, with the conceptual territory of *pe'a pe'a* (illness or fatigue) in Tahitian.

or troubled. In short, he described his condition as an illness, not as an emotion. Here we see the differences and similarities between the concept of illness in Tahitian and sadness in English. They have much in common but belong in different categories. See Figure 3.2 for a visual diagram of the relationship between these words. Similarly, culturally Chinese individuals are more likely to describe their reaction to an emotional situation (by Western standards) in bodily terms, rather than in terms emphasizing emotional feelings (Tsai, Simeonova, & Watanabe, 2004). In Chapter 1 we defined emotion in terms of four aspects of emotional responding: subjective feelings, cognitions/appraisals, physiological changes, and behaviors including nonverbal expressions. Different cultures emphasize different aspects of this territory, and this shapes both how we experience and talk about our emotions.

It's easy to think of culture as something other people have, and to define culture in terms of how other societies differ from our own. However, mainstream North American concepts of emotion are equally shaped by culture. Let's consider an example. When you think about romantic love, what images come to mind, what stories, which memories? According to Ann Swidler (2001), people's answers to this question reflect their culture's network of meanings, ideas, and beliefs about intimate relationships. In her study, Swidler interviewed 88 middle-class Californian men and women of many ages. She asked these people what *real love* means, what their experiences with love had been, where their ideas of love came from, what makes a romantic relationship good or bad, and so forth.

Swidler (2001) found that North American culture promotes two distinct concepts of romantic love. One concept is the Hollywood, bolt-of-lightning kind of love that turns your world over in an instant and lasts a lifetime. As Swidler summarizes it, "They met, and it was love at first sight. There would never be another girl (boy) for him (her). No one could come between them. They overcame obstacles and lived happily ever after." In this image of love, the beloved is "the one," there is a feeling of destiny, of being meant for each other, and the beloved is irreplaceable.

The other concept of love is more prosaic and practical. This kind of love, often espoused by those who are skeptical of the Hollywood version, grows slowly over time rather than happening in an instant. The couple's story revolves around compatibility of personality, social connections, and activities, rather than obstacles to overcome.

FIGURE 3.3. Two versions of the romantic love narrative in middle-class US culture, as represented in popular films.

This kind of love does not require finding your one perfect mate. You may find many people for whom this kind of love has the potential to develop, given the opportunity. People who advocate this image of love say that this love is slow to grow, but deep and sure, whereas Hollywood love is flashy and shallow.

The important point, to Swidler (2001), is that neither of these versions of romantic love is objectively more real or valid than the other. Both are socially constructed narratives, stories we tell about how romantic relationships are supposed to work, and what experiences and feelings should be involved. Many American movies emphasize the love-at-first-sight version, but in societies where arranged marriages are the norm, and among Western couples who have been together for many years, people tend to talk more about the slow-growing, steady kind of love. Swidler also points out that many Americans include both concepts of love in their worldview, moving back and forth between them as needed to explain their experience. A couple might even move from one type of love to the other over time, although in Western popular culture a given relationship is typically depicted in just one way. The key point is that each of these ways of thinking about love is, at least in part, a social construction (Figure 3.3).

Do All Cultures Name the Same Emotions?

Recall from Chapter 1 that one proposed criterion for a basic emotion is that it should occur among people everywhere. Happiness, sadness, fear, anger, surprise, and disgust are considered good candidates for basic emotions, and researchers study other possibilities as well. A social construction perspective leads researchers to ask a different question: Are there emotions that occur in some cultures but not in others?

There are certainly emotion *words* that exist in some languages, but not in others. The English language offers more than 2,000 emotion words, although most are seldom used (Wallace & Carson, 1973). Taiwanese includes about 750 emotion words (Boucher, 1979). The Chewong language of Malaysia only includes 7 words that could be translated into English emotion words (Howell, 1981). However, the number of words in a language is not the same as the number of emotion *concepts*. English has many synonyms or near-synonyms for emotions—English dictionaries have accumulated more words than other languages for almost everything. Also, a culture with fewer words could recognize and even discuss an emotion without having a word for it; for example, someone with no word

TABLE 3.1 **Languages that lack words for certain emotions**

English emotion words absent in other languages. Summarized from Russell (1991).					
SADNESS	**SURPRISE**	**GUILT**	**LOVE**	**ANXIETY**	**DEPRESSION**
Chewong (Malaysia)	Chewong (Malaysia)	Chewong (Malaysia)	Nyinba (Nepal)	Eskimo	Chewong (Malaysia)
Tahitian	Ifaluk (Micronesia)	Ifaluk (Micronesia)		Machiguenga (Peru)	Inuit Fulani (Africa)
		Ilongot (Philippines)		Yoruba (Nigeria)	Kaluli (New Guinea)
		Pintupi (Australia)			Malay Mandarin
		Quichua (Ecuador)			Xhosa (Africa)
		Samoan			Yoruba (Nigeria)
		Sinhalese (Sri Lanka)			
		Tahitian			

for embarrassment could say "the way you feel when you have made a mistake and others are staring at you." Still, to study cultural differences, one place to begin is to examine the emotions identified by one language and not by another.

James Russell (1991) reviewed dozens of ethnographies—rich, detailed descriptions of life in a particular society—that described the emotional lives of people in different cultures. He identified English emotion concepts that various other languages lack, as well as emotion terms in other languages that English lacks (Table 3.1). We have already mentioned one example: the Tahitian language has no word for sadness, so the Tahitian man whose family was away described himself as ill or fatigued instead.

Many languages also contain emotion words that have no English counterpart. Consider the description of *litost* offered by Milan Kundera ([1979] 1980) in the *Book of Laughter and Forgetting* (pp. 121–122; edited version from Russell, 1991):

> *Litost* is a Czech word with no exact translation into any other language. It designates a feeling as infinite as an open accordion, a feeling that is the synthesis of many others: grief, sympathy, remorse, and an indefinable longing. ... Under certain circumstances, however, it can have a very narrow meaning, a meaning as definite, precise, and sharp as a well-honed cutting edge. I have never found an equivalent in other languages for this sense of the word either, though I do not see how anyone can understand the human soul without it. ... *Litost* is a state of torment caused by a sudden insight into one's own miserable self ... *Litost* works like a two-stroke motor. First comes a feeling of torment, then the desire for revenge.

Litost is hardly the only example. English also has no equivalent to the German word *schadenfreude*, meaning the enjoyment of another person's suffering (Leach et al., 2003; Smith & Van Dijk, 2018). The Ilongot speak of the emotion *liget*, which, like anger, can be a response to insult or injury, but can also be evoked by mass celebrations, by a successful hunt, or by the death of a loved one (Rosaldo, 1980). Also unlike anger, *liget* is considered a positive force that contributes to society.

Another emotion that researchers often describe as culture-specific is the Japanese feeling of **amae**. This feeling has been described as pleasurable dependence on another person, like the feeling an infant has toward its mother (Doi, 1973). In Japan, one feels *amae* when one receives a gift, is cared for, or is allowed to be dependent and childlike (even childish), without any obligation to reciprocate. It is a core characteristic of relationships between spouses and among family and close friends.

In his description of *amae*, Doi (1973) says it is a foundation of the Japanese social structure, and that Japanese individuals expect this unconditional nurturance in most close relationships. It arises in many situations. Studies have suggested that Japanese people rely on social support for getting through a stressful experience more than Americans do (Morling, Kitayama, & Miyamoto, 2003). Japanese mothers talk with their infants more about relatedness than American mothers do (Dennis et al., 2002). Japanese people are also more likely to define happiness and success in terms of interpersonal relationships, rather than individual accomplishments (Ford et al., 2015). That is, happiness relates more to intimacy than it does to pride or self-esteem (Kitayama, Markus, & Kurokawa, 2000; Uchida, Norasakkunkit, & Kitayama, 2004).

To many Americans, however, the concept of enjoying dependence on other people seems alien. Americans expect adults to take care of themselves without depending on others. Imagine yourself as a guest in an American home. Your host says there are snacks in the refrigerator and invites you to help yourself. An American might like that message, interpreting it as an invitation to treat the host's home as one's own. A Japanese individual might take it as the slightly insulting message: no one is going to help you!

Is *amae* a culture-specific emotion? Or is it perhaps a culturally defined situation for feeling a pleasant, loving emotion? Not necessarily. In fact, according to Doi (1973), *amae* is a basic, universal emotion, but one that many Americans are uncomfortable acknowledging beyond childhood, and that Japanese may rely on as a cornerstone of close relationships. In other words, people have the capacity to feel *amae* around the world, and do so as children, but by adulthood this emotion is modulated in ways that reflect expectations of the surrounding culture. We'll return to this example later, when we discuss individualism and collectivism as important aspects of culture.

Emotion Vocabulary Around the World

It is one thing to ask whether different languages have a single word for some emotional state, and another to ask how the concepts captured by words relate to each other across different languages. A team of researchers led by Joshua Conrad Jackson and Kristen Lindquist took a crack at the latter question by examining patterns of emotion words in a database of 2474 languages from around the world (Jackson et al., 2019). This database holds information on how English-language concepts are represented in other languages in terms of **colexification**—combination of concepts captured by distinct words in one language into a single word in another language. Here's an example to which we'll return several times in this chapter: in the language spoken by the Oriya people of India, the term *lajya* covers the content of both "embarrassment" and "shame" in English—the two English terms are colexified into one Oriya word. English is not the only possible starting language, of course, but because it contains such a huge number of distinct words, it's not a bad choice. The database included 24 emotion words, so the researchers used statistical analyses to document the frequency with which every possible pair of English emotion words was colexified in every other language, and to identify "communities" or clusters of English-language emotion terms that were highly likely to be combined in other languages. Figure 3.4 illustrates these communities across all languages studied, as well as in the five largest language families.

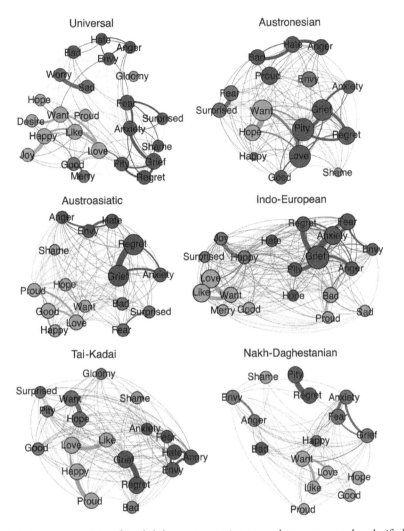

FIGURE 3.4. Communities of English-language emotion terms that are commonly colexified in a total sample of 2474 languages ("Universal"), as well as in the five largest language families. Larger circles indicate emotion terms that were combined with terms in other languages at higher frequencies overall; thicker lines indicate higher colexification frequency for a specific pair of terms. Colors indicate communities, or groups of terms that showed high rates of colexification. To access the colorized version of this image visit: www.oup.com/he/shiota-cavanagh4e/shiota-cavanagh-image-3-4/. Jackson et al. (2019).

What patterns do you see in Figure 3.4? How similar are the color-coded communities to basic emotion concepts previously proposed (fear, anger, sadness, and so forth)? How similar versus different are the communities, and terms within the communities, across the five language families shown? We notice a few interesting points. Positive-valence, pleasant emotions are generally grouped into one or two communities, with like and love often (but not always) in a different community from concepts such as happy and joy. Grief and regret are often (but not always) combined into a single term in other languages, as are anxiety and fear, and anger and hate. Shame is often off by itself, occasionally colexified but rarely part of a community. You might detect other trends as well.

Across all languages in the database, there was significantly more similarity in emotion word community structures than would be expected by chance. In other words, English-language terms were clustered together in more consistent groupings in other languages around the world than you would see if the other languages simply combined English terms at random. However, this consistency was modest; for comparison, running the same series of analyses with English-language color words as the starting point resulted in considerably higher cross-language consistency. Also, some consistency was accounted for by geographical distance. New languages split off from older languages through an evolutionary process of their own, as groups of people who speak them split up and move apart, resulting in a language family tree in which new languages sharing the same "parent" language are fairly similar. Groups of people living near each other often have languages that split off from the same parent language, and to subsequently adopt each other's words as well, leading to more similarity than groups far apart. In these data, the less geographical distance there was between regions where two languages had emerged (suggesting closer relatedness on the language family tree), the more similar their emotion concept community structures ($r = -.26$). This accounts for some of the cross-cultural consistency. These data suggest that even if there is some evolved, universal basis for emotion categories such as fear, sadness, love, et cetera, this plays only a small part in determining the words used to talk about emotion in day-to-day life around the world.

What Do Cultural Differences in Emotion Vocabulary Mean?

What do these language differences mean for emotional experience? In considering the relationship between language and experience generally, Edward Sapir (1921) and Benjamin Whorf (1956) each proposed what came to be known as the **Sapir–Whorf hypothesis**: humans require language to think, and therefore have only those experiences, thoughts, and perceptions for which they have words. In the emotion domain, the consequence would be that people cannot experience an emotion for which they have no word.

This seems unlikely. For example, even before you learned the term *schadenfreude*, did you ever feel pleased at seeing someone suffer? Never? Not even when a rich, unethical person is arrested for fraud? Not even when a politician you dislike is caught in a scandal? Maybe you are a saint and never feel that way, but most people can relate to the concept, agree that it differs from other types of enjoyment, and are pleased to learn a word for it. In the last decade or so, the term has caught on and been incorporated into English colloquial speech, and researchers have begun to study *schadenfreude* in English-speaking participants as well as in speakers of German (Combs et al., 2009). Similarly, Russell (1991) describes an Arab woman who was delighted to learn the word "frustration." Because her language did not include a corresponding word, she had never been able to label the feeling, though she readily related to it.

According to a weaker form of the Sapir–Whorf hypothesis, people might more readily experience or express an emotion for which they have a word than one for which they lack a word. Another way of stating the weaker hypothesis is that the way people express something in words influences the way we think about it. For example, it used to be customary in English to refer to a person of unknown gender as masculine, as in "A physician should take good care of his patients." Over time it become more typical to say "his or her patients," both acknowledging and reminding people that the medical profession includes women as well as men. In recent years, the use of the plural (e.g., "their patients") to refer to individuals of any gender has become more common and encouraged, reflecting growing cultural recognition of a variety of gender identities.

A subtler influence of language on perception, memory, or reasoning is consistent with Shweder's (1993) definition of culture, discussed earlier: culture (including language) helps define the categories of experience people use to make sense of the world around them. It influences the ways in which individuals think about their experience, and communicate it to others, but it does not restrict one's perception of the world, and people may make conceptual distinctions that are not reflected explicitly in their vocabulary. A study by Jonathan Haidt and Dacher Keltner (1999) offers evidence to this effect in the domain of emotion. Haidt and Keltner showed photographs of several emotional facial expressions to participants in the United States and in Eastern India, where people speak the Oriya language. The expressions included an embarrassment display (a smile with the lips pressed together, averted glance, and a face touch) as well as a photo of a person covering her face with one hand, suggesting shame (see Figure 3.5). Researchers then asked participants to tell a story about what event caused the person to make each face.

As expected, American participants labeled one expression embarrassment and the other shame, and they described different situations in which each would be felt. But as we noted earlier, Oriya has only a single word—*lajya*—that combines the meanings of both embarrassment and shame (embarrassment and shame are colexified). Accordingly, most Indian participants labeled both facial expressions *lajya*. Nevertheless, they typically said the person covering her face (in what Americans called shame) had probably done something wrong or had failed at something. They said the person smiling and looking away (in what Americans called embarrassment) had done nothing wrong, but was the focus of awkward social attention, such as public praise or winning an award. These descriptions are consistent with the different meanings of shame and embarrassment in English (Tangney et al., 1996). The implication is that although the Indian participants did not have separate words for embarrassment and shame, they still recognized the

FIGURE 3.5.   Prototypical facial expressions of embarrassment and shame, similar to those used in the study by Haidt and Keltner (1999).

situations that prompted different expressions. They knew the difference and could describe it, even if was not explicit in the Oriya vocabulary.

Why do different languages and cultures have different emotion vocabularies at all? Based on his extensive field research on Tahitian life and language, Levy (1984) offered one plausible explanation. The Tahitian language has 46 words for anger, yet (as noted earlier) no word for what we call sadness (Levy, 1973). After getting to know this culture, Levy (1973) concluded that Tahitians do experience sadness. He proposed that cultures **hypercognize** emotions that are considered important in that society, creating an elaborate network of definitions, conceptual associations, and distinctions leading to an increase in vocabulary. According to this idea, the 46 Tahitian words for anger probably distinguish among different degrees of anger: anger at someone in particular versus general grumpiness; anger at a fish that got away from you versus anger at the idiot who bumped into you while you were trying to catch the fish; the kind of anger that makes you trudge home in silence versus the kind of anger that makes you yell at the person who bumped into you, and so on. You get the idea.

Other emotions in a culture might be **hypocognized**, lacking much cognitive elaboration or detail. In Tahiti, sadness may be a "real" emotion in the sense that it is a coherent package of observable responses to loss or separation, but it is of so little social interest that it is lumped linguistically with illness and fatigue (there's that colexification again). The lumping of unrecognized emotions with other kinds of states is not arbitrary. For example, Tahitians are not wrong in lumping sadness with sickness, because the two states have much in common. But presumably it is less valuable in Tahitian culture to distinguish the states themselves, and/or their causes, than is the case for cultures in which English is the primary language.

Cultural differences in emotion vocabulary lead to a tricky methodological problem. How can researchers study emotions in different cultures if the emotion words of one language don't translate into the other language? One solution is to study the concepts underlying the words. For example, Usha Menon and Richard Shweder (1994) studied *lajya* by asking participants to describe the meaning of a commonly portrayed facial expression of that emotion by the goddess Kali—a core cultural symbol. This approach allowed Menon and Shweder to examine differences between the concept of *lajya* and the English-language concept of shame, as well as similarities.

What if researchers want to study a proposed basic or discrete emotion in some culture with no word for that emotion? In this case, they can move away from emotion vocabulary to study whether evidence of the hypothesized emotion packages—like the superordinate neural programs described in Chapter 2—can be observed in the other culture. For example, if we wanted to study sadness in Tahiti, we might ask the following questions. When does one feel *pe'a pe'a*? How does one behave? What does one's face look like? The more these and other features of *pe'a pe'a* resemble those of sadness, the more confident we might be that the two words refer to pretty much the same state. If we found that Tahitians reliably look sad, sound sad, show sad physiology, and appear sad when a loved one dies in ways similar to people in Western countries, we might conclude that Tahitians do experience sadness whether they have a word for it or not. Alternatively, we might find that the different aspects of sadness (as defined in the English language) do not combine reliably among Tahitians. Such research might help us to understand better which aspects of various emotions are universal, and which are primarily influenced by culture.

ASPECTS OF CULTURE THAT PREDICT DIFFERENCES IN EMOTION

Learning Objectives

- Define individualism and collectivism, identify aspects of the self-concept associated with each, and describe one way in which individualism/collectivism shapes people's emotions.
- Differentiate vertical and horizontal societies, and describe one way in which emotional expression tends to differ across these cultural contexts.
- Define emotional complexity, and summarize the data linking it to cultural differences in epistemology—beliefs about what it means to know or understand something.
- Define ideal affect, and analyze cultural differences in the implications of motivation to pursue happiness for actual well-being.

Many differences in emotion among cultures have been identified—they can be difficult to keep track of, and even more so to explain. Most early studies of culture and emotion simply noted a difference between the United States and some other culture and left it at that. Frustrated with the hodgepodge of findings produced in this way, several researchers suggested a new approach. They argued that although every culture is unique, researchers can compare cultures to one another along a few dimensions that are relevant to social behavior and emotional experience. We next discuss four examples of this approach.

Individualism versus Collectivism

First, cultures have been described as varying along a continuum from individualism to collectivism (Hofstede, 2001; Markus & Kitayama, 1991). According to many cultural psychologists, people in Western cultures (especially in the United States) tend to be high in **individualism**, which emphasizes individual uniqueness, autonomy, being true to one's self, and independence from others. People high in individualism generally agree with statements such as the following (Triandis & Gelfand, 1998):

- My personal identity, independent of others, is very important to me.
- I'd rather depend on myself than others.
- It is important that I do my job better than others.

Many other cultures, including most cultures in South and East Asia and Latin America, emphasize **collectivism**, valuing group identification, social harmony, and interdependence. Each person has a role, aspires to be a good member of the groups to which they belong, and places a strong priority on the needs of relationship partners and group members. People who have a collectivist attitude tend to agree with statements like these:

- The well-being of my coworkers is important to me.
- I feel good when I cooperate with others.
- It is important to me that I respect the decisions made by my groups.

In one classic study, Chinese and US participants were asked to complete the phrase "I am . . ." 20 times, in any way they wanted (Triandis, McCusker, & Hui, 1990). Chinese participants were three times more likely than those in the United States to list group membership as part of their identity. Whereas people in the United States tended to list things that made them different from others, Chinese participants were more likely to list similarities. Of course, these differences pertain to average frequencies across many people. Americans listed some group memberships, and Chinese participants described some unusual aspects about themselves, but the proportions differed across the two cultures. Another example of the difference between relatively individualist versus collectivist cultures is that Chinese people tend to talk more about their friends and family, whereas people in the United States tend to talk more about themselves. For example, when asked to describe experiences from memory, North Americans in one study tended to focus on how *they* felt in the situation, and participants from Asia were more likely to describe how they thought *the people around them* felt (Cohen & Gunz, 2002).

In another study, researchers asked people to describe the behavior of the fish in Figure 3.6. Most people in the United States say the fish on the right is leading the others. Among Chinese people, a common answer is that the other fish are chasing this one (Hong et al., 2000). That is, the Chinese put more emphasis on group influences and context in interpreting ambiguous situations. Such differences in appraisal can lead to differences in emotional experience. Someone who thinks the fish is a leader would probably think the fish is happy, whereas someone who thinks the fish is being chased would likely infer that it is afraid.

A more complex example can be found in the emotion *amae*, introduced earlier in this chapter. According to Takeo Doi (1973), the Japanese psychologist who richly described this emotion for an academic audience, *amae* is a universal emotional experience associated with pleasurable dependence on another person. However, it was

FIGURE 3.6.   Chinese people are more likely than people in the United States to say the group of fish to the left is chasing the fish on the right; Americans typically say the fish on the right is leading the others.

unfamiliar to a Western, especially North American, audience. In a highly individualist cultural context such as the United States, depending on other people is kind of shameful—by adulthood you really should be able to take care of yourself, not depending on anyone. In a highly collectivist cultural context, as Japan was in the mid-twentieth century, depending on others and allowing them to depend on you is desirable and appropriate. In hinting that people in the United States might benefit from allowing a little more *amae* into their lives, and that Japanese people could dial it down a notch or two, Doi was really suggesting that hyper-individualist and hyper-collectivist ways of relating to close others might both be a bit problematic. As a thought exercise, you might consider where you fall on the *amae* spectrum, and contemplate the advantages and disadvantages of being at either end of that spectrum.

A word of caution is needed: it is an oversimplification to equate Western cultures with individualism and Eastern cultures with collectivism. First, although people may prioritize one over the other, and many studies do treat individualism-collectivism as a single, bipolar scale (see Figure 3.7), individualism and collectivism are not mutually exclusive. Cultures, and the individuals within them, can be described as holding some combination of these two systems of meaning (Singelis, 1994). Looking at the items above, you might well agree that your personal identity is important to you *and* that it feels good to cooperate with other people. Similarly, you can try a version of a task described above to see how your self-concept might involve both senses of "self." Write down 20 words or phrases that say who you are; you can begin with "I am ..." if you like, but what matters is that the answers describe you. Next, go through your list and note the entries that emphasize you are separate from other people—unique, special, or different in some way—versus those that emphasize group memberships or relationships with

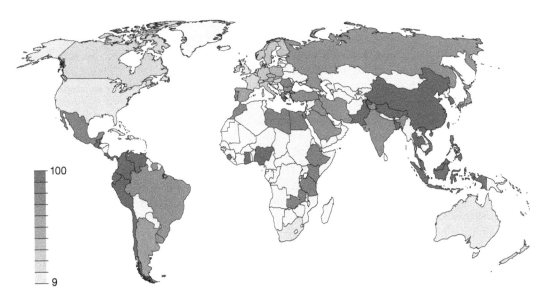

FIGURE 3.7. Hofstede's original ratings of countries around the world on a single individualism-collectivism dimension. Higher numbers indicate more extreme collectivism, lower numbers more extreme individualism; white indicates data were not available for that country. Chiao & Blizinsky (2010).

other people. You might discuss these answers with an instructor, teaching assistant, or classmate to see if you agree with the classifications. How many statements did you have of each type? Do you see yourself as primarily individualist, primarily collectivist, or a combination of the two?

Second, although researchers often study cultural differences by comparing people in different countries, culture does not follow tidy national borders. Individualist and collectivist attitudes vary from region to region, person to person (Fiske, 2002; Yamawaki, 2012), and even within one person from one situation to another (Bond, 2002). In many ways, people in Tokyo, Beijing, London, and New York more closely resemble each other than those in rural areas of their respective countries. Moreover, cultures change over time. Researchers find that Japanese people of the twenty-first century are about as individually competitive as people in the United States, and in some ways more so (Bond, 2002; Oyserman, Coon, & Kemmelmeier, 2002; Takano & Osaka, 1999). Japanese culture was described as highly collectivist shortly after World War II, but almost any country develops more collectivist attitudes in the face of danger, or after a disastrous loss (Takano & Osaka, 1999). People in the United States were strongly united as well, shortly after the terrorist attacks of September 11, 2001. Moreover, research suggests that as societies become wealthier, they tend to become more individualistic (Grossman & Varnum, 2015; Hamamura, 2012). Japan today has customs and attitudes that differ vastly from those of the mid-twentieth century, and they are also vastly different from those of today's China.

What causes a cultural group to develop collectivist or individualist attitudes? One hypothesis is that cultural worldviews are shaped, at least in part, by constraints of the local ecology and economic base (Oishi, 2014). For example, some research has linked collectivism to a history of rice farming which, unlike wheat farming, requires prolonged group coordination and cooperation. Because harvesting rice requires massive effort, especially before the days of tractors and similar machinery, farmers needed to plant their crops at different times so that each would be available to help his or her neighbors at harvesting time. One study found that collectivist attitudes are stronger in southern China, which has a long history of rice farming, than in northern China, where wheat farming (which can be accomplished by a single family) has been more common (Talhelm et al., 2014; see Figure 3.8).

How might cultural differences in individualism versus collectivism affect emotional life? As one example, such differences have been proposed as an explanation for variability across cultures in how people display and interpret facial expressions. For example, people in more collectivist societies tend to discourage open expression of negative emotion as a way of preserving group harmony (Matsumoto, Yoo, & Fontaine, 2008; Mauss et al., 2010; Senft et al., 2021). Collectivism and individualism may also facilitate experience of different kinds of emotion or encourage emotions in different situations. One striking example occurs in regard to the situations that arouse *self-conscious* emotions such as pride, shame, and guilt, which involve an appraisal of oneself as good or bad. Research in North America suggests that people experience pride when they have accomplished something and their social status is on the rise (Mercadante, Witkower, & Tracy, 2021; Seidner, Stipek, & Feshbach, 1988; Tiedens, Ellsworth, & Mesquita, 2000). Americans experience shame and guilt after doing something wrong, when others are likely to express disapproval (Tangney, Miller et al., 1996). Thus, pride, shame, and guilt all appear

FIGURE 3.8. Collectivism may be more likely to emerge in societies whose economic base requires intense cooperation, as in Asian regions with long histories of rice farming.

to require an interpretation of whether the self is good or bad. However, *self* means different things to people in different cultures. In individualistic cultures, my "self" is distinct from the people around me. In collectivistic cultures, self is more closely tied to group memberships and relationships with friends and family (Triandis et al., 1990). Thus, we might predict that people in collectivist cultures would experience pride and shame in response to their friends' and relatives' actions, not just their own.

Deborah Stipek (1998) tested this hypothesis in a study of United States and Chinese university students. She asked participants in each country to read several scenarios and to rate how proud, guilty, and ashamed they would feel in each situation. In two of the scenarios, someone was accepted to a prestigious university, but in one scenario it was the participant and in the other it was the participant's child. In two other scenarios, a person is caught cheating, but in one scenario it was the participant and in the other it was the participant's brother. Participants in the United States reported that they would be equally proud if they or their child was accepted to a prestigious university, but Chinese participants reported that they would be prouder to have their child accepted. Chinese participants reported that they would feel more guilt and shame than Americans in the cheating scenario regardless of who did it, and participants in both countries said they would feel more guilt and shame if they were caught than if the brother were caught. However, Chinese participants reported that they would feel more guilt and shame in the "brother cheated" scenario than did those in the United States.

Note that this study suggests both similarities and differences between Chinese and mainstream United States culture. In both countries, participants expected to feel pride if they accomplished something, and guilt and shame if they did something morally wrong. The difference is that US participants felt these emotions more strongly if they did these things themselves, whereas in China, the activities of one's family reflect strongly enough on one's own identity that those activities can produce comparable levels of self-conscious emotion. In fact, participants in China said that it is more appropriate to feel pride for other people's accomplishments than for one's own (Stipek, 1998).

Power Distance: Vertical versus Horizontal Societies

Another major difference among cultures is the degree to which they emphasize power distance, or social hierarchy (Hofstede, 2001; see Figure 3.9). Harry Triandis (1995) defined a **vertical society** as one that emphasizes the social hierarchy, encouraging emotions and behaviors that advertise and reinforce status differences. A **horizontal society** is one in which people tend to minimize attention to status differences, and seldom acknowledge them publicly. For illustration, consider various nonhuman species. Most monkey troops have a rigid vertical structure in which one monkey, usually a large male, dominates the others. Deer and cattle have a more horizontal structure, in which all members of the herd have approximately the same status.

As an example, Nancy Much (1997) contrasts the social structure she observed in Hindu Indian households with typical American social interaction. Traditional Indian society is a prototypical vertical society, with a firm class structure and detailed rules for how people interact with others within and between classes. Even within a family, people observe rules of hierarchy, often addressing one another by title (such as older brother) rather than by name. Younger family members were expected to prostrate themselves (touching their head to the feet of a higher-ranking, older family member) as a standard display of respect. Failure to use the proper title or gesture of respect is a breach of propriety, reflecting badly on both parties. For instance, your father's friend would never invite you to call him by his first name, and you would never agree to do so.

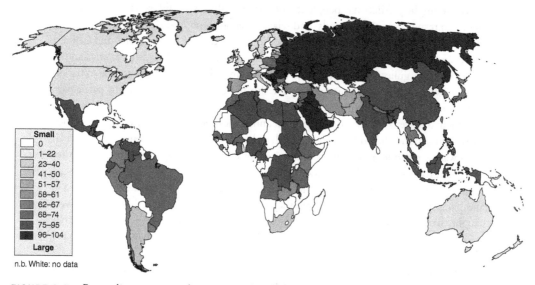

FIGURE 3.9. Power distance, or emphasis on social hierarchy, is another cultural variable that differs around the world. G. J. Hofstede (n.d.).

United States culture is more horizontal, although no human society is completely status free. People in the mainstream United States recognize status differences and acknowledge the authority of parents, bosses, elected leaders, and such, but this authority is limited to certain domains. A worker acknowledges the boss's right to give orders at the office, but not to command what meal to order at a restaurant or how to interact with one's spouse. The United States has no hereditary aristocracy, and North Americans treasure the idea that someone born poor can ascend to a position of power and success. An American student invited to address a professor by their first name might not think that particularly odd, interpreting it as a welcoming and friendly gesture rather than a breach of appropriate social behavior.

Like individualism/collectivism, power distance can facilitate or discourage the experience of certain kinds of emotion. For example, certain vertical societies have an emotion concept that the English language does not recognize, although it is often translated as shame. In the Orissa language in India, this is the *lajya* we discussed earlier, and among the Bedouin it is called *hasham*. It's helpful to think of this concept as a combination of embarrassment, shame, admiration, shyness, and gratitude (e.g., Abu-Lughod, 1986; Menon & Shweder, 1994; Russell, 1991). People feel this emotion in the presence of a higher-status person and show their respect by displaying it. For people in more horizontal societies, such as the United States, this feeling is difficult to relate to. It may seem unfamiliar, but imagine meeting in person an actor, musician, political figure, or someone else you deeply respect. The feeling you would have toward that person might be something like *lajya* or *hasham*.

Power distance can make the expression of certain emotions more or less appropriate as well. Researchers Hyisung Hwang and David Matsumoto (2014) examined the behavior of judo competitors in the Olympics, right after learning they had either won a medal or lost. They found that competitors from more hierarchical cultures—countries high on power distance—showed stronger displays of triumph (Figure 3.10) when they won, although power distance was unrelated to behavior among those who lost. This suggests that the overt display of dominance after success is encouraged more strongly in cultures where the social hierarchy is salient.

Cultural emphasis on power distance can also predict who displays which emotions. In Japan, for example, it is appropriate for a high-status person such as a coach of a sports team to express anger at a player, but deeply inappropriate for the player to show anger to the coach (Matsumoto, 1996). Anger implies high status, and for the player to express anger toward the coach would undermine the group's structure (Matsumoto, 1990). By contrast, group leaders are expected not to show sadness or fear, which might convey weakness. Note that these are guidelines for emotional *display*, not necessarily for emotional *experience*. Inevitably, players will sometimes feel angry toward their coaches, and leaders will sometimes feel sad or afraid. They can, however, stifle expression of these feelings to maintain the functioning of the group.

Similarly, investigators found differences among Nepali children in their willingness to express anger, based partly on status. In rural Nepal, Brahman Hindu children have relatively high status compared to Tamang children, who follow Tibetan Buddhism. When psychologists interviewed children about how they would feel and act in various difficult situations, the Brahman children said they would feel and express anger in many situations; the Tamang children almost never said they

FIGURE 3.10. Researchers found that Olympic judo competitors from high power distance cultures showed stronger dominance displays, such as this, after winning a medal than those from low power distance cultures.

would feel anger. In contrast, the Tamang children were far more likely to say they would feel shame or just okay. These contrasts relate partly to status and partly to religion; Buddhism praises a calm, balanced attitude as highly desirable (Cole, Bruschi, & Tamang, 2002; Cole & Tamang, 1998).

As with individualism and collectivism, these differences among cultures are relative, not absolute (Hofstede 2001). The United States is not a purely horizontal culture, and a coach is still more likely to yell at a player than vice versa. Similarly, an employer will show anger toward an employee, and a professor toward a student, more often than the reverse. However, the implications of status for emotional expression are less pronounced than in many other cultures.

Linear versus Dialectical Epistemology

Cultural differences in individualism/collectivism and power distance emphasize different ways to think about the relationships between people. Cultures can also differ in *epistemology*, or theories about what it means to know or understand something. According to Kaiping Peng and Richard Nisbett (1999), Western cultures such as the United States have a different epistemology than East Asian cultures such as China and Japan. In Western culture, epistemology has been heavily influenced by the theories of Aristotle. In this **linear epistemology**, knowing something means knowing what is constant and unchanging about it, knowing how it differs from other things, and knowing what is true and what is false. In contrast, East Asian epistemology has been heavily influenced by Confucianism, Taoism, and Buddhism. This **dialectical epistemology** emphasizes that true knowledge involves understanding that reality is changing rather than constant, that all things are interrelated rather than separate, and that the same proposition can be both true and false, from different perspectives. Although not many people in a given culture read the works of Aristotle or Confucius, psychologists believe that their ideas have become infused into the broader culture.

What implications might this have for emotion? You might remember that in Chapter 1 when we discussed dimensional models of emotion, we introduced a debate about whether positive and negative emotions can be experienced at the same time. Mixed positive and negative emotions are uncommon among people in the mainstream United States, although people do report them sometimes (Larsen & McGraw, 2014). **Emotional complexity**—the simultaneous experience of positive and negative emotions—is more common in highly collectivist/interdependent cultural contexts (Grossmann, Huynh, & Ellsworth, 2016). Researchers have asked whether the infrequency of mixed emotions in the United States might also be related to linear epistemology, which encourages Western thinkers to conceive of positive and negative emotion as mutually exclusive opposites. In contrast, people from cultures emphasizing dialectical epistemology may be less likely to think of emotions in terms of opposites such as happy *or* sad and loving *or* angry, and therefore may feel mixed emotions more often.

Studies suggest that this may be the case. For example, in one study researchers asked participants to report on their emotions frequently as they went about their daily lives. They found that participants in East Asia were more likely than those in the United States to report feeling positive and negative emotions at the same time (Scollon et al., 2004). Especially in predominantly positive situations, Japanese people are more likely than people in the United States to report mixed emotions (Miyamoto, Uchida, & Ellsworth, 2010). Another study found that Asian-American biculturals who had been encouraged to think about the Asian aspect of their identities reported more mixed emotions in diaries over a two-week period, compared with those encouraged to think about the American aspect of their identities (Perunovic, Heller, & Rafaeli, 2007).

In each of these studies, it is difficult to know whether participants in different cultures experienced emotion differently because of the way they saw the world or because they were encountering different experiences. To tease these possibilities apart, researchers in one study asked whether United States residents of East Asian ethnicity would experience more mixed emotions than those of European ancestry when engaged in the same task (Shiota et al., 2010). They invited same-ethnicity Asian American and European American dating couples to come to the laboratory for a series of structured conversations, which were videotaped. After every conversation, each member of the couple rated his or her emotions during the conversation. In the first conversation, each partner teased the other, making up a nickname and telling a story explaining the nickname. In the second, each partner shared a concern or worry about something outside the relationship. In the third, each partner talked about a previous romantic partner. In the fourth, the couple talked about their first date. In each conversation participants might reasonably have felt loving toward their partners, but could also have felt a negative emotion, such as shame at being teased, anger at hearing about the partner's ex, and so forth. The research question was: Would Asian American partners be more likely than white partners to report feeling love and a negative emotion *at the same time* during the conversations?

The conversations themselves were similar. For example, Asian and white couples showed similar patterns of criticizing versus praising each other during the teasing task, taking responsibility versus acting helpless during the current concern conversation, and so forth. However, participants in the two groups reported different patterns of emotional experience. In almost every conversation, European Americans reported *either* love *or* the target negative emotion, but not both—love and negative emotion were negatively correlated. In contrast, the Asian American participants were more likely to report feeling love and a negative emotion at the same time; in some conversations love and negative emotion were positively correlated. Although it is hard to be certain that these effects were a result of cultural differences in epistemology rather than some other cultural factor, it was consistent with predictions suggested by the linear versus dialectical distinction.

Culture and Ideal Affect

The three aspects of culture discussed above have implications for the emotions people are expected to feel and show, and actually do feel and show, in different cultural contexts. Researcher Jeanne Tsai has shown that **ideal affect**, the profile of emotional states that people ideally *want* to feel, also varies from person to person and culture to culture. In fact, some research suggests that the effects of cultural variables such as individualism-collectivism and power distance on *ideal* affect may be even stronger than they are on people's *actual* emotional experience (Tsai, Knutson, & Fung, 2006; Tsai et al., 2007).

Across gender and culture lines, most people say they would like to feel more positive emotion than negative emotion (Tsai, 2007; Senft et al., 2021). However, people in the United States show a preference for high-arousal positive affect states such as excitement and enthusiasm, whereas people in East Asian cultures tend to show a stronger preference for low-arousal positive affect, such as contentment and tranquility (Tsai et al., 2006). Ideal affect shapes our behavior in important ways (Figure 3.11). For example, European Americans are more likely to say that opportunities for exploration and excitement are important for their vacations and other leisure activities, whereas Chinese people are more likely to prefer relaxation (Tsai, 2007). Preference for high-arousal positive affect is

FIGURE 3.11.   Whereas people in mainstream United States culture tend to seek experiences that evoke high-arousal positive emotions, such as excitement, people in Chinese culture are more likely to prefer activities that promote low-arousal positive emotion, such as contentment and relaxation.

associated with purchasing consumer products that increase arousal, whereas preference for low-arousal positive affect is associated with preference for relaxing products (Tsai, Chim, & Sims, 2015). Moreover, studies suggest that we are more likely to feel comfortable with and trust other people who display the kind of positive affect we consider ideal. Preferring people who express open-mouthed, toothy smiles versus closed-mouth, contented smiles tracks with preference for high- versus low-arousal positive affect social interaction partners (Park et al., 2016), physicians (Sims & Tsai, 2015), and job applicants (Tsai et al., 2019), respectively.

Ideal affect varies across cultural groups within the United States as well. A team of researchers examined ratings of the desirability of 19 specific emotions, provided by more than 1,600 undergraduate participants of European, Latino, or Asian heritage enrolled at US universities (Senft et al., 2022). The researchers used a statistical technique called latent class analysis to try to reveal common profiles of ideal affect that accounted for most participants' ratings. As seen in prior research, nearly all people rated positive emotions as generally desirable, and negative emotions as generally undesirable. Against this backdrop, however, four main classes or profiles of ideal affect emerged: (1) in the *polarized* profile, participants reported strong desirability of positive emotions and undesirability of negative emotions; (2) in the *hyperpolarized* profile participants reported even more extreme desirability of positive and aversion to negative emotions; (3) in the *positive focus* profile, participants reported extremely high desirability of positive emotions, but were relatively tolerant of negative emotions, rating them as only moderately undesirable; (4) in the *moderate* profile participants reported less extreme ideal affect in general, rating positive emotions as only moderately desirable and negative emotions as moderately undesirable.

Notably, people's cultural background predicted which of these profiles best matched their own pattern of desirability ratings. European Americans' ratings typically fit either the polarized or hyperpolarized profile. Among Latinos, the polarized profile was most common. For Asian-Americans, the best-fit profile depended on whether participants were born in the United States or immigrated to the United States after spending much of their lives in another country. Whereas Asian immigrants were most likely to report moderate ideal affect profiles (commonly observed in other research as well, e.g., Smith et al., 2016), US-born Asians tended to report positive focus ideal affect profiles. This latter distinction is striking because the profiles of US-born Asians were not somewhere midway between those of mainstream Americans and those of immigrants. Rather, they suggest a new subculture within the United States with a distinct sense of the ideal emotional life.

Cultural differences in ideal affect may have important implications for people's emotional well-being. One recurring finding in US samples is that extreme **motivation to pursue happiness**, defined as the desire and expectation to feel very happy nearly all the time, may ironically make us unhappy. In US samples, very high scores on a questionnaire measure of motivation to pursue happiness have been linked to lower scores on psychological well-being, and higher risk for depression (e.g., Ford et al., 2014; Mauss et al., 2011). These results suggest that expecting to feel happy all the time will inevitably lead to disappointment, as normal life setbacks and demands for not-fun activity will feel like something is wrong with your life. In an interesting twist, however, the intensity and even the direction of this effect may depend on culture. In a study of nearly 800 participants in several countries, Brett Ford and colleagues (2015) found that motivation to pursue happiness had no relationship with well-being in Germany, and was *positively* associated with well-being in Russia, Japan, and Taiwan. Moreover, the positive effects seen in the last three countries were accounted for by their tendency to define "happiness" in terms of positive social connection, rather than individual achievement or exciting positive experiences. In other words, the data suggest that strong motivation to pursue happiness may be good for well-being provided that your definition of "happiness" emphasizes the lower-arousal, connected-to-loved-ones variety of positive affect.

Other research suggests that high-arousal positive affect ideals might confer some benefits as well as risk, at least in certain cultural contexts. Researchers Jiquan Lin and Julia Dmitrieva (2019) examined ideal affect, actual affect, acculturation to mainstream US culture, and depressive symptoms among Chinese college students attending universities in the United States. Using structural equation modeling (a fancy statistical technique that evaluates relationships among variables) to estimate the pathways connecting these variables, the researchers found that participants who were more acculturated to mainstream US culture reported higher valuation of high-arousal positive effect, which directly predicted stronger symptoms of depression. Through a separate pathway, however, ideal high-arousal positive affect also predicted more *actual* experience of high-arousal positive affect, which predicted *lower* levels of depression. Thus, at least for these Chinese students visiting the United States, increased high-arousal positive affect ideals seemed to have both positive and negative implications for well-being, through different pathways (see Figure 3.12).

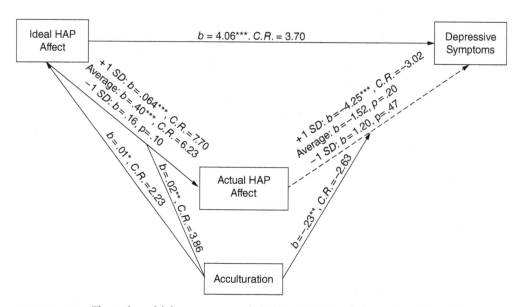

FIGURE 3.12. This path model shows separate paths linking ideal high-arousal positive affect with depressive symptoms, with a direct path predicting higher depression, but a path mediated by actual experience of high-arousal positive affect predicting lower depressive symptoms. Lin & Dmitrieva, 2019 (Figure 1).

METHODOLOGICAL CONSIDERATIONS

Learning Objectives

- List and explain three limitations to studying culture by comparing the survey responses of people in two different countries.
- Define cultural priming, and summarize an example of this alternative approach to studying culture.

In this chapter we introduced the question of how culture shapes our emotions in terms of language, experience, and expression. Most studies of culture and emotion have examined differences (or similarities) between people in two or more countries, or between people of different ethnicities within the same country. This is the common strategy used in cultural psychology, and it can be a good start to a program of research. However, there are several limitations to this strategy, and to the way it has been applied so far.

The first limitation is a practical one. Most psychology researchers come from prosperous, Western countries—especially the United States and Canada—and when they study culture it usually involves going to some other country and comparing that place with home. They might choose the other country because of its theoretical significance, such as being a good example of a collectivist culture, but they also consider how easily they can gain access. Many cross-cultural studies contrast the United States or Canada with Japan, China, Hong Kong, or Taiwan—all prosperous, modern countries where many psychology researchers have their roots. There is nothing wrong with these comparisons, which have greatly enriched our understanding of how and why cultures vary in emotion, but many other cultures have been overlooked.

In particular, researchers' understanding of how collectivism shapes emotion may be biased by the strong emphasis on East Asian collectivist contexts. Researchers have begun to show greater interest in Latin American culture, where collectivism is also highly valued, and its implications for emotion. One distinct feature of Latin American culture is its emphasis on ***simpatía***, defined as a relational value of warmth, compassion, and prioritization of group harmony (Acevedo et al., 2020; Figure 3.13). The ideal affect profiles reported by young adults of Latino heritage within the United States, in which positive emotions are highly desired and negative emotions rather discouraged, are consistent with *simpatía*. In contrast, participants of Asian heritage tended to report more moderate profiles, reflecting a cultural concern that both positive and negative emotions have the potential to disrupt relationships and affect others' feelings. Both profiles are geared toward preserving relationship harmony, but they do so in different ways.

A second problem is that cultures do not follow clear national boundaries. Within the United States, cultures differ greatly between people of different ethnic backgrounds, religions, and regions of the country (Cohen, 2009). People moving from one part of the United States to another often experience culture shock, as if they had moved to another country. Even within one city at one point in time—Minneapolis, Minnesota—researchers found that young adults of Scandinavian ancestry expressed their emotions with more restraint than those of Irish ancestry (Tsai & Chentsova-Dutton, 2003). Also, cultures change over time. As we noted earlier, Japan has become less collectivist since the mid-twentieth century, likely due to economic growth and increased urbanization (Matsumoto et al., 1998; Varnum & Grossmann, 2017). Differences in social class within countries have been linked to cultural variables as well, such as individualism-collectivism and the extent

FIGURE 3.13. *Simpatía*, a quality of interpersonal relations characterized by warmth, compassion, and prioritization of social harmony, is highly valued in Latin American culture.

to which explanations of other people's actions emphasize their situation rather than dispositional factors (Kraus, Piff, & Keltner, 2011). Cultural or subcultural differences are probably even greater within countries where transportation and communication are more difficult. For example, more than 20 languages are recognized as official across the states of India.

Odd as it sounds, culture itself is the third major difficulty in interpreting differences between two countries. Suppose researchers ask people of various cultures to rate how openly they express their emotions on a 1 to 7 scale. Rating yourself on such a scale implies a comparison of yourself to others. So, if you rate your expressivity as 4 (average), you mean average with respect to the other people you know, presumably of your own culture. If the mean expressivity rating for people in both your and some other culture is 4, can we conclude that people in the two cultures are equally expressive? Not necessarily. If the average differs between cultures, then the 4 will have different meaning in each—and presumably that difference is exactly what the researcher aims to reveal. Moreover, people across cultures differ in how they use rating scales in general. For example, people from some Asian cultures are more likely to give answers in the middle range of a several-point scale, regardless of the scale's content, whereas people in the United States and Canada tend to give more extreme ratings (Smith et al., 2016). In short, cultural comparisons based on self-ratings are fraught with difficulties of interpretation (Heine et al., 2002).

Example: Effects of Priming Culture on Emotion

Aside from the practical concerns discussed above, there is a conceptual problem with studying culture by comparing two countries or distinct groups. Look back at the definition of culture offered at the beginning of the chapter. Is studying differences between two groups the same as studying culture? Not really. When we compare, say, China and the United States, we measure some outcome in each country and try to infer the cultural process behind any differences that we find. We can't even be sure that anything about culture is the reason behind the differences we find, because we can't randomly assign people to one culture or another.

Or can we? One clever technique in cultural psychology involves **cultural priming**—studying **bicultural** people who have deep experience with two distinct cultural contexts and using an experimental manipulation to make one of each participant's cultural identities especially salient before proceeding to the rest of the study. For example, a researcher might ask some Asian-American participants to think of a time when they felt very Asian, and others to think of a time when they felt very American. This approach can also be used to examine the effects of specific aspects of culture on various psychological processes, including emotion. For example, researchers might ask some participants to think about a time they accomplished a goal alone, to prime individualism; others would think about a time they accomplished something as part of a team, priming collectivism. This helps to isolate the aspect of culture thought to be important, and the experimental approach also allows researchers to draw conclusions about cause–effect relationships that would not be possible in a cross-sectional research design.

Here's an example. Recall a finding discussed earlier that contrary to the pattern seen in the United States, motivation to pursue happiness and well-being were positively correlated among participants in Russia, Japan, and Taiwan, and this effect was accounted for by a tendency in these cultures to define "happiness" in terms of positive relationships with others (Ford et al., 2015). A team of researchers led by Lillian Shin and Sonja Lyubomirsky (Shin et al., 2021) addressed a similar phenomenon using cultural priming. Participants were undergraduates in Hong Kong, fluent in both Chinese and English. As discussed earlier, language is one mechanism through which culture is transmitted, so having people communicate in one language versus the other should make the associated cultural worldview more salient. Participants were asked to write brief essays about two separate acts of kindness, with a one-week interval in between. One essay was about kindness toward a close other, whereas the other was about kindness to a stranger; half of the participants wrote the "close other" essay in Chinese and the "stranger" one in English, and the remaining participants did the reverse. This is called a **within-subjects design**—each participant is in multiple conditions of an experiment. Priming studies can assign different participants to different conditions instead, but there are statistical advantages to the within-subjects approach. After writing each essay, participants rated their mood. Results showed that the effect of relationship type depended on the language in which participants wrote: when writing in Chinese, mood was more positive after writing about kindness toward a loved one rather than a stranger, but this was not the case when writing in English. This pattern is consistent with heightened collectivism, in which in-group–out-group distinctions tend to be more pronounced.

Here's another example. Russian culture is reputed to be rather pessimistic, brooding, and dark. Consistent with this, research shows that both actual and ideal negative affect are rated more highly by people in Russia than among North Americans (e.g., Chentsova-Dutton, Choi, & Ryder, 2014; Grossmann & Kross, 2010). Russian children's

Cultural Prime   followed immediately by...   **Lexical Decision**
Is it a word?

FIGURE 3.14.   In the lexical decision task, participants complete many trials in which they first view a visual image, and then decide whether the string of letters immediately after is (or is not) a word. Analyses ask whether word recognition is faster after seeing images intended to "prime" a related concept than after control images. This technique can be used to experimentally activate different cultural systems of meaning in people who are bicultural.

picture books depict anger, sadness, and fear more often than these are seen in US books, and Russian parents report reading books with more negative content to their kids (Chentsova-Dutton et al., 2021).

Researchers Igor Grossmann, Phoebe Ellsworth, and Ying-Yi Hong (2012) conducted a study with ethnic Russians living in Latvia—a country with a culture more strongly influenced by Western European worldviews. As with the bilingual participants in Hong Kong, Russian Latvians were expected to be bicultural, able to relate to both Russian and Latvian cultural worldviews. Study participants performed a series of trials, first briefly viewing an image evoking a Russian or Latvian mindset, or neither; and then deciding whether the string of letters that followed was or was not a real word. This **lexical decision task** method presumes that if the conceptual meaning of some word is already somewhat activated, that concept should be accessible to consciousness, thereby accelerating recognition of the word (Figure 3.14). Nonword letter strings are included in some trials so that "yes" is not always the correct answer. Results showed that after viewing Russian primes participants were faster to detect negative-valence words, and slower to detect positive-valence words, relative to their reaction times after neutral image primes. The opposite was true after prime images evoking Latvian culture: detection of positive-valence words sped up, while slowing down for negative-valence words. These kinds of findings add powerful experimental evidence to address the effects of culture per se on people's emotions and experience.

INTEGRATING EVOLUTIONARY AND CULTURAL APPROACHES
Learning Objectives
- Define display rules, and explain how they illustrate a way in which evolved responses and cultural shaping can interact.

- Summarize an emotion script from your own language, analyzing which (if any) aspects of that script might be observed across cultures, and which are likely to be specific to your culture.
- Define historical heterogeneity, and explain its association with facial expressions of emotion around the world.

On one hand, certain aspects of emotion share common features across cultures. On the other hand, culture has a powerful influence on our emotional lives. Although both positions are supported by research, some researchers mainly emphasize the universal aspect, whereas others emphasize cultural differences. Is there any way to integrate both aspects in one theory? Here are three examples of proposed ways to meet this goal.

The Neurocultural Theory of Emotion

Paul Ekman's (1972) neurocultural theory was the first explicit attempt to combine evolutionary and cultural forces shaping emotion. In this model (see Figure 3.15), events in the environment (as well as memories or imagined events) are appraised or interpreted by individuals in specific ways, leading to nervous system activity triggering an emotional response. This neural activity sets in motion a variety of physiological changes, cognitive processing biases, and motivational changes, as well as activating facial expression templates generated by an innate and universal *facial action program*. In the absence of cultural influence, these responses will lead to prototypical, coherent, observable emotional behavior.

Neurocultural theory presumes, however, that cultural influence *is* present, altering the output of the process as well as aspects of the input. Because Ekman's own area of expertise lies in nonverbal expression, his articulation of neurocultural theory was geared mainly toward explaining both universality and cultural variation in facial expressions of

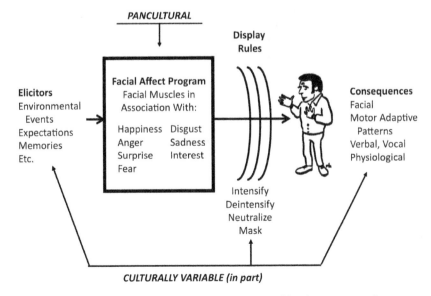

FIGURE 3.15. Paul Ekman's (1972) neurocultural theory of facial expressions of emotion.

emotion. Ekman proposed that different cultural groups have **display rules** that specify which emotions are appropriate to express in various situations and social contexts. Early in life, learning and following these rules should require effort, but with growing experience in a particular cultural context, the rules may become habitual, and followed automatically.

Display rules are prominent parts of cultural systems, helping to guide a consistent pattern of social interaction. For example, we noted earlier that in cultures characterized by strong power distance, in which the social hierarchy is prominently displayed and enforced, it is okay for a high-status person such as a coach to show anger toward a lower-status person, such as a player, but very inappropriate for anger to be displayed in the other direction. This display rule reinforces the roles of various people within the group, allowing the group to function effectively. In another example, Olympic judo competitors from countries around the world all tended to show a pride or triumph posture upon winning a match, but these were more subtle and briefer among those from relatively egalitarian cultures than among those from highly hierarchical cultures (Hwang & Matsumoto, 2014). This example highlights both the universality (in the form of the emotional display) and cultural variability (in the intensity and duration of the display) predicted by Ekman's neurocultural theory.

Figure 3.15 suggests that cultures provide feeling rules as well as display rules. In addition to adjusting the observable output of an emotional response, culture also shapes how different situations are appraised or interpreted, so that an event might lead to different emotions among people from different cultures. We saw an example of cultural feeling rules in Stipek's (1998) work on the events that elicit self-conscious emotions, such as pride and shame, in China versus the United States. In that case, distinct cultural meanings of "self" led to different appraisals of whether a close other's behavior was self-relevant or not. In another example, researcher Dov Cohen and colleagues (1996) showed in several studies that young men who had grown up in the American South—a **culture of honor** in which one's reputation for strength, self-reliance, personal integrity, and toughness is an important basis for social standing, and protected fiercely—responded to an insult from a stranger after an accidental bump in a hallway with considerable anger, whereas men from Northern states often found the interaction amusing. By situating the same eliciting event within different systems of meaning, cultures may greatly alter how we respond emotionally to that event.

Emotion Episodes as Socially Constructed Scripts

Another way to integrate universal and cultural aspects of emotion has been offered by James Russell (1991). To understand his explanation, it will help to think back to the definition of emotion we tentatively proposed in Chapter 1. This definition included several events: person X perceives some event in the environment and interprets it in a certain way; X's physiology changes, perhaps with increased heart rate and blood pressure; X reports having a certain feeling; X displays a particular facial expression; X wants a certain outcome in the situation and takes action to try to bring about that outcome. We called this series of events an emotion, as have many researchers.

Researchers working from the assumption that emotions are evolved adaptations think of sequences such as these as innate and universal. Russell (1991) offers a different interpretation—that such sequences are socially constructed scripts or cultural beliefs about what events, thoughts, sensations feelings, and behaviors go together. In Chapter 1 we described the process of psychological construction of emotion concepts (Barrett, 2006). In this case, the **emotion scripts** reflect not only individuals' idiosyncratic memories, but also systems of meaning shared by people in the same culture. Some scripts are more common than others, due to cross-culturally important features of the environments in which we live (e.g., the presence of predators or other source of mortal danger, or social hierarchy), to which we have some limited set of instinctive responses. These cases might be the basis for a rough emotion concept likely to receive universal recognition. However, there is ample room for cultures to tinker with components of the scripts, and even create new ones, defining and encouraging unique emotion concepts. According to Russell, emotion scripts can be broad or precise, and can emphasize some aspects of emotional responding over others.

Based on this framework, Russell (1991) proposes that it is possible to identify aspects of emotion scripts that are more likely to be universal, and those that are more likely to be culture specific. The universal aspects may include such components as prototypical antecedents or objective eliciting situations, facial expressions, physiological changes, and action tendencies. The perceived cause of an emotion, however, may vary tremendously from one culture to the next. In some societies, the perceived cause may be an interpersonal event, in others it may be a physical illness, and in yet others it may be supernatural events such as curses, possession, or ghosts. Note the difference between an *actual* prototypical eliciting situation and the *perceived* cause embedded in the meaning system of the person in some culture. Russell says they may be very different.

Also, the expected consequences of emotion in the script may vary considerably. This statement takes Ekman's (1972) notion of display rules, and says that they are incorporated into the very emotion concepts recognized by a society. As an example of these differences, we can take *litost*, the Czech emotion described by Milan Kundera (1980) earlier in this chapter. *Litost* is caused by a sudden insight into one's own misery—a completely internal event that may or may not reflect some universally recognizable or objective event in the environment. The outcome of *litost* is a desire for revenge—a consequence that might manifest differently in another society with another set of feeling and display rules.

Socioecological Determinants of Culture

Throughout this chapter we have discussed various ways in which culture might influence our experience of emotion. This begs the question of the origins of culture itself. Can we understand and predict the nature of cultural worldviews and their implications for emotion around the globe? According to the **socioecological perspective** (Oishi, 2014; Sng et al., 2018), many cultural characteristics can be explained in part by features of the local physical and social environment. The idea is that culture is not random, but rather reflects an appropriate response to the constraints of ecological factors such as population density, the types and distribution of material resources, the kinds and prevalence of disease-causing pathogens, the extent to which people in your community are reasonably stable over time versus moving around a lot, and other factors with implications for people's lives.

If evolution has bestowed on human nature certain algorithms linking important properties of the environment to behavior, then we would expect behavior to look very different across distinct ecologies. Moreover, culture itself may "evolve" in response to properties of the local physical environment, such as climate, but also to human-created features, such as the kind of crops grown locally. Genetic evolution typically occurs over millennia. Individual learning can happen in a matter of seconds. Cultures, on the other hand, are likely to keep pace with changes in ecology on time scales ranging from years to centuries.

Paula Niedenthal, Magdalena Rychlowska, and their colleagues have published a series of studies documenting a fascinating socioecological effect in the domain of emotion. They asked whether **historical heterogeneity**—the extent to which a country's current population reflects immigration from a wide range of other geographical regions over the last 500 years—is a predictor of various aspects of facial expressions of emotion. Figure 3.16 shows the distribution of historical heterogeneity around the world. The United States is an example of very high historical heterogeneity, because people have been migrating to the United States from around the globe for hundreds of years. At the other extreme, the vast majority of people living in Japan are . . . Japanese, so Japan scores very low in historical heterogeneity. Would you expect that people in high historical heterogeneity cultures would show facial expressions that are relatively strong, or relatively subtle, and why?

The researchers predicted that historical heterogeneity would be positively correlated with expressive intensity, as people coming from different cultural backgrounds had to communicate their feelings clearly and without ambiguity. Consistent with this hypothesis, they found evidence that higher historical heterogeneity predicts display rules encouraging more intense facial expressions, even after controlling for possible confounds such as income, population density/urbanity, and individualism/collectivism (Rychlowska et al., 2015). Present-day ethnic diversity did not have this effect, suggesting that the primary

FIGURE 3.16. Historical heterogeneity of countries around the world. Niedenthal et al. (2019).

mechanism is cultural rather than an individual response to diversity in the environment. Spontaneous displays of emotion by people in high-historical heterogeneity cultures are also more easily recognized around the world, suggesting that they better represent whatever universal expression prototypes humans have (Wood, Rychlowska, & Niedenthal, 2016).

Other studies have found that higher historical heterogeneity predicts more intense smiling—both self-reported and observed in people watching film clips—as well as reports of affiliation (rather than dominance) as the main motivation for smiling (Girard & McDuff, 2017; Niedenthal et al., 2018; Rychlowska et al., 2015). Have you ever heard that outside the United States, Americans have a reputation for smiling way too much? Well, (a) it's based on a kernel of truth, and (b) there's a good reason for it! As we shall discuss further in Chapter 9, smiling invites safe social interaction, essentially saying "I'm not going to hurt you, so please don't yell at/kick me!" This is arguably less important where high genetic relatedness and long history in the same, homogeneous community provide a foundation for cooperation, as well as some protection against aggression. Where that foundation is absent, making it extremely clear that you are not a threat and just want to get along has important benefits.

SUMMARY

Some mechanisms of emotion may be part of human nature, yet cultures differ greatly in what emotions they encourage or discourage, in who is expected to express what emotions in what situations, and in how emotions play out in daily life. People in different cultures talk about emotion in very different ways, carving up the space of affective/emotional experience into concepts that make sense for that social and ecological context, and assigning a word label to each slice. Analyses of language across cultures suggest some similarities in key emotion concepts, but a lot more differences. Beyond vocabulary, cultural systems of meaning shape our experience and expression of emotion in a wide range of ways—often without our realizing it.

According to all three proposals for integrating the evolutionary and social construction approaches to emotion, culture influences emotion because emotion is profoundly social, and people in different ecological and cultural contexts endorse different patterns of social interaction. We hope we have convinced you that evolutionary and social construction approaches to emotion are fully compatible with each other. We still have much to learn about the mechanisms of culture and evolution, but clearly both make large contributions to our emotional lives.

KEY TERMS

amae: Japanese term describing the feeling of pleasurable dependence on another person, like the feeling an infant has toward its mother (p. 87)

bicultural: an individual with the ability to alternate between membership in one culture and membership in another (p. 107)

colexification: combination of concepts captured by separate words in one language into a single word in another language (p. 88)

collectivism: prioritizing the group over the individual, valuing group identification, deference, social harmony, and interdependence (p. 93)

cultural priming: an experimental manipulation that makes one of a bicultural person's cultural identities especially salient for a short period of time (p. 107)

culture: the meanings, conceptions, and interpretive schemes that are activated by participation in social practices (including language) (p. 82)

culture of honor: a culture in which one's reputation for strength, self-reliance, pride, personal integrity, and toughness is an important basis for social standing (p. 110)

dialectical epistemology: belief that reality is always changing, that all things are interrelated, and that the same proposition can be both true and false from different perspectives (p. 100)

display rules: a cultural group's rules about when and with whom it is appropriate to display certain kinds of emotional expressions (p. 110)

emotional complexity: the simultaneous experience of positive and negative emotions (p. 101)

emotion scripts: socially constructed, cultural beliefs that certain events, thoughts, sensations, feelings, and behaviors cluster together in an emotion-like concept (p. 111)

historical heterogeneity: the extent to which a country's population reflects immigration from a wide range of other geographical regions over the last 500 years (p. 112)

horizontal society: one in which people typically minimize attention to status differences and seldom acknowledge those differences publicly (p. 98)

hypercognize: to create an elaborate network of associations and distinctions that lead to an increase in the vocabulary for some emotion (p. 92)

hypocognize: to fail to give an emotion much cognitive elaboration or detail (p. 92)

ideal affect: the profile of emotions that is considered most desirable; varies from individual to individual and across cultures (p. 102)

individualism: emphasis on individual uniqueness, personal rights, being true to one's self, and independence from others (p. 93)

lexical decision task: a task used to assess concept activation, with many trials in which participants see a prime image followed by a string of letters; they decide as quickly as possible whether or not the letters form a word (p. 108)

linear epistemology: belief that knowing something means knowing what is constant and unchanging about it, how it differs from other things, and what is true and what is false about it (p. 100)

motivation to pursue happiness: the extent of one's desire and expectation to feel very happy nearly all of the time (p. 103)

Sapir–Whorf hypothesis: proposal that humans require language to think and therefore we have only those experiences, thoughts, and perceptions for which we have words (p. 90)

simpatía: a relational value of warmth, compassion, and prioritization of group harmony, strongly emphasized in Latin American culture (p. 105)

social construction of emotion: process by which societies create culture-specific ways of thinking about, experiencing, and expressing emotion (p. 81)

socioecological perspective: a theoretical perspective proposing that cultural characteristics can be explained, at least in part, by features of the local physical and social environment (p. 111)

vertical society: one that pays particular attention to the social hierarchy and encourages emotions and behaviors that respect status differences (p. 98)

within-subjects design: an experimental design in which each subject participates in multiple conditions, rather than just one; analyses compare performance of the same subjects across these conditions (p. 107)

THOUGHT/DISCUSSION QUESTIONS

1. What emotion concepts are hypercognized versus hypocognized in your language? How do you see this in its vocabulary, and in the ways people talk about emotions? If you are fluent in more than one language, consider how the two languages compare.

2. Of the various cultures and subcultures in which you participate, do some have a more horizontal social structure and others a more vertical structure? Does this affect the way emotions are expressed in those groups?

3. Talk with friends born in different countries, or to immigrant parents who are fluent in different languages as well as English. Do those languages have emotion words not present in English? Does English have emotion words that do not translate? How does emotional life in other countries differ from that in mainstream American culture?

4. What are some cultural display rules in your larger culture, as well as in the subcultures of your local community, family, and friends? Are people consciously aware of these rules, or are they more implicit?

SUGGESTIONS FOR FURTHER READING

Abu-Lughod, L. (2000). *Veiled sentiments: Honor and poetry in a Bedouin society.* University of California Press. A rich description of the relationship between social structure and emotion in Bedouin culture, as observed by a Palestinian-American anthropologist.

Coontz, S. (2006). *Marriage, a history: How love conquered marriage.* Penguin. In modern Western society, marriage is presumed to be based on love. In this popular press book Coontz offers a rich historical and cross-cultural tour of marriage, highlighting the novelty of the love-marriage link and describing the forces that produced it.

Markus, H. R., & Kitayama, S. (1991). Culture and the self: Implications for cognition, emotion, and motivation. *Psychological Review, 98*(2), 224–253. The original literature review arguing that culturally shaped aspects of self-concept have powerful implications for emotion, this paper has had enormous impact on affective science as well as cultural psychology.

Niedenthal, P. M., Rychlowska, M., Zhao, F., & Wood, A. (2019). Historical migration patterns shape contemporary cultures of emotion. *Perspectives on Psychological Science, 14*(4), 560–573. This fascinating paper summarizes the implications of historical heterogeneity for cultural differences in how people express their emotions through the face.

CHAPTER 4

What Activates Motivation and Emotion?

Think about the last time you really wanted to eat something. Why did you feel that way? Was it because you were actually physically hungry? Perhaps you hadn't eaten in a while, or were late for a meal you usually have at a certain time of day. Had you recently engaged in intense physical exercise that used up a lot of energy? Alternatively, was it because you saw and/or smelled some food that you find especially delicious? Were you feeling stressed or upset about something? You may have been aware of any of these causes, or some combination of them, but not others.

Now think about the last time you felt a strong emotion. What caused you to feel that way? On the surface, the answer may seem obvious. In many cases we can easily identify a specific object or event that elicited our own emotion or that of another person—a spider caused fear; a filthy refrigerator caused disgust; a friend moving away to a new city made us sad; an A+ on an exam made us feel proud; a funny joke made us laugh; a cup of hot cocoa elicited contentment. With more careful thought, however, some complexities emerge. Let's take the filthy fridge example. Let's say you're visiting a friend's house, they invite you to grab a cold drink, and you open the door to see a bunch of rotting food (Figure 4.1). Why do you care? Why should this elicit an emotion from you? What is your emotional response *about*?

At least most people can agree on the appropriate emotional reaction to a dirty refrigerator. In many cases, we are baffled by other people's emotions. Think about a time when another person became angry with you, and you had no idea why. Perhaps you said something innocuous, or were minding your own business, and suddenly your friend, or romantic partner, or whoever, was yelling at you or giving you the cold shoulder. All you could think was, "What did I do?" Similarly, think of a time when a friend of yours was really frightened, or despondent, and you thought they were being silly—the friend's emotions seemed inappropriate or out of proportion to the situation.

Sometimes even our own emotions are a mystery. Imagine waking up one morning, and for no reason you're in a grumpy mood. As you drive to class, the traffic is moving slowly; not much more slowly than usual, but somehow today it really bothers you.

FIGURE 4.1. Why do the contents of someone else's refrigerator elicit an emotional response from you—in this case, disgust? This chapter discusses the role of appraisal—cognitive evaluation of what some stimulus or situation means for one's own goals, concerns, and well-being—in evoking emotions.

In addition, it's hot out, and your car's air conditioner is broken, and you're getting uncomfortable. When you finally get to class, you find yourself snapping irritably at another student. Realizing what you've done, you think, "what is wrong with me today?"

Our own motivation can be a mystery as well. You might be struggling just to make it through your classes this semester; your roommate is in the same classes, yet *also* manages to work a part-time job, is President of the student wellness club, and plays lacrosse. Where does she get all her energy? Perhaps you have yet to choose a major that fires you up, while your friends are already charging headlong toward their dream careers and lives. Where do they get their clear sense of direction?

One of the challenges faced by those who study emotion and motivation has been to explain how and why these states are activated, including why people can have such different reactions to the same situation, and the same response to completely different situations. Even simple physical drives such as hunger can be activated in a variety of ways, as we just discussed. Activating emotions is even more complicated. Most researchers have concluded that there must be some psychological process between perception of the eliciting stimulus and the emotional reaction. In Chapter 1 we introduced the term "appraisal," which we defined as a cognitive evaluation of what a stimulus or situation means for the self. In the remainder of this chapter we will dig into that concept more deeply, explaining the general idea as well as how different theorists use the term. We will also present the case made by a smaller number of theorists that at least in some cases, no appraisal is necessary to have an emotional response.

PROXIMAL CAUSES OF DRIVES, INSTINCTS, AND EMOTIONS

Learning Objectives

- Summarize the general process by which deficits in the body's basic needs generate motivational drives.
- Explain the role of classical conditioning in developing automatic emotional and motivational responses to specific external stimuli (cues).
- Define "appraisal," differentiate appraisal from the objective features of an emotion-eliciting stimulus/event, and identify the appraisal in an example emotion episode.

In Chapters 2 and 3 we discussed broad evolutionary and cultural functions served by emotions and other motivational states, asking why people have the capacity for such responses at all; these are the **distal causes** of emotion and motivation. In this chapter we ask how emotions and motivational states are activated within a particular person, at a particular time. These are the **proximal causes** of emotion and motivation—those causing the state to occur in the moment. It would be nice and tidy if instincts were activated by one kind of proximal cause; drives were activated by another kind; and emotions by a third kind. As we shall see, it's not that simple. However, it's useful to begin by differentiating among three broad classes of proximal causes, so we can see how they work on their own and ask questions about how they influence each other.

Messages from the Body

In Chapter 2 we defined drives as motivational states reflecting unmet deficits in the demands of the physical body. As we shall discuss in detail in Chapter 6, humans have sophisticated neural circuitry for keeping track of circulating glucose levels, hydration, blood oxygen, core temperature, and other bodily factors crucial for staying alive, as well as a complex neural and hormonal messaging system that helps make whatever corrections are needed. Because behavior is sometimes required to make the necessary adjustments, we may experience these messages as motivational states such as hunger, thirst, or another form of physical discomfort. In this case, the proximal cause of the motivational state is within the body.

For example, the hypothalamus and brainstem constantly receive messages from the rest of the body about the amount of usable energy present, relative to current and anticipated physical demands (Murphy & Bloom, 2006; see Figure 4.2). Fatty tissue cells produce a hormone called **leptin** that tends to reduce the sense of hunger, communicating that a good amount of energy is already stored. **Ghrelin** is a peptide hormone produced by the stomach, as well as some other parts of the digestive system and structures in the brain, that generally increases feelings of hunger. While leptin release into the bloodstream changes slowly depending on fat stores, ghrelin secretion can change more quickly based on how full the stomach is, the time of day, and other aspects of one's physical and psychological state.

Do you tend to feel hungrier when you haven't been getting enough sleep? Lots of people do, and studies have linked sleep deprivation to increased ghrelin and reduced leptin circulating in the bloodstream (Chaput et al., 2007; Spiegel et al., 2004). One study even detected increased ghrelin after a single night with no sleep (Schmid et al., 2008). These hormones are signaling a need for more energy to compensate for the added time

Hunger hormones

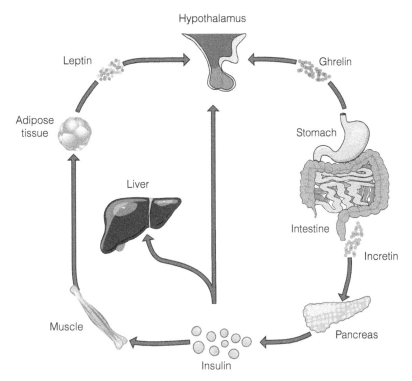

FIGURE 4.2. The hormones leptin and ghrelin help regulate feelings of hunger and the drive to eat, based upon the amount of energy stored in fat cells, the amount of food currently being digested, the time of day, and other factors.

spent awake, and the stress of losing sleep, but people may eat more than the body requires as a result. One study asked whether getting enough sleep would help overweight women participating in a clinical weight-loss program to shed some pounds; sure enough, participants who got at least seven hours of sleep per night and reported better sleep quality were more likely to have lost at least 10% of their starting body weight by the end of the study, relative to women who were getting less sleep (Thomson et al., 2012).

Can simple physiological states influence our emotions? Both anecdotal and empirical evidence suggest that they can. Have you ever felt "hangry"—more angry or annoyed than seemed justified by the situation, because you were hungry? In one study researchers found that participants who were had not eaten for at least five hours before starting the study reported more intense negative emotions, greater feelings of hate toward the experimenter, and greater perception of the experimenter as judgmental after a frustrating task in which the study computer crashed, and the experimenter blamed the participant for the problem (MacCormack & Lindquist, 2019). One possible interpretation is that being hungry really does increase the likelihood of becoming angry, assuming one is in an annoying situation. Another is that hungry people aren't actually more anger-prone, but may misinterpret their feelings of discomfort as an emotional response (we'll discuss the relationship between discomfort and anger in more detail later in the chapter). Which interpretation you accept depends on how you define "real" anger. In an interesting twist, the effect was eliminated for participants who were asked just beforehand to write about the feelings—and what caused those feelings—of a man showing an angry or sad facial expression in a photograph. This pattern of results suggests that the effects of hunger on emotional feelings are wiped out if one is actively thinking about emotions and their causes. In later chapters we'll see other examples in which drawing attention to people's emotions tends to eliminate some of the effects they might otherwise have.

Instinctive and Habitual Responses to Cues

As one of us writes these words (MNS), it's approaching 2:00 in the afternoon, and she can smell pizza heating up in the toaster oven. Although she wasn't hungry when her husband offered to prepare a slice for her 10 minutes ago, her stomach is starting to grumble now.

In Chapter 2 we defined instincts as evolutionarily programmed patterns of behavior elicited by stimuli or events in the environment. Like other animals, humans do have innate instinctive responses to certain stimuli—responses that require little or no learning. For example, almost everybody flinches and shows a spike in fight-flight sympathetic nervous system activation when they hear an unexpected, very loud noise (Figure 4.3; Yeomans & Frankland, 1996). Newborn babies have a **rooting reflex** in which they turn their head and begin to suck when something gently touches the corner of their mouth— a response crucial for feeding. Evidence from a wide range of modern and indigenous

FIGURE 4.3. In the acoustic startle response, people flinch, tighten their eyes, and show a quick increase in fight-flight sympathetic nervous system activation when they hear an unexpected loud noise.

cultural groups suggests that disgust may be an instinctive response to feces (Curtis & Biran, 2001), although developmentally the full-blown disgust response does not typically appear until children are around five years of age—later than would be predicted for an evolved instinct to avoid contamination by the various pathogens feces may contain (Rottman, 2014).

People may also develop automatic responses to stimuli after being exposed to them so many times that the response becomes a habit. For example, after eating a particularly tasty food enough times, people may form conditioned responses in which the sight or smell of that food can evoke salivation, as well as desire to eat (Volkow, Wang, & Bler, 2011). Some research suggests that people who are chronically worried about their weight and trying to diet all the time may be particularly reactive to external food cues (rather than internal hunger signals) as causes of eating (Polivy & Herman, 2017). This is based on correlational data rather than experiments (it would be difficult, not to mention somewhat cruel, to experimentally manipulate people's concerns about their weight), so it's not clear whether people who react strongly to environmental temptation end up worrying more about their weight, or constantly trying to restrain your eating tends to backfire once you're faced with a piece of cake.

In a related phenomenon called **cue reactivity**, people develop conditioned responses to objects, places, and other stimuli associated with prior use of addictive drugs (including nicotine and alcohol), such that exposure to these cues can evoke intense craving. Seeing these cues activates dopaminergic reward circuitry that promotes appetitive behavior (Jasinska et al., 2014), and several studies have found that individuals who show stronger cue-evoked neural activity tend to have more a difficult time quitting the substance, and are more prone to relapse (Courtney et al., 2016).

People can form conditioned fears as well. In the original, rather nasty demonstration of this phenomenon, researchers John Watson and Rosalie Rayner (1920) worked with an infant who lived at a local hospital. "Little Albert" initially showed no fear of various animals, including rats, dogs, or rabbits, or masks depicting any of these. The researchers wanted to know if they could create a new fear in Albert, just by connecting an animal with danger in his mind. In the key phase of the study Albert was shown a white rat several times, and each time the researchers hit a steel bar with a hammer right behind his head, making a startling noise. Before long Albert started to show terror of the rat, crying and trying to get away whenever he saw it. According the researchers, he soon began to generalize this fear to other furry animals (Figure 4.4).

The Little Albert study has been criticized widely on scientific as well as ethical grounds. Who was this Albert kid, anyway? The report says that prior to the study, at 11 months of age "no one had ever seen him in a state of fear and rage . . . [and he] practically never cried." Most people who have spent time with infants would agree this is a bit odd. Was he a typically developing child, or did he have some kind of developmental disorder? Would the same effects have been seen in other children? What on Earth were the researchers thinking? Despite these contemporary critiques of this classic research, the underlying phenomenon of developing a conditioned fear response to previously neutral stimuli (e.g., by giving someone a small electric shock whenever they see a particular shape) is now so well-established that fear conditioning is a commonly used technique in research on memory, decision-making, and emotion (Lonsdorf et al., 2017).

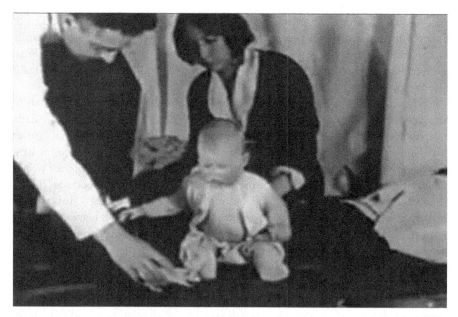

FIGURE 4.4. In the original demonstration of fear conditioning, "Little Albert" learned to be terrified of rats after researchers startled him with a sudden, loud noise every time he saw one.

Appraisal: The Generator of Emotion

Make a list of everything that scares you. The evidence suggests that very few fears are completely innate, requiring no learning at all. It's unlikely that the rest of your fears can be explained by some kind of Little Albert-like torture during your childhood, though traumatic experiences may account for a few of them. How do you explain the rest of the things you fear? This is where the phenomenon of appraisal becomes important. Because appraisal is so central to theorists' understanding of what emotions are and why we experience them at a particular time, we discuss this topic in detail.

Recall the bear example used by William James to explain his theory of emotion, as described in Chapter 1. In the original paper presenting his theory, James (1884) proposed that when you see a bear, your body instinctively prepares you to run away, and you run; your feeling of fear is just your conscious perception of these physiological changes and the act of flight. Before long, critics raised a problem with this account: you don't *always* run away from a bear. If you saw a bear in an enclosure in the zoo, you probably would not run away. If you were in a vacation cabin in the mountains and saw a bear walking by outside the window, you might even be excited and run toward that window rather than away from it. It's not the bear per se that is eliciting your emotional response. In a later publication, James (1894) amended his theory to account for this phenomenon, proposing that what makes people run is not the bear, but their interpretation of the bear as being dangerous.

This is the core idea of appraisal—that what elicits an emotional response is not the objective stimulus, but our subjective interpretation of what the stimulus means for our goals, concerns, and well-being (we can have goals and concerns that involve other people, or the state of the world, so emotion-eliciting appraisals needn't be completely selfish).

Appraisal is different from the habitual, conditioned responses to stimuli described above, because it explains how we can have an emotional response to a complex, unfamiliar, abstract, or even hypothetical situation. Although learning and prior experience likely play important roles in explaining people's appraisals, and the difference between cue reactivity and appraisal of a new event's emotional meaning may be one of degree, it's useful to focus on appraisal as a distinct psychological process.

Although the implications of James's proposal were neglected through much of the mid-twentieth century, as the behaviorist movement discouraged research on the "black box" of the inner workings of the mind, Magda Arnold (1960) and Richard Lazarus (1977) later revitalized appraisal theory and made major contributions to its development (Figure 4.5). These two theorists' approaches are not identical. Diverging from James's initial proposal, in which instinctive physical reactions are the basis of emotional feelings, Arnold's theory prioritizes cognitive appraisal as the defining feature of emotional experience and the cause of emotional behavior. Her ideas have strongly influenced philosophical theories of emotion, which often hold that cognitive appraisal *is* the emotion (Nussbaum, 2003). Lazarus was more closely aligned with James on this point, arguing that appraisal causes emotions, but is not *the* emotion; emotions include physiological, motivational, and behavioral responses as well (Lazarus, 1991b). However, the two approaches have many important points in common, and we shall emphasize them in this chapter.

One crucial implication of appraisal theory is that emotions are not about isolated things out there in the world; instead, they are about our "ongoing relationships with the environment" (Lazarus, 1991a, p. 5), our evaluation of whether a given stimulus is a likely source of benefit or harm. If you are on a wildlife expedition in Alaska and you see a baby bear off in the distance, it's reasonable to assume that you are in no danger (Figure 4.6). In this case, there is no reason for fear. If the bear is a fully grown adult, and it starts charging toward your group, then you would (we hope) begin to feel some anxiety, and

FIGURE 4.5. Magda Arnold and Richard Lazarus each made major contributions to appraisal theories of emotion.

FIGURE 4.6.   According to appraisal theory, a bear should only elicit fear if it is perceived as an immediate source of danger. Few people would be frightened by the sight of a baby bear some distance away.

your body would probably start preparing a response. The bear is still a bear, but now it has completely different implications for your well-being.

This explanation sheds light on some of the examples we discussed at the beginning of this chapter. Why does someone else's filthy refrigerator elicit disgust? According to Paul Rozin and April Fallon (1987), disgust is a response to anything that we perceive as a potential source of contamination, likely to make us sick. If you feel disgusted by the contents of your friend's refrigerator, this is probably because it looks (and smells) like a haven for sickness and disease. Appraisal might also help explain the time when another person was angry with you and you didn't understand why. From the other person's perspective, you had presumably said or done something that was disrespectful, inconsiderate, or rude. Even if that was not your intent, it's the other person's interpretation of your actions that determine his or her emotions.

A key point is that it's not always clear whether a given emotional response is right or wrong, in the sense of being justified or not. On one hand, you and your angry friend or partner may each have a legitimate perspective on the situation: you may not have intended any disrespect, but the other person thought that your words or actions communicated a lack of the consideration they deserve (this happens sometimes in any close relationship). On the other hand, the diagnostic criteria of several clinical disorders include emotional reactions that do not reflect a reasonable response to the situation, such as ongoing sadness in the absence of a major loss (depression), or extreme fear about a situation that poses little or no objective threat (phobias and other anxiety disorders). In these cases, appraisal biases may be part of the problem.

The Speed of Emotional Appraisals

When you experience an event, how quickly do you appraise it? According to the James–Lange theory, described in Chapter 1, you begin by assessing the overall situation and classifying it as calling for some kind of action (escape, attack) or no action at all. This classification triggers physiological changes and behaviors. The term "appraisal" is used here in a general sense. You don't necessarily analyze the situation consciously enough to put it into words. What is necessary is that your brain identifies certain implications of the object, such as being dangerous or insulting, or at least good or bad, right away. From an evolutionary standpoint, we should expect this appraisal to be quick. In the presence of a threat, the faster you react, the greater your chance of survival. For this reason, researchers have been interested in how quickly appraisals happen.

As predicted by the updated James–Lange theory, the brain shows signs of identifying the emotional quality of a stimulus extremely fast. In one case, physicians studied a man who was undergoing brain surgery for severe epilepsy. As is often the case, the surgery was conducted with local anesthesia to the scalp, so the man was awake and alert throughout the procedure. (Keeping the patient awake during brain surgery is helpful. As surgeons probe one brain area after another, eventually the patient says, "That makes me feel the way I do when I'm about to have a seizure." The surgeons then know they are close to the area causing the seizures.) In this study, while they had the patient's brain exposed, the physicians inserted electrodes into his prefrontal cortex, an area important for certain aspects of memory and emotion. Then they asked him to look at pictures of pleasant and unpleasant scenes, as well as happy and frightened faces. Cells in the prefrontal cortex responded within 120 milliseconds, and they showed a different pattern of activity in response to happy faces and pleasant pictures than in response to frightened faces and unpleasant pictures (Kawasaki et al., 2001). This quick response is consistent with the idea that cognitive appraisal precedes the reactions of the body, which take a bit longer.

In another study, college students looked at photographs of faces with happy, angry, or neutral expressions while the investigators recorded brain activity with an EEG. Looking at an angry, threatening face evoked a strong response 200 to 300 milliseconds after the onset of the photograph, whereas seeing a happy or neutral face did not evoke that response (Schupp et al., 2004). Again, the evidence indicates that the brain categorizes the emotional quality of a scene quickly, at least for certain kinds of emotions (Robinson, 1998).

In other studies, researchers have recorded movements of facial muscles while participants looked at photos of people with various facial expressions. A smiling face slightly activated the muscles responsible for smiling, and an angry face activated the muscles responsible for frowning. The muscles reacted less than half a second after onset of a photo, even if the viewer was paying attention to something other than the expression (Cannon, Hayes, & Tipper, 2009; Dimberg & Thunberg, 1998). Another experiment found that a photo of a fearful face caused slight sweating and trembling, even if the photo was presented so briefly that people did not report awareness of seeing it at all (Kubota et al., 2000; Vuilleumier et al., 2001). These results suggest that the brain classifies the emotional quality of an expression rapidly, and that people need not be aware of this appraisal to show appropriate behaviors and physiological changes. When you think about it, these results are stunning. They reveal that before you have figured out what you are seeing, even before you realize that you have seen anything at all, your brain has already begun to classify images as good or bad, threatening or harmless.

The research just described indicates that classification as good versus bad is often quick enough to precede and guide emotional actions and feelings. However, we are not in a position to say that emotional appraisal is *always* that fast, or that it always causes feelings and actions. Suppose you are in a bad mood because of an event a few hours ago. Then, someone takes your chair where you wanted to sit, and you yell angrily. Your anger is way out of proportion to the offense, so you look for an explanation—an appraisal—to explain your anger. You say, "You're always so inconsiderate!" or something like that. In such cases, the appraisal apparently comes after the feeling and action, or carries over from one emotional situation to another. This process is consistent with Schachter and Singer's theory of emotion. Many studies provide empirical evidence for this process, finding that appraisals associated with a prior emotion can influence people's interpretation of a new, completely unrelated situation (e.g., Keltner, Ellsworth, & Edwards, 1993; Lerner & Keltner, 2001). That is, cognitive appraisals may lead to behaviors and feelings, but sometimes the feelings may influence future appraisals too.

WHAT IS THE CONTENT OF APPRAISAL?

Learning Objectives
- Define the term "core relational theme," and give and identify examples.
- Analyze the difference between core relational themes and appraisal dimensions, linking each to a major modern theory of emotion.
- List several appraisal dimensions, and apply them to describe appraisal in an example situation.
- Differentiate primary from secondary appraisal and their elements, and apply this distinction in an example.

Most researchers would agree with the general description of appraisal that we offered above, assuming that they endorse the concept of appraisal at all (Moors et al., 2013). However, researchers describe the content of appraisals—the ingredients of our evaluations of emotional stimuli and what they mean for us—in different ways. Although many researchers study appraisal, each taking a different approach, they can be divided into two main camps: those using a more categorical approach, emphasizing the prototypical theme associated with each emotion, and those using a multidimensional approach, emphasizing ratings of each stimulus on several common dimensions. Each of these was introduced briefly in Chapter 1, but we explain them in more detail here.

Core Relational Themes

We have alluded to the first kind of appraisal several times throughout this chapter so far. Someone who is frightened by a bear evidently perceives the bear as dangerous. If you feel disgusted by a refrigerator, it's because you perceive it as a probable source of disease. If your friend is angry with you, it likely reflects that person's appraisal that you are not treating them with the respect and consideration they deserve. In each case, the appraisal takes the form of a basic, prototypical type of problem or benefit that people can encounter in their transactions with the environment. Richard Lazarus (1991a) referred to these as **core relational themes**.

TABLE 4.1 | Core relational themes for several emotions

Core relational themes associated with 15 emotions, as proposed by Richard Lazarus (1991a).

EMOTION	CORE RELATIONAL THEME
Anger	Demeaning offense against me and mine
Anxiety	An uncertain, existential threat
Fear	Immediate, concrete, overwhelming physical danger
Guilt	Having transgressed a moral imperative
Shame	Failing to live up to an ego-ideal
Sadness	Experiencing an irrevocable loss
Envy	Wanting something someone else has
Jealousy	Resenting a third person for loss of or threat to another's affection
Disgust	An indigestible object or idea
Happiness	Progress toward achieving a goal
Pride	Taking credit for a highly valued object or accomplishment
Relief	Distressing condition that has improved or gone away
Hope	Fearing the worst, but yearning for the better
Love	Desiring reciprocated affection from another person
Compassion	Being moved by another's suffering and wanting to help

This approach to describing appraisal content is closely linked to the assumptions of basic/discrete emotion theory. According to Lazarus (1991b), core relational themes reflect fundamental kinds of events humans encounter in moving through the world, and the implications those events have for our well-being (Table 4.1). He argues that the importance of these themes, and our ability to detect them and respond to them with the appropriate emotion, is universal and does not depend on language. Consider the case we described in Chapter 3, of a Tahitian man whose wife had gone away and was acting sad, but who had no word for sadness and instead described himself as *pe'a pe'a* or ill. Lazarus (1991b) says that although the man did not have a conscious concept of sadness, he was still able to experience his wife's departure as an important loss, and the result was a cognitive, biological, and motivational sadness response.

Appraisal Dimensions

The other major approach to describing appraisal content proposes that we evaluate the meaning of stimuli using a common set of criteria, rather than holding each experience up to a categorical meaning template to see whether it fits. We introduced the idea of **appraisal dimensions** in Chapter 1 when describing the component process model, because appraisals play such a central role in that theory of emotion. Appraisal dimensions reflect questions people are thought to ask about every object and experience they encounter, such as: Was I expecting this? Have I ever encountered this situation before? Is it consistent with my goals? What caused this situation? How certain am I of its outcome? How much control do I have? The answer to each of these questions has its own set of cognitive, physiological, motivational, and (potentially) behavioral consequences; when combined, these consequences explain the emotion as it is experienced. Different researchers have proposed different sets of appraisal dimensions (in fact, sometimes the same researcher uses different sets of dimensions in different publications), but there is a fair amount of overlap, and the basic idea is still the same (Table 4.2).

....

TABLE 4.2 | **Several appraisal dimensions commonly used in emotion research**

APPRAISAL DIMENSION	QUESTION
Novelty	Have I ever encountered this before?
Expectedness	Was I expecting this to happen?
Pleasantness	How pleasant versus unpleasant is this for me?
Responsible agent	Who caused this situation—self or other?
Goal conduciveness	Is this good or bad for my goals?
Fairness	Is this situation fair and just?
Control	How much control do I have over this situation?
Certainty	How certain am I of what the outcome will be?
Morality	Is this situation consistent with my views of morality?
Self-concept relevance	Does this situation impact my feelings about myself?

....

In this approach, emotions such as fear, sadness, hope, and so forth are linked not to a single relational theme, but to a profile across the various appraisal dimensions. Let's return to our refrigerator example. Describing your appraisal from a dimensional standpoint, you would likely evaluate the filthy fridge as moderately novel (depending on how many particularly gross refrigerators you've seen before); somewhat unexpected (unless you already knew your friend was a slob); very unpleasant; caused by someone else; low on goal conduciveness, assuming that disease avoidance is one of your goals (you have to reach in there to get your drink); moderately unfair; and low on self-concept relevance (it's not your refrigerator). People might have different appraisals of control in this situation, and this would shape their emotional response. You might get to morality and think, what does morality have to do with anything? For people in Western cultures, this situation may have nothing to do with morality, but as we shall soon see, different cultures have different rules about what is and is not morally relevant.

The dimensional approach to appraisal has important implications for the way emotions can be experienced, and maps to key differences between basic/discrete emotions theory and the component process model. If emotions are elicited by core relational themes, then people either will or will not experience a given emotion to some extent, based on their appraisal of the relevant theme in the current situation. Also, the only emotions people should be able to experience are those associated with core relational themes. One might experience multiple emotions at the same time, an **emotion blend**, caused by simultaneous appraisal of multiple core relational themes, but there is no gray area between the emotions. In contrast, the appraisal dimension approach indicates that people are theoretically capable of emotional experiences reflecting all possible points in X-dimensional space, where X is the number of dimensions. Although we can identify certain appraisal profiles that are prototypical of emotions such as fear and sadness, there is a lot of room for emotional responses between these prototypes as well.

Which Approach Is Correct?

Which description of appraisal content is correct—the one emphasizing categorical core relational themes, or the one emphasizing continuous dimensions? Possibly both approaches are right. Some researchers think of dimensions as "molecular" appraisal content that can be aggregated in to the "molar" content of core relational themes (e.g., Lazarus, 1991b; Smith & Lazarus, 1993). Put another way, it may be that core relational themes are just aggregate profiles created by several dimensional appraisals. Lazarus (1991a) describes core relational themes as composites made up of two stages of appraisal that take place in rapid succession. **Primary appraisal** includes assessments of the eliciting situation's goal relevance (does this matter to me?), goal congruence (is this good or bad for me?), and *ego-involvement*, or the specific way in which the situation might matter for one's goals and well-being. This is followed by **secondary appraisal**, in which an individual evaluates his or her ability to cope with the situation. Secondary appraisals include three elements: an assessment of who or what is responsible for causing the situation (blame or credit); an assessment of the amount and type of control one has over the situation (coping potential); and the extent to which one expects the situation to change (future expectations).

One way to think about the relationship between primary and secondary appraisal is that primary appraisals determine one's emotional response, whereas secondary appraisals are more important for coping and emotion regulation—they determine how intensely an emotion is experienced, as well as how one responds behaviorally to the situation. However, you may have noted that when taken together, the various appraisals in Lazarus's model look a lot like the appraisal dimensions in the other approach—particularly goal conduciveness, responsible agent, control, and certainty. In this sense, the two approaches are not that different. They just focus on different levels of description.

Nonetheless, one important difference remains. The appraisal dimension approach has a goal conduciveness dimension, but is agnostic as to which goal is at stake; there's no mechanism by which your emotional response would differ between a situation interfering with your goal to avoid pathogens and one interfering with your goal to be treated with respect by other people. In Lazarus's model, the ego-involvement aspect of primary appraisal is specific this way, giving each core relational theme a unique flavor. The question is whether this unique flavor matters for the specific quality of a person's emotional response. So far, no study has convincingly shown that one approach is better than the other.

Although it's important to recognize how these approaches differ, it's also important to appreciate what they have in common. In both approaches, appraisals are thought necessary to experience emotion and cause the emotional response, although emotion is not reducible to appraisal. Also, in both approaches different people can appraise the same event in different ways, and this is strongly influenced by culture and learning, but the arrows from appraisals to the resulting emotions do not depend on language or culture—they are innate and should be universal. Now we turn to empirical evidence addressing these hypotheses.

EVIDENCE LINKING APPRAISAL TO EMOTION
Learning Objective
- Differentiate challenge versus threat appraisal, and effects of these appraisals on emotional experience, cardiovascular physiology, and task performance.
- Define the mere exposure effect, and analyze the evidence on whether emotions can occur without appraisal.

William James's revised theory stated that appraisals are necessary for the experience of emotion, and many modern researchers agree. Intuitively, this proposal makes sense, but intuition is not the same as scientific data. Let's consider the evidence relating appraisal to emotion.

Does Appraisal Cause Emotion?

To what extent do appraisals influence the emotions that people experience? Do appraisals even predict what emotion (if any) a person will feel? To address this question, Craig Smith and colleagues (Smith et al., 1993) randomly assigned participants in one study to remember and describe a personal experience with one of eight situations: receiving an important honor; getting a high grade on an exam; having a meaningful discussion with parents on a topic they cared about; finding out someone they liked had a crush on them; questioning whether their career plans were right for them; receiving a low grade on a course; parents not letting them do something they cared about; and having the person they were dating criticize something they cared about. Each of these situations might plausibly elicit a variety of emotional responses.

Participants were asked to answer a battery of questions about their experience. These questions included rating a series of statements intended to capture the core relational themes hypothesized for anger, guilt, fear–anxiety, sadness, hope, and happiness, as well as items measuring subjective experience of each of these emotions. As predicted using appraisal theory, ratings of the core relational themes accounted for a large proportion of variability in the emotion ratings across eliciting situations, ranging from a low of 34% for hope to a high of 60% for happiness. Thus, the core relational themes did a good job of predicting which emotions people reported, although this effect was stronger for some emotions than for others. Moreover, the ratings of each core relational theme correlated more strongly with ratings of the intended emotion than with those of any other emotion, indicating that the core relational theme–emotion relationships were reasonably specific.

Even stronger evidence comes from experimental studies in which researchers instruct participants to think about stimuli in specific ways, and examine effects on various aspects of emotional responding. In one study using a fairly typical approach (Ray et al., 2010), participants watched a series of 162 photographs. Half of these photos showed something unpleasant or upsetting, such as a plane crash, wounded animal, or a gun aimed at the viewer; and the other half showed neutral images of people, objects, and outdoor scenes. For each photo, participants were instructed either to "think about the picture in a way that increases your negative response"; to "be aware of your response and respond naturally"; or to "think about the picture in a way that decreases your negative response," with each photo assigned at random to one of these three instructions. Participants not only reported feeling more negative affect after being asked to think negatively about a given image, but also showed more contraction of the brow muscles, as seen in expressions of some negative emotions. Importantly, these effects held true not only for the negative photos, but also the objectively neutral ones (Figure 4.7); people were able to *think* themselves into being upset even by innocuous images, when instructed to do so.

One limitation of the study is that the instructions were a bit leading—they basically told participants how they should feel after each image. However, many studies using variants of this general approach have given more specific instructions about appraisal

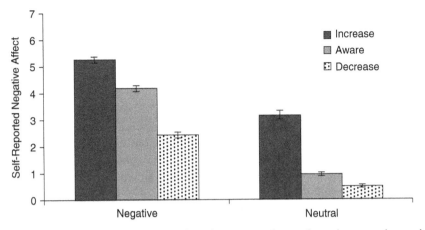

FIGURE 4.7. Self-reports of negative affect after viewing objectively unpleasant and neutral photographs, after receiving instructions to increase or decrease thoughts that make people feel bad, or simply to be aware of feelings. From Ray et al. (2010).

FIGURE 4.8. How does this image make you feel? Try thinking about it in a positive way, such as focusing on the women's relationship. Changes in appraisal can impact the emotional response.

content, such as thinking about positive aspects of negative images (e.g., Shiota & Levenson, 2012, Figure 4.8), and remembering past experiences of rejection from the perspective of a "fly on the wall" (Ayduk & Kross, 2010), demonstrating effects on emotional physiology and nonverbal expression as well as feelings. Studies have also shown that appraisal instructions can modulate people's experience of positive emotions, as well as reducing distress (e.g., Gruber, Hay, & Gross, 2014; Kalokerinos, Greenaway, & Denson, 2015). We will consider the merits of cognitive reappraisal as an emotion regulation strategy in Chapter 15.

An interesting series of studies suggests that one particular aspect of appraisal can have striking effects on people's physiological responses and task performance, as well as subjective aspects of emotional experience (Tomaka et al., 1997). Imagine that you are a participant in the following study: after arriving at the lab, several sensors are attached to your chest and back to measure your physiological responses. Then the experimenter instructs you to do the mental arithmetic task described earlier, counting back in increments of 13 or 17 from a high starting number, such as 1,162. The importance of doing the task as quickly and accurately as possible is emphasized, and you're told that your performance will be scored for speed as well as the number of times you are correct. By this time you might be thinking, "Ugh, why math? Why didn't I sign up for the study with all the personality questionnaires?" Before you do the task, you're asked to rate both how threatening you expect the task to be, and how well you think you'll be able to cope with it—your appraisals of the situation ahead.

Participants in this condition rated their threat appraisals as higher than their coping appraisals, about 50% higher on average. Physiologically, they showed consistent signs of a *fight–flight* sympathetic nervous system response: their hearts beat more quickly, contracted more quickly with each beat, and pumped more blood, and their blood vessels constricted, providing more resistance against the blood coming through (similar to an increase in blood pressure). This is comparable to the profile seen in laboratory studies of fear (Kreibig, 2010), and researchers concluded it was a response to **threat**.

However, participants randomly assigned to another condition received a different set of instructions. They were asked to do the same mental arithmetic task, but instead of the threatening instructions, they were encouraged to think of the task as a challenge and of themselves as someone capable of meeting that challenge. This was referred to as the **challenge** condition, but if you think about it, it's really a manipulation of control appraisal. Participants in this condition still appraised the task as threatening, but their appraisals of challenge were comparable—they thought their coping ability was matched to the difficult task at hand.

A striking difference appeared in these participants' physiological responses (Figure 4.9). They showed an even stronger increase in cardiac activity than participants in the threat condition. However, their arteries relaxed somewhat overall rather than contracting, allowing blood to travel more freely. This suggests that the body was still mobilizing to deal with the task ahead, but without preparing for danger. Other studies have linked these physiological profiles to threat and challenge appraisal as well (e.g., Tomaka et al., 1993). In subsequent research, challenge appraisals and physiology have been found to predict higher exam performance (Skinner & Brewer, 2002), better academic outcomes (Seery et al., 2010), and better performance on a motor task (Moore et al., 2012).

Studies have also found that people randomly assigned to high-power roles show challenge physiological profiles, whereas those in low-power roles are more likely to show threat (Scheepers et al., 2012). In an extension of this work to intergroup relations research, studies have found that upper-middle class white participants tend to show threat profiles when talking with Black or economically disadvantaged interaction partners, but

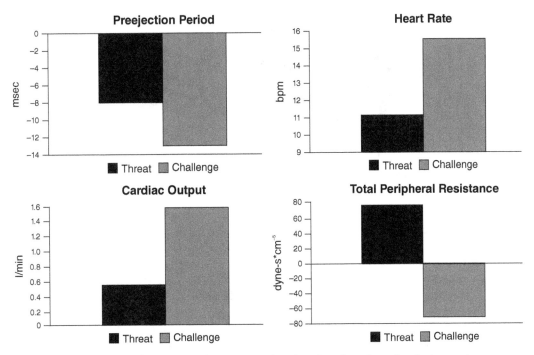

FIGURE 4.9. Cardiovascular responses during a mental arithmetic task performed under instructions emphasizing threat versus challenge. Although cardiac activity increases in both conditions, the blood vessels contract in threat and relax in challenge. From Tomaka et al. (1997).

challenge profiles when interacting with partners who are more similar to themselves (Mendes et al., 2002). This is one finding in a cluster that suggests people experience interactions with out-group members as anxiety-provoking, leading to exploration of ways to reduce this anxiety and promote intergroup interaction (e.g., Page-Gould, Mendes, & Major, 2010; Page-Gould, Mendoza-Denton, & Tropp, 2008; Schultz et al., 2015). The threat-challenge literature is part of a growing body of evidence that control appraisals may be particularly important for well-being (DeNeve & Cooper, 1988).

Is Appraisal Necessary for Emotion?

The theories we have discussed so far assume that a fair amount of cognitive interpretation must take place for people to experience emotion. Some researchers have challenged this assumption, and they offer intriguing research findings to support their case. In a classic paper, Robert Zajonc (1980) argues that "preferences need no inferences" (p. 151)—that at least some kinds of emotional responses do not require appraisal at all. Let's consider his argument and the evidence.

Here's another study to imagine (Moreland & Zajonc, 1976). In this case, you go to the lab at the assigned time and you're asked to watch a series of slides showing Japanese characters, like those shown in Figure 4.10. Japanese writing uses characters such as these, adopted from Chinese writing, to denote whole words—they're often referred to as ideograms, but in Japanese they are called *kanji*. Your job is just to watch these images go by.

FIGURE 4.10. Studies of the mere exposure effect suggest that simply seeing simple, novel stimuli like these Japanese ideograms many times is enough for people to develop a liking for them.

Sounds much better than the mental arithmetic study, right? You've never seen any of these before, not often enough to recognize anyway, so they have no inherent meaning for you. They're reasonably pleasant to look at, but you don't have the expertise to tell them apart. You just watch a long line of these images go by—anywhere from 9 to 81 in total—with some ideograms appearing more often than others over the course of the slide show. At the end you are asked to rate how much you like each of several ideograms, relying on your first impressions rather than thinking about it too hard.

Analyses of the data showed that the more often a participant had seen a particular ideogram in the slide show, the more he or she reported liking it on the questionnaire measures. These effects could not be accounted for by the total number of slides people had seen, or by the number of different ideograms they had seen—liking was only related to the number of exposures to a given ideogram. Participants seemed unaware of this effect; when asked whether they could guess the purpose of the study, only two participants mentioned anything linking ideogram frequency to liking.

This effect, which Zajonc dubbed the **mere exposure effect**, has been replicated with a wide range of other novel stimuli including Turkish words, random sequences of tones, and geometric shapes (Zajonc, 1980). In one experiment, researchers even rigged a supposed study of taste perception in such a way that participants stood near each of several other participants once, twice, five times, ten times, or not at all, without ever talking or interacting with them (Saegert, Swap, & Zajonc, 1973). Afterward, the more often they had seen a given person over the course of the session, the more likable they thought that person to be. In follow-up studies researchers have demonstrated that mere exposure effects can occur even when stimuli have been presented subliminally, showing that the effect does not depend on conscious awareness or memory (Bornstein, Leone, & Galley, 1987; Monahan, Murphy, & Zajonc, 2000).

How much of a threat do these studies pose to appraisal theories of emotion? It depends on what you mean by "emotion" and "appraisal." The mere exposure effect predicts the simple response of liking, which counts as a meaningful aspect of core affect (assuming that one likes things that one finds pleasant), but might not count as an emotion to someone representing basic emotion theory or the component process model. Also, the "preferences need no inferences" approach implicitly defines cognitive appraisal in terms of thoughts that are accessible to the conscious mind. As we have seen, however, appraisals need not be conscious. We may be able to report on them after the fact, but they do not require awareness, and they begin a fraction of a second after we perceive a stimulus. Perhaps some kind of stimulus conditioning could be taking place, as discussed earlier in this chapter, but conditioning to what? The ideograms (or whatever) were not paired with anything else in these studies, positive or otherwise, so it's not clear how positive associations could have formed. Although the mere exposure effect was first reported decades ago, the mechanism behind it has not yet been revealed.

Liking is not the only affective response that need not, according to some researchers, require appraisal. Anger is another. We will review the evidence on this case later in the chapter.

UNIVERSALITY AND DIVERSITY IN APPRAISAL

Learning Objective

- Summarize Klaus Scherer's (1997) cross-cultural study of emotional appraisals, and evaluate the evidence for the proposal that dimensional appraisals are associated with experience of emotions in similar ways around the world.
- Analyze gender-related similarities and differences in emotional experience.

From an evolutionary perspective, appraisals should be functionally related to the emotional feelings, physiology, and behavior that follow. This suggests that although people from different backgrounds may interpret the same event in different ways, based on their social context and life experience, the links between appraisals and the resulting emotions should be universal. Does the evidence support this proposal?

Emotional Appraisals Across Cultures

Researchers conducting cross-cultural studies on emotional appraisal typically ask two questions. First, do particular emotions accompany the same appraisals, or different ones, from culture to culture? Second, do people in different cultures appraise the same kind of event in similar or different ways? Said another way, do emotional responses to the same event differ across cultures mainly because we interpret that event differently?

The first question was addressed in an extraordinary study by Klaus Scherer (1997) with the help of dozens of colleagues around the world. In Scherer's study, participants in 37 countries on 5 continents were asked to think of a time they felt each of the following emotions: joy, anger, fear, sadness, disgust, shame, and guilt (these emotion words were translated and back-translated[1] to try to identify the best word possible in each language). Then participants were asked to describe a situation in which they felt the emotion, and to rate that situation on several appraisal dimensions. Analyses asked whether participants around the world associated the same appraisal profile with each emotion. Figure 4.11 shows the average appraisals associated with each emotion by people in six major cultural regions: Northern/Central Europe, the New World (the United States, Australia, and New Zealand), Asia (including India), the Mediterranean countries, and Africa. Each region is represented by a line. When the lines are on top of each other,

---

[1] The procedure for back-translation is that one person translates something from Language A to Language B and then someone else translates the translation from B to A to see how closely it matches the original.

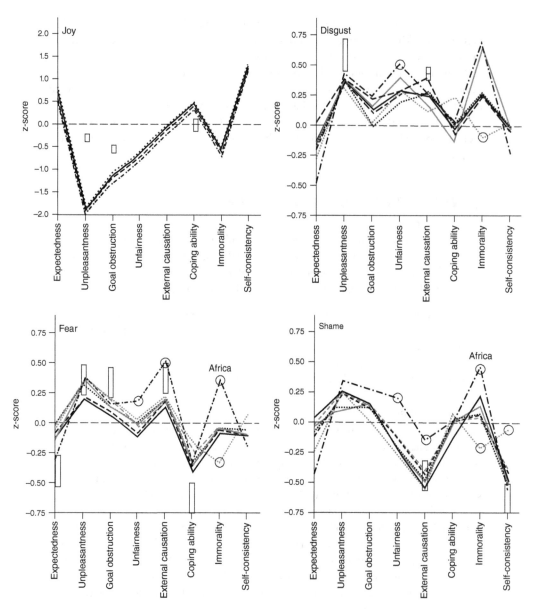

FIGURE 4.11. Appraisal patterns associated with the experience of seven emotions by people in major geopolitical regions around the world. From Scherer (1997).

people in different regions offered similar appraisal ratings, on average, for situations in which they had felt that emotion.

Overall, this study suggests that certain emotions are associated with pretty much the same appraisal profiles throughout the world. Across regions, similarities were much greater than differences regarding which appraisal pattern fits a given emotion. For example, people said they felt happy in response to an event that was somewhat expected,

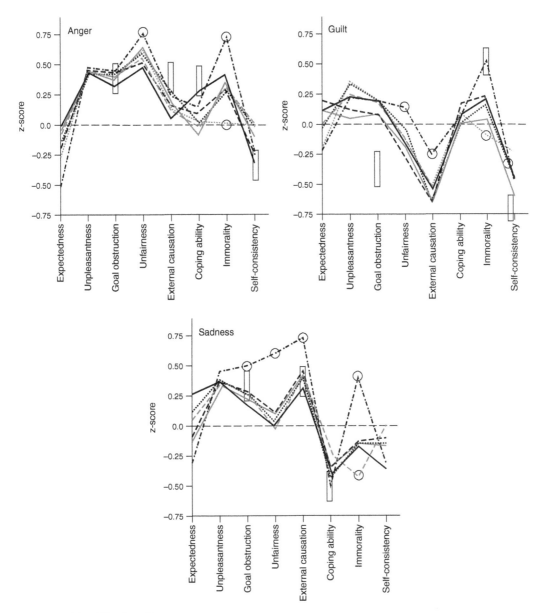

FIGURE 4.11.   (Continued)

pleasant, consistent with their goals, fair, and that made them feel good about themselves; and frightened in response to an event that what somewhat unexpected, unpleasant, goal obstructive, caused to some extent by someone or something other than the self, and that they felt was out of their control (low coping ability).

It is also interesting to note where cultural differences emerge. One major difference involved the roles of fairness and morality in emotional appraisals. African participants were most likely to describe any sadness-eliciting event as unfair and immoral, an idea that sounds odd to most Americans, Europeans, and Asians. Think of it this way: You are sad when your dog passes away, but how does fairness come into it? In what way is the event morally wrong? In general, participants in Africa rated the events eliciting most negative emotions as immoral, externally caused, and unfair. By contrast, Latin American participants tended to rate events that elicited negative emotions as less immoral than did participants from other continents.

Interpreting these differences among cultures is difficult, but we can imagine a few plausible explanations. Scherer (1997) notes that among the regions studied, those in Africa were the least urbanized and the most traditional. Rural communities are often close-knit and interdependent, with strict conventions for how to go about daily life. In urban communities, people of diverse experience and philosophy interact a great deal, but more superficially, so shared morality is not as crucial. It may be that rural communities depend more on shared morality to survive, so issues of fairness and morality may generally be more prominent in rural than in urban communities. It would be interesting to test this explanation with new data from, say, urban versus rural regions of North America, to see if the same pattern emerges.

Also, Africa is the least powerful and most politically unstable of the six regions in the study. Although all participants in all of the regions were college students, and therefore of relatively high status within their cultures, their sense that negative events were outside their control might reflect a general sense of powerlessness and unpredictability. Because Scherer did not measure appraisals of unemotional situations, it may be that these cultural differences in appraisal are not specific to emotions. Perhaps African cultures place greater emphasis on the immorality and unfairness of all situations, emotion-producing or not, whereas Latin American cultures are generally more likely to think of the world as morally right.

Importantly, Scherer (1997) did not examine the specific events that participants appraised in their descriptions of emotional experiences. One major influence culture can have on emotion lies in the meaning we attribute to various events. People in different cultures may appraise the same event in different ways, depending on each culture's system of meaning. Think back to the example we used in Chapter 3 of being a guest in someone's home, and being invited to help yourself at the refrigerator. An American would probably interpret this as pleasant (an invitation to feel at home), fair (it is reasonable to ask you to get the food for yourself), goal conducive (allowing you to eat), and controllable (you can choose whatever you want). Thus, an American might feel happy in this situation.

By contrast, a Japanese person might interpret the event as unpleasant (the host has just told you he will not take care of you), unfair (what did you do to be treated in this rude way?), uncontrollable (surely there are things in the refrigerator the host does not wish you to eat—how are you supposed to know what they are?), and goal obstructing (now you cannot eat anything!). Thus, using the same formula for converting appraisals into emotion, but appraising the event in a very different way, a Japanese person might experience sadness or anger.

Some researchers have suggested that culturally encouraged biases in emotional appraisal may help explain differences in emotional aspects of personality—differences in the frequency with which people tend to experience various emotions, both within and between cultures (Scherer & Brosch, 2009). There is good evidence supporting this proposal at the individual level. For example, children who show a bias toward appraising their peers' actions as motivated by hostile intent tend to be more aggressive (De Castro et al., 2002). Although aggressive behavior is the outcome in these studies, it's reasonable to assume that this aggression is motivated by anger. Similarly, highly anxious people show a bias toward interpreting innocuous events as threats (Britton, Lissek, Grillon, Norcross, & Pine, 2011). However, few studies have addressed the hypothesis that cultural differences in emotion can be explained in this way. In one promising exception, Ira Roseman and colleagues (Roseman et al., 1995) reported that participants in India tended to appraise events as less goal-discrepant than did participants in the United States, and this accounted for cultural differences in sadness and anger (Indian participants reported feeling less of each emotion). Expanding this approach to more appraisal dimensions and more cultural groups may be an interesting direction for future research.

Gender and Emotional Experience

Think about the men and women you see in television shows, movies, and other popular media in your culture. How do they compare in terms of their emotions? At least in the Western world, gender stereotypes are rife with assumptions about emotion (Ellemers, 2018). One common stereotype is that women are simply "more emotional" than men overall (Figure 4.12). Other stereotypes assign some emotions to women, and others to men. Are these stereotypes objectively true? If so, why? This is a complicated question. Even asking about the emotions of "women versus men" oversimplifies

FIGURE 4.12. Common stereotypes about gender and emotion describe women as more emotional than men. However, the data indicate a more complicated pattern.

biological sex, which reflects a variety of genetic, hormonal, neural, and anatomical variables that do not split tidily into two bins; and gender, which reflects culturally defined constructs and individual identities that are even more diverse (Hyde et al., 2019). For now—recognizing that more and better data are needed—let's take one version of this question: How do the emotions of people who identify primarily as women versus men compare?

For questions such as these, it is important to ensure that data come from large, diverse samples of people whose characteristics are similar to those of the broad population. In one particularly large study, Robert Simon and Leda Nath (2004) used data from the 1996 US General Social Survey to achieve this goal. The General Social Survey is conducted every other year, completed by thousands of adults in the United States who are representative of the demographic and geographic distribution of that country. Each year the survey includes a variety of questions about attitudes, preferences, behaviors, and so forth, but in 1996 participants also answered questions about the number of days during the previous week they had felt each of 19 different emotions.

When all the different types of emotion were added together, did women report feeling emotions more often than men? Nope. Younger people reported more frequent emotions than older people, and high-income people reported feeling emotions less often than lower-income people, on average, but the totals for men and women were almost identical (around 44 emotion episodes per week). The stereotype that women are more emotional than men overall was not supported by the data.

Gender differences *were* observed, however, for different categories of emotions. Men reported experiencing positive emotions more often than women, and this effect remained after controlling for other demographic variables. Women reported feeling more frequent negative emotions than men overall. However, this difference was accounted for by household income. On average, women's household income was lower than men's, and lower household income was associated with more negative emotion; once this effect was controlled, the difference between men and women on overall negative emotions was no longer significant.

Further gender differences emerged for more specific emotions. Rather than studying every emotion term separately, the researchers asked whether participants tended to rate certain emotions in similar ways, suggesting that they could be grouped together. Based on these analyses, Simon and Nath (2004) created averages for calm positive feelings, excited positive feelings, anxious feelings, sad feelings, angry feelings, and feelings related to embarrassment and shame. Again, men reported feeling positive emotions more often than women—this was true for both calm and excited positive feelings. Women reported feeling fear and sadness more often than men. No gender differences were observed for frequencies of anger and embarrassment/shame (see Figure 4.13).

Is the pattern in other cultures similar or different? Agneta Fischer and colleagues (2004) examined data from Klaus Scherer's cross-cultural study of appraisal and emotion, described earlier, to address this question. The study included men's and women's ratings of the intensity of their emotional feelings during personal experiences of fear, sadness, anger, disgust, shame, and guilt from participants in 37 countries around the world. Women and men reported similar intensity of anger and disgust; this did not differ across cultural groups. However, women reported more intense experiences of fear, sadness, shame, and guilt. Although this analysis included a different set of emotions than Simon

FIGURE 4.13. In a large, nationally representative sample of US adults, men reported more frequent positive emotion feelings, whereas women reported more frequent fear and sadness. Men and women reported equal amounts of anger and embarrassment/shame.

and Nath's (2004) study in the United States (positive emotions in particular were omitted) and emphasized intensity rather than frequency of emotions, the results are consistent in important ways. Men and women did not differ in their experience of anger, but women reported higher levels of fear and sadness.

What might explain these differences? Theorists have pointed out that men and women live in different worlds in terms of social status and power—even in the United States, where gender roles are more egalitarian than in many other cultures (Brody & Hall, 2008; Simon & Nath, 2004). Positive emotions are experienced when the environment brings rewards and things are going well, and status and power increase access to many rewards. To the extent that men have higher status, on average, they are likely to encounter more positive emotion-eliciting rewards. Alternatively (or in addition), men may be more likely to perceive or appraise the environment as containing many rewards, even in cases where men's and women's environments are objectively the same. Future research teasing apart this distinction would be valuable. The gender differences in fear and sadness may reflect differences in power and status as well. In the appraisal profiles associated with these two emotions, appraisal of control or coping ability is low (Scherer, 1997). If women generally have less power over their environment, or if they feel less control even if the objective environment is the same (again, we can't tell based on these data, and each may be true at different times), then fear and sadness are more likely.

This raises an interesting question for the cross-cultural data: Do women experience less sadness and fear in cultures where, objectively speaking, they have more power? Because a measure of societal gender equality was available in the data set (e.g., proportion of women in political office and in managerial or professional roles at work), Fischer and colleagues (2004) were able to address this question. Women's levels of sadness and fear was not significantly related to level of gender equality. In an interesting twist, however, men experienced less intense sadness and fear (also shame and guilt) in countries that were more egalitarian. Thus, relatively high gender equality did not appear to influence women's experience of these emotions as much as it created a climate in which *men* felt less negative, low-power emotion. This is inconsistent with the idea that when women have more power in society, men feel more threatened and are less happy.

EXAMPLE: WHAT CAUSES ANGER?
Learning Objectives
- Differentiate explanations of what causes anger from the core relational theme, appraisal dimensions, and cognitive neoassociationistic approaches.
- Summarize the cognitive neoassociationistic model of anger, and evaluate the evidence that anger can occur without a preceding cognitive appraisal.

Like hunger, discussed in the early sections of this chapter, anger offers an interesting case study on the proximal causes of emotions and other motivational states. People may be angered by a wide range of situations and events. Not only will an event that infuriates one person elicit a shrug or a laugh from someone else, the same event might elicit either of these responses from the *same* person under different conditions. Imagine being in your car in a parking lot, hunting for a spot, and seeing one up ahead; just as you drive toward it someone turns into the aisle and takes it for themselves. If you've had a bad day, or are running late, or for any of a dozen other reasons, you might be furious. On another day you might just sigh and look for a different spot.

This poses a practical problem for researchers, especially those who want to study emotions in a laboratory or other controlled setting. However, it is also a challenge for theories of anger, and there has been considerable controversy over what exactly elicits this emotion. Let's take a look at the different sides of this debate.

Core Relational Theme Approach
Richard Lazarus (1991) defined the prototypical *core relational theme* eliciting anger as a demeaning offense against me and mine (see Table 4.1). Consistent with this idea, many studies indicate that anger arises against someone who has insulted or harmed you, either intentionally or carelessly. If someone steps in front of you and knocks you off balance, your degree of anger depends on why you think the person stepped in front of you. You probably would not feel angry with a toddler or a blind person. You might become angry with someone who had no excuse for carelessness, but just wasn't paying attention to where he or she was going. You would become even angrier if you thought someone was intentionally trying to block your way. In one study, American, European, and Asian students all reported anger most strongly when someone treated them unfairly (Ohbuchi et al., 2004). In another study, people reported recent events in which things went badly for them. They reported feeling anger only when they had someone to blame for their misfortune (Kuppens et al., 2003).

Much research points to the importance of blame in anger, but the nature of the relationship is unclear. Consider this study: high school students read descriptions of several situations, rated various aspects of the situations, and then stated how angry they would feel in those situations. They also reported how often they feel angry overall. In general, when students perceived a situation as blameworthy, they said they would feel angry. The students who tended to feel angry most often in everyday life were also most likely to interpret unpleasant situations as situations in which someone was to blame (Kuppens, Van Mechelen, & Rijmen, 2008). Another study indicated that participants made to feel angry earlier in the study were more likely to interpret ambiguous words as threats (Barazzone & Davey, 2009). So, does having someone to blame lead to anger? Or does being angry make you look for someone to blame? Research suggests that the causal arrow might go in both directions.

Appraisal Dimension Approach

Studies of appraisal from the component process model perspective yield compatible results. In the cross-cultural study of appraisal by Scherer (1997), described earlier, people said they usually felt angry in unexpected, unpleasant, and unfair situations that interfered with their goals and were caused by someone else. Participants also described anger-inducing situations as potentially changeable—at least partly under their control. An uncontrollable bad situation elicits more sadness or fear than anger. The intentionality factor was not included in this study, so it would be interesting to know whether it was crucial for situations evoking anger.

In the United States, anger often arises when people are driving, and people can be openly aggressive (Figure 4.14). Why? One obvious reason is that driving can be unpleasant, interfering with the goal of getting wherever we're trying to go, and there is frequently someone to blame. You are trying to get somewhere in a hurry and someone slows to a crawl, straddles two lanes, or takes their time when the light turns green. But frustration is not the whole explanation. Another factor is that in the safety of your car, you can

FIGURE 4.14. Anger and aggression are common while people are driving, likely because we feel protected from any consequences.

honk, yell, or make a fist without much fear of retaliation (unless you are on a Los Angeles freeway, in which case it's an extremely bad idea). You likely feel a stronger sense of control than you would if you were not separated from the person you're insulting by your two cars and a bunch of traffic.

Scherer's (1997) findings suggest that we typically become angry about another person's actions. If you did something careless or foolish that caused problems for you later—such as locking yourself out of your house—might you be angry with yourself? Many people say that they are. Self-anger is different from other-anger in several ways. When you are angry toward someone else, you might seek revenge in some way. You don't attack yourself. Self-anger is often mixed with sadness and guilt or embarrassment (Ellsworth & Tong, 2006). The phenomenon of being angry with yourself is not well explained by the core relational theme approach, but appraisal dimensions allow for more ambiguous, less prototypical emotional experiences, and may support a better explanation.

No-Cognition Approach: The Cognitive Neoassociationistic Model

What about the no-appraisal approach? Can you feel anger, despite having no one to blame? As an example, have you ever found yourself furious with a broken copy machine? The copy machine isn't deliberately trying to annoy you, but you still feel an overwhelming desire to kick it until it does what you want. Taking this question even further, can you feel cranky for no apparent reason?

According to Leonard Berkowitz's (1990) **cognitive-neoassociationistic (CNA) model of anger generation**, any unpleasant event or sensation facilitates anger and aggressive behavior. The unpleasant thing might be frustration, but it could also be pain, an aversive odor, or almost anything. For example, the probability of aggression increases when the weather is hot (Preti et al., 2002) or when people themselves feel uncomfortably hot (Anderson, 2001). If two rats or mice are together when they both get a foot shock, they attack each other. Do they really blame each other, or do they feel aggressive just because they are uncomfortable? If a rat gets a foot shock and then sees something unusual, like a plastic hedgehog, it attacks the apparent intruder (Keith-Lucas & Guttman, 1975).

Note that this proposal contradicts the idea that anger requires an attribution. Berkowitz (1990) suggests that being too hot, feeling crowded, having a headache, being hungry or in pain, smelling something foul, or any other discomfort by itself provokes anger, even if you don't attribute it to anyone or interpret it. In fact, blame may be something we invent after the fact: you feel angry, you yell at someone, and then you quickly rationalize, "I was angry at that person because . . ." Like the mere exposure effect, Berkowitz's proposal forces us to question what we mean by emotion. Remember the definition offered in Chapter 1: emotion is a complex sequence of reactions to a stimulus (Plutchik, 1982). Berkowitz suggests that an emotion can arise directly from an unfulfilled biological drive, including states of hunger or fatigue, without any external stimulus (Berkowitz & Harmon-Jones, 2004). If there is no stimulus, then there is no need for appraisal.

What evidence supports Berkowitz's theory? To give a few examples, rates of violent crime are higher during the summers, when temperatures peak, than during the winter, and the likelihood of rioting increases with temperature as well (Carlsmith & Anderson,

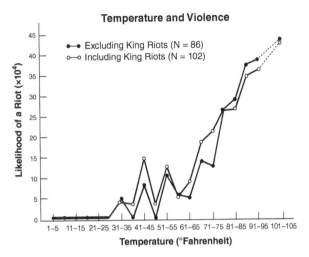

FIGURE 4.15.   People are more likely to riot when temperatures rise, consistent with the cognitive neoassociationistic model of anger generation.

1979; see Figure 4.15). These are correlational studies, which means we can't be confident about a causal relationship; perhaps people riot more and commit more crime when it's warm simply because they're more likely to be outside. In laboratory experiments, however, study participants who were subjected to physical pain (Berkowitz, Cochran, & Embree, 1981), trapped with an extremely unpleasant noise (Geen, 1978), or exposed to secondhand cigarette smoke (Zillmann, Baron, & Tamborini, 1981) all tended to behave more aggressively toward convenient target people, although the targets were not responsible for the conditions. Each study included a stimulus, but not of the kind suggested by most appraisal theories of anger. These findings are consistent with the CNA model.

Even within the CNA model, however, appraisals influence the tone of emotional experience, particularly appraisals of control. Frustration, pain, and other kinds of discomfort often lead to anger and aggression, but not always. According to Berkowitz (1990), if you think you are in danger and have no control, fear will trump anger. If you are not sure what would happen if you express anger, you vacillate between attack and escape. Have you ever watched a cat approach a mouse? If the cat is an experienced mouser and the mouse is small, the cat makes a quick kill. But if the cat is less accomplished and the mouse is large, the mouse hisses and bares its teeth. Under these conditions, the cat retreats. In an intermediate case, the cat approaches cautiously. It bats at the mouse with its paws again and again until it weakens the mouse enough to bite it safely. Observers sometimes think the cat is playing with the mouse, but the behavior is in deadly earnest. Give the cat a tranquilizer to reduce its fears and a cat that would have played with the mouse goes for a quicker attack (Adamec, Stark-Adamec, & Livingston, 1980; Biben, 1979; Pellis et al., 1988). Something similar is true in humans: people who have drunk alcohol or taken tranquilizers sometimes get into fights because they have suppressed their fear. Much larger doses calm them enough to become inactive and cease fighting (Valzelli, 1979). These examples suggest that even within the relatively "cognition-free" CNA model, appraisals direct our emotional responses in important ways.

SUMMARY

In Chapter 1 we defined drives as motivational states reflecting basic biological needs, and emotions as more complex responses to events with implications for our goals and well-being. Based on these definitions you might expect a clear-cut distinction between the forces that activate drives and those that elicit emotions. As we'll say often in this book, it's not that simple. The drive of hunger can be activated by environmental stimuli, even stimuli that have no inherent relationship to food. In contrast, the emotion of anger can be potentiated by hunger, pain, and physical discomfort. Elicitors of these different kinds of motivational states overlap in ways researchers are still trying to understand.

Nonetheless, research on why we feel these states in the moment has produced valuable insights, with powerful implications for efforts to understand our emotions and improve people's lives. Most emotion researchers agree that to have an emotional response to some situation, you must appraise or interpret it as having implications for your goals and welfare. Different researchers emphasize different appraisal content, with some focusing on specific kinds of goals in a categorical approach, and others taking a dimensional approach in which specific goals are less important. However, these different approaches are not incompatible. Even the "no-cognition" CNA model of anger acknowledges that appraisals of unpleasantness and high control are necessary for this emotion to occur.

Although the approaches described in this chapter differ in subtle ways, considering these subtleties and their implications has been helpful in advancing theory, and translating the basic research into practical settings. Is liking an emotion? If so, does the absence of an obvious appraisal-based explanation of the mere exposure effect spell doom for appraisal theories, or is there a way to reconcile the two sets of findings? Different approaches also lead to different hypotheses about what people's emotions might look like beyond the prototypical examples of sadness, anger, fear, and so forth. Knowing that cues previously associated with addictive substances and unhealthy foods can evoke craving, researchers can advise people trying to lead healthier lives to avoid those cues. Appraisal theories have proved extremely important for clinical psychology, where appraisals play a key role in our understanding of emotional disorders and emotion regulation techniques. Appraisals provide a tool for making better sense of our own emotional lives, and those of other people.

KEY TERMS

appraisal dimensions: a common set of questions used to evaluate the meaning of every stimulus or situation we encounter; appraisal profiles, rather than individual themes, are associated with specific emotions (p. 127)

challenge appraisal: a state in which one's coping resources are appraised as adequate for dealing with the threat posed by a situation;

associated with increased cardiac activity, but reduced vascular resistance (p. 132)

cognitive-neoassociationistic (CNA) model of anger: theory that anger and reactive aggression are enhanced by any unpleasant event or aversive condition (p. 144)

core relational theme: a basic, prototypical type of problem or benefit that people can encounter in their transactions with the environment (p. 126)

cue reactivity: a conditioned response to objects, places, and other stimuli previously associated with rewards (including addictive substances), such that exposure to these cues evokes craving and appetitive motivation (p. 121)

distal causes: causes of some event that are removed in terms of time or process; in the cases of emotion and motivation, these include evolutionary, cultural, and other causes that explain why humans have the *capacity* for experiencing a given state (p. 118)

emotion blend: in basic/discrete emotions theory, the simultaneous experience of more than one emotion (p. 128)

ghrelin: a peptide hormone produced by the stomach, as well as other parts of the digestive system and structures in the brain, that generally increases feelings of hunger (p. 118)

leptin: a hormone produced by fat cells that generally reduces feelings of hunger (p. 118)

mere exposure effect: an effect in which people develop liking or fondness toward targets only because of being exposed to them a large number of times (p. 134)

primary appraisal: In Richard Lazarus's theory, the way in which some event is relevant to the individual's needs and well-being (p. 129)

proximal causes: causes of some event that are close in terms of time or process; in the cases of emotion and motivation, these include the immediate reasons why a state was activated *in the moment* (p. 118)

rooting reflex: an innate behavioral response crucial for feeding, in which newborn infants turn their head and begin to suck when something gently touches the corner of their mouth (p. 120)

secondary appraisal: In Lazarus's theory, the individual's appraisal of his or her ability to cope with the situation, including who caused the situation, how much control one has over the situation, and the extent to which the situation is expected to change (p. 129)

threat appraisal: contrasted with challenge; a state in which the threat posed by a situation is appraised as exceeding one's ability to cope; associated with increased cardiac activity and overall vascular constriction (p. 132)

THOUGHT/DISCUSSION QUESTIONS

1. What elicits pain? Based on your experience, how much of the experience of pain can be explained by physical harm, environmental factors, and psychological state? How might you test your theory of the cause(s) of pain scientifically?

2. Think of a time when a friend of yours was going through a romantic breakup and was very sad (you may even know someone in this situation now; if it's you, we hope this exercise will help). How was this person appraising the breakup—what did it mean for him or her? Can you suggest some other appraisals that might help the person feel better?

3. We noted that it's difficult to characterize people's appraisals and emotional responses as right or wrong, yet symptoms of psychological disorders often involve dysfunctional emotions. What criteria might you use to judge whether someone's appraisal of a situation (and the resulting emotion) is reasonable?

4. Appraisals can be quick or slow. Can you think of a time when your appraisal of some situation developed or changed over the course of hours, days, or even longer? How did your appraisal change? How did your emotions change?

5. Using Table 4.2, what appraisal profile might you expect for the emotion pride?

6. Is there an appraisal that might explain the mere exposure effect? What do we learn about some object or person simply from seeing it over and over again?

SUGGESTIONS FOR FURTHER READING

Glassner, B. (2018). *The culture of fear: Why Americans are afraid of the wrong things*. Basic Books. Well-documented critique of the role that mass media—and increasingly social media—play in constructing targets of fear.

Moors, A., Ellsworth, P. C., Scherer, K. R., & Frijda, N. H. (2013). Appraisal theories of emotion: State of the art and future development. *Emotion Review*, 5(2), 119–124. This review article is a collaboration by four major thinkers in appraisal theory, summarizing current points of agreement and considering where it needs to go next.

Scherer, K. R. (1997). The role of culture in emotion-antecedent appraisal. *Journal of Personality and Social Psychology*, 73(5), 902–922. The original paper reporting Klaus Scherer's major cross-cultural study linking appraisal dimensions to the experience of specific emotions.

CHAPTER 5

Expression in the Face, Posture, and Voice

In this first section of the book we have asked what emotions and motivations are, and why people experience them. We have considered the distal origins of key motivational states, as well as both evolutionary and cultural perspectives on the functions emotions serve. We also discussed the central role our interpretation of a situation plays in determining the emotions we feel in the moment and activating motivations. In the final chapter of this section, we consider how people express emotions and other motivational states nonverbally, through facial expressions, posture, and voice.

All the complex issues we have considered thus far are vividly illustrated in the research on nonverbal expression, offering our first chance to see how the theoretical perspectives we've reviewed play out in a relatable aspect of real-life experience. Many big arguments in the field were raised first, and are still debated most contentiously, in the context of facial expressions. To what extent are people's facial expressions part of human nature, and to what extent are they shaped by cultural learning? How much agreement must there be across cultures to declare that some aspect of nonverbal expression is "universal?" What does "universal" even mean in this context? Is the research on nonverbal expressions consistent with the proposal that emotions exist as a limited number of discrete categories, rather than a series of continuous, intersecting dimensions? Do motivational and emotional states beyond Ekman's six proposed basic emotions also have characteristic nonverbal expressions? How do nonverbal expressions relate to emotional and motivational feelings?

The three modern theories of emotion described in Chapter 1 lead to distinct hypotheses about nonverbal expression. According to basic emotions theory, human nature provides a template for the expression of each emotion. Although cultural learning may add new elements and culture-specific expressions, and individuals may conceal or fake expressions intentionally, the uninhibited expression of each basic emotion should be displayed in a similar form, recognizable all over the world (Ekman, 1992). According to the component process model, human nature does provide a "code" for emotional expression, but it codes for aspects of emotional appraisal, such as novelty, unexpectedness, pleasantness, and control, rather than emotion categories (Scherer, 1992). Psychological construction theories instead note

FIGURE 5.1.   The facial expression of people in pain often includes lowered eyebrows, tightened muscles surrounding the eyes, and raised upper lip.

that nonverbal expressions of the same emotional state may vary widely from person to person and situation to situation, and propose these expressions are mostly learned from the social environment (Barrett, 2006). Facial expressions provided the first battleground on which these theories competed for evidence, and there's still no sign of a definitive winner.

Modern research on nonverbal expression examines facial configurations, postures, and vocal qualities associated with a wide range of emotional and motivational states. Researchers have proposed characteristic expressions for contempt (Matsumoto, 1992), pride (Tracy & Robins, 2007), embarrassment and amusement (Keltner, 1995), romantic love and sexual desire (Gonzaga et al., 2006), pain (see Figure 5.1), sensory pleasure, confusion, and boredom, among many other states (e.g., Campos et al., 2013; Cordaro et al., 2018; Dael et al., 2012). However, the first modern studies of facial expressions focused on just six emotions. These studies are the reason emotion is now a respected and important topic within psychology, and their methods and findings shaped the direction of future research in profound ways. We could even claim that these studies are the reason you're reading this textbook right now! The history behind this assertion deserves some attention. Read on and see for yourself.

HISTORICAL IMPORTANCE OF FACIAL EXPRESSION RESEARCH
Learning Objectives
- Explain the origin of the facial expression prototypes used in Paul Ekman's and Carroll Izard's initial cross-cultural expression-recognition studies.
- Summarize the methods and results of Ekman's study with participants in New Guinea.

- Interpret the implications of Ekman's and Izard's initial expression recognition study, relative to prevailing beliefs about facial expression in the social sciences in the mid-twentieth century.

Research on emotional expression began with Darwin's ([1872] 1998) studies of facial and postural expressions, which he conducted soon after developing his theory of evolution. Darwin's observations, although neglected by psychology for several decades, went on to powerfully influence the questions asked and hypotheses eventually posed by pioneering researchers in emotion.

Over the course of Darwin's travels on the H. M. S. *Beagle*, as well as in his daily life at home in England, he noted similarities in the physical behaviors exhibited by animals of many species in situations that, if they were experienced by a human, would evoke a particular emotion. For example, many species react to a physical threat by changing their posture to appear larger. Birds raise their feathers and spread their wings, cats arch their backs and their hair stands on end, and primates stand on their hind legs and lift their arms. Darwin also noted that some of the most common human expressions of emotion resemble those of monkeys, chimpanzees, and apes in similar kinds of situations (Figure 5.2).

In *The Expression of the Emotions in Man and Animals,* Darwin ([1872] 1998) provided detailed evidence for these similarities and argued that expressions of emotion probably evolved because they conferred some kind of survival or reproductive advantage on individuals who displayed them. For instance, animals that react to threats by making themselves look larger increase their chance of survival, because the change in appearance might scare off an attacker. In much of the book, Darwin argues that human expressions of emotion are also the result of evolutionary processes that link us to our closest primate relatives.

Darwin recognized that if facial expressions were inherited from primate ancestors, they should look the same (or at least very similar) in all human cultures. In his era, the mid-1800s, photography was awkward and expensive, so to test his hypothesis he had to rely on written reports from missionaries and others who had traveled to other continents. Darwin wrote to anyone he knew who was living in another part of the world; described typical facial expressions of particular emotions; and asked his correspondents whether natives of that culture expressed each emotion in the same way.

Darwin's correspondents replied that people throughout the world did show similar expressions of many feelings. When they were surprised or astonished, his correspondents agreed, they open their eyes widely—sometimes their mouths as well. When puzzled or

FIGURE 5.2. Nonhuman primates have some nonverbal expressions that clearly resemble those of humans, and they display them in similar situations.

perplexed, they frown. When determined, they frown and close their mouths tightly. When they feel helpless, they shrug their shoulders. In this way, Darwin documented intriguing similarities in the nonverbal gestures and expressions people were seen to display around the world.

His ideas influenced some early psychologists, including William James, whose theory of emotion also reflects an assumption that emotions are innate responses inherited from our ancestors. Before long, however, some problems with Darwin's research strategy were noted. First, consider the nature of the questions he asked his far-flung assistants. The question was not "Can you describe the way people's faces look when they are astonished?" A typical question read more like this: "Is astonishment expressed by the eyes and mouth being opened wide, and by the eyebrows being raised?" Darwin's correspondents simply said yes or no. People sometimes agree with a description such as this even if the description is not completely accurate, or if they are not sure, especially when it is clear what hypothesis the researcher is testing. Today, well-trained researchers would avoid such a constraining question and let the correspondents describe expressions in their own words. Alternatively, they might offer a series of choices without indicating which is the expected answer. Another problem is that Darwin's question required that his correspondents infer people's emotions by some other means than facial expressions, and it's not clear how they did so.

By the end of the nineteenth century and the early decades of the twentieth, social scientists were traveling throughout the world to study the lives and customs of people in different cultures. Their observations included comments about the local people's behavior in emotional situations, often emphasizing differences from typical behavior in the West. For example, Lafcadio Hearn ([1894] 2011) described a Japanese woman who laughed when showing her employer her recently deceased husband's ashes (we'll let you contemplate the possible explanations of this). Otto Klineberg (1938) analyzed descriptions of emotional expression in Chinese literature, noting differences as well as similarities. Characters would be described as clapping their hands when they were angry, or as scratching their ears and cheeks when they are happy. As discussed in Chapter 3, ethnographic reports of cultural differences in emotional language and behavior, as well as expression, were pouring in from around the globe. By the middle of the twentieth century it was widely accepted in the social sciences that emotion, and its expression, were largely the product of cultural learning (Birdwhistell, 1970; Ekman, 1972; Klineberg, 1940).

In the 1960s, however, the psychologist Silvan Tomkins began to ask whether Darwin might have been right after all. Tomkins had examined thousands of photographs of people's emotional expressions, some in naturalistic settings and others posed by actors. He found that for some emotions, many of the expressions had a common set of elements, defining a prototype for each emotion (see Figure 5.3). When participants in the United States were shown photographs of expressions closely resembling this prototype, they tended to agree strongly as to what emotion was being portrayed (Tomkins, 1963). However, Tomkins knew this was not great evidence for the argument that emotional expressions are part of universal human nature—his participants could simply have learned the same cultural code for displaying emotions as the actors in the photos, just as they all learned the English language as children.

At this point, Tomkins pulled a sneaky move (Ekman, 1999). He was mentoring two young researchers, Paul Ekman and Carroll Izard, each of whom was interested in

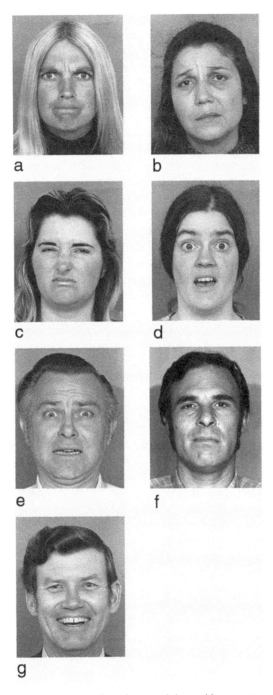

FIGURE 5.3. While looking at photographs of people around the world in certain emotional situations, Silvan Tomkins noticed common elements among their facial expressions. Prototype expressions, such as those shown here, have been used in much research on the nonverbal expression of emotion. People in many cultures have been asked to identify which face shown here goes with each of the following emotions: anger, disgust, fear, happiness, sadness, and surprise (one expression is neutral). Can you tell which is which? The answer is on page (184).

emotion. To each researcher, Tomkins suggested that the way to find out whether facial expressions of some emotions were determined by human nature rather than cultural learning was to go to people in a variety of cultures—preferably with little or no exposure to Westerners—and ask them to interpret the meaning of these prototypical expressions. The sneaky part is that Tomkins did not tell either Ekman or Izard that he was giving the same advice to the other researcher as well. As a result, each researcher went off to do the study in question, having no idea that the other was doing the same thing.

Although we do not recommend this as a mentoring technique, or as a strategy for winning friends, from a scientific standpoint Tomkins's move made sense. He knew that if the results supported his hypotheses about universality, they would be highly contro-versial; having two independent researchers do the same study, and report the same find-ings, provides more convincing evidence than one study alone. Ekman himself was skeptical of Tomkins's predictions, thinking it more likely that facial expressions were learned and culture-specific rather than innate. In the end, Tomkins's trick paid off. Izard selected for his studies those photographed expressions that were most consistently identi-fied as expressing the target emotions by people in the United States, and went on to show that these were also recognized at remarkably high rates in a variety of other Western and non-Western societies (Izard, 1971). Ekman took the point even further, traveling with colleagues Richard Sorenson and Wallace Friesen and a translator to New Guinea, where they had access to participants in small, isolated villages who had previously had little or no contact with people from the West (Sorenson, 1975).

For his study, Ekman chose photographs from Tomkins's files that closely matched the prototype expressions, as described with a new system called the **Facial Action Coding System** or FACS (Ekman & Friesen, 1978). Figure 5.4 shows many of the muscles underlying the facial skin; FACS assigns an **action unit** to the change in appearance created by moving each muscle. The expressions in the photos Ekman used looked like the ones in Figure 5.3, although the photos in that figure were taken much later. Because the local language was so different, and because the indigenous partici-pants were extremely uncomfortable with direct questions such as "What emotion is this person expressing?" (Sorenson, 1975), Ekman and colleagues developed an alterna-tive method for linking facial expressions to emotions—they told short stories about situations expected to elicit that emotion (e.g., someone in the village has stolen your pig) and asked participants which of two or three photographed facial expressions was most appropriate for each situation. This way, all the participants had to do was point to the chosen picture.

This study has many limitations (Russell, 1994). The stories were told by a translator, and the researchers had no idea what the translator was saying. For all they knew, the translator might have said, "Hey, these guys want you to point to the photo on the left; just do it." To the researchers' knowledge, however, the translator was reasonably consis-tent in conveying the stories and did not do anything obvious to give the expected answer away. Also, this situation bore no relationship to the participants' typical social interac-tion (villages in New Guinea did not have formal tests or even a practice of asking direct questions, much less research participation pools for psychology experiments), and par-ticipants appeared uncomfortable (Sorenson, 1975). Also, for each story, participants only had two or three photos to choose from; in each case, they may have chosen the closest available option if the expression they would typically expect was not available.

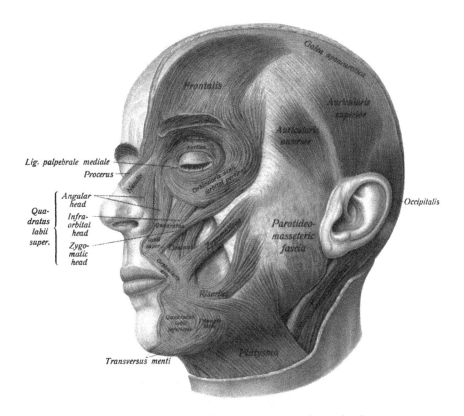

Lig. palpebrale mediale
Procerus

Qua-
dratus
labii
super.
— Angular head
— Infra-orbital head
— Zygo-matic head

Frontalis

Galea aponeurotica

Auricularis superior

Auricularis anterior

Occipitalis

Parotideo-masseteric fascia

Risorius

Transversus menti

Platysma

FIGURE 5.4. The Facial Action Coding System assigns a number to the change in appearance caused by moving each muscle in the face. From Sobotta (1906).

Despite these limitations, the results were remarkable. Participants chose the "correct" or predicted pictures at very high rates: 92% for happiness, 84% for anger, 81% for disgust, 80% for fear, and 79% for sadness (Sorenson, 1975). In a related set of studies, Ekman and colleagues (Ekman, Sorenson, & Friesen, 1969) reported that upward of 70% of participants in the United States, Brazil, and Japan chose the intended label for expressions of these same emotions, plus surprise (chance in these studies was 1 in 6, or about 17%). People in Borneo also had accuracy rates well above chance. The idea of cross-cultural generality of facial expressions received further support from the research of Irenäus Eibl-Eibesfeldt, who photographed expressions in many remote cultures. One of his more surprising findings was that people throughout the world raise their eyebrows as a friendly greeting (Figure 5.5) and that this eyebrow-raising greeting lasts about one-third of a second, from relaxed to raised and back to relaxed, in every culture (Eibl-Eibesfeldt, 1973).

Recall that most psychologists and anthropologists of the time assumed that emotions and their expressions were completely culturally learned. Ekman's, Izard's, and Eibl-Eibesfeldt's findings changed everything. Although intense argument took place along the way—and is still going on—these findings convinced many within psychology that *something* about emotional expression must be innate and universal, at least for some

FIGURE 5.5.   People throughout the world greet one another by raising their eyebrows and sometimes also slightly opening their mouths.

emotions. This made emotion a legitimate topic for psychology research, and the field of affective science was born.

EMOTION IN POSTURE AND THE VOICE

Learning Objectives

- Summarize the methods and results of Aviezer and colleagues' (2012) study of facial and postural/bodily cues in positive versus negative affect, and analyze implications.
- Describe the prototypical pride posture examined in prior research, and explain its association with a comparable pose seen in nonhuman primates.
- Define the term "vocal burst," and explain its relevance to research on the vocal expression of emotions.
- Analyze which emotion/affect states are most easily recognized through facial expression, posture, or nonverbal vocal expression, according to existing data.

Ekman's and Izard's early studies of facial expressions shaped future research in many ways. For example, many studies have examined the same set of emotions that had been included in this early work. A more subtle effect was the intensity of focus on the face as the main channel of emotional expression, rather than other ways of communicating emotion such as posture (Aviezer, Trope, & Todorov, 2012), voice (Laukka & Elfenbein, 2012; Sauter et al., 2010; Simon-Thomas et al., 2009), and touch (Hertenstein et al., 2006). In fact, recognition rates for facial expressions are increased if information about posture or the voice is included (Martinez et al., 2016; Van den Stock et al., 2007). But what about posture and voice on their own? Do they reliably communicate emotions?

Posture and Emotion

One set of studies suggests that at least for intense emotional experiences, posture may be even more important than the face in communicating emotional valence—whether one feels good or bad (Aviezer et al., 2012). Look at the faces in Figure 5.6. These are photographs of real people playing tennis, right after either winning or losing a point. Can you tell which is which? It turns out that most people are uncertain, and when they guess, they are often wrong. How can that be? In Ekman's research, happiness was consistently the easiest emotion for participants around the world to identify, presumably because it was so clearly different from all of the negative emotions. Even in dimensional models of emotion, valence is supposed to be the most important way in which emotions differ. Of all the judgments one should need to make about another's expression, the difference between positive and negative emotion should be the easiest.

It turns out that people can make the distinction reliably, but not based on the face. Hillel Aviezer and colleagues (2012) asked participants to guess whether tennis players

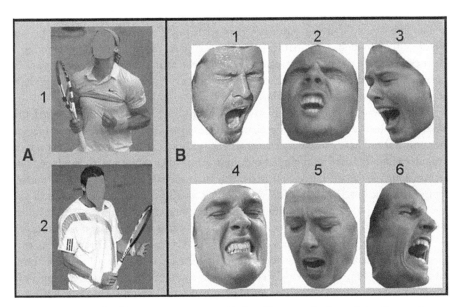

FIGURE 5.6. Each of these expressions was displayed by a tennis player right after a point was scored. Can you tell who won the point, and who lost? From Aviezer, Trope, & Todorov (2012).

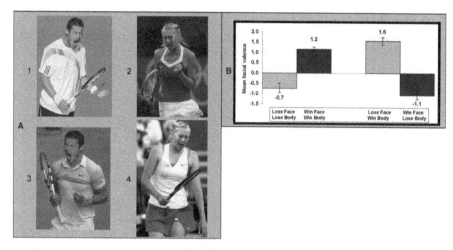

FIGURE 5.7. In these photos, some face–body pairs were altered to send mixed messages about whether the person had won or lost a tennis point. Pictures 1 and 3 include losers' faces; pictures 2 and 4 show winners' faces. However, picture 3 has a loser's face on a winner's body, and the opposite is true for picture 4. Participants' guesses about the players' affect valence clearly tracked the expressions of the bodies, although they had been instructed to focus on the face. From Aviezer, Trope, & Todorov (2012).

had won or lost based on the face only (as in Figure 5.6b); the body only (as in 5.6a); or the face and body combined. When participants could see the body, with or without the face, they answered correctly, but with the face alone they could not tell the difference. In a follow-up study these researchers asked what would happen if they paired faces with bodies incorrectly, putting winners' faces with losers' bodies and vice versa (see Figure 5.7). Although participants had been instructed to rate the players' emotional valence based on the facial expression (with higher ratings indicating more positive valence), their ratings clearly tracked the emotion expression in the body, accurately identifying the winners based on the postural cue.

Can postures reliably communicate *specific* emotions? This is more complicated. On one hand, evidence suggests that the characteristic expressions of some emotions include key postural and head movement elements. For example, the typical expression of pride includes a slightly raised head, puffed-out chest, arms either akimbo (with hands on hips) or raised high in the air, and feet planted firmly in a wide-legged stance, as well as a small smile (Tracy & Robins, 2007, 2008b; see Figure 5.8). This display looks a great deal like the dominance pose shown by nonhuman primates, suggesting that we may have inherited this way of claiming and advertising high social status from common ancestors.

Research by Belinda Campos and colleagues (Campos et al., 2013) suggests that posture and head movement may be especially important for differentiating various positive emotions. You may have noted that among the six emotions studied by Ekman, only happiness was clearly positive. The prototypical happiness expression includes upturned lip corners and contraction of the orbicularis oculi muscles surrounding the eyes; it's referred to as a **Duchenne smile** in honor of Guillaume-Benjamin-Amand Duchenne, the French neurologist who described this expression in detail in the eighteenth century.

FIGURE 5.8. The prototypical pride expression includes a slightly raised head, expanded chest, arms akimbo, legs in a wide stance, and a small smile. From Tracy & Robins (2008b).

FIGURE 5.9. Prototypical expressions of amusement, affectionate love, and sexual attraction all include a smile, but are more easily distinguished from each other by head movements and/or posture.

Campos and colleagues wanted to determine whether people might display specific positive emotions through more distinct expressions. They asked undergraduates in the United States to tell personal stories of their experiences with several positive emotions— amusement, love, pride, contentment, awe, and others—and then to pose what that emotion would look like if they were to express it nonverbally to someone else.

Although many positive emotion poses did include a Duchenne smile, head and posture movements were more distinctive (see Figure 5.9). For example, in amusement poses the head was typically tilted back or to the side, or bobbled around as though the person were laughing. In love poses participants often hugged themselves, and in interest they tended to lean forward. In pride poses participants sat up straight, puffed out their chests, and lifted their heads. Other studies have found that people often turn their head away slightly while looking toward their interaction partner when feeling sexual attraction (e.g., Cordaro et al., 2018; Gonzaga et al., 2006).

What about negative emotions? Anger and sadness, in particular, may be detected relatively easily based on full-body postural cues (e.g., Dael et al., 2012; Martinez et al., 2016; Visch, Goudbeek, & Mortillaro, 2014). However, research has not clearly revealed distinct, reliable postures for specific negative emotions. In one study researchers asked trained actors to portray postures for the negative emotion states of hot anger/rage, panic fear, despair, cold anger/irritation, anxiety/worry, and depression, as well as the positive states of elated joy, amusement, pride, pleasure, relief, and interest. They coded 49 postural behaviors, and used a statistical technique called principal components analysis to identify sets of behaviors that tended to occur at the same time. They then used a technique called cluster analysis to identify clusters of individual postures, across actors and emotions, that included similar sets of behaviors from the previous analysis. (We know— this is a lot of complicated statistics; just focus on the gist of the study.) For hot anger, amusement, and pleasure, most actors' postures ended up in the same cluster, indicating a fairly consistent combination of postural elements for each emotion (Dael, Mortillaro, & Scherer, 2012). The other emotions were expressed in more diverse ways, however. This variability may not stop observers from recognizing the emotion being displayed. At least one study has found that spontaneous postural expressions of fear and anger were recognized at even higher rates than postures posed based on researchers' instructions (Abramson et al., 2017); however, this study had a very small number of participants (only 25) so more research is needed to support this claim.

Vocal Expression of Emotion

Try saying, "Are you sure?" with enthusiasm. Then say the same words sounding frightened, or amused, or sad. You can convey a good deal of emotion through your tone of voice. Casual experience suggests that we interpret tone of voice easily, even without words. While writing this paragraph, one of us (MNS) heard a burst of distinctive, high-pitched shrieking from a hallway near her office, made a silent bet about what was going on, and went to investigate. Sure enough, the hallway contained several colleagues clustered around a young, extremely cute puppy. But anecdotal evidence is not a good basis for scientific claims—people are too prone to confirming their own biases in observing the world, without even realizing it. How would researchers go about collecting hard evidence on the nonverbal vocal expression of emotion?

First, they would need to obtain a wide range of vocal expressions intended to communicate emotion states. In several studies, researchers have asked actors and/or research participants to produce **vocal bursts**—wordless vocalizations such as *ah* or *mmm* intended to express a particular emotion—and recorded these bursts to analyze and play to participants in future studies. Researcher Emiliana Simon-Thomas and colleagues (2009) used this approach to record one set of undergraduate students' vocalizations expressing 9 negative and 13 positive emotions. In a procedure similar to that used by Ekman to study recognition of facial expressions, these researchers then played the vocal bursts for a new set of participants and asked them to guess which emotion (or none of the above) from a list of terms was being expressed; positive and negative emotions were examined in different studies.

The vocal bursts expressing disgust, anger, sadness, and surprise were all recognized at high levels, with mean accuracy rates from 60% to 83%. For fear, 37% chose the correct label, on average, but 46% chose surprise, reflecting confusion between these two emotions that is often seen in facial expression research as well. For contempt, embarrassment, guilt, and shame, more people chose "none of the above" than the intended label. Amusement, interest, and relief were recognized at rates from 66 to 81%. Rates for enthusiasm (42%), pleasure (35%), awe (30%), and compassion (24%) vocal bursts were lower, but the intended label was still the most common choice. Not surprisingly, pleasure was most commonly chosen for the sexual desire vocal burst, with the intended label close behind. For love, gratitude, contentment, and pride, the option "none of the above" was chosen by at least as many people as the intended emotion label.

Although most research on expression has focused on the face, these and many other studies show that humans have several nonverbal channels for expressing their emotional and motivational states. As we have seen, a feeling that is easily recognized in the face may not be communicated as clearly through tone of voice or posture, and vice versa. Intense positive and negative emotion appears easier to decode from posture than from the face. Posture and head position may play particularly important roles in communicating positive emotions, but negative emotions are more clearly differentiated in the face. Feelings about events out there in the environment are identified more readily through vocal bursts and tone of voice, whereas feelings likely to be expressed in close relationships, such as love and gratitude, are more easily communicated through touch (Hertenstein et al., 2006). Each channel plays an important role in communicating our feelings, but we still have a lot to learn about which states are best expressed through each channel, and which states may not by expressed nonverbally at all.

Before we draw any conclusions, we must consider a lot more evidence. The claim at stake is that human nature includes some kind of template or code for facial and other nonverbal expressions of emotions—at least some emotions. Supporting this claim requires evidence that people around the world produce similar expressions in similar emotional states. Presumably they should also interpret an innate emotional expression in similar ways, regardless of whether the person displaying that expression is from the same culture or not. Researchers approaching the issue of nonverbal expression from both evolutionary and cultural perspectives have had plenty to say, and each offers strong evidence for their case. Let's take a look, and then return to the question about universality of emotional expressions.

EVOLUTIONARY PERSPECTIVES ON NONVERBAL EXPRESSION

Learning Objectives
- Summarize and evaluate the evidence regarding cross-cultural agreement on the meaning of Ekman's prototypical facial expressions of fear, anger, sadness, disgust, happiness, and surprise.
- Describe common inferences made about individuals displaying the prototypical pride posture, as observed in cross-cultural research.
- Define the term "meta-analysis," and explain the results of Laukka & Elfenbein's meta-analysis of vocal burst recognition.
- Differentiate possible meanings of universality in the context of nonverbal expressions, and analyze the evidence regarding universality in facial expressions of emotion.

There are good reasons to propose that at least some aspects of nonverbal expression are shaped by our evolutionary heritage. Although Charles Darwin ([1872] 1998) proposed that some aspects of expressions may reflect behavioral strategies for self-protection—for example, sticking out your tongue in a disgust expression serves to remove something offensive that you may have put into your mouth—the primary function of nonverbal expression is to communicate our inner states and intentions to others, and to "read" their own states and intentions. As we noted in Chapter 2, humans live in fairly large, complex, interdependent communities, working together to acquire food, protect against predators and other threats, and raise children. The ability to quickly, intuitively, and silently (in the case of facial and postural expression) communicate internal emotional and motivational states would have played an important role in coordinating activities and navigating this complex network of relationships (we'll discuss this in detail in Chapter 9). If the earliest modern humans already had an innate set of expressions for such states, perhaps inherited in part from even older primate ancestors, these expression templates would have been carried throughout human populations as they grew and spread throughout the world.

The inherent sociality of emotional expression also creates interesting complexities for research methods. We must distinguish between the *production* of nonverbal expressions and the ways in which other people *interpret* these expressions, and recognize that these are distinct psychological processes. We must also distinguish between *deliberately posed* expressions and *spontaneous* responses to emotional situations. Demonstrating similarity across cultural contexts and people of different backgrounds in one kind of expression does not necessarily demonstrate universality in the other. For example, one review of studies on emotional expressions found that blind and sighted individuals showed very similar spontaneous expressions in response to emotion stimuli, but quite different intentional poses of emotion states (Valente, Theurel, & Gentaz, 2018). Also, people can exert control over their expressions for social purposes, concealing some emotions and faking others. These are important processes in their own right and must be considered in interpreting any research on expression. Even acknowledging these complications, research on cross-cultural similarities and differences in nonverbal expressions of emotions and other motivational states has come a long way.

Cross-Cultural Studies of Facial Expression

After his initial studies, Ekman continued to focus on gathering evidence for cross-cultural agreement on the emotional meaning of his six prototype expressions. With the help of colleagues around the world he gathered data from participants in more than a dozen countries, including Estonia, Germany, Greece, Hong Kong, Italy, Japan, Scotland, Sumatra, and Turkey, as well as the United States. The basic test differed slightly from the method he had used in New Guinea. Participants would see a photographed expression similar to the ones in Figure 5.3, and then decide which emotion was displayed: anger, disgust, fear, happiness, sadness, surprise, or neutral (Ekman & Friesen, 1984). For participants speaking a language other than English, the researchers had the six emotion words translated by fluent speakers of that language.

Figure 5.10 shows the results, averaged across many studies and almost 2,000 people (Russell, 1994). The light-gray bar represents the percentage of times, on average, that non-Western observers chose the expected emotion word for the facial expression of an

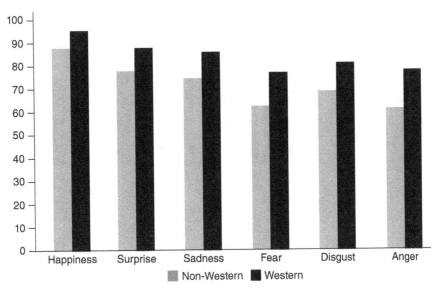

FIGURE 5.10. Mean accuracies for pairing the expressions in Figure 5.3 with their emotion labels. Adapted from data in Russell (1994).

emotion. The black bar represents the corresponding statistic for Western participants. Random guessing would produce 1 of 6 or about 17% correct for each emotion, and clearly results were better than that. Although the photographs were of people of European ancestry, people from other countries and cultural contexts identified most of the expressions correctly. These findings strongly suggest that most people throughout the world give similar interpretations to certain facial expressions of emotion.

What about expressions beyond the "Ekman 6" (sounds like a gang of bank robbers, doesn't it)? Daniel Cordaro and colleagues (2019) used a technique similar to Ekman's original methods, asking participants in Germany, Poland, China, South Korea, Japan, India, Pakistan, Turkey, and the United States to identify the one of four photographed expressions that best matched situations relevant to 18 different emotional and motivational states. Figure 5.11 shows the results across cultures. With the exception of sympathy and interest, participants selected the intended expression for every situation at above-chance levels in every country for each emotion; averaging across the whole sample, recognition rates often exceeded 70%.

These studies suggest at least the potential for high recognition of facial expressions across cultures. Does this mean that people from every culture share the same mental template for such expressions, allowing them to decide whether a given expression that they observe matches that template? One study investigated this in a clever way. Rachael Jack and colleagues (2012) used computer software to generate video expressions for all possible combinations of FACS action units. They then asked 15 participants from European countries and 15 participants from East Asian countries—all of whom had recently arrived in the country where the study was conducted—to decide whether each expression reflected fear, anger, sadness, disgust, surprise, happiness, or none of these. Data analyses used a version of correlation to see which FACS action units predicted assigning

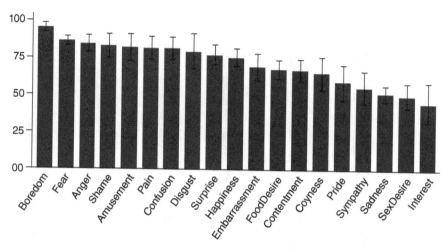

FIGURE 5.11. Mean accuracies for choosing the predicted expressions as the best fit for situations eliciting 18 different emotional and motivational states. Participants had four photos to choose from, so chance would be 25%. From Cordaro et al. (2019).

a given emotion for each participant, allowing them to see whether each participant's pattern of ratings indicated a prototype set of action units leading them to infer each emotion. Although the European participants seemed to have similar prototypes for most emotions, this was not the case for the Asian participants; with the exception of happiness, clear, shared prototypes of each emotion could not be identified for the latter group. This study is small, so evidence from more cultural groups and larger numbers of people is needed for a compelling case, but these findings do question the notion of a universal mental template for facial expressions of these six emotions.

Cross-Cultural Studies of Postural and Vocal Expressions

As noted earlier, the importance of posture is especially well established for the expression of one emotion: pride. In one impressive study, Jessica Tracy and David Matsumoto (2008) recorded the reactions of Olympic and Paralympic judo contestants from around the world after either winning or losing a match. (Fun fact: in addition to being a prominent emotion researcher, Matsumoto has had another life as an Olympic-level judo coach. Impressive, right?). Coding the athletes' postures revealed that regardless of culture, gender, or sightedness (some athletes were blind), Olympians who had just won a match were more likely to lift their heads, expand their arms and chest, and make fists with their hands than those who lost. Interestingly, there was more cultural variability in the extent to which the athletes displayed shame postures, lowering their heads and hunching after losing; at least among sighted athletes, displays were less common among athletes from highly individualistic cultures.

Beyond documenting common features of the pride or victory display, Tracy and colleagues have gathered evidence that this posture is recognized as a sign of dominance and high social status across cultures as well. In one study it was recognized as an expression of pride by 74% of people in the United States, 80% of people in Italy, and 57% of people in a rural tribe in West Africa, regardless of the ethnicity of the poser (Tracy & Robins, 2008b). In later research, Tracy and colleagues (2013) found not only that Fijians also easily recognized the pride display at high rates, but also that like North Americans, Fijians implicitly assumed that a person displaying pride likely has high social status (although interestingly, in explicit measures participants from both cultural groups rated a person showing simple Duchenne smile as having even higher status than the person displaying pride). Unfortunately, no other postural expression of emotion has received nearly the level of attention as the pride display, so more research is needed to see whether other meanings of posture may be universally recognized as well.

What about nonverbal vocal expressions? In the study described earlier, both the people who produced the vocal bursts and the participants decoding them were from the United States. Would these same sounds be recognized by people in other parts of the world? Disa Sauter and colleagues (2010) began to address this problem by obtaining vocal bursts for several emotional and motivational states from people in two cultures: English speakers in London and people from small, isolated settlements in Namibia who had little or no exposure to Western voices. Then, with new sets of participants, the researchers described situations thought to elicit those emotional/motivational states and played two vocal bursts, asking which was more likely (see Figure 5.12). This approach was similar to the methods used by Ekman with villagers in New Guinea. Vocal bursts produced by both English and Namibian posers were rated by participants in both cultures to determine whether there was a systematic in-group advantage.

FIGURE 5.12. A Namibian participant in Sauter and colleagues' (Sauter, Eisner, Ekman, & Scott, 2010) study, listening to two vocal bursts and then choosing the one that best fits an emotional situation.

English participants easily interpreted the bursts produced by English vocalizers, achieving almost perfect scores for each of nine states: fear, anger, disgust, sadness, surprise, achievement, amusement, pleasure, and relief. Namibian participants interpreting bursts by Namibian vocalizers did somewhat worse (probably because this kind of task was so unfamiliar), but still well above chance for all states except relief. Participants from both cultures showed a modest in-group advantage, choosing the intended vocal burst for each situation at lower rates when the vocalizer and participant were from different cultures than when they were from the same culture. Nonetheless, English participants still scored above chance in selecting Namibian vocal bursts for all states. Namibian participants scored above chance for all negative emotions and surprise, but only for amusement among the positive emotions.

In another study, Daniel Cordaro and colleagues (Cordaro et al., 2016) recorded prototype vocal bursts for 16 different states, produced by six individuals in the United States (see Table 5.1). College student participants from 10 different countries representing East Asia, South Asia, and the Middle East as well as Western nations then attempted to identify which of three vocal bursts (all of the same valence) or "none of the above" best matched the situation.

With the exceptions of desire for food and sympathy in South Korea, and surprise in India, every vocal burst was recognized at above-chance (25%) levels in every country, with overall mean accuracy around 80%. There was a main effect of country, with participants in South Korea generally doing worse than those in other countries, but on the whole recognition rates were very high. Cordaro and colleagues (2016) repeated the task with participants in a small, isolated village in Bhutan with no electricity and thus no access to Western media. Although the proportion of participants choosing the intended vocal burst for each emotion story was considerably lower than that among college

TABLE 5.1   Sounds included in vocal bursts for several emotions

Descriptions of sounds in highly recognized vocal bursts for several emotions studied by Cordaro and colleagues (Cordaro et al., 2016).

EMOTION	VOCAL BURST
Amusement	Laughter
Anger	Growl
Awe	"Wow"
Contempt	"Thuh," spit sound
Contentment	"Ahhh," long sigh
Desire	"Mmm," savoring sound
Disgust	"Ughh," retching
Embarrassment	Self-conscious laughter, groan
Fear	Scream
Interest	"Mmhmm"
Pain	"Ouch"
Relief	"Whew," short sigh
Sadness	Crying
Surprise	Gasp
Sympathy	"Aww"
Triumph	"Woo-hoo"

students in developed countries, it was significantly above chance for all emotions except contempt and relief. In one recent paper, researchers conducted a **meta-analysis** of 37 studies, with vocalizers from 26 different cultural groups and participants from 44 groups. This statistical technique combines the results of many different studies as if they were a single, very large study. All of the 12 positive and negative emotion states included in the meta-analysis were recognized at rates significantly higher than chance (Laukka & Elfenbein, 2021).

How Strong Is the Evidence For Universality?

As Darwin's original study did, the research summarized above has important limitations. One is that in most studies, the photographs of facial and postural expressions were carefully posed to be very strong examples of the intended expressions. With such photos, recognition rates tend to be high (Tracy & Robins, 2008a). However, in everyday life we seldom encounter such perfect, intense prototypes. One of us (MNS) frequently videotapes participants while they watch emotional film clips, and as a general rule, strong expressions are rare; subtle ones are more common. With everyday expressions, our accuracy of identifying emotions is considerably less impressive (Kayval & Russell, 2013; Naab & Russell, 2007).

Another problem is that the multiple-choice matching procedure likely overestimates people's accuracy (Russell, 1994). When you look at Figure 5.3, presumably you identify face (g) as happy. Almost everyone does. Now you are left with five faces to pair with five labels. Suppose you are unsure whether face (d) represents surprise or fear. If you decide that face (e) is a better expression of fear, you choose (d) for surprise. Suppose you have no idea what to call face (c). If you identify (a) as anger and (b) as sadness, you label (c) as disgust just by process of elimination. If this is how participants typically approach the task, the recognition rates in these kinds of studies may be inflated by skillful test-taking techniques.

One way to get around this limitation is to present photos one at a time and ask what emotion (if any) each face expresses, allowing participants to use their own words—this is referred to as **free labeling**. The difficulty of this method is that people sometimes give answers that are not what the researchers expect (Ekman, 1994a). For face (e), the intended answer is "fear." Various people call this expression terror, horror, panic, or "she looks like she just saw a ghost." Presumably we would count all those answers as correct, as near-synonyms for fear. But what if someone called the expression worry? Is worry close enough to fear that we should consider it correct? Also, some people have more elaborate, nuanced emotion vocabularies than others (Smidt & Suvak, 2015). Someone who sees a disgust expression and labels it "upset" may still recognize it as the expression you'd probably show if you found a bunch of rotting food in the refrigerator, without the word "disgust" coming readily to mind. Despite these difficulties, researchers find that people are reasonably accurate at freely labeling facial expressions, even in faces from other cultures, but to a lesser extent than seen with multiple-choice measures (Frank & Stennett, 2001). Figure 5.13 shows the accuracy of one group of college students in free labeling the emotions portrayed by six faces (Ekman, 1994b).

Overall, how strong is the evidence for the "universality" of facial, postural, and nonverbal vocal expressions of emotion? The answer to this question depends on the exact claim one is trying to make. Even considering their many limitations, it is hard to explain

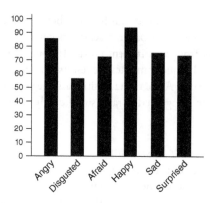

FIGURE 5.13. Accuracy of one group of college students in free labeling six emotional expressions. The students were not given labels to choose from, or any other suggestions about their answers. From data in Ekman (1994a).

results from the recognition studies above without acknowledging that *some* aspect of our emotional expression is innate. If emotional expressions were completely culturally learned, trying to read the expression of someone in a very different culture would be like dropping into another country with no knowledge of the language beyond what you've heard on TV, and trying to understand what everyone is saying. People identify many expressions far better than that. A meta-analysis of cross-cultural facial expression studies revealed an average recognition rate of 58% - far higher than plausible by chance (Elfenbein & Ambady, 2002). This suggests that humans do have some kind of universal decoder ring they use in interpreting other people's facial expressions, and it's hard to see how this could be if the expressions themselves were not influenced in some way by evolution. A similar body of evidence is now emerging for tone of voice.

Having said that, we do not yet have anything close to compelling evidence as to what exactly the universal code is—what the decoder ring actually says. We can't assume it contains full-blown templates for fear, anger, and so forth just because those were the states examined in Ekman's and Izard's studies, and the study discussed above by Rachael Jack and colleagues (2012) was unable to find templates shared by European and East Asian participants. It's possible that a process aligned with Scherer's component process model, with the decoder ring mapping specific facial muscle movements to individual appraisal dimensions such as novelty, pleasantness, and coping potential, would account for the observed expressions and recognition rates. However, studies aimed at document-ing these associations have not yet produced a simple, convincing map. The most rigorous studies so far have identified several action units linked in similar ways with inferences of novelty, pleasantness, and goal conduciveness appraisals, but these are nonspecific, complex, many-to-many associations (Scherer et al., 2018).

It's possible that the decoder ring can only distinguish between pleasant and unpleas-ant emotions, but then why is agreement so high across cultures on expressions associated with fear, anger, sadness, and disgust? And these complexities are just about recognition. We can't assume that everyone feeling Ekman's six emotions *shows* the same, intense expressions used in his studies—they clearly don't (and he never expected that they would; Ekman, 1972). Real-life expressions are more subtle, murkier, and difficult to interpret. Presumably the variability in people's actual expressions is caused by a combination of cultural learning and individual differences in expressivity. Let's turn to some of those factors now.

CULTURE, GENDER, AND NONVERBAL EXPRESSION

Learning Objectives

- Define "display rule" in the context of emotional expression, and identify and describe example display rules.
- Summarize the methods, results, and theoretical implications of Elfenbein and colleagues' (2007) study of facial expression "dialects."
- Describe gender differences in emotional expression, as documented by research, and analyze in relation to typical gender roles.

Although the research suggests that some facial expressions of emotion are interpreted in similar ways across cultures, other expressions are clearly culture-specific. For example, the prototypical expression of *lajya*, an Orissa Hindu emotion combining aspects of embarrassment and shame, includes biting one's tongue—a display not commonly observed in the United States (Menon & Shweder, 1994). In many cultures people indicate *no* by shaking their heads back and forth, and *yes* by nodding it up and down. In Greece and Turkey, however, people typically indicate *yes* by tilting their heads back, and in Sri Lanka they express *I understand* by shaking their heads back and forth. In the United States, people often give a gesture of joining the tip of the thumb with the tip of the index finger to make a circle to indicate *we're in agreement*, or *OK*. In many other cultures, that gesture is meaningless; and in some it is considered an invitation to have sex.

Some researchers distinguish **gestures** such as these—head and hand movements that convey verbal meaning—from emotional expressions. As with the vocabulary of spoken language, gestures are expected to vary widely from culture to culture. Yet even for Ekman's original six emotions, expressions vary across individuals and cultures as well. In this section we will consider two processes that contribute to this variability: cultural display rules for when expressions off certain emotional states are and are not appropriate; and dialects with which people in different cultures may accent their nonverbal expressions. We will also consider ways in which people's nonverbal expression of emotion is modulated by gender.

Cultural Display Rules

People learn from their culture when it is appropriate to amplify or conceal certain emotional expressions. Just as you do not always say in words everything that you are thinking, you sometimes feel emotions without wanting to show them. Cultures differ somewhat in their rules for which emotions should be shown and which hidden, and in what circumstances. These cultural **display rules** are an important tool in any society. In a job interview, you try not to act nervous. If a guest spills something on your carpet, you try not to show anger. If a friend says something stupid, you try not to laugh. Other display rules require us to express emotions even if we do not feel them. Have you ever laughed politely at a joke that wasn't especially funny, or displayed more sorrow than you really felt over someone else's loss?

We learn these rules from the people around us, and cultures vary in their expectations. Some display rules are fairly specific. For example, European and North American adults, especially men, are discouraged from crying in public, but this prohibition is even stronger in other cultures, such as China. Some cultures discourage emotional expression in general. One study of Hmong immigrants to the United States found that the immigrants who were more assimilated into US culture expressed a number of emotions more visibly than did those who were more traditional (Tsai et al., 2002). However, some of the most interesting demonstrations of display rules come from studies linking cultural differences in emotional expression to particular aspects of culture, and/or expectations for relationships within different cultures.

Wallace Friesen (1972) conducted a classic study of this kind, comparing the behavior of Japanese and American undergraduate participants while they watched disgusting videos of surgical procedures. Participants first watched the videos alone, and then watched them again in the presence of an experimenter, introduced as a graduate student and wearing a lab coat. Although participants from both countries showed considerable disgust when they watched the video alone, Japanese participants masked this disgust with a polite smile when the experimenter was in the room (Friesen, 1972). Japan emphasizes the social hierarchy much more than the United States, and the Japanese consider it inappropriate to show negative emotion to a high-status person. American participants were evidently less intimidated by the experimenter and saw no reason to hide their feelings. Similarly, another study found that when displaying fear, anger, or sadness, Japanese and Russian participants often added a slight smile to soften the expression, as if saying "although I am distressed, it isn't really that bad" (Matsumoto et al., 2005). In the United States, moderate displays of anger are common. In Japan, a high-status person can display anger toward subordinates, but almost any other display of anger is considered shockingly inappropriate (Matsumoto, 1996).

Why are people in some cultures more expressive than those in others, especially in terms of negative emotion? David Matsumoto and his colleagues (Matsumoto et al., 1998) analyzed data from a large, international study of emotions and attitudes to find out. Their analyses showed that both at the individual and at the cultural level, higher collectivism was linked to stronger display rules for controlling the expression of negative emotions. This finding was later replicated in a study with new data from 32 countries (Matsumoto, Yoo, & Fontaine, 2008). However, display rules depend to some extent on the person with whom someone is interacting. In Japan, it is more appropriate to show negative emotions to acquaintances than to close friends and family, whereas the reverse is true for people in the United States (Matsumoto, 1990; Matsumoto et al., 2008). In each country this makes sense in terms of cultural values around emotions and their role in relationships. In East Asia, people emphasize preserving harmony in close relationships (Kwan, Bond, & Singelis, 1997), so it is safer to express negative emotions elsewhere, toward people who are less important to you. In the United States, people expect emotional authenticity in their close relationships (Kim & Sherman, 2007), so it is considered appropriate to express negative emotions honestly to loved ones, but less appropriate toward acquaintances.

Display rules are not limited to negative emotions. Although the postural expression of pride or dominance shares common elements around the world, as we saw earlier, this expression is modulated in some cultures and some contexts. Consider the study discussed earlier of expressions by Olympians after judo matches. While winners across cultures all tended to show a strong smile at first, participants from certain cultures—mostly Asian—restrained their expressions a moment or two later (Matsumoto & Willingham, 2009; Matsumoto, Willingham, & Olide, 2009). Another study asked whether different postural expressions of pride are considered equally appropriate in North America and Japan. Participants in this study were asked to take one of four seated poses: sitting upright with chest expanded; sitting upright with their hands spread wide apart on the desk in front of them; leaning back in the chair with their feet up on the desk; or sitting in a somewhat slumped position (see Figure 5.14). The first three postures are all physically expansive, suggesting dominance or pride, and US participants associated a sense of power with all of them. The two postures on the left led to associations with power among Japanese participants as well. The feet-on-desk pose was rated as inconsistent with Japanese expectations for self-discipline, however, and was not associated with power in the same way as the other expansive postures (Park et al., 2013). These studies suggest that unbridled expressions of pride are acceptable in the United States, but that Japanese culture encourages balancing pride with politeness and humility.

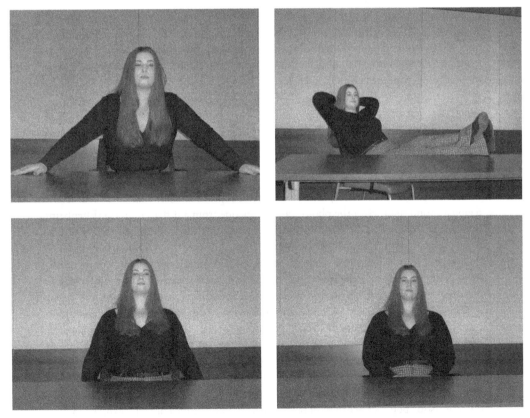

FIGURE 5.14. Although postural expansion generally communicates power across cultures, certain forms may be perceived as culturally inappropriate. The feet-on-desk pose shown here appears undisciplined in Japan, and is not associated with power.

You might get the impression from these examples that other cultures have display rules, but not people in North America. However, those in North American cultural contexts have display rules as well. Unless you think it's totally appropriate to burst out laughing while looking at a horrible car accident, you are aware of display rules. People in the United States typically think they are supposed to show their feelings honestly—a display rule of its own—and emotional authenticity is valued as a desirable trait (Kim & Sherman, 2007). In many countries, people consider the strong facial expressions displayed by Americans to be inauthentic and rather silly. One fascinating study suggests, however, that historical factors may have promoted this intensity of expression. Researchers in this study examined **historical heterogeneity**—defined as the estimated number of source countries from which immigrants to a modern country had come over the past 500 years, based on genetic data—as a predictor of facial expressions of emotion. For example, an isolated indigenous cultural group would score only 1 on historical heterogeneity, because the entire modern population had ancestors from the same place. In contrast, the score for the United States is 83, because the ancestors of the current population moved to the United States from many countries around the world. The analyses showed that facial expressions of emotion posed by people in countries with high historical heterogeneity were recognized more easily by people in *other* cultures than was the case for expressions by people in low-historical-heterogeneity countries (Wood, Rychlowska, & Niedenthal, 2016). In other words, countries with historically high immigration rates tend to encourage more intense and/or prototypical facial expressions of emotion, presumably so that people from different cultures and languages can communicate through one available channel clearly.

Expression Dialects

So far we have emphasized cultural differences in the *intensity* of emotional expressions, but the *content* of expressions also varies from culture to culture. This appears to be true even of the emotions studied by Ekman, Izard, and colleagues. In the meta-analysis of facial expression recognition studies discussed earlier, researchers found that accuracy was consistently higher when participants rated people of the same national, ethnic, or regional group than when the photo was of someone from a different group (Elfenbein & Ambady, 2002). This difference was especially notable when the photograph was of a freely posed emotion ("now show me an expression of disgust") or a spontaneous expression, rather than an expression based on instructed muscle movements. This result strongly suggests that people from different cultures show somewhat different facial expressions, even of possible basic emotions such as anger, fear, sadness, and disgust.

Based on these results, the researchers proposed that people living in different cultures have different **dialects** for facial expressions, while still having some elements of expressions in common. Taking an analogy from language, people in different regions of a country pronounce the same words somewhat differently, and even use some different words. For example, people in some parts of the United States refer to carbonated soft drinks as pop, whereas people in other regions call it soda. Both are correct, and in fact, the term "soda pop" is the origin of both terms. To test the idea of facial expression dialects, Hilary Elfenbein and colleagues asked participants from two French-speaking regions—Quebec in Canada and Gabon in sub-Saharan Africa—to pose expressions of anger, fear, sadness, disgust, happiness, surprise, contempt, shame, embarrassment, and serenity (Elfenbein et al., 2007). Rather than asking the posers to move specific facial muscles, the researchers gave the posers each emotion word and asked them to pose an expression their friends could easily understand. All of the emotion words were in French to avoid translation problems.

As expected, expressions posed by people from the two cultures had subtle but consistent differences. For example, displays of happiness by the Quebecois were more likely to include contraction of the orbicularis oculi muscles surrounding the eyes (try this in front of a mirror—if "crow's feet" wrinkles appear, then you're doing it right), whereas displays of happiness by the Gabonese were more likely to involve an open mouth. In expressing anger, the Quebecois were more likely to tighten their lips and squint, whereas the Gabonese were somewhat more likely to widen their eyes. The elements of each posed expression across the two cultures were characteristic of the prototypical expressions used in Ekman's research; it's just that some muscle movements were more pronounced in one culture than in the other. In a follow-up study, the researchers showed these posed expressions to new participants in each culture, along with expressions that were matched to be morphologically identical. They found an in-group bias in recognizing the free poses of the expressions, but not the matched poses. Both findings are consistent with the notion of dialects in facial expressions of emotion.

Recently, another meta-analysis indicated that nonverbal vocal expressions of emotion may have a combination of universal elements and cultural accents as well. Petri Laukka and Hilary Elfenbein (2021) found that just as with facial expressions, vocal expressions were consistently recognized at higher rates by people from the same cultural group than by people from other cultures. This cannot be explained in terms of language differences, because the stimuli did not include emotion words; they were either vocal bursts with no words at all, or words with no overt emotional content. This study also revealed another interesting pattern. The researchers used a database of ratings for individualism, power distance, preference for masculinity, and another cultural dimension called uncertainty avoidance of different countries around the world, and calculated an overall cultural distance for each pair of cultures in their meta-analysis. The greater this distance, the more the in-group advantage each culture had in terms of recognizing expressions, and the greater the accuracy penalty across cultures. This finding suggests not only that cultures have different accents in vocal expressions of emotion, but that the accents themselves may be linked to aspects of culture in meaningful ways.

Gender and Emotional Expression

Much research suggests that even within the same cultural context, men and women express emotions in somewhat different ways. Often these differences can be linked to power. Agneta Fischer and colleagues (2004) compared how often women and men around the world reported expressing open antagonism or anger, and crying in emotional situations. As you might expect, men reported more openly angry behavior than women did, and women reported crying more often. These effects could not be explained in terms of gender differences in subjective experience; men and women reported feeling sad and angry with similar frequency. Moreover, the effect of gender on anger expression was moderated by the country's level of gender equality; women in more egalitarian countries reported expressing anger more often. In another study, participants were covertly posed in either an upright or slumped position, then told they had performed particularly well on a previous task. Men rated their own performance as higher when in the upright rather than slumped position, but adopting the more expansive, dominant one did not have this effect for women (Roberts & Arefi-Afshar, 2007).

Despite a widespread finding that men experience positive emotion more often than women, studies consistently show that women smile more often than men (Brody & Hall, 2008). Like the expression of anger, this gender difference has been linked in part to status and power. In one study by Marvin Hecht and Marianne LaFrance (1998), same-sex pairs of participants engaged in a conversation in the lab and their smiling behavior was measured. Some pairs conducted a mock job interview, in which one partner asked the other questions about their qualifications and work experience, and subsequently rated the applicant for the position; other pairs engaged in a more egalitarian conversation about each person's work experience and career goals. Women tended to smile more than men in all conditions; in fact, this sex difference was greatest when the two partners were of equal power. However, smiling behavior and self-reported positive affect were strongly correlated for study participants in high-power roles (i.e., the interviewer, $r = .55$), moderately correlated for people in egalitarian roles (just getting to know each other, $r = .38$), and unrelated among people in low-power roles (the job applicant, $r = -.16$). This result suggests that women may smile more than men for a variety of reasons, but that smiling may become detached from feelings when people are in low-power positions.

The compiled evidence indicates that there are real differences in men's and women's expressions of emotion, but that these are complex and influenced by power dynamics in society rather than a reflection of innate sex differences. Because they tend to have somewhat lower status in society, women may feel pressured to show less anger than they feel, and to smile when they do not feel happy. (A side note to the guys: if you are ever tempted to call out, "Hey beautiful, why don't you smile?" to a strange woman, please don't. You may intend it as a friendly comment, but to the woman it communicates that you expect her to display an emotion she doesn't feel for your benefit.) These status dynamics do not affect women alone. As we noted earlier, men in most cultures report crying less often than women, and this likely reflects gender differences in the acceptability of showing weakness and vulnerability. Just as with different cultures, each gender role is associated with rules about what expressions are appropriate, and these rules do not always reflect the patterns for underlying feelings.

HOW DO WE DECODE NONVERBAL EXPRESSIONS?

Learning Objectives

- Compare and contrast narrowing down the options, identifying appraisal profiles, attending to context, and combining across expressive modalities as possible processes by which people decode nonverbal expressions of emotion.

Most of the studies discussed so far have examined either the typical nonverbal expression of some emotional or motivational state, as displayed by participants in various cultures, or the rates at which such expressions are recognized within and across cultural groups. Studies such as these have had tremendous impact, strongly suggesting that *something* about the way we produce and interpret nonverbal expressions is part of our inherited human nature. However, they do not address *how* we decide which emotion another person is feeling, in the absence of words. Increasingly, researchers are beginning to investigate these processes.

Narrowing Down the Options

Imagine that you are a participant in this study (Jack, Garrod, & Schyns, 2014). On each trial, the computer shows you a short video of a facial expression based on a random selection of action units, each emerging over one of six time windows (e.g., peaking 300 milliseconds into the video versus 650 milliseconds in). For example, Figure 5.15 shows a computer-generated model of an expression combining action units 4 (the eyebrows pull down and together in a frown), 5 (eyelids raise to open the eyes more widely), and 20 (the muscles on the sides of the chin contract, stretching the lower lip down and to each side) that plays out over 1.25 seconds (these same stimuli were used in a study discussed earlier). Your job is to decide which of six emotions—happiness, fear, anger, sadness, disgust, or surprise—best fits the expression.

In addition to asking which action units were associated with each emotion in general, the researchers asked when each action unit appeared most important—whether it had the greatest impact on people's ratings early in the expression versus relatively late. They found that four action units were most important early on: action units 5 (upper eyelid raiser), 9 (nose wrinkler), 22 (lip funneler), and 27 (mouth stretch). These action units combined allowed participants to distinguish among four categories: happiness, sadness, fear/surprise, and anger/disgust. Action units that helped people make

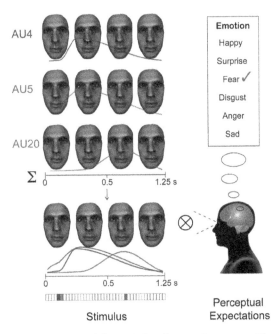

FIGURE 5.15. Computer-generated dynamic facial expressions, created by combining the effects of three randomly selected Facial Action Coding System units over the course of 1.25 seconds. From Jack, Garrod, & Schyns (2014).

finer-grained distinctions were more important later in the expression. This suggests that people might initially narrow down the possible meanings of an expression based on a few, easy-to-see elements, and then use other action units to decide among the remaining options.

Identifying Appraisal Profiles

As we have seen, most of the work on nonverbal expression has adopted a basic or discrete emotion perspective, asking whether people agree on specific emotion labels for various expressions. The component process model suggests that people might arrive at these labels by associating nonverbal expressions first with appraisals such as novelty/unexpectedness, pleasantness, controllability, and so forth, and then converting the appraisal profiles into emotion categories. Petri Laukka and Hillary Elfenbein (2012) asked whether interpretations of emotional tones of voice could be explained in this way. The researchers used a database of recordings by actors in the United States, who had been asked to express 15 emotions while describing a personal experience with a relevant situation. To retain tone of voice without giving the situation away to participants, the researchers only used short clips of these tales with neutral verbal content, such as "That's the way it happened."

The vocal clips were then played for participants in a new study. Instead of deciding which emotion was expressed, participants were asked to rate each burst in terms of the likely novelty, pleasantness, goal conduciveness, urgency, power, and norm compatibility of the situation eliciting that tone of voice. Reliability among participants was high (greater than .80) for each dimension, indicating that participants agreed in their ratings. In general, the appraisal profiles for the vocal clips were consistent with appraisal profiles for each of the emotions being expressed, as identified in earlier research. Similar research has found that participants agree on the appraisal-related meaning of facial expressions of emotion as well, in ways that correspond to inferences about specific emotions (Scherer et al., 2018). Actually mapping individual action units to individual appraisal dimensions has remained elusive, however. It's clear that people can infer appraisals from others' expressions, but it's not so clear what code they're using to do so. Documenting the details of that code would strengthen the support for this theoretical proposal.

Effects of Context

In a typical study of facial expression recognition, participants are asked to match an expression to a label for an emotional/motivational state, with no information about the situation in which that expression was displayed. Of course, this is not what happens in real life; when we encounter a noteworthy facial expression we nearly always have *some* information about the context, if not all the details. Researchers have made this point for decades, and conducted small studies finding that participants rely primarily on the eliciting situation to guess how a person is feeling, even if the facial expression and situational context suggest quite different emotions (e.g., Aviezer et al., 2008; Carroll & Russell, 1996).

For example, in one study participants examined photographs of Olympians who had either won or lost an important match, and rated each target's experience of several emotions. These ratings were aggregated into an overall positive-negative valence ratio. When participants were told the truth about which Olympian had won or lost, or were

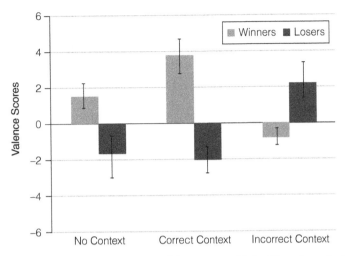

FIGURE 5.16. Ratings of inferred valence of the emotions felt by Olympians who had won or lost a match, depending on whether participants were told true, false, or no information about the match outcome. Results show that contextual information can override inferences based on facial expressions alone. From Kayyal, Widen, & Russell (2015).

told nothing at all, their ratings accurately tracked the match outcomes: winners were rated as feeling more positive than losers. This effect was reversed, however, when participants were misled about the match outcomes, told that the actual winners had lost and vice versa (Kayyal, Widen, & Russell, 2015; see Figure 5.16). In other words, the contextual information dominated participants' judgments, overriding information from the face itself.

Another study suggests people might be biased toward inferring negative-valence emotion when *any* strong expression is present (other than a big smile, which is easily recognized as positive). In this study, participants watched videos of people responding to real-life positive situations. Some participants saw videos edited to show only the person displaying the emotion, with the situation edited out; others saw the original videos showing the situation as well. In reality, all of the videos showed an unexpected reunion of the target individual with a beloved soldier who had been away for a long time, so the expressions were pretty intense. Participants seeing the original videos naturally rated the target's feelings as very positive. When participants could only see the face, however, they tended to rate the person's emotions as *negative* rather than positive (Israelashvili, Hassin, & Aviezer, 2019). Of course, this is a complex situation, and the people in the videos may have been experiencing more mixed emotions than pure, grinning happiness at the time. However, this adds to a substantial and growing body of evidence that real-life expressions may be harder to read than those commonly used in research, and that we rely a great deal on context to interpret what expressions mean.

Combining Across Expressive Modalities

In everyday life we rarely try to read someone's emotion based solely on a static facial expression. We note facial movement as well as posture, eye blinks, trembling, shoulder shrugging, head turns, speed of walking, hand gestures, and direction of gaze (Ambadar,

Schooler, & Cohn, 2005; Bould, Morris, & Wink, 2008; Edwards, 1998; Van den Stock, Righart, & de Gelder, 2007). Some people are able to detect fear from another person's smell (de Groot, Semin, & Smeets, 2014; Leppänen & Hietanen, 2003; Zhou & Chen, 2009). Combining information across these sensory modalities increases the chance that we will accurate infer someone's emotional state.

One study demonstrating this effect used stimuli posed by six actors, who were filmed expressing naturalistic full-body responses to hypothetical situations eliciting fear, anger, sadness, disgust, happiness, and surprise (Martinez et al., 2016). These films were edited to show either the face alone, the body alone, or both face and body; participants were randomly assigned one type to film, and asked to identify the emotion for each pose. Regardless of modality, participants were very good at this; recognition rates were significantly greater than chance even when participants saw videos that were only 250 milliseconds long. However, recognition rates were consistently higher when participants could see both the face and the body than when seeing either on its own.

What does this all mean? On one hand, the early studies used methods that may have inflated participants' ability to decode specific emotions based on static facial expressions alone. On the other hand, we hardly ever try to do that in real life. For a variety of reasons, figuring out what another person is feeling based on their nonverbal expression may be either easier or harder than in many studies. At this point, the question of *how* people make these judgments—the processes they use to infer others' emotions—is arguably more intriguing the yes-or-no question of cross-cultural universality.

CAN NONVERBAL EXPRESSIONS INFLUENCE FEELINGS?

Learning Objectives

- Summarize and evaluate the evidence that information from the body (awareness of emotional expression and behavior; sensing visceral changes) is necessary for people to experience emotional feelings, as William James proposed.
- State the facial feedback hypothesis, and analyze the current evidence regarding this hypothesis.
- Differentiate direct and conceptual replication, and identify examples of each.

One important topic remains in our discussion of the nonverbal expression of emotional and motivational states, and it goes back to one of the earliest theories of emotion. As you may recall from Chapter 1, William James proposed that our emotional feelings are caused by instinctive behavioral and physiological responses to emotional situations; his classic example was that of running away from a bear and therefore feeling fear. Are emotional behaviors, such as nonverbal expressions of emotion, necessary for emotional feeling? If not, can these behaviors at least intensify emotional feelings?

An extreme hypothesis based on James's theory is that if you were unable to make facial expressions, you would no longer be able to experience emotional feelings. This hypothesis is not supported by the available data. People with permanent paralysis of the facial muscles adjust to their condition over time and report feeling normal emotions (Keillor et al., 2002). People with **Möbius syndrome** (a rare congenital condition) are unable to smile. They nevertheless report feeling happy and amused in the expected situations. The condition does have serious consequences, but these are mediated by social

FIGURE 5.17. This girl with Möbius syndrome could not smile before a surgical procedure created an artificial expression. She could feel happiness, however, and had a sense of humor.

factors rather than being a direct effect of the condition on emotional experience; inability to smile can make relationships with people awkward. The girl in Figure 5.17 underwent surgery to give her an artificial smile (Miller, 2007). However, the evidence suggests that facial expressions are not necessary for emotional feelings.

A more moderate hypothesis might be that people who cannot make facial expressions still feel emotions, just less intensely. In one study, researchers temporarily paralyzed participants' frown muscles with botulinum toxin (Botox). Until the toxin wore off, people had weaker than normal brain responses to the sight of other people's angry expressions, apparently because they could not frown back at people frowning at them (Hennenlotter et al., 2009). However, the brain responses did not necessarily reflect feelings of anger.

Facial expressions and other nonverbal behaviors may not be necessary for feelings of emotion, but they could still help create such feelings. This proposal is referred to as the **facial feedback hypothesis** (as we shall see, the hypothesis extends to posture as well). Does smiling make you feel happy, and does frowning make you feel annoyed? A popular proverb encourages people to "turn that frown upside down" as a way of improving mood, but does that actually work? To test this hypotheses, researchers can't simply tell people to smile or frown and then ask them how they feel (they could, but it wouldn't be rigorous science). If you were in that study, you would probably guess what hypothesis the experimenters were testing, and you might say you were feeling an emotion just because it was what you thought they wanted you to say. Psychological researchers call this problem one of **demand characteristics**, meaning the cues that tell participants what the experimenter hopes to see.

FIGURE 5.18.   Holding a pen with your teeth forces you to smile; holding it with your lips prevents smiling.

To avoid demand characteristics, researchers use methods that disguise the intention of the study. Here is one clever procedure, which you can try with a friend as your participant: ask them to hold a pen with their lips, as illustrated in Figure 5.18. Later, repeat the procedure holding the pen with their teeth. In each case, have your "participant" look at a series of funny memes, rating each one as very funny (+), somewhat funny (√), or not funny (-). When holding the pen with your teeth you are virtually forced to smile; when holding it with your lips, you press your lips together in a way that people often do when they are angry or annoyed. In the initial study using this method (with comic strips instead of memes), participants holding the pen in a smiling position rated the comics as slightly funnier than did those who held it in the annoyed position (Strack, Martin, & Stepper, 1988); that is, the sensation of smiling appeared to increase amusement.

Since Strack and colleagues' (1988) initial study, the basic principle of the facial feedback hypothesis has been supported by dozens of additional studies using similar, though not identical, methods (e.g., Dimberg & Söderkvist, 2011; Duclos & Laird, 2001; Hess, Kappas, McHugo, Lanzetta, & Kleck, 1992; Larsen, Kasimatis, & Frey, 1992; McIntosh, 1996; Mori & Mori, 2009; Soussignan, 2002). Studies have indicated that injecting Botox into people's facial muscles can not only alter their own subjective experience of emotions (e.g., Davis et al., 2010), but also reduce their ability to recognize *other people's* emotions, presumably because it inhibits the ability to mimic others' expressions (Neal & Chartrand, 2011).

The studies above are referred to as **conceptual replications**; they address the same theoretical principle as an original study, but using different methods. Although there are slightly different versions of the facial feedback hypothesis (e.g., can facial muscle movements initiate an emotional feeling, or only intensify one you have anyway?), the basic idea was supported by several published, conceptual replications and has been widely accepted for many years; so much so, in fact, that Strack suggested it would be a good test case for a large-scale replication effort, in which several researchers agree to conduct the same study independently (a **direct replication**) and assess whether the new results are consistent with the original findings. In recent years, several other studies had failed to pass this kind of replication test, but in these cases the original studies offered findings many had thought implausible to begin with. In contrast, here was a rock-solid finding with lots of evidence—it should replicate with no problem, right?

Another psychologist, E. J. Wagenmakers, took up the challenge, preparing instructions for a study that was as similar as possible to the original and inviting researchers from other labs to participate. Ultimately, 17 identical studies were conducted, with nearly 2,000 participants. What did they find? Nothing. Across studies, the pen-in-the-mouth manipulation had essentially zero effect on participants' ratings of how funny the cartoons were (Wagenmakers et al., 2016). What does this mean for the facial feedback hypothesis?

We don't really know. Researchers are not ready to discard the theory because of one set of failed replications, using only one method to test the predictions. There are many reasons why the new studies might not have worked. The cartoons in the new studies differed from those in the original, and although they were carefully pretested, it's possible that something about them did not work. A substantial number of participants in the replication studies may have heard of the effect before and were somehow on guard against it. Maybe the facial feedback effect is real, but this specific technique is not able to capture it consistently. The point is, we don't know. Any explanation must account for *both* the failed replication studies and the large number of successful studies that have been published. Facial feedback most likely modulates emotional experience sometimes and in some circumstances, but not always; future research will need to solve the puzzle of when the effect is reliable and when it disappears.

In general, it's important to interpret the results of any single study with caution. Although popular magazines, websites, and other news media may report some new study finding with huge excitement, any one study will inevitably have limitations and may only have examined a small number of people. When all of the studies relevant to some question are examined, their findings sometimes point to a clear answer, but in other cases they may contradict each other and be difficult to interpret. As we shall see throughout this book, this happens fairly often; welcome to science with humans. In some cases, the methods producing one set of findings are simply more rigorous, or more valid for the question at stake, than the methods producing the alternative findings. In that case one of the findings is probably right, and the other is wrong. An alternative is that both findings are partially right, and it depends on details of the situation. Good science is slow to make final decisions based on limited information, and takes the time to investigate these more subtle possibilities instead.

Here's another example of a finding that has become controversial due to inconsistent results. Earlier we described the postural expression of pride, in which the body expands to take up more space, typical of the behavior of other mammals expressing dominance. In an early study researchers randomly assigned participants to adopt either a "power pose," with open, expanded limbs, or a more contracted pose, with arms and legs held close to the body. After holding the pose for a couple of minutes, participants completed a financial gambling task, rated their subjective feelings of power, and even provided a blood sample so their hormone levels could be measured. Consistent with the facial (postural) feedback hypothesis, those in the power pose condition reported feeling more powerful than those given the less expansive pose. They also made riskier decisions in the gambling task, and showed hormonal changes consistent with increased dominance (higher testosterone) and decreased stress (lower cortisol) after the task (Carney, Cuddy, & Yap, 2010). That's a remarkable finding!

However, the original study included only 42 participants across the two posture conditions. In any single study, scientists worry that the results may be a fluke, reflecting features of a few people who happen to be in this sample that might not appear in the larger population of interest; when a sample is this small, it's of particular concern. Another team of researchers attempted to replicate the study, this time with 200 participants. Although they were able to replicate the effect of the power pose on subjective feelings of power, the effects on risk-taking behavior and on hormones disappeared (Ranehill et al., 2015). Other studies have also found that participants instructed to adopt an expansive pose feel more powerful; report a more positive mood in general, and more pride in particular; and show implicit activation of thoughts involving high status and power (e.g., Park et al., 2013; Stepper & Strack, 1993; Veenstra, Schneider, & Koole, 2017). In a meta-analysis of the available studies, the early findings regarding physiological and behavioral effects of power posing were not found to replicate, but effects of expansive posture on positive affect, positive self-evaluation, and subjective feelings of power had consistent support (Cuddy, Schultz, & Fosse, 2018).

Does the power pose increase pride and dominance or not? Good psychology researchers are careful about giving simple answers to all-or-none questions such as this. The power pose has some effect, but based on the evidence we have now, it's more limited than suggested by the initial study. As is often the case, more research is needed to determine which effects are consistently observed and under what conditions. When we encounter situations such as this throughout this book, we'll be honest with you about the complexities of the evidence, and encourage you to decide for yourself what it might mean.

SUMMARY

At the beginning of this chapter, we asserted that the modern field of affective science exists in large part because of research on facial expression. We hope that you now understand the reasons for this claim. Darwin's ideas about emotional expression laid the foundation for thinking of emotion as an evolved aspect of human nature, and Ekman's and Izard's early studies on facial expression recognition revolutionized the status of emotion in psychology. For better and/or for worse, the six emotions included in Ekman's studies were the only ones studied for decades, although the nonverbal expressions of many more emotional and motivational states have been studied in recent years. Researchers have not reached a consensus about whether nonverbal expressions communicate basic emotions or continuous dimensions, and we still have a great deal to learn about the specific psychological processes supporting expression and interpretation of others' expressions. None of the theories discussed in Chapter 1 adequately accounts for all the available evidence on its own; whatever is going on, it's more complicated than these individual theories can explain. Evidence strongly suggests that some inherited, universal language exists for facial, postural, and nonverbal expressions of some emotional and motivational states, but studies have not yet provided a clear dictionary mapping expressions to these states.

What are the other take-home lessons from this chapter? One is that emotions can be reliably expressed in channels beyond the face, including posture, voice, and touch. Another is that rather than a battle between nature and nurture, the research on emotional expression suggests that evolutionary and cultural forces interact with each other in complex ways to produce our expressions; display rules and expressive dialects are just two examples. The principle of nature/nurture interaction applies in many other aspects of emotion as well (and throughout psychology more broadly), so we shall encounter it again in later chapters of this book.

We also introduced a discussion of the need for caution in interpreting research results, especially when they come from a single study. We recommend applying a critical eye to all of the research on facial expressions, asking carefully what each study does and does not mean and realizing how much we still have to learn. In several places in this book, we'll encounter situations in which one body of research reaches one conclusion and another body of research reaches the opposite conclusion. Our response to this is not to throw our hands in the air and give up on science altogether, but instead to look carefully at the methods used in different studies and ask whether they might account for the discrepancy. We don't know the answer to every question that we'll raise, but we'll be honest with you about controversies that are out there and how researchers are moving forward.

KEY TERMS

action unit: in the Facial Action Coding System, the number and name assigned to the visible effects of contracting a specific facial muscle (p. 154)

conceptual replication: a study that attempts to support the theoretical implications of a previous study's findings, but using slightly different methods (p. 180)

demand characteristics: cues in a research study that reveal what the experimenters hope to find; participants may knowingly or unconsciously comply with these wishes (p. 179)

dialect: group differences in accent and vocabulary within a language (in this case, facial expression of emotion), such that people from different groups can understand each other, but still find it easier to understand in-group than out-group members (p. 172)

direct replication: a new study that uses the same methods as a previous study to see whether the original findings are repeated (p. 181)

display rules: cultural norms about when and with whom it is appropriate to display certain kinds of emotional expressions (p. 169)

Duchenne smile: a smile that includes contraction of the orbicularis oculi muscles surrounding the eyes, as well as raised lip corners (p. 158)

Facial Action Coding System (FACS): a system for coding the specific muscles that contract in a person's facial expression (p. 154)

facial feedback hypothesis: the hypothesis that a posed facial expression of emotion can help generate an emotional feeling (p. 179)

free labeling: a method in which participants see a facial expression and come up with their own label for the emotion rather than choosing one from a predefined set of options (p. 167)

gesture: deliberate head and hand movements that convey semantic content and are often culture specific (p. 169)

historical heterogeneity: the extent to which the ancestors of a country's or cultural group's modern population lived originally in a variety of other countries (p. 172)

meta-analysis: a statistical technique that combines the results of many different studies into a single analysis (p. 167)

Möbius syndrome: a rare, congenital condition in which people are physically unable to smile (p. 178)

vocal bursts: wordless vocalizations such as *ah* or *mmm*, intended to express a particular emotion (p. 160)

THOUGHT/DISCUSSION QUESTIONS

1. Most research on facial expressions of emotion has studied people's interpretations of expressions. If you wanted to study the expressions people actually produce during various emotional and motivational states, what task might you use? What are the strengths and limitations of different approaches?

2. People frown (contract the muscle that pulls the eyebrows together and down toward the top of the nose) as part of many negative emotion expressions. However, not all negative expressions include a frown, and people often frown when they are not feeling negative. What are other situations in which people frown? What explanation might the component process model offer for this muscle movement?

3. Think about the ways that emotion is expressed in music. What acoustic properties convey cheerfulness, sadness, fear, anger, and so forth? Do they map onto the properties of these emotions in human voices as well?

4. We noted in this chapter that different emotions may be communicated best through different expressive channels. What kinds of emotional and motivational states might be communicated most effectively through facial expression, posture, vocal expression, and touch? Explain your answer.

SUGGESTIONS FOR FURTHER READING

Ekman, P. et al. (1987). Universals and cultural differences in the judgments of facial expressions of emotion. *Journal of Personality and Social Psychology, 51,* 712–717. Ekman's original paper reporting a large study of facial expression recognition in countries around the world.

Elfenbein, H. A., Beaupré, M., Lévesque, M., & Hess, U. (2007). Toward a dialect theory: Cultural differences in the expression and recognition of posed facial expressions. *Emotion, 7*(1), 131–146. The original empirical paper defining and documenting facial expression "dialects" in African and Canadian communities sharing the same language.

Rosenberg, E. L., & Ekman, P. (2020). *What the face reveals: Basic and applied studies of spontaneous expression using the Facial Action Coding System (FACS)* (3rd ed.). Oxford University Press. A collection of chapters addressing a wide range of questions about emotional expression, including the relationship of expression and feeling, developmental trajectories, and applications to clinical and health psychology.

Russell, J. A. (1994). Is there universal recognition of emotion from facial expression? A review of the cross-cultural studies. *Psychological Bulletin, 115*(1), 102–141. Russell's classic analysis and critique of cross-cultural data on recognition of facial expressions of specific emotions.

Sorenson, E. R. (1975). Culture and the expression of emotion. In T. R. Williams (Ed.), *Psychological Anthropology* (pp. 361–372). Mouton & Co. A vivid, compelling description of the backstory of Ekman and colleagues' classic study of facial expression recognition in New Guinea.

ANSWERS

Figure 5.3: a) anger; b) sadness; c) disgust; d) surprise; e) fear; f) neutral; g) happiness.

PART II

How Do Motivations and Emotions Affect Our Lives?

CHAPTER 6

Emotion, Motivation, and the Central Nervous System

We now enter the second major section of the textbook, asking how emotion and motivation affect our lives. Emotions are vivid, highly salient experiences. Motivation underlies and drives our choices and behaviors. Both phenomena are interesting to study in their own right. However, they also have implications for many other aspects of human experience, including biology, development, relationships, and cognition. In one chapter we discuss the bodily changes that often accompany strong emotion and stress, touching on the nervous system mechanisms of these responses as well as implications for physical health and motivated behavior. In another chapter we examine the ways in which emotion and motivation change over the life course, emphasizing how emotional development interacts with biological, cognitive, and social changes over time. In further chapters we consider the powerful ways in which emotion and motivation shape our relationships with others, as well as our cognition and decision-making. Across these chapters, we will see that these core concepts connect with many subdisciplines of psychology.

We begin with this chapter on emotion, motivation, and the **central nervous system**, defined as the brain and spinal cord. What can we learn about emotion and motivation by studying the brain? Potentially, we might learn a great deal. For one thing, the brain circuits underlying emotion and motivation overlap greatly. Just as the concepts themselves are hard to tease apart (as discussed in Chapter 1), it is hard to distinguish emotion and motivation clearly within the brain. Research on the neuroscience of emotion and motivation is one of the major reasons we have decided to include both topics in the same textbook.

Other potentially revealing questions we could ask at the level of the brain relate to the theories of emotion we covered at the start of our intellectual journey together, back in Chapter 1. Different theories of emotion make different claims about how emotions should be represented in brain activity. If researchers found that happiness depended on activity in one brain area, neurotransmitter, or network of connections; anger in another; fear in another; and so on, then that would support calling each of these a basic emotion. Alternatively, researchers might find that brain activation during emotions closely resembles activation during what we call motivation more generally, driving us toward situations that hold promise for reward and away from those that spell punishment or harm. As a further possibility, it may be that most neural activity during emotion takes place in brain regions that support language, awareness of situational context, and interpretation; this finding would be most consistent with a psychological construction model of emotion.

Research on emotion in the brain has practical implications as well. If researchers link some aspect of emotion to a particular neurotransmitter or brain circuit, for example, this information might inform the development of treatments for emotional disorders such as anxiety, depression, and post-traumatic stress disorder. Understanding the central nervous system mechanisms of emotion and its regulation has legal implications as well. In certain cases, attorneys have argued that a defendant cannot be held fully responsible for violent acts because of brain injury, brain immaturity, genetic abnormalities affecting the brain, and so forth. To evaluate such arguments, we must understand how emotional processes are supported by activity in the brain.

Is there an "emotion region of the brain," generally speaking? Probably not, although there are several regions that play important roles in aspects of emotional experience. In an early attempt to define the emotional brain, Paul MacLean (1952) proposed that a network of structures he called the **limbic system** was the source of emotion. In his triune brain model, MacLean divided the brain into three regions: first, a central "reptilian" area (presumably inherited with minor modifications from our ancient reptilian ancestors) controlled sensory, survival, and reflex actions. A "mammalian" area, also called the limbic system, surrounded the reptilian area and controlled emotion. Surrounding all of that was the neocortex, responsible for complex cognition and reasoning in humans and other primates (see Figure 6.1). Later evidence showed that this idea has several problems. First, all three regions proposed by MacLean are activated during and help mediate sensation, emotion, and reasoning, and they communicate extensively with each other—they aren't specific to emotion.

Second, some of the evolutionary aspects of the model contradict available evidence. In a journal article amusingly titled "Your Brain is Not an Onion with a Tiny Reptile Inside," Joseph Cesario, David Johnson, and Heather Eisthen (2020) reviewed the problems regarding MacLean's triune theory of brain function. They note that it is a scientific misconception that animals on Earth evolved linearly in complexity, from seaworms on up to human beings, adding new layers of the brain as they evolved. Instead, new species radiate (evolve from) common ancestors (see Figure 6.1). Most nonhuman animals possess some similar brain structures and divisions that we could conceive of as the hindbrain, midbrain, and forebrain—it isn't that "simpler" creatures have just a hindbrain and only human beings and a few other lucky mammals get forebrains. All modern animals have brains that reflect intertwining of ancient structures with more recently evolved ones, and the ancient structures have themselves continued to evolve in each species.

Also, as Tor Wager, Anjali Krishnan, and Emma Hitchcock (2018) point out, if we really were to define an "emotion area" in the brain, it would be no less than the entirety of the brain. In addition to the midbrain areas commonly named as important for

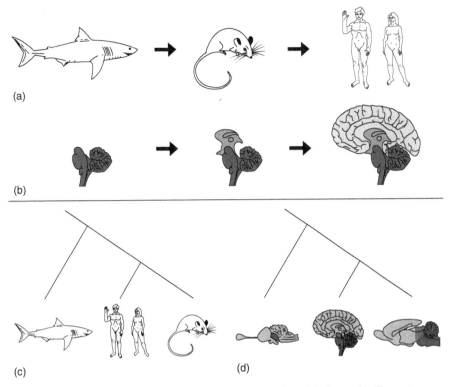

FIGURE 6.1. Top Panel: An incorrect view of evolution (a) and the brain (b), illustrating that earlier species lacked outer, more recent brain structures. Just as species did not evolve linearly (a), neither did neural structures (b). Although psychologists understand (a) is incorrect, the corresponding neural view (b) is still widely endorsed. Bottom Panel: A correct view of evolution (c) and organization of the brain (d). From Cesario, Johnson, & Eisthen (2020).

emotion, parts of the brainstem support withdrawal from noxious or painful stimuli, and the entire cortex aids in processing and interpreting emotional situations. That all said, several of the structures in MacLean's limbic system are particularly important in emotional processes, and term limbic system continues to be in use.

The goal of this chapter is to introduce the major techniques and current state of knowledge in affective neuroscience. We first describe several research methods specific to understanding the emotional and motivated brain, examining their strengths and limitations. We then discuss the research on several brain structures and circuits that are especially important to the study of emotion and motivation. This will include areas involved in approach and avoidance motivation; areas relevant to the generation and perception of bodily changes in emotion; and a network crucial for controlling cognition and inhibiting impulses (this network is highly relevant for both emotion regulation and goal-directed behavior). We will focus particularly on the amygdala—an area of great interest in emotion, and a strong example of the possible pitfalls as well as the promise of neuroscientific approaches to understanding affect. Finally, we consider the overall state of the field, relating the existing evidence from affective neuroscience to theories of emotion introduced in Chapter 1.

METHODS TO STUDY EMOTION, MOTIVATION, AND THE BRAIN

Learning Objectives

- Describe the major tools we have for investigating emotion and motivation at the level of the brain, and compare the strengths and limitations of these methods.
- Explain what the reverse inference problem is, and provide and recognize examples.

Studying the brain is difficult. The brain is a complex organ made up of microscopic cells that respond to minute variations in certain chemicals, yet many of our measures depend on patterns of activity distributed over a wide area of brain real estate. This remarkable organ is also constantly changing—it must balance its internal functions and predictions of what may happen next based on past experiences against a constantly updating flow of new information from the external environment.

Furthermore, both practical and ethical restraints limit the sorts of research we can do that intrudes into a human brain. For a long time, the only way to study brain mechanisms of human behavior was to find people with brain injuries, observe their behavior, and then do autopsies after they died. Research with nonhuman animals legally allows for more invasive methods, but relating brain activity to emotions requires that we infer what emotion some animal is or is not experiencing. Measuring emotions in humans is difficult enough, and with nonhumans it is far more so . . . some say it is impossible.

Luckily, a bevy of new technologies have made it possible for researchers to noninvasively measure human brain activity in close to real time. However, each of these technologies has limitations. Advances in our understanding depend on convergent evidence from studies using different methods, where the strengths of one method help compensate for the limitations of another. Let's consider some of those methods.

Brain Damage

One difficulty in research on human brain damage is that the damage (usually from a stroke or accident) is in different locations for different people, generally overlaps several brain areas, and almost never affects exactly the area that some researcher would like to study. Therefore, for many purposes, researchers turn to laboratory animals (mostly rats and mice) and intentionally create a **lesion**—that is, damage—to an area of interest. Researchers can create a lesion by either surgical or chemical methods, as certain drugs can inactivate certain brain regions. However, interpreting the results of an intentional lesion is often difficult, and an overeager researcher can jump to a wrong conclusion. Suppose an extraterrestrial being who did not understand people made a lesion in your tongue, and found that you now avoid most conversations with others (after all, you can hardly speak). Hence, the extraterrestrial concludes that the tongue is the organ that governs your desire to socialize with others. Or the extraterrestrial makes a lesion of all your fingers except the middle one. Now whenever you raise your hand (gesturing only with that remaining middle finger), someone punches you in the nose. The extraterrestrial decides the function of those other fingers must be to deter aggression. You can imagine other ridiculous conclusions an alien might reach after making lesions to body parts and then observing behavior superficially. When researchers study brain damage, they risk making similar kinds of mistakes.

When dealing with human brain damage, researchers also encounter problems because brain damage does not happen to people completely at random. Consider this example: patients with damage to the ventromedial prefrontal cortex (Figure 6.2) show greater risk-taking behavior in a gambling task than patients with no lesion or with lesions in other areas (e.g., Clark et al., 2008). A common cause of damage to this area is head trauma. While of course anyone can suffer head trauma at any time, some people may be

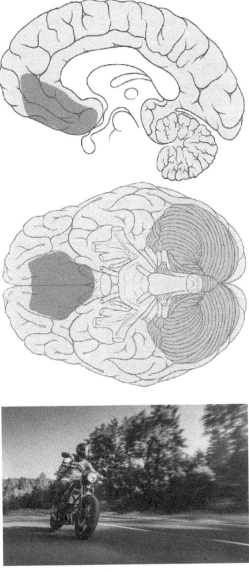

FIGURE 6.2. The ventromedial prefrontal cortex is in an area of the brain that is often damaged by head trauma. Damage in this area is associated with later risk-taking tendencies, but which way does the causal arrow point?

especially likely to encounter head trauma. Who might this be? People who take a lot of risks, such as motorcycle riding and extreme sports, right? Might the risky behavior be the cause of brain damage, rather than the result of it?

Despite these limitations, gains in knowledge can come from using multiple methods of studying the brain that cancel out each other's weaknesses. In this case, researchers rely on neuroimaging studies with people who have never had brain damage. The results show increased activity of the ventromedial prefrontal cortex when people resist the temptation to take a risky action, such as gambling (e.g., Eshel et al., 2007). Studies like this give researchers more confidence in the interpretation that the ventromedial prefrontal cortex may be involved in risk assessment or inhibition than they would have from the brain damage studies alone.

Electroencephalography (EEG)

The method of **electroencephalography (EEG)** relies on the fact that neurons generate an electrical potential (or charge) in the process of communicating information from one neuron to another. The potential generated by one neuron is weak, but when many nearby neurons activate at the same time, electrodes (sensors) at the scalp can detect this activity. Researchers place electrodes at many points on someone's head and compare responses to a reference electrode somewhere else (Figure 6.3). They can then measure spontaneous patterns of activity or responses to sights, sounds, or other stimuli. Such EEG responses to stimuli are called **evoked potentials** or **event-related potentials**. A closely related method is magnetoencephalography (MEG), which records momentary changes in brain cells' magnetic activity instead of electrical activity. (The passage of an electrical current generates a magnetic field.)

Research using EEG or MEG is not easy for participants, who must remain as motionless as possible during a lengthy procedure (even eyeblinks introduce noise to the signal and must be deleted from the data before processing!). The stimuli and tasks used in EEG studies must be simple (and often boring) to isolate specific mental processes. It's not unusual for undergraduates to begin getting sleepy during EEG studies—an effect readily visible to researchers watching incoming data. Researchers using this technology also face other types of difficulties. Because the results on any single trial include a fair amount of noise, the

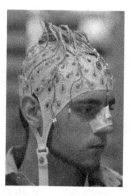

FIGURE 6.3. The use of electroencephalography allows researchers to measure the average activity of neurons in the area under an electrode.

researcher takes an average over many trials. Because EEG and MEG summarize activity over an area at the level of the scalp, they do not yield precise information about the location of activity, especially if it is generated deeper in the brain. However, for many purposes we do not need great precision. On the other hand, the advantage of these methods is that they measure rapid changes on a millisecond-by-millisecond basis. As we will see, some of the methods that are better at measuring the specific brain structures that are responsible for the neural activity are poorer in terms of timing precision—it's a bit of a balancing act. EEG and MEG can indicate how soon the brain begins to respond to an emotional stimulus, how long the response lasts, and which large brain areas respond before others. We might want to test whether activity in one area encourages or inhibits activity in another, and the timing of activity in the two areas helps answer that question.

Here is an example of research related to emotion that uses EEG: researchers can detect a distinctive change in the electrical potential at electrodes over the frontal lobes about 100 milliseconds after a person makes a mistake on some task, an effect called *error-related negativity*. This negative deflection in the waveform is greater in individuals with anxiety disorders than in other people (e.g., Hajcak, McDonald, & Simons, 2003; Figure 6.4). That is, people with anxiety disorders react more strongly than average when they make a mistake.

Functional Magnetic Resonance Imaging (fMRI)

Studies using EEG and MEG mostly record activity near the surface of the brain, simply because they are closer to the electrodes. One method used to localize brain activity more precisely, and to measure the activity of areas deeper in the brain, is positron emission tomography, generally known as PET scanning. To produce a PET scan, a researcher injects a chemical such as radioactively labeled glucose and then uses a device that measures the radioactivity emanating from various areas. Because glucose is the brain's main source of fuel, the brain's most active areas take up the most glucose and therefore show the highest level of radioactivity. While ingesting radioactivity can sound scary, PET uses a very minute amount of radioactivity—about the amount that a flight attendant would be exposed to in a few months of work. Still, you would not want to undergo PET repeatedly unless you have a medical reason to do so.

Today, a more common method (which doesn't require injecting anything) is **functional magnetic resonance imaging (fMRI)**. The physics of the technique is complex, but the basic idea is this: hemoglobin, the molecule that delivers oxygen to the cells, reacts differently to a magnetic field depending on whether it still has oxygen or has already released it. The most active brain areas use oxygen more rapidly than other areas. Therefore, a device that measures how hemoglobin reacts to a magnetic field can identify the brain areas that have been more versus less active in the preceding couple of seconds. The device provides a measure of brain activity with spatial accuracy to 1–3 millimeters and temporal accuracy of about 1 second. The result is a series of pictures showing activity in each "slice" of the brain. Each picture is composed of *voxels* (like pixels on a computer monitor, but in three rather than two dimensions) of brain. Typically, the readout uses a color code to show activity. For example, red voxels might indicate the highest activity, followed by yellow voxels and uncolored voxels (those with no more activity than average). An fMRI scan can also indicate areas that decrease their activity during some stimulus or task, often depicted in cool colors like blue.

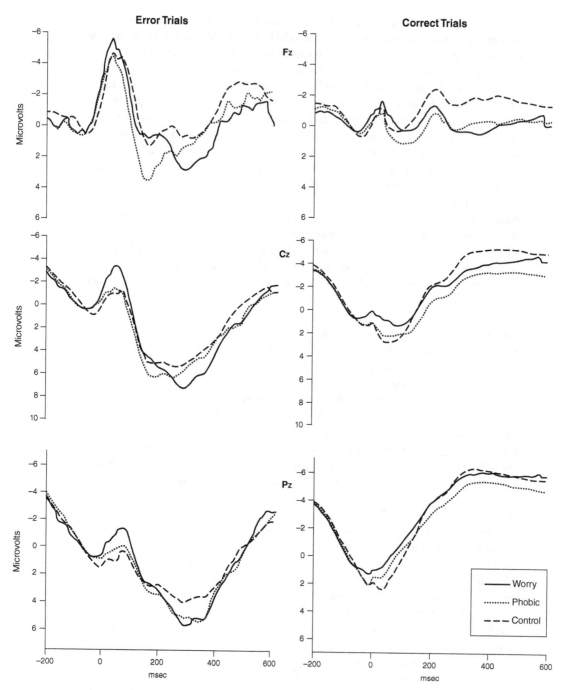

FIGURE 6.4. The negative deflection (note that negative is up, not down) in the electrical waveform about 100 milliseconds after a participant makes an error is stronger in participants who report strong anxiety-related symptoms (the worry group). From Hajcak, McDonald, & Simons, 2003.

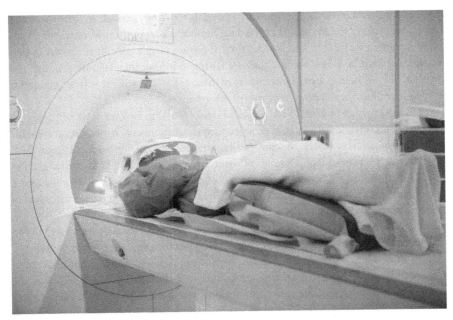

FIGURE 6.5. During a functional magnetic resonance imaging scan, people must lie very still in a tiny space, and the machine itself generates a lot of noise; eliciting strong emotions may be difficult.

Current fMRI technology can be used to examine relationships among brain activity, emotional feelings, and simple behavior in live, healthy humans in ways that were never possible before—a truly remarkable development. Just like any method for studying emotion, however, fMRI has important limitations. The participant must lie with his or her head motionless for many minutes inside a large metal device (Figure 6.5). Individuals who suffer from claustrophobia (fear of enclosed places) have difficulty with this procedure. Children are difficult to study because they have a hard time holding still. Furthermore, the machine makes loud noises that probably induce emotional responses by themselves. There is also some evidence that lying prone and still may change the nature of people's emotional response (Harmon-Jones & Peterson, 2009). Most fMRI studies of emotion record people's responses to photographs of other people's facial expressions, more emotionally complex photos or films, or ask people to engage in processes related to attention, memory, or decision-making with emotional elements. Many researchers question whether a typical person is able to have a normal (for them) emotional experience in this kind of situation.

fMRI produces many valuable results, but people (including psychology researchers) sometimes become so awestruck by the beautiful pictures such scans produce that they overlook the challenges of interpretation. Here is an example: the amygdala is considered important for interpreting emotional expressions. We can use fMRI to measure how someone's amygdala reacts to photos of people's emotional expressions. If the amygdala reacts weakly to a photo, what does that mean? Did the person not detect any emotion in the expression? Or did they activate the amygdala so weakly because so little effort was needed to interpret the emotional expression? Similarly, part of the prefrontal cortex appears important for inhibiting risky impulses. If certain people show little activity in that area during some task, is it because they are failing to inhibit their impulses, or because they had only weak impulses that were easy to inhibit? fMRI results are often ambiguous until we combine them with other types of information.

Here is a further problem: a researcher who uses fMRI to look for any brain area that increases or decreases its activity is, in effect, testing a huge number of hypotheses at the same time—one for each brain area. In some studies, data are analyzed one voxel at a time, which means researchers are asking thousands of research questions at once. With any other kind of outcome measure, this would be considered highly inappropriate for statistical reasons. Some areas might show increased activity by chance, or because of some irrelevant aspect of the experiment, and the more areas you examine, the more likely this is to occur.

To point out the seriousness of this problem, one group of researchers used fMRI to scan a dead Atlantic salmon while ostensibly having it complete an *interspecies perspective-taking task* and found that several small regions of its brain and spinal column appeared more active during this task than during a control task (Bennett et al., 2010). Naturally, this evidence did not indicate that those regions were contributing to the perspective-taking task, which the fish could not have performed even if it were still alive; the finding simply represented measurement noise. Researchers now typically use statistical techniques that avoid these kinds of mistakes, but in older publications such mistakes are not uncommon.

Please do not think that the message here is to give up, or to ignore fMRI studies or other brain data. The point is to be cautious, and to replicate any finding with other populations and other procedures. As we noted at the end of Chapter 5, it's important to avoid jumping to conclusions based on any one study, or even one type of study.

Neurochemistry Techniques

An alternative approach emphasizes **neurotransmitters**, the chemicals that neurons release to communicate with one another. The human brain uses dozens of chemicals with various distributions in the nervous system. The most abundant neurotransmitters can attach to multiple receptor types with different functions. For example, the neurotransmitter **serotonin** has at least seven families of receptors, one of which is responsible for nausea. A drug that blocks that receptor prevents nausea without strongly affecting other processes involving serotonin—a great benefit for cancer patients undergoing chemotherapy.

Neurochemistry research focuses on either measuring the activity at a particular type of synapse or using procedures that increase or decrease activity at a type of synapse. For example, drugs can be used to increase or decrease production of a neurotransmitter, directly stimulate certain receptors, block their stimulation, or prolong the presence of a neurotransmitter at the synapse by preventing the first cell from reabsorbing it. Another approach is to examine the effects of genetic mutations that alter synaptic receptors.

A more refined technique is *optogenetics*, in which a researcher uses a specially manipulated virus to insert light-sensitive proteins into the membrane of certain neurons, and then implants a thin optical fiber into the brain to shine light and thereby control the activity of just one type of neuron, in just one brain area. As you can imagine, this procedure is used mostly with laboratory animals.

The Reverse Inference Problem

We have alluded already to some kinds of mistakes one can make in interpreting data from neuroscience studies. One additional mistake seems to be especially pervasive. This mistake is an example of a more general logical error, but it is particularly common when researchers try to relate psychological processes to biological ones. To illustrate the general form of the error, here is a question:

> Given: If A, then B. (In psychology this often means if you manipulate A, this causes B.)
> Question: If B, therefore A? (If B is present, can you presume A is as well?)
> We'll give you a minute to think about this one. Read on when you have your answer.

Ready? Okay. The correct answer is no. Showing that A causes B, even definitively, does not mean that if B is present, A must be present as well. B could be caused by many things other than A. You have no way of knowing whether A is present unless you've ruled out all other plausible causes of B, which is extremely difficult. This logical error is referred to as *affirming the consequent*, a classic fallacy.

As an example, if you go outside when it's raining, your hair will probably get wet. Does this mean that if your hair is wet, you must have been outside? Of course not. Maybe you took a shower and washed your hair. Maybe you were in an indoor swimming pool. Maybe your roommate got too playful with their new water gun. You can't conclude the cause based on the effect because there are other possible causes. In a more subtle point, you also can't conclude that going outdoors was what caused your hair to get wet, or that this will happen every time you go outside. Being outdoors per se was not the problem; the rain was. Usually if you went outdoors your hair would stay dry.

Here is an example of what this error looks like in neuroscience. One researcher shows participants scary pictures during an fMRI scan and finds that the amygdala becomes more active. Another researcher shows participants photos of balloons and finds that the amygdala becomes more active in response to these images; this researcher concludes that people must be afraid of balloons.

In this context it sounds more reasonable, right? And yet the inference is just as questionable as in the simpler, more abstract form of the fallacy described above. Showing that the amygdala is activated during a scary task does not necessarily mean that the amygdala becomes active *only* during fear. In psychology research this is referred to as **reverse inference**: concluding that because a known effect of some cause is present, that specific cause must be present as well (rather than some other cause). This error is often made when researchers conclude that some brain region is the "*X* area" of the brain because that area became more active during psychological process *X*. It is even more pervasive in popular media accounts of neuroscience findings. In reading this chapter, as well as in future encounters with neuroscience research, we encourage you to be cautious about this potential problem.

New Directions in Affective Neuroscience Methods

Existing tools such as EEG and fMRI have illuminated a great deal about the emotional and motivated brain. However, as we have also discussed, these tools have limitations in terms of how much information they convey, and the sorts of research questions we can ask. The fMRI environment largely requires that human beings lie passive and motionless in a long tube, which is a sharp contrast to most of the situations we encounter in daily life, especially those situations that evoke emotion and engender motivation. You cannot, after all, approach or avoid anything while lying down. You also cannot engage in conversation, or debate, or flirtation with other human beings.

Leading voices in the field have called for the development of designs and tools to allow for more "real-life neuroscience." For instance, Simone Shamay-Tsoory and Avi Mendelsohn (2019) propose a paradigm shift in how human neuroscience approaches studying brain and behavior. They argue that we must develop portable technologies and new research designs to better allow for the study of brain activation patterns during real-life encounters (see Figure 6.6).

Encouragingly, some of these developments are already happening. A new neuroimaging technique called **functional near-infared spectroscopy (fNIRS)** allows for the measurement of blood oxygenation changes, much like fMRI, but is based on measuring changes in the absorption of light at the level of the scalp. This technique thus allows for a person to be much more mobile than fMRI, somewhat like wearing an EEG cap. For

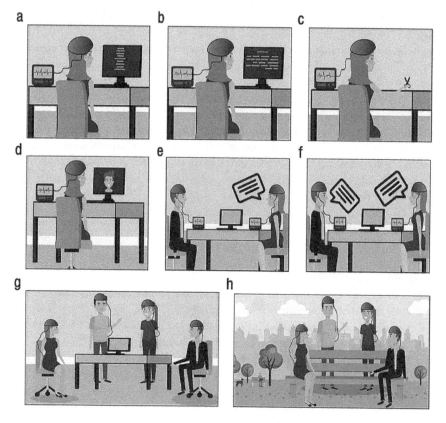

FIGURE 6.6. Progression of increasingly real-life neuroscience methods, from (a) typical neuroscience paradigms today, where a single human being interacts with lists of simple computerized stimuli, to (h) a scenario where brain activation patterns are measured in multiple human beings interacting in a realistic environment and social encounter. From Shamay-Tsoory & Mendelsohn (2019).

instance, researchers Reindl, Gerloff, Scharke, and Konrad, (2018) used fNIRS to measure brain activation patterns in parents and children while they cooperated on a task to study associations between their brain synchrony and how they regulated their emotions. Another technique called **hyperscanning** allows for simultaneous measurement of fMRI from two or more people engaged in social interaction (Misaki et al., 2021). Together, greater portability of neuroimaging methods and more focus on measuring people in real-life interactions promise truly exciting developments in our understanding of the emotional and motivated brain over the next few decades.

THE NEURAL CIRCUITRY OF APPROACH AND AVOIDANCE
Learning Objectives
- Differentiate the behavioral activation and inhibition systems (BAS and BIS) proposed by Jeffrey Gray, and summarize the proposed roles of these systems in motivation.
- Analyze the amygdala's roles in the subjective experience of fear, fear conditioning, and emotional memory, summarizing relevant experimental evidence.
- Describe the reward circuit of the brain, including its relevant structures and differentiating anticipatory from consummatory pleasure.

Why did brains evolve? It isn't to make life possible, as plenty of organisms on our planet do just fine without one of those heavy masses in their skulls. Take a moment and jot down some thoughts: What is the purpose of a brain?

In a widely viewed TED talk, neuroscientist Daniel Wolpert makes the claim that brains evolved to support movement. He uses the example of a sea creature that has two stages to its life, one where it moves around like an animal, and one where it plants itself in the sea floor and acts a lot more like a plant. The first thing this creature does upon planting itself, he claims, is digest its own brain. It doesn't need it anymore. (He jokes that a similar process happens once a professor is awarded tenure).

Whether movement is the *entire* purpose of having brains is up for debate, but movement is certainly a marvelous feat when you stop to think about it. (SRC: See what I did there? MNS: Yes, very funny. ☺) Movement is how we act on the world. We can navigate space, reach out and manipulate objects, and avoid dangers. We use movement in two main ways: to approach situations, objects, and people that promise pleasure and/or are likely to increase our adaptive fitness; and to avoid situations, objects, and people likely to bring displeasure and/or threats to adaptive fitness.

Recall from our early introduction to motivation that in some of the first considerations of motivation in the scholarly record, Ancient Greek philosophers argued that tendencies to approach pleasure and avoid pain are *the* major drivers of human behavior. In a more modern account, neuroscientist Jeffrey Gray (1982) proposed that the brain might be wired for these same two categories of behavior. Our ancient ancestors were presented with a wide range of opportunities that must be approached to take advantage of them: food and other material resources, potential sex partners, babies, and other kin are examples. Their environment also presented a wide range of threats: predators, toxic foods, environmental hazards, and even dangerous people. Someone who failed to avoid these threats would not manage to pass his or her genes to the next generation. According to Gray, the mammalian brain includes a **behavioral activation system** that motivates approaching opportunities, and a **behavioral inhibition system** that motivates threat detection and avoidance.

The evidence regarding the exact systems Gray proposed is complicated. On one hand, behavioral and EEG studies make a compelling case that the approach–avoidance distinction is important among mammals. Questionnaire measures of behavioral avoidance and inhibition are largely uncorrelated with each other (Carver & White, 1994). This suggests that at least at the individual-differences level, these traits are independent (both can be high or low in the same people) rather than opposite ends of the same dimension (being high in one means being low in the other). Experiments also find that instructing people to adopt approach- versus avoidance- related motions (such as postures and movements) can have quite different, often opposing, effects on information processing and behavior (e.g., Krpan & Fasolo, 2019; Neumann & Strack, 2000; Rougier et al., 2018). Research using electroencephalography methods has consistently indicated that when people are in a heightened approach-motivation state they tend to show greater activation of the left frontal cortex than of the right, whereas the reverse is true for avoidance motivation (Davidson, 2004; Harmon-Jones & Gable, 2018). Researchers have even identified structures that are arguably specialized for reward pursuit or threat avoidance, although, as we shall soon see, it has proved more difficult to identify whole networks associated exclusively with one or the other motivational direction.

Approach and avoidance also connect motivation and emotion. In one recent review of the neural systems underlying emotion and motivation, the authors concluded that they had no choice but to adopt a "view that emphasizes integration of emotion and motivation, to the point that they merge into a single process and involve overlapping brain substrates" (Cromwell et al., 2020, p. 204). Let's review some of the evidence behind this proposal.

Avoidance and Fear

The early years of psychology focused largely on what can go wrong in human experience: depression, anxiety, violence, and unrealized potential. This early focus on difficulty was followed by a later renaissance of interest in what can go *right*, exemplified by a movement known as "positive psychology." Affective and motivation neuroscience followed a similar trajectory, first focusing primarily on how the brain manages avoidance and withdrawal, and later turning to how it manages approach and reward. We shall follow the same path here.

The study of avoidance motivation in the human brain has been dominated by interest in a small structure in the temporal lobe known as the **amygdala** (pronounced uh-MIG-duh-luh; Figure 6.7). The brain has two amygdalae (the plural of amygdala), one in the left hemisphere and one in the right, but for simplicity we will use the singular. *Amygdala* is the Greek word for almond; the amygdala is shaped somewhat like an almond, if you use a little imagination. The amygdala receives input representing vision, hearing, other senses, and pain, so it is in a position to associate various stimuli with outcomes that follow them. It sends information to the pons and other areas controlling the startle reflex, and it exchanges information back and forth with the thalamus (a sort of "central relay station" for sensory information coming into the brain) and several areas of the cerebral cortex. Because the history of research on the amygdala offers a great example of the complexity and potential pitfalls of affective neuroscience, we review it in detail.

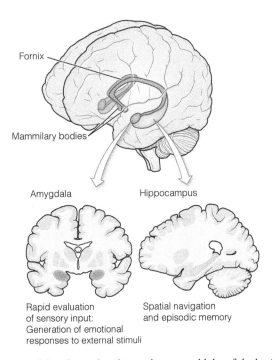

FIGURE 6.7. The amygdala is located within each temporal lobe of the brain, with one in each hemisphere. It is connected with the hippocampus, an important structure in the formation of episodic memories.

Effects of Amygdala Damage

The amygdala first attracted research attention because of what happened after brain damage to this area. Animal research in this case is relevant to humans, because the structure of the amygdala and its connections to other brain areas are highly similar across species.

In the 1930s, two researchers who were studying monkeys identified what came to be known as **Klüver–Bucy syndrome**, a pattern of emotional changes after removal of the anterior part of the temporal cortex in both hemispheres, including the amygdala. Animals with such damage seemed not to recognize the emotional implications of objects. For example, they would approach snakes, try to pick up lighted matches, and put feces into their mouths (Klüver & Bucy, 1939). Monkeys with damage to the amygdala would also fearlessly approach aggressive monkeys and unfamiliar humans (Kalin, Shelton, & Davidson, 2004), sometimes getting injured as a result (Rosvold, Mirsky, & Pribram, 1954). In laboratory studies, such animals are impaired at learning to avoid shock or other pain (Kazama et al., 2012). In other words, amygdala-damaged monkeys engaged blithely with objects and situations other monkeys tried hard to avoid.

Research in other species indicates a similar pattern. Normal rats and mice show an inborn fear of cats, including the odor of cats. Those with damage to the amygdala show no such fear, even approaching cats with curiosity (Berdoy, Webster, &

Macdonald, 2000; McGregor et al., 2004). Like the monkeys, they do not easily learn to avoid shock or other danger (Hitchcock & Davis, 1991).

Humans with damage limited to just the amygdala are rare. Nevertheless, we can examine the differences between brain damage that does or does not include the amygdala. People whose damage includes the amygdala can classify photographs as pleasant or unpleasant, showing the cognitive aspect of emotion, but they show little or no arousal (the feeling aspect) when they view unpleasant photos (Berntson et al., 2007). They will approach strangers virtually at random when they need help, instead of trying to choose someone who looks safe. If they are asked to look at faces and rate which ones look friendliest or most trustworthy, they rate all faces as almost equal (Adolphs, Tranel, & Damasio, 1998). When soldiers in the Vietnam War suffered wounds causing brain damage that did not include the amygdala, 40% developed posttraumatic stress disorder. If the damage did include the amygdala, none of the soldiers developed posttraumatic stress disorder (Koenigs et al., 2008). This evidence suggests that activation in the amygdala may be related to anxiety in some way, and researchers began to suggest that it might be the "fear area of the brain."

What happens with damage more localized to the amygdala? In a rare condition called Urbach–Wiethe disease, calcium accumulates in the amygdala and damages it, without much damage to surrounding tissues. Much interesting research focuses on these few patients, especially a woman known in the literature as patient SM. SM describes herself as fearless and consistently acts fearlessly, often to her detriment. She has been attacked and assaulted repeatedly after wandering into dangerous situations that other people would avoid. When she describes those events, she recalls anger but not fear. Although she reports hating snakes and spiders, when researchers took her to an exotic pet shop, she repeatedly tried to touch the tarantulas and venomous snakes. When viewing clips from frightening movies, she reported feeling only excitement, not fear. At a haunted house, she led the way down dark hallways, and when someone dressed as a monster jumped out, she only laughed (Feinstein et al., 2011).

From these observations, it might appear that SM is incapable of feeling fear, consistent with the proposal that the amygdala is the brain structure supporting this emotion. However, a later study found that she and two others with the same condition panicked while breathing 35% carbon dioxide. (Concentrated carbon dioxide makes you feel like you are suffocating). On the other hand, although all three participants described the experience as terrifying, they readily agreed to do it again a week later, and reported that they did not think about it during that time (Feinstein et al., 2013). So, they were capable of feeling intense fear, but something in the system has clearly gone wrong. If you found some experience frightening, shouldn't you be hesitant about doing it again?

Laboratory Studies of Fear Conditioning

Another type of research on the amygdala uses **fear conditioning**. Here is the procedure: a rat hears a distinctive tone, followed quickly by an electrical shock to the floor of the cage. After several pairings, a rat will tense up or freeze when it hears that tone. The rat also shows increased blood pressure and other physiological responses that people typically show when they are afraid. In a control condition, rats hear the tone and get the same shocks, but at separate times so that they do not associate the two.

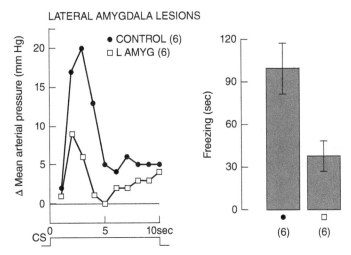

FIGURE 6.8. Rats with intact brains quickly learn that a sound tone means an electrical shock is coming, and show physiological and behavioral responses suggesting fear when they hear the tone. Rats with amygdala damage show a much weaker response to the tone. From LeDoux et al. (1990).

Joseph LeDoux and colleagues (LeDoux et al., 1990) compared rats with amygdala damage to similar rats without damage. Figure 6.8 illustrates the results. After the same training, the amygdala-damaged rats showed much weaker freezing responses and increases in blood pressure after hearing the danger tone than did brain-intact rats. Similarly, if a rat has learned that one tone predicts a shock and a different tone predicts a period of safety, its startle reflex is stronger just after hearing the first tone—an effect consistent with fear—and weaker after the second (Schmid, Koch, & Schnitzler, 1995). However, if the rat has lesions to the amygdala in both hemispheres, the danger signal and the safety signal have almost no influence, and the startle reflex is the same in both cases (Hitchcock & Davis, 1991). Rats with amygdala damage not only fail to learn new signs of danger, but also lose conditioned fears that they had previously learned (Gale et al., 2004). Similar results occur after chemical injections that temporarily disable the amygdala (e.g., Schafe et al., 2000). Much later research indicated specific pathways within the amygdala that are responsible for fear conditioning (Likhtik et al., 2014).

Fear conditioning in people with amygdala damage yields an interesting result. Physiological measures such as heart rate indicate little response, as if the person had not learned. However, the person reports knowing that the conditioned stimulus (in this case, a colored image) predicts the unpleasant stimulus (Bechara et al., 1995). This suggests that the amygdala is not necessary for people to consciously recognize the association between the conditioned stimulus and the unpleasant outcome, although it may be necessary for a more implicit, emotional response.

Experiences That Activate the Human Amygdala

If the amygdala is the fear area of the brain, it should activate in response to scary stimuli but *not* other kinds of stimuli. If it is generally associated with avoidance, it might activate in response to a wider range of aversive situations. Recordings of brain activity with fMRI show increased amygdala activity when people view a variety of emotional stimuli, such as faces with emotional expressions. The amygdala reacts even to brief presentations that the viewer may not identify consciously (Kubota et al., 2000; Vuilleumier et al., 2001). The response increases if the expression is difficult to interpret. For example, the response to an expression is strong at first, but weakens after repeated presentations (Breiter et al., 1996; Büchel et al., 1998). Fearful expressions elicit greater responses if the reason for fear is uncertain (Adams & Kleck, 2005).

The amygdala responds to stimuli eliciting other emotions as well. Some cells within the amygdala even respond to pleasant stimuli (Namburi et al., 2015; Wang et al., 2014), although the amygdala as a whole seldom responds strongly. Your amygdala might respond especially strongly to a happy face if you have an extraverted personality, or if a task requires attention to happy faces. Even so, unpleasant stimuli provoke a stronger response (Canli et al., 2002; Stillman, Van Bavel, & Cunningham, 2015). One fMRI study indicated clear amygdala responses only to facial expressions of fear and anger (Mattavelli et al., 2014). How shall we interpret that result? When you see an expression of anger, do you also feel anger? Perhaps, but you might reasonably react with fear instead.

Some people show stronger amygdala responses than others, and the differences correlate with feelings of anxiety in daily life. College students in one study recorded their emotions for 28 days. A year later, their amygdala responses to frightening pictures were measured in the scanner. The students with the greatest amygdala activation had previously reported the greatest number of unpleasant emotional experiences (Barrett et al., 2007). In another study, researchers started by measuring amygdala responses in newly inducted Israeli soldiers as they viewed briefly flashed unpleasant photos. Soldiers with the greatest amygdala responses were most likely to report highly stressful experiences during their military service (Admon et al., 2009).

As discussed in Chapter 4, your level of fear depends on how you appraise a situation. For example, if someone scowls at you, you could think either, "too bad he is in such a bad mood" or "I guess he really doesn't like me!" If you have an overdue credit card bill, you could think about ways to deal with it, or you could start to imagine everything that could go wrong (Ruined credit rating! Bill collectors! Jail!). Amygdala activation is modulated by other brain regions thought to be involved in appraisal (Figure 6.9). For example, parts of the prefrontal cortex become more active while someone is consciously reassessing or "reappraising" a situation in a more neutral way. During this activity, projections from the prefrontal cortex appear to restrain the amygdala (Buhle et al., 2014; Marek et al., 2013; Moscarello & LeDoux, 2013). People with below-average activity in the prefrontal cortex, including most people with depression, tend toward more anxiety-inducing interpretations, and they show less inhibition of amygdala activity as well (Holmes et al., 2012).

Another brain area whose activity modulates that of the amygdala is the **cingulate cortex** (Figure 6.9). This area, which wraps around part of the corpus callosum in the center of the brain, is linked to a variety of processes that relate to memory, cognition, and emotion. For example, if you are playing a game in which you must choose between attacking your opponent or defending against attack, the anterior part of the cingulate cortex is more active while you evaluate defensive moves, and the posterior part is more active while you evaluate offensive moves (Wan, Cheng, & Tanaka, 2015). Parts of the

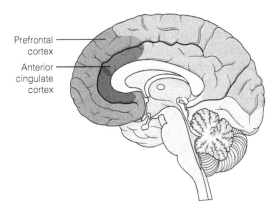

FIGURE 6.9. Activity in the prefrontal cortex and the anterior cingulate cortex has been linked to appraisal processes, and both regions modulate activity within the amygdala.

anterior cingulate cortex respond strongly to painful stimuli (Gu et al., 2015). They are also active when evaluating a situation as threatening (the opposite of the pattern in the prefrontal cortex). Telling a research participant to expect possible shocks produces increased activity in the anterior cingulate cortex, and this leads to increased activity in the amygdala (Kalisch & Gerlicher, 2014). People with stronger connections between the anterior cingulate and the amygdala tend to pay more attention than average to threatening stimuli (Carlson, Cha, & Mujica-Parodi, 2013).

Another way to probe the role of the amygdala in emotional experience, increasingly possible for researchers, is to stimulate activity in the amygdala and observe the effects on the person's feelings. While we noted earlier that it is difficult to interfere directly with brain function in live human beings, one exception is when patients are undergoing brain surgery. Some of these patients are willing to do additional tasks, while their brain is exposed, for the sake of science. (An interesting question to ponder: If you were undergoing brain surgery or electrode placement for epilepsy treatment, would you agree to be a neuroscience research participant?)

One group of researchers recruited patients with temporal lobe epilepsy who agreed to have their amygdala electrically stimulated (that is, activated) and report on their emotional experiences during and after stimulation (Inman et al., 2020). Some patients received "active" stimulation of the amygdala; others "sham" stimulation (no actual stimulation, although the researchers pretended to do so); and a third group received stimulation in a nearby control area. The results indicated that amygdala stimulation led to a clear increase in skin conductance, along with a decrease in heart rate. These physiological effects are commonly shown in people whose attention is suddenly grabbed by some stimulus (Bradley, 2009). Most patients reported no corresponding change in emotional experience—no sudden rush of fear or apprehension, or any other general or specific emotional feelings.

Complicating the matter, however, two of the nine amygdala-stimulation patients *did* report an increase in negative emotion, and it was intense—a participant compared it to a moment where a vicious dog was about to leap on you in attack. One patient said that when his right amygdala was stimulated: "It just felt like, um, half of my body was scared. You know when you get scared and you get that attack. It pretty much just goes down the back of your neck, throughout the rest of your body. It's just only on my left side." The brain is structured contralaterally, so the right side of the brain governs the left side of the body and vice versa. Feeling these effects on the opposite side of the body from the amygdala stimulation is consistent with that principle. Fascinating! Clearly this is a small sample size with many individual differences adding noise to the results, but such a precise and striking effect suggests more research is warranted.

Does this all mean that amygdala activation *causes* fear? The evidence is not that clear-cut. Also, remember the reverse inference problem defined earlier. Research largely suggests that tasks evoking fear may cause amygdala activity, not the other way around. The findings that the amygdala becomes more active in response to other kinds of emotional stimuli, as well as frightening ones, and that patient SM could experience intense fear although she did not have amygdalae, indicate that amygdala activity is neither limited to nor necessary for subjective feelings of fear. A stronger case can be made for the amygdala's role in avoidance, although even that does not account for its (admittedly weak) responses to smiles and other positive stimuli. What alternative explanation might account for the evidence we have discussed so far?

The Amygdala and Emotional Memory

Suppose you hear a story that includes commonplace, unemotional details, plus a gruesome description of a child's injury. Almost certainly, you would remember the gruesome part more than the rest. Similarly, if you read a list of words that includes one highly emotional word, such as *murder*, you are more likely to remember that word than most of the others. People with amygdala damage do not show this emotional facilitation of memory, remembering the everyday content approximately as well as the emotional items (Cahill et al., 1994; LaBar & Phelps, 1998). Also, studies using fMRI indicate that amygdala activation while viewing emotional stimuli predicts later memory of those stimuli (Canli et al., 2000; Canli et al., 1999).

According to Elizabeth Phelps (2004; 2005), the amygdala serves two functions related to memory. First, it directs attention toward stimuli with emotional implications, such as the expression that the eyes show. Second, amygdala activation associated with the experience of a strong emotion facilitates activity in the hippocampus, a brain area known to be important for storing vivid memories of personal experience. In this way, amygdala activation "tags" particular memories as having strong emotional significance and instigates processes that enhance these memories for future reference. This explanation is consistent with the findings that the amygdala is more active when people are frightened, that amygdala lesions interfere with fear conditioning and emotional enhancement of memory, and that patients such as SM fail to learn from previous dangerous experiences, while also accounting for amygdala activation in emotional situations that do not involve fear.

Is it settled then—can we now be confident that the amygdala mediates attention to emotional stimuli and enhancement of emotional memories? It is a better explanation of the current evidence than the amygdala being the "fear area" of the brain. There may still be alternative explanations, however, and the research does suggest some degree of amygdala specialization for recognizing and avoiding bad situations. Moreover, even a structure as small as the amygdala may support several related psychological processes, rather than just one. For example, studies suggest that one part of the amygdala is important when an animal learns to avoid a dangerous area (because of shocks or other pain received there); another part is important for learning that a different area is safe; and still another part leads to the heavy breathing that occurs when in the dangerous area (Kim et al., 2013). When an animal learns that some light or sound signals probable shock, activation in one part of the amygdala triggers a change in heart rate, but another is responsible for the freezing response typical of a frightened animal (Viviani et al., 2011). Researchers are just beginning to understand how complex the brain is, and our measures are still crude relative to the tiny scale on which the brain operates—especially in humans.

Approach, Pleasure, and Reward

Human beings sometimes move toward unpleasant or threatening situations when doing so is consistent with their goals—witness the firefighter rushing into a burning building, the bodybuilder enduring physical agony to pursue a higher level of fitness, or the college students studying late into the night to achieve their goals. For the most part, though, when we think about approach behavior, we think about actively pursuing pleasant, enjoyable experiences. One of the first challenges facing researchers studying the neural basis of approach motivation has been to *define* pleasure and identify appropriate stimuli to use in experiments, both with humans and with nonhuman animals. This turns out to be more complicated than you might expect, and the process of disentangling different aspects of pleasure has led to valuable research on the brain's circuitry for both approach behavior and enjoyment.

As you will have noticed by this point in the chapter, much of what we know about emotion, motivation, and the brain comes from studies of nonhuman animals. The problem is that these creatures cannot tell us how they are feeling, and pleasure is not a state we can objectively measure. We can only make inferences based on how they behave—whether they approach or avoid certain stimuli or situations. For this reason, animal work on approach motivation is much more likely to use the word "reward" than the word "pleasure." Reward is easier to define through observable behavior. If an animal is willing to work or expend effort to acquire some stimulus (e.g., running a complex maze to earn a piece of cheese), that stimulus (the cheese) is a reward. The rewarding properties of a stimulus can also be demonstrated by giving it to an animal after a behavior you are trying to encourage. For example, you tell a dog to sit and then give it a small piece of bacon when it does. If giving the bacon increases the dog's probability of sitting upon command, the bacon has demonstrated its property as a reward (MNS: mmm, bacon!).

Early work observing nonhuman animals' approach behavior revealed several brain areas that appear critical for reward processing. For instance, researchers observed that rats will work to deliver electrical shocks to several brain areas, and before long discovered that these areas directly or indirectly increase release of the neurotransmitter dopamine in the **nucleus accumbens**. Later research indicated that many addictive drugs also release dopamine in the nucleus accumbens (Wise, 1996). In humans, sexual excitement activates the nucleus accumbens as well, as do pleasant music, the taste of sugar, or even imagining something pleasant (Costa et al., 2010; Damsma et al., 1992; Lorrain et al., 1999; Mueller et al., 2015). Gambling activates the area for habitual gamblers, and video games activate it for habitual video-game players (Breiter et al., 2001; Ko et al., 2009; Koepp et al., 1998). For these reasons the nucleus accumbens and one of its primary input structures, the ventral tegmental area, are often referred to as core structures of the brain's **reward circuit** (Figure 6.10).

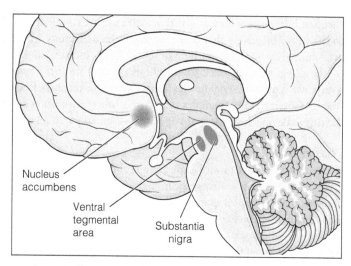

FIGURE 6.10.   The nucleus accumbens and ventral tegmental area are part of a neural circuit that appears important for anticipating rewards.

As with the amygdala and fear, the relationship between the nucleus accumbens and reward is complex. Some cells in this structure begin to fire when a reward is anticipated, more intensely for larger rewards, and their firing is inhibited when an expected reward does not arrive (Day, Jones, & Carelli, 2011; Schultz, Dayan, & Montague, 1997; Sugam et al., 2012). Dopamine activity in the nucleus accumbens also appears necessary for animals to approach stimuli that signal a reward is coming, such as a light that indicates a food treat will be delivered shortly. Injecting dopamine into the nucleus accumbens increases this behavior, and lesioning the nucleus accumbens, or blocking its dopamine receptors, will inhibit it (Blaiss & Janak 2009; J. Hoffmann & Nicola, 2014; Saunders & Robinson, 2012). However, nucleus accumbens activity is not necessary for all aspects of reward. Damage to this structure does not prevent eating, nor does it interfere with learning to self-administer cocaine or similar drugs (Ito, Robbins, & Everitt, 2004). Blocking dopamine input does not prevent a rodent from learning how to get a larger instead of a smaller reward (Floresco et al., 2006). Moreover, some cells in the nucleus accumbens respond to punishment as well as reward, supporting fear conditioning in a manner similar to the amygdala (Wendler et al., 2014).

Another important area for reward is the ventral caudate, part of the caudate nucleus. The caudate nucleus is located near the center the brain, close to the thalamus (see Figure 6.11). The caudate regulates movement, but has also been implicated in reward, motivation, and romantic love. In one fun study researchers investigated reward-related processing in the caudate and its associations with real-life behavioral choices in dogs (Cook et al., 2016). These researchers wanted to amass neuroscientific clues to the age-old question: Do our dogs truly love us, or do they just love the food we provide?

Their participants were a very select group of dogs who first went through extensive training to stay still in the fMRI scanner. They also went through training to learn that certain cues predicted the appearance of either food, their owner's praise, or no reward (see Figure 6.12). For food training, the dogs received pieces of hot dog after a toy horse

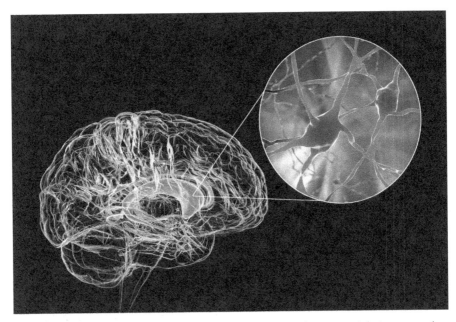

FIGURE 6.11. The ventral portion of the caudate nucleus is also activated during approach motivation.

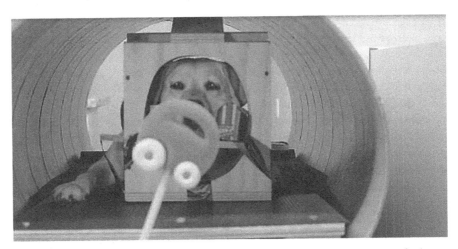

FIGURE 6.12. Subject Kady is viewing the car object (predicting owner praise was forthcoming) during her training sessions in a mock fMRI scanner.

was shown. (As a long-time dog owner and kennel volunteer, SRC assures you that hot dogs are extremely desirable treats for most dogs.) For praise training, the owner would emerge and praise the dog after a toy car was shown. No reward was given after the hairbrush was shown.

After this training the dogs entered the fMRI scanner and were shown these objects in different orders, while the researchers observed activation in their ventral caudates.

On another day the researchers brought the dogs out to a real room with a Y-shaped maze, and repeatedly let the dogs choose between going down one arm with food at the end, versus another with their owner at the end. If you have a dog, which do you predict they would choose?

Across different imaging days dogs showed a stable, greater ventral caudate response to cues predicting either food or praise, relative to the boring hairbrush. That is, some dogs consistently showed more caudate activation upon seeing the toy car (associated with praise), whereas others consistently showed more caudate activation in response to the toy horse (associated with food). Even more striking, the dogs' patterns of caudate activation to food versus praise cues successfully predicted the probability they would choose either the food or owner arms of the maze. In other words, dogs who showed greater caudate activation to cues predicting praise were more likely to run to greet their owner and ignore the food—and dogs who activated more to food cues were more likely to seek out the snack. There were only fifteen dogs in this study, and you might already be thinking that a dog who can tolerate all that training and also the experience of fMRI might not be your typical dog. This was not a representative sample. Still, it is compelling evidence that reward circuit activity may be linked to real-world choices in a social species other than our own.

Wanting, Liking, and the Nucleus Accumbens

We *can* ask humans how they are feeling as well as observing their behavior, so there is an opportunity to understand how more subjective aspects of motivation and emotional experience are linked to neural activity. Even at the level of subjective experience, however, pleasure and reward are a bit complicated. Let's take something most people seem to find pleasant: eating chocolate. Sounds delightful, right? What if you have just finished a huge holiday meal, and the prospect of eating another bite of *anything* is aversive rather than exciting? Or what if you are one of those rare people who don't enjoy chocolate at all? (SRC has a dear friend who experiences a full disgust response when she sees a picture of molten chocolate cake—she hates imagining burying her fork into a mountain of cake and having its guts ooze out on the plate.) The extent to which any particular stimulus is perceived as pleasant depends on the individual's preferences, needs, and goals, their current homeostatic balance, and the situational context (Sander & Nummenmaa, 2021).

Putting individual differences and extreme fullness aside, say that we successfully get a bunch of hungry chocoholics into the scanner. We then expose them to chocolate versus control stimuli, and observe brain activation differences across the two conditions. Here's a question, though: Should the chocolate stimuli be photographs of chocolate, or actual slivers of chocolate they get to taste? Would you expect these two chocolate stimuli to lead to identical reward circuit activation, or would you expect differences? In each case, the nucleus accumbens does become more active (e.g., Thomas et al., 2012). However, there are reasons from research with rodents to bet that even finer-grained measures of neural activity might show a difference.

Although we cannot ask laboratory rats how they are feeling, we can examine their brain's activity in different situations, such as when they first see a cue that they've learned means a treat is on the way, versus while they are eating the treat. Despite the tiny size of this brain region, evidence from research with rodents indicates that even the nucleus accumbens contains sub-regions or *microcircuits* supporting at least three distinct psychological processes (Berridge & Kringelbach, 2013; Floresco, 2015). The first microcircuit is active during anticipation of and movement toward a likely reward (Floresco, 2015; Hoffmann & Nicola, 2014). The word "likely" is important here. This region of the nucleus accumbens is more active while expecting or predicting a reward than when consuming it. For example, if you bought a ticket for a multimillion-dollar lottery, the nucleus accumbens would react strongly while you wait to see whether you have the winning number (Knutson et al., 2005). This microcircuit relies on the neurotransmitter dopamine for activation and communication with other brain structures. In humans the associated feeling is **anticipatory pleasure** associated with wanting, craving, and appetitive motivation.

The second microcircuit is active while a reward is being consumed (Berridge & Kringelbach, 2013). In humans this is experienced as **consummatory pleasure**, sensory enjoyment or liking. The distinction between *wanting* and *liking/enjoying* some reward is important. To return to our chocolate example, imagine eating many pieces of chocolate in one sitting. As you anticipate eating the first couple of pieces, you probably look forward to each one in an excited way. Once the chocolate is in your mouth, you savor its taste. The two experiences can be separated; after the first several pieces you may not anticipate the next so eagerly, but if another piece is placed in your mouth, it still tastes good. According to much research by Kent Berridge and his colleagues (2013), the nucleus accumbens contains several spots that mediate the subjective experience of liking. Importantly, however, these regions communicate primarily through opioid neurotransmitters rather than dopamine; this aspect of reward responding is not altered by techniques that manipulate dopamine activity.

Finally, further microcircuits of the nucleus accumbens are involved in learning to predict future rewards and punishments (Cox et al., 2015; Lammel, Lim, & Malenka, 2014). Cells in this region fire in response to unpredicted outcomes, detecting errors in prediction and updating expectations for the future. Even within this microcircuit, different dopamine receptors may mediate learning for predictors of positive versus negative outcomes (Cox et al., 2015).

This is a lot of activity in one small structure of the brain. There are many parallels to what we learned earlier about the amygdala. Like the amygdala, the nucleus accumbens appears to have multiple substructures or circuits that mediate different psychological processes. These are so small, and in some cases so intertwined, that we cannot yet distinguish them on an fMRI scan; the most recent work is done with cutting-edge technology for injecting neurotransmitters and/or receptor blockers into the brains of lab rodents (whose nucleus accumbens is sufficiently similar to our own). As with the amygdala, people argued for several years over which of these processes is really going on in the nucleus accumbens, until the evidence suggested that they all are. Both examples highlight that rather than jumping to quick conclusions about what a particular brain structure does, researchers must take their time to test many possibilities, and consider that multiple possibilities may all be correct.

BRAIN MECHANISMS OF EMOTION IN THE BODY

Learning Objectives

- Discuss the hypothalamus' role in maintaining the body's homeostasis, and analyze its role in the body's response to emotion-eliciting situations.
- Define interoception, and describe the insula's role in supporting interoception.

The amygdala and nucleus accumbens are far from the only brain structures supporting motivation and emotion. As we noted earlier, many structures communicate with the amygdala during fear and other states characterized by avoidance motivation, such as the anterior cingulate cortex and prefrontal cortex. Neuroimaging work has also revealed important roles in reward processing for the thalamus, some brainstem nuclei, anterior cingulate, and orbitofrontal and lateral frontal cortices—even our friend the amygdala (Sander & Nummenmaa, 2021). Moreover, not all structures important for emotion and motivation fall neatly into the approach/avoid/regulate divide, or are even specific to emotion or motivation.

However, some structures seem particularly important for what we experience as emotion, even if they are often active during not obviously emotional experience as well. Consider William James's proposal, discussed in Chapter 1, that the subjective feeling of emotion is caused by your perception of instinctive changes in the body upon perceiving some exciting stimulus. Examples included a pounding heart, sweating, and trembling. James never claimed that these visceral changes *only* occur during emotion, but he did propose that they were *necessary* for emotional feelings to occur. Many theorists agree that such visceral changes are at least a common and very salient aspect of subjective emotional experience. Fortunately, we know quite a bit about the brain regions supporting these changes and our ability to perceive them.

The Hypothalamus

The **hypothalamus** is a small structure located just above the brain stem and below the larger thalamus (see Figure 6.13). This little structure—yet again about the size of an almond—is critical for many life-or-death processes, regulating many motivational drives as well as generating aspects of our "fight-flight" and "rest-digest" responses (these will be described in detail in Chapter 7). The hypothalamus is often described as the body's thermostat, and it functions in that way, but it regulates more than temperature. Mammalian bodies are picky—they can function only when their body temperature, hydration, oxygen levels, sugar levels, salt levels, and other factors are all within a narrow range. The job of the hypothalamus is to monitor these factors and then initiate corrective change when some factor is out of range—to maintain **homeostasis** (a concept we first introduced in Chapter 4). The hypothalamus also collects sensory information coming from outside the body (e.g., pheromones in the air) as well as input from within the body (e.g., stomach fullness) and helps promote behaviors appropriate given the situation.

The hypothalamus initiates changes in the body for many reasons unrelated to emotion and motivational state: when your temperature is too high, the hypothalamus sends instructions to activate sweat glands, and when temperature is too low, it sends instructions to constrict blood vessels to the extremities so you conserve heat. When you exercise

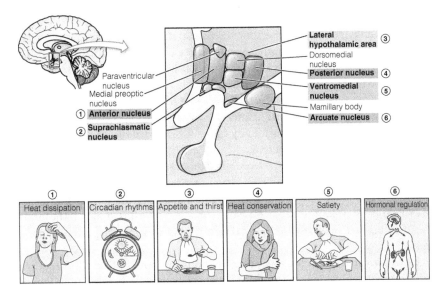

FIGURE 6.13. The hypothalamus regulates temperature, blood chemistry, hydration, and other processes via influence on the autonomic nervous system and endocrine system. From Cook et al. (2016).

and muscles consume more oxygen and glucose, you breathe faster to bring in more oxygen, organs release more glucose into the bloodstream, and the heart beats faster and harder to move all this stuff around. The hypothalamus initiates these changes when it detects that homeostasis has already been disrupted. However, the hypothalamus also receives cues that homeostasis is *likely* to be disrupted by upcoming activities, and it prepares the body accordingly. For example, it reacts to a frightening sight by increasing heart rate and sweating in preparation for possible fight-or-flight activities.

Hypothalamic control of hormones has similar flexibility. After prolonged psychological stress, the hypothalamus triggers the pituitary's release of cortisol, which increases blood sugar and speeds up metabolism. So, the hypothalamus controls many of the changes in the body that we experience during strong negative emotion and stress. However, the hypothalamus directs changes associated with pleasant motivational and emotional states as well. It has receptors for both leptin and ghrelin, two hormones discussed in Chapter 4, and it activates some physiological aspects of hunger and satiety. The hypothalamus also plays an important role in sexuality by controlling the profile of autonomic nervous system activation associated with sexual arousal and orgasm, and by triggering the pituitary gland's release of sex hormones into the bloodstream. One substructure within the hypothalamus appears to be important for sexual behavior and is sexually dimorphic—that is, different between males and females. In many species, the "sexually dimorphic nucleus" is nearly twice the size on average in males than in females (Swaab & Fliers, 1985) because of higher testosterone exposure during fetal development (Pei et al., 2006). Lesion studies with rats and mice also indicate the importance of this area for male sexual behavior (Balthazart & Ball, 2007).

The Insular Cortex: Processing Signals from the Body

The hypothalamus is central to generating the visceral changes that characterize emotion, but how do we become consciously aware of those changes? The **insular cortex**, or **insula**, is a region of the cortex tucked inside the fold between the temporal and parietal lobes (Figure 6.14). When human research had to rely almost entirely on observations of brain damage, researchers had trouble learning about the insula. Although many strokes damage the insula (because of a major artery coursing through the area), stroke damage is rarely limited to just this structure. Early consensus regarded the insula as the primary site in the cortex for perception of taste.

Given that view, psychologists were excited by an fMRI study indicating that viewing facial expressions of disgust produces strong activation of the insula (Phillips et al., 1997). Reports also indicated that people with insula damage did not react strongly to sights that usually evoke disgust, such as vomit, maggots, or a dirty toilet. If the insula is devoted to taste, it makes sense that damage to this area might specifically impair disgust.

However, later research using other methods did not confirm this tantalizing possibility (Gasquoine, 2014). A study of patients who had the insula removed on one side of the brain indicated impaired recognition of many facial expressions of emotion, but not much effect on recognition of disgust (Boucher et al., 2015). Researchers sometimes found an effect on disgust recognition and sometimes not. Furthermore, the insula is not limited to taste sensations. Fewer than 10% of neurons in the insula respond to taste.

Further research has shown that the insula *is* important for emotions, just in a different way. Activation of the insula largely reflects **interoception**—perception of the body itself, especially organs such as the heart, digestive system, bladder, muscles, and the skin. As the James–Lange theory predicts, people who perform better on an

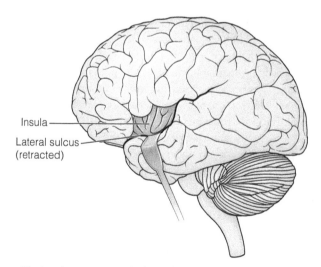

Insula
Lateral sulcus (retracted)

FIGURE 6.14. The insular cortex is tucked in a fold between the temporal and parietal lobes of the brain. It appears to mediate awareness of one's internal physical state and is strongly activated during disgust and fear.

interoception task (counting their own heartbeats), and who show stronger insula activity during this task, tend to report stronger subjective experiences of negative emotion (Critchley et al., 2004). People with damage to the insula tend to report weaker than average emotional feelings; they also report feeling less empathy when they see other people in distress (Boucher et al., 2015).

For instance, researchers for one study recruited 40 healthy university students in China to participate in an fMRI study of the relationship between interoception, the insula, and anxiety (Tan et al., 2018). Before the fMRI portion of the study, participants completed a heartbeat counting task in which they silently estimated their own heart rate while their actual heartbeats were measured using a device. This allowed for assessment of how accurate they were at estimating their heart rate—how good their interoception was. Participants also self-reported their levels of current anxiety (state anxiety), their typical levels of anxiety (trait anxiety), and wrote about anxious events occurring in the last five years. This writing exercise was in preparation for an anxiety-focus condition in the scans that occurred next.

During fMRI, the participants alternated between focusing their attention on their heartbeats, focusing their attention on their previously described anxious events, and focusing their attention on the noise of the scanner. The results revealed many significant associations among insula activation, interoception, and anxiety. Most interesting, however, was that mid-insular activation during the heartbeat attention condition predicted both how accurate participants were at counting their own heartbeats, and also their levels of state and trait anxiety. This finding led the researchers to conclude that mid-insula activity may be a critical link between heart-related interoception and anxiety.

CIRCUITRY FOR EMOTION REGULATION, SELF-REGULATION, AND INHIBITORY CONTROL

Learning Objectives
- Describe the role of the prefrontal cortex in inhibition of impulses and other aspects of self-regulation.
- Define frontotemporal lobar degeneration/dementia, and relate symptoms of this disorder to psychological processes supported by the prefrontal cortex.

Do you always do exactly what you feel like doing? Do you allow every emotional reaction to roll out in full force, without reconsideration or restraint? Do you give free rein to every impulse you have?

We really hope not. We can reasonably assume the descriptions above do not characterize you well. If you are reading this book you are probably in college, and people with no self-control or ability to regulate their emotions generally do not make it into higher education (congrats on that, by the way—it is a big deal!).

Think back to the last time you had a very strong emotion or undesirable motivational impulse, and you didn't act on it. Maybe a customer at work said something that got your blood boiling with fury, but you took a deep breath and smiled at them. Or your alarm went off in the morning and, despite your desire to hit the snooze button and go back to sleep, you hauled out of bed and got ready for class. Perhaps someone did something that initially made you feel hurt and upset, but you stopped to think about the action from their perspective, considered their feelings, and then decided what they had done was reasonable and fair. Each of these requires some degree and kind of self-regulation. We will consider the cognitive and behavioral processes involved in self-regulation in much more detail in Chapters 14 (where we discuss setting and pursuing goals) and 15 (where we explore emotion regulation). For now, let's focus on the brain circuits most critical for supporting this self-regulation.

The Prefrontal Cortex

The **prefrontal cortex**—the part of the brain forward of the motor and premotor areas of the frontal cortex—is important for "executive" cognitive functions such as planning, working memory, and the inhibition of impulses (Figure 6.15). This is a pretty huge chunk of real estate, by brain standards. Most of the structures we've discussed thus far are around the size of an almond, but the prefrontal cortex is more like the size of a small fist. A lot is going on in there: the mental activity supported by the prefrontal cortex is not easily reduced to a single phenomenon, and researchers are still trying to sort out how the circuitry works (Dixon et al., 2017; Friedman & Robbins, 2022). Regions of the prefrontal cortex appear crucial for the ability to inhibit impulsive behavior (Munakata et al., 2011). The ventromedial prefrontal cortex, in particular, is activated when people are asked to reinterpret or reappraise some stimulus in a less emotional way (Etkin, Büchel, & Gross, 2015). This activation inhibits the amygdala, and the overall effect is reduced emotional intensity (Goldin et al., 2008; Ochsner et al., 2002). The amygdala communicates with the prefrontal cortex as well, informing it of the possible emotional consequences of a decision and enabling selection of a good outcome (Shenhav & Greene, 2014).

A famous early case of brain injury was that of Phineas Gage, who in 1848 survived an explosion that sent an iron rod flying into his left cheek and out the top of his forehead. More than a century and a half later, researchers studied Gage's skull and determined that the rod had gone through the prefrontal cortex—specifically a region called the orbitofrontal cortex, which sits stop the bony casing around the back of the

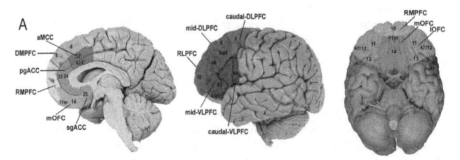

FIGURE 6.15. Subdivisions of the prefrontal cortex, as suggested by Dixon et al. (2017): sgACC, subgenual anterior cingulate cortex; pgACC, pregenual anterior cingulate cortex; aMCC, anterior mid-cingulate cortex; lOFC, lateral orbitofrontal cortex; mOFC, medial orbitofrontal cortex; RMPFC, rostromedial prefrontal cortex; DMPFC, dorsomedial prefrontal cortex; RLPFC, rostrolateral prefrontal cortex; VLPFC, ventrolateral prefrontal cortex; DLPFC, dorsolateral prefrontal cortex.

eyeballs—presumably causing major damage (Ratiu & Talos, 2004). Gage survived the accident and seemed to be in good physical health, but his personality changed. For example, he began dropping profanities all over, where previously his language had been more polite. Unfortunately, observers at the time published only brief, superficial reports about him. Later descriptions of the case grew more and more dramatic, and less and less based on fact. Gage apparently recovered enough to live a reasonably normal life, although we do not know nearly as much as we would like (Kotowicz, 2007).

In the 1990s, researchers reported extensive tests on a new patient, "Elliot," with prefrontal cortex damage caused by surgery to remove a tumor (Damasio, 1994; Damasio, 2002). After the surgery Elliot seemed normal in many regards, but he consistently had trouble making decisions. He deliberated endlessly about unimportant details, only to make a haphazard and often harmful choice in the end. He could neither plan for the future, nor follow plans that others suggested. He often put trivial tasks ahead of important tasks. For example, at work, when he was supposed to be sorting documents, he once stopped to read one of the documents for the rest of the afternoon. Everyone is distracted occasionally, but for Elliot this was a pattern. As a result, he could not hold a job. He divorced his first wife, married a woman who was clearly a bad choice, and then divorced her. He invested all his savings in a project that seemed sure to fail, and it did.

When people who knew Elliot noticed how much his behavior had deteriorated, they brought him to psychologists for testing (Damasio, 1994). Tests of vision, memory, language, and intelligence yielded mostly normal results. His only prominent abnormality was a lack of emotional reactivity. Even when he looked at photos of people injured in gory accidents, he showed none of the revulsion or distress that most people display.

The researchers tried to identify more precisely where Elliot's decision-making process went wrong. They presented him with hypothetical situations, such as "Imagine you went to a bank and the teller gave you too much change," or "Suppose you owned stock in a company and you learned that it was doing badly." In each case, Elliot was asked to suggest actions that he might take and then to predict the consequences of each action. He seemed to understand the possible courses of action and their consequences as well as anyone else. However, after describing all the possible actions he might take and all the probable consequences, he remarked, "And after all this, I still wouldn't know what to do!" (Damasio, 1994, p. 49).

What might cause this pattern? Studies with other patients who show damage in the same region can help pinpoint what is going on in the orbitofrontal cortex. Suppose you must choose between two decks of cards, each of which produces a gain or loss of money. You try both decks, and discover that Deck A has larger rewards than Deck B. However, Deck A also has larger losses, so in the long run you would do better with the slow, steady gains from Deck B. Most people gradually shift their preference to Deck B, but many people with prefrontal damage continue choosing mostly from Deck A (Bechara, 2004; Bechara et al., 1999).

The problem seems not to be with knowing the rewards and punishments that are likely to follow from one's actions. Like Elliot, most patients with orbitofrontal cortex damage can describe the likely consequences of their behavior, even when they are making bad decisions. One hypothesis is that they do not anticipate how they will *feel* after one outcome or another. According to this interpretation, Elliot makes poor decisions because he cannot imagine whether an outcome would make him feel good or bad. If you cannot imagine your future feelings, one outcome seems as good as another. In short, imagining both the possible outcomes of some situation, and your emotional outcomes to those outcomes, is an essential basis for making a good decision.

Many (but by no means all) patients with damage to the prefrontal cortex display flat emotions, coupled with poor, impulsive decision-making. They express less empathy than average for people in distress (Shamay-Tsoory et al., 2004), show less ability to interpret people's facial expressions (Jenkins et al., 2014), and experience less sense of guilt after hurting someone. Would you be willing to kill one person if you thought doing so would save the lives of five others? Patients with this type of brain damage say yes, as do many other people, but unlike most people, the patients typically say so with no hesitation and no evidence of mixed feelings (Ciaramelli et al., 2007). Some calmly say it would be okay even if the person you had to kill was your own daughter (Thomas, Croft, & Tranel, 2011). Some say it would be okay to kill an annoying boss if they thought they could get away with it (Taber-Thomas et al., 2014). So, the ability to imagine hypothetical situations, and generate an emotional response is central to moral decision-making as well as good practical judgment.

Researchers have also used fMRI to study the role of the prefrontal cortex in decision-making in people with an intact brain. In one study, individuals who showed greater prefrontal activation while considering a financial gamble were especially responsive to the size of the potential loss (Tom et al., 2007). In other studies, prefrontal activation tracked the subjective value of a possible reward, based on both the possible size of the reward and the probability of winning (Peters & Büchel, 2009; Pine et al., 2009). In short, parts of the prefrontal cortex appear to respond to the probable outcomes of a decision.

Frontotemporal Dementia

In a condition called **frontotemporal lobar dementia** (or **frontotemporal degeneration**), parts of the frontal and temporal lobes of the cerebral cortex gradually degenerate (Figure 6.16). A common early effect is serious impairment of social behavior. These patients have much trouble interpreting others' nonverbal expressions, such as facial expression, tone of voice, or body posture (Van den Stock et al., 2015). Unable to discern people's emotions, they show a lack of empathy or concern for others (Oliver et al., 2015). In an interesting twist on this effect, patients with frontotemporal dementia also show deficits in ability to understand emotional messages in music and art without words (Shiota et al., 2019). For example, most people, at least in Western countries, recognize that slow music, played in a minor key, sounds sad, whereas quick-paced music in a major key sounds cheerful. Patients with frontotemporal dementia are much less likely to make these connections.

They also show a lack of embarrassment. Suppose an experimenter asks you to sing, karaoke style, in a room by yourself. Without warning you, the experimenter videotapes your performance and later shows that videotape while you watch. If your singing skills are, like most people's, not up to *American Idol* standards, you would feel embarrassed, right? People with frontotemporal lobar degeneration seem unperturbed, no matter how bad their singing (Sturm et al., 2008).

What ties these different effects together? One theme seems to involve being oblivious to other people's feelings and perspective—an effect that might be due to

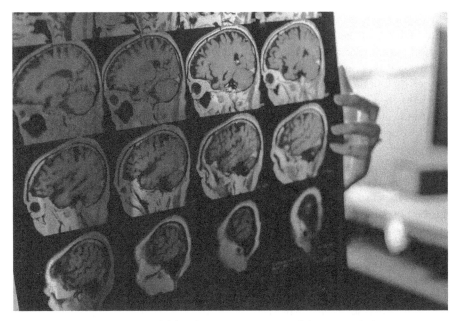

FIGURE 6.16. Frontotemporal lobar degeneration-associated damage to the brain.

deterioration of regions of the temporal cortex, as well as the prefrontal cortex. However, consequences for experience and behavior vary depending on the exact location and extent of damage. This is one example where studying specific patterns of symptoms in people with lesions in varying locations can actually help us decode the psychological processes supported by specific regions and circuits of the brain.

EMOTION NEUROCHEMISTRY

Learning Objectives
- Identify important functions of dopamine, opioids, serotonin, and oxytocin, critically evaluating claims seen in popular media.

Saying that the amygdala responds to threatening information, or that the nucleus accumbens responds to rewards, is somewhat like saying that people in Iowa grow corn. This is true, but not *everyone* in Iowa grows corn. Similarly, not every synapse in the amygdala or every synapse in the nucleus accumbens has the same function. For more detailed information, it helps to study neurotransmitters and their receptors. Here we briefly review a few neurotransmitters that seem to play key roles in emotional experience.

Dopamine
Several pathways in the brain release **dopamine**, including much of the reward circuit we discussed earlier in this chapter. The dopamine pathway from the ventral tegmental area to the nucleus accumbens is highly active after an unpredicted reward, and activity decreases when an expected reward fails to appear (Pignatelli & Bonci, 2015). Activity in

this path serves to increase attention and facilitate learning about how to get some reward. A set of dopaminergic axons leading from an area called the *substantia nigra* contributes to any behavior related to active approach (Ikemoto, Yang, & Tan, 2015). This path deteriorates in Parkinson's disease, a condition marked by difficulty in initiating movements, lack of vigor in most movements, and depressed mood. Dopamine axons also become less active than normal in people with major depression, and most effective pharmaceutical treatments for depression increase dopamine release. Dopamine is also important for cognitive operations in the frontal lobes, and typical antipsychotic drugs (those used to alleviate schizophrenia) act by blocking dopamine synapses. However, drugs that block dopamine in one place also block it in other places, and so a common side effect is a feeling of "flat" emotion (Arana, 2000).

The use of stimulant drugs such as cocaine and amphetamine causes a substantial increase in dopamine receptor activity in the nucleus accumbens. Cocaine binds to the transporters that would normally facilitate reuptake of dopamine (as well as serotonin) into the axon of the presynaptic neuron, so that dopamine remains longer in the synapse, prolonging its effect. Amphetamines block reuptake and increase dopamine release. Most other drugs of abuse also serve to increase dopamine activity, sometimes indirectly by blocking something that inhibits dopamine release. Furthermore, as noted previously, gambling and habitual video-game playing can also yield an increase dopamine activity. From these observations, psychologists and neuroscientists formed the hypothesis that addictive behaviors depend on dopamine.

However, when we think some aspect of brain functioning is simple, we are often wrong. Heroin and nicotine are highly addictive drugs, but their use results in only small increases in dopamine activity, and sometimes none. Methylphenidate (Ritalin), when used in therapeutic doses for attention deficit disorder, produces much more dopamine activity with less potential for addiction. In short, the amount of dopamine activity caused by some substance correlates only moderately with its potential for addiction, and it's not clear that dopamine per se is the problem (Nutt et al., 2015). The good news is that researchers are working hard to understand the relationship between dopamine and addiction in a more nuanced way, with the hope of finding more effective treatments.

β-Endorphin and the Opioid Peptides

The opioid peptides are another class of neurotransmitters that relate to pleasure and reinforcement. The best known of these is **β-endorphin**, a neurotransmitter that serves as a natural painkiller. The term "endorphin" is a contraction of *endogenous morphine* because it acts like a self-produced morphine. Pain does not always release endorphins, but when it does, the endorphins put on the brakes to limit pain. Many types of pleasant activity also release endorphins, including sex, a "runner's high," or listening to music that thrills you (Goldstein, 1980). Endorphin receptors contribute to the pleasant sensations and addictive potential of alcohol, cocaine, nicotine, and other abused drugs (Roth-Deri, Green-Sadan, & Yadid, 2008; Tseng et al., 2013).

Could the neurotransmitter that relieves physical pain also relieve social pain? When people talk about "hurt feelings," is it like hurt in any literal sense? In one study, infant guinea pigs cried when separated from their mothers (presumably indicating distress), but if they were given a mild dose of morphine (stimulating endorphin receptors), the crying stopped. When given naloxone, a drug that blocks endorphin activity, they cried harder than usual (Herman & Panksepp, 1978). This effect has been repeated with several other mammalian species, suggesting that the pain of social loss and rejection may be alleviated by the same mechanisms that help manage physical pain (MacDonald & Leary, 2005). Among humans, researchers have demonstrated that variations in the gene for an endorphin receptor predict individual differences in social rejection sensitivity, as well as the intensity of responses to rejection in pain-related brain areas such as the anterior cingulate cortex (Way, Taylor, & Eisenberger, 2009).

Oxytocin

The pituitary gland releases the neuropeptide **oxytocin**, which serves several purposes throughout the body (Figure 6.17). It causes contractions during labor and delivery of children. It also facilitates nursing. Oxytocin levels increase during sexual arousal and orgasm. In many animal species, evidently including humans, oxytocin and the similar hormone *vasopressin* promote pair-bonding between mates and between parents and offspring (Avinun, Ebstein, & Knafo, 2012; McCall & Singer, 2012; Walum et al., 2012). One study indicated that men with a less active form of the vasopressin receptor were less likely to marry, less likely to show affection, and more likely to consider divorce (Walum et al., 2008).

Oxytocin also occurs in the brain, as a neurotransmitter (many chemicals occur both as hormones and as neurotransmitters). Because of the effects just described, some researchers have called oxytocin the *love hormone* or *love neurotransmitter*. However, that description is overstated and misleading, at best. Let's consider the research.

Researchers sometimes give people oxytocin as a nasal spray and compare the results to people given a placebo. In one study, heterosexual men who reported being in love rated the attractiveness of their partners and other women, before and after the nasal spray. Oxytocin increased their attractiveness rating of the loved partner, but not of the other women (Scheele et al., 2013). That is, oxytocin use resulted in magnified love only if love was already present. (You can't use this as a love potion to make someone fall in love with you.) In a related study, researchers gave oxytocin or placebo to heterosexual men shortly before they met an attractive woman. Men who were in a monogamous relationship reacted to the oxytocin by standing farther away from the attractive woman, compared to results in men who were not given oxytocin (Scheele et al., 2012). These results suggest the oxytocin made the men even more loyal to their partners.

Would you expect oxytocin to increase trust? Perhaps, and several studies suggest that it does so, at least toward people you already trusted (Olff et al., 2013; Poulin, Holman, & Buffone, 2012; Van Ijzendoorn & Bakermans-Kranenburg, 2012). On the

FIGURE 6.17. Activities involving the neuropeptide oxytocin.

other hand, other researchers began expanding the questions they asked in their research studies to conditions under which oxytocin might affect trust in other ways. These studies have shown that oxytocin also may increase defensive aggression against out-groups (De Dreu, et al., 2010) and in patients with a psychiatric diagnosis called borderline personality disorder, oxytocin *decreased* rather than increased trust (Bartz et al., 2011). Researchers in such studies suggest the hypothesis that oxytocin increases attention to social cues, magnifying the inclinations that are already felt. This interpretation is a lot different than oxytocin being a simple "moral molecule" everyone should go around sniffing!

Moreover, many studies on oxytocin in humans have some serious methodological challenges (Nave, Camerer, & McCullough, 2015; Mierop et al., 2020). Unlike studies with laboratory animals, in which researchers inject oxytocin directly into the brain or measure its levels in the brain, human research relies mostly on nasal sprays, and it is unclear how much oxytocin reaches the brain or how soon, if at all. Other researchers have measured oxytocin levels in the blood or saliva, hoping that those levels indicate brain levels as well, but that assumption is also uncertain. Furthermore, the results concerning trust and other social behaviors are highly variable from one study to another, indicating either that the effects are small or that they depend on specific conditions. For the time being, we should reserve judgment about the specific effects of oxytocin on human emotion and social behavior.

THEORIES OF EMOTION: EVIDENCE FROM NEUROSCIENCE

Learning Objectives

- Evaluate the current neuroimaging evidence for and against the main theories of emotion: basic/discrete emotions, dimensional accounts, and social construction.

We noted at the beginning of this chapter that each major theory of emotion leads to specific predictions about what emotion should look like in the brain. Many researchers have addressed these predictions, questioning whether different emotions are linked to activation in different regions or networks in the brain. According to basic/discrete emotions theory, it should be possible to identify these distinctions. Psychological construction theory posits that these distinctions should not exist, and instead, all emotions should involve activation of common brain regions mediating conscious experience, conceptualization, and language (Barrett, 2006). Which theory has better support?

You might think that researchers would have agreed on a clear answer to this question by now, but alas, they have not. In the last chapter we introduced the technique of meta-analysis, a statistical procedure for combining effects across many different studies and asking whether the total evidence indicates the presence of some effect. Two separate meta-analyses by two teams of researchers, published just two years apart and including comparable sets of studies, reached opposing conclusions on this point. Katherine Vytal and Stephen Hamann (2010) concluded that their meta-analysis did find support for basic emotions in the brain. Kristen Lindquist and colleagues (Lindquist et al., 2012) concluded that their analysis failed to provide any such evidence, and argued instead for a psychological construction approach. How can this be?

The discrepancy occurred because the two sets of researchers asked different questions. The use of meta-analysis helps to pull different studies together to answer a specific question, but the researcher must decide exactly how the question will be framed. Lindquist and colleagues (2012) pointed to previously published suggestions that four basic emotions were located in particular structures in the brain: fear in the amygdala, disgust in the insula, sadness in the anterior cingulate cortex, and anger in the orbitofrontal cortex. We discussed each of these structures earlier in the chapter, and if you were reading carefully, you should already be skeptical about these associations. The researchers asked whether each structure was more active during the hypothesized emotion than during all other emotions combined. They failed to find evidence for this, instead showing that many different emotions are associated with activation in regions previously linked to language, attentional control, and visualization.

Others have argued, however, that these analyses were asking the wrong question (Buck, 2012; Hamann, 2012; Pessoa, 2012). Recall our description of basic emotions theory from Chapters 1 and 2. According to proponents of this theory, emotions serve to coordinate many sensory, cognitive, physiological, and behavioral processes that otherwise tend to operate separately (Ekman, 1992; Levenson, 1999; Tooby & Cosmides, 2008). Such researchers suggest that emotions should involve different patterns of activity across the various structures and substructures supporting these psychological processes, not that all aspects of a given emotion should be localized in a single chunk of brain. In general, neuroscientists are leery of claims that any complex psychological phenomenon can be pinned down to a single structure, and instead emphasize the importance of networks connecting many structures and the precise processes they support. Thus, even if the basic emotions view is correct, emotions should emerge from coordinated activity across many regions—often referred to as a circuit—rather than activity in one large region (Pessoa, 2012).

Researchers conducting the other meta-analysis asked a question more consistent with this proposal. Vytal and Hamann (2010) aggregated findings across studies for every voxel in the brain (a voxel is like a pixel, but in three dimensions) for every contrast between a specific emotion and a neutral reference condition. They then asked two questions: (1) For each emotion, is it possible to identify regions that are *consistently activated*? (2) For each pair of emotions, is it possible to identify regions that are *more active in one emotion than in the other*? In both cases, the answer was yes, with several regions for each emotion or contrast between emotions. This finding indicates that different emotions are associated with different patterns of activation in the brain.

The Vytal and Hamann (2010) meta-analysis has strengths, but also important limitations. First, it's not clear that all studies really evoked emotional responses, or that what one study called sadness was the same as sadness in another study. Most researchers used photos of other people's facial expressions as the stimuli. As we noted in Chapter 5, looking at someone else's expression may or may not elicit the same emotion in the viewer. Second, Vytal and Hamann (2010) caution that showing some brain area is *active* during an emotion is not the same as showing it is *necessary* for that emotion, or that it causes or defines that emotion's experience. For example, their analysis indicated that an area of the prefrontal cortex is often activated during anger, but given what is already known about the prefrontal cortex, it's more likely that this activation reflects attempts to regulate anger rather than a cause of anger itself.

Third, the specific regions associated with each emotion in this analysis did not make obvious sense—it was not easy to look at the patterns and think, "of course, that is what we'd expect for emotion *X*." This is not surprising, since the analyses were completely data driven rather than tests of hypotheses linking emotions to particular structures on theoretical grounds, but it does make the findings hard to interpret.

Fourth, although the researchers did examine different structures for each emotion, rather than just one, they did not study brain networks. To do this, Vytal and Hamann (2010) would need to use techniques to figure out which structures were active at the same time, which was not possible with the data they had. Finally, the imaging technology and analysis strategy yielded crude spatial resolution relative to the level of resolution in the brain. As we saw with the amygdala and nucleus accumbens, even tiny structures can support several distinguishable processes, which could not have been teased apart in these analyses.

Recent investigations have offered a more circuit-based account, taking advantage of new statistical techniques to analyze brain activation patterns in existing data. Again, they found evidence both for and against the idea that basic emotions are discernable in patterns of brain activation. For instance, Zhou and colleagues (2021) examined fMRI data from three separate samples of participants undergoing fear induction, using a computerized analysis technique called machine learning. Participants in these studies viewed dangerous or scary visual images, and tried to imagine being in these situations in real life (see Figure 6.18). The researchers also evaluated activation patterns related to learning about threat cues, as well as patterns related to general negative affect; this is important because, as we saw earlier, these latter psychological processes often accompany fear without actually *being* fear. Analyses revealed a reliable network of brain regions (including the prefrontal cortex, insula, and amygdala, among others) associated with participants' self-reports of fear. These activation patterns were specific to fear as compared with threat detection or generally unpleasant feelings. The researchers concluded that the activation serves as a "brain signature" for feeling subjectively fearful, which probably sounds a lot like basic emotion theory to you.

However, another recent study used fMRI to measure brain activity as people watched the emotionally charged movie *Forrest Gump*, while also reporting on their subjective feelings of fear, anger, sadness, disgust, happiness, and surprise (Lettieri et al., 2019). The researchers attempted to correlate the emotional reactions with the brain activity, focusing on several regions including the right temporoparietal junction—a region important in social and emotional processing. Within the temporoparietal junction they found evidence for three "gradients" or patterns of activity linked to participants' emotional experience. The first appeared to reflect degree of positivity versus negativity, what we previously called valence. The second reflected intensity of feeling, what we sometimes called arousal. The third they called "complexity," which ranged from events that caused a quick emotional response (mostly fear) to events that were ambiguous or ambivalent, and required more thinking and interpretation. They found no evidence for basic emotions, except insofar as happiness equates to one direction of the valence dimension.

(a) Fear induction fMRI paradigm used in the discovery cohort (80 stimuli in total, distributed over 4 runs)

(b) Fear induction fMRI paradigm used in the validation cohort (60 stimuli in total, distributed over 2 runs)

(c) Analysis stages

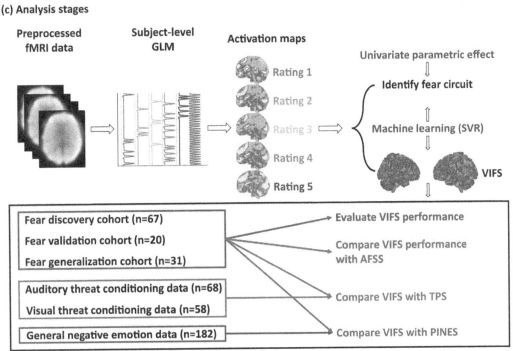

FIGURE 6.18.   Model of the fear induction research design in which participants were asked to view dangerous images and imagine themselves into the situations depicted, and then rate how fearful they felt. From Zhou et al. (2021).

In short, this study provided more evidence for a gradient or dimensional theory of emotions, not a list of basic emotions.

Why do the two studies disagree? Again, they're asking different questions—one about feeling emotion, the other about responding to another's emotions as depicted in a movie (this interpretation is most consistent with other evidence about the temporoparietal junction)—so it's not all that surprising they point toward different answers. Clearly, the jury is still out! Researchers have a long way to go before neuroscience methods can yield information about which theory of emotion is "right." Moreover, much as we concluded when first introducing these theories, it's highly possible that each is right in its own way and for different aspects of the emotional experience.

SUMMARY

When fMRI technology first became widely available in the 1980s and 1990s, affective scientists were very excited. Here, finally, was the technique needed to answer difficult questions about the nature and structure of emotion, once and for all! It has not proved so simple. Even cutting-edge human neuroscience methods are crude relative to the scale of activity in the brain; more precise techniques can be used with small animals, but not with people. Researchers have argued extensively about how to test various theories, and because different researchers try to elicit emotions in different ways, it's difficult to aggregate their findings. The data clearly contradict the notion that any one emotion can be localized to a single structure in the brain, but no theory of emotion insists that should be the case.

If you take one core message away from this chapter, we hope it's that claims based on neuroscience should be evaluated as critically as claims based on any other kind of evidence—perhaps even more so. Despite its promise, neuroscience is just another method. It may seem more daunting than other common methods in psychology, but that's largely because it's so new, and there is so much about the brain that we still don't know. The brain is extremely complex—far more so than researchers appreciated even a decade ago. Even the best-informed experts know little about how neurons create psychological experience and behavior.

Rather than being either intimidated or unduly entranced by neuroscience methods, we hope you will apply the same critical analysis to study methods and findings that you would for any other study. What exactly was the research question? Was emotion manipulated in a reasonably valid way, given that question? Are the conclusions drawn from the findings consistent with core principles of logic, or are the researchers committing logical fallacies? Have we learned anything about psychological processes from the study, beyond what areas of the brain "light up" while they take place? Are alternative interpretations of the findings adequately considered? Are conclusions consistent with findings from other study methods, both within and outside neuroscience? Affective neuroscience has enormous promise, but it will take patience and many mistakes along to way to realize researchers' goals.

KEY TERMS

amygdala: a structure within the brain's temporal lobe important for evaluating emotional information, especially threatening information, and for enhancing emotional memories (p. 200)

anticipatory pleasure: positive feelings in anticipation of a reward, characterized by wanting, craving, and appetitive motivation (p. 211)

behavioral activation system: a hypothesized system of neural structures thought to support approach toward opportunities and important resources (p. 200)

behavioral inhibition system: a hypothesized system of neural structures thought to support avoidance of threats (p. 200)

β-endorphin: a neurotransmitter that serves as a natural painkiller (p. 220)

central nervous system: the brain and spinal cord (p. 187)

cingulate cortex: an area that surrounds part of the corpus callosum near the center of the brain, important for a variety of cognitive, memory, and emotional functions (p. 204)

consummatory pleasure: positive feelings during the enjoyment of a reward, characterized by sensory enjoyment or liking (p. 211)

dopamine: one of the brain's neurotransmitters, important for appetitive behaviors and positive mood, among other functions (p. 219)

electroencephalography (EEG): technique that uses electrodes on the scalp to measure electrical potentials generated by neurons (p. 192)

evoked potentials or **event-related potentials:** rapid changes in the electroencephalogram signal in response to particular stimuli (p. 192)

fear conditioning: a procedure in which one learns that a new stimulus, such as a tone or color, predicts an electrical shock or other aversive event (p. 202)

frontotemporal lobar degeneration or **dementia:** gradual deterioration of the frontal and temporal lobes of the cerebral cortex, producing variable effects that sometimes include greatly impaired social behaviors (p. 218)

functional magnetic resonance imaging (fMRI): a technique used to measure changes in blood oxygenation, indicated by changes in the magnetic properties of hemoglobin, as a way of assessing where neurons have recently been active (p. 193)

functional near-infared spectroscopy (fNIRS): a technique used to measure changes in blood oxygenation, much like fMRI, but is based on measuring changes in the absorption of light at the level of the scalp (p. 198)

homeostasis: the body's regulation of temperature, blood chemistry, hydration, and other variables, keeping them within a healthy range (p. 212)

hypothalamus: a structure located just above the brain stem and below the thalamus; directs the pituitary gland and regulates variables such as body temperature, hunger, and thirst (p. 212)

hyperscanning: a neuroimaging research design in which two or more human beings are scanned at the same time, often during social interaction (p. 199)

insular cortex, or **insula:** a region of the cortex tucked between the temporal and parietal lobes; important for perception of visceral sensations (p. 214)

interoception: perception of the body itself, especially its interior (p. 214)

Klüver–Bucy syndrome: a pattern of emotional changes accompanying removal of both anterior temporal lobes, including the amygdalae (p. 201)

lesion: damage to part of the brain (p. 190)

limbic system: a set of neural structures originally proposed by Paul MacLean (1952) as the emotion network of the brain (p. 188)

neurotransmitters: the chemicals that neurons use to communicate with one another (p. 196)

nucleus accumbens: a structure that receives information relating to reward, focuses attention, and energizes behaviors that might lead to reward (p. 207)

oxytocin: a hormone and neurotransmitter that facilitates bonding and may increase attention to social cues (p. 221)

prefrontal cortex: the region forward of the motor areas of the frontal cortex, associated with self-regulation, memory, effortful cognition, and some emotion-related processes (p. 216)

reverse inference: a logical fallacy in which evidence that Predictor A causes Outcome B is taken to mean that if B is present, A must be as well. This often happens in psychology when A is a psychological process and B is a biological one (p. 197)

reward circuit: an interconnected set of brain structures, including the nucleus accumbens and ventral tegmental area, that play important roles in approach motivation, enjoyment, and behavioral responses to reward (p. 207)

serotonin: a neurotransmitter involved in many sensory, cognitive, and emotional processes (p. 196)

THOUGHT/DISCUSSION QUESTIONS

1. What evidence would convince you that activation in some brain region *Y* causes some psychological process *X* or is at least necessary for it? For example, if researchers claim that one tiny location is responsible for detecting faces (Kanwisher, McDermott, & Chun, 1997), what evidence would convince you they are right?

2. Many neuroscience researchers have addressed hypotheses from basic emotions theory, but fewer have tested other major theories of emotion. What do you think an fMRI study testing the component process model might look like?

3. An fMRI study has indicated that people reading sentences meant to evoke embarrassment showed greater activation in part of the right temporal cortex than people reading neutral control sentences. Think of several explanations of this finding (i.e., what psychological process might be mediated by the right temporal cortex) other than concluding that this region is the "embarrassment center of the brain."

4. Before reading this chapter, which theory of emotion did you find most compelling or convincing? Has the evidence reviewed above shifted your opinion?

SUGGESTIONS FOR FURTHER READING

Barrett, L. F. (2017). *How emotions are made: The secret life of the brain.* Houghton Mifflin Harcourt. A comprehensive overview of the history and current controversies in not just affective neuroscience, but also emotion science in general.

Lieberman, M. D. (2013). *Social: Why our brains are wired to connect.* Crown. An engaging, early review of the growing field of social and affective neuroscience with continuing relevance.

Poldrack, R. A. (2018). *The new mind readers: What neuroimaging can and cannot reveal about our thoughts.* Princeton University Press. A cogent overview of both the promise and limitations of neuroimaging to understand human experience.

Shackman, A. J., & Wager, T. D. (2019). The emotional brain: Fundamental questions and strategies for future research. *Neuroscience Letters, 693*, 68–74. This article introduces and offers an overview of a multiarticle special issue on the neuroscience of emotion.

CHAPTER 7

The Autonomic Nervous System and Hormones

Think about a time when you were really nervous about something. Maybe you were about to take an important test, or perhaps you had to stand before a large audience to give a speech. Maybe you were worried about a loved one who was sick or hurt. Perhaps you were working up the nerve to ask someone out on a date. Remember that experience vividly. How did your body feel?

See how well this describes your experience: your heart was pounding faster and harder than usual. Your hands were cold and a little damp. Your stomach churned and felt queasy. Your mouth was dry. Your muscles were tense, and your hands trembled. Maybe you were even afraid you would wet your pants. Does any of this sound familiar?

In his book *The Feeling of What Happens*, Antonio Damasio (1999) wrote that "emotions use the body as their theater" (p. 51). As we noted in an earlier chapter, many other emotion theorists have also emphasized the body's central role in emotional feelings. William James (1884) wrote that an individual's perception of physiological and behavioral changes *is* his or her feeling of emotion. Think back on the intensely emotional experiences you've had throughout your life. How did your body feel during those experiences? Can you think of any strong emotions that did *not* include a bodily reaction?

As you know from previous chapters, many scientists theorize that emotions evolved to prepare us for actions that are likely to be adaptive in certain circumstances. Many of the physical changes associated with emotion are carried out by the branch of the nervous system known as the autonomic nervous system, as well as by hormones running through the bloodstream. In this chapter, we consider these systems that communicate commands from the brain to the rest of the body. We also consider evidence regarding the importance of physiological aspects of emotion for emotional feelings. Finally, we will highlight the physiological aspects of stress, and explain why prolonged or severe stress sometimes threatens not just emotional well-being, but also physical health.

THE AUTONOMIC NERVOUS SYSTEM
Learning Objectives
- Define the autonomic nervous system and its functions.
- Explain why the sympathetic nervous system is often called the "fight or flight" system and the parasympathetic the "rest and digest" system. Elaborate on how these two systems work together to support the body.

Think back to the physical sensations associated with nervousness, as described above. Although these diverse sensations are spread throughout the body, a single system directs them. The **autonomic nervous system** consists of two chains of neurons (one on the left and one on the right) alongside the spinal cord with connections to organs such as the heart, lungs, stomach, intestines, genitals, and even the smooth muscle surrounding the arteries (Figure 7.1). The autonomic nervous system both sends information to the organs and receives information from them. That is, it has both input and output functions.

The autonomic nervous system plays an important role in regulating heart rate, breathing, and other functions that keep the body alive and functioning. When you stand up after sitting down for a while, your autonomic system adjusts your blood pressure to prevent you from fainting. When you walk up a flight of stairs, you're able to make it to the top because the same system has caused an increase in your heart rate to deliver more blood sugar and oxygen to your muscles. When you are hot, the autonomic nervous system serves to increase sweating. When you get cold, blood flow to your skin is reduced to help conserve heat at your core. Also, the hairs on your body stand up, giving you goose bumps. The function is to trap warm air close to your skin and increase insulation. (That function accomplishes almost nothing for humans because our body hairs are so short, but it was important to our ancient, hairier ancestors and still is to dogs, cats, and many other mammals.)

Figure 7.1 shows the structure of the autonomic nervous system. The autonomic nervous system's two major branches, the sympathetic and parasympathetic nervous systems, connect to many of the same organs, although some receive input from only the sympathetic system. In some cases (but not all!), the sympathetic and parasympathetic systems have opposing effects. Let's examine these branches and their functions.

Fight or Flight: The Sympathetic Nervous System
The sensations we associate with nervousness and other types of arousal largely reflect increased activation of the **sympathetic nervous system**. This system increases heart rate, increases breathing rate and expands the bronchioles (sacs) in the lungs, inhibits digestion, dilates the pupils, increases sweating, and increases blood flow to the muscles while decreasing flow to the stomach and intestines, among a variety of other effects. Early investigators wondered what all these functions had in common. Then a famous physiologist, Walter Cannon (1915), had an *a-ha* insight: all these changes prepare the body for vigorous activity! In an emergency, you need to be ready for "fight or flight." You need more heart activity, more blood and fuel to the muscles, and more sweat to prevent overheating. You save energy by cutting back on digestive activities, you provide more blood to the muscles by providing less to the stomach and intestines, and while you are fighting for your life, it is not a good time to get distracted by sex.

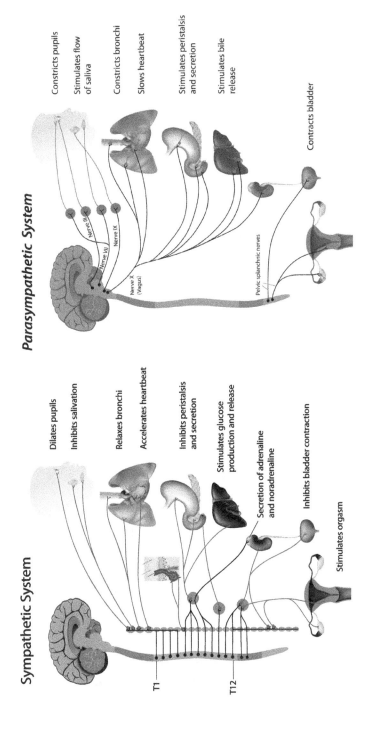

Sympathetic System

- Dilates pupils
- Inhibits salivation
- Relaxes bronchi
- Accelerates heartbeat
- Inhibits peristalsis and secretion
- Stimulates glucose production and release
- Secretion of adrenaline and noradrenaline
- Inhibits bladder contraction
- Stimulates orgasm

T1
T12

Parasympathetic System

- Constricts pupils
- Stimulates flow of saliva
- Constricts bronchi
- Slows heartbeat
- Stimulates peristalsis and secretion
- Stimulates bile release
- Contracts bladder

Nerve III
Nerve VII
Nerve IX
Nerve X (Vagus)
Pelvic splanchnic nerves

FIGURE 7.1.   The autonomic nervous system consists of two branches. The sympathetic nervous system prepares the body for intense muscular action. The parasympathetic nervous system facilitates digestion, growth, and reproduction.

The sympathetic nervous system causes blood flow to shift from some body parts to others by controlling vasoconstriction (tightening) of the smooth muscles surrounding the arteries. Arteries leading to the digestive system and genitals are tightened, whereas arteries leading to the large muscles and brain remain relaxed. The result is more blood for your muscles and your brain. You also need to avoid losing too much blood if you are wounded. Consistent with this, the sympathetic nervous system constricts the smooth muscles around the arteries to your hands, feet, and skin as well. This is why you have cold, clammy hands when you are nervous or upset.

Although your hands are cold, they might sweat when you are nervous. Why? In an emergency, you are likely to become highly active, and if so, you will generate much body heat. Through sweating, the sympathetic nervous system is preparing you to prevent overheating before your activity has even started.

Several actions of the sympathetic nervous system serve to slow down digestion. The salivary glands turn off, leading to a dry-mouth feeling. The smooth muscles in your intestines stop their pulsing, called **peristalsis**, which keeps food going in the right direction. Your stomach and intestines stop secreting enzymes that digest food. If you're *really* upset, sympathetic activation even constricts the muscles needed to kick food out of your stomach (i.e., vomiting) to slightly decrease your body weight.

Another effect of sympathetic nervous system activation is **piloerection**—making the body's hairs stand up on end. Piloerection happens through the contraction of tiny muscles attached to the hair follicles in the skin. For many species, one consequence is that the raised hairs make an animal look larger and more intimidating (Figure 7.2). People also get goose bumps (erected hairs) when frightened. Our body hairs are so small

FIGURE 7.2.   The erected hairs of a frightened animal make it look larger and potentially more threatening.

that fluffing them out doesn't make us look any bigger or scarier, but we still have this reflexive response as an evolutionary relic from our ancient mammalian ancestors.

One of the subtlest effects of sympathetic nervous system activation is on the eyes. The pupils dilate, allowing more light into the retina. The effect is similar to opening the aperture in a camera, increasing the overall brightness and detail of the visual image. This can be useful if you are watching for possible danger or looking for a potential meal. Dilated pupils can also simply indicate interest. If you date someone whose pupils dilate at seeing you, it is probably a good sign.

Finally, sympathetic nervous system activation leads to some effects that are important for long-term activity. Sympathetic innervation of the liver stimulates the release of more glucose to the bloodstream, supplying plenty of energy to the hard-working skeletal muscles, brain, and heart. Other changes increase the breakdown of fats to create more energy and stimulate overall cellular metabolism. Finally, sympathetic activation changes the chemicals in the blood to promote coagulation—again preparing for a possible wound.

The term "sympathetic" was chosen for this branch of the autonomic nervous system because neurons leading to different organs travel alongside each other for long distances, and synapses connecting different neurons are typically clustered together. This differs from the parasympathetic branch, where neurons split off and head for different organs closer to the spinal cord. As a result, researchers assumed that neurons within the sympathetic branch would usually be active at the same time, acting in "sympathy" with each other. The result would be a highly coordinated response, in which all of the changes described in the preceding paragraphs happened together or none of them happened at all. If you have taken an introductory psychology class, this *all-or-none* principle is probably what you were taught.

Sometimes this coordination does happen, so that your heart starts to pound, you begin to sweat, your blood pressure goes up, and your stomach feels queasy all at the same time. However, later research has indicated that activation within the sympathetic system is much more differentiated than early researchers realized, with different visceral organs controlled by different combinations of neurotransmitters and receptor subtypes (Folkow, 2000; Jänig & Häbler, 2000; Kreibig, 2010). As a result, the effects described above can and do happen separately, with some occurring and some not at any given time. Thus, the sympathetic nervous system is capable of creating more complex, interesting patterns in the body than the old all-or-none maxim suggests.

Rest and Digest: The Parasympathetic Nervous System

If the effects of sympathetic nervous system activation generally help prepare the body for intense activity, activation of the **parasympathetic nervous system** has largely the opposite effects. Think of how you feel when you relax after a big meal. Many of your sensations at this time reflect parasympathetic nervous system activation. For this reason, researchers often refer to the parasympathetic system as the *rest-and-digest* system.

Many effects of parasympathetic activation are geared toward digesting food. Even during a meal, parasympathetic activation promotes the secretion of saliva, helping to process the food while you chew. Have you ever seen cats or dogs drool when they are relaxed? Salivation reflects increased parasympathetic activation. Parasympathetic activation also stimulates the secretion of various digestive chemicals into the stomach, and increases peristalsis so that food moves smoothly through the intestines. Insulin secretion at this time facilitates the storage of energy in fatty tissues and in the liver. Parasympathetic activation also decreases heart rate, thereby conserving energy for the digestive system (the heart is itself a hungry, demanding muscle in terms of energy). Similarly, whereas sympathetic activation speeds up breathing and expands the size of bronchioles in the lungs, parasympathetic activation slows down breathing and constricts the bronchioles.

With one exception, discussed below, parasympathetic activity does not affect the blood vessels directly. However, if sympathetic activation decreases while parasympathetic activation increases (such as right after a meal), then many of the smooth muscles surrounding blood vessels relax. Less blood flows to the brain and muscles simply because so much is going to the digestive system. Have you ever tried to exercise right after a big meal? Bad idea, right? While the body is devoting so much energy to digestion, it does not have much available for intense muscular activity. Because less blood flows to the brain, you might feel sleepy as well—the "food coma" people often experience after a particularly large feast (Figure 7.3).

Parasympathetic activation also promotes bodily conditions favorable for sexual activity. Parasympathetic nerves dilate the blood vessels leading into the genitals, causing the erections and swelling of vaginal tissue associated with sexual arousal. However, do not assume that eating a large meal results in sexual arousal. Like the sympathetic system, the parasympathetic system does not act as an all-or-none unit. The stimuli that activate one part of the system may or may not activate other parts.

Historically, emotion researchers have been far less interested in the rest-and-digest system than in the fight-or-flight system, which supports easily observed, highly active emotional behavior. However, researchers have become increasingly interested in the role of parasympathetic activation in emotion as well. A certain degree of calming is valuable for social relationships, and perhaps for some positive emotions (Porges, 1997). People with higher resting parasympathetic activation tend to be better than average at regulating their emotions (Butler, Wilhelm, & Gross, 2006; Eisenberg et al., 1989; Gyurak & Ayduk, 2008; Vasilev et al., 2009). They also report more positive affect in their daily lives (e.g., Bhattacharyya et al., 2008; Oveis et al., 2009), although experimental studies often find that parasympathetic influence on the heart *decreases* during some

FIGURE 7.3.   Parasympathetic activation is associated with relaxation and digestion. People often experience a strong parasympathetic response after a big meal.

positive emotions rather than increasing (Kreibig, 2010), and in one investigation the researchers found a link between parasympathetic activation, positive affect, and daily activities only for those activities that were social in nature (Isgett et al., 2017).

Although the link between parasympathetic activation and positive emotion is inconsistent, the link with social engagement is more robust. When your heart is beating fast, you tend to care about yourself and your own problems. Slowing your heart rate helps you focus on others. Several studies have indicated that parasympathetic input to the heart predicts the amount of compassion people feel and show when someone else is suffering (e.g., Stellar et al., 2015), an effect that was supported by a meta-analysis of sixteen research studies on the topic (Di Bello et al., 2020). However, that tendency may be true only within a certain range of parasympathetic activity (Kogan et al., 2014). It may be that with a moderate calming of the heart, you stop worrying so much about your own troubles and you can relate well to others. With too much calming, you could stop worrying about other people's troubles as well.

In one intriguing study, Desiree Delgadillo and colleagues (Delgadillo et al., 2021) found a significant link between mothers' positive emotional responses to their children and the children's parasympathetic activation both at rest and while recovering from frustration. This work suggests that caregivers may help tune their children's developing autonomic nervous system. However, hopefully you are thinking to yourself that to be sure of such a link, we'd need more research. More compelling studies would be ones that randomly assigned caregivers to have positive versus neutral interactions and evaluated the effects of each type of interaction, and/or longitudinal studies that carefully followed caregiver-child pairs over time.

How the Sympathetic and Parasympathetic Systems Work Together

Because many effects of the sympathetic and parasympathetic nervous systems oppose each other, it is easy to imagine that you are activating only one or the other at a given time, and unfortunately the system is sometimes described this way in introductory psychology textbooks. However, both systems are continuously active, with the relative balance between them shifting from time to time. Moreover, many situations activate part of one system and part of the other (Wolf, 1995). For example, when you experience nausea, your sympathetic nervous system decreases stomach contractions and produces retching, whereas your parasympathetic system stimulates your intestines and salivary glands and slows your heart rate. As we noted earlier, parasympathetic activation is needed for the early stages of sexual arousal because it allows more blood to flow to the genitalia. However, sympathetic activation promotes vaginal lubrication as well as the muscle contractions involved in orgasm and ejaculation.

Even where both systems have opposing effects on the same organs, such as the heart, their combined input produces more precise control. A common analogy is to the gas pedal and brake in a car. The amount of pressure you apply to the gas pedal can control your speed; if you want to slow down, you can just take some pressure off, right? However, if you need to stop quickly, you apply the brake. There are certain circumstances when using both the gas pedal and the brake in quick sequence is handy. For example, one of us (MNS) spends a lot of time driving up and down hills in San Francisco. Sometimes she gets stopped at a traffic light while her car is still pointed steeply uphill, with another car right behind her. Anyone who lives in that city knows a trick: apply the brake (the

FIGURE 7.4.   The sympathetic nervous system is somewhat like the gas pedal in a car, with the parasympathetic system akin to the brake. In some situations, such as when you are stopped on a steep hill and need to start again without rolling into the car behind you, the combination of the two systems can be helpful.

parking brake is fine and keeps your feet from getting confused), and when you're ready to go, release the brake quickly while stepping on the gas at the same time. This way the car gets momentum quickly, so you don't roll into the car behind you (Figure 7.4).

This is a long analogy, but it resembles what the body does when a threat is encountered. Imagine a rabbit at rest when it suddenly hears a noise. It freezes and looks around to find out whether a predator is nearby. At this time, parts of each system increase their activity (Lang, 2014). The sympathetic nervous system dilates the pupils (helpful for visual attention) and slightly increases sweating (in preparation for cooling the body, in case of vigorous running that might start at any moment). Meanwhile, the parasympathetic system decreases heart rate. The rabbit might need increased heart rate if it starts running, but not now, while it is simply focusing its attention. In fact, moving at all could be dangerous because it could attract a predator's attention. A moment later, when the predator starts approaching, the rabbit releases the parasympathetic "brake" and presses the sympathetic "gas pedal" to accelerate at once. The key point is that both the sympathetic and the parasympathetic nervous systems are always active, but the degree of activation in each is constantly fine-tuned to meet current needs.

The same is true for people. If you look at pictures of dangerous or unpleasant situations, your heart rate probably decreases. Suppose you read a list of objects while evaluating how useful each object might be in a life-or-death situation. Thinking about threats (but not yet doing anything about them) produces a sympathetic system-mediated increase in pupil dilation as well as a parasympathetic system-mediated drop in your heart rate, much like the effect on the rabbit. The effect of this combination is increased attention and a much-increased probability of remembering the words on that list (Fiacconi, Dekraker, & Koehler, 2015).

Similarly, imagine yourself in this experiment: you are playing a video game in which you sometimes have an opportunity to win some money, and sometimes face the threat of losing money. When you see an image of a gun, it means you will be at risk of losing some money, unless you react quickly enough when a signal appears. As the gun image gets larger (and presumably closer), you know the time for action is approaching. You will pay close attention to the gun, but while it is small and distant, your heart rate decreases. When the gun grows larger and closer, you shift to high arousal, increased activation of the sympathetic nervous system, and readiness for a vigorous response (Löw et al., 2008).

A key message of this section is that the autonomic nervous system is sophisticated and capable of producing complex, finely tuned patterns in the body. Although the all-or-none principle of sympathetic activation is still commonly taught in biology and psychology classes, along with an image of the sympathetic and parasympathetic nervous systems as a single, up-or-down switch, neither principle is entirely accurate. The effects of sympathetic and parasympathetic activation do generally oppose each other. However, the autonomic nervous system contains many different neural pathways for regulating the organs in the body and can adjust them selectively, just as a sound mixer might be used to adjust the relative volume of different instruments in recording a band in the studio (Figure 7.5).

FIGURE 7.5. The combined mechanisms of the sympathetic and parasympathetic nervous systems are like a sound board for mixing the volume of different instruments in a band. Different organs are controlled separately, allowing many complex patterns throughout the body.

HORMONES AND THE ENDOCRINE SYSTEM
Learning Objectives

- Identify effects of the hormone cortisol on the body, and analyze the conflicting research on the links between cortisol increases after awakening and emotional well-being.
- Summarize effects of the sex hormones estrogen and testosterone on emotions and behavior.

In addition to the autonomic nervous system, control of the interior of your body depends on **hormones**, chemicals produced and released by glands in one part of your body and carried by the bloodstream to cells in other areas. The **endocrine system** (the glands and hormones combined) affects a wide range of physiological functions. For example, the hormone insulin, produced and released by the pancreas, causes cells throughout the body to take in more glucose as a source of energy. Growth hormone, manufactured by the pituitary gland, promotes cell reproduction.

We considered the hormone and neurotransmitter oxytocin in Chapter 6. Emotion researchers are also highly interested in the hormones epinephrine (aka, adrenaline) and cortisol, which play central roles in our responses to stress, as we shall discuss shortly. Epinephrine has effects similar to that of sympathetic nervous system activation, but lasts longer because the hormone stays in the bloodstream for a while after it is released. **Cortisol** leads to an increase in blood sugar, encouraging the liver to release glucose into the bloodstream; cortisol may prompt the breakdown of muscle and fat to produce more glucose as well (although in long-term stress, cortisol may also stimulate storage of fat, especially around the waist). Cortisol increases blood pressure, partly by retaining sodium and fluids, increasing the total amount of blood plasma pumping through the system, but also by increasing resistance from the arteries. We will describe additional effects of cortisol later in the chapter.

Although cortisol is well described as a "stress hormone," it is not inherently bad. In most people, cortisol peaks soon after waking in the morning and slowly declines through the afternoon and evening (Edwards et al., 2001). The morning cortisol response presumably helps provide a burst of energy, so that people can get up and start their day. Several studies have linked disruption of this normal rhythm to severe stress and mental health concerns. A smaller cortisol response on waking is seen among women suffering from depression (Stetler & Miller, 2005), women living with severe economic hardship (Ranjit, Young, & Kaplan, 2005), and adults who experienced severe and/or chronic stress as children (Gunnar & Vazquez, 2001). On the other hand, a *larger* cortisol response after awakening has been linked to high tendency to experience negative daily emotions in men (Polk et al., 2005) as well as women (Kunz-Ebrecht et al., 2004). An increased morning cortisol response has also been linked with higher depression scores at the end of an exercise program for patients with major depressive disorder (Refsgaard, Schmedes, & Martiny, 2022). What could be going on? Is a larger cortisol response after awakening a good thing or a bad thing (Figure 7.6)?

Like so many other topics we cover in this book, it looks like it depends on several different factors. People tend to have higher cortisol responses on workdays than the weekend (Kunz-Ebrecht et al., 2004). Higher morning cortisol response also seems to linked to feeling overworked and worried on weekdays—but not on the weekends

FIGURE 7.6. Are higher cortisol increases in the morning a measure of being excited to meet the day's demands, or of higher stress? As with many other questions regarding emotion, motivation, and physiology, research is still sorting out the answer.

(Schlotz et al., 2004). Thus, this variable may track both how efficiently your body gets you ready to greet the day *and* the degree to which you are anticipating stressors that same day. You can imagine that the former predicts good emotional functioning, and the latter the opposite. It may also be that over time, people who repeatedly have intense morning cortisol bursts related to anticipated stressors begin to experience a blunting of this same response (Dedovic & Ngiam, 2015). It's a bit as though your body gives up trying to prepare for yet *another* stressful day. This hypothesis might explain why we sometimes observe links between depression and high morning cortisol response, and sometimes the opposite. Are you tired of hearing this yet? More research is clearly needed.

Other investigators have examined cortisol responses to stressful experiences later in the day, finding that some cortisol response in such situations is healthy. Blunting of this response is seen in children who have been abused or severely bullied (Ouellet-Morin et al., 2011) or who are experiencing chronic stress (Gunnar & Vazquez, 2001), as well as adults who experienced greater stress as children (Lovallo et al., 2012). Blunting of this response in puberty has also been linked to higher levels of early life stress (Kircanski et al., 2019). Although researchers are still trying to understand what these patterns mean, the lack of responsiveness suggests that under severe, ongoing stress, especially early in life, people's bodies may begin to give up on responding to challenging situations.

Other hormones related to emotion include the sex hormones estrogen, progesterone, and testosterone. Although these hormones are somewhat sex differentiated, with cisgender women having more of the first two and cisgender men more of the third, all human beings have some of each. The relationships among estrogen, mood, and risk for depression are . . . you guessed it, complex. Some studies indicate that higher levels of estrogens appear to have mood-enhancing effects (Walf & Frye, 2006), and sharp drops have been linked to depressive symptoms in women (Payne, 2003). One study indicated that women taking birth-control pills (which introduce extra estrogens into the system) were less prone to depression than other women, on average. However, another study examined over one million Danish women's medical records and found that women who began taking oral contraceptives (e.g., "the pill") were more likely in the following months to begin taking an antidepressant, to be diagnosed with a first episode of depression, and even to attempt suicide, as compared to women who had either never used or had long used oral contraception (Skovlund et al., 2016; Skovlund et al., 2018).

Does this indicate that oral contraception causes these effects? Not necessarily—we can think of many ways that women who take oral contraception differ from women who don't, that might account for some of these "effects." Can you hypothesize a few? To truly understand whether these effects are being caused by hormonal changes, we would need to recruit a group of women and randomly assign them to take either an oral contraceptive or a placebo pill, and then measure how mood differed across these two groups.

In one of the only such studies on this topic, over two hundred women were assigned to take the pill or a placebo for three consecutive menstrual cycles while reporting on their anxiety, irritability, and mood swings (Lundin et al., 2017). Interestingly, the results indicated that taking oral contraceptives led to *worse* mood during the middle phase between periods, but to *better* moods during the premenstrual phase. Two caveats are needed—first, although these overall effects were statistically significant, they were tiny, suggesting that oral contraceptives do not on average have very strong effects on mood in either a negative or positive direction. Second, there was a high degree of variability in the women's experiences. For instance, some women reported very dramatic changes in mood (up to 30% worse!) whereas others reported positive changes. In responding to almost any drug or medication, people vary. Importantly, it appears mood responds to a *change* in estrogen levels, rather than the *absolute* levels. This may be why the intense moment-to-moment fluctuations in estrogen typical of puberty and menopause are associated with mood swings.

Testosterone also has a wide range of emotional implications. In addition to a role in sexual motivation, testosterone appears to have mood-enhancing effects for men with minor symptoms of depression (Walther, Breidenstein, & Miller, 2019), especially if they had low testosterone levels before treatment (Amanatkar et al., 2014). Extra testosterone does little good for those who already had normal levels.

Given the fact that cisgender adult males are responsible for most of the aggressive behavior in humans as well as almost all other animal species, one might expect a strong correlation between testosterone levels and all types of angry and aggressive behavior. Researchers do find a relationship, if they test for it carefully. For example, certain children react to mistreatment with a burst of testosterone release, matched by an outburst of disruptive or violent behavior. Training these children to control their emotions lowers their testosterone responses as well as their behavioral outbursts (Carré et al., 2014).

However, most studies indicate only a low, and sometimes nonsignificant, correlation between testosterone and aggression, measured both at resting baseline and as reactions to challenges (for a review of this work, see: Geniole et al., 2020). The reason is that behavior depends on many other influences, including certain biological factors. Whereas testosterone tends to increase aggression, the hormone cortisol tends to decrease it. In both men and women, a high ratio of testosterone to cortisol correlates with increased aggressive behavior (Platje et al., 2015) and increased risk-taking behavior (Mehta et al., 2015). Another influence is the arousal of the sympathetic nervous system. For most people, the thought of doing something to hurt another person arouses strong emotions—guilt, fear, and so forth—associated with arousal of the sympathetic nervous system. People with weak autonomic responses feel less guilt and fear, and therefore less restraint against antisocial acts (Herpetz et al., 2007).

MEASURING PHYSIOLOGICAL ASPECTS OF MOTIVATION AND EMOTION

Learning Objectives

- Identify physiological measures that reflect a combination of sympathetic and parasympathetic influence, as well as those that reflect one or the other branch of the autonomic nervous system.
- Analyze the strengths, weaknesses, and challenges inherent to physiological measures in research on emotion.

So far, we have outlined the functions of the autonomic nervous system and the hormones. To conduct research on how they relate to emotions, we need good, practical ways to measure physiological responses. The physiological responses that we care about occur inside the body. As a result, most researchers measure autonomic changes by attaching sensors to the skin to record the transmission of electricity, pressure, or other energies.

Commonly Used Measures

Heart rate is the best known and most widely used physiological measure of emotion. When you take your own heart rate (say, by laying your pointer finger against the inside of your wrist, near the base of the thumb, and counting the number of beats in a minute), you are relying on pressure changes to let you know when each heartbeat happens. In the laboratory, however, researchers detect electrical signals generated by the heart while it contracts, rather than changes in blood pressure.

In rough outline, your heart generates small but detectable electrical signals when the atria (the upper chambers of the heart) and the ventricles (the lower chambers) begin to contract. These signals can be detected by putting sensors that detect changes in electrical potential on a person's chest, on a diagonal across the heart. The signal measured using this approach is called an electrocardiogram, or ECG. (Some authorities use the abbreviation EKG.) Figure 7.7 shows a typical ECG recording.

Cardiologists can describe the parts of the ECG signal in great detail, but for our purposes we care about just a few points. Note the big spike in each heartbeat, followed by a dip, and then a return to the straight line. This sequence, called the QRS complex, indicates the contraction and relaxation of the ventricles. The Q point indicates the beginning of the contraction, the R point indicates the peak of electrical activity, and the S point indicates recovery.

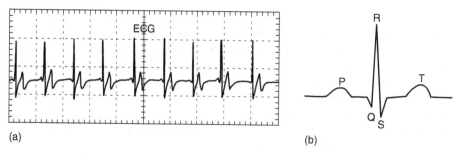

FIGURE 7.7. (a) An electrocardiogram signal reflects patterns of electrical activity associated with the heartbeat. (b) The letters P through T designate several stages in a single heartbeat.

Researchers can analyze these signals in one of two ways. One option is just to measure heart rate, in terms of number of beats per minute. They can do this by measuring the *number* of R peaks in a given period of time and scaling to a minute. However, the changes in heart rate evoked by an emotion may be just a couple of beats per minute and may happen too briefly to capture with such a crude measure. Emotion researchers often measure the average **interbeat interval** instead. To do this, they calculate the time in milliseconds between each of the R peaks in the ECG signal and then average those numbers for the period of interest. This finer measurement allows researchers to detect changes on a second-by-second basis.

Another common physiological measure is blood pressure, which reflects the volume of blood in each heartbeat as well as the constriction of the muscles surrounding the arteries. You've probably had your blood pressure measured many times. Unfortunately, researchers can't just keep taking a new blood pressure every few seconds using a sphygmomanometer (isn't that a great word?) and stethoscope, like your doctor. This would clearly distract attention from any emotion manipulations the researcher is trying to use. However, computer-controlled blood pressure monitors are available that control a sensor strapped to the wrist or finger, taking a new measure every few seconds. Just like the system in your doctor's office, these monitors apply and release pressure to your pulse, and then examine the effects on blood flow at that point. Researchers distinguish between **systolic blood pressure**, while your heartbeat is actively pushing blood through your arteries, and **diastolic blood pressure**, while the heart is between beats.

Another way to assess vasoconstriction is by measuring finger temperature. Sympathetic nervous system activation reduces blood flow to the skin, while shunting more blood toward the heart and brain. Because less blood is being delivered to the hands, they get cooler—an effect that can be measured with a simple temperature-recording sensor.

Respiration rate, or breathing rate, is also typically measured using a pressure-sensitive device. In this case, researchers strap an elastic belt with a tension- or pressure-sensitive component around the participant's diaphragm, and measure changes in pressure associated with breathing. This allows measurement not only of respiration *rate*, but also of respiration *depth*, or the volume of each breath.

Another physiologic measure that tracks with emotion and motivation is the extent to which your pupils are dilated. While you might think about pupil size as reflecting the amount of available light in a setting (and they certainly are responsive to changes in light),

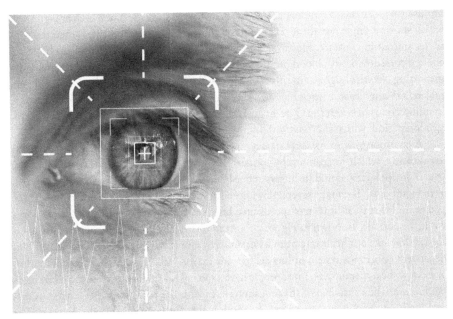

FIGURE 7.8. Researchers can measure changes in pupil diameter with a device that also measures gaze direction.

they also dilate when you are more versus less physiologically aroused or activated. You might think it would be easy to measure pupil diameter, because it is at the surface of the body. However, a typical video camera cannot detect subtle changes in the size of the pupil, especially if the head is moving. Researchers who are interested in measuring where an individual is looking, as well as the size of the pupil, use an eye-tracking device that provides a chin rest for the participant, as well as a camera that closely follows the eye (Figure 7.8).

The measures just discussed all indicate the relative balance between the sympathetic and parasympathetic systems—each is influenced by both systems, which makes it difficult to tease influence of the two systems apart. **Electrodermal activity** (changes in how well the skin conducts electricity) detects the increased sweat gland activity resulting specifically from sympathetic activation. (The parasympathetic system has no connection to the sweat glands.) To measure electrodermal activity, a researcher puts electrodes at two places on someone's skin and then passes an electrical current between them. Don't worry; The current is so weak that people do not even feel it. Your skin is constantly sweating to a slight degree that you do not notice. When you become aroused—even slightly—the result is a momentary increase in sweating, and therefore greater flow of the electricity along your skin (moist skin conducts with less resistance than dry skin). Measuring the strength of the current flow gives an indirect measurement of sweating, and therefore a measurement of sympathetic nervous system arousal.

Cardiac pre-ejection period is yet another measure of sympathetic activation. Sympathetic nervous system activation not only increases the number of beats per minute, but also makes the heart beat more forcefully, pushing blood harder through the arteries. It does this in part by speeding up every contraction of the ventricles, just as a fast kick against a wooden board is more likely to break it than a slow kick. Look back at Figure 7.7, which shows a single heartbeat on an ECG signal. The Q point indicates when the ventricles started to contract. However, the ventricles need a few milliseconds to build up enough pressure to push blood out through the valve leading to the rest of the body. By measuring electrical signals (in this case with sensors on the front and back of the torso), researchers can measure when blood has been expelled through the aortic valve. The time in milliseconds between the Q point and the expulsion of blood into the aorta is the pre-ejection period, which shortens with increasing sympathetic activation.

A common way to measure parasympathetic activation is called **respiratory sinus arrhythmia**, which you can test by yourself. If you're sitting quietly and comfortably, use your index/pointer and middle fingers of one hand to measure your pulse on the other wrist, as in Figure 7.9a. Then take several slow, deep breaths in and out. Notice anything? Many people find that their heart rate speeds up a little while they are inhaling and slows down while they exhale, as shown in Figure 7.9b. At rest, the parasympathetic nervous system is always slowing your heart rate from its natural rhythm (determined by a "pacemaker" independent of nervous system influence) to some extent. Whereas the pacemaker's rhythm is about 90 beats per minute, most people have a resting heart rate between 70 and 80 beats per minute. The expansion of the lungs interferes with the parasympathetic nervous system's ability to slow down the heart. The result is that the heart rate briefly increases. The extent of the difference in heart rate between inhalation and exhalation thus indicates how strongly the parasympathetic system is trying to slow the heart down at any given time.

Think of it this way. Have you ever used a light switch with both a switch and a rheostat, where the switch controlled whether the light was on at all, and the rheostat controlled the amount of light if it was on? If the rheostat was low, then flipping the switch on and off wouldn't have much impact. If the rheostat was high, flipping the

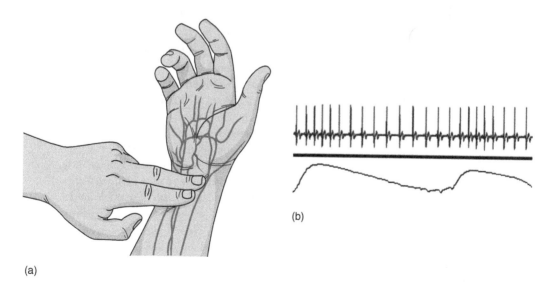

(a)

(b)

FIGURE 7.9. (a) How to take your pulse at the wrist. (b) The variability in heart rate (top) associated with breathing (bottom) is called respiratory sinus arrhythmia.

switch on and off would have a more dramatic effect. In this analogy, the rheostat reflects the level of parasympathetic activation, and the lungs are the switch alternately blocking that signal or allowing it to pass, thereby slowing your heart rate.

Finally, how do we measure hormone levels? Because hormones are in the bloodstream, the most accurate way to measure them is by a blood sample. A less intrusive measure is to take measurements from saliva. That procedure works well for cortisol, estrogen, and testosterone, all of which enter the saliva in amounts roughly proportional to the blood levels, but it is less reliable when measuring some other hormones. Researchers interested in how cortisol might relate to stress over longer periods of time sometimes also measure cortisol from hair samples.

Measurement Challenges

People differ from one another in their resting heart rate, blood pressure, cortisol level, and other physiological measures. Therefore, to measure the physiological response associated with an emotional state, we must compare a measurement during the emotion with a measurement taken beforehand, called the *baseline*. We measure the effect of the emotion by the change from baseline to the target period. Because the baseline itself changes over time, it is best to record the baseline anew before each emotional task.

That idea brings us to our next point. The autonomic nervous system is constantly adjusting in response to all kinds of events, both within and outside the body. Almost every physiological variable changes when people stand up, jiggle their feet, or move, and especially when they talk. A researcher must discard data every time a participant sneezes, because a sneeze changes autonomic physiology in striking ways. The mere fact of attaching sensors to someone's body produces a certain amount of anxiety, for some people more than others, and more at the start of the study than later. Once they're on, sensors can become dislodged or start to slip off, especially in long laboratory sessions; this will alter the signal they produce. Before trying to analyze physiological data, researchers must carefully inspect and "clean" obvious sources of error from the signals, and at least be aware of the problems that may be created by other sources.

Another problem is that the autonomic nervous system may take one to two seconds to react measurably to certain stimuli, depending on the stimulus and the type of measurement. Changes in salivary hormones can take 15 minutes or more to detect. When designing an experiment, researchers must be alert to what they can measure accurately and promptly, and what they cannot.

Despite these limitations, physiological measures have the advantage of objectivity. You don't have to rely on people's self-reports, and you don't have to worry about possible biases of someone's observations of behavior. Physiological recordings do not answer all our questions, but at least they provide reliable, precise measurements of bodily changes that people cannot describe clearly on their own.

THE AUTONOMIC NERVOUS SYSTEM, EMOTION, AND MOTIVATION

Learning Objectives
- Summarize the arousal theory of motivation, explaining its claim about the relationship between arousal and performance.

- Describe the effects of some forms of nervous system damage (e.g., pure autonomic failure, locked-in syndrome) on subjective feelings of emotion, and analyze implications for William James's proposal about the relationship between physiology and emotion.
- Evaluate the evidence regarding the autonomic specificity hypothesis—the proposal that different emotions have distinct physiological "fingerprints."
- Define kama muta, and summarize results of a study examining the physiology of this emotional state.

Recall from Chapter 1 that our proposed definitions of emotion, as well as the James–Lange and Schachter–Singer theories, include the assumption that a physiological change is an essential part of any emotional experience. Recall also the assertions that emotions prepare us for action, and that motivation is all about the energy and direction that animates behavior. Energy and preparation for action both involve a state of arousal, which as we have discussed in this chapter thus far, is largely governed by our autonomic nervous system.

Arousal Theory of Motivation

You might recall from Chapter 2 our extensive discussion of homeostasis, drives, and the motivating nature of physiological drives such as hunger, sex, and sleep. All these concepts are relevant here in our discussion of the physiological basis of motivation, but we'd like to add another historically important theory of motivation to the mix: **arousal theory**. As drive theory fell a bit out of favor, motivation researchers turned to the study of physiological arousal.

Arousal refers to the overall degree of energy, alertness, and activity within one's physiology. You might consider arousal to be on a continuum from unconscious to drowsy to calm to alert to anxious. We can measure a person's level of arousal using many of the variables we've considered thus far in this chapter—heart activity, electrodermal response, and muscle tension. As we've noted, these are not always strongly correlated with each other, but you can average across them to approximate general arousal.

One early question that arousal theory tackled was: What is the best level of arousal for performance? Consider your own behaviors and experiences. If you must take an exam, shoot a goal on the playing field, or be interviewed for a job, at what level of arousal do you think you would perform best? If you answered that you would want a medium-high level of arousal for these tasks, your answer would be supported by a lot of research. One of the most famous effects in all of psychology is called the Yerkes–Dodson Law (named for its coiners) and it argues that the relationship between arousal and performance is curvilinear (Yerkes & Dodson, 1908). If you must go to a job interview or take an exam, both very low and very high levels of arousal are likely to result in poor performance. After all, if you are drowsy and too calm, you will respond slowly and sluggishly and perhaps answer poorly. If you are hovering on a panic attack, on the other hand, you may have trouble collecting your thoughts. The ideal state may be one that is alert, focused, but reasonably calm.

Like so many other early findings we have covered in this book, this law has come under greater scrutiny. For one thing, Yerkes and Dodson were studying mice, not humans. For another, so much about the best level of arousal for performance depends

TABLE 7.1   Physiological changes in motivational states

Changes in physiology at rest and in response to various challenges, separated by type of motivational state (approach, avoidance, and effort). Adapted from Mendes & Park (2014).

	Approach	Avoidance	Effort
Synonyms/related constructs	Challenge Activation Appetitive	Threat Inhibition Withdrawal Defensive	Attention Mental demand Engagement Vigilance
Measurements at rest or baseline			
Autonomic nervous system		Lower heart rate variability	
Hormones	Higher testosterone Lower cortisol	Lower Dehydroepiandrosterone (DHEA)	
Measurements during reactivity or challenge			
Autonomic nervous system	Large increases in sympathetic nervous system (SNS; e.g., heart rate, skin conductance)	Immediate SNS decreases Delayed, moderate SNS increases Decreased heart rate variability	Moderate increases in SNS Decreases in heart rate variability
Hormones	Moderate cortisol increases Testosterone increases	Cortisol increases	Moderate cortisol increases Moderate testosterone increases

on the person being considered, the type of task being performed, how arousal is measured, one's degree of motivation, and so on. For this and other reasons, arousal theory also fell out of favor as the primary way that motivation researchers think about how motivation affects behavior. But that's not to say that motivation researchers stopped caring about arousal and its effects. Far from it. For just a brief overview, consider Table 7.1, adapted from a literature review on the physiology of motivational states by psychologists Wendy Berry Mendes and Jiyoung Park (2014). As you can see, the systems of our bodies track our motivational states of approach, arousal, and the summoning of effort. When we talked back in Chapter 1 about motivation being energy plus direction, the recruitment of these biological systems is what makes up the energy component.

You might notice from this table that a lot of the physiological effects of approach, avoidance, and effort motivation are not *that* different from each other—all involve some level of increase in sympathetic nervous system activity, increase in cortisol, and so on. This is probably because summoning the energy to move a body into action is a similar process whether that action is approach or avoidance. It is at the levels of appraisal, thought, and understanding of context that many of the directional aspects of motivation come into play.

What about emotion? Do emotions differ in their physiology? The theory of basic/discrete emotions predicts that different emotions will have different physiological signatures, and because they are part of evolved human nature, these signatures should be similar for people in different cultures. In contrast, the Schachter–Singer theory and dimensional theories propose that all emotions simply include some degree of arousal.

The relationship between the physiological and feeling aspects of emotion is important for emotion theory. There are three questions: (1) Are physiological changes necessary for the feeling aspects of emotion? (2) Do different emotions have qualitatively different physiological profiles? (3) Do physiological changes in emotion look similar from one culture to another? Where do the data stand on these issues? As with research on the central nervous system, the results of existing studies appear to rule out both the extreme version of the dimensional hypothesis and the extreme version of the basic emotion hypothesis.

Here are the relevant data.

Are Bodily Sensations Necessary for Emotional Feelings?

If you had no sensations from your organs, would you still feel emotions? According to the James–Lange theory, and to some extent the Schachter–Singer theory, you might still appraise the situation cognitively ("well that's annoying"), but you should not *feel* an emotion. Furthermore, if physiological sensations are critical for emotional feelings, then people with weak feedback from their organs should experience only weak emotions, and people who are especially sensitive to feedback from their organs might experience intense emotions. We can examine these proposals by comparing various kinds of people.

In one study, people were asked to report whether they thought their heart rate was increasing or decreasing while researchers measured the actual heart rate. The participants also reported how sensitive they were to visceral (gut) sensations in general, and how intensely they felt moments of fear and sadness. The people who were most accurate at judging their heart rate tended to be those who reported high sensitivity to visceral sensations, and great intensity of unpleasant emotions (Critchley et al., 2004). That is, the more you notice your own arousal level, the more intensely you feel emotions, especially the negative ones. You may recall from last chapter that this ability to notice your internal bodily aspects of emotion is called interoception, and it applies not just to cardiac measures but also changes in breathing and stomach movements (Critchley & Garfinkel, 2017). Higher interoceptive ability may be linked with not just intensity of emotion, but also how well you manage or regulate your emotions (Füstös et al., 2013).

At the opposite extreme are people with diminished responses. **Pure autonomic failure** is a medical condition in which the autonomic nervous system ceases to influence the body. The causes of this uncommon, incurable condition are unknown. Usually, its onset occurs when people reach middle age. One prominent symptom occurs when people stand up: the blood sinks rapidly from the head to the trunk, and the person faints. (The medical term for this symptom is *orthostatic hypotension*.) This would happen to everyone without the action of the sympathetic nervous system. When you stand up, you reflexively trigger mechanisms that increase heart rate and constrict (tighten) the veins leading from your head back to the heart. People with pure autonomic failure lose this reflex and therefore must stand up slowly to prevent blood from sinking out of their head. Physical or mental stresses also have no effect on their heart rate, breathing rate, sweating, and other autonomic responses.

What about emotions? In objectively emotional situations these people report the same type of emotions as other people, but feel them less intensely (Critchley, Mathias, & Dolan, 2001). Presumably, the appraisal part of their emotion is intact, but the feeling part is weakened. Even someone with few or no emotional feelings can say, "I recognize this as a situation that calls for fear" (or anger or so on). But as the without autonomic changes, they may have less to feel.

Locked-in syndrome is an even more extreme condition in which people lose almost all output from the brain to the muscles and the autonomic nervous system (that is, no commands from the brain reach the body), although they continue to feel sensations like touch or pressure. The cause usually is a stroke or other damage to part of the brainstem. Most people with spinal cord damage retain control of some of their muscles, depending on the location of the damage. Even those who are paralyzed from the neck down have output to the heart and other organs because the nerves of the parasympathetic nervous system originate in the pons and medulla, not in the spinal cord. In locked-in syndrome, however, key areas of the pons and medulla themselves are damaged. In these areas, axons travel from the brain to the spinal cord. A few clusters of neurons above the damaged area control eye muscles, so the person retains the ability for eye movement. Otherwise, the person is totally paralyzed while remaining intellectually alert and capable of surviving for many years.

What happens to their emotions? They can tell us, although not easily. First, a specialist must teach them to spell out words by a code in which different patterns of eye movements or blinks represent different letters of the alphabet. This process is often aided by the use of "spell boards" which have letters or symbols represented on them. When these patients give their first message, you might expect a message of terror or despair. After all, the person is permanently paralyzed except for the eye muscles, and most of us imagine that we would feel overwhelming distress at that prospect. The James–Lange theory, however, predicts greatly weakened emotion because of the virtual lack of feedback from the body.

Unfortunately, the results are sparse on this point. Communication with these people is slow and laborious. Most of what they say is remarkably unemotional, without any sign of panic or despair. One woman's first message after learning an eye-blinking code was, "Why do I wear such an ugly shirt?" (Kübler et al., 2001). Many of the reports by locked-in patients are described as tranquil, or calm (Damasio, 1999). A plausible interpretation is that they do not experience fidgeting, heart palpitations, stomach churning, or any of the other bodily responses that ordinarily accompany emotions.

However, an autobiography by a locked-in patient (dictated by blinks of one eyelid) does refer to sadness, disappointment, frustration, and similar emotional terms (Bauby, 1997). Other memoirs and literary creations of people with locked-in syndrome suggest surprisingly high quality of life as well (Vidal, 2020). But the majority of locked-in patients do not write or even respond to survey questions, so how can we know whether this subset of people who are capable of art under such conditions are truly representative? We would like to know more: Do people experiencing this syndrome feel emotions, and do they feel them as intensely as before, or are they talking primarily about the cognitive/appraisal aspect of emotions? This distinction is theoretically important to psychologists studying emotions, although it might be obscure to anyone else. The few research studies currently available do not provide enough information to answer our questions about emotional feelings.

Autonomic Nervous System Specificity of Emotions

Basic/discrete emotions theory predicts that different emotions should be associated with different profiles of activity in the organs of the body, or **autonomic specificity**.

According to the idea, we should expect consistent differences among emotions (Ekman, 1992). Evolutionary approaches also tend to emphasize the different adaptive functions served by specific emotions, suggesting that different emotions should have different physiological effects (Tooby & Cosmides, 2008). In contrast, according to the idea that emotions vary only across dimensions of valence and arousal (*core affect* theory), we should expect some differences of degree, but also a great deal of similarity from one emotion to another. According to the Schachter–Singer theory of emotions, physiological arousal determines the intensity of an emotional feeling, but the identification of one emotion from another (such as the difference between fear and anger) depends on an individual's cognitive appraisal of the situation, not what's happening in their body. What does the evidence suggest?

In an early and extensive study, Paul Ekman, Robert Levenson, and Wallace Friesen (1983) asked whether anger, fear, sadness, happiness, surprise, and disgust could be differentiated in terms of their autonomic nervous system effects. You will recognize this as the same list of emotions Ekman and colleagues (1969) used in their studies of facial expressions. In this study, the researchers had sets of participants engage in two emotion-eliciting tasks: (1) posing facial expressions of each emotion, following muscle-by-muscle instructions; and (2) reliving strong emotional memories. This procedure is important, because demonstrating something in more than one way increases confidence in the conclusions. In an interesting twist, the researchers used professional actors and researchers who study facial movements as participants to ensure that they would be able to follow the facial movement instructions accurately. Only data from trials where the participant reported a moderately strong experience of the target emotion were used. Physiological variables in the study were heart rate, finger temperature, skin conductance, and muscle tension.

The researchers found that in both emotion tasks, the six emotions showed different (and consistent) results for heart rate and finger temperature. The results for these variables are shown in Figure 7.10. Each graph shows baseline-to-trial change scores on a physiological variable for each of the six emotions. Heart rate increased substantially from baseline during anger, fear, and sadness, but not during happiness or surprise. The graph showing changes in finger temperature adds to the picture. This shows that finger temperature increased dramatically during anger, and somewhat during happiness, but decreased a little during fear and disgust. This pattern across the two variables suggests that at least anger, fear, and disgust can be differentiated in terms of their autonomic effects, although the status of sadness, happiness, and surprise remains uncertain.

In later research, the same team of researchers replicated this pattern of results using facial expression instruction to elicit the emotions (Levenson, Ekman, & Friesen, 1990). However, other researchers, using other methods, have found different patterns. In an attempt to resolve the confusion, John Cacioppo and colleagues conducted a meta-analysis of studies about autonomic specificity (Cacioppo et al., 2000). Using a meta-analysis allows researchers to consolidate the results of many studies by different researchers as if they were one large study. The results of the meta-analysis confirmed some of Levenson's (1992) original claims about differences between specific emotions, failed to support others, and indicated some new differences as well. What do you expect they found? Some of the differences confirmed by the meta-analysis were the following: (1) Happiness generally produces less arousal than anger, fear, sadness, or disgust. (2) Heart rate accelerates more during anger, fear, and sadness than during disgust. Nausea produces both sympathetic and

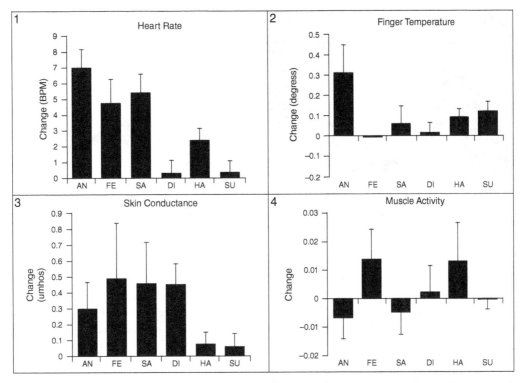

FIGURE 7.10.   These baseline-to-trial change scores in heart rate, finger temperature skin conductance, and muscle activity suggest different physiological profiles for a few different emotions.

parasympathetic activation, and it is possible that these two influences cancel each other out somewhat in disgust. (3) Compared to fear, anger produces higher blood pressure, smaller increases in heart rate and stroke volume, and greater finger pulse volume and temperature. These patterns distinguish the negative emotions from happiness, disgust from the other negative emotions, and anger from fear, but the status of sadness is uncertain.

Note that the researchers who conducted this meta-analysis examined one aspect of physiology at a time. Recall the meta-analyses used to test basic emotion theory in the previous chapter, on emotion in the brain. We noted that the real question is whether different emotions are associated with different *patterns* in brain activity across many areas, not just whether they differ for individual areas. A similar question is appropriate here: Do different emotions evoke different profiles of activation across organs in the body and their nervous system mechanisms (Figure 7.11)?

A few researchers have taken a more explicit approach to measuring the profiles of autonomic activity in different emotions, using complex statistical techniques. Gerhard Stemmler and colleagues compared the effects of anger and fear on 24 different physiological variables, and distinguished the two emotions using a technique called *multivariate analysis* that examines all of the variables at once (Stemmler, Aue, & Wacker, 2007). Israel Christie and Bruce Friedman (2003) used a technique called *pattern classification analysis*

FIGURE 7.11. Would you expect these emotions to be associated with different, distinct patterns of changes in heart rate, stomach movements, skin sweating? Or would you expect similar changes for all? Emotion researchers disagree, and there is some evidence for each possibility.

that works backward from the usual analysis. Instead of asking whether different emotion conditions produce different physiological profiles, researchers using this analysis ask whether the program can identify the emotion in each trial based on the pattern of physiological effects after looking at data from the whole study. Christie and Friedman found that their analysis correctly classified just over a third of trials across seven emotions (including a neutral-emotion condition)—significantly better than chance, but far from perfect.

More recently, many studies have found small differences, but also much similarity in physiological responding across emotions (Quigley & Barrett, 2014). For example, in most regards the responses to fear resemble those for anger. Even amusement and disgust produce many similarities of response (Kreibig, Samson, & Gross, 2015), and so do pain and surprise (Jang et al., 2015). An updated meta-analysis of all the research on autonomic specificity thus far (202 studies!) asked whether a basic emotion approach (which predicted what the researchers called "emotion fingerprints") or a more psychological construction-focused approach better fit the available data, and concluded that the weight of the evidence lay with the latter (Siegel et al., 2018). Their analyses indicated great variation in autonomic patterns among the different emotions, did not replicate Cacioppo's finding of differences between anger and fear, and highlighted the importance of good experimental methods. They also included some fancy statistics to account for what is called "publication bias" (basically, studies are much more likely to be published when they claim strong effects than weak or no effects) and found that accounting for such bias reduced variation between emotion categories even more.

Overall, it is possible to argue about whether we should be more impressed with the autonomic differences among emotions, or with the similarities. For example, when heart rate or finger temperature increases more during one emotion than another, do we consider that an important distinction or not? Should we be more impressed with the fact that someone could use your autonomic responses to identify your emotion one-third of the time, or should we be more struck by the fact that the identification would fail two-thirds of the time? As Siegel and colleagues (2018) point out in their meta-analysis, what if there are "emotional fingerprints" for the different emotions, but the exact fingerprint varies from person to person? (Y'know, kind of like . . . . fingerprints?) Maybe your heart rate always drops when you are surprised, but your friend's speeds up. Our current methods aren't set up to detect such possibilities.

If emotions are evolved adaptations, we should expect people raised in different cultures to be similar at the physiological level, at least to some extent. Do people around the world show similar physiological responses during the same emotional experiences? This is a difficult question to study, but a few researchers have tried. In one major study, described in detail in Chapter 2, researchers Robert Levenson, Paul Ekman, Karl Heider, and Wallace Friesen (1992) asked whether participants from an indigenous community in Indonesia showed physiological responses in emotional situations similar to the responses of young adults in the United States and found that overall, physiological responses were similar in the two samples (see Figure 2.17). A statistical analysis called multivariate analysis of variance, which allows researchers to compare two or more groups on several different outcome variables, did not detect a difference in the two groups' patterns of physiological responding across the five emotions and three physiological variables. However, cultural differences did exist. Statistical tests suggested that the magnitude of responses during the facial expression task was smaller among the Minangkabau than among the Americans. This may be because the Minangkabau have smaller physiological responses during emotion, or because the facial expression task was less effective at eliciting emotion in this group—there's no way to know.

To continue exploring this issue, Jeanne Tsai and colleagues (2002) examined several aspects of emotional responding—including physiology—in two different cultural groups in the United States. One sample consisted of college students of European American descent. The other sample consisted of students who were ethnically Hmong (pronounced with a silent *h*)—a distinct Southeast Asian culture originally from Laos. The Hmong students were born either in Laos or Thailand or in the United States to two parents born and raised in Laos. Hmong participants also had to be fluent speakers of both Hmong and English. (Language fluency is a common criterion for cultural affiliation.)

Each participant was asked to describe and try to relive experiences in which they felt happiness, pride, love, anger, disgust, and sadness. Participants briefly described a specific event in which they felt a particular emotion and then tried to reexperience the event as vividly as they could. Throughout the study, Tsai and colleagues (2002) measured participants' skin conductance. They found that skin conductance increased slightly during all six emotions and that these increases were similar between the European American and ethnic Hmong groups.

It's best to think of these two studies as intriguing first steps on a long and difficult road. Each study only included people from two cultural groups. The two studies showed some similarities in physiological responding across cultures, but this does not constitute a full test of universality. We can say with some confidence that the physiological responses in emotion show similar patterns for a few emotions in a few cultures. However, a great deal of work must still be done before a claim of universality in physiological aspects of emotion can be justified.

Robert Levenson (2014) has argued that the research on the question of whether different emotions have distinct physiological fingerprints so far has been inadequate to allow a firm conclusion (see also Behnke et al., 2022; Norman, Berntson, & Cacioppo, 2014;

Quigley & Barrett, 2014). The methods in previous research have had important limitations. First and most important, we should expect a distinctive autonomic response only for strong fear, strong anger, or any other strong emotion. Because of ethical restraints, most investigators use weak, sometimes pathetically weak, manipulations. They might ask participants to remember the last time they felt anger, fear, sadness, or some other emotion. Depending on how intense and recent the experience, and how vividly someone recollects that experience, this instruction might induce strong emotion or not much at all. The other common procedure is to ask people to look at photos or watch film clips. If you watched a film of someone eating live insects or cleaning a filthy toilet, would you feel disgust? Probably, but some people laugh instead (and MNS has videos of research participants to prove it!). If many of the participants are feeling only a weak emotion, or some emotion different from or blended with the intended one, we cannot expect a clear and distinctive autonomic profile.

A second problem is that many researchers examine only a limited range of physiological responses. The most common are heart rate and skin conductance, because they are the easiest to measure. When people describe their emotional feelings, they frequently mention a sensation of "butterflies in the stomach" or churning in the intestines (they almost never mention changes in skin conductance), but hardly any researchers have measured digestive system activity during emotion. You may have noted that some of the measures we described earlier in the chapter, such as cardiac pre-ejection period and respiratory sinus arrhythmia, are not even discussed in these studies of autonomic specificity. This is because they are relatively new and not available in much of the earlier research.

A third problem is that most emotional reactions are intense for only a few seconds. It is important to measure responses as they are happening, and not to take an average over half a minute or more. New technologies make it possible for people to wear a device that monitors autonomic responses moment by moment throughout the day as they engage in normal life (Wac & Tsiourti, 2014). Perhaps we shall see better, more definitive research in the future.

Physiological Aspects of Positive Emotions

Most research on emotion in the body has focused on negative emotions. In the Cacioppo et al. (2000) meta-analysis, happiness was easily distinguished from fear, anger, and disgust by virtue of showing little physiological effect. If positive emotions are real emotions, shouldn't we expect some sort of physiological response? On closer examination, however, the effects of positive emotion are not as bland.

Many studies find little or no effect of positive emotion on autonomic physiology. However, all autonomic responses are a matter of degree, and many studies of happiness have used weak stimuli. You will probably say that looking at photos of puppies or kittens makes you feel "happy," but it is likely not an intense experience. A study of responses to humorous videos indicated increased heart rate when people watched the most intensely amusing videos, but little effect from the others (Lackner et al., 2014).

Also, most emotion researchers have distinguished among fear, anger, disgust, and sadness while lumping together happiness and all other pleasant states as positive emotions. Far fewer studies compare specific positive emotion states against each other. In one such study, researchers examined five states: enthusiasm, attachment, nurturance, amusement, and awe. Enthusiasm is eagerness for food or other rewards. Attachment is

TABLE 7.2 | Physiological changes in five positive emotions

Changes in physiology while viewing images eliciting five positive emotions studied by Shiota and colleagues (Shiota et al., 2011).

	CARDIAC INTERBEAT INTERVAL	CARDIAC PRE-EJECTION PERIOD	SKIN CONDUCTANCE	RESPIRATORY SINUS ARRHYTHMIA	MEAN ARTERIAL PRESSURE
Enthusiasm	−	O	+	−	+
Attachment	−	O	O	−	O
Nurturance	−	O	O	−	O
Amusement	O	O	O	O	O
Awe	O	+	O	−	O

love and trust for a parent, friend, or loving partner. Nurturance is a tendency to care for the young or other helpless beings. Amusement is play and humor. Awe is a response to novel, amazing sights or experiences. Table 7.2 shows autonomic responses to photos intended to evoke each of these experiences. In each case, a 0 means no difference from the effects of a neutral, unemotional photo, whereas + indicates an increase and − indicates a decrease. Without worrying too much about the details, note that the pattern differs from one positive emotion to another (Shiota et al., 2011).

A recent meta-analysis attempted to consolidate all the existing evidence on physiological reactivity during specific positive emotions (Behnke et al., 2022). On one hand, the researchers found very little evidence of autonomic specificity for positive emotions. On the other hand, the evidence available—despite being heroically scoured from the available literature—was far from sufficient to address the question at stake. The data not only suffered from the limitations discussed above, but also were scattered in terms of which positive emotions and physiological measures were included in a given study, such that very few data points were available for many tests (e.g., changes in respiratory sinus arrhythmia during awe).

Some newer, exciting work has examined physiological changes during positive emotion associated with powerful social experiences. One such study found that *moral elevation*, the reaction to observing heroic, altruistic acts by other people, produces an unusual combination of increased heart rate (consistent with a sympathetic nervous system response) and increased respiratory sinus arrhythmia (a parasympathetic response) (Piper, Saslow, & Saturn, 2015).

Have you ever said to someone that you felt *moved* by an experience? Or *touched?* People sometimes use such terms when they are describing an emotional reaction to circumstances of unusual kindness or interpersonal closeness (Figure 7.12). You might feel such a way when you see a usually cranky teenager in your neighborhood shoveling an elderly neighbor's driveway. You might also feel this way when a good friend calls you on the anniversary of your mother's death, and you realize that they must have noted down the date and set a reminder because they knew it would be a hard day for you. People often describe the feeling as involving a feeling of warmth or glow, and sometimes even tear up or get goosebumps. Well, it turns out this feeling has a name, and it is **kama muta** (Fiske, Seibt, & Schubert, 2019).

FIGURE 7.12. A feeling of being moved or touched by someone's generosity or thoughtfulness is called kama muta.

One intriguing research study took a cross-cultural perspective on understanding the physiological responses involved in kama muta (Zickfeld et al., 2020). Approximately a hundred and fifty Portuguese and Norwegian participants watched videos piloted to evoke feelings of sadness, awe, and kama muta while sensors and devices measured various aspects of their physiological response—including cardiovascular measures, electrodermal activity, respiration, and facial muscle movements. They even measured whether people experienced piloerection and tears using cameras! The results revealed that stronger self-reported kama muta responses were associated with increases in certain physiological variables (e.g., cheek tension, skin temperature, piloerection) and decreases in others (heart rate, respiration). These patterns were distinct from sadness and awe.

Other researchers have found that positive emotions can help people recover after an intense negative emotion, physiologically as well as emotionally. This is known as the **undoing effect of positive emotion**. Imagine participants who watch a frightening or sad film clip and then watch either a neutral clip or a clip eliciting contentment or amusement. The first film clip elicits increases in heart rate, blood pressure, and sweating that tend to persist. However, participants who subsequently watch a more positive film recover faster, returning more quickly to their baseline physiology (Fredrickson et al., 2000). In this context, even a relatively calm reaction can be highly adaptive. The undoing effect has also been observed for high-intensity positive emotions like desire (Kaczmarek et al., 2019), suggesting that it is the positive valence rather than the calm that might be important in driving the effects. In sum, positive emotions can elicit a variety of responses, depending on the nature of the positive experience and its intensity.

STRESS AND ITS HEALTH CONSEQUENCES

Learning Objectives

- Summarize Hans Selye's classic theory of stress, listing and defining the three stages of the general adaptation syndrome.
- Describe the role of the hypothalamus-pituitary-adrenal (HPA) axis in the stress response.
- Differentiate short- versus long-term physiological effects of the stress response, and analyze implications for effects of chronic stress on health.

Wait (you may wonder), why are we going to talk about stress? Stress is not an emotion. That's true, but stress has enormous impact on emotions. It is an experience that produces emotion, especially in the cases of fear, anger, and grief. After all, the term "fight or flight" was first coined by Walter Cannon to describe the typical physical reactions to stressful conditions.

Have you ever noticed how often people say they are under stress? As Robert Sapolsky (1998) has pointed out, the prime stressors for humans today differ from those of our ancestors. Long ago, our remote ancestors faced many life-or-death crises requiring brief, emergency responses. If a fox is chasing a rabbit, the next few seconds will determine whether the rabbit lives or dies and whether the fox eats. It is a desperate crisis, but when it's over, it's over, and if you survived (or got your meal) you could relax.

For people in technologically advanced societies today—such as, presumably, the readers of this book—the common stressors are less immediate, less life-threatening, but more prolonged, such as paying bills, dealing with a troubled romantic or family relationship, or taking care of a relative with a long-term health problem. Such problems might persist for months or years without much relief. Many people show a stress response even from watching television coverage of major disasters (Silver et al., 2013). Because the human fight-or-flight response evolved to deal with scenarios like the fox–rabbit chase, rather than credit card bills, our bodies react to these prolonged, daily problems as if we were readying for a fight-or-flight emergency. When our reactions are inappropriate, our health suffers.

Hans Selye and the Concept of Stress

Unlike the concept of emotion, the biological and psychological concept of stress is relatively recent. The story is a great one and offers lessons about the importance of observation and ingenuity in science, as well as about stress.

Hundreds of years ago, medical doctors treated most illnesses in the same way. When someone was ill, doctors recommended bed rest, perhaps applied leeches to withdraw "excess" blood, and used herbs or other cure-all tonics. The great progress of scientific medicine depended on distinguishing one disease from another, so that today the recommended treatment depends on which disease you have.

Despite the differences among diseases, when Hans Selye (Figure 7.13) was in medical school, he noted that almost all patients have many symptoms in common. Regardless of their specific symptoms, nearly all have a fever. Nearly all lose their appetite, feel sleepy most of the time, have little energy, and feel little sex drive. They also show increased activity in the immune system. Years later, Selye was doing research with laboratory rats, testing whether a particular kind of substance tended to cause cancer. Like a good scientist,

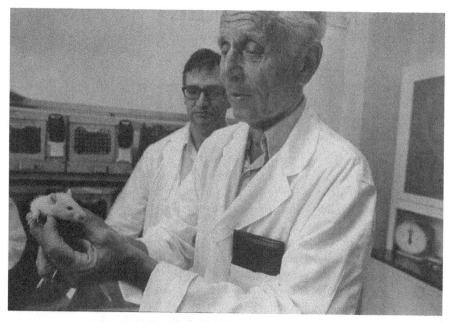

FIGURE 7.13. Hans Selye (1907–1982) was an Austrian-born Canadian physician who became a great pioneer in the study of stress.

he administered the substance (by injection) into half of the rats on a regular basis, and injected a saline solution into the remaining rats as a control group. He was expecting that when he checked the rats for cancer after some months, the group given the experimental treatment would have an unusually high rate of cancer. He was right, but he was surprised to find that his control rats had a remarkably high rate of cancer as well!

It turns out that Selye, although a brilliant scientist, was not good at giving injections to rats. When trying to administer the shots to either group of rats, he sometimes missed the injection spot, got bitten, dropped the rat, chased it around the room, and generally (although unintentionally) tormented the poor creature. When he compared rats he had injected with the rats a more adept research assistant had injected, he found that his own rats were more likely to have developed cancer.

In following up on this lead, Selye noted that either prolonged heat or prolonged cold increased the rats' heart rate and breathing rate, enlarged their adrenal glands, weakened their immune system, and increased their risk of stomach ulcers and other illnesses. He found the same pattern after rats were exposed to pain, poisons, enforced activity (such as confinement to a motorized running wheel), or frightening stimuli (such as a cat, a more aggressive rat, or a clueless researcher chasing it around the room).

Selye concluded that each kind of challenge to the body not only produced specific effects, but also more general effects, which were a result of the body's efforts to fight the problem. He described the body's reaction to any threat as the **general adaptation syndrome**, which he said progressed through three stages—alarm, resistance, and exhaustion. Eventually, Selye introduced the term "stress" to refer to the general adaptation syndrome. Selye was not the first to use the term "stress," but he greatly popularized it and changed what people meant by the term. **Stress**, according to Selye's definition, is the nonspecific response of the body to any demand made on it. The analogy is to a metal: every time you bend a metal, you weaken it. After you have bent it, bending it back weakens it further. Similarly, according to Selye, any major alteration in your life stresses you by changing you in some way, just like bending a metal.

Alarm, the first stage of the general adaptation syndrome, is a brief period of high arousal of the sympathetic nervous system. The adrenal glands secrete epinephrine (also known as adrenaline), which readies the body for vigorous activity, and the hormone cortisol, which increases blood sugar to provide extra energy. Occasional, short-term stress is not a health hazard. In fact, it is probably good for you. Brief, mild stress stimulates attention, memory, and immune system activity (Sapolsky, 2015). You should not try to eliminate all stress from your life, even if that were possible. However, more severe or more prolonged stress begins to pose problems. During the stage of **resistance** the body maintains prolonged but moderate arousal. The sympathetic response declines, because it is not capable of permanent arousal, but the adrenal cortex continues secreting cortisol, enabling the body to be ready for response at any time. After even more prolonged and severe challenges, the body enters the stage of **exhaustion**, characterized by weakness, fatigue, loss of appetite, and lack of motivation. The body's prolonged fight against its threats has weakened its ability to do anything else. The immune system becomes less active and the individual becomes more vulnerable to illness. Exactly when someone moves from one stage of response to another is difficult to predict, and the transition between one stage and the next is gradual, but the data confirm the idea that short-term responses to stress differ from long-term responses.

Defining and Measuring Stress

If Selye's definition is useful, then a good way to measure stress is to examine all the changes that have occurred in someone's life. Researchers have developed several questionnaires based on this assumption. We shall consider one of them in detail, as an example of the others.

Researchers in a pioneering study devised a checklist to measure people's stress by how many life-change items they checked (Holmes & Rahe, 1977). The researchers began by assembling a list of major life changes, including both undesirable events (such as death of a loved one, divorce, or losing one's job) and desirable events that cause upheaval (such as marriage, birth of a child, or taking a vacation). They also included items such as change in financial state, where *change* could refer to either an increase or a decrease. Again, the assumption was that changing something in life is like bending a metal—a movement in either direction is stressful.

Because all life changes are not equally stressful, they should not count equally. The researchers asked more than 300 people to rate the stressfulness of various events relative to one another. Then they used the averages to develop the Social Readjustment Rating Scale. Table 7.3 presents a revised and updated version (Hobson et al., 1998). The instruction is to check the items you have experienced in the past 12 months and then add up the corresponding points. For a large representative sample of US adults, the median total score was 145 (Hobson & Delunas, 2001). Therefore, if your total is above 145, you have had more stress in your life than most other people; if your score is below 145, you have had less stress. However, the distribution of scores is not a neat bell-shape curve.

TABLE 7.3 | Revised social readjustment rating scale

The Revised Social Readjustment Rating Scale (Hobson et al., 1998). To measure your stress level, check the events you have experienced in the past 12 months and total their point values.

LIFE EVENT	MEAN	LIFE EVENT	MEAN
1. Death of spouse/mate	87	27. Experiencing employment discrimination/ sexual harassment	48
2. Death of close family member	79	28. Attempting to modify addictive behavior of self	47
3. Major injury/illness to self	78		
4. Detention in jail or other institution	76	29. Discovering/attempting to modify addictive behavior of close family member	46
5. Major injury/illness to close family member	72		
6. Foreclosure on loan/mortgage	71	30. Employer reorganization/downsizing	45
7. Divorce	71	31. Dealing with infertility/miscarriage	44
8. Being a victim of crime	70	32. Getting married/remarried	43
9. Being a victim of police brutality	69	33. Changing employers/careers	43
10. Infidelity	69	34. Failure to obtain/qualify for a mortgage	42
11. Experiencing domestic violence/sexual abuse	69	35. Pregnancy of self/spouse/mate	41
		36. Experiencing discrimination/harassment outside the workplace	39
12. Separation or reconciliation with spouse/mate	66		
13. Being fired/laid off/unemployed	64	37. Release from jail	39
14. Experiencing financial problems/difficulties	62	38. Spouse/mate begins/ceases work outside the home	38
15. Death of close friend	61		
16. Surviving a disaster	59	39. Major disagreement with boss/coworker	37
17. Becoming a single parent	59	40. Change in residence	35
18. Assuming responsibility for sick or elderly loved one	56	41. Finding appropriate child care/day care	34
		42. Experiencing a large unexpected monetary gain	33
19. Loss of or major reduction in health insurance/benefits	56		
		43. Changing positions (transfer, promotion)	33
20. Self/close family member being arrested for violating the law	56	44. Gaining a new family member	33
		45. Changing work responsibilities	32
21. Major disagreement over child support/ custody/visitation	53	46. Child leaving home	30
		47. Obtaining a home mortgage	30
22. Experiencing/involved in auto accident	53	48. Obtaining a major loan other than home mortgage	30
23. Being disciplined at work/demoted	53		
24. Dealing with unwanted pregnancy	51	49. Retirement	28
25. Adult child moving in with parent/parent moving in with adult child	50	50. Beginning/ceasing formal education	26
26. Child develops behavior or learning problem	49	51. Receiving a ticket for violating the law	22

About one-fourth of all people report scores of zero, and more than 5% report scores above 1,000. Although the median (i.e., the 50th percentile) is 145, the statistical average is 278.

The scale does not include every major stressor we could imagine—note for example the absence of "global pandemic" from the list—but it includes a wide sample. However, it is open to some serious objections. First, the instrument is devised so that points are added for various stressful events, including relatively minor ones. Suppose you graduate from college (26 points), get some unexpected money (33), move to a new address (35), and then start a new job (43). Those events give you a total of 137 points—far more than you would get for a divorce (71) or the death of a husband or wife (87). Does that seem reasonable?

Another problem is the ambiguity of certain items. Consider, for example, the item *Major disagreement with boss/coworker*. How do you decide what is major or minor? The stressfulness of an event also depends on individual circumstances. For example, being laid off from work can be a catastrophe for a 50-year-old who loved his or her job and expects to have trouble finding another one. It may mean little to an 18-year-old who was planning to quit next week to start college. As we noted in earlier chapters, the stressfulness of an event depends on how people appraise the event, and what they think they can do about it. Measuring the stressfulness of an event to the individual is critical, but it is virtually impossible using a brief questionnaire.

Perhaps the most serious problem is that based on the questionnaire, all types of stress are presumed to pose similar health problems. Evidence suggests, however, that the greatest threats to physical and mental health derive from feelings of personal rejection, such as from a divorce or romantic break-up (Murphy et al., 2015).

Because of the conceptual issues raised by these problems, contemporary theorists have been moving away from Selye's definition and calling for more careful and rigorous measurement of stress. For instance, researcher George Slavich (2019) calls out stress research for lumping together stressors that vary significantly in terms of severity, duration, life stage, and frequency. He goes so far as to label this type of research "stressnology," like the ancient practice of phrenology (see Figure 7.14). Phrenology involved feeling for bumps on a person's skull and making statements about their personality based on the size or location of these bumps—this is not a rigorous, or remotely valid, scientific measure. Slavich notes that there have been several improvements in stress measurement, and calls for more researchers to adopt these finer-grained instruments. According to Bruce McEwen (2018) and others, we also need to focus more on how the body's stress response systems become overloaded and less efficient under chronic, repeated stress, rather than focusing on what's going on at one point in time. Teasing out these variations in stressors can help settle some of the contradictory findings in the field of stress research, such as the controversy over whether increased cortisol upon awakening is an adaptive response or a maladaptive one.

How Stress Can Affect Health

However we define stress, researchers can easily identify some events that people regard as stressful, and then test how those events alter physiology and health. For example, people have long observed that the death of a spouse leaves the survivor more vulnerable than usual to a wide variety of illnesses, ranging from dental problems (Hugoson, Ljungquist, & Breivik, 2002) to stroke, heart attack (Carey et al., 2014), and depression (Sasson & Umberson, 2014). After the death of one spouse, the other has an increased probability of dying in the next few months, compared to other people of the same age (Manor & Eisenbach, 2003; Moon et al., 2014). What would be an explanation?

One possibility has nothing to do with stress: maybe both spouses were in the same automobile accident, or got food poisoning from the same meal, or caught the same

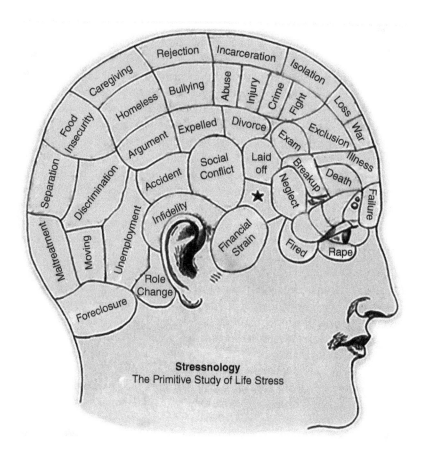

FIGURE 7.14. Stressnology is the primitive (and problematic) study of life stress exposure that involves measuring only the surface features of various forms of life stresses, and which count as similar stressors that vary significantly in terms of severity, timing, duration, and frequency. Is the stress of taking an exam the same as the stress of being imprisoned? From Slavich (2019).

illness. Then, one died shortly after the other. Another possibility is that a grieving spouse does not eat properly, exercise properly, show up for doctors' exams, or take other steps to protect health. Stress affects our behaviors, and if we're not taking care of ourselves, then illness and accidents are more likely.

Other explanations relate more directly to stress physiology. Severe or prolonged stress can be harmful to health, especially if the stressful event seems unpredictable or uncontrollable (Kubzansky et al., 2009). Activity increases in the **hypothalamus–pituitary–adrenal (HPA) axis,** composed of the hypothalamus, pituitary gland, and adrenal gland. Like the sympathetic nervous system, the HPA axis readies the body for vigorous action, but compared to the sympathetic nervous system, the HPA axis responds more slowly and lasts longer, through adrenaline, cortisol, and other hormonal mechanisms. It readies the body for a more prolonged struggle, such as an unpleasant job, a tense relationship with someone you meet every day, living near a war zone, or simply

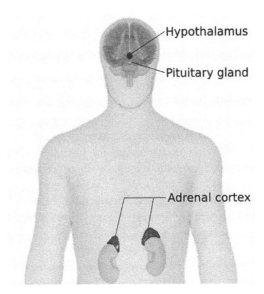

FIGURE 7.15.   The hypothalamus–pituitary–adrenal axis. Stress leads to secretion of the hormone cortisol from the adrenal gland. Cortisol elevates blood sugar and increases metabolism.

worrying about anything that might go wrong. Although the HPA axis prepares the body for a prolonged struggle, people fighting a prolonged struggle do not feel constantly vigorous. Frequently they feel withdrawn or depressed, their performance is inconsistent, and they complain of decreased quality of life (Evans, Bullinger, & Hygge, 1998).

Figure 7.15 illustrates the HPA axis. The hypothalamus reacts to a stressful event by sending a releasing hormone to the anterior pituitary gland, which in turn secretes the hormone adrenocorticotropic hormone. Adrenocorticotropic hormone travels through the bloodstream to the adrenal gland (part of the adrenal gland, located adjacent to each kidney). The adrenal gland responds to adrenocorticotropic hormone by releasing cortisol, which enhances metabolism and increases the availability of fuels. The body stores fuels in the form of carbohydrates, fats, and proteins. Cortisol mobilizes all three types of fuel to come out of storage and enter the blood stream. That activity is helpful to a point, but muscles are the source of protein. That is, when cortisol provides your circulation with extra protein, it does so by breaking down your muscles. You don't want that process to continue for long.

A brief or moderate elevation of cortisol not only elevates blood sugar levels, but also mobilizes parts of the immune system, helping to fight off illness. You can see how that tendency is adaptive because many stressful events that elevate cortisol are potentially injurious, leading to infections and illness. However, we also react with increased cortisol to other events we regard as stressful, although they pose little threat of injury. For example, many college students have increased immune system activity during final exams (Liu et al., 2002; Turner et al., 2020).

The immune system includes natural killer cells, leukocytes (white blood cells), and small proteins called **cytokines** (Segerstrom & Miller, 2004). The body has several types of cytokines. Some of these produce inflammation, such as what forms around a wound in your skin. Although the process of inflammation helps to heal a wound, excessive or prolonged inflammation is linked to increased risk of psychological depression, diabetes, and other disorders (Hodes et al., 2015).

The immune response fights infections directly, but cytokines also stimulate the brain to initiate certain adaptive responses, such as fever, sleepiness, inactivity, decreased appetite, and decreased sex drive. Many people think of fever as something that an infection does to us. In fact, the brain produces fever to try to fight the infection, by inducing reactions of shivering, increased metabolism, and so forth. A moderate fever is adaptive, because many types of bacteria reproduce more slowly at increased temperatures. A fever up to 39°C (103°F) increases one's probability of surviving an infection (Kluger, 1991). Sleepiness, decreased activity, and decreased motivations are also adaptive because they save energy. You will recognize this list of symptoms—fever, sleepiness, decreased activity, and decreased motivation—as the symptoms that Selye noted as a medical student. We now see why so many illnesses share these symptoms: almost any illness activates the immune system, and the immune system produces these symptoms. Severe stress also activates the immune system, producing many of the same symptoms as an illness. If you have been under severe stress and now you feel listless, sleepy, and feverish, you might not be sick. You might be showing effects that result from stress itself.

More serious problems develop with long-term stress, when the body enters the exhaustion stage of the general adaptation syndrome. Although a brief stress activates your immune system, severe or prolonged stress weakens it (Segerstrom & Miller, 2004). For example, production of natural killer cells is suppressed in women taking care of a husband with terminal cancer, women who became widows recently, and survivors of a major earthquake (Glaser et al., 1986; Inoue-Sakurai, Maruyama, & Morimoto, 2000; Irwin et al., 1988). The result of impaired immune response is an increased chance of illness. In one study, volunteers reported their recent stressful experiences and then received injections of a common cold virus. People who reported serious and prolonged stressful experiences were more likely than others to become ill, presumably because their prolonged coping had weakened their immune response (Cohen et al., 1998). In a follow-up study by the same lead researcher, perceived social support (that is, the sense that the people in your life are there for you when you need them) acted as a buffer between stress and greater risk of infection (Cohen et al., 2015). For people reporting low levels of support, increased social stress was associated with higher risk of illness. For people with high levels of support, increased social stress had no such effect on health. And for those who did get sick, both perceived support and receipt of hugs predicted less severe signs of illness. Get your hugs!

Part of the increased health risk is caused by cortisol. Because prolonged cortisol provides more energy for the body to use at the moment and because it increases the breakdown of the body's proteins for extra fuel, it leaves less energy available for synthesis of the proteins that the immune system needs. However, depending on the type of stress, its intensity, and its duration, cortisol levels and immune system responses can vary over a wide range.

Prolonged cortisol elevation also produces direct effects on the brain. Cortisol increases metabolic rate, and in doing so, it causes cells in the hippocampus to become more vulnerable to damage by either toxins or overstimulation. Hippocampal cells that are highly active take in more blood, including any toxins that might be in the blood, and are also more subject to damage by overstimulation than are other brain cells. The result of high cortisol levels is damage to many neurons in the hippocampus, an area important for storing memory (Sapolsky, 1992). In one study, baby rats were separated from their mothers—a stressful event for infant mammals—for 3 hours each day for the first 2 weeks of life. They were treated normally from then on. As adults, the production of new neurons in the hippocampus was less than normal (Mirescu, Peters, & Gould, 2004). This result is interesting because the stress was social rather than physically painful, and the effects lasted a lifetime.

Cortisol also has direct effects on the expression of many genes in brain cells, producing a variety of effects that vary from one brain area to another. In some brain areas cortisol causes shrinkage of dendrites and loss of synapses, but in other areas it expands dendrites and increases synapses (McEwen et al., 2015). In particular, stress impairs functioning in the prefrontal cortex while strengthening activity in the amygdala and an area called the striatum, part of the basal ganglia (Arnsten, 2015). The prefrontal cortex is important for planning, attention, working memory, and inhibiting risky impulses. Severe stress impairs attention, working memory, and performance on complex tasks, with similar results in rodents, monkeys, and humans. The amygdala, as you know from Chapter 6, processes emotional information, especially information relevant to threats. The striatum, an area not previously discussed in this book, is especially important for learned habits.

Imagine what happens if stress strengthens your amygdala and striatum while it weakens your prefrontal cortex. You react strongly to any sign of threat, you stick with your habitual responses, you don't think things through, and you don't inhibit your impulses. In many emergencies, that approach is helpful. If someone or something is about to attack you, you should note the danger and take action immediately, not stopping to contemplate possible strategies. However, if the danger is less immediate, your reaction to stress may block you from finding the best possible decision.

Given that stress makes it difficult to inhibit your impulses, one bit of advice is to develop good impulses. While you are at rest, imagine what you should do in potential dangerous situations, so you can react quickly without much thought if the situation arises.

The same advice applies to people like airplane pilots and professional athletes who must act quickly under pressure: in a high-stress situation, you may not be thinking clearly about strategy. Therefore, it is important to practice good responses to likely situations under realistic conditions, so that if the need arises, you can act quickly, habitually, automatically.

SUMMARY

When we describe or imagine emotional feelings, we commonly refer to bodily sensations. Yet despite the apparently obvious role of the body in emotion, researchers have long struggled with core questions about the relationship between physiological changes and emotional experience. How strongly do changes in physiology correlate with changes in feeling, or other aspects of emotion? Does each emotion really have a unique physiological signature? Do stressful emotions affect health, and if so, how? In this chapter you have seen—if you had not already noted from previous chapters—that definitive research on emotions is difficult. For ethical reasons, researchers have limited control over people's emotions, and for practical and technical reasons, they can measure behavior and physiology with only limited accuracy.

Still, a few conclusions emerge. Both approach and avoidance motivation seem linked with arousal and activation of the body, serving as the energy part of the "energy + direction" equation for motivation. With regard to the autonomic specificity hypothesis, we can rule out the two most extreme positions. No named emotion (such as fear, anger, or disgust) has a sufficiently unique physiological signature that we could identify it in someone just by measuring physiology. (MNS often gets requests from tech companies asking for her help with this, and she has to say no!) At least, that is true with our current sophistication of measurement and the evidence we have so far. Even if we could measure all the physiological changes in each emotion perfectly, the patterns are not exact, and we would face the reverse inference problem described in Chapter 6. However, it would also be wrong to say that all emotions differ only in level of arousal. Overall, if we compare two emotional states, we find some degree of similarity and some degree of difference.

Second, changes in the body associated with emotion are neither inherently good nor inherently bad. Fight–flight sympathetic nervous system activation is seen in positive emotions as well as in negative emotions. Increases in cortisol occur in response to stressful situations, but also when healthy people living relatively low-stress lives wake in the morning, encouraging us to get up, go out, and make use of the day. Physiological changes in emotion are about allocating energy when and where it is needed. This is a problem when the system is disturbed, and cues meant to help us survive threats to life and limb backfire in the face of modern stressors.

Finally, our review of research on stress shows important differences between brief, mild stress and prolonged, severe stress. Mild stress is harmless or even healthy, but severe stress poses dangers to both physical and mental health. As researchers continue to explore the mechanisms of these effects, we may gain better ways to control stress reactions.

KEY TERMS

alarm: a brief period of high arousal of the sympathetic nervous system, readying the body for vigorous activity (p. 259)

arousal theory: early theory of motivation which emphasized the role of physiological activation in motivational states (p. 246)

autonomic nervous system: a set of neurons by which the central nervous system influences the visceral organs (p. 230)

autonomic specificity: the extent to which each emotion has a distinct, recognizable pattern of autonomic nervous system response (p. 249)

cardiac pre-ejection period: the time in milliseconds between the beginning of ventricular contraction and the expulsion of blood into the aorta (p. 243)

cortisol: an adrenal gland hormone that enhances metabolism and increases the availability of fuels in the body (p. 238)

cytokines: small proteins that contribute to the immune process by regulating inflammation at the site of an injury and by communicating to the brain to initiate appropriate responses by the brain (p. 263)

diastolic blood pressure: the pressure exerted by blood against the arteries while the heart is not contracting (p. 242)

electrodermal activity: changes in the ability of the skin to conduct electricity (p. 243)

endocrine system: the hormones and the glands that produce them (p. 238)

exhaustion: the final stage of reaction to a prolonged stressor, characterized by weakness, fatigue, loss of appetite, and lack of interest (p. 259)

general adaptation syndrome: Hans Selye's term for the body's reaction to any change (p. 258)

hormone: a chemical produced by an endocrine gland and released into the bloodstream, with effects on one or more organs elsewhere in the body (p. 238)

hypothalamus–pituitary–adrenal (HPA) axis: the hypothalamus, pituitary gland, and adrenal gland (p. 262)

interbeat interval: the average time in milliseconds between heartbeats (p. 242)

kama muta: an emotion characterized by feelings of warmth, often evoked by acts of extreme generosity or kindness (p. 255)

locked-in syndrome: condition in which people lose almost all output from the brain to both the muscles and the autonomic nervous system, although they continue to receive sensations (p. 249)

parasympathetic nervous system: the rest-and-digest branch of the autonomic nervous system, which diverts resources to maintenance and growth activities (p. 233)

peristalsis: smooth muscle contractions than move food through the digestive system; caused by parasympathetic nervous system activation (p. 232)

piloerection: contraction of smooth muscles around the base of hairs, making them stand up; caused by sympathetic nervous system activation (p. 232)

pure autonomic failure: medical condition in which the autonomic nervous system ceases to influence the body (p. 248)

resistance: the stage of prolonged but moderate arousal in response to some stressor (p. 259)

respiratory sinus arrhythmia: the change in heart rate associated with breathing in versus out; used as a measure of parasympathetic nervous system activation (p. 244)

stress (McEwen's definition): an event or events that are interpreted as threatening to an individual and which elicit physiological and behavioral responses (p. 261)

stress (Selye's definition): the nonspecific response of the body to any demand made on it (p. 259)

sympathetic nervous system: the fight-or-flight branch of the autonomic nervous system, which prepares the body for vigorous activity (p. 230)

systolic blood pressure: pressure exerted by blood against the arteries while the heart is contracting (p. 242)

undoing effect of positive emotion: an effect where positive emotions facilitate recovery from sympathetic arousal associated with negative emotion (p. 256)

THOUGHT/DISCUSSION QUESTIONS

1. The English language includes many physical metaphors for emotion, such as "blowing your top" and "melting." Think of other such metaphors. What do they imply about the physiological changes we should expect to see in particular emotions?

2. Think about the last time you felt a powerful emotion. What were the physical sensations that accompanied that feeling? Imagine you had not experienced those physical sensations, but everything else about the experience was the same. What is left over? Would you still be feeling an emotion?

3. When someone is stressed or upset, we often tell them to take a deep breath in an effort to calm down. What happens to the rest of your body when you take a deep breath? Design a simple study you can conduct in class or with a group of friends, examining the effect of a few deep breaths on heart rate. You can also use an online search engine to learn about other physiological effects of deep breathing and the mechanisms by which these occur. Why might these changes help people regulate their emotions?

4. In a later chapter, we will discuss physical exercise as another valuable emotion regulation strategy. Given what you have learned about the physiological stress response in this chapter, explain why physical exercise might be helpful.

SUGGESTIONS FOR FURTHER READING

Damasio, A. (1999). *The feeling of what happens: Body and emotion in the making of consciousness.* Harcourt College. A thoughtful analysis of the relationship between physiological aspects of emotion and conscious experience, written by a prominent neuroscientist.

Levenson, R. W. (2014). The autonomic nervous system and emotion. *Emotion Review, 6*(2), 100–112. An accessible, balanced summary of the evidence on autonomic physiology-related hypotheses rooted in basic/discrete emotion theory, including a critique of the available data.

O'Connor, D.B., Thayer, J.F., & Vedhara, K. (2021). Stress and health: A review of psychobiological processes. *Annual Review of Psychology, 72,* 663–688. A comprehensive overview of the current state of play in stress and health research.

Sapolsky, R. M. (2004). *Why zebras don't get ulcers, 3rd edition.* Holt. An excellent review of physiological changes in stress and why they are such a problem in modern life, written in a highly engaging style.

CHAPTER 8

Emotional and Motivational Development

What is your earliest memory of an emotional experience? How old were you? To what were you reacting? What did you want or need from the situation? How did other people around you react? How would you have described your emotion to others at the time, and how would you describe it now? Did you get the impression that it was okay to feel the way you did, or that your feelings were frowned upon by those around you?

Can you remember when and how you began to learn words for emotions? Can you remember the first time you were strongly aware of someone else's emotions? How did you respond? How have your emotions and motivations changed as you went through childhood, adolescence, and now (for most readers) young adulthood? How do you think your emotions and motivational priorities will change in the future?

Developmental psychologists with interests in emotion and motivation address questions such as these, and many others, in their research. Studying emotional and motivational development is important for both practical and theoretical reasons. At a practical level, if you spend time with toddlers, teenagers, people in the throes of midlife, or those entering old age, it's helpful if you can understand the perspective underlying their emotional reactions and goals. Parents are often concerned about whether their child is developing "on schedule" in various ways, and emotion is no exception. Also, good research can help identify the mechanisms that underlie developmental changes in emotion and motivation. This knowledge is important for those who want to develop interventions. For example, the onset of psychological disorders involving disruption of emotion often occurs during adolescence or the transition to adulthood (Kessler et al., 2005); understanding why this is the case could help point toward effective treatments. Similarly, if public health officials want to support older adults' well-being, it helps to know that loneliness is a common cause of distress in late life and that loneliness has detrimental effects on physical as well as mental health (Hawkley et al., 2019).

Learning how emotion develops may also help us understand more about emotion itself. We learn about the causes of emotion by seeing how emotional development relates to changes in the body, in cognition, and in one's social world. As we shall see, developmental trajectory sometimes provides information about the function served by some aspect of emotion, or about other abilities needed for the emotion to occur. Understanding the developmental trajectories of people's motivational goals can help inform interventions supporting well-being across the lifespan. Moreover, researchers studying the socialization patterns by which children learn rules about emotional feelings and displays contribute to our understanding of how emotion is shaped by culture.

However, research on emotion and motivation, difficult enough with adults, is even more challenging with young children. For most of their first year children don't talk at all, and for the next year or so they don't talk much. Infants have very expressive faces, and they certainly use their voices to make their feelings known, but their range of specific facial expressions is more limited than is true of adults. Some preverbal children use hand gestures to indicate their feelings, such as drawing the forefinger from an eye down the cheek (like a flowing tear) to indicate sadness (Vallotton, 2008). However, gestures convey limited information.

Even when children do begin to talk, we can't expect them to communicate their emotions clearly until they learn what words to use and what those words mean. Researchers are still debating how exactly this happens, but whatever the process, it takes a while. Children do not reliably use words for specific emotions such as "angry" or "excited" until they are two or more years old, and it takes years for emotion vocabulary to develop (Ridgeway, Waters, & Kuczaj, 1985). Anyone who has spent much time with infants and toddlers has wondered, "what on earth is the baby crying about?" You might be able to guess these things based on the situation, but not always. Even if you do know what event elicited an emotional reaction, it can be difficult to determine how the child is appraising that event. So adults are trying to interpret young children's emotions and motivational needs at the same time that children are trying to learn the words and concepts to communicate all this. Confusion is inevitable.

For ethical and practical reasons, researchers studying babies and very young children can't use many of the methods they would use with adults. For the most part, researchers observe infants' spontaneous behaviors or their reactions to simple situations, and see how those reactions change over time. This approach leaves substantial room for debate over how to interpret study results, but that's part of the fun.

EMOTION AND MOTIVATION IN INFANCY

Let's start by exploring the displays of emotion and motivation we can see during the first months of life. Later we discuss the changes that continue through childhood, adolescence, adulthood, and into old age.

Learning Objectives
- Differentiate the situations in which newborns and babies in the first weeks of life are likely to cry and smile from the situations in which older children and adults show these expressions.
- Define the Moro reflex, and analyze whether this behavior reflects the experience of an emotion versus a more general motivational state.
- Summarize the theorized role of social smiling in parent-infant bonding.

Crying

One nonverbal expression readily apparent from birth is crying (see Figure 8.1). Newborns cry when they are hungry, sleepy, gassy, or uncomfortable. For very young babies, crying usually means that a core motivational need is unmet; it's not an emotional response to some event out there in the world. One meta-analysis of several studies compared babies with **colic**—fussing or crying more than three hours per day, at least three days per week—who'd been randomly assigned to consume doses of *Lactobacillus reuteri* against babies in placebo control groups. *Lactobacillus reuteri* is a **probiotic**, a type of microorganism such as bacteria and yeast, commonly used in making yogurt and kombucha. Probiotics are thought to help humans maintain a healthy digestive tract, encouraging the inner bacterial life needed to digest food appropriately and thereby reducing discomfort (Verna & Lucak, 2010). Sure enough, the babies in the probiotic conditions showed substantially reduced crying as compared to the control groups, especially among breast-fed babies (Sung et al., 2018). These babies weren't crying because of a loss, or a failure, or because someone had hurt their feelings—their tummies were just upset!

Newborns also cry when they hear other newborns cry; this is called **contagious crying**. Tape-recorded cries of older children, monkeys, or the infants themselves evoke little reaction; only the cry of another newborn will produce a major effect (Dondi, Simion, & Caltran, 1999; Martin & Clark, 1982). We might be tempted to think that the newborn sympathizes with the other infant and assumes that something awful for babies is happening. However, much argues against that interpretation. The newborn almost certainly does not understand the existence of other newborns similar to itself. Over the next few months, infants gradually increase their social responses to others, but meanwhile the probability of contagious crying

FIGURE 8.1. Newborn infants cry when they are uncomfortable or distressed, but they are not yet able to communicate discrete negative emotions.

decreases rather than increasing (Geangu et al., 2010). Not until the age of eight months do infants show any sign of understanding that another infant is in distress, and even then the reaction looks more like interest than real concern (Davidov et al., 2013). Furthermore, contagious crying is not immediate, but generally begins after listening to another infant cry for two or three minutes. Contagious crying may just mean that hearing a loud, prolonged cry is arousing and unpleasant.

Young babies do sometimes cry when they hear a loud, unexpected noise (Schmidt & Fox, 1998). However, crying in response to a sudden loud noise (scary) sounds about the same as crying in response to someone holding the infant's hands immobile (uncomfortable and annoying), so we cannot distinguish specific emotions such as fear and anger based on the sound of babies' cries (Chóliz, Fernández-Abascal, & Martínez-Sánchez, 2012). The facial expressions babies show in scary versus annoying situations do not differ reliably either (Camras et al., 2007). For this reason, researchers say a newborn's cry expresses **distress**—an undifferentiated protest against anything unpleasant or threatening.

Crying has an immediate and powerful effect on people nearby, especially the baby's parents: suddenly everybody wants to know why this tiny thing is howling, and how to make it stop! Studies using fMRI methods have found that both mothers and fathers show heightened activation in brain regions supporting approach motivation, perspective-taking, and empathy when hearing a recording of their baby's cry (Li et al., 2018; Lorberbaum et al., 2002). In one impressive study with hundreds of participants from 11 countries around the world, researchers videotaped an hour of interaction between mothers and babies at home, and coded the moms' behavior in response to their baby crying. The most common responses involved picking the baby up and either holding it or talking to it, engaging actively with the baby (Bornstein et al., 2017). The advantage to the infant is clear: crying is its first way of getting attention and care. Later, the addition of smiling and laughter offers a second message: I like that, keep doing it!

Smiling and Laughing

When newborns relax, sometimes the corners of their mouths curl up. By about the age of three weeks, their eyelids begin to crinkle as well, and infants may open their mouths into a full grin (Emde & Koenig, 1969; Wolff, 1987). These expressions occur occasionally throughout the day, but most commonly during "active" or rapid eye movement sleep (Challamel et al., 2021). The expressions have little or no connection to the social situation, unless we assume that the babies are having happy dreams, so it's a matter of definition as to whether we want to call them smiles.

By about two months of age infants begin **social smiling**—smiling in response to seeing someone else smile (Figure 8.2). At first, social smiling is exhibited mainly with parents and other regular caregivers (Mendes, Seidl-de-Moura, & Siqueira, 2009). Social smiling occurs much more frequently in some mother–infant pairs than in others, although it is not obvious how much the mother influences the infant and how much the infant influences the mother (Bigelow & Power, 2014).

Why does the social smile emerge at this time? Many psychologists relate the transition to the development of visual acuity and to changes in how the infant looks at people's faces. For the first few weeks of life, infants have only blurry vision, and they tend to look toward the top of the face (the eyes) rather than the bottom, including the mouth (Cassia,

FIGURE 8.2.   Social smiling, which begins around the second month of life, makes it more rewarding for adults to interact with babies.

Turati, & Simion, 2004). At six to eight weeks, infants begin to look more closely at people's features and to see smiles more clearly. However, you don't have to learn how to smile. People blind from birth smile about as much as sighted people do, and in the same situations (Matsumoto & Willingham, 2009). They don't smile in response to seeing someone else smile (because they do not see), but they smile in appropriate situations nevertheless.

Whatever the reason for the onset of social smiling, its function is clear: back-and-forth exchanges of smiling and cooing help support affective coordination and bonding between babies and their caregivers (Lavelli & Fogel, 2013). This coordination is thought to be the basis for **coregulation**—a process by which two or more individuals (in this case a baby and its caregiver) reciprocally influence each other's emotions, helping both move toward the desired state. Mother-infant coregulation when infants are six months old has been found to predict higher infant cardiac vagal tone, a physiological marker of developing self-regulation ability (Porter, 2003), as well as higher motor and cognitive functioning later in the first year of life (Evans & Porter, 2009).

Although social smiling helps to strengthen the relationship between parent and child, it is not necessary. Children who are blind from birth can establish an attachment to their parents that is just as strong as that of any other child (Demir et al., 2014).

On average, the parents of blind children play physically with their babies (tickling, bouncing, and so on) more than parents of sighted children, and blind babies often smile in response to this play, as well as in response to sounds (Fraiberg, 1974; Rogers & Puchalski, 1986). Indeed, tactile cues, especially skin-to-skin contact, are an important basis of bonding for everyone (Takeuchi et al., 2010).

Parents in different cultures may create affective reciprocity in a variety of ways, using vocalizations and/or touch instead of face-to-face social smiling. In one study researchers coded the behavior of mother-infant dyads: some in middle-class Italian families; some in families from a traditional rural community in Cameroon, Africa; and some from West African immigrant families living in Italy. Whereas the expected face-to-face exchanges were observed often in the Italian sample, the other samples showed more reciprocal patterns of vocalizing and affectionate touch (Lavelli, Carra, Rossi, & Keller, 2019). This study offers a great example of interaction between an evolved mechanism (parent-infant coordination of nonverbal positive affect) and shaping by cultural context (which expressive modalities are emphasized) in understanding emotional processes.

Responses to Danger

Another infant behavior that we might consider an emotional expression is the **Moro reflex**—a sequence in which the infant flings out its arms and spreads its fingers, then contracts quickly into a fetal position with fingers bent (Figure 8.3). Some babies exhibit this reflex while they are still making their way out of the womb, and in the first few seconds of life (Rousseau et al., 2017). The Moro reflex has been described as an *infant startle*, and the second part of it does resemble the adult startle response. Babies display

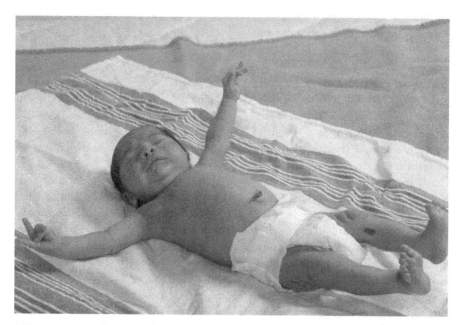

FIGURE 8.3. In the Moro reflex babies fling their arms wide with fingers spread and then contract into the fetal position, bending their fingers. This reflex may help babies grab onto a caregiver in a potentially dangerous situation.

the Moro reflex in situations that suggest danger, such as being dropped, hearing a sudden loud noise, or seeing a large figure moving quickly toward them. Infants probably don't understand that these signals mean danger, any more than a bird understands why it sits on eggs or why it feels an urge to fly south for the winter. Rather, the human nervous system has developed to produce a startle response in situations that during our evolutionary history, have usually been dangerous.

The utility of the Moro reflex is clear. In a potentially dangerous situation, an infant reaches out and grabs onto whatever it can, pulling in tightly. Grabbing something might prevent an infant from falling. Grabbing an adult might mean that the adult will carry the infant away from danger. Some researchers have suggested that the Moro reflex might also be an innate communicative gesture, evoking attention and contact from caregivers, but this proposal has not yet been investigated with strong research (Rousseau et al., 2017).

Does the Moro reflex indicate that newborns experience fear? Not necessarily. The reflex does not include the prototypical facial expression of fear. Also, adult fear depends on a cognitive appraisal of the situation as dangerous. If a loud noise or sudden flash of light startles us, we might flinch, but if we examine the situation and find no danger, the startle might give way to laughter and amusement, anger, or indifference, rather than fear. After a Moro reflex, infants start crying regardless of what else is happening. If they start to cry at the sound of fireworks, for example, their crying continues despite the lack of any other sign of danger. In contrast, they fail to show fear in many situations adults find dangerous. Infants are not afraid of heights until they begin to crawl (Adolph, 2000; Campos, Bertenthal, & Kermoian, 1992). In short, the newborn's Moro reflex is related to certain kinds of dangerous situations, but fear itself develops more gradually.

One consistent trend emerges from these lines of research. In newborns, expressions such as crying, smiling, and startle are mostly responses to simple biological states, more aligned with basic motivational needs than emotional reactions to events in the outside world. Newborns cry because they are hungry or in pain, not because they miss their stuffed animals. Newborns smile when they feel comfortable. They exhibit the Moro reflex in response to sudden bright lights or loud noises, or when they are dropped. Emotions in response to cognitive appraisals of events—especially social events—come later.

HOW DO EMOTIONS DEVELOP?

By about three years of age, children express a wide range of emotions. Across childhood they develop greater understanding of other people's emotions, greater ability to talk about emotions, and greater ability to regulate their emotions. How do these transitions occur? Research suggests that physical maturation, cognitive development, and social interaction all play important roles in this process.

Learning Objectives
- List three aspects of development and experience beyond emotion that play important roles in supporting emotional development, and provide an example of each.
- Define theory of mind, intersubjectivity, and social referencing, and recognize hypothetical/unfamiliar examples of each.

Physical Maturation

The capacity to experience and display emotions requires a certain degree of physical maturation. For example, newborn infants have poor vision, especially in the center of the eye where adults' visual acuity is best (Abramov et al., 1982). For the first six months they have trouble shifting visual attention from one object to another, yet a moving object will capture their attention so thoroughly that they literally cannot look away from it (Clohessy et al., 1991; Johnson, Posner, & Rothbart, 1991). Their immature vision does not limit their emotions, but it does limit their ability to respond to visual stimuli.

Similarly, developing abilities to crawl and walk introduce new situations with implications for emotion. An infant who is newly able to crawl also must face a new risk of getting lost, or encountering danger. An infant who is newly able to stand and walk suddenly must cope with the risk of falling. These changes in motor ability may trigger the development of new emotion systems, or they may stimulate emotion systems that were present but dormant.

Increasing motor maturation also enables the infant to express emotions more clearly. A newborn human cannot make a fist in anger or run away in fright, and in many ways resembles a computer that is not attached to a screen or printer. Much may be going on inside, but no one knows about it. Muscle control increases greatly in the first year or two of life, and with it comes a great increase in the capacity for emotional and other communication.

Cognitive Maturation

In Chapter 4 we emphasized the importance of appraisal, one's cognitive interpretation of an event, in determining emotional experience. Appraisal requires cognitive abilities that develop across the early months and years of life, rather than being present at birth. Learning continues throughout life, but the most obvious and dramatic changes occur in the first few years. Children develop many cognitive abilities that adults typically take for granted—after all, we can't remember a time when we did not have them—and these abilities have important implications for how we experience emotion.

In one classic study researchers compared the reactions of infants of one, four, and seven months of age to a procedure in which someone held down one of the infant's arms firmly, so that it could not be moved (Sternberg & Campos, 1990). An adult would presumably find this annoying, and would express anger toward the person restraining their arm (see Figure 8.4; we don't recommend trying this technique at home, certainly not with your roommate). The one-month-old infants did not show a prototypical anger display, but they did lower their brows and raise their cheeks in an expression somewhat different from both generic distress and anger, with their eyes tightly closed and their tongues stuck out of their mouths. At four months infants showed a more characteristic anger expression, narrowing their eyes, pulling back their lips, frowning, and raising their cheeks. At this age they looked primarily at the arm that was being restrained during their protest. At seven months, infants showed an even more prototypical anger expression and looked at the face of the experimenter doing the restraining—and at their mothers, who were in the room. In short, the anger expression emerged gradually across the first several months.

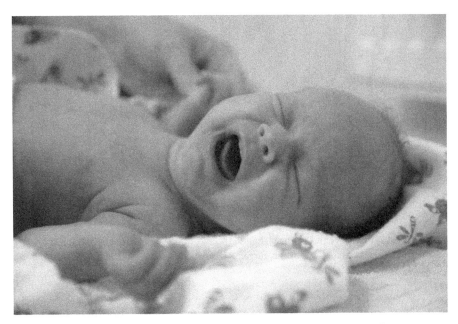

FIGURE 8.4. The arm restraint procedure is used to examine babies' emotional response to an uncomfortable, annoying situation.

According to Sternberg and Campos (1990), this sequence reflects development from a fuzzy sense of frustration to prototypical anger directed at the experimenter, as the baby's capacity for appraising or understanding the situation becomes more sophisticated. At one month the infant can't move its arms and presumably doesn't understand why. By four months the infant localizes his or her discomfort to the arm restraint, but still cannot attribute the event to the actions of another person. By seven months, the infant appears to blame the experimenter (and mom) for the situation. By this interpretation, infants are beginning to feel different kinds of distress even in the first month of life, but they become more prototypically angry as they develop the cognitive ability to attribute their frustration to a particular cause, especially another person.

One important cognitive ability that develops late in the second year of life is having a self-concept. Most psychologists believe that infants lack a clear sense of self, and Lewis and Brooks-Gunn (1979) designed a clever study to determine when this ability emerges. They asked the mothers of nine- to 24-month-old children to put a spot of rouge on the children's noses, while pretending to wipe off their faces. The mothers then held the children up to a large mirror. Infants younger than about 16 months of age typically reached out to the mirror, as though it were another child. By contrast, children 18 to 24 months of age consistently did what adults would do—reach up to their own noses to wipe off the spot (Figure 8.5). They recognized "The child I see in the mirror is me." Modifications of this test have shown apparent self-recognition in several nonhuman species as well, including chimpanzees, certain monkey species, dolphins, elephants, and magpies (Heschl & Burkhart, 2006; Plotnik, de Waal, & Reiss, 2006; Prior, Schwarz, & Gunturkun, 2008). At the age when children first start to recognize themselves in the

FIGURE 8.5.   A typical child younger than 16 months of age sees the red dot on his or her nose or forehead and points at it in the mirror. An older child points to his or her own head, indicating self-recognition.

mirror, they also begin to show signs of embarrassment, shame, and guilt, all of which require seeing yourself through other people's eyes and/or comparing yourself to their expectations (Lewis, 1992; Lewis et al., 1991). These emotions continue to emerge over at least the next few years.

Gradually children begin to develop **theory of mind**, the understanding that other people have minds too and that some people, including yourself, might know something that other people don't know. Depending on how we test for this ability, it may seem to emerge as early as age 1½ or as late as 4½ to 6 years old (Rubio-Fernández & Geurts, 2013; Senju et al., 2011; Wellman, Cross, & Watson, 2001; Wimmer & Perner, 1983). This suggests that rudimentary theory of mind becomes more sophisticated with time and/or experience. Theory of mind is thought to serve as an important foundation for empathy, sharing another person's feelings (Preckel, Kanske, & Singer, 2018). Theory of mind is important for emotions such as shame, embarrassment, and guilt as well; for this reason, some researchers refer to these as *other-conscious* emotions, rather than self-conscious emotions (e.g., Witherington, Campos, & Hertenstein, 2001).

Social Interaction

As social constructivists have pointed out, humans learn a great deal about emotion from their social environment. Children and their parents begin to synchronize their attention to objects, and their emotional responses to them, late in the first year of life (Leclere et al., 2014). The result is **intersubjectivity,** the sharing of experience. Not only does the parent copy the child's response, but the child copies the parent, thereby learning the proper emotional reactions. At first infants just respond to the parent's emotions (*primary intersubjectivity*), but later they notice what caused the parent's reaction and then adjust their own reaction to that object or event (*secondary intersubjectivity*). Infants begin looking to trusted caregivers to find out how they should feel about novel objects or events sometime late in the first year of life. This is called **social referencing**: observing other people's behavior as a guide to your own reaction. When an infant meets someone new, the parent's pleasure says "this person is okay." If the infant falls, whether they start to cry or stand up and continue playing depends in part on whether the caregiver shows panic or nonchalance. Intersubjectivity and social referencing begin in infancy and become increasingly prominent as children grow (Perez Burriel & Sadurni Brugue, 2014).

Like theory of mind, social referencing emerges over time. An early sign of social referencing appears at about nine months, in the **visual cliff**: researchers place an infant on a table with plates of clear glass on either side. On the "shallow" side, the infant sees a floor that is just a short step down. On the "deep" side the floor appears to be much farther away (Figure 8.6). Infants who have had some experience with crawling, and therefore some experience with falling down, usually turn toward the shallow side, indicating the ability to detect depth (and a preference for avoiding injury).

Suppose researchers place an infant on the shallow side while the mother stands on the other side of the table, beyond the deep end. The mother is instructed either to look frightened or to smile and encourage the infant to cross. Starting at about nine months of age, most infants use their mothers' cues to decide whether to cross. An infant stays put when the mother looks frightened, but tests the glass and then crosses when the mother looks happy (Sorce et al., 1985).

Consider some other situations. A parent blows "air raspberries" toward a baby. Infants as young as five months old smile and laugh more if they see the parent

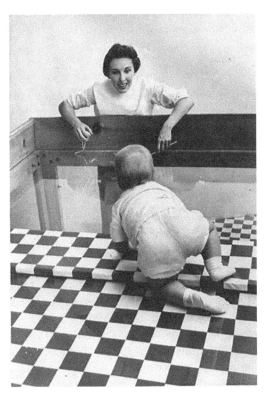

FIGURE 8.6.   Infants late in their first year of life look to caregivers' emotions to decide how to respond to novel situations, such as the visual cliff.

smiling and laughing too (Mireault et al., 2015). In another study, an infant sees some unfamiliar toys, and the mother acts afraid of one of them. Here, we see 11-month-olds copying the mother's fear (Blackford & Walden, 1998). In yet another study, infants watch an actress in a video display an emotional reaction to an object. When permitted to play with the object, 16- to 18-month-old infants approached it if the actress had shown happiness or surprise, and avoided it if the actress had shown fear or anger. Infants aged 12 to 14 months seemed unaffected by the actress's display (Martin et al., 2014).

Physical maturation, cognitive development, and changes in social interaction and other aspects of the environment are often intertwined. Some aspects of emotional development may be explained by one of these factors, but in other cases a more complex set of causes is involved. We will see an example of this later in the chapter, as we discuss emotion in adolescence.

EMOTIONAL DEVELOPMENT IN CHILDREN

The period between infancy and adolescence brings striking development in every aspect of emotion. A rich array of distinct emotional experiences and expressions emerges from the baby's global distress and pleasure. Children become increasingly able to understand and talk about other people's emotions, as well as their own. Childhood is also a crucial period for learning cultural norms and expectations around emotion: what emotions are valued and discouraged, how to appraise the meaning of various events, and how emotions may be expressed.

Learning Objectives
- Summarize the trajectories of development from infancy to age 12 in emotional (a) facial expression display and recognition, (b) vocabulary, (c) conceptual knowledge, and (d) emotion regulation, and analyze the pattern that emerges.
- Generate hypotheses regarding the role of physical maturation, cognitive development, and/or social interaction in supporting different aspects of child emotional development.
- Summarize three ways in which parents and other adults socialize, or help shape, children's emotions.

Experience, Nonverbal Expression, and Language

How does children's experience of emotion change over time? When does the capacity for more differentiated emotions emerge, and how? As we noted earlier, these questions are inextricably tied to children's development of emotion vocabulary and nonverbal expression; without these we have no way of knowing specifically what a child is feeling. There is little sign of such specificity during the first several months of infancy. If your baby is crying, probably it is hungry, or sleepy, or uncomfortable, or it needs a diaper change. Those are the multiple-choice options. For all practical purposes, you do not really need to know whether the baby is sad, annoyed, frightened, or some combination of these, because regardless the correct response is to pick up the baby, hold it, and figure out what it needs.

The theoretical issues at stake in understanding when the capacity for more specific emotions emerge are not trivial, however. For those who advocate for the basic or discrete emotion perspective, one criterion is that such emotions should emerge early in life. Anything we see in newborns is, by definition, something they were born with, part of human nature. Some emotional capacity that emerges years later could be a product of learning, though this is not a logical necessity. Many aspects of our inherited human nature do not emerge for some years into life. Language is one such aspect, and sexual desire is another. Still, if we could demonstrate distinct emotions early in life, we would strengthen the case that they are innate. For that reason, several investigators have sought to identify facial expressions for distinct emotions in infants as young as possible.

In one set of studies, researchers obtained photographs of strong facial expressions by dozens of infants, most of whom were less than seven months old (Oster, Hegley, & Nagel, 1992). These expressions had previously been coded by a system similar to FACS, but specific to babies' faces, called Max (Izard, 1983). According to this coding system, the expressions were thought to convey joy, interest, surprise, disgust, fear, anger, sadness, or generic distress. The researchers first wanted to know whether untrained adults would recognize these supposedly distinct expressions, labeling them with the intended emotion terms. Participants did well for positive and neutral emotions: more than 70% correctly labeled each expression of joy and surprise. Results for negative emotions were much less impressive. People did slightly better than chance for some photos of some emotions, but not by much, and participants were more likely to choose the label *distress* or *sadness* than the intended label for most photographs.

Moreover, when the same photos were coded using a new, FACS-based system called Baby FACS, the Max and Baby FACS conclusions about which emotion was expressed differed for almost all of the negative emotions. Even at 11 months, infants' facial expressions do not consistently differ in response to the arm-restraint procedure described earlier (which should make the baby angry or annoyed) versus seeing a scary gorilla head that makes growling noises while its eyes light up and its lips move (Camras et al., 2007).

Facial expression is not the only nonverbal behavior researchers can observe to document an emotional response, but the alternatives are controversial as well as sneaky. Consider the difficulty in determining the age when babies first experience surprise. Experimenters in a study show an infant two objects, cover them with a screen, and then retrieve one of the objects from behind the screen, as shown in Figure 8.7. Then they remove the screen to show either one object (the possible outcome) or two objects (the impossible outcome). Even infants just a few months old stare longer at the impossible outcome (Wakely, Rivera, & Langer, 2000; Wynn & Chiang, 1998). When they do, some psychologists infer that the infants were surprised by the impossible outcome, suggesting a primitive understanding of number. However, the infants don't *look* surprised. Yes, they stare (sometimes), but they don't show the facial expression of surprise (which includes lifted eyebrows and widened eyes). As we saw earlier, researchers have been able to capture these expressions in photographs, typically when babies are looking high above themselves, and they are interpreted correctly by many adults (Oster et al., 1992). Still, few babies show this expression in situations adults would consider surprising before they are close to two years old.

Researchers used follow-up studies to examine infants' and toddlers' reactions when an experimenter's voice suddenly changed to a squeaky, metallic sound (because the

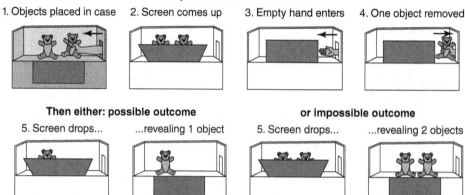

FIGURE 8.7. Experimenters show infants a possible or impossible outcome of removing one doll. Infants stare longer at the impossible event; does this mean they feel surprise?

experimenter was speaking into a microphone connected to a sound distorter). Even up to age 14 months, the children almost never made any vocal or facial expressions resembling adult surprise. They did, however, stop what they were doing and stare at the experimenter (Scherer, Zentner, & Stern, 2004). So, do infants feel surprise or not? We might say they are showing interest, rather than surprise, but that raises a debate regarding whether interest is an emotional experience. In short, it is not clear whether infants experience surprise in anything like the way that adults do, or that what the infants experience qualifies as an emotion. All of this suggests that at least before one year of age, babies have limited ability to express specific emotions—particularly negative emotions (Camras & Shutter, 2010).

It becomes easier to understand what emotion a child is feeling once the necessary vocabulary is in place. Various studies with children speaking English, German, or Chinese as their first language have found that emotion vocabulary increases steadily from the ages of four to 11 years (Baron-Cohen et al., 2010; Grosse et al., 2021; Li & Yu, 2015; Nook et al., 2020). The earliest terms children learn are for generic positive and negative feelings. German children typically used the words for happiness, sadness, and fear by four to five years, adding anger by around the sixth year (Grosse et al., 2021). Emotion vocabulary typically plateaus by age 11, at least among English-speaking children (see Figure 8.8; Baron-Cohen et al., 2010; Nook et al., 2020).

How children develop their emotion vocabulary is another question. Some propose that children learn emotion concepts and vocabulary when adults say things such as, "I'm sorry you're feeling sad," or "that person is angry," labeling the emotion and using it to describe the child's or another person's experience (Hoemann, Xu, & Barrett, 2019). One of us (MNS) was firmly told by her six-year-old goddaughter "No more books about feelings!" (In MNS's defense, she was not the one who had purchased said books.) An alternative is that children pick up on statistical patterns in the emotional situations, expressions, and actions of the people around them, and form specific emotion concepts (such as happiness and fear) on their own, attaching words to those concepts later on. Surprisingly little work has addressed these two alternatives, so we must await further research to see.

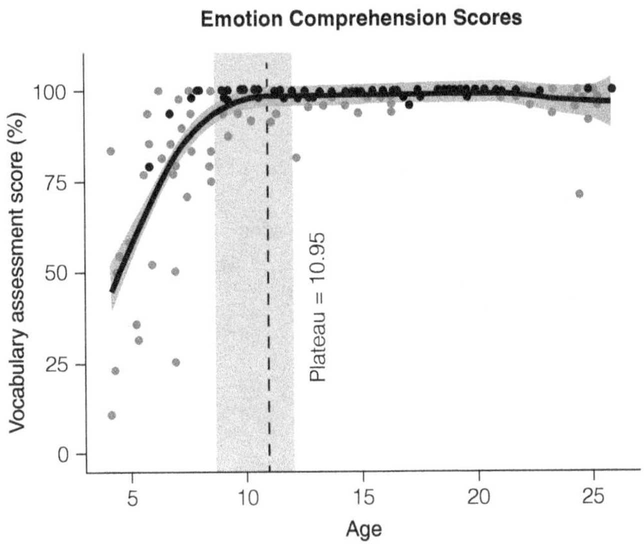

FIGURE 8.8. Children's emotion vocabulary grows steadily over the course of childhood, plateauing at around age 11 years. From Nook et al. (2020).

Whatever is driving the development of emotion vocabulary, children's increasingly sophisticated language has implications for how they experience emotion. In one clever study, researchers asked participants aged six to 25 years to rate the similarity of every possible pair among 10 emotion words. Using a version of the multidimensional scaling technique described in Chapter 1, the researchers showed that the youngest children's perception of emotion space relied almost entirely on positive-to-negative valence (Figure 8.9). Differentiation of the emotions in terms of arousal, creating a two-dimensional circumplex similar to that seen when adults do the task, occurred gradually across childhood, and this effect was statistically mediated by growing overall vocabulary and verbal knowledge (Nook et al., 2017).

Emotion Understanding and Recognition

It's one thing to learn emotion words, and another to understand emotion concepts with any depth, and relate to other people's emotions as well as your own. The fact that young children use words like *angry* or *sad* does not tell us how thoroughly they understand these terms. To test how well toddlers understand emotions as internal experiences, Judy Dunn and colleagues (Dunn, Bretherton, & Munn, 1987) examined the situations in which preschool children use emotion words. They found that even two-year-old children use some emotion words in accurate ways. In play, they attribute emotions to dolls and stuffed animals in appropriate situations. Toddlers also talk about what they and others have felt in the past and what they expect to feel in the future, not just in the present (Wellman et al., 1995).

This emotion talk is a good predictor of healthy social development. In one study, 1½- to two-year-old children who used more emotion words also showed more empathy and helping behaviors toward other children (Gross, 2015). In another study,

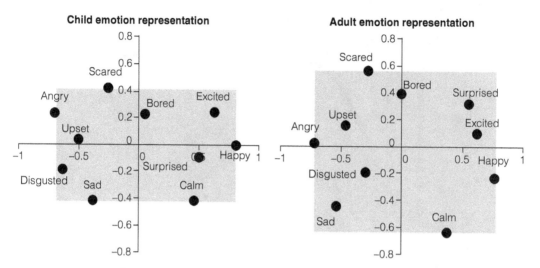

FIGURE 8.9. Young children define emotion space primarily in terms of positive-to-negative valence. The dimension of arousal emerges gradually, as children develop more sophisticated verbal knowledge. From Nook et al. (2017).

three-year-old children who talked more with their families about emotional experiences showed better ability to determine other people's emotions when they reached first grade (Dunn, Brown, & Maguire, 1995). These findings reflect correlations, however, rather than experiments where researchers randomly assigned participants to one condition or another. As a result, we do not know for sure whether emotion language skills caused these desirable outcomes; another possible explanation is that both language and social skills depend on overall cognitive maturation, and some children mature faster than others.

The development of emotion concept understanding continues well beyond the preschool years. One study with English-speaking participants in the United States examined teenagers' and young adults' open-ended descriptions of emotion terms. Although performance on emotion vocabulary tests peaked by age 11 or so, participants' conceptual descriptions became less concrete and more abstract across the teenage years, plateauing around age 17 (Nook et al., 2020). Younger children's descriptions of emotion tended to rely more on specific situations that might elicit an emotion (e.g., a friend moved away), and concrete behaviors someone might show when feeling that emotion. These features became less prominent across adolescence, with greater reliance on abstract appraisals (e.g., loss), internal feelings, and synonyms for emotion terms (Figure 8.10).

Beyond conceptual understanding, at what point do children recognize and respond appropriately to emotions expressed by other people? Children begin to recognize other people's nonverbal emotional expressions by about three years of age. However, their accuracy depends on the test we use. If children are asked to look at still photographs and name the emotion expressed (without options provided by the researcher), seven-year-olds still make many mistakes (Wang et al., 2014). In a more natural setting, however, infants use context, gestures, tone of voice, and other cues to

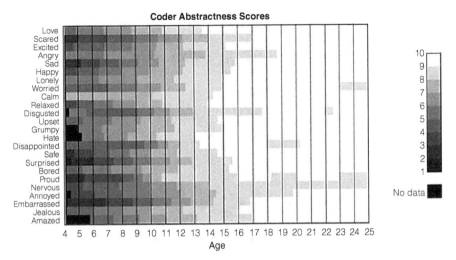

FIGURE 8.10. Across childhood and adolescence, conceptual descriptions of emotion grow more abstract and less concrete. From Nook et al. (2020).

recognize emotions easily and accurately (Otte et al., 2015). Even seven-month-olds become uneasy if you stare at them with an angry face (Hoehl & Striano, 2008). If a parent shows fear at the sight of a new toy, infants and toddlers become frightened too, approaching the toy with caution, if at all (Vaish, Grossman, & Woodward, 2008). These responses would not make sense if the babies did not understand the meaning of their parents' expressions.

Children learn gradually to recognize emotional expressions, rather than acquiring the skill all at once. Even children just beginning to talk can label faces as happy. By around age six they can label faces as angry or sad. Fear and surprise come later still, and disgust comes last, for both English- and French-speaking children (e.g., Lawrence, Campbell, & Skuse, 2015; Maassarani et al., 2014; Widen & Russell, 2003). Even 11-year-old children generally find it difficult to differentiate the expression of disgust from other negative emotions, and some research suggests that ability to tell disgust and anger apart increases with puberty, independent of exact age (Lawrence et al., 2015).

How do children learn that a smile means someone is happy? How do they learn what frowns mean? At this point we have clues, rather than clear answers. One possibility is that an infant automatically knows what smiles and frowns mean through an inherited mechanism. That hypothesis is plausible from an evolutionary standpoint, because this kind of communication is so important. However, opportunities for learning abound as well. Infants and their parents tend to have similar emotional experiences and expressions at the same time (Figure 8.11). One reason is that they react to the same events (Kokkinaki, 2003); another is that they sometimes copy each other's expressions. An infant who smiles, feels happy, and sees someone else smile at the same time has the opportunity to associate a happy feeling with the sight of a smiling face.

As early as seven months of age, babies learn to attend to the regions of the face that are most important for understanding expressions in their culture; for example, babies in

FIGURE 8.11. Young children and their parents often have the same emotional expression at the same time because they are reacting to the same event. This provides one opportunity for children to learn what different expressions mean.

the United Kingdom pay more attention to the mouth, and Japanese babies to the eyes (Figure 8.12; Geangu et al., 2016). Preschool-age children who have experienced neglect are generally worse at differentiating the expressions of negative emotions, and those who have experienced abuse are especially adept at detecting another's expression of anger (Pollak et al., 2000). This all suggests some effect of learning, but fully separating the roles of heredity and environment is difficult, as usual.

Although very young infants display sympathetic crying, the development of truly empathetic responses to another's feelings comes later. In one rigorous study researchers followed 400 pairs of twins over a two-year period, with laboratory sessions at 14, 20, 24, and 36 months of age. During each session the babies encountered events intended to evoke empathy or compassion, such as their mother pretending to hurt her knee when standing up from the floor, or the experimenter pretending to shut their finger in a case. At each event the child's behavior was coded for nonverbal signs of concern; "hypothesis testing" such as asking if the person was hurt; and trying to comfort or help the person. Expressions of concern peaked by around age two, but the hypothesis testing and helping behaviors continued to emerge over the course of the study (Knafo et al., 2008). Interestingly, analyses comparing patterns among identical versus nonidentical twins suggested that heritability of empathy was very low in the youngest infants, but increased substantially from 18 months to three years of age. This suggests that genetic contributions to empathy were more apparent a bit later in development than at the beginning—a trajectory that is not uncommon among psychological characteristics.

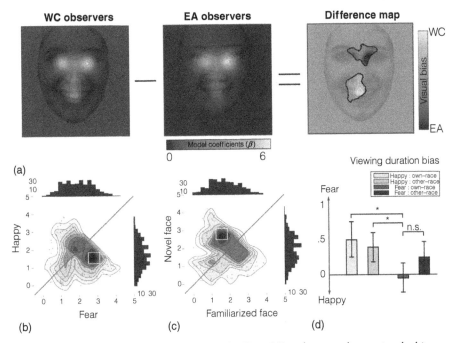

FIGURE 8.12. By 7 months of age, babies in the United Kingdom spend more time looking at people's mouths, whereas babies in Japan look more closely at people's eyes. This suggests early attunement to key regions of facial expressions in a given culture. From Geangu et al. (2016).

One possible explanation is that some ability that supports empathy, with a strong genetic component, typically comes online at around 18 months. One good candidate for this is self-regulation. Although the brain mechanisms of self-regulation show a spurt of development around three to four years of age (Rothbart et al., 2011), capacities for emotional self-regulation are visible earlier, during the second year of life. One study found that **ego resiliency**, the ability to bounce back and recover easily from stress or distress, as rated by parents at 18 months predicted children's empathetic concern for others (also parent-rated), not only at the same time, but as it increased over the new few years (Taylor et al., 2013). It possible that the strength of this association partly reflects the fact that both measures were provided by parents—who could be just a little biased when describing their own children. However, the finding is consistent with other research supporting the idea that self-regulation is needed to respond to another's distress with concern and helping, rather than feeling overwhelmed by one's own discomfort—a point to which we return in Chapter 9.

Emotion Regulation and Socialization
Babies may express their emotions freely, but older children's and adults' emotional behavior is more constrained by societal expectations. In order to get along with others, and be effective in the world, we must learn to regulate our emotions and learn the emotion norms of the culture in which we live. Even two-year-olds are so aware of how their emotions affect other people that they may begin faking emotion to get what they want (Bretherton

et al., 1986). At this age, children use emotion to "train" their parents just as much as parents use emotion to train their children. Because the development of emotion regulation and the socialization of cultural emotion norms are intertwined, we discuss both here.

Early signs of emotional self-regulation can be seen in the second year of life (e.g., Mangelsdorf, Shapiro, & Malzorf, 1995; Morales et al., 2005). At the individual level, children vary substantially in their ability to regulate or conceal their emotions. One rule of polite behavior in the United States is to express thanks for any gift and never show disappointment. Preschool children in one study were asked to rank-order five small presents from best to worst, and experimenters promised to give them one of the presents after the children performed a task. When the time came, the experimenters first gave each child their *least* preferred gift, waited a few seconds, and then apologized and gave the most preferred gift. During that brief delay, the experimenter recorded the children's reactions. Some children cried, threw the unwanted present, and demanded a better one. Others politely accepted it and hid their disappointment. As you might guess, those who vigorously displayed their frustration were rated by their teachers and others as more lacking in social skills, whereas those who hid their disappointment were considered good at controlling their emotions in a variety of situations (Liew, Eisenberg, & Reiser, 2004). In a study using the same task, children who hid their disappointment scored higher on understanding other people's emotions and understanding cultural rules for displaying emotions (Hudson & Jacques, 2014).

By the time children are toddlers they receive frequent messages about the emotions expected by parents, peers, and the rest of their social world. Some expectations for children's emotion are seen consistently across cultures and contexts. A survey of 48 countries found that parents in all locations wanted their children to be happy, not too fearful, and capable of controlling their anger (Diener & Lucas, 2004). Most people expect and tolerate occasional impulsive and aggressive behaviors by two- and three-year-olds (thus the expression "the terrible twos"), but after that, they expect children to restrain themselves, and peers ostracize those who don't (Trentacosta & Shaw, 2009). These expectations are largely similar from one culture to another (Eisenberg, Liew, & Pidada, 2001; Eisenberg, Pidada, & Liew, 2001; Hanish et al., 2004).

Emotional expectations also vary across gender and culture, however, and the effects of these differing norms become increasingly visible over the course of childhood (e.g., Chaplin & Aldao, 2013; Much, 1997). From birth to 18 months boys and girls show few if any differences in the emotions they express. Differences emerge and grow during preschool, childhood, and adolescence, with girls showing more happiness, sadness, anxiety, and sympathy, and boys showing more anger (Chaplin & Aldao, 2013). Across cultures, most parents work harder to control their sons' anger than that of their daughters (Chaplin, Cole, & Zahn-Waxler, 2005). Meanwhile, they strongly reinforce daughters' expressions of happiness (Diener & Lucas, 2004). In the disappointing gift laboratory protocol discussed earlier, girls display more positive emotion than boys, presumably covering up their negative feelings about the gift with a smile (Chaplin & Aldao, 2013).

How do children learn and internalize the emotional norms of their social world? This may occur in part as children observe the emotions of those around them, especially their parents, and model the behavior they see. On the whole, parents who express mostly positive emotions have children who also express positive emotions, whereas parents who express much negative emotion have children who also vigorously express their fears and anger

(Cole, Teti, & Zahn-Waxler, 2003; Denham et al., 2000; Valiente et al., 2004). These studies are correlational, so we cannot draw cause-and-effect conclusions. Perhaps the parents are reacting to their children's emotional outbursts. Perhaps parent and child show similar emotional displays because of shared genetic profiles. A study with adopted children suggested that all three of these explanations are valid to some extent (Rosen et al., 2015).

Parental emotional displays vary across cultures, and children learn from them. In one study, researchers asked Japanese and American mothers to yell angrily while their 11-month-old infants crawled toward a toy (Miyake et al., 1986). The American babies typically paused briefly but then kept approaching the toy, whereas Japanese babies paused far longer. According to the researchers, the American babies had heard their mothers yell so often that they did not take them seriously ("Mom's yelling at me again. Oh well."). For Japanese babies, however, an angry voice was a rare and mysterious event. Even in the first year of life, many American babies learn that anger is acceptable, whereas Japanese infants learn that anger is rare and generally inappropriate.

Children also learn cultural rules when parents and other caregivers reinforce or discourage their emotion displays. Sometimes parents give lessons in emotion without realizing what they are doing. In one study, researchers asked Japanese and American mothers of three- and four-year-olds how they would respond to various kinds of misbehavior, such as drawing with crayons on the wall or knocking products off the shelves at the supermarket (Conroy et al., 1980). Mothers in the United States often said they would demand that the child stop the behavior, or that they would physically force the child to stop. These strategies trigger a clash of wills between parent and child, encouraging the child to argue and become angry. If the parent then gives in, the behavior is reinforced— if you don't get what you want, get angry, fight, and you will win. Japanese mothers said they were more likely to explain why the misbehavior hurt other people, appealing to their children's desire to please and cooperate (Figure 8.13). In training children to interpret such situations from other people's perspectives, they aim to encourage development of prosocial emotions and discourage self-focused appraisals that may lead to anger.

Simply validating and engaging with a child's emotion can reinforce it. Much research has documented gender and cultural differences in the ways parents respond to their children's emotions, particularly their negative emotions. Parents tend to discuss emotions with their preschool daughters more than with their sons, but this may be because the girls initiate such conversations more often (Fivush et al., 2000). In one study looking at intersecting implications of gender and culture for emotion socialization, researchers asked the parents of European American, African American, and Lumbee Native American children how likely they would be to respond in various ways to scenarios in which their child was upset. In the European-American families, mothers were much more likely than fathers to respond to their children's sadness and fear in supportive ways, talking openly about feelings and the situation that elicited them. This gender difference was less dramatic among Lumbee families, and actually reversed in African American families, in which dads tended to report more supportive engagement with their children's emotions (Brown, Craig, & Halberstadt, 2015).

Parents' beliefs about and engagement with their kids' emotions have consequences for healthy development. In one study with several hundred children in the United States, five-year-olds whose moms talked with them about negative emotions in more supportive ways grew into 10-year olds who showed better emotion regulation skills, and from there

FIGURE 8.13. Children learn their culture's display rules when parents reinforce certain emotional expressions. Explaining how a misbehaving child is hurting other people encourages compassion and discourages anger.

into 15-year-olds with lower risk for anxiety, depression, and problematic risk-taking as well as higher social competence (Perry et al., 2020). Another study found that third-grade students whose mothers believed that emotions can be dangerous, leading to out-of-control behavior, were less able to identify emotions felt by characters in short vignettes, and displayed less appropriate behavior in the classroom (Garrett-Peters, Castro, & Halberstadt, 2017). This all suggests that talking with children about emotion, including negative emotions, can play an important role in helping them learn to manage their own emotions and understand those of other people.

While studies such as these add much to our understanding of emotional development and socialization, they have important limitations. Most studies have been conducted in the United States or the United Kingdom, and the typical sample is either mostly white or a mix of white and Black children. Fully understanding the socialization of emotion will require studies with more diverse populations, both within and beyond the United States and Europe.

ADOLESCENCE AND TRANSITION TO ADULTHOOD

Learning Objective

- Summarize the changes in emotional experience and behavior that are (and are not) supported by empirical evidence, and analyze the roles of physical maturation, cognitive development, and social interaction in accounting for these changes.

When we talk about adolescence, we generally mean the teenage years between the beginning of puberty and the onset of full adult responsibilities. When you think of adolescent emotions, what comes to mind? Many people consider adolescence a period of "storm and stress." That is a little like saying that the Caribbean is a place of hurricanes. Yes, hurricanes happen in the Caribbean, but not all the time. Contrary to popular stereotype, **ecological momentary assessment** studies—in which participants report on their experiences and feelings multiple times per day while going about their normal lives—find no evidence that overall negative emotion intensity increases across adolescence, though positive emotion intensity does decrease (Bailen, Green, & Thompson, 2019). The overall frequency of negative moods increases from early to late adolescence (although frequency of *strong* negative emotion decreases), and as with intensity positive mood frequency drops to some extent (Frost et al., 2015). This may in part reflect an age-related change in emotion ideals (recall this term from Chapter 3). As compared with adults, teenagers report *wanting* to experience negative emotions to a greater extent (Riediger et al., 2009); a preference perhaps related to the development of more complex and nuanced emotion concepts, discussed earlier.

Against the backdrop of these average trends, individuals vary greatly in how much their emotions change during the teenage years. Most adolescents experience a moderate amount of conflict with their parents, especially in early adolescence, plus occasional periods of depression, anxiety, or anger (Laursen, Coy, & Collins, 1998). Some have more serious problems than that, and some have almost none. Part of this variation in outcome is genetic in origin (McGue et al., 2005), and part relates to the amount of sympathy and understanding that adolescents receive from their parents (Lee, Su, & Yoshida, 2005).

What is driving the shifts in emotion during the teenage years? During this time adolescents are experiencing a great deal of change, in their bodies, their cognitive abilities, and in their environment (Bailen et al., 2019). First, new hormones are surging, and some effects may reflect the relative timing of puberty, increases in sex hormones, and development of brain mechanisms for self-regulation. Researchers find that the onset of puberty is a better predictor of increased emotional intensity than age itself (Forbes & Dahl, 2010). Emotional instability, with unpredictable bursts of sadness, anger, happiness, and anxiety, tends to peak right around the ages of 13 to 14 years, and may be linked to hormonal changes as well (Bailen et al., 2019).

However, these hormonal changes interact with changes in cognition and emotion-related conceptual development to produce some interesting patterns over time. For example, in a study of several hundred Black and white American teenagers, girls showed declining clarity in understanding their own emotions over a five-year period, whereas boys started with higher clarity and remained more stable across adolescence (Haas et al., 2019). In another study, participants rating their emotional responses to photographs depicting various unpleasant scenes showed a decrease from age five to around age 15 in **emotion granularity**—the extent to which they used different emotion words to describe their feelings in different situations—which was followed by an *increase* in granularity from age 16 to 25 (Nook et al., 2018). Further analyses suggested that the younger children simply tended to describe their emotions with one word at a time, leading to moderate specificity, whereas the older teens and young adults reported more complex patterns of emotional response. During the mid-adolescent years teens may be increasingly aware of complex emotions, but still be developing the conceptual depth needed to understand and articulate their feelings (Nook et al., 2020).

FIGURE 8.14. Risk-taking behavior tends to peak during mid-to-late adolescence and the first years of adulthood. The reasons for this are not easily reduced to a single cause.

One very consistent finding in research on adolescents is that of a sharp increase in risky behavior (Figure 8.14). This research offers a great example of the challenge of teasing apart biological, cognitive, and social forces driving developmental change. It may simply be that teenagers have substantially increased freedom and independence relative to childhood, at least in Western cultures. Adolescents have new opportunities to engage in unprotected sex, fast driving, extreme sports, use of alcohol or other drugs, and other potentially dangerous activities that provide thrills but may have costly consequences (Steinberg et al., 2009). Adolescents of other species, including rodents, show increased exploration and risk taking as well, however, in ways that cannot be accounted for by changes in social environment (Spear, 2000). Studies have found that the hormones testosterone and cortisol interact to predict greater risk-taking among both women and men, consistent with a proposal that hormonal changes in adolescence may play a role (Mehta et al., 2015).

Let's address one popular explanation right now—that teenagers can't or don't think before they act. While this may be an issue sometimes, in most cases adolescents *do* think about their decisions. Suppose we ask people about possible decisions:

Swimming with sharks: Good idea or bad idea?
Eating a well-balanced diet: Good idea or bad idea?
Setting your hair on fire: Good idea or bad idea?

In laboratory studies adolescents make the same decisions that adults do, on average, just more slowly. Adults know immediately that they don't want to swim with sharks. Adolescents weigh the pros and cons more deliberately (Reyna & Farley, 2006). Maybe swimming with sharks could be fun! Are we talking about a hungry shark, or one that's recently been fed? Well-balanced diets are healthy, but poorly balanced diets can be delicious. Setting your hair on fire will harm your appearance for a while and could be dangerous, but will go down in history as one of the epic memories of high school. If you think about it, adolescents are being quite logical, though adults may frown on their analysis of the potential benefits of risky behaviors.

One hypothesis is that adolescents engage in risky behavior because the prefrontal cortex of the brain does not reach full maturity until the early twenties (Sowell et al., 1999; Sowell et al., 2001). Because the prefrontal cortex is important for inhibiting automatic behaviors, adolescents may have less "brake" on their impulses. Here is one easy test of inhibitory control: a light flashes to the left or right, and the viewer's task is to inhibit the tendency to look at it and instead look the *opposite* direction. (You can try a similar task yourself: put your hands to the sides of someone's head and tell them to look toward the hand in which you do *not* wiggle one finger.) Young children find this task difficult, and even adults are quicker to look toward the light than to look away from it. The ability to inhibit the reflex to look toward the light gradually improves over the teenage years, along with maturation of the prefrontal cortex (Luna, Padmanabhan, & O'Hearn, 2010). Ability to inhibit impulsive appetitive behavior follows a similar trajectory (e.g., Somerville, Hare, & Casey, 2011).

The evidence linking immaturity of the prefrontal cortex to adolescent risk taking is complicated. The most direct test of the hypothesis did indicate a correlation, but not in the way we might guess. In a longitudinal study, adolescents who grew more successful at inhibiting risky activities over time showed *less* activation in the prefrontal cortex during inhibition tasks in the scanner (Qu et al., 2015). As with many findings correlating neural activity to behavior, this is difficult to interpret. Does this mean that participants who took fewer risks in real life were less able to inhibit their impulses? Probably not. A more likely explanation is that these individuals showed less activation there because they found it easier to inhibit their impulses—possibly their impulses were less strong than those of other adolescents. Moreover, if immaturity of the prefrontal cortex were the sole reason for adolescent impulsive behavior, we should expect risky behaviors to decrease gradually across the teenage years, as brain maturation progresses. In fact, risky behavior *increases* between the ages of 10 and 20 years (Shulman, 2014).

At this point, the evidence suggests that adolescent risk-taking reflects a complex interplay of biological, cognitive, and social factors. Beyond the prefrontal cortex, the brain areas responsible for reward also develop and show increased reactivity during the teenage years (Larsen & Luna, 2015; Peters & Crone, 2017). Risks often come with a possibility of material reward, but risky behavior can elicit social rewards in the form of attention from other people as well. Indeed, risky and impulsive acts are more likely to occur under peer observation or pressure (Figure 8.15; Cohen & Prinstein, 2006; de Boer, Peeters, & Koning, 2017; Gardner & Steinberg, 2005; Prinstein, Boergers, & Spirito, 2001; Van Hoorn, Crone, & Van Lijenhorst, 2017). Layered upon these developmental changes are lasting individual differences. In most cases, adolescents who are responsible for seriously dangerous and destructive behaviors are people with

FIGURE 8.15.   Teenagers are more likely to engage in risky, impulsive acts when they are observed by their peers.

lifelong impairments, who continue to engage in risky behaviors long after adolescence (Bjork & Pardini, 2015; Vassallo et al., 2014). The interactions among sensitivity to reward, developmental trajectories and individual differences in self-regulation mediated by prefrontal cortex activity, and peers who may encourage or discourage risky behavior helps explain why adolescents show such varying profiles of risk-taking as well as emotion over the teenage years.

The analysis above adds layers of complexity to the idea that adolescents are just emotionally difficult. From the perspective of parents and other adults, the changes in emotional experience, behavior, and expression may be frustrating, even scary at times. However, these changes may reflect important processes in maturation from the relative protection of childhood toward richer emotional experience, skill, and understanding that will support resilience throughout adulthood (Somerville & McLaughlin, 2018).

EMOTION AND MOTIVATION ACROSS ADULTHOOD

Until now we have focused on how emotion develops early in life. What happens later? Although most research has addressed emotional development in children, emotions continue to change throughout adulthood as well. As the Western population grows older, with the baby boomer generation entering retirement, researchers are especially interested in the changes that accompany normal aging. Let's first consider aspects of continuity in emotion across the adult years; then we'll examine the ways and reasons that emotions may change.

Learning Objectives

- Analyze the evidence on emotion in midlife, debating whether "midlife crisis" is a common occurrence or not.
- Summarize the average trajectory of emotional experience from midlife through late adulthood, and describe different explanations of these changes in terms of (a) life circumstances, (b) motivation, and (c) self-regulation skill.

Individual Consistency Across the Lifespan

Emotional characteristics tend to be consistent throughout a person's life for many reasons. For example, people who tend to be happy form close relationships with others, and forming close relationships helps people become or stay happy (Ramsey & Gentzler, 2015). In one study, investigators observed hundreds of seven-year-olds and later followed up on them at age 35. Proneness to distress in childhood correlated $r = .24$ with adult measures of anger, indicating a small-to-moderate-size relationship (Kubzansky, Martin, & Buka, 2004). In another study, children who were highly impulsive at age seven were three times as likely as others to become problem gamblers in adulthood (Shenassa et al., 2012). Aggressive behavior in childhood has a low but significant correlation with adult hostility and anger (Hakulinen et al., 2013).

In one study researchers coded the quality and intensity of smiles posed by young women in their college yearbooks, and then asked whether these single expressions of emotion could predict outcomes of the women's lives decades later (Harker & Keltner, 2001). They found that women who had displayed stronger and more "felt" smiles (Duchenne smiles) in the college photographs were more likely to have married and less likely to have divorced. They described themselves as more competent, more emotionally stable, and more agreeable with other people than did women with less intense or less genuine smiles in their photographs. Results of a follow-up study indicated that both men and women who showed a strong smile in their yearbook photos were less likely than average to divorce later in life (Hertenstein et al., 2009). In short, the emotions you feel right now are a moderately good predictor of the emotions you will feel throughout life, in part because they are good predictors of some major choices and life events with implications for emotion.

Midlife and Aging

The studies we have just described asked whether people who were above or below average in some regard remained above or below average years later, compared to others of their own age. A corresponding question is how emotions change, on average, from young adulthood to old age. On the whole, the news is good. Panic disorder, social phobia, and some other anxiety disorders are most prevalent in young people; they become less common, and on average less intense, as people grow older (Miloyan et al., 2014; Rubio & López-Ibor, 2007; Swoboda et al., 2003). As people grow older, they also feel anger less often and less intensely, and express it less vigorously (Birditt & Fingerman, 2003; Blanchard-Fields & Coats, 2008; Zimprich & Mascherek, 2012). This trend makes sense if we consider the function of anger. Young and midlife adults are competing with one another for mates, jobs, promotions, status, and so forth. If someone treats them badly, and they don't stand up for themselves, it could have consequences for their long-term success. For older people, the cost of a fight may be more than what they could gain from it.

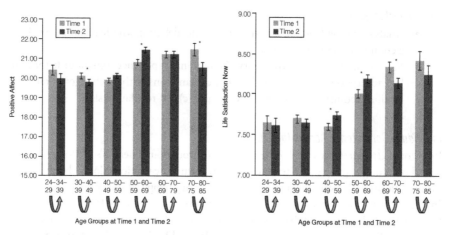

FIGURE 8.16. Assessed in terms of positive affect and life satisfaction, happiness declines slightly from young adulthood through the 40s, then rises considerably until very late in life, when health and cognitive problems become more severe. Arrows indicate longitudinal changes among the same cohort, from Time 1 to Time 2 of the study. From Lachman, Teshale, & Agrigoroaei (2015).

Who would you guess is happiest: young adults (say in their twenties), middle-aged people (in their 40s), or older people (aged 60+ years)? Much evidence suggests it is the older adults! In both cross-sectional and longitudinal studies, reported satisfaction with life declines slightly from age 18 until about age 50, and then begins to rise quite a bit (Lachman, Teshale, & Agrigoroaei, 2015; see Figure 8.16). Rates of subjective stress and clinically significant depression and anxiety show the opposite pattern, peaking in midlife and steadily declining until very old age (Infurna, Gerstorf, & Lachman, 2020). Little evidence supports the stereotype of a universal "midlife crisis," with emotional upheaval and a return to adolescent pleasure-seeking and risk-taking (Lachman et al., 2015). However, people in their 40s and 50s are often "sandwiched" between responsibilities for raising children, caring for aging parents, managing peak career demands, and obligations to the community that, while rewarding, combine to create considerable stress (Almeida & Horn, 2004).

On average, healthy people over 70 years old report the highest subjective well-being (Mroczek, 2004; Mroczek & Spiro, 2005; Stone et al., 2010). That tendency interacts with a cohort effect: People born in more recent decades tend to report greater happiness than the people born in previous decades did, when they were at the same age (Sutin et al., 2013). What accounts for these trends? First, people's situations change. Most older adults are either established in their careers or retired, and therefore face fewer work-related conflicts. At least in the United States, where most of the surveys have been done, most aging people are also financially secure. Retirees no longer have the obligations of a job, and many have both the time and the money for entertainment and travel. They can enjoy their children and grandchildren without the full responsibility of day-to-day care. Laura Carstensen and Susan Turk Charles (1998) distributed pagers to adults of various ages and paged them several times a day, asking about their current emotional experience. The oldest adults reported the fewest situations evoking unpleasant emotions.

In addition, growing older changes your priorities. When you are young, your goal is to build toward the future. Sometimes this means putting up with difficult, even unpleasant situations. Older adults are less concerned with the future and more motivated to enjoy the present. In surveys older adults report being less motivated to acquire higher status and new mates, worrying less about being excluded, and being more motivated to maintain strong relationships with their partners and families than do young adults (Neel et al., 2016).

According to **socioemotional selectivity theory**, midlife triggers an increase in adults' motivation to make the most of their remaining time (Carstensen, Isaacowitz, & Charles, 1999). For example, would you prefer to spend this weekend meeting interesting new people, strengthening relationships with acquaintances at work, or getting together with friends and family members you have known for most of your life? Younger people are more likely to choose the new relationships, whereas older people prefer to be with family and long-term friends (Carstensen, 1992; Carstensen & Charles, 1998). Older adults also behave differently when interacting with loved ones. For example, when talking about an area of conflict in their marriage, older adults are less likely to quarrel (Levenson, Carstensen, & Gottman, 1994) and more likely to express affection during the discussion (Carstensen, Gottman, & Levenson, 1995).

A related possibility is that older adults are more adept at regulating their emotions. Some research suggests that older people may deliberately control their attention to maintain a positive outlook on life. They try to maintain a favorable mood (Riediger et al., 2009), and several studies suggest that older people in the United States (though evidently not in Japan) deliberately shift their attention away from unpleasant events and toward positive ones (Grossmann et al., 2014). Recall from earlier chapters that emotional images, especially threatening ones, tend to capture and hold our attention strongly. Older adults do not show this bias as strongly, and may be biased toward more positive stimuli. This effect has been referred to as a **positivity bias**.

Here is a complex study that supports this idea: participants stared at a point in the center of a computer screen, and then two faces appeared for one second, to the left and right of this fixation point. One face had a neutral expression, whereas the other had either a pleasant or an unpleasant emotional expression. Then the faces disappeared and a small dot appeared on either the left or the right side. The participant's task was to indicate the position of the dot as quickly as possible. Whereas young adults responded to the dot about equally rapidly regardless of its location, older adults (mean age 74) responded more slowly if the dot appeared where a sad or angry face had been, and faster if it replaced a smiling face (Mather & Carstensen, 2003). Evidently, the smiling faces exerted more pull on the older participants' attention, so they found the dot quickly when it replaced the smile, and sad and angry faces showed the opposite pattern.

Similar effects have been observed in other studies. For example, one study found that older adults selectively recount positive information from autobiographical memories, to a greater degree than young adults (Kennedy, Mather, & Carstensen, 2004). However, most research showing that older people shift their attention toward more favorable stimuli is based on highly constrained laboratory experiments, in which people had to focus on just one stimulus or the other. In a more complex room with a wider variety of positive, negative, and neutral stimuli, older and younger people divide their attention among the stimuli in similar proportions (Isaacowitz et al., 2015). It's not yet clear how much impact this positivity bias has in real life.

Older adults may restrain their expressions of emotion more often as well. When James Gross and colleagues (1997) asked American and Norwegian participants about their emotions, they found that older adults rated themselves as less emotionally expressive, less impulsive, and better able to control their emotions than younger adults. Other studies have also found that older adults report suppressing their emotional expressions (e.g., Eldesouky & English, 2018), and avoiding situations that are likely to be unpleasant (Livingstone & Isaacowitz, 2021), to a greater extent than younger adults. This is striking because overreliance on expressive suppression and avoidance-based coping is typically associated with *worse* mental health and well-being, as we shall see in Chapter 15 (Aldao, Nolen-Hoeksema, & Schweizer, 2010; Srivastava et al., 2009). It may be that later in life, however, it makes more sense to pick your battles than to keep fighting them.

SUMMARY

Emotions change considerably throughout the life span, from early infancy through late adulthood. The emotions of infancy are interesting for theorists because they shed light on the structure of affect space before babies have had the time or cognitive ability to learn much about emotion concepts. As you have seen, the evidence on this point is somewhat difficult to interpret. Babies show little more specificity beyond distress and contentment. The ability to display particular emotions develops gradually over the first year or so, and the ability to recognize facial expressions of emotion and talk about specific emotions develops even more slowly. Is that because basic or discrete emotions are only concepts learned through language and culture, as suggested by psychological construction theories? Or is it because babies are not yet paying attention to the outside world, or capable of understanding what it means for them? Is an innate capacity for basic/discrete emotions waiting inside them for the necessary cognitive abilities to emerge? These questions are controversial, and we still don't know the answers.

Regardless of whether the capacity for different emotions is evolutionarily built in, it's clear that many important aspects of emotional development depend on the environment. Given our limited ability to experiment on the lives of babies and young children in any deep and lasting way, researchers are constrained in their ability to tease apart the influences of human nature, physical and cognitive development, and social learning. It is likely that these influences interact with each other, just as you were born with the capacity to develop language, but whether you speak English, Chinese, or Swahili depends on social and cultural influences. Is language innate or learned? Clearly it is both. Similarly, your biological nature gave you the capacity to feel emotions, and your genes influence how intensely you feel them, but at a minimum, you have learned from your culture the appropriate ways to express them and the situations in which you should suppress or modify them.

Emotional development does not end with early childhood. Although the storm-and-stress image of the teenage years is an exaggeration, adolescents do sometimes experience more intense emotions and tend to take greater risks, for a complex set of biological and social reasons. Emotions also change later in life. The idea that people become more mellow with age has some merit. On average, anxiety and anger become less intense, and people tend to experience more positive moods. As at other stages of life, these changes reflect internal changes in biology, changes in people's external environments, but also conscious decisions about how we want to feel and how best to achieve that state.

KEY TERMS

colic: in infants, fussing or crying more than three hours per day, at least three days per week (p. 271)

contagious crying: crying in response to the sound of another newborn's cry (p. 271)

coregulation: a process by which two or more individuals influence each other's emotions, helping both move toward a desired emotional state (p. 273)

distress: an undifferentiated protest against anything unpleasant or aversive (p. 272)

ecological momentary assessment: a research method in which participants report on their experiences and feelings multiple times per day while going about their normal lives (p. 291)

ego resiliency: the ability to bounce back and recover easily from stress or distress (p. 287)

emotion granularity: the diversity of a person's emotion vocabulary and concepts, measured by the extent to which they use different emotion words to describe feelings in different situations (p. 291)

intersubjectivity: two or more people sharing attention and experience (p. 278)

Moro reflex: a sequence in which the infant flings out its arms and spreads its fingers, and then contracts quickly into a fetal position with fingers bent (p. 274)

positivity bias: a tendency to direct attention toward positive rather than neutral or negative stimuli, more common in older than in younger adults (p. 297)

probiotics: microorganisms including bacteria and yeast that live in the human gut and support healthy digestion (p. 271)

social referencing: looking at the emotional expressions of trusted caregivers before responding to novel objects, people, or situations (p. 278)

social smiling: exchanging smiles with another person (p. 272)

socioemotional selectivity theory: view that midlife triggers an increase in adults' motivation to make the most of their remaining time and that consequently, older adults put a high priority on emotional quality of life (p. 297)

theory of mind: the understanding that other people have minds too, and the ability to discern what other people know or think (p. 278)

visual cliff: A protocol in which researchers place an infant on a table with plates of clear glass on either side. On the "shallow" side, the infant sees a floor that is just a short step down; on the "deep" side the floor appears to be much farther away (p. 279)

THOUGHT/DISCUSSION QUESTIONS

1. Early in this chapter, we noted that crying is an infant's way of getting care and attention from adults. If so, why don't infants cry all the time, to get even more care and attention? Consider this question first from an evolutionary perspective, next from a cultural perspective, and then try to integrate the two perspectives.

2. What evidence would convince you that nine-month-old babies are able to feel disgust? What evidence would convince you that babies this age are *not* yet able to feel disgust?

3. Think of a recent experience of strong emotion and write down as much detail as you can about it. Then, think of your earliest memory of strong emotion and write down as much detail as you can remember. Compare the two memories—what do they have in common, and how are they different? What are some explanations for the differences you identify (try to think of more than one explanation)? What study or studies could you design to test your theories of the development of emotional memory?

4. Do you have any memories from your own childhood of emotion socialization—caregivers or others teaching you what emotions are appropriate and valued? These

lessons might have been explicit, with someone telling you what to feel or express; or implicit, responding positively or negatively to your emotions without explicitly talking about them. Think of as many examples as you can, and try to come up with a taxonomy or classification system for emotion socialization strategies, identifying several different categories.

5. As people age, their arteries tend to harden, becoming less flexible. As a result, blood pressure tends to increase, both at rest and during exercise and strong emotion. In Chapter 4 we described the threat versus challenge distinction in appraisal and physiology. What implications might older adults' reduced arterial flexibility have for the subjective experience of emotion?

SUGGESTIONS FOR FURTHER READING

Bailen, N. H., Green, L. M., & Thompson, R. J. (2019). Understanding emotion in adolescents: A review of emotional frequency, intensity, instability, and clarity. *Emotion Review, 11*(1), 63–73.

Gopnik, A. (2009). *The philosophical baby: What children's minds tell us about truth, love, and the meaning of life*. Farrar, Straus & Giroux. What is consciousness like for a baby? This book brings together empirical psychology and philosophy, arguing that infants' capacities for understanding and emotion are far more complex than we think.

Infurna, F. J., Gerstorf, D., & Lachman, M. E. (2020). Midlife in the 2020s: Opportunities and challenges. *American Psychologist, 75*(4), 470–485. This accessible review of the research on midlife both debunks common misunderstandings and explains the challenges—and opportunities—encountered by those in middle adulthood.

CHAPTER 9

Emotion in Relationships and Society

In the last few chapters we have mostly emphasized emotional and motivational processes that take place within the individual: how emotion and motivation are linked to activity in the brain; the roles of bodily responses and visceral sensations in emotional and motivational states; and how people develop emotionally throughout their lives. Think, however, about the last several times you were intensely motivated toward some end, and/or felt some strong emotion. Were you alone, or were other people present? Was a current, anticipated, or imagined interaction with someone else the cause of your emotion? Did the situation have implications for your relationships with loved ones, or for your standing and reputation in society more broadly?

Most emotional experience happens in a social context (Parkinson, Fischer, & Manstead, 2005). Much of our motivation has roots in the social world as well. Roy Baumeister and Mark Leary (1995) have proposed that belonging or social connectedness is one of our most deep-seated psychological needs, accounting for a wide range of behaviors. As we saw in Chapter 2, Douglas Kenrick and colleagues (2010) have proposed a series of fundamental social motives as part of evolved human nature, reflecting the selection pressures of our ancestors' complex and highly interdependent social environment. In this chapter, we will highlight emotions' roles in expressing and fulfilling those motives.

We begin with the earliest relationship experienced by humans—that of an infant with its parents and other frequent caregivers. We then consider romantic relationships, asking what attracts partners to each other initially, how long-term bonds form, and what factors predict satisfaction and stability in marriages and similar committed partnerships. We discuss research on how we respond to other people's emotions, including others' distress. Finally, we consider a few examples of ways in which emotions help us navigate relationships with others in the larger society.

EARLY EMOTIONAL BONDS: INFANT ATTACHMENT

Learning Objectives

- Define attachment, including its three main behavioral manifestations—proximity-seeking, safe haven, and secure base—and explain how these behaviors emerge in the strange situation laboratory protocol.
- Summarize the adaptive function of attachment in infants, as theorized by John Bowlby, linking attachment behavior to the infant's developing motor skills.
- Describe one behavioral and one biological mechanism of parent-infant attachment formation.
- Summarize the behavioral profiles of the secure, anxious-ambivalent, and avoidant infant attachment styles in the strange situation, and describe the caregiver characteristics associated with each style in prior research.

People's first experience of emotion in relationships is almost always with their parents—those who nurture us from the first days of life. Humans appear hard-wired to figure out who will take care of us, as quickly as possible. This is crucial; human babies are born completely helpless, unable to fulfill their own basic physiological needs. They would soon die without extensive, committed care. Just hours after birth, babies recognize and prefer their mothers' voices over those of other women (DeCasper & Fifer, 1980). Within a few days, they recognize their mothers' faces as well (Field et al., 1984). Still, newborn infants are not terribly selective about the people with whom they interact. As long as they are warm, comfortable, and well-fed, they are content to be held by just about anyone. At this point, of course, they don't have much choice.

Things change at around six to nine months of age. Infants develop the capacity to form more intense and selective emotional bonds with a few special people. A baby who would lie calmly in a stranger's arms just a few weeks earlier suddenly becomes hysterical when Mom leaves the room. Rather than playing freely with new objects and people, the infant now checks in with parents often, to see whether they're around and paying attention. Developmental psychologists refer to this new pattern of behavior as **attachment**—a lasting emotional bond between the individual and a few regular caregivers, producing a desire to be near that person (proximity-seeking), an instinct to turn to that person when threatened (safe haven), and a sense of security and confidence in exploring new things (secure base). Hand in hand with attachment comes **stranger anxiety**—a fear of unfamiliar people.

The concept of attachment was first developed in the 1950s by John Bowlby and Mary Ainsworth (Figure 9.1). Over many years working as a psychiatrist in hospitals and a mental health clinic in London, Bowlby had become increasingly doubtful of his field's assumption that children only require food, protection from disease, and physical safety to develop normally, and of the psychoanalytic mantra that children's emotional distress must be caused by anxiety over sexual and aggressive drives rather than aspects of their relationships with parents (Bretherton, 1992). Meanwhile, Mary Ainsworth was writing a dissertation on the importance of *familial security* as a foundation for adults' sense of confidence and independence. In 1950, she moved to London, and their collaboration began (Bretherton, 1992).

FIGURE 9.1. John Bowlby and Mary Ainsworth pioneered the study of infants' attachment to their parents, proposing that babies have an innate need for these emotional bonds.

It seems bizarre, now, to think that less than a century ago scientists believed bonds between parents and children were based entirely on fulfillment of physical needs, especially food. Because infectious disease was considered the primary threat, the staff in hospitals and nurseries were instructed to touch children in their care as little as possible, and parents were often kept away as well. In the late 1940s, Bowlby recruited a research assistant named James Robertson to take extensive notes on the behavior of children hospitalized in these settings. Robertson's notes documented the children's depression, anxiety, and failure to thrive despite perfectly adequate medical care. Within a few years, he also went on to make a documentary film depicting their plight. The film, combined with Bowlby's formal report to the World Health Organization on the consequences of separating young children from their mothers, began to convince some researchers that separation of a young child from its parents was itself emotionally devastating.

To understand the intensity of young children's responses to separation and the selectiveness of their bonds with parents, Bowlby turned to the work of Konrad Lorenz and others who had documented imprinting in a variety of bird species (Figure 9.2). Newly hatched chicks would fixate on the first moving thing they saw, and follow it closely throughout their youth. Although the birds would imprint on any moving object—even Lorenz himself—the target would normally be the chicks' own mother. Bowlby concluded that human children must go through a similar process, instinctively identifying their parents and remaining close to them for care and protection. Among others, Bowlby soon convinced the young American researcher Harry Harlow (1958), whose famous studies of baby monkeys also confirmed the dramatic consequences of maternal separation and the importance of warmth and comfort, rather than food, as the basis for maternal–infant bonding (Figure 9.3).

FIGURE 9.2. Soon after they hatch, the chicks of many bird species imprint on the first moving object they see and will follow it everywhere.

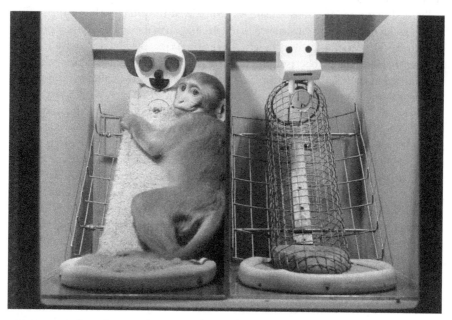

FIGURE 9.3. In a classic study by Harry Harlow (1958), baby rhesus macaques were allowed to move freely around a cage containing one plain wire "mother" and another covered in terrycloth, only one of which held a bottle of food. The monkeys spent the majority of their time clinging to the fuzzy mother, regardless of which mother provided nourishment.

Ainsworth went on to document the time course and features of typical infant attachment, first in a sample of mothers and babies in Uganda, and later in the United States. After years of observing families in the home and similar unstructured contexts, Ainsworth and colleagues (Ainsworth et al., 1978) developed a standardized laboratory task that would elicit attachment behavior. This **strange situation** consists of the following series of events: (1) an infant and parent enter an unfamiliar, toy-filled room and the infant is allowed to play; (2) a stranger enters the room, talks with the parent, and engages the infant for a few minutes; (3) the parent leaves, is gone for three minutes while the stranger remains in the room, and then returns for a few minutes; (4) both the stranger and the parent leave the room; (5) the stranger returns alone and tries to comfort and play with the infant; and finally (6) the parent returns.

Between around six months and two years of age, a typical infant will play freely during the first stage, exploring the room, yet checking in visually to make sure the parent is still there and watching. As soon as the parent leaves the room, most infants cry loudly and protest, sometimes trying to follow. Although the stranger may provide some comfort, only the parent can fully alleviate the distress. Once the parent returns, however, the infant is soothed quickly and easily and is able to return to play.

What Is the Function of Attachment?

In adopting an ethological approach to understanding attachment behavior, Bowlby and Ainsworth emphasized the nature of attachment as an instinct—an evolved aspect of human nature. Bowlby (1969) proposed that humans, and likely most other mammals, have a neural *attachment program* that kicks in at a particular developmental stage and is activated thereafter by particular situations. What function might such an instinct serve?

One important clue to the function of attachment is the time course of its appearance. Attachment behaviors begin to emerge in most infants soon after their sixth month of life. Why six months? Several theories have been proposed, and as usual, they probably all have some element of truth. First, infants' vision improves substantially over the first six months, and some researchers have suggested that this is the first time infants can recognize parents and other caregivers well enough to know when they have come or gone. Another explanation relates to cognitive maturation. Developmentalist Jean Piaget argued that infants less than nine months old lack **object permanence**—the understanding that objects continue to exist even when we do not see or hear them (Piaget, [1937] 1954). Later researchers using different research methods have found indications of object permanence much earlier. Still, the tendency of very young infants to respond mainly to what they can see at the moment would decrease their response to someone leaving the room.

A third explanation is, however, the most commonly accepted. Between six and nine months of age, most babies learn to crawl, and they begin their rush to explore the world. This new skill opens doors to all sorts of new experiences including, unfortunately, getting lost, tumbling down the stairs, touching something sharp or hot, putting something poisonous in one's mouth, and encountering less-than-gentle animals. Previously, the baby could rely on caregivers to keep the immediate environment safe. Now it must balance the thrill of exploration with the risk of wandering away and getting into serious trouble. According to Bowlby (1969), the attachment system helps newly mobile babies balance these two competing needs. As long as a trusted caregiver is nearby and in regular contact, the child plays happily. As soon as the caregiver is out of sight, the child does something to bring them back. The emotions and behaviors necessary for this regulation constitute attachment.

This explanation means that attachment behavior—especially the protest when a caregiver leaves—has the specific purpose of keeping caregivers close enough to help when needed, while allowing the infant space to do some exploring. Before six months, that vigilance is unnecessary, because infants are not yet able to move around on their own. It gradually becomes less important as the child grows old enough and competent enough to roam without constant supervision. In the strange situation, children continue protesting the caregiver's departure until they're around two years old, but their protests become less intense as the child becomes more capable and self-confident (Izard & Abe, 2004).

Behavioral and Biological Mechanisms of Attachment

How do infants even decide who their caregivers are? They might recognize mom's voice or her smell right after birth, and dad is probably the guy who's around most often, but what about other people? Ruth Feldman (2007) has emphasized the importance of synchrony between two individuals' behaviors as a possible trigger for the attachment system (Figure 9.4). Newborn infants experience alternating periods of alertness and withdrawal. Mothers typically try to interact with their infants when they become alert, but let them rest at other times. Newborns are especially attuned to this contingent responding, and become particularly interested in mothers who are sensitive to their cues for play versus quiet (Feldman & Eidelman, 2007). By the time infants are three months old, they contribute to behavioral synchrony as well, matching facial expressions and turn-taking with vocalizations. One study found that greater behavioral synchrony between the infant and its father predicted more secure attachment (Feldman, 2003), although this relationship was not observed for mothers.

FIGURE 9.4. Behavioral synchrony is one mechanism by which children identify committed caregivers and form attachment bonds.

Strong evidence suggests that the pituitary hormone **oxytocin** is one biological mechanism for bonding between infants and their caregivers. Oxytocin stimulates the uterus to contract while a mother is giving birth. It also stimulates the mammary glands to produce and release milk, and the brain uses it as a neurotransmitter to facilitate maternal behaviors. Skin-to-skin touch releases oxytocin, which in turn facilitates attachment and bonding (Dunbar, 2010; Feldman et al., 2007; Keverne & Kendrick, 1992; Klaus & Kennell, 1976). Because the hormone makes its way easily into breast milk, and from there into the infant, babies may get a strong dose of oxytocin during nursing. Baby rats injected with a chemical that interferes with oxytocin fail to develop preference for their mother's smell (Nelson & Panksepp, 1996), suggesting that oxytocin helps mediate infant attachment to the mother.

The effects of oxytocin are not limited to bonding between mothers and infants. In one study, Ruth Feldman and colleagues watched fathers interacting with their five-month-old babies twice: once after snorting a nasal spray containing oxytocin; and once after snorting a placebo. The fathers did not know which spray was which, so this knowledge could not influence their behavior. Even so, the fathers touched their babies for longer periods of time and showed more reciprocity (similar to synchrony, in that Dad's behavior is closely responsive to his baby's) under the influence of oxytocin compared to placebo. Moreover, their babies also showed more oxytocin in their saliva after the fathers had been given the oxytocin, and they spent more time looking at their fathers' faces (Weisman, Zagoory-Sharon, & Feldman, 2012). Oxytocin may be an important mechanism for attachment and bonding with a wide range of frequent caregivers, not just Mom.

Several studies suggest that the endorphins and other opioid neurotransmitters, which have effects similar to heroin and morphine and are often referred to as the body's natural painkillers, play an important role in infants' attachment behavior as well. One of the core features of attachment is distress at being separated from the attachment figure. Baby rats, chicks, kittens, puppies, and monkeys all cry in distinctive ways when separated from their mothers, much as human infants do. Researchers have found that these **separation distress** cries are associated with a sudden decrease in endorphins (Nelson & Panksepp, 1998). When young rhesus monkeys are separated from their mothers, a small amount of morphine reduces their cries, and the drug naloxone, which blocks opioid receptors, increases their cries (Kalin, Shelton, & Barksdale, 1988). Francesca D'Amato and her colleagues studied mice that lacked the gene for the μ (mu) type of endorphin receptor. The researchers reasoned that if endorphins are important for attachment, then animals insensitive to endorphins should develop only weak attachments. Indeed, these mice made far fewer than the normal number of cries when they were separated from their mothers (Moles, Kieffer, & D'Amato, 2004).

In another study, researchers examined the behavior of rhesus macaques with different versions of the μ-type endorphin receptor gene, one of which leads to enhanced receptor function. They found that monkeys with the allele for more efficient receptors not only cried more persistently than those with normal receptor genes when separated from their mothers, but also spent more time with their mothers when other monkeys were present, suggesting a strong preference for their mother's company (Barr et al., 2008).

Types of Attachment: Secure, Anxious-Ambivalent, and Avoidant

Bowlby and Ainsworth argued that the attachment instinct is a universal, biological program emerging at a specific point in development, and that all infants form attachments to their primary caregivers. When placed in the strange situation, do all babies show the behavioral profile we described earlier? Although this is the most common profile, it's not the only one. Averaging across studies from around the world, about 65% of babies show this **secure attachment** pattern (Van Ijzendoorn & Kroonenberg, 1988). What about the other babies?

About 20% of babies show a similar pattern, but cling to the parent more while he or she is present and are less easily soothed when the parent returns from an absence (Ainsworth & Bell, 1970). During the first phase of the strange situation, before the parent leaves the room, these babies show more reluctance to explore and play on their own. When the parent leaves, the babies panic and become extremely upset, but when the parent returns the babies are more difficult to calm, simultaneously clinging and pushing or twisting away. Although different researchers use different terms for this category, **anxious-ambivalent attachment** is common.

About 15% of babies show a third pattern, referred to as **avoidant attachment** or anxious-avoidant attachment. These babies seem to show little interest in the coming and going of their caregivers. While the parent is present, they play on their own. When the parent leaves, they may look toward the door and play less, but they do not cry or protest. They do not show obvious interest when the parent returns, and do not turn to the parent for comfort. You may be thinking, "That's great! These babies are probably more mature and independent than the 'secure' ones!" To test this hypothesis, researchers in one study compared changes in heart rate and cortisol reactivity during the separation phase of the strange situation in babies classified as secure versus avoidant based on their behavior. If the avoidant babies really were less distressed by their parents' absence, they should have shown little or no increase in these biological measures of stress. Instead, the avoidant babies' increases in heart rate and salivary cortisol were just as strong as those of the secure babies, suggesting that they were just as upset, but handling their distress in a different way (Spangler & Grossmann, 1993).

The attachment style proportions given above are averages from a meta-analysis of studies conducted in eight countries including the United States, Japan, China, Israel, and a few Western European countries (Van Ijzendoorn & Kroonenberg, 1988). The analyses revealed some cultural differences in the proportions as well, which may reflect different norms around parenting. For example, rates of babies classified as anxiously attached were higher in Japan and Israel than in the other samples. Many Japanese mothers stay with their infants almost constantly during the first year of life. In the strange situation, a mother may be leaving her infant alone or with a stranger for the first time ever, and the infant reacts with horror—it's a much stranger situation than it would be for most babies in North America (Rothbaum et al., 2000). It may be that behaviors indicating anxious-ambivalent attachment in most other countries have a different meaning in Japan and Israel, or that more babies really are anxiously attached. In contrast, a higher proportion of the Western European (German, Dutch, Swedish, and English) babies were classified as avoidant based on their behavior in the strange situation. Again, it's not clear whether this is because parents in these countries explicitly encourage independence in babies, leading to earlier maturation and confidence during the strange situation, or more babies really are learning an avoidant way of handling their distress.

Importantly, Ainsworth and Bowlby would say that babies showing any of these three styles are attached to their caregivers. There is a fourth category, although it is rare. **Disorganized attachment** may be coded if the infant displays open, intense anxiety even when the caregiver is present, such as freezing in place, nervously pulling at their own hair, or rocking back and forth. These babies seem paralyzed by the situation, frightened, yet unable to turn to the caregiver for comfort. In these cases, there is a higher chance that the caregiver is emotionally volatile, suffering from depression or trauma, or even abusive.

What predicts these individual differences in attachment style? One possibility is that they are innate—people are born with a predisposition to one attachment style or another. Attachment insecurity has been linked statistically with polymorphism of a serotonin receptor gene in multiple studies (Fraley et al., 2013; Gillath et al., 2008), but the effect is small, and study results are not always consistent. Given the same caregiver, attachment style is generally consistent from one observation to another, and it predicts the warmth of child–parent relationships, years and even decades later (Ding et al., 2014; Waters et al., 2000). However, infants can show different attachment styles to different caregivers (Steele, Steele, & Fonagy, 1996), suggesting that attachment type is determined at least in part by the environment.

The function of attachment is to regulate proximity so that the baby has some freedom to explore on its own, but caregivers are easily summoned if the baby needs help. Just like babies, however, not all caregivers are the same. Babies seem to adapt their approach to what is most effective for striking the balance between independence and safety, given the caregiver's typical behavior (Isabella & Belsky, 1991). When caregivers are highly attuned and responsive to the baby's signals, letting the baby explore when he or she wants to, but attending quickly if the baby wants to engage or becomes upset, babies are more likely to be classified as secure (De Wolff & van IJzendoorn, 1997; Lucassen et al., 2011). Caregivers' ability to remain calm, relaxed, and connected with the baby, even or especially when the baby is crying, may be a particularly important predictor of secure attachment (Woodhouse et al., 2020; Figure 9.5). If a caregiver is smothering, ignoring the infant's need for independence, or becomes anxious and upset themselves when the infant cries, the infant may find separation particularly frightening, and be difficult to soothe. This pattern can be seen in anxious-ambivalent attachment. With distant, unresponsive caregivers, seeking their attention during play and crying for their return if they leave are pointless. These caregivers are more likely to have infants showing avoidant attachment. According to Ainsworth and Bowlby, each attachment style can be thought of as a reasonable strategy, given the characteristics of the parent.

The different attachment profiles are related to important long-term outcomes. Infants with a secure attachment tend to develop into young children who show higher cognitive functioning (Ranson & Urichuk, 2008), teens who are rated as more socially mature (Murray et al., 2006), and adults who maintain good relationships (Salvatore et al., 2011). Children showing avoidant attachment are at increased risk for aggressive, antisocial behaviors later in life (Burgess et al., 2003). Infants classified as insecurely attached (either anxious-ambivalent or avoidant) are more likely to suffer from psychopathology as adults (Sroufe et al., 2005), and have even been found to report more physical illness symptoms (Puig et al., 2013). Researchers emphasize, however, that it's not the infant attachment per se that is necessarily the problem. Rather, it's the ongoing environment in which the child is being raised, and the extent to which behaviors learned in

FIGURE 9.5. Caregivers' ability to remain calm, responsive, and comforting when the infant is distressed has been found to predict the baby's security of attachment.

infancy (e.g., panicking at the idea of separation from loved ones; not asking for help; hiding emotions rather than showing them) carry forward into adulthood and become problematic down the road.

Attachment Across the Lifespan

Although attachment-related behaviors appear in the first year of life, Bowlby (1969) argued that the attachment system is active in close relationships "from the cradle to the grave." Beyond attachments to parents, people develop attachments to other family members, close friends, and—as we discuss in detail soon—romantic partners (Ainsworth, 1989). Data from a study with over 86,000 participants suggests some changes in attachment style across adolescence and adulthood, on average, with attachment anxiety highest in young adulthood and avoidance highest in midlife (Figure 9.6; Chopik, Edelstein, & Fraley, 2013). Note that in this study, anxiety and avoidance were measured using a questionnaire that captures degrees of anxiety and avoidance, rather than classifying people into one attachment style or another. When people choose one of three descriptions that best reflects their attachment style, however, the overall proportions of attachment security, anxiety, and avoidance are similar among adults and infants.

People begin to form friendship bonds early in childhood, and as children mature into their teens, friends become an increasingly important source of emotional and practical support (Furman & Buhrmester, 1992). Warm, secure friendships in adolescence may be crucial building blocks for healthy adult lives. In one study, researchers measured the number and quality of friendships in early adolescence, and found that those with more and closer friends had higher self-esteem and fewer symptoms of psychological disorders (such as depression

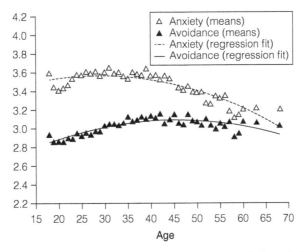

FIGURE 9.6. In a study with more than 86,000 participants, mostly from the United States, Canada, and the United Kingdom, attachment anxiety was highest in young adulthood, declining with age, and attachment avoidance peaked in midlife. From Chopik, Edelstein, & Fraley (2013).

and anxiety) 12 years later (Bagwell, Newcomb, & Bukowski, 1998). As you can probably guess, this was a correlational study (you can't randomly assign teenagers to have lots of friends or no friends), so it is difficult to know whether the friendships caused people to thrive emotionally in adulthood, or people who were already on track for healthy adult lives tended to form more friendships as teenagers. Both explanations are probably true.

Some studies do suggest, however, that healthy childhood and adolescent friendships can help buffer people from the effects of other negative influences. In one, researchers found that although children from abusive home environments in early childhood were more likely than others to be the victims of bullying in the third and fourth grade, this correlation was weaker among children who reported having many friends (Schwartz et al., 2000). In another study, researchers asked whether the security of relationships with parents or that with friends was the better predictor of adolescents' overall adjustment (Laible, Carlo, & Raffaelli, 2000). As expected, adolescents who reported secure relationships with both parents and peers were the best adjusted. However, teens who had secure relationships with peers, but insecure relationships with parents, were better adjusted than teens for whom the reverse was true. The buffering effect of friendships in adolescence is particularly strong for girls, and is most associated with close, warm, and supportive friendships rather than casual or activity-based friendships (Rubin et al., 2004). A longitudinal study following a cohort of more than 700 participants from birth through the teen years also found that that friendship quality during childhood and adolescence was a better predictor of attachment style at age 18 than some aspects of parental behavior (Fraley et al., 2013). Although less research has examined implications of attachment to friends in adulthood, these findings indicate that close friendships do confer distinct benefits of their own, and that attachment may be an important part of this process.

ROMANTIC LOVE AND MARRIAGE

Learning Objectives

- Summarize the research on characteristics people find most important/attractive in a potential romantic partner, and describe behaviors associated with flirting.
- Differentiate passionate and companionate love in the context of romantic relationships.
- Analyze the behavioral and other characteristics associated with secure, anxious, and avoidant attachment styles in infants and adults, identifying themes that show continuity for each style, and summarize the evidence that both infants and adults with avoidant attachment styles do experience attachment-related needs.
- List several established predictors of long-term relationship satisfaction and stability, analyzing the likelihood that each effect is causal rather than reflecting a third variable's causal effects.

For many people, the relationship with a spouse or similar, committed partner will be the most intimate one in their lives. People often wonder, "How will I know when I'm in love?" or "How will I recognize the person who is right for me?" There is no easy answer to these questions, and the fact that about half of all US marriages end in divorce suggests that many people either don't know how to choose the right partner, or don't know how to maintain love once the sparks have died down and they have to figure out whose job it is to clean the garage. Although we wish science had more definitive advice to offer on this subject, psychologists studying emotion in marriages and other romantic relationships have identified some features of typical romantic relationships, as well as some predictors of couples' happiness and stability.

Much of the discussion that follows applies mainly to Western cultures where young people may date a variety of partners, virtually unsupervised, before committing to marriage. In many Arab, Asian, and Latin American cultures it would be scandalous for an unmarried couple to spend time together without a chaperone; having a series of flirtations and/or love affairs before settling down is unthinkable. So, from the start we must admit that "typical" romantic relationships and marriages vary across cultures, and have changed throughout history as well (Coontz, 2005). The relationship between romantic love and marriage itself differs from culture to culture. Romantic love is not considered a prerequisite for marriage and reproduction in all cultures, and it may even be seen as a threat to the extended family relationships that provide the foundation of many cultures' social structures (Dion & Dion, 1993). In some societies, parents arrange young people's marriages for economic or other practical considerations and virtually ignore romantic love. Spouses in these societies manage to mate and rear their children quite successfully, and often develop close, intimate bonds (Figure 9.7). "Yes," you might say, "but are those marriages happy?" Some are and some aren't. In the United States, where partners typically choose each other based on romantic love, some marriages are happy and some aren't. Studies have compared marital satisfaction in arranged versus love marriages in societies where both are reasonably common, and the results are inconsistent as to which kind of marriage is happier, if either.

Our discussion also focuses on heterosexual dating and marriage. The research on homosexual couples is still relatively meager. The available studies suggest that many of the important issues are similar for homosexual and heterosexual relationships. For

FIGURE 9.7. Although modern Western cultures emphasize romantic love between spouses as the main prerequisite for marriage, other cultures encourage marriages based on compatibility and the implications for uniting the spouses' extended families.

example, in either case, people seek a partner with similar attitudes, who will be honest, supportive, and trustworthy (Bäccman, Folkesson, & Norlander, 1999). The variables that predict relationship satisfaction are similar for homosexual and heterosexual couples as well (Kurdek, 2005). Some communication dynamics, such as the **demand-withdraw** pattern in which one partner escalates their insistence on discussing some topic while the other retreats further and further into themselves, can be observed in both heterosexual and homosexual couples (Christensen & Heavey, 1990; Holley, Sturm, & Levenson, 2010). With these caveats in mind, let's consider the trajectory of a prototypical North American romantic relationship.

Romantic Attraction and Falling in Love

This story begins when two people meet, find each other attractive, and start spending more time together. It is fascinating to see who finds whom attractive, and what constitutes a "turn-on" varies considerably from person to person (Morse & Gruzen, 1976). Still, most people, even across cultures, agree on a few features that enhance attractiveness (Buss, 1989; Cunningham et al., 1995). One of the most consistent is health. Other things being equal, healthy people are sexier than unhealthy people. In women, features such as long, shiny hair and clear, rosy skin are considered attractive, perhaps because problems with hair and skin are often early signs of malnutrition or illness (Rushton, 2002).

Statistically average features are also attractive. For example, if you photograph many people with their faces in the same position and then use a computer to average the faces, most observers rate the resulting average as very attractive (Donohoe, von Hippel, & Brooks, 2009; Langlois & Roggman, 1990). Why? Average features are familiar, so they may make us feel comfortable. They may also represent genes that have succeeded in past generations. A nose, mouth, or other feature notably larger or smaller than usual is questionable. The genes responsible have not stood the test of time.

In addition to good looks, we are also attracted to people with certain personality characteristics. People seek a happy disposition and kindness toward others (Cunningham et al., 1995; Evans & Brase, 2007; Gross & Crofton, 1977; Langlois & Roggman, 1990). We are also attracted to intelligence (Evans & Brase, 2007; Shackelford, Schmitt,

& Buss, 2005) and a sense of humor (Li et al., 2002; Sprecher & Regan, 2002). Humor may be a sign of high intelligence and good mate value, but humor is also used to show interest in another person, so it can be an important part of flirting (Li et al., 2009). Both men and women value these features to a comparable degree.

Perceptions of physical attractiveness and personality are not independent (Kniffin & Wilson, 2004; Lewandowski, Aron, & Gee, 2007). After you come to like and respect someone, you might find that person better looking than before. Similarly, you may find yourself repulsed by the appearance of someone you dislike. Personality has a slightly stronger impact on women's perception of men's attractiveness than the other way around, although the effect occurs in both genders (Lewandowski et al., 2007).

How do people behave when they are attracted to another person? You probably have some ideas about this—if you've gotten all the way to college without noticing how people flirt, you haven't been paying attention! Researcher Monica Moore (1985) went to an ideal place to observe flirting—a bar near a college campus—and took careful notes recording women's behavior. Women seemed to display initial interest in a man through a darting glance, looking at him for a couple of seconds and then quickly looking away. Some women also tossed their heads and flipped their hair with their hands, tilted their heads, licked their lips, and caressed the objects around them.

A recent study suggests a similar display. Researchers Parnia Haj-Mohamadi, Omri Gillath, and Erika Rosenberg (2021) asked college-age American men to rate the affect shown by women in several hundred posed photos, with many different combinations of facial muscle, head, and eye movements. In the two expressions identified as flirtatious by over 70% of men, the women showed a closed-mouth Duchenne smile (recall from Chapter 5 that the eye corners crinkle in this smile), with the head lowered and turned away, but the eyes looking toward the viewer. Keep in mind that this was what researchers call an "expression recognition" study, rather than a "production" study; finding that some expression is easily recognized is not the same as showing it is widely displayed. However, the similarities in the "coy glance" documented by the two studies suggests some continuity over the decades in women's nonverbal signs of attraction. Another limitation was that only US participants were studied, so future research is needed to examine similarities and differences in flirtatious behaviors across cultures.

Does anything strike you as odd about these studies? They investigated how women flirt, but did not study men's behavior at all! Some researchers have suggested that men display fewer nonverbal flirting behaviors than women because when they are interested, they simply approach a woman and talk with her (Grammer et al., 2000). Women may prefer a less direct way of expressing their interest. One reason is to slow down courtship while they gather more information. Another is that even when women flirt in subtle ways, men tend to overestimate women's interest, so a more direct approach would be risky (Abbey, 1982). Unfortunately, men are capable of misunderstanding in both directions (Farris et al., 2008): many men think women are flirting when really they are not, and often think women are not flirting when really they are.

Not all signs of attraction are associated with gender. A meta-analysis of studies linking behaviors to self-reported attraction found that both men and women smile, make eye contact, and stand or sit closer to a person toward whom they are attracted (Montoya, Kershaw, & Prosser, 2018). They also subtly match each other's nonverbal cues, in unconscious mimicry—one signals, the other copies, and so forth (Figure 9.8;

FIGURE 9.8. Both men and women show attraction by matching each other's posture and movements.

Lakin & Chartrand, 2003; Montoya et al., 2018). However, these signals may not be specific to romantic or sexual attraction, but simply how we behave when we like someone (Montoya et al., 2018).

The early stages of a romantic relationship are typically marked by **passionate love**, with frequent thoughts about the other person, intense desire to be together, and excitement from the partner's attention (Hatfield & Rapson, 1993). At this stage, each person is likely to idealize the other—to be well aware of the other's positive qualities, but less aware of flaws and limitations. Passionate love is intensely rewarding, even at the neurological level. One study examined 17 young adults who professed to be deeply and madly in love. Each viewed photographs of friends and of the person he or she was in love with, while researchers used fMRI to measure brain activity. Viewing the loved person activated a variety of brain areas, including dopamine-laden reward centers such as the nucleus accumbens. During this stage, just the sight of the loved one produces anticipation and excitement (Bartels & Zeki, 2000).

Many people report that they changed dramatically when they fell in love. Some of this change is the emotional rush we just described, but some may be in actual identity and behavior. In one study, Art Aron asked college students five times over the course of a semester to answer the question, Who are you today? (Aron, Paris, & Aron, 1995). Each time, Aron also asked whether each participant had fallen in love since the last report. People who said they had recently fallen in love described themselves in more diverse ways than they had prior to falling in love in terms of traits, feelings, and social roles. Why might this be? Aron believes that when people fall in love, they begin to incorporate into themselves various aspects of the partner's personality, activities, and attitudes—a process he describes as self-expansion.

As a relationship continues, partners may grow even more alike (Anderson, Keltner, & John, 2003; Davis & Rusbult, 2001). However, couples often overestimate their similarity in attitudes and preferences, as they emphasize shared feelings over differences and each projects his or her own feelings onto the other partner (Murray et al., 2002). As couples dated, their estimates of each other's attitudes and behaviors may became more confident without necessarily becoming more accurate (Swann & Gill, 1997).

Attachment in Adult Romantic Relationships

If the relationship continues, partners may increase their integration into each other's lives. Lovers are introduced to each other's families, and they may begin to share resources, live together, or make some other long-term commitment. Over the course of this process, relationships move toward **companionate love**, with an emphasis on security and mutual care and protection as well as affection and shared fun (Hatfield & Rapson, 1993). However, we should not overstate this transformation. In a study of people who had been married for more than 30 years, researchers found that more than one-third said they were still intensely, passionately in love, and brain scans showed the same reward circuit arousal that couples show in the early stage of romance (Acevedo et al., 2012; O'Leary et al., 2012). Strong companionate love is usually related to high satisfaction with life, more so than passionate love.

If the term "security" in the paragraph above caught your attention, you are astute! Recognizing that a sense of security is an important part of healthy romantic relationships, just as in infant–parent relationships, researchers Cindy Hazan and Philip Shaver (1987) asked whether the attachment system might be activated in the former as well as the latter relationship type. Like infants' attachments to their caregivers, adult attachments are relationships in which one or both people prefer to be in close contact and experience distress during extended separation (proximity-seeking), turn to the partner for support in times of stress or danger (safe haven), and derive security and confidence from the partner, facilitating a confident approach to the rest of the world (secure base; Fraley & Shaver, 2000). A strong body of research now documents the role of attachment in long-term romantic relationships (Fraley & Shaver, 2000). For example, a key feature of infant attachment is that a child who feels threatened or stressed turns to the attachment figure for protection and comfort. Mario Mikulincer and colleagues (Mikulincer et al., 2000) wanted to know whether adults showed these same tendencies. People report that they do, but can we measure this tendency? In the strange situation, the mother takes the baby into an unfamiliar room, leaves, and comes back; researchers measure how hard the baby cries and how easily it is soothed by the mother's return. You're welcome to try this with adults, but we don't think it will work.

To get around this problem, Mikulincer and colleagues developed an indirect measure of the "safe haven" aspect of attachment behavior, asking whether people are quicker to detect words of closeness or separation when they feel threatened. The idea was that if certain kinds of thoughts are already in a person's mind, they should be able to identify words related to those thoughts more quickly. In an ingenious experiment, they asked participants to watch a computer screen (see Figure 9.9). Right after seeing one word (a "prime") flash on the screen for a second, they had to decide whether the next string of letters was a word or not. Sometimes the prime word was "failure," and sometimes it was a neutral word. The following string of letters might be a proximity-related word like

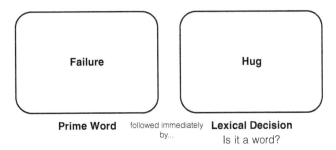

FIGURE 9.9. To see whether adults' minds turn instinctively to thoughts of closeness and love when they are threatened, reflecting the "safe haven" aspect of attachment, Mario Mikulincer and colleagues examined reaction time to recognize closeness-themed words right after seeing a threatening or neutral prime.

"closeness" or "love"; a distance-related word like "rejection" or "abandonment"; a neutral word; or a nonword string of letters. Results showed that in general, people identified proximity-related words faster after seeing the word "failure" than after a neutral prime word. It was as though the tiny threat of thinking about failure made people want to feel close to someone. In another study, the same effect was found using the names of participants' particular attachment figures rather than generic proximity words (Mikulincer et al., 2002).

These studies suggest that, as predicted by Bowlby and Ainsworth decades earlier, adults' attachment systems are awake and going strong. Adults also appear to have different attachment styles, just like small children. Think about how you generally feel in romantic relationships. Then read the three paragraphs in Figure 9.10—which describes you best?

These paragraphs were designed by Cindy Hazan and Phil Shaver (1987) to represent what secure, anxious, and avoidant attachment might feel like in the context of adult

Secure (N = 319, 56%): I find it relatively easy to get close to others and am comfortable depending on them and having them depend on me. I don't often worry about being abandoned or about someone getting too close to me.

Avoidant (N = 145, 25%): I am somewhat uncomfortable being close to others; I find it difficult to trust them completely, difficult to allow myself to depend on them. I am nervous when anyone gets too close, and often, love partners want me to be more intimate than I feel comfortable being.

Anxious/Ambivalent (N = 100, 19%): I find that others are reluctant to get as close as I would like. I often worry that my partner doesn't really love me or won't want to stay with me. I want to merge completely with another person, and this desire sometimes scares people away.

FIGURE 9.10. These paragraphs describe secure, avoidant, and anxious/ambivalent attachment styles in adult romantic relationships. Which one describes you best?

romantic relationships. Hazan and Shaver had these paragraphs printed in a local newspaper, along with dozens of self-report items measuring beliefs about relationships, attitudes toward the respondent's most important relationship partner, and characteristics of the respondent's relationships with parents and important romantic partners. Readers were asked to complete the questionnaire, cut it out, and mail it back to the researchers.

Hazan and Shaver (1987) found that adults classified themselves into attachment styles in proportions similar to those observed in studies of infants: 56% of the sample said the secure paragraph described them best, 25% chose the avoidant paragraph, and 19% said the anxious paragraph described them best (of course, these labels were not given in the newspaper). People endorsing different attachment styles had different relationship histories, and different beliefs about relationships. Those endorsing the secure paragraph had had longer relationships than participants who chose the anxious or avoidant paragraph; were less likely to have been divorced; and typically described their most important love experience as happy, friendly, and trusting. They tended to endorse the belief that ups and downs are normal in relationships—sometimes the romance will cool down, but then it will flare up again. They were unlikely to say that it was easy to fall in love, or that they fell in love frequently.

By contrast, people endorsing the anxious paragraph tended to describe themselves as obsessively preoccupied with their partners, and experiencing intense emotional highs and lows in relationships. They were more likely than secure and avoidant individuals to agree that their love experiences were "love at first sight," and that an intense feeling of oneness with their partner was important. They were most likely to say that they fell in love easily and often. They also agreed most strongly of the three groups that they experienced much self-doubt, were misunderstood or unappreciated, and were more able than most people to commit to a long-term relationship.

Finally, people endorsing the avoidant paragraph described being afraid of closeness in their most important relationships, and unable to accept their partner's imperfections. They were more likely than secure and anxious participants to agree that romantic love does not last forever, and less likely to agree that romantic feelings grow and wane repeatedly over the course of a relationship. They were also most likely to endorse a statement that they were independent and able to get along by themselves.

How do the three adult styles relate to the attachment types observed in infants? According to Chris Fraley and Philip Shaver, adult styles reflect the same kinds of deeply ingrained expectations about caregiver/partner relationships that are the basis for infant styles (Fraley & Shaver, 2000). Securely attached infants expect that caregivers will be responsive, protective, and warm; securely attached adults think of themselves as lovable and worthy, and of their lovers as kind, trustworthy, and dependable. Anxiously attached infants seem to expect inconsistency from caregivers, and are terrified of separation. Attachment-anxious adults want to be in a deep, intense relationship and think such relationships are possible, but they don't really trust others, don't think of themselves as lovable, and are constantly afraid of being abandoned. Avoidant infants appear to have given up on their caregivers, playing on their own and showing little reaction when the caregiver leaves; attachment-avoidant adults seem to have given up on committed, intimate relationships in a similar way.

Or have they? Have attachment-avoidant people really turned off their attachment needs in the way their self-reports and surface behaviors suggest? In the Mikulincer et al. (2000) word-recognition study described earlier, researchers found that people with more anxious attachment styles were quick to detect proximity-related words regardless of whether the prime was "failure" or the neutral word. They seemed to be thinking about attachment needs at all times, stressed or not. Also, attachment-anxious people were quicker to recognize distance-related words after the failure prime, as though the stress made them worry about rejection.

Because attachment-avoidant people should also expect rejection from others, one might have expected them to show a similar pattern, but they did not. To determine whether avoidant people were suppressing these attachment anxieties, Mikulincer and colleagues (2000) repeated their study, but this time participants had to complete the word-detection task while listening to a loud and annoying story over a set of headphones. This time, the stressful prime had an even bigger effect on the avoidant participants' distance word recognition than it did on the anxious participants! It was as though avoidant participants usually put mental effort into suppressing their fears of rejection, but when they were overloaded these fears were released.

You may be wondering, do people really fall neatly into one attachment style or another? Are adult feelings about romantic relationships that easy to categorize? It's a good question. Toddlers can't tell us in detail about their feelings, so we must rely on their behavior in the strange situation to measure their attachment to caregivers. Behavior in the strange situation is easy to categorize, so the three-type model is the one used most often in studying small children. Adults, however, may describe themselves as "mostly secure, but kind of anxious," "somewhat avoidant," or even "both anxious and avoidant." When you read the three newspaper paragraphs used by Hazan and Shaver (1987), you may have identified with two or more paragraphs as well.

According to Kim Bartholomew (1990; Bartholomew & Horowitz, 1991), this is because attachment styles represent the interaction between two *working models* or implicit internal beliefs—one about the value of the self, and one about the value of other people. As a result, adult attachment is best measured in terms of two dimensions, rather than three categories (Fraley & Waller, 1998). The anxiety dimension measures whether a person generally has positive or negative feelings of self-worth and desirability as a partner. People who think of themselves as less worthy and desirable thus score higher on attachment anxiety. The avoidance dimension measures whether a person generally has positive or negative beliefs about other people. People who think others are less trustworthy, and who see less value in intimate relationships, score higher on attachment avoidance. Attachment questionnaires based on the two-dimensional model have proved to be reliable and useful in measuring adults' attachment styles (e.g., Brennan, Clark, & Shaver, 1998; Griffin & Bartholomew, 1994).

The critical test of a questionnaire measure is whether it predicts people's thoughts, feelings, and behavior in the way that it should. In a creative study, Chris Fraley and Philip Shaver (1998) went to a local airport and surreptitiously recorded the behavior of couples waiting at the gate until either both partners got on the plane, or one got on the plane and the other left (Figure 9.11). (This study was done while you could still go to the gate without a ticket—can you imagine?) If one person was left behind, the researchers asked that person to complete an attachment style questionnaire. For women anticipating

FIGURE 9.11. In a clever study of adult attachment, researchers measured the feelings and behaviors shown by a person waiting at an airport gate—for their partner to leave without them.

separation from their partners, the results were striking. Those who scored higher on attachment anxiety reported feeling more upset about the separation. Women who scored higher on avoidance had shown fewer contact and caregiving behaviors (such as kissing, hugging, gently touching, and whispering to the partner) and more avoidance behaviors (such as looking away from the partner and breaking off physical contact).

One interesting feature of this study is that it showed the independence of attachment anxiety and avoidance as separate dimensions, just as Bartholomew had suggested. Attachment anxiety most effectively predicted how women *felt* when facing a separation, with more anxious women feeling more distress. By contrast, attachment avoidance best predicted women's *behavior* in terms of avoiding contact or closeness when separation was imminent. Thus, a very anxious woman could be feeling very distressed at the idea of separation, but her avoidance score would predict whether she handled the distress by seeking or avoiding contact. Similarly, an avoidant woman might or might not feel particularly sad about the separation, but was likely to disengage from her partner regardless.

The questionnaire measure of attachment did not predict men's behavior or feelings as accurately, and it's not clear why. One plausible reason is that there are different constraints on men's affectionate behavior in public than on women's behavior. Men may also have been more reluctant to say they were distressed, or perhaps even less aware of distress. The study is now about a quarter-century old. Although researchers can no longer hang out at airport gates waiting to chat with a partner left behind, there should be other ways to study separation-related feelings and behaviors, and it would be interesting to see whether attachment style effects are still more powerful among women than among men. There's still a great deal to learn about the role of attachment processes in adulthood, but Bowlby's original ideas have proved remarkably helpful in our understanding of romantic relationships.

Are the biological mechanisms of attachment in adult romantic relationships similar to those in infants? Earlier we discussed the role of oxytocin in maternal-infant bonding. Studies comparing different animal species have identified a fascinating role for oxytocin in attachment between mates as well. In particular, consider little rodents called voles, which are similar to mice. Prairie voles and meadow voles (Figure 9.12) are closely related species, but prairie voles develop long-term pair-bonds after mating, whereas meadow voles do not. If a male meadow vole is given a choice between the female he recently mated with or some other female, he shows a 50–50 preference. Sue Carter and her colleagues found that injecting oxytocin directly into a female prairie vole's brain caused her to form an attachment to a nearby male, even without mating; blocking oxytocin receptors prevented formation of pair-bonds, even after voles did mate (Williams et al., 1994). Researchers genetically engineered some male meadow voles, which ordinarily do not form pair-bonds, to produce more vasopressin receptors (vasopressin and oxytocin are very similar hormones, with vasopressin somewhat more prominent in males). The result: each male developed a strong attachment to the female with which he mated. He spent as much time with her as possible, and even helped take care of her babies (Lim et al., 2004).

Research suggests that oxytocin and vasopressin play important roles in human behavior as well. A study of married couples found that men with more vasopressin receptors have closer relationships with their wives and are less likely to have considered divorce (Walum et al., 2008). In another study, researchers took measures of oxytocin in the blood while participants remembered an experience of strong romantic love. Participants who showed more facial displays of romantic love and affiliation while verbally describing the experience also tended to show greater increases in oxytocin levels while vividly remembering that experience (Gonzaga et al., 2006). In yet another study, researchers administered oxytocin nasal spray or a placebo to romantic partners 45 minutes before they had a conversation about a conflict in their relationship. Couples who had received the oxytocin spray showed a significantly higher ratio of positive behavior during the conversation (eye contact, emotional disclosure, caring, validating the partner's perspective, etc.)

FIGURE 9.12. Prairie and meadow voles are closely related species, but their relationships after mating look different. Researchers believe that oxytocin and vasopressin facilitate prairie voles' tendency to pair-bond.

to negative behavior (e.g., criticism, contempt, defensiveness) than couples who had received the placebo (Ditzen et al., 2009).

By now you may be wondering: If the same attachment system is involved in both infant–parent and romantic relationships, are people who started out with insecure attachments doomed to a life of misery? It's complicated, but not hopeless! Researcher Chris Fraley (2002) tested several models of how attachment style might change over time to see which model offered the best fit to data from 27 longitudinal studies. The results indicated some stability in attachment styles between infancy and adulthood, but with a correlation of .39. To get a sense of what this means in practical terms, you can square the correlation and estimate a percentage of individual differences in people's adult attachment style that is explained in terms of infant style—in this case, only 15%. Across different periods of adulthood, correlations tend to be higher, around $r = .70$ (Davila, Karney, & Bradbury, 1999), but this still means only half of variability in later ages is predicted by earlier ages (.70 squared = .49). Longitudinal studies continue to find that although infant attachment style does predict attachment style in adulthood, the effect is weak, and as we noted earlier, close friendships in childhood and adolescence can play important roles in modulating the attachment system's set point (Fraley & Roisman, 2019). Moreover, at least in reasonably healthy, satisfying marriages, spouses' attachment styles tend to become more secure over time (Davila et al., 1999). There is continuity, but there's also ample room for change.

Marriage: Predicting Satisfaction and Stability

Many love stories end with the couple getting married. Marriage rates in the United States and many other developed countries have declined to some extent since the 1970s, and people are older on average at their first marriage (Schneider, Harknett, & Stimpson, 2018). Still, about 90% of people will marry at some point, and many of those who do not will be in a comparable long-term, committed relationship with a romantic partner (Figure 9.13; Karney & Bradbury, 2020). What happens beyond the wedding day?

Although many marriages do last "as long as we both shall live," about half of them end in divorce, at least in the United States (Kreider & Ellis, 2011). The United States is the most divorce-prone country in the world, and this rate has not changed much since its initial rise in the 1970s and 1980s. It's normal for people's marital satisfaction to fluctuate over the course of a long life together. On average, satisfaction decreases somewhat from the heights of newlywed bliss over the next ten years (a period that often coincides with having small children at home), bottoms out around age 40, and then steadily increases well into old age (Bühler, Krauss, & Orth, 2021; Hirschberger et al., 2009). Recall the lifespan trajectories of life satisfaction and positive affect we examined in Chapter 8. The trajectory of marital satisfaction looks quite similar, and evidence suggests that the midlife low points in marital as well as life satisfaction may reflect the heightened stress common during this life stage.

Importantly, the mean trajectory conceals a great deal of variability among couples in how their marital satisfaction changes over time. A review of longitudinal studies, in which individual couples' change over time can be examined, suggested that while several different trajectories can be described, many or even most couples show fairly little decline in marital satisfaction over the years (Proulx et al., 2017). The question is this: What predicts whether a marriage will survive and flourish, or end with unhappy spouses parting ways?

FIGURE 9.13. Although marriage rates in the United States and other developed countries have declined in recent decades, around 90% of people will marry at some point.

Some predictors of marital stability involve simple demographic characteristics (Harker & Keltner, 2001; Howard & Dawes, 1976; Karney & Bradbury, 1995; Myers, 2000b; Thornton, 1977; Tzeng, 1992). Marriages are most likely to last if the spouses:

- Were over 20 when they married;
- Grew up in two-parent homes;
- Dated for a long time before marrying, but did not live together;
- Have a similar level of education, especially a high level of education;
- Have a good income;
- Have a long-term happy disposition;
- Live in a small town or a rural area;
- Are religious and of the same religious affiliation;
- Are approximately the same age and have similar attitudes; and
- Have sex often and arguments rarely.

Some of these effects are plausibly causal in nature. For example, a great deal of evidence indicates that economic stress is bad for marital satisfaction and stability (Falconier & Jackson, 2020), so it makes sense that couples with higher incomes should be somewhat protected from divorce. Earlier we described the evidence linking oxytocin to pair bonding, and given that oxytocin is typically released during sex (Carmichael et al., 1987), this is a mechanism by which sex might promote relationship satisfaction (it seems likely that happy couples have more sex as well).

Does this mean that if you don't go to church you are doomed to split up? Or that you should give up now on the partner you've been living with for a year? Should you move to a farm to keep your marriage alive? Of course not. Each of these factors *correlates* with, or tends to predict, whether a couple divorces or stays married. A correlation does not necessarily demonstrate a *causal* relationship. For example, why would living together before marriage cause divorce? Marriages do better when people have dated for a long time and already know each other's quirks and flaws. Living together is a great way to learn about each other, so you'd expect it to be good for marriages, right? Think of it this way. Who doesn't live together? Many religions specifically prohibit living together outside of marriage, and these same religions tend to prohibit (or at least seriously discourage) divorce; religiosity accounts for most, though not all, of the apparent effect of cohabitation on divorce (Kerrigan & Bailey, 2021). Another possibility is that some couples decide too quickly to live together, and then drift into a decision to marry rather than making a careful choice. In either case, living together may not cause marriages to end, but is linked to factors that may make divorce easier or more likely years later.

The effects of similarity beyond the initial flush of attraction are complicated as well. The early evidence that partner similarity is generally conducive to relationship satisfaction and stability was based on evidence of **assortative mating** in marriages and other intimate relationships (Figure 9.14). Assortative mating is the tendency of people to marry people who are more similar to themselves than you'd expect by chance. One study of nearly 300 newlywed couples in Iowa found considerable similarity between spouses on age, religiosity, political orientation, education level, and verbal intelligence (Watson et al., 2004). The couples were more similar than you'd expect by chance on personality and social values as well, though not by a lot. A study with a sample of thousands of German couples found similar results (Arránz Becker, 2012).

FIGURE 9.14.   Evidence suggests that people tend to marry partners who are somewhat similar to themselves, a phenomenon called assortative mating.

Whether similarity predicts marital satisfaction and stability is a different question. As you've read so many times already in this textbook (let's all say it together, shall we?), it depends! In the German study described above, couples' alignment on desire to have children, the importance of career, life goals, and values was associated with higher satisfaction, although the effect sizes were small. Similarity on demographic variables may not matter as much as previously thought. For example, a recent meta-analysis found that spouses from different ethnic/cultural backgrounds did not differ in relationship satisfaction from those of the same background (Henderson & Braithwaite, 2021).

The implications of personality similarity may depend on the couples' age and/or the length of their relationship. In two large studies, one with dating couples and one with newlyweds, similarity on the Big Five personality factors of Extraversion, Agreeableness, Conscientiousness, Neuroticism, and Openness to Experience was associated with higher relationship satisfaction (Gonzaga, Campos, & Bradbury, 2007). This effect was largely accounted for by similar spouses' tendency to share emotional experiences in response to events in their lives; as we saw in Chapter 8, shared emotional experience can support bonding in valuable ways. In another study published the same year, however, it was *differences* in Big Five personality that predicted more positive marital satisfaction trajectories over a 12-year period (Shiota & Levenson, 2007). Why the discrepancy? Couples joined this latter study when they were in their 40s or 60s, and had already been married for decades. Perhaps by the time couples have been together for many years they have already established that they're on the same wavelength, and the benefits of complementarity—with different partners offering different strengths and fulfilling different relationship roles—become increasingly apparent.

One factor that does stand out as important is commitment to the relationship. All long-term relationships go through rough patches—times when mutual adoration is at low tide. The results of one national survey in the United States indicated that among people who reported being unhappily married during the first wave of the study but did *not* divorce, 86% reported being happily married to the same person 5 years later (Popenoe, 2002). Over the years of a new marriage couples learn about big and small incompatibilities, differences they must negotiate to get along. In general, people tend to be more satisfied with their relationship if they consider their partner's flaws specific to particular situations, or see them as related to virtues (Murray & Holmes, 1999). For instance, a woman may tolerate her husband's unwillingness to try new activities if she thinks of it as being related to his stability and consistency.

As time goes on, spouses can simply get a bit bored with each other. However, they may be able to reignite their spark by doing novel and exciting activities together. Art Aron and his colleagues (Aron et al., 2000) brought long-term romantic couples into the lab and assigned them to work together either on a boring task or on an arousing task, such as having two of their legs tied together and crossing a large room on "three legs." Participants not only had more fun with the second task, but also reported that their relationship improved afterward. Expressing gratitude toward your partner can help facilitate satisfaction as well. In one study, some couples were randomly assigned to a gratitude-expression task in which one partner thanked the other for a specific kind or thoughtful act; other couples did a control activity. A month later, the gratitude-condition couples still reported significantly higher satisfaction with the relationship (Algoe, Fredrickson, & Gable, 2013).

In one meta-analysis of nonmarried but committed couples, the strongest predictors of staying together were love, commitment, high sense of investment in the relationship, and low perceived availability of attractive alternative partners (Le et al., 2010). In other words, there are times in almost any relationship when it's worth sticking around to see if things improve, rather than trading your trusty old partner in for a flashy new one.

Yet another factor that predicts marital satisfaction is equity, especially in terms of the skills, effort, and resources each spouse brings to their shared life. People who feel, in general, that they get about as much as they give in their relationships tend to be happier, and people who feel like they are doing all the work are less satisfied (Van Yperen & Buunk, 1990). Individuals tend to feel more trust in a relationship if they perceive that the partner is willing to make some sacrifices for them (Wieselquist et al., 1999). That is, both should feel they are getting a fair deal. This does not mean that couples should keep score about who did what for whom. In fact, one sign of closeness in both close friends and married couples is that they *don't* expect instant repayment for favors, or explicit exchanges of one favor for another (Buunk & Van Yperen, 1991).

Some predictors of marital satisfaction concern how spouses communicate with each other. Couples with happy relationships generally have high levels of self-disclosure—the sharing of personal, intimate, and confidential information (Hendrick, Hendrick, & Adler, 1988; Sanderson & Cantor, 2001). In strong relationships, this process develops gradually over time. As a general rule, people like others who self-disclose to them (Aron et al., 1997), although they feel uneasy if someone discloses deep secrets too early in a relationship. We also tend to like people to whom we have disclosed personal information and feelings (Collins & Miller, 1994). Do not assume that you need to tell your partner everything about yourself. But anything that you think your partner should know about you, or is likely to find out anyway, you should tell. If your partner discovers that you have lied or withheld important information, you will lose a great deal of trust.

John Gottman (1994; Gottman et al., 1998) has spent decades studying the ways in which married couples communicate with each other. To determine which relationships will succeed, he has observed couples at their worst—when they are arguing about some area of disagreement in their lives. Gottman and colleagues first work with a couple to identify an aspect of their lives that causes conflict—such as money, how to raise the kids, or who is doing more of the housework. Then they videotape the couple during a 15-minute discussion about that topic by themselves. This procedure has uncovered emotional components of these conversations that predict the future of the couple's relationship.

You might think that anger would be the biggest risk factor for a relationship. However, Gottman and colleagues' research (1998) indicates that anger is not always a major problem. Mild anger (not screaming or throwing things) may even let a partner know that you are serious about your concern, and give the partner a chance to make changes. Gottman has identified four emotional patterns that predict serious problems for a relationship, however, that he calls "the four horsemen of the apocalypse." These are as follows:

1. *Criticism*: Suggesting changes in behavior can be constructive, but complaining about personal flaws is destructive. Criticism at its most destructive includes attacking the spouse (or the spouse's relatives), listing the spouse's flaws, and blaming the spouse for problems in the relationship. (For example, "You never help me with the housework! You're so lazy!")

2. *Defensiveness*: This is usually a response to criticism, in which one defends one-self by denying that the complaint is valid, giving an excuse for the behavior, or countercriticizing the spouse. (For example, "You're such a perfectionist that you think I never do anything right, so why should I try?")
3. *Contempt*: This includes behaviors like rolling one's eyes, being sarcastic, or insulting the spouse—any message suggesting that the spouse is worthless, in-competent, or beneath the speaker.
4. *Stonewalling*: A spouse stonewalls when they ignore or shut out the spouse who is trying to communicate something, either sitting stone faced and not saying anything or looking away or closing his or her eyes (Figure 9.15).

Couples who showed more of these behaviors were more likely to divorce during the years that followed. In contrast, couples who expressed affection, validated each other's perspectives, and enjoyed shared humor (not making fun of your partner—this is obvi-ously not helpful) even while discussing an area of conflict were happier.

Does this necessarily indicate that communication behaviors *cause* marital satisfac-tion to rise or fall? Certainly many studies document correlations. However, one study asks whether the causal arrow might go the other way as well (Lavner, Karney, & Brad-bury, 2016). In this study over 400 newlywed couples in the Los Angeles, California area completed three videotaped conversations at home every nine months for three years. One conversation was about an area of conflict; the others were on something each spouse would like to change about themselves. Partners rated their marital satisfaction at each time point, and their conversation behavior was coded for positivity (e.g., warmth, humor, attentiveness toward the partner) as well as negativity (e.g., the "four horsemen" above).

FIGURE 9.15.   In stonewalling, one partner ignores or tunes out the other, who is trying to communicate.

Analyses predicting changes in each variable from one time point to the next showed that for the most part, marital satisfaction predicted positive communication behavior, rather than the other way around. Effects linking negative communication behaviors to marital satisfaction were a bit sparse, and went in both directions.

At this point, some previously accepted dogma about marital satisfaction and stability is being challenged, new predictors are being identified, and much work is needed to advance our understanding further (Karney & Bradbury, 2020). This work is extremely important, as there is a need for interventions that can help both young couples getting started, and couples in distress. The next decade of research will be even more sophisticated than the last, and we look forward to seeing what it reveals.

CARING EMOTIONS AND EMPATHY

Learning Objectives

- Differentiate sympathy, personal distress, nurturant love, empathic accuracy, and emotional empathy, and summarize the way in which each is associated with prosocial/helping behavior.
- Summarize research highlighting the role of motivation in empathy.
- Analyze the extent and likely causes of gender differences in empathy, as reflected in research studies.

So far we have emphasized emotions related to feeling secure and knowing others care for our needs, as well as emotions in romantic relationships. We also experience strong emotions in the context of caring for other people. Emotion researchers have described several emotion states associated with caregiving toward others in distress. **Sympathy** has been defined as concerned attention toward someone who is suffering (Eisenberg et al., 1989). **Compassion** has been defined in a similar way, as a feeling experienced in response to another's suffering that motivates helping behavior (Goetz et al., 2010). The two terms are often used interchangeably, and both states can be contrasted with **personal distress**, or self-focused anxiety in the face of another's suffering.

Do sympathy and compassion promote helping? Nancy Eisenberg and her colleagues have addressed this question, contrasting the implications of sympathy and personal distress. The researchers brought elementary school–age children and college students into the lab, and showed them a short local community news program (Eisenberg et al., 1989). The program showed a single mom and her two children in a hospital room, and described a car accident in which the kids had been seriously injured. The mom talked about the kids' fears of falling behind in school, and about her own stressful feelings about supporting the household and still spending time at the hospital. As participants watched this program, experimenters videotaped their facial expressions and measured their heart rates.

After the news program, participants received an envelope supposedly from the professor in charge of the study. In the envelope was a letter from the mother portrayed in the news clip, asking for the participants' assistance, along with a note from the professor saying she had encouraged the mother to write the letter. Adult participants were asked to spend some time helping the mother with housework; child participants were asked to help collect the injured children's homework assignments during their own recess breaks. Then, participants were left alone for a few minutes with a slip of paper. Adults could write the number of hours they were willing to help; children could mark on a calendar the days they would collect homework.

As you've probably guessed, the news story was really designed to see how participants would respond to this opportunity to help. What did the researchers find? Eisenberg and colleagues (1989) split participants into *low helper* and *high helper* groups to see whether their heart rates, facial expressions, and self-reports of emotion differed. Both groups showed expressions of sadness. However, high helpers' heart rates dropped when the segment showing the hospital scene began, whereas low helpers' heart rates tended to speed up; this suggests that helpers were less personally upset, although they were paying close attention to the film. Consistent with this, high helpers tended to show more concerned attention (leaning forward with eyebrows contracted and lowered, as though concentrating) while watching the news story.

Why do some people respond to another's suffering with sympathy, whereas others respond with personal distress? In the study described above, sad expressions were associated with both sympathy and personal distress, so both feelings seemed to start with empathic sadness. In a study of children between four and eight years old, Eisenberg's team found that those who were high on *effortful control* (the ability to regulate one's attention and behavior) reported stronger sympathy and less personal distress (Valiente et al., 2004). In another study, Eisenberg's team found that high helping was predicted by greater respiratory sinus arrhythmia, the fluctuation in heart rate associated with breathing (Fabes, Eisenberg, & Eisenbud, 1993). In Chapter 7 we noted that this measure of parasympathetic nervous system activation has been linked to emotion regulation ability (e.g., Butler et al., 2006; Vasilev et al., 2009). So it may be that helping someone in distress is most likely when you empathize with that person's sadness, but are able to regulate the emotion so it doesn't become overwhelming.

Feelings of sympathy and compassion presume that the person (or animal) toward whom your feelings are directed is in pain or distress. However, we often feel a pleasurable desire to cuddle and care for others who are not in distress at all—they're just really, really cute. **Nurturant love** has been defined as an emotion elicited by cues of youth, vulnerability, and helplessness, which motivates caregiving intended to enhance the other's overall well-being (Griskevicius, Shiota, & Neufeld, 2010). The term "maternal love" is often used in the research literature, but we prefer this more gender-neutral term. Think about a time when you were around a small baby and how you felt, sounded, and acted (Figure 9.16). If the idea of being around a human baby is anxiety-provoking rather than pleasant, imagine how you feel being in a room with a puppy, or kitten, or some other baby animal, stumbling around, whimpering for attention, playing incompetently, and just generally being adorable. That's nurturant love.

How does nurturant love affect our behavior? Across mammalian species, mothers and other caregivers nurture their young by grooming, licking, rubbing, and carrying, as well as feeding and protecting them (Dunbar, 2010). One striking effect is that people seem to respond to cuteness by becoming a bit more careful. In one study, researchers showed women photos of babies and toddlers, and then had them complete a task where they traced a line on a computer screen using a mouse. Half of the women saw photos that had been manipulated to exaggerate the babies' cuteness; the others saw the original photos. Among women who identified strongly with prosocial motivations, those who

FIGURE 9.16.   Whereas sympathy and compassion are felt toward others in distress, nurturant love is a pleasurable response to others who are young, helpless, vulnerable, and/or cute.

had been randomly assigned to the extremely cute babies were more accurate in tracing the line than those who had seen the less-cute babies (Sherman et al., 2013). Despite these intriguing advances, we still have a great deal to learn about nurturant love. Although many studies have examined people's responses to others' pain and distress, remarkably few have looked at people's responses to cuteness. Fortunately, the research should be fun!

Empathy

The various emotions related to caring for others, discussed above, can be differentiated from empathy. The term "empathy" has a muddled history in psychology because people have used it in so many ways, but researchers are finally settling on useful definitions and distinctions. Rather than being a distinct emotion, **empathic accuracy** is the ability to decode what another person is thinking and feeling (Ickes et al., 1990; Levenson & Ruef, 1992). **Emotional empathy** is actually *feeling* what another person is feeling, often including similar physiology and expression as well as subjective experience.

Is empathy good for relationships? Research indicates that the answer to this question depends on at least two things: (1) whether we are talking about empathic accuracy or emotional empathy and (2) what the target is thinking and feeling. Empathic accuracy is generally a good thing, associated with higher relationship satisfaction (Sened et al., 2017), prosocial behavior (Eckland, Huang, & Berenbaum, 2020), and greater numbers of friends (Kardos et al., 2017). On the whole, knowing what someone else is feeling provides a great deal of information about how they interpret the current situation, what their motives and priorities are, what they need, and what they are likely to do next—all helpful if you are going to interact with them in a positive way.

In some circumstances, however, empathic accuracy may have drawbacks. Researchers in one study brought romantic couples into the lab and told them they were participating in a study of physical attractiveness. The couple was shown 12 photographs of more and less attractive men and women, and told that in a follow-up study they might be asked to talk for a while with the people they rated most attractive. It turns out that the couples who were closest showed the least empathic accuracy in guessing what their partners were thinking and feeling when they later watched a videotape of the task, especially if the partners were rating very attractive people (Simpson, Ickes, & Blackstone, 1995). In another study, researchers found that empathic accuracy was associated with *decreased* relationship satisfaction when the target partner was thinking about something that threatened the relationship. When the target partner's thoughts and feelings were nonthreatening, however, empathic accuracy was associated with higher relationship satisfaction (Simpson et al., 2003). In short, when your partner is thinking something favorable to your relationship, you want to know about it. If he or she is thinking something that might annoy you, you might not want to pay close attention.

Emotional empathy is more of a mixed bag. On one hand, it can promote cooperation (Rumble, Van Lange, & Parks, 2010) and as noted earlier, regulated empathetic distress or "sympathy" can promote helping (Eisenberg et al., 1989). Empathy experienced by medical professionals can lead to better care (Decety, 2020). Certainly a lack of emotional empathy is problematic, linked to psychopathic traits and antisocial behavior (Dadds et al., 2009). On the other hand, empathy can be hazardous in situations where one or both partners might become upset, perhaps leading to escalation of conflict and distress (Levenson & Gottman, 1983).

Empathy is not always fun, and an increasing body of research suggests that it takes some effort—effort we may not always be inclined to expend. Consider a series of studies by Daryl Cameron, Michael Inzlicht, and their colleagues (Cameron et al., 2019). Participants in these studies did a series of trials in which they chose between empathizing with a person based on their facial expression, or simply describing that person's demographics, clothes, and whatnot (see Figure 9.17). Across studies, participants only chose the "feel" option about a third of the time, and they were less likely to make this choice as the study went on. The "feel" task was also rated by participants as more effortful and unpleasant than the "describe" task. Remarkably, participants' empathy aversion was not limited to expressions of distress. It makes sense that they might prefer not to feel someone else's sadness or fear, but people tended to choose the "describe" option even when they knew the expression would be a happy one!

In a series of follow-up studies participants viewed an emotion-eliciting photograph, and were allowed to choose on each trial whether they would describe how they (i.e., the participant) felt in response to the photo, or how a hypothetical other person would feel. Again, the default response was to avoid empathy; participants chose to estimate another person's feelings on only a third of trials, on average. However, paying a tiny bonus for choosing the empathy task—even a penny—dramatically increased participants' willingness to do so, as did inviting empathic estimates of a close other's feelings, rather than those of a stranger (Ferguson, Cameron, & Inzlicht, 2020). The message across these and

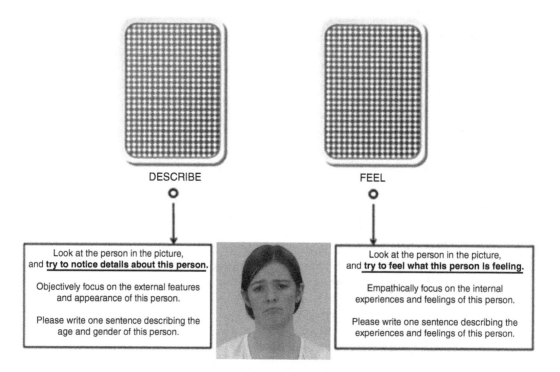

FIGURE 9.17. In the task used by Daryl Cameron, Michael Inzlicht, and colleagues, participants chose on each trial whether to simply describe a person showing a facial expression of emotion, or to empathize with their feelings. On average, participants chose the "feel" version of the task only a third of the time.

other recent studies is clear: empathy takes effort, and some motivation is needed for it to be worth our while.

Gender and Empathy

Some people are more empathetic than others. To what extent does this fall along gender lines? People believe that men and women differ greatly on this aspect of emotional life. Women rate their own empathetic feelings as far more intense than do men (Eisenberg & Lennon, 1983). Beyond self-reports, however, the evidence is more complicated. In infancy, baby girls cry in response to another baby's cry more often than baby boys do, yet there is little evidence of sex differences in older children's and young adults' self-reported feelings in response to a target's emotion, ability to identify the emotions of people in pictures or stories, or global physiological responses to the emotions of someone in a film clip (Eisenberg & Lennon, 1983).

Tania Singer and colleagues (2006) conducted a study suggesting a more complex relationship between gender and empathy. They used fMRI to scan the brains of women and men who watched videos of other people receiving a painful electric shock. Before the fMRI task, each participant had played two prisoner's dilemma games, each with a confederate shown in a later video. In the **prisoner's dilemma**, each player has the opportunity to cooperate or defect—the best outcome is if both people cooperate, but if your partner defects, you're better off if you also defect than if you cooperate. In this situation, the nice thing to do from your partner's perspective is to cooperate. In this study, one of the research confederates had cooperated with the participant, but the other had defected.

Both men and women showed increased activation in regions of the insular cortex and anterior cingulate cortex while they saw the confederate who had cooperated receiving shocks. These areas are typically active during one's own pain, suggesting that in this condition, both men and women experienced empathy. The gender difference appeared in response to the confederate who had defected; women still showed pain-like brain responses while watching the "cheaters" receive a shock, but men did not. In fact, men were more likely to show activation in areas of the brain associated with reward. These data indicate that women are more likely to empathize with others' pain regardless of the relationship, whereas men tend to empathize only with people they like, approve of, and/or trust (Singer et al., 2006).

Klein and Hodges (2001) explain why gender differences in empathy might emerge in some situations, but not in others. Participants watched a five-minute video of a real young woman who had just learned that she performed poorly on the math portion of the Graduate Record Examination (a standardized test required in applications for some graduate school programs in the United States). The video was stopped four times; each time, the participant was asked to guess what the woman in the video was thinking and feeling. These reports were coded for accuracy, and the four time points were summed to form a total accuracy score for each participant. Note that this is a complex empathy task—participants were scored not on feeling badly for the woman in the video, but on their ability to correctly infer her inner state (i.e., empathic accuracy)—and better scores reflect performance, not self-reports.

This study included a consideration of possible moderators as well. In one condition, participants simply did the rating task; in this condition, women did much better than men. Another set of participants were told that the more accurate they were, the more they would be paid for participating in the study; in this condition, women did slightly better than men, but not significantly so. A third set of participants did the same task with a practice video first, and received feedback on their performance; in this condition, men and women performed equally well (Klein & Hodges, 2001). These studies do not support the idea that men and women have inherently different capacities for empathy. Rather, men may tend to empathize with others more selectively, requiring greater motivation to have this response (Figure 9.18).

EMOTIONS IN SOCIETY

Learning Objective

- Summarize the social functions of gratitude, embarrassment, and pride, and describe one study illustrating each function.

The roles of emotions in our close relationships, such as those with parents, romantic partners, and children, are easy to see. Emotions also guide our relationships in the broader society, although not always in obvious ways. Let's consider some examples.

FIGURE 9.18. Contrary to popular belief, research indicates that men can be just as empathetic as women, provided that they have sufficient motivation.

Gratitude: Find, Remind, and Bind

Imagine that you're really sick and you desperately need some cold medication, but you've run out. In one scenario, you call your romantic partner and ask them to pick some up and bring it over. When the partner and the medicine arrive, you are appreciative and happy, but it's not that big a deal—it's what partners do for each other, right? Now imagine the same situation, but this time your neighbor, who you barely know but who seems nice, runs out to buy you the medicine and brings it back with flowers and a can of soup. How does that feel?

According to Sara Algoe (2012), **gratitude** is experienced when someone does something unexpectedly kind for us, and does not seem to expect us to reciprocate. We experience gratitude when we believe that our benefactor's actions were motivated by our need, rather than the promise of future repayment. This tells us something important about the benefactor: he or she cares about us, understands our needs, and, most important, sees the relationship as communal rather than exchange-oriented. This helps us find good relationship partners and invest in them. People who report higher dispositional gratitude are less lonely, have higher self-esteem, and experience less stress than those who feel gratitude less often (Corona et al., 2020). Experimentally elicited gratitude leads to an increase in people's willingness to cooperate in economic games, even when this comes at some cost to the self (DeSteno et al., 2010).

Although the feeling of gratitude may help bind the beneficiary to the giver, receiving an expression of gratitude can also motivate the giver to continue investing in the beneficiary. College students in one study were asked to provide thoughtful feedback on a supposed high school senior's college application essay; a week later, they received either an effusive thank you note or a more generic one, by random assignment. Participants were then asked whether they would be willing to spend more time mentoring the student, introducing the student to the campus, answering questions by email, and so forth. Those who had received more elaborate expressions of gratitude reported greater willingness to help the mentee in the future (Williams & Bartlett, 2015). The benefits of gratitude can spread even further, as third parties who observe gratitude expression are later more inclined to affiliate with, and to help, both the giver and the beneficiary (Algoe et al., 2020).

The Appeasement Function of Embarrassment

Embarrassment can be defined as the emotion felt when one violates a social convention, attracting unexpected and unwanted social attention. What function might embarrassment serve? Although the experience of embarrassment is unpleasant, your display of it lets other people know you care about their opinion, and that you hope for their understanding after you have done something clumsy, awkward, or inappropriate (Keltner & Buswell, 1997).

If you feel embarrassed, what is the first thing you do? Most people avoid eye contact and hide their face, either by covering their eyes with their hands or by turning their head down and to the side. The message is, "I don't want you to see me right now" (Figure 9.19). People who feel embarrassed often smile, although their lips also tense up as though they were trying to suppress the smile. The expression of embarrassment is similar from one human culture to another. Researchers have noted that the display of embarrassment resembles the bashful behaviors of a child or subordinate (Keltner, 1995; Miller, 2001a). The embarrassment expression serves as an appeasement gesture, similar to the way a weak, young animal deters an attack from a superior. The gesture says, "I know I made a mistake. I'm sorry. Please don't be angry."

FIGURE 9.19. The expression of embarrassment makes the person seem smaller and less conspicuous. The smile says "please be nice to me," whereas the gaze aversion and face touch say "I don't want you to see me right now."

To illustrate the usefulness of the embarrassment display, imagine this scenario. You are in a grocery store carrying a large, heavy box of kitty litter. As you walk through a crowded aisle, you trip and knock over a display of bottled salsa, breaking several bottles and spewing a ghastly mixture of salsa and kitty litter on a couple of people's clothes. If you just walk away casually as if nothing happened, how will other people react? Most likely, they'll be angry and consider you rude as well as clumsy. If you apologize and look embarrassed, however, they might laugh and tell you not to worry—they might even start to like you a little bit (Semin & Manstead, 1982). People particularly improve their opinion of you if you blush, perhaps because it is so difficult to fake (Dijk, De Jong, & Peters, 2009).

Research indicates that embarrassment helps repair awkward social situations in just this way. People say they would be more likely to forgive someone who broke a valuable item if they looked embarrassed (Miller, 2001b). Children who display embarrassment after breaking a rule are punished less severely than children who don't (Semin & Papadopoulou, 1990). People are also more likely to help a person who looks embarrassed, and to feel affection toward that person (Keltner, Young, & Buswell, 1997; Levin & Arluke, 1982). Overall, your display of embarrassment transforms a potentially tense, aggressive situation into a polite and friendly one.

Pride and Social Status

Now let's consider an emotion that is more pleasant to experience—pride. Jessica Tracy and Rick Robins (2004) define **pride** as the emotion you feel when you accept credit for causing a positive outcome that supports a positive aspect of your self-concept. Let's break this definition down. You feel pride when something good happens. That's no surprise because positive emotions should result from positive events. What makes pride special is (1) when you are proud, you feel that you caused the good event and can take the credit for it, and (2) the good event confirms your social value, to yourself and others. In a study with more than 2000 people from 16 countries around the world, Daniel Sznycer and colleagues (2017) asked participants to rate either how much other people value various actions or characteristics, or how much pride they would feel if they performed each act or had that characteristic. Although the specific acts/characteristics that were most valued varied from country to country, the appraisal of others' value consistently predicted anticipated pride. This is a good example of a universal link between an appraisal ("I did something valuable") and experience of a specific emotion (pride), even when the target of that appraisal differs across cultural contexts.

As we first noted in Chapter 5, pride has been linked to a distinct nonverbal expression—an expanded posture with the chest puffed out, head lifted, and arms held in a way that takes up more space (Figure 9.20). Earlier we noted that the embarrassment expression closely resembles the behavior of a low-status individual. In contrast, the expression of pride looks like the behavior of high-status people, and people who display pride are assumed to hold high-status positions in society (Tiedens et al., 2000; Tracy et al., 2013).

Although no one likes pride that leads to bragging, pride in the sense of self-confidence is generally helpful. In one study, researchers asked people to do two tasks, the first as individuals and the second as a group. After the first task, they privately told certain individuals (chosen randomly) that they had performed unusually well. In the group task that followed, people who believed they had done well on the first task took a

FIGURE 9.20. Pride is expressed by a combination of face and posture. The pride display makes you seem larger and more powerful, helping others to notice and admire you. From Tracy & Robins (2004).

more prominent role in the group activity, and other members of their group described them as very likeable (Williams & DeSteno, 2009). Evidently, self-confidence based on actual (or perceived) achievement promotes additional success. Observers seem aware of this as well; studies show that people are more likely to copy the behavior of individuals displaying pride than those displaying neutral or generic happy affect (Martens & Tracy, 2013).

Status comes with enormous benefits to adaptive fitness, including greater control over material resources, wider territory, and more and better mating opportunities (Van Vugt & Tybur, 2016). In one study, participants induced to feel pride, contentment, or no emotion were asked how desirable they found several different kinds of consumer products, given a limited amount of money. Those in the pride condition tended to rate flashy products for display, such as watches and shoes, as more desirable than nice home products such as a new bed, suggesting that they were motivated to gain others' attention; in a follow-up study, this effect was mediated by self-reported desire to "have other people notice you" (Griskevicius, Shiota, & Nowlis, 2010). Thus, pride seems geared toward helping us advertise our value to others, and take advantage of all the benefits high social status can bring.

SUMMARY

John Bowlby once wrote, "Intimate attachments to other human beings are the hub around which a person's life revolves, not only when he is an infant or a toddler or a school-child, but throughout his adolescence and his years of maturity as well, and on into old age" (Bowlby, 1980, p. 422). Our close relationships are fraught with emotion and can be a tremendous source of reward, a source of stress and pain, or both. On the one hand, social contact is rewarding even at the level of the brain's chemistry. On the other hand, intimacy and closeness do entail risk. There are some things we'd prefer not to know about a partner's thoughts and feelings, and if we are so linked that we absorb a partner's good moods, we may absorb their bad moods as well.

Emotions appear to play important roles in supporting a wide variety of human relationships, not only those within the family. The human social environment is extraordinarily complex, and emotions help us to navigate it. From individual friendships to larger group alliances, from new affiliations to status hierarchies, emotions help us identify promising relationship partners and figure out what we can expect from each other. The mechanisms of emotion across these different contexts may overlap. For example, behavioral synchrony and mirroring appear to facilitate relationship development between mothers and their infants, people who find each other romantically attractive, and groups that need to cooperate. Scientists are just beginning to understand the complex ways in which emotions facilitate our relationships, but the importance is substantial.

KEY TERMS

anxious-ambivalent attachment: a profile in which babies are hesitant to explore even when the attachment figure is present, become intensely distressed when the attachment figure leaves, and are difficult to soothe when the attachment figure returns (p. 308)

assortative mating: people's tendency to marry partners who are more like themselves than would be expected due to chance (p. 324)

attachment: a long-lasting emotional bond to a regular caregiver, producing a desire to be near that person (and distress when separated), a tendency to turn to that person when threatened, and a sense of being supported in exploring new things (p. 302)

avoidant attachment: a behavioral profile in which babies seem unconcerned with the caregiver's presence or absence, playing quietly and independently either way (p. 308)

companionate love: strong attachment with an emphasis on security, mutual care, affection, and shared fun (p. 316)

compassion: a caring and concerned response to another person's distress (p. 328)

demand-withdraw: a marital interaction pattern in which one partner escalates their insistence on discussing some topic (typically an area of conflict) while the other retreats further and further to avoid the conversation (p. 313)

disorganized attachment: the infant displays intense anxiety even when the caregiver is present; frightened, yet unable to turn to the caregiver for comfort (p. 309)

embarrassment: the emotion felt when one violates a social convention, attracting unexpected and unwanted social attention (p. 335)

empathic accuracy: ability to figure out what another person is thinking and feeling (p. 330)

emotional empathy: feeling what another person is feeling (p. 330)

gratitude: emotion experienced when someone does something unexpectedly kind for us and does not seem to expect us to reciprocate (p. 334)

nurturant love: an emotion elicited by cues of youth and vulnerability that motivates caregiving behavior (p. 329)

object permanence: the understanding that objects continue to exist even when we do not see or hear them (p. 305)

oxytocin: a pituitary hormone released by female mammals while giving birth and while nursing, and by both males and females during sex (p. 307)

passionate love: experience frequent thoughts about the other person, intense desire to be together, and excitement from the partner's attention (p. 315)

personal distress: self-focused anxiety in the face of another's suffering (p. 328)

pride: the emotion felt when you accept credit for causing a positive outcome that supports a positive aspect of your self-concept (p. 336)

prisoner's dilemma: a dyadic task often used in research, in which each player has the opportunity to cooperate or defect; the best outcome is if both people cooperate, but if your partner defects, you're better off if you also defect than if you cooperate (p. 332)

secure attachment: a behavioral profile including exploration when the attachment figure is present, crying and protest when the attachment figure leaves, and easy soothing when the figure returns (p. 308)

separation distress: emotional distress experienced and/or displayed when one is separated from an attachment figure (p. 307)

stranger anxiety: a fear of unfamiliar people (p. 302)

strange situation: a research procedure for studying attachment in which a child is repeatedly separated from and reunited with the attachment figure (p. 305)

sympathy: concern, attention, and empathic sadness for another person who is suffering (p. 328)

THOUGHT/DISCUSSION QUESTIONS

1. During the stage of passionate love, early in a dating relationship, each partner tends to be more aware of the other's strengths than of his or her weaknesses. Why might this occur? Think about possible explanations from the standpoint of both the perceiver and the person being perceived.

2. Which of the adult attachment style paragraphs describes you best: secure, anxious, or avoidant? Make a list of the characteristics of that style that fit you well, as described in this chapter. Do any typical characteristics of that attachment style fit you less well? Are you a combination of two styles? Think of other people you know well who fit each of these styles and give examples of their relevant characteristics.

3. In this chapter we distinguished among sympathy, compassion, nurturant love, and personal distress. What do these have in common, and how do they differ? Under what circumstances might you experience one of these without the others—for example, nurturant love without sympathy or compassion?

4. Several studies have found that people experience more empathy toward members of their own groups (e.g., ethnic groups, cultural groups) than toward members of outgroups. Why might this be? Design a study that would test your hypothesis.

5. Remember a time when you felt really embarrassed. What is most vivid about that memory: the event that occurred, your internal feelings, or the behavior of the people around you? Did you notice how people responded to your display of embarrassment?

SUGGESTIONS FOR FURTHER READING

Beall, A. T., & Tracy, J. L. (2017). Emotivational psychology: How distinct emotions facilitate fundamental motives. *Social and Personality Psychology Compass*, *11*(2), e12303. https://doi.org/10.1111/spc3.12303 This thoughtful article analyzes the relationship between fundamental social motives and specific emotions in a way that is accessible to an undergraduate audience.

Coontz, S. (2006). *Marriage, a history: How love conquered marriage*. Penguin. A fascinating overview of marriage throughout human history and across cultures, arguing that the expectation of love-based marriage is very recent.

Hrdy, S. B. (1999). *Mother nature: Maternal instincts and how they shape the human species*. Ballantine. Written by a renowned primatologist, this book views the complexity of maternal behavior through an evolutionary lens.

Parker-Pope, T. (2010). *For better: The science of a good marriage*. Dutton. An up-to-date and fun-to-read synthesis of the research on martial stability and satisfaction.

CHAPTER 10

Emotion, Motivation, and Cognition

You're in a good mood, and you decide to walk instead of driving to a store a few blocks away. You notice the sunshine, the trees, the birds singing, the smiling faces of people you see along the way. Ah, what a glorious day!

A few days later, you're walking the same route in similar weather but you're in a bad mood. Now you hardly notice the trees, birds, or smiling people. Instead, you notice the litter on the street, the filthy smell of an uncovered trash can, and the sounds of the traffic. What a lousy day! Emotions influence what we notice, what we remember, and how we reason.

When we are facing an important decision, people often advise us to think calmly and rationally, not to let our emotions get in the way of our logic. Sometimes emotions do lead to bad decisions. For example, during the first three months after the terrorist attacks of September 11, 2001, many people were afraid to get onto planes, so they drove to their destinations instead. During those months, the number of people killed in US traffic accidents increased enormously. The increase in the number of traffic fatalities during those few months was greater than the number of people killed in the terrorist attacks themselves (Gigerenzer, 2004).

However, as the evolutionary approach to emotion emphasizes, emotions are ordinarily *functional*. We evolved the tendency to experience emotions because they quite often lead to useful actions. As it turned out, avoiding airplane flights after September 11, 2001 was a mistake, but no one knew that at the time. Perhaps the lesson from the increase in automobile fatalities during the months after 9/11 is not that we should fear airplanes less, but that we should fear cars more. Overall, do emotions help us make good decisions, or do they interfere?

The answer is (can you guess?), it depends! But it depends on what? One hypothesis is that mild or moderate emotion helps reasoning, whereas higher amounts hurt. Emotion is often accompanied by physiological arousal. As discussed in Chapter 7, the **Yerkes–Dodson law** claims learning is at its best when stimulation or arousal is neither too strong nor too weak (Yerkes & Dodson, 1908). Later psychologists broadened this idea to propose that learning, memory, performance, and reasoning are most enhanced under medium levels of arousal, motivation, or emotion (Teigen, 1994). The idea strikes most people as reasonable: I do my best if I'm somewhat aroused, but not too much. However, within a huge intermediate range between sloth-like lethargy and absolute frenzy, no one can predict the best level of arousal for any given task. Although the Yerkes–Dodson law isn't necessarily wrong, it isn't terribly useful, either.

Another possibility is that emotion affects different cognitive processes in different ways. "Cognition" is an umbrella term that includes functions of the thinking mind like attention, memory, reasoning, and decision-making. Let us consider the research about emotional influences on each of these types of cognition, and how motivation influences our cognition in some powerful ways.

EMOTIONS AND ATTENTION

Learning Objectives

- Describe the effect of emotionally evocative stimuli on attention, as well as a piece of research evidence demonstrating this effect.
- Explain the dot-probe and eye-tracking methods of studying attentional bias, and analyze the strengths and limitations of these methods.
- Summarize and critique the evidence regarding effects of positive/pleasant emotion versus pre-goal, high-approach motivation on breadth of attention.

There are several ways in which emotional feelings increase attention, and in which emotional stimuli draw and hold attention more than neutral stimuli. For instance, a strong emotion, such as anger, increases overall attention just by increasing arousal and alertness (Techer et al., 2015). Furthermore, an emotional stimulus draws attention to itself, at least momentarily, at the expense of your attention to something else. Imagine yourself in this study: on each trial, the screen displays a pair of one-digit numbers separated by a word, like this:

5 chart 8

Your task is to press one key if both numbers are odd or both are even (such as 3 and 5, or 2 and 8), and a different key if one number is odd and the other is even (such as 5 and 8). You are supposed to ignore the word between them. However, if that word is an emotion-eliciting one, such as "kill," it grabs your attention, so you take longer to make the decision and press the correct key. Although the emotional word is irrelevant to your task, it distracts your attention and slows your response more than neutral words such as "chart" (Harris & Pashler, 2004).

Other researchers have found similar results using different kinds of emotion stimuli (see Figure 10.1). For example, you might be asked to answer quickly whether two pictures are the same or different, while ignoring a third picture of a face, which might or might not show an emotional expression. Most studies show interference in the picture-comparison task when an intense emotional expression is present (Carriet́e, 2014). Presence of a visual image previously paired with shock also distracts attention from the main task at hand (Schmidt, Belopolsky, & Theeuwes, 2015). Emotional stimuli are more distracting for people who are habitually prone to strong emotions, such as those with strong social anxiety (Yoon et al., 2015). This tendency for emotionally evocative stimuli to draw more attention than neutral stimuli has been called **attentional bias**.

FIGURE 10.1. Which of these photographs draws your first attention? Which does your gaze linger upon? People tend to pay more attention to emotional over neutral information.

Attentional bias is often measured using a method called the "dot-probe" task (see Figure 10.2). In this task people sit in front of a screen that displays two or more pictures at once, either or both of which might include emotional content. One of the two pictures is then replaced by a small probe (often a dot, giving the task its name, but sometimes another symbol such as a letter or number); the participant's job is to find the dot as quickly as possible and press a key indicating that they have done so. People often detect the dot replacing an emotional picture faster than one behind a neutral picture, because the emotional picture is where they were already looking. By measuring the difference in how quickly participants respond to a probe replacing an emotional versus neutral image, researchers try to capture attentional bias toward certain types of stimuli (e.g., negative, positive, anxiety-related). A wealth of research has demonstrated that people higher in anxiety exhibited an attentional bias toward threat-related stimuli when compared to those lower in anxiety (for a meta-analysis of much of this work, see Bar-Haim et al., 2007).

Researchers can also use eye-tracking devices to record people's shifts of visual attention from one image to another. An image that grabs immediate attention does not necessarily hold it for long (Waechter et al., 2014). Attentional bias for positive information is more often observed in studies that examine early attention, rather than later attention (Pool et al., 2016). People who are prone to strong anxiety are likely to orient their vision quickly toward a disturbing image, but then look away as soon as a

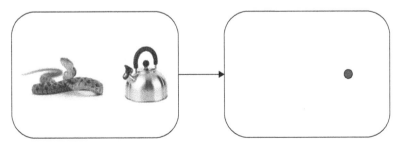

FIGURE 10.2. In the dot-probe task researchers examine individual differences in the extent to which emotion-eliciting images distract participants from finding a dot on the screen, as compared to the effect of neutral images. Some studies suggests that anxiety-prone individuals show more intense attentional bias on this task, but the research is inconsistent.

half-second later (Calvo & Avero, 2005; Holas et al., 2014). For people with major depression, unpleasant images do not capture attention any faster than they do for nondepressed people, but they hold attention longer. That is, people with depression continue staring at an unpleasant image for a longer than average time instead of looking away to regulate their emotions, as most people would (Armstrong & Olatunji, 2012; Sanchez et al., 2014).

Although dot-probe and eye-tracking tasks are clever ways of capturing people's moment-to-moment changes in attention, they have limitations. Dot-probe reaction time effects can fluctuate substantially from one task or trial to another, even within the same person. That is, these measures of attention tend to have low reliability, or repeatability (Waechter et al., 2014). Meta-analyses of eye-tracking studies have led researchers to question how robust attentional bias for emotional information really is (e.g., Jones et al., 2021), though reliability over time may be better for emotional scenes than emotional faces (Sears, et al., 2019). As with any other type of research, researchers have less confidence in the results if they are not based on reliable measurements. These and other measurement issues have led leading researchers in the field to call for better statistics and reporting in studies using dot probes and other cognitive-emotional measures (MacLeod, Grafton, & Notebart, 2019; Parsons, Krujit, & Fox, 2019).

Attentional bias studies often focus on people's attention to unpleasant images, and negative feelings such as anxiety. How do you suppose a happy mood would affect your attention? According to the **broaden and build theory** of positive emotions (Fredrickson, 2001), positive emotions expand the focus of your attention, helping you survey the environment broadly and notice opportunities you might otherwise have overlooked. Several studies have found that after positive emotion induction people are more likely than usual to attend to the "big picture" rather than focusing on small details, and to think creatively (Bolte, Goschke, & Kuhl, 2003; Fredrickson & Joiner, 2002; Fredrickson & Losada, 2005). The phrase "can't see the forest for the trees" refers to this tension between focusing on the larger pattern and the elements that make up that pattern.

Several of these studies use a procedure similar to the following. In each trial of this task, people look at a display of a large letter composed of smaller letters, and state as quickly as possible which of two letters is present. For example, you are asked to press a key on the left if you see an *H* and a key on the right if you see an *F*. Here's your first trial (you can just tap your left hand for *H* and your right hand for *F*):

```
L L L L L
L
L L L
L
```

The correct answer was *F*, so you should have tapped your right hand. How long did that take you? Was it easy or difficult? Now here's the next trial—remember, tap your left hand for *H* and your right for *F*:

```
H H H H H
   H
   H
   H
   H
```

This time the correct answer was *H*, so you should have tapped your left hand (if you don't believe us, look at the smaller letters making up the *T*). In this trial was it easier or harder to identify the correct letter than in the first trial? Which trial took longer?

Results for each trial type are averaged across many trials. Responding faster when the correct answer lies in the larger letter (as in the first trial above) indicates *broadened* attention, because you are looking at the overall shape made of tiny elements. If you respond faster when the correct answer is determined by the elements (as in the second trial), you are considered to have *narrowed* your attention, because you are attending to details instead of the whole pattern. Evidence suggests that when we are in a positive mood, the first kind of trial is easier than the second; attention tends to be more global.

Some researchers have asked whether emotional valence (the positive–negative dimension) is the determining factor in this effect. Sadness tends to broaden attention, as happiness does, whereas anger narrows attention (Gable & Harmon-Jones, 2010; Gable, Poole, & Harmon-Jones, 2015). Why might this be the case? If you think about it, both sadness and happiness are linked to outcomes that have already happened—they are both "post-goal." You are sad when things didn't turn out the way you wanted them to, or when your life is missing something you desire. You are happy when things *have* turned out how you wanted them to, or when your life is full of those things you desire.

In contrast, when you are feeling angry, you are usually pre-goal, not yet certain what will happen. Anger is about fixing wrongs, gearing you up for confrontation. According to researchers Philip Gable and Eddie Harmon-Jones (2008), pre-goal and post-goal emotions are very different in **motivational intensity**—how badly you want to achieve (or prevent) some outcome that still lies in the future. Sadness and happiness are low in motivational intensity, and anger is high. Other emotional and motivational states that are pre-goal, and therefore high in motivational intensity are hunger and sexual desire. Studies show that stimuli eliciting more intense pre-goal emotion, such as the image on the right in Figure 10.3, tend to *narrow* attention rather than broadening it (Gable & Harmon-Jones, 2008). You haven't eaten that ice cream yet! Gable and Harmon-Jones

FIGURE 10.3. Valence of emotion may not be the best predictor of attentional scope. Whereas the pleasant image on the left tends to elicit global attention, the one on the right tends to elicit more focused attention to detail.

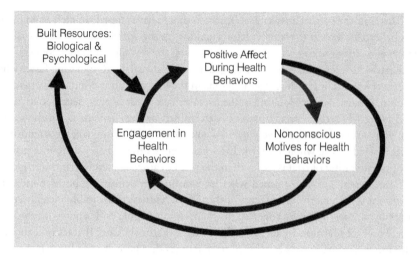

FIGURE 10.4. The upward spiral theory of lifestyle change (from Fredrickson & Joiner, 2018).

suggest that the key aspect of emotion is the extent to which it involves strong approach motivation, the impulse to move toward something rather than moving away or watching it passively. According to this interpretation, the stronger one's approach motivation, the more detail-oriented attention will become (Gable & Harmon-Jones, 2010).

Elaborating on the connections among positive emotion, approach motivation, and the building of resources, Barbara Fredrickson has recently expanded and applied broaden and build theory to consider ways in which positive emotion might help people develop health-promoting habits (Fredrickson & Joiner, 2018, see Figure 10.4). This model proposes an "upward spiral" in which positive emotions encourage a first step of behavior change, this change generates positive affect and outcomes, which then reinforce the new behavior and increase the likelihood it will be repeated.

For instance, you might be feeling cheerful one day and decide to start walking every morning before work. You go for the walk; you feel good because your blood is moving and you are proud of following through on your intention. These immediate rewards increase the likelihood you'll go for a walk again the following morning. Over time, cues you associate with walking—your phone with its fitness app, your walking sneakers, your dog's leash—elicit positive feelings and you are drawn to them in subtle, even unconscious ways. Early laboratory research demonstrates evidence for each part of this spiral (Rice & Fredrickson, 2017a, Rice & Fredrickson, 2017b).

EMOTIONS AND MEMORY
Learning Objectives
- Differentiate memory encoding, consolidation, and retrieval.
- Identify the specific aspect of emotion that promotes encoding of new memories, and summarize the methods, results, and implications of Cahill and colleagues' (1994) demonstrating this effect.

- Evaluate the proposal that we have "flashbulb memories"—remarkably strong and accurate memories for unusual events—based on the research evidence.
- Summarize the synaptic tag-and-capture hypothesis, describe one study demonstrating the effect of emotion on memory consolidation, and identify the key brain structure thought to support the emotional facilitation of memory.
- Describe the ways in which current emotion affects the content you are most likely to remember.

Suppose your history professor spends an hour describing details about some part of the world that you have never visited, and in which you have no interest. The professor repeats the information several times, and uses the best audiovisual materials to improve learning, but you find the material unexciting. At the end of the lecture the professor announces that the upcoming exam has been postponed a few days to give you more time to prepare, and warns you against using the east exit from the building because some venomous snakes have nested in the bushes there. How well will you remember the history lecture (which you are paying tuition money to hear), the good news about the postponed test, and the scary news about snakes?

Immediately after class, you will likely remember all three—even a surprising amount of the boring history lecture. As time passes, however, you forget the uninteresting material while continuing to remember the emotionally arousing material, both the good and the bad (Yonelinas & Ritchey, 2015). Indeed, you will remember many of your highly emotional experiences vividly for the rest of your life.

For a simple laboratory demonstration of how emotion influences memory, researchers show people a variety of photos and later test which ones they remember. On average, people remember best any items that evoked an emotional reaction. For example, you would be more likely to remember a photo of a snake than one of a fish, unless these are a vicious piranha fish and a harmless garter snake, in which case you remember the fish better than the snake (Meyer, Bell, & Buchner, 2015). When people describe from memory a photo including an emotional element, such as the one in Figure 10.5, they describe the emotional part in great detail, but usually forget the details in the background (Adolphs, Denburg, & Tranel, 2001).

Emotion affects memory partly through its effects on attention—the more attention we pay to some stimulus or event, the more we mentally elaborate on the details and the more likely we are to remember it—but not entirely. Emotion also influences the stages of memory encoding, storage, and retrieval. Let's discuss these three stages in order.

Emotion and Memory Encoding

Your emotion at the time of an event strongly enhances your initial formation of memories, called **encoding**. Although extreme arousal bordering on panic interferes with memory storage, a moderate degree of arousal improves memory storage. In one classic study of this phenomenon, Margaret Bradley and colleagues (Bradley et al., 1992) showed participants 60 photographs of objects and events, ranging from everyday pictures of hair dryers and umbrellas to emotionally intense pictures of dangerous animals, mutilations, and extreme sports (see Figure 10.6 for examples). They asked the participants to rate each picture on how pleasant or unpleasant it was, and how calm or aroused it made them feel. After viewing all 60 pictures, participants were asked to name or briefly describe as many

FIGURE 10.5. Just as the emotionally arousing element of a complex image tends to capture the most attention, it is also the most memorable. Most people remember the central aspect of such photos, but forget the background details.

FIGURE 10.6. When people view large numbers of emotional and nonemotional images like these, they are more likely to remember the emotional ones—even as much as a year later.

pictures as possible. People were more likely to remember pictures that they had rated as arousing than pictures they had rated as calming, regardless of whether the photographs were pleasant or unpleasant. Previous studies showed that the pictures rated as highly arousing also elicited stronger skin conductance responses, so the sense of arousal was not merely subjective (Greenwald, Cook, & Lang, 1989). In short, emotional arousal promoted encoding pictures into memory.

When the researchers contacted the same participants a year later and asked them to describe as many of the slides as they could, people were still more likely to remember the intense, arousal-producing ones than the more ordinary ones (Bradley et al., 1992). People remember emotionally arousing pictures better than average even when they see the pictures rapidly, with little or no opportunity for rehearsal (Harris & Pashler, 2004).

In contrast, weakening physiological arousal weakens memory storage. Researchers in one study examined this hypothesis by giving participants one of two pills—either a **beta-blocker**, a drug that temporarily disables some aspects of sympathetic nervous system-mediated arousal, or a placebo with no physiological effects. Then participants viewed a slideshow depicting some wrecked cars, an emergency room, a brain scan, and a surgery. While watching the slide show, participants heard one of two stories. In the neutral version, a young boy walks by a junkyard, then goes to the hospital where his dad works, looks curiously at a brain scan, and watches a surgical team doing a practice drill. In the arousal version, the boy is hit by a car on the way to visit his dad, is rushed to the hospital, has a brain scan that shows his brain is bleeding badly, and undergoes surgery (Cahill et al., 1994). All participants watched the same set of images, but their emotions were manipulated both by the content of the story that accompanied the pictures and by the pill that they took before the slide show.

One week later, participants were asked to answer 80 multiple-choice questions about the slides and the stories that had accompanied them. As expected, people who had heard the neutral version of the story received modest scores on the test—on average, they answered about two-thirds of the questions correctly. For participants in the arousal version, memory depended on whether they had taken the beta-blocker pill or the placebo. Participants who had been given the beta-blocker (and therefore would not have experienced a racing heart or similar symptoms, even if they recognized that the story was upsetting) performed no better on the memory test than participants in the "neutral" condition. Participants who had been given the placebo did far better, on average answering more than 85% of the questions correctly (see Figure 10.7). This suggests that interrupting the arousal associated with strong emotion will disrupt the emotional facilitation of memory.

We introduced the emotional facilitation of memory earlier in this textbook, when discussing the amygdala in Chapter 6. Why did we evolve in such a way that emotions enhance memory formation at all? The kinds of events that produce emotion are usually more important than most other events. After all, emotions accompany events that have serious implications for your life—a time you were in danger, the day you were accepted into your dream college, the time someone cheated you out of some money, the day you first met someone special in your life. Sometimes your success in life depends on remembering these events—what led up to them, how they played out, which people were helpful or harmful, and what happened afterward. This kind of memory allows you to predict important events and improve the outcome the next time you face a similar situation.

Think about where you were and what you were doing when you first heard some extremely distressing news, either world news or news about some friend or relative. You could also try remembering a uniquely exciting pleasant experience, such as your first kiss. Whichever memory you have chosen, how vivid and detailed is it? Can you remember where you were, who else was around, what you were doing, how you felt, and what

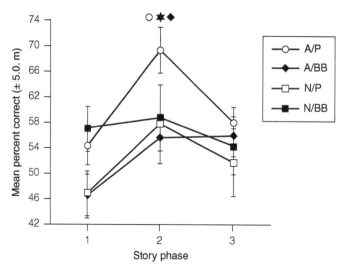

FIGURE 10.7. In this study, participants given a placebo remembered the emotionally distressing part of a story (Phase 2) especially well. This effect was blunted among participants who had taken a β-blocker—a drug that interferes with sympathetic nervous system functioning. *Key*: A = arousing story, N = neutral story, P = placebo, BB = beta-blocker. From Cahill et al. (1994).

your first thoughts were? Can you remember what happened just before and after this moment? Can you remember the weather and the time of day? Now try to remember an unemotional event, like the last time you bought toothpaste in a store. How long does it take to remember, specifically, the last time—do you remember immediately or do you have to think about it? Were you with someone or alone? What time of day was it, and what was the weather? What else did you buy? What did the person at the checkout counter say and do?

For most people, highly emotional memories seem drastically different from those of everyday events. Psychologists refer to these emotion-laden, vivid, and highly detailed memories as **flashbulb memories** because they seem to have a clear, almost photographic quality. This vividness seems especially to characterize such events when they are negative in nature (e.g., Cooper, Kensinger, & Ritchey, 2019). Although flashbulb memories are vivid and imagelike, however, research indicates that they are not always as accurate as they feel. For example, shortly after the terrorist attacks of September 11, 2001, researchers asked Americans to recall details of what they were doing when they heard that news. At various later times, researchers asked the same questions. Long after the event, people continued to report having a clear, vivid memory, but in many cases it was a *different* vivid memory from the one they had originally described (Talarico & Rubin, 2003). One person had originally reported hearing about the event on a car radio; two years later he reported hearing about it while standing in line at the airport (Kvavilashvili et al., 2009).

How can flashbulb memories be so vivid, yet partly inaccurate? If many of the details we remember are untrue, where did they come from? Most research on flashbulb memories has focused on highly publicized national or international events, such as assassinations or terrorist attacks. These are the kind of events we sit around discussing with friends and family. Perhaps we confuse our own reports with other people's descriptions of the event, or our memory of one event with the memory of another. Also, sometimes when we report something, we embellish for emphasis or leave out details that seem unimportant, and eventually we confuse the story we told with what really happened. When we retrieve memories from storage, we can change them in the process, altering what goes back into storage for the future (Kensinger & Ford, 2020; Inda, Muravieva, & Alberini, 2011). It's possible that telling the story right after an event has the effect of sealing the correct version more firmly in memory. A recent study collected memories from students within hours after terrorist attacks in Brussels in March 2016, and then conducted in-depth interviews 15 months later (Cordonnier & Luminet, 2021). Unlike previous studies, the memories across the two time periods showed relatively high consistency over time.

Here's an implication of all this: suppose you were a witness or victim of a crime. Later you describe the event to the police, identify the guilty person from a lineup, and testify in court. You may say that you remember the event vividly, that you are sure of the facts, and that you can identify the guilty person confidently. Should a jury trust your self-assurance? Research consistently indicates that if you say you are highly confident while you report a memory of a very recent event, then what you say is probably correct, especially the first time you describe it. However, your confidence about an older memory, especially one you have discussed repeatedly, can be sadly misplaced (Wixted et al., 2015).

Emotion and Memory Consolidation

You soon forget many of the memories you form, but some of them develop into long-term memories. We say that they undergo **consolidation**. Sleep helps consolidate memories (Figure 10.8). During the process of forming a memory, the relevant synapses

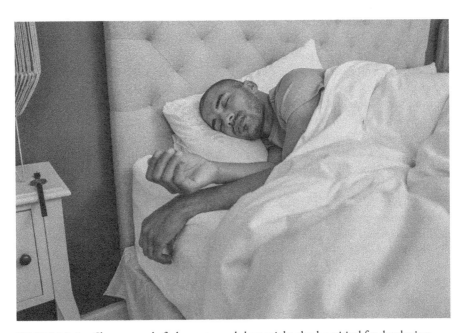

FIGURE 10.8. Sleep not only feels great, good sleep might also be critical for developing long-term memories.

strengthen. During sleep, the brain weakens some of the irrelevant synapses, enabling the strengthened ones to stand out by contrast (Maret et al., 2011). Varied brain rhythms during the different stages of sleep may support these processes of memory strengthening (Girardeau & Lopes-dos-Santos, 2021).

Emotional arousal also facilitates consolidation, resulting in greater long-term persistence of emotional memories. This is partly caused by activation of the amygdala, as discussed in Chapter 6. When people view a series of images, they remember most accurately the ones that produced the greatest degree of amygdala activation (Canli et al., 2000). Memory consolidation also relates to a small brain area called the locus coeruleus. Important, emotionally arousing events activate the locus coeruleus, which then sends messages via its widely branching axons, releasing the neurotransmitter norepinephrine throughout the cortex. Norepinephrine magnifies the response of the neurons that were already active and suppresses the response of those that were less active. The result is to increase attention and memory about important information (Eldar, Cohen, & Niv, 2013).

Emotional excitement also increases the release of the hormones epinephrine (adrenaline) and cortisol from the adrenal gland. Studies on both humans and laboratory animals have indicated that a direct injection of a low to moderate amount of epinephrine or cortisol strengthens the memory of an event, although larger amounts interfere (Colciago et al., 2015). Importantly, these hormones can be effective even when administered right *after* the event to be remembered (Cahill & McGaugh, 1998). Epinephrine and cortisol stimulate the vagus nerve, which in turn excites the amygdala. That said, there may be a trade-off between cortisol and memory such that higher cortisol promotes better memory for negative details, but also poorer memory for neutral details of the same scenes (Cunningham et al., 2021).

Why did we evolve in such a way that arousal even after the event can help us remember it? One proposal is the **synaptic tag-and-capture hypothesis** (Dunsmoor et al., 2015). According to this idea, when you form a memory, the brain puts a tag on it for potential consolidation later. A later—but not too much later—event can indicate, that was important! Keep it! For example, imagine that you meet someone at your company's holiday party and talk with her for a few minutes. After you walk away, someone says, "Hey, did you know that woman you were just talking to is the daughter of the president of the company?" Your heart rate increases, your adrenal gland secretes some epinephrine, and you focus on remembering the woman's name and everything she said.

Here is a laboratory experiment to illustrate the point: first, people look at 60 pictures and classify each one as being either an animal or a tool, with no instruction about remembering them for later. In the second stage, these people look at new pictures of animals and tools; for each person, either some of the animal pictures or some of the tool pictures are paired with electric shocks. Hours later, people return to the laboratory for the third task, in which—to their surprise—they are asked to examine more pictures and remember which ones they had seen in the earlier sessions. Naturally, they remember well the pictures that were paired with shock in the second stage. More important, if animals were paired with shock in the second stage, people also remembered the animals from the first stage. If tools were paired with shock, then people remembered tools from the first stage (Dunsmoor et al., 2015). That is, you tag initial memories, and if you later discover that some of them might be important—that is, you later experience emotional arousal—you can go back and strengthen them.

One interesting implication of the effects of emotion on memory encoding and consolidation is that in summarizing your emotions over some extended period, you concentrate mainly on specific events that had the strongest impact at the time. Suppose you take a trip on spring break. You take a device that beeps at unpredictable times, telling you to record your emotion at that moment. At the end of the trip, you rate how much you enjoyed the trip as a whole. Your overall rating will probably be close to the highest rating you gave at any of the individual moments, rather than the overall average (Wirtz et al., 2003). That is, one or two wonderful moments make the whole trip seem wonderful. However, if one of your friends got badly injured at the end of the trip, that single bad moment would likely ruin the whole trip for you. In short, the strongest emotional event, positive or negative, outweighs all the ordinary moments in your memory.

Something similar applies to the joys of parenthood. On average, when parents report the emotions associated with each event of the day, they describe child-care activities as only slightly better than household chores, especially while the children are young (Kahneman, et al., 2006). Changing diapers is not fun, and neither is staying up all night with a sick child. Nevertheless, most parents say that their children are one of their greatest sources of joy in life and a sense of meaningfulness (Nelson et al., 2013). The occasional high points, such as when a child gives a hug and says, "I love you," outweigh the tedious and trying moments.

Emotion and Memory Retrieval

Current emotions also modify what events we are most likely to pull out of stored memory, known as **retrieval**. A general principle is that people tend to remember events that resemble in some way whatever they are doing or thinking about at the moment. For example, if you are at a ball game, you remember other ball games. If you are discussing politics, you remember other discussions of politics.

Similarly, when you are in a good mood, you are more likely than usual to remember events that previously happened when you were in a good mood, and when you are sad, you are more likely than usual to recall other events that made you sad. When you are frightened, you tend to remember frightening information, and when you are angry, you remember information consistent with being angry (Levine & Pizarro, 2004). However, this only occurs to some extent. Research results range from robust (you can count on seeing it in a wide variety of circumstances) to fragile (now you see it, now you don't). Mood-specific memory is a fragile effect, especially in laboratory studies that weakly elicit a mood by having you look at pictures, listen to music, or imagine past events. If you are in a strong mood because of something you have just done, the effect on memory is stronger (Eich, 1995).

Research also shows that our goals at the time of memory retrieval have strong effects on how memories are recalled, guiding both the vividness of the memory and which specific details are recalled (Kensinger & Ford, 2020). Moreover, emotion at the time of retrieval also affects both how the event is remembered and how it will be remembered in the future.

EMOTIONS AND INFORMATION PROCESSING

Learning Objectives

- Differentiate systematic and heuristic cognition, and analyze the evidence regarding effects of emotion on these aspects of information processing.
- Contrast the effects of positive and negative moods on creativity.

Beyond attention and memory, emotions influence how we think in many ways, some subtle and some not so subtle. For one example, your current emotion affects how you appraise the meaning of a new situation. To illustrate, first think about how you are feeling right now. If you had to choose, would you say you are feeling more angry, sad, or neither? Second, consider the following situation:

> You and your housemates are having a party for about 10 people, one of whom you just met at a coffee house. This person was attractive and seemed interested in you, and was excited by your invitation. You are really looking forward to getting to know this person, and hope that a more romantic relationship might develop.
>
> You tell your housemates about this person, hoping they will make him/her feel comfortable and welcome. Your new friend arrives at the party after everyone else is there, and when you open the door, you see that this person has brought a date. To make things worse, the date is a good friend of your housemates.
>
> The room suddenly becomes quiet, and you hear one of your housemates chuckle and say, "So there's the new love." Your new friend is silent, and the date seems upset. You try to create a more relaxed atmosphere, and your housemates attempt to keep everyone entertained, but as you go into the kitchen you hear your new friend and his/her date whispering to each other uncomfortably.[1]

Why was this situation so uncomfortable? Were your roommates to blame, or was it the situation itself? On average, people who have just imagined themselves in an anger-producing situation (in a supposed preliminary or warm-up to the real study) are more likely to blame the roommates, whereas people who have just imagined themselves in a sad situation are more likely to blame it on bad luck. Angry people blame most negatively valenced events on people (such as a bad cab driver) instead of blaming them on chance circumstances (bad traffic), whereas the reverse is true for sad people (Keltner et al., 1993).

Here's a similar experiment: two months after the terrorist attacks on the US Pentagon and World Trade Center, more than 1,700 US adults were randomly assigned to three groups who were asked to write different kinds of short essays. One group was asked to write about how the attacks made them feel angry. A second group was to write about how the attacks made them sad, and a third group was to write about how the attacks made them afraid. Then all were asked how much danger they foresaw for themselves personally and for the United States in general in the coming year. Those who had just finished writing about fear estimated greater probabilities of danger for both themselves and the country (Lerner et al., 2003).

These studies and others indicate that anger increases confidence. In that regard, anger is like happiness, although we typically think of anger as a negative emotion and

---

[1] Adapted from Keltner, Ellsworth, & Edwards (1993).

happiness as a positive emotion. Both anger and happiness imply certainty, which leads to confident, optimistic predictions about almost anything, ranging from world events to your probability of getting a good job or your probability of winning a bet. Worryingly, this connection between anger and confidence means that feeling angry may set one up to be more susceptible to misinformation (Greenstein & Franklin, 2020). On the other hand, sadness, fear, or worry imply uncertainty, which leads to low confidence, pessimism, and a tendency to avoid most risks—because, you assume, they would probably turn out badly (Lerner & Keltner, 2001; Lerner et al., 2015; Raghunathan & Pham, 1999; Tiedens & Linton, 2001). Together, these findings suggest we should be wary about making strong judgments about information when we're feeling highly emotional.

Systematic versus Heuristic Processing

Imagine that someone is trying to persuade you of something—perhaps to vote for a particular candidate, to purchase some product, or to change your diet. How carefully would you listen to the evidence and try to evaluate the facts and logic? Would your mood at the time influence your evaluation? Before we discuss the possible effects of mood, let's distinguish two types of cognition.

Psychologists distinguish between **systematic cognition** and **heuristic cognition**. Systematic cognition relies on collecting relevant information, and evaluating it as carefully and logically as you can. For a serious decision, such as buying a car or a new home, you take time to consider many relevant features and weigh all the pros and cons. Heuristic cognition relies on easy, superficial considerations such as agreeing with people you like, or choosing a product that you associate with pleasant images. For example, you might buy a brand of beer or soda because your favorite movie star or sports hero endorsed it. You rely on heuristic cognition for decisions that seem too unimportant to bother considering carefully, or when the factual details are unimportant. (For example, few people choose a beer or soda based on the nutritional label.) You also use heuristic cognition when you are too tired, busy, or distracted to spend much time making a careful decision.

It might seem that heuristic cognition depends on emotion, and systematic cognition depends on logic. However, that is an oversimplification. Systematic cognition also includes the emotional aspects of a decision, but only when they are relevant. For example, if you are buying a car, you consider not only the cost and the safety features, but also how much you will enjoy driving one car or another—a relevant emotional factor. In heuristic cognition you might choose a car just because the showroom was attractive and pleasant to be in, or because the salesperson was smiling and well dressed—these are irrelevant emotional factors. Of course, car dealers are trying very hard to make sure you enjoy yourself and are in a good mood, to take advantage of the latter effect, but it's the systematic consideration of how much you will enjoy the car that is better grounds for the decision.

What is the effect of mood on heuristic versus systematic cognition? Several studies have indicated that people in a happy mood are more likely than average to engage in heuristic cognition, accepting some type of persuasion without evaluating it carefully. Sad people are more cautious, paying more attention to the quality of the evidence. The evidence derives from studies such as this: students were randomly assigned to writing for 15 minutes about either one of the most pleasant or one of the least pleasant events that ever happened to them, to induce a happy or a sad mood. Then they listened to either

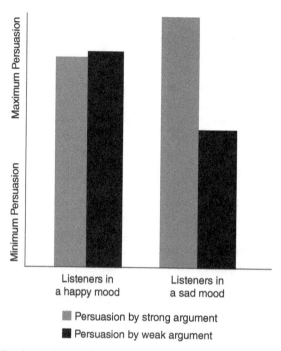

FIGURE 10.9. People in a happy mood were equally persuaded by strong evidence or weak, superficial arguments. People in a sad mood paid more attention to the quality of the evidence. Based on data from Bless et al. (1990).

several strong, factual arguments or several weak, superficial arguments in favor of raising student fees at their university (most students are opposed to this initially, so if they later agree, researchers can reasonably assume they were persuaded). As shown in Figure 10.9, the strong argument was more persuasive to those in a sad mood than to those in a happy mood. The weak argument was more persuasive to those in a happy mood. Said another way, the students in a happy mood were about equally persuaded by the strong or the weak arguments, whereas those in a sad mood were persuaded by the strong arguments but not by the weak ones (Bless et al., 1990).

Stereotypes also offer a way to shortcut decision-making and use heuristics instead of analyzing the evidence carefully. Suppose you are given a list of names and asked to identify which ones are famous basketball players, famous politicians, or dangerous criminals. Some of the names (none of which is in fact famous) sound like they are probably the names of white people, such as Steven Olsen. Some are names that you would guess probably belong to Black people, such as Karanja Jackson. If you resist the stereotypes and answer only on the basis of actual knowledge, you will say you have never heard of any of these names. In fact, people who have just watched a sad or neutral movie make few errors in name identification. However, people who have just watched a humorous movie identify many of the Black names as either basketball players or criminals, and many of the white names as politicians, relying on racist stereotypes to make their decisions (Park & Banaji, 2000). Can you think of ways we could use knowledge of this effect to educate people about their underlying biases and how to counteract them?

Here is a related phenomenon: to induce a happy or sad mood, students were first randomly assigned to write about a pleasant or unpleasant life event. Second, they listened to a story titled "Going out for Dinner." Third, they were given a list of sentences and asked to identify which sentences had been part of the story. Of the sentences not in the story, some were typical going-out-for-dinner items that would have made sense (e.g., "He called a friend of his, who recommended several restaurants") and some were irrelevant (e.g., "Jack cleaned his glasses"). Students in a happy mood were more likely than the others to make the mistake of "remembering" the typical sentences that were not actually in the story (Bless et al., 1996). That is, they relied more on their script of what usually happens or what seems likely. Relying on a preconceived script is similar to relying on stereotypes.

These are just a few examples of the effects of emotion on heuristic versus systematic processing. There are several dozen more documenting these and similar effects of happy versus sad mood (Fiedler, 2001; Forgas, 2013). Recently, however two new twists to the story have appeared. The first is that the effects typically attributed to overall pleasant or unpleasant mood may not generalize to all emotions of the same valence. For example, studies comparing the effects of several specific positive emotions in the persuasive-argument and romantic-dinner protocols described earlier have found that many, but not all, pleasant emotions promote heuristic processing. Notably, experimentally elicited awe or wonder showed the opposite effect, seemingly pushing people toward more systematic processing of the persuasive message (Griskevicius, Shiota, & Neufeld, 2010) and story memory that was less influenced by what people expected to hear (Danvers & Shiota, 2017), even relative to neutral control conditions. Because most of this research was done with sadness as the only negative emotion, it's also not clear whether the effects generalize to anger, fear, or other unpleasant emotion states.

The other wrinkle is that mood may not alter systematic or heuristic processing, per se. Instead, researchers Gerald Clore, Linda Isbell, Jeffrey Huntsinger, and others have suggested that negative mood may simply make us question our current processing strategy and switch to a different one, whereas positive mood encourages continuing on with whatever strategy we're already using. Because most of the time our default strategy is heuristic, the effects always seem to be happy-sloppy and sad-careful. In several studies, however, the researchers sneakily induced systematic processing as the baseline state, and only then introduced the mood manipulation. Results revealed the opposite of previously observed effects, such that sad mood now prompted people to switch to heuristic processing, while happy-mood folks kept being systematic (Clore, Schiller, & Shaked, 2018; Huntsinger, Isbell, & Clore, 2014).

Sometimes in science you think you've got something completely figured out, and new data come along and mess it up. It happens regularly! Each time, it opens a new door to richer understanding, and we accept the evidence and go through that door.

Positive Affect and Creativity

Western culture offers a popular image of the tortured artist, whose misery and depression nonetheless facilitate great creativity. However, research suggests the opposite may be true—that a happy mood frees people to see new possibilities and to be more creative. In one early study, Alice Isen and colleagues showed a funny film clip to one group of participants, and an emotionally neutral clip to a control group. Then, to test creative thinking, they offered participants the items shown in Figure 10.10 and asked them to

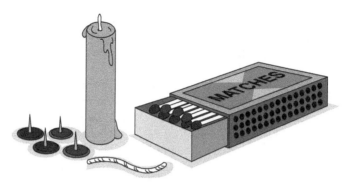

FIGURE 10.10.   Using just the materials shown here, how could you affix the candle to the wall so that it would burn without dripping wax on the table or floor? Think creatively, and then check the answer at the end of this chapter.

find a way to affix the candle to a corkboard on the wall in such a way that it would burn without dripping wax onto the table or the floor (Isen, Daubman, & Nowicki, 1987).

Can you find a solution? To complete the task, you must think about using one or more of the objects in a way that's different from the way they are normally used—a classic aspect of creativity. Think about it and then check the solution given at the end of this chapter.

In this study, people who had watched the funny film clip were more likely to solve the problem (and solved it faster) than people in the neutral condition. This result suggests that positive affect promotes creative thinking (Isen et al., 1987).

How general is this effect? Would any positive affect, as opposed to amusement, also enhance creativity? Can we see benefits with a different type of creativity task? Investigators induced a positive mood by asking Japanese college students to think happy thoughts while listening to cheerful music for 10 minutes. Students in the control group spent the same time listening to a reading of the Japanese constitution, which should induce no emotion, unless you count mild boredom as an emotion. Then the students performed the task of generating new names for types of rice. The result was that on average, the happy students generated more creative and unusual ideas (Yamada & Nagai, 2015).

In another study, young adults reported daily records of the emotions they felt and all their creative activities of the day, such as knitting a scarf, creating a new recipe, playing music, or generating a new idea. Their reports of creative activities correlated most strongly with reports of emotional excitement and enthusiasm. They also correlated positively, but more weakly, with reports of happiness and relaxation (Conner & Silvia, 2015). These results suggest a contribution from positive mood, and a larger contribution from energetic activity. These relationships between positive mood and creativity have implications not just for enjoyment of life but also for performance at work, where creativity can lead to innovative solutions (Diener, Thapa, & Tay, 2020).

Contrary to popular belief, the negative emotions of sadness and anxiety either inhibit creativity or have no apparent effect, according to most studies. The results for anger are more mixed. Some studies indicate little or no effect on creativity, but under some circumstances anger may increase creativity. For example, in a group situation, hostility toward other people's suggestions may facilitate generating your own ideas (Yang & Hung, 2015).

EMOTIONS AND DECISION-MAKING

Learning Objectives

- Summarize the affect infusion model, explaining the effects of positive versus negative mood on judgment and decision-making.
- Summarize the somatic-marker hypothesis, and explain how research on patients with brain damage helped develop this theory.
- Using research based on the trolley dilemma as an example, describe the role of emotions in moral judgment and reasoning.
- Analyze the limitations of relying on emotion in risky decisions involving large but statistically unlikely rewards.

Do emotions influence the decisions you make? Should they? It depends. Are human activities contributing to climate change? Your answer to that question should depend on the facts, not on which answer you like or what emotions it evokes. But change the question to ask what action we should take to address climate change, and suddenly we have values at stake. Any possible action will have costs, different actions have different costs and benefits, and we can't decide without considering which outcome we want. For another example, which is bigger, six or seven? That is a trivially easy question, unrelated to emotions. But let's change the question: Which would you prefer, a six-day skiing vacation or a seven-day beach vacation? Now the decision depends on how much you like skiing and how much you like beaches. You can't answer the question except on the basis of emotions. Indeed, most decisions depend on your emotions in some way. You decide which of two or more choices probably would make you feel better.

According to the **affect infusion model**, people use their current emotion as information in reaching a decision, even if the decision pertains to something unrelated to the source of the emotion (Forgas, 1995). For example, how satisfied are you with the way your life has been going, overall? Researchers find that on average, people give higher ratings on sunny days than on cloudy days (Cunningham, 1979). Similarly, stock market prices show a slight tendency to go up on sunny days and down on cloudy days (Goetzmann et al., 2015). That is, feeling happy at the moment carries over into optimism about unrelated matters.

Curiously, the cloudy-day effect disappears if you pay attention to the weather and recognize the possibility that it might affect you. If someone had asked you what you think of the weather today, and afterward asked you how satisfied you are with your life, today's weather would no longer have much effect on your answer. In another study, volunteers who had a cold were assigned to remember vividly an event that made them feel happy, sad, or neutral. When asked about their physical cold symptoms, participants in the "sad" condition reported more severe symptoms, and less confidence that they could do things to make themselves feel better, than participants in the other two conditions (Salovey & Birnbaum, 1989). The authors cautioned that mood may influence people's decisions about whether to seek medical care when they're ill.

Decisions about buying, selling, and taking financial risks also yield to emotions. Suppose we ask you to estimate the value of some object, such as a set of highlighter pens. Perhaps you estimate a value of $10. Now we give you the pens to keep, but ask whether you would be willing to sell them back to us for $10, the price you said they were worth. Most people in a neutral or happy mood refuse, saying they would prefer to keep the pens. Sad people are more inclined to sell; they would prefer the money (Lerner, Small, &

Loewenstein, 2004). If we feel good, then whatever we are currently contemplating (for example, pens) seems good and valuable. If we feel bad, then we assume the object is also bad. In another study, participants recalled a variety of personal experiences that elicited both positive and negative emotions before taking part in a simple gambling task (Yang et al., 2020). Interestingly from an approach/avoidance perspective, feeling fearful was linked to greater avoidance of possible risk compared to feeling angry, happy, or neutral. These results make sense, right? When you are feeling fearful, there are other potential risks about—best to play it safe.

So, emotions influence your choices. Does anybody ever use this idea for practical purposes? You bet they do! Stores arrange cheerful decorations and play happy music, hoping to entice you into a happy mood so you will be more likely to buy things. Television advertisers try to associate their product with happy scenes, especially if they are advertising something like cola beverages, where there aren't many facts to separate one brand from another. The influences are quick and implicit. If you thought it out, you wouldn't conclude that one kind of cola or potato chip will make you more fun or popular or attractive than another cola or potato chip. Political candidates want you to like them and dislike their opponents. In the constraints of a brief television advertisement, they can't explain the complexities of a difficult issue, so they try to associate themselves with smiles, confidence, and cheerful music while associating their opponents with frightening, unpleasant images.

The Somatic Marker Hypothesis

Some of the examples just discussed suggest that emotions distort our decisions, leading us to irrational decisions (Figure 10.11). Nevertheless, as Antonio Damasio (1999) has argued, emotional guidance is not only helpful but necessary for many of our everyday

FIGURE 10.11. The character Spock on Star Trek insisted that all decisions should be rational and not emotional. In fact, people have trouble making good decisions if they cannot imagine the emotional consequences of those decisions.

decisions. In Chapter 6 we encountered patients who had trouble making appropriate decisions after brain damage that impaired their emotions. Although they could describe the probable consequences of various acts, they seemed puzzled at how to choose the preferred outcome.

According to Damasio's **somatic marker hypothesis**, when you make a decision, you quickly estimate the likely outcome of each option, imagine your emotional response to each outcome, and use those imagined responses to guide your choice (Damasio, 1999). The term "somatic marker" refers to your brain's representation of the physiological response you would feel in each possible outcome.

Consider a possible situation: you drive to campus later than usual, you need to get to class quickly, and you are struggling to find a parking place. You do see one place where you could park, but it is next to a fire hydrant. What a dilemma. You quickly imagine the possible consequences of taking the spot. You make it to class on time (good), you might get a parking ticket (bad), and your car might get towed (even worse). According to the somatic marker hypothesis, the last option probably evoked such a strong emotional response that you steer away from the risky parking spot. The outcome could vary, however. The prospect of the parking ticket alone might dissuade you from parking there, especially if your bank account is close to empty. Or, if this is not just a normal class but the final exam, and you need to do well to pass the course, and you need to pass the course to graduate, and the professor locks the door after the exam starts . . . wow, the consequences of being late become worse than having your car towed. In short, the decision depends on your personal circumstances, your preferences, and how likely you consider each of these outcomes. The key point is that you imagine each of the possible consequences and make your decision based on the emotion aroused by imagining each outcome. If you couldn't imagine the emotional responses, you would have no way to decide.

One implication of the somatic marker hypothesis is that the intensity of your emotional reaction to some dilemma might change your decision, even when the actual outcomes are the same. In one study, investigators asked people how much they would decrease their consumption of beef if they thought it had a small possibility of contamination with mad cow disease. They asked other people how much they would decrease consumption of beef if they thought it had a small possibility of contamination with bovine spongiform encephalopathy. People expressed a stronger avoidance based on mad cow disease than on bovine spongiform encephalopathy, although these well-educated participants knew perfectly well that mad cow disease and bovine spongiform encephalopathy are the same thing (Sinaceur, Heath, & Cole, 2005). Mad cow disease sounds scarier, so it leads to more avoidance.

These influences of framing and emotion on decisions have led psychologists to ask how they can best frame important messages about health behavior. For instance, one study examined messaging about dental health in rural regions of the Appalachian region of the United States, where more than half the population are at risk for severe dental disease (Dragojevic et al., 2018). Several hundred participants from this region listened to audio messages about oral health promotion that either used the words "tooth decay" or "Mountain Dew Mouth" and delivered these messages in either a standard American accent or a Southern one. Participants then rated perception of threat, acceptance of the health message, and other responses to the radio message. The results revealed that listeners agreed with the speaker more when she spoke in a standard American accent, and felt more threat and acceptance of the importance of oral health when the threat was described as tooth decay. It appears that listeners were more open to messages conveyed in a way that was perceived as higher status—more official terms for dental hygiene and a more standard than a local accent. Whether these perceptions of the message would lead to changes in oral health behaviors was not assessed, but one can hope that feeling convinced by a health message would affect motivation and behavioral change.

As you might imagine, research on the framing of health messaging became of particular interest during the early years of the COVID-19 pandemic, when researchers were eager to evaluate how to most effectively communicate with the public about the importance of vaccination (Chou & Budenz, 2020) and mask-wearing (Capraro & Barcelo, 2021). Reading this, you might think: but wait! What about all those times you told us about exciting new research failing to replicate, or scientists discovering the story was more complex than first thought, or even new research turning the original finding upside down? What if the research is wrong, and we have gone and given people potentially life-altering advice based on it? If you thought along these lines, you are not alone. There are active, fascinating, and important debates occurring right now among psychological scientists about to what degree psychologists should and should not publicly promote changes in policy and public health based on evolving research (IJzerman et al., 2020; Van Bavel et al., 2020).

Emotions and Moral Reasoning

Emotions influence relatively unimportant choices, like where to park, but they are just as critical for moral reasoning. Let's begin with two examples that have interested both philosophers and psychological researchers.

The Trolley Dilemma

A trolley car's brakes have failed, and it is plunging toward five people. Let's assume some evil person has tied them to the tracks so that they cannot move. You are standing at a switch that controls which track the trolley will enter at a junction. If you leave the switch alone, the five people will be killed. If you pull the switch, you send the trolley onto another track, where it will kill just one person. Should you pull the switch to kill one person but save five? Compare this dilemma to . . .

The Footbridge Dilemma

An out-of-control trolley is again plunging downhill toward five people. Again, there is no hope that they will jump out of the way. This time, there is no switch and only one track, but you are standing on a footbridge above the track. For a split second, you consider diving onto the trolley track to stop the trolley, sacrificing your life to save the five people. Unfortunately (or fortunately, depending on your point of view), you are not heavy enough to stop the trolley, so your sacrifice would accomplish nothing. However, standing right next to you is a hefty wrestler, whose mass would surely stop the trolley. Should you push him off the bridge to stop the trolley, and save five people's lives (see Figure 10.12)?

From a purely logical standpoint these are the same dilemma, because you would be killing one person to save five. Nonetheless, far more people say it is okay to pull the switch than say it is okay to push the stranger off the bridge. (One reason is that you may not feel certain that pushing that man to his death will save the other five, but for the sake of argument, let's pretend you are certain.) Some people do decide that it is morally

FIGURE 10.12. Would it be right to flip a switch to divert the trolley to a different track in the trolley dilemma? Would it be right to push a stranger off a bridge to block a trolley in the footbridge dilemma? In either case, your action would kill one person but save five others.

right to push the stranger off the footbridge, but they are typically slow and hesitant about that decision, as if they are fighting hard against an impulse to say no (Greene et al., 2001). Why do most people find it unacceptable to push the stranger in front of the trolley?

One major reason is the expectation of guilty feelings. If you push someone to his death, you know you will feel extremely guilty afterward . . . even assuming that you don't face murder charges. If you do nothing, you will feel some guilt about not saving five people, but it would be much weaker guilt. People feel much more guilt after committing harm by commission than harm by omission (DeScioli, Christner, & Kurzban, 2011; Miller, Hannikainen, & Cushman, 2014). For example, right now you could probably save the life of a starving child somewhere in the world by contributing to an appropriate charity, but how much guilt do you feel from not contributing? Probably not much. How much guilt would you feel if you actively took food away from a starving child? Vastly more, we assume, unless something is very wrong with you. Another way of putting this point is that you would feel a moral repulsion if you actually put your hands onto someone to force him to his death.

Perhaps through their role in moral "reasoning," emotions influence our political attitudes. Consider the death penalty. Are you for it or against it? How much do you know about it? Is the murder rate lower in states that have the death penalty? Does the murder rate drop after a highly publicized execution? How often have people been sentenced to death and later found to be innocent? How much more likely are poor people to get the death penalty than rich people, for similar crimes? With regard to questions such as these, most people admit they don't know many of the answers, and even when they think they do know, they are almost as likely to be wrong as they are to be right. Providing people with accurate information tends to decrease support for the death penalty (Lambert et al., 2011). However, most people make their decision first, and later look for facts to support the decision they already made (Haidt, 2001). The same pattern holds for many other controversial issues, and has been called **motivated reasoning.** In essence, you evaluate new information not purely on its merits but rather in a slanted way, depending on whether it supports or contradicts your already-held beliefs (e.g., Su, 2022).

Is it wrong to rely on emotions in decisions like these? That is a philosophical question, rather than a scientific one. If you think the right moral decision is the one that a computer would have reached (say, that it is morally right to save five lives by sacrificing one, even if it means shoving someone off a bridge), then emotions are getting in the way of the right decision. Keep in mind, however, that scenarios like the footbridge dilemma describe unusual situations, designed so that carefully reasoned logic opposes our instincts. It feels wrong to push someone off a bridge, and almost always it really is a bad idea. Your emotions are not always right, but often they prepare you for a quick response that is likely to be accurate most of the time.

The Downside of Relying on Emotions

Let's reverse the order of that last sentence: your emotions often prepare you for a quick, probably useful response, but they are not *always* right. They are especially misleading when we don't know, or don't pay attention to, the probabilities of the possible outcomes.

Gambling is a particularly good example. Would you risk $1 on a 50% chance of winning $2? Most people would not. What about betting $1 on a 1% chance of winning $100? Statistically, this is the same as the first bet, because you should come out even in the long run. But most people find this second bet more appealing, because winning $100 sounds like much more fun than winning $2. Would you bet $1 on a 0.0001% (that is, one in a million) chance of winning $1 million? Again, statistically this is a break-even bet in the long run; however, far more people find this bet more attractive than the 50% chance of winning $2. If you buy a ticket in a Powerball lottery (in the United States), your chance of winning is less than 1 in 175 million, but many people buy Powerball tickets regularly (Figure 10.13).

FIGURE 10.13.   Lotteries and other forms of gambling entice people with the lure of a high (although unlikely) payoff. People's emotional responses correspond more closely to the size of a possible reward than to its probability.

Almost half of US college students say they would bet $10 on a one-in-a-million chance of winning $1 million (Rachlin, Siegel, & Cross, 1994). Statistically, this is a terrible bet. You would have to take a one-in-a-million bet about 700,000 times to have a 50% chance of winning at least once, and by that time you would have already lost close to $7 million. People in other countries show the same tendency to prefer bets with a small chance of a high payoff (Birnbaum, 1999). The low-probability, high-payoff bet seems appealing because we anticipate enormous pleasure from the possible win, and the low probabilities do not weaken our emotions.

How would your emotional state influence your reactions to risky choices? The results are mixed. Many studies indicate that happy people tend to be confident, optimistic, and therefore willing to take more risk than they might have otherwise. Even feeling happy for an irrelevant reason—such as because your favorite sports team just won a big game—makes people more likely to make a risky investment (Kaplansky et al., 2015). This effect is consistent with the affect infusion model, described earlier. However, other studies show weak or mixed effects (Nguyen & Noussair, 2014) or find that happy people tend to avoid risks, especially if the risk might lead to a large loss (Nygren et al., 1996).

Research also shows either that sad people accept more risk in order to gain a big reward and cheer themselves up quickly, or that sad people become more aware of risks and therefore become more cautious (Lerner, Li, & Weber, 2013; Tixier et al., 2014). A recent meta-analysis on emotions and risk-taking revealed that introducing negative moods in the laboratory increased risk-taking to a small degree, but introducing positive moods did not (though there were many fewer studies on the positive side; Um et al., 2022). We have noted in earlier chapters that in situations like these, one or more third variables probably moderate some of these effects. Research is needed to figure out what those moderators might be.

EMOTIONAL INTELLIGENCE

Learning Objectives
- Define emotional intelligence, and analyze the strengths and limitations of tests used to measure it.
- Critically assess research on outcomes predicted by high emotional intelligence, and whether it is a trait that can be intentionally improved.

So far this chapter has focused on the role emotion can play in cognition, influencing what we notice and remember, and how we process information and make decisions. What about cognition about emotion itself? Some people seem almost always to know the right way to regulate their own emotions, and how to handle emotional situations with other people. No doubt you also know someone who seems either unable to handle emotional situations, or uninterested in trying. Consider the following examples.

> You are walking down the street when you notice a young woman sitting alone and crying on a park bench (Figure 10.14). You pause and look at her. She looks up briefly, curtly says "hello," and resumes crying. Should you go over and offer to help, or would she prefer to be left alone?

FIGURE 10.14. If you saw someone quietly crying in public, what would you do? People's answers to hypothetical situations like this are sometimes used to measure emotional intelligence.

You need to get to an appointment fast, and your roommate has promised to drive you. But your roommate is slow in getting ready, and you are starting to feel tense. Do you try to speed up your roommate or do you try to calm yourself down? In either case, how do you do it?

Someone has just told a joke that you find insulting or offensive. What do you say, if anything? And what tone of voice do you use?

In each of these cases, the correct answer is obviously "it depends." In the first example, before you decide whether to offer help to the woman crying on the park bench, you might consider her facial expression, body language, tone of voice, and any clues you can see as to why she is crying. The right answer also depends on who you are. For example, she might be more willing to talk with a woman her own age than with someone else. Similarly, in any of the other situations, you would assess the situation before deciding what to do. The point is that you must care enough to try, you must attend to the most relevant cues, and you must weigh the information quickly to find the right answer.

Beginning in the 1990s, psychologists began discussing the idea of **emotional intelligence** (Mayer, Caruso, & Salovey, 2000). Definitions of emotional intelligence vary, but the term generally includes perceiving emotional signals, understanding emotions, and managing emotions, such as calming oneself down or relieving someone else's anxiety. Some psychologists also include the ability to communicate emotions effectively. The term "emotional intelligence" implies that it is enough like academic intelligence to merit the term "intelligence," but that it is also different enough that we need a separate term to describe it. Casual observations are consistent with those assumptions. The people we recognize as having excellent emotional intelligence are, in most cases, above average in other types of intelligence.

The idea of emotional intelligence has become popular among psychologists, corporate executives, and laypeople alike, but fundamental questions remain. First, although we use the term "emotional intelligence," how much of it is an ability, like other types of intelligence? And how much of it is a personality variable? For example, if someone does not detect other people's emotions accurately, does that failure represent a lack of ability, or a lack of interest? Consider a second question: Is emotional intelligence separate from other psychological variables, or it is a combination of academic-type intelligence and certain aspects of personality? To answer questions like these, we must measure emotional intelligence.

Measuring Emotional Intelligence

As we have seen so often in this book, understanding any concept and measuring it support each other: the better we understand a concept, the better we know what to measure; and as we make better measurements, we increase our understanding. If we find that we cannot measure something effectively, we have reason to question the concept itself. How has emotional intelligence been measured, and what do results indicate about the concept?

One way to measure emotional intelligence is to ask people to rate themselves, as researchers typically do for personality. Here are a few true–false items from one questionnaire designed to measure emotional intelligence (Austin et al., 2004):

> I sometimes can't tell whether someone is serious or joking.
> Other people find it easy to confide in me.
> I know what other people are feeling just by looking at them.

As you would guess, a "false" answer on the first item counts the same as a "true" answer on the next two. One problem with any self-report measure is that we don't know whether someone's answers are accurate. Some people who claim to be sensitive to other's feelings and skilled at handling emotional situations are actually wrong, at least according to their friends' and associates' judgments (Carney & Harrigan, 2003; Elfenbein, Barsade, & Eisenkraft, 2015). Overall, however, people with high self-reported emotional intelligence also rate themselves high on social adjustment (Engelberg & Sjöberg, 2004). They tend to be extraverted and agreeable (Siegling et al., 2015; Warwick & Nettelbeck, 2004), and they recover better than most people do after a traumatic experience (Hunt & Evans, 2004). According to most studies, people who rate themselves high on emotional intelligence are more successful than other people on the job. However, many of the items on emotional intelligence questionnaires ask about self-confidence, ability to deal with others, industriousness, and ability to achieve goals (Joseph et al., 2015). Thus, it is hardly surprising that people who in fact do their jobs well also report confidence in their ability to do the jobs well.

A few researchers have related scores to actual (as opposed to self-reported) performance on emotional tasks. On average, people with higher self-reported emotional intelligence do well at recognizing facial expressions of emotion (Austin, 2004). They are also above average in academic performance, mental health, physical health, and ability to restrain aggressive impulses (Di Fabio & Palazzeschi, 2015; García-Sancho, Salguero, & Fernández-Berrocal, 2014; Hall, Andrzejewski, & Yopchick, 2009; Mikolajczak et al., 2015). A meta-analysis of 158 studies on the relationship between emotional intelligence and academic performance found a significant link between the two variables.

(MacCann et al., 2020). The link was stronger when emotional intelligence was measured by a scale that assessed ability rather than relying on self-report.

The authors proposed that higher emotional intelligence might predict stronger academic performance in three different ways. First, better emotional intelligence might lead to better regulation of emotions in academic situations. You can imagine someone high in emotional intelligence dialing down their panic about an upcoming deadline in order to focus and get to work. Students with higher emotional intelligence might also be more successful building helpful social relationships with fellow students—think study partners, and people to borrow notes from. Finally, there might be some overlap between one's academic work and emotional intelligence. After all, what is writing a literature essay if not clearly understanding the emotions and motivations of both the characters and the author?

The other approach to measuring emotional intelligence is to develop an ability test, comparable to IQ tests or other standardized tests. The best known and most widely used test of this type is the Mayer–Salovey–Caruso Emotional Intelligence Test (MSCEIT, pronounced mes-keet). Here are examples, revised slightly from items in actual use (Mayer et al., 2000):

(1) A middle-aged man says his work has been piling up and he is falling behind. He works late at night and spends little time with his family. His relationship with his wife and daughter has suffered. He feels guilty for spending so little time with them, and they feel left out. Recently a relative moved in with them after he got divorced and lost his job. After a while, they told him he had to leave because they needed their privacy, but they felt bad about kicking him out.

On a scale from 1 to 5, where 5 is highest, rate how much this man feels:
Depressed _____
Frustrated _____
Guilty _____
Energetic _____
Joyous _____

(2) A dog runs into the street and gets hit by a car. The driver stops and the dog's owner hurries to check on the dog.

On a scale from 1 to 5, where 5 is the highest, how would the driver and the dog's owner probably feel?
The owner would feel angry at the driver._____
The owner would feel embarrassed at not training the dog better._____
The driver would feel guilty for not driving more carefully._____
The driver would feel relieved that it was a dog and not a child._____

(3) Someone you know at work looks upset. He asks you to have lunch with him, alone, in a quiet place. After a few minutes, he confides in you that he got his job by lying on his application. Now he feels guilty and he is afraid of getting caught. What do you do?

Scoring these questions faces a serious problem: What are the correct answers? On each item, you might like to answer, "It depends! I need more information!" But that answer is not allowed. You must do your best with the limited information provided. We can imagine several ways of determining the right answers, but each poses serious problems (Conzelmann & Goerke, 2015). One method is **expert scoring**, relying on the answers chosen by experts in the field. Researchers use expert scoring for mathematics tests, because in mathematics they can easily identify the experts, and the experts fully agree with one another. The experts on emotional intelligence are harder to identify, and even those regarded as experts do not always agree.

Another way to determine the correct answers is by **consensus scoring**—using the answer given by the largest number of people. That is, the most common answer is considered correct. In most cases, consensus scoring gives partial credit for each possible answer, depending on how many people choose it. Consensus scoring poses three problems. The first is that if 99% of people give the same (and therefore correct) answer on an easy question, you get .99 point for that answer. On a more difficult question, where perhaps only 40% give the most common answer, you would get only .4 point for that answer. Thus, the easiest questions account for the biggest differences in people's scores. People with psychopathy, schizophrenia, and substance abuse issues generally show impairments on almost any aspect of emotional intelligence (Blair et al., 2004; Edwards, Jackson, & Pattison, 2002; Kohler et al., 2003; Kornreich et al., 2001; Townshend & Duka, 2003).

The second problem with consensus scoring is that if the right answer is whatever the majority says, then the test can't include any difficult items that only emotional geniuses answer correctly. The third is that the consensus answer varies from one culture to another. Especially for questions about how to control your emotions, the most common answers differ among the United States, Japan, China, India, and Argentina (Shao, Doucet, & Caruso, 2015). Researchers concede that in consensus scoring, no answer is objectively correct. For most items, the best answer as chosen by the consensus method is the same as the answer chosen by the experts. However, the meaning of this agreement is not clear. Perhaps the majority of experts and the majority of the public are both right, or perhaps they are both wrong.

The third method of scoring is to base the correct answers on **target scoring**—answers from people who had the experiences described in the test questions. For example, for the item about how a driver would feel after accidentally hitting someone's dog, researchers could find and question people who had that experience. Target-based scoring has great potential, but so far it has not been used extensively. And it is not perfect. When we ask people what emotions they felt when they had some experience, often they do not remember clearly, and sometimes they do not answer honestly.

Do Emotional Intelligence Tests Predict Important Outcomes?

Despite the known limitations of emotional intelligence tests, people are very interested in the idea that they might predict important social and life outcomes. A test has **predictive validity** if scores accurately predict people's behavior in another setting. In the case of emotional intelligence, valid test scores might predict behavior in emotional and social situations. Researchers have found positive validity for predicting life satisfaction, quality of friendships and romantic relationships, forgiveness, gratitude, optimism, obedience to the law, academic performance, and ability to restrain anxiety (Ivcevic & Brackett, 2014; Lopes et al., 2004; MacCann et al., 2020; Maul, 2012; Rey & Extremera, 2014). However, the correlation is low in most cases. One study indicated that someone could predict the quality of your friendships and romantic relationships better by asking people who know you than by asking you or using your MSCEIT scores (Choi & Kluemper, 2012).

In principle, the most important criterion for evaluating emotional intelligence tests is **incremental validity**, the extent to which the test scores improve prediction of behavior beyond what researchers could already predict with established variables, such as academic intelligence and personality tests. Scores on the MSCEIT correlate moderately well with scores on IQ tests (Kong, 2014), and they also correlate moderately well with personality tests that measure extraversion, neuroticism, conscientiousness, agreeableness, and openness to experience (Siegling et al., 2015). The IQ scores and personality scores serve to predict life satisfaction, quality of friendships and romantic relationships, and everything else predicted by MSCEIT scores. If emotional intelligence is a separate ability, it should serve to predict certain aspects of behavior better than researchers could from a combination of IQ tests and personality tests.

Most of the research on this point has ranged from slightly positive results to no demonstrable benefit. Several studies have indicated that a combination of emotional intelligence and the personality factors served to predict life satisfaction slightly better than the personality factors alone (Gannon & Ranzijn, 2005; Siegling et al., 2015), but other studies indicated that emotional intelligence added nothing to what was predicted using IQ and personality (Karim & Weisz, 2010; Rossen & Kranzler, 2009). One study indicated that adding emotional intelligence scores to personality scores improved the predictions of ability to deal with stress and anxiety by 1 or 2% (Siegling et al., 2015). At most, emotional intelligence scores seem to show slight incremental validity.

Can Emotional Intelligence Be Taught?

Poor emotional intelligence leads to obvious harm. A spouse says something, the other spouse incorrectly interprets it as hostile, and suddenly a fight erupts (Flury & Ickes, 2001). A child on a playground misinterprets another child's facial expression or tone of voice, and retreats from the playground in tears (Halberstadt, Denham, & Dunsmore, 2001). Someone smiles at someone else in a professional setting, hoping to make a useful contact, and the receiver of the smile misinterprets it as romantic flirting. No doubt you can think of other examples.

As the concept of emotional intelligence became popular, many people set up programs to teach it or urged the schools to teach it (Elias, Hunter, & Kress, 2001). Given that researchers are not sure what emotional intelligence is or how to measure it, it is not surprising that the early attempts to teach it produced no apparent benefits (Izard, 2001). Both a systematic review of the literature (Kotsou et al., 2019) and a meta-analysis (Mattingly & Kraiger, 2019) revealed that later research on emotional intelligence training produced more promising results, indicating training effects above and beyond that of control groups. However, these investigations also revealed significant limitations in the research designs of these studies, ranging from poorly designed control groups to small sample sizes to neglecting to randomize participants to experimental conditions.

Is emotional intelligence worth the hype? By now you've probably detected our skepticism on this point, but we retain an open mind. Certainly the ability to understand, and effectively engage with, your own and other people's emotions is valuable in moving through life with success. However, the use of self-report measures and tests with questionable validity has hampered good research, and more rigorous experimental designs are needed to provide a fair test of the effects of emotional intelligence training. Hopefully the years ahead will see such work.

INTERACTIVE EFFECTS OF MOTIVATION AND COGNITION
Learning Objectives
- Differentiate fixed and growth mindsets, and summarize the evidence as to which is associated with better outcomes.
- Define achievement motivation, and contrast performance versus mastery goals.

In earlier sections of this chapter we asked how emotions influence cognition. In the section above we considered how people understand and reason about emotion. As we turn to the interactive effects of motivation and cognition, we flip the equation again, asking: How does the way we think about some activity or task affect our motivation?

Fixed versus Growth Mindset
We are willing to bet that you have either said yourself, or heard someone say, the words "I'm just not a math person." Or perhaps, if you have always been pro-math: "I don't have an artistic bone in my body." Both statements reflect an assumption about your ability and potential that is static, immovable, and determined by forces outside of yourself (e.g., your genes, your upbringing). This way of thinking about ability is known as a **fixed mindset**. We can contrast it with **growth mindset**—a way of thinking about ability and potential that is fluid, changing, and determined mostly by effort. We could change the statements above from fixed to growth mindset by rephrasing them as, "I have struggled with math in the past, but that means I have a lot of room to improve and develop my skills" and "I've never really engaged with art before, but I'm excited for this new opportunity to learn."

Imagine that we measured people's fixed versus growth mindsets at one point in time, and then followed them through some sort of learning challenge—a college course, a full semester, or a degree program. What would your hypothesis be about the implications of the two mindsets for how well people performed over the course of this learning challenge? Would people with fixed mindsets excel more than growth, growth more than fixed, or would it be a draw?

If you bet that growth mindset is associated with all sorts of good outcomes (higher grades, better retention, more satisfaction), then you would find a mountain of research studies to support your prediction. Some of these studies have demonstrated correlations between current mindsets and future outcomes. Others randomly assigned participants to an intervention promoting one mindset or the other, relative to a control condition, and then examined differences among the groups on outcomes of interest. The mindset interventions in these studies often involved worksheets, explanatory videos, and brief lessons on the power of a growth mindset to enhance performance.

The earliest, most important, and ongoing work on mindsets has been done by the psychologist Carol Dweck (2008). Let's consider just one study, as an example. Along with collaborators, Dweck recruited more than 1500 students from 13 different high schools to participate in an experiment testing the effects of an intervention aimed at encouraging a growth mindset (Paunesku et al., 2015). Students were randomly assigned to one of three conditions. In the intervention condition students read an article about the benefits of growth mindset, and then completed a writing assignment applying what they had learned to a fictional student case. In one control condition students read an article about the value of understanding the underlying or broader purpose of some assignment, course, or assessment; they too completed the writing assignment applying these ideas to a fictional case. In a second control condition, students completed a reading and writing assignment unrelated to either mindsets or purpose in learning. The researchers then followed the students over a semester. Results revealed that among those students whose grades were initially in the bottom third of their classes, the mindset intervention led to significantly improved grades and successful completion of core classes. The authors raise this compelling question: "Among the 4.93 million students who constitute the lowest-performing third of high school students nationwide, could this translate into a proportional 1.18 million additional successfully completed courses?" (p .8).

This is a grand question! It is also indicative of the excitement that marked the early days of work on mindsets. As in many areas of psychology, this early enthusiasm was tempered by questions about the strength of the effects, as well as failures to replicate the findings in larger, even more rigorous research studies (e.g., Brez et al., 2020; Li & Bates, 2019). Nonetheless, ongoing work suggests that while the effect of mindset interventions on academic performance may not be as large as the first study suggested, there is still an interesting effect to be examined (Yeager & Dweck, 2020). One critical improvement would involve calibrating the depth and length of mindset interventions with care. Some of the early work suggested that a single worksheet could have a lasting effect on academic performance—this seems awfully unlikely, given how difficult it can be to significantly alter cognition (Moreau, 2021). Future work in this area will likely explore the conditions under which mindsets are and are not alterable, and the most effective and efficient ways of encouraging a focus on growth.

Achievement Motivation

Some people seem to have endless motivation or drive, moving constantly from one accomplishment or ambition to the next. This is actually a *specific* form of motivation known as **achievement motivation.** The achievements in question don't have to be in the form of medals or degrees; rather, achievement motivation refers to a striving for excellence in some form, often in reference to or competition with a standard (McClelland, Atkinson, Clark, & Lowell, 1976). This standard can be external (e.g., a student striving for an A) but it can also be internal (e.g., a runner training to reach a certain number of miles).

In Chapter 2 we discussed the psychologist Henry Murray and his list of psychological needs—evolved predispositions to fulfill certain psychological requirements, such as power and affection. Murray listed achievement among these needs, and he had an unorthodox method of measuring people's degree of need for achievement (along with the other needs), called the Thematic Apperception Test (TAT; Murray, 1938). In Murray's test participants looked at drawings of people in complex scenes, and were asked to tell a story that explained what was happening. Murray then coded their stories for the presence of themes reflecting his theorized needs, such as power and achievement. For instance, one card shows a small boy sitting alone in a large doorway of a log cabin. One could tell a story about the young boy being rejected from his peers, sitting lonely and pensive in the doorway ruminating about his loss of social connection. Such a story might be coded for high need for affiliation and social belongingness. Alternatively, one could tell a story that the boy is daydreaming about future accomplishments, that he has ambitions to be a famous inventor who lives in a skyscraper. Such a story might be coded for high need for achievement.

Since these early days, achievement is measured in more valid and reliable ways, and theories of achievement motivation have evolved as well. One influential theory—achievement goal theory—was introduced by several researchers, including Carol Dweck of mindset-theory fame (Urdan & Kaplan, 2020). Achievement goal theory proposes that one's achievement goals are focused on either **mastery** (individual development of competence and satisfaction) or on **performance** (motivated by social comparison and competition). Emphasis on mastery goals (rather than performance goals) has been linked to all manner of positive outcomes such as interest, persistence, and use effective learning strategies (Senko, 2016). That said, more recent research has indicated that in some circumstances (e.g., simple tasks, tests of simple knowledge), performance goals can be linked to better outcomes than mastery goals (Senko, 2019).

You might be wondering—where does achievement motivation fit in the spectrum of extrinsic to intrinsic motivation, first discussed in Chapter 1? Two influential researchers have proposed that achievement is actually a third, distinct type of motivation (Locke & Schattke, 2019). They define intrinsic motivation as pursuing an activity purely for enjoyment, or "liking the doing." When you're sort of rubbish at tennis, but you play it anyway because you love the rhythm and activity of the game, that's intrinsic motivation. When you play piano in the comfort of your own home, with no one listening, just for the feel of the music rushing through you, that's intrinsic motivation. In contrast to both intrinsic and extrinsic motivation, Locke and Schattke (2019) argue, achievement motivation is "wanting to do well"—to feel competent, masterful, and satisfied. Wanting to do well can be rooted in both social comparison/performance *and* in the enjoyment of internal mastery (see Figure 10.15). They write, "all three types of motivation are independent yet related concepts (all are sources of pleasure) that can mutually facilitate, compensate, or be in conflict with one another" (p. 287), and call for a rigorous program of research to assess and investigate these concepts.

Locke and Schattke (2019) agree that extrinsic motivation comprises carrot-and-stick motivations—working a job you don't enjoy for a paycheck; not speeding to avoid a ticket. They also argue that extrinsic motivation has been unfairly demonized. If we are motivated to pursue some activity (the "means") because we desire the result (the "ends"), it probably indicates that we truly value those ends. That paycheck pays for enriching summer camps for our children, a gym membership to stay physically healthy, and degree programs to further our education. Put this way, pursuing activities for extrinsic ends is just part of being an effective human being.

As a college student, achievement motivation likely plays a large role in your life. You probably notice elements of both performance goals (e.g., studying for that A) and mastery goals (e.g., endlessly tweaking your lab experiments to reach success in your

FIGURE 10.15.   A proposal for how the intrinsic/extrinsic motivation dichotomy could be reconceptualized as a "trichotomy." From Locke and Schattke (2019).

independent research work) in your work. A rich literature on the interactions of emotion, motivation, teaching, and learning in higher education suggests that the college classroom is a setting where some of the topics we've considered this chapter have important and real-life implications (Camacho-Morles et al., 2021; Cavanagh et al., 2021; Hulleman et al., 2016).

SUMMARY

Throughout this chapter, we have encountered many ways in which emotions and motivation can influence cognition. Emotional stimuli tend to grab attention quickly, and varieties of emotional experience may either broaden or narrow your attention to details. Emotional arousal enhances both the storage of memory and its consolidation. When you retrieve your memories, the most emotion-laden memories tend to dominate your attention. Certain emotion states, such as happiness and anger, tend to increase confidence, and emotions can nudge us toward more systematic or heuristic ways of processing information.

As suggested by the affect infusion model, the emotion you feel at any moment influences how you react to subsequent events, even if they are unrelated to whatever evoked your emotion. As suggested by the somatic marker hypothesis, you make many decisions by imagining the emotional consequences of each possible outcome. Moral decisions necessarily rely on emotions, and we often make our moral decisions impulsively and then try justify them with a rational explanation afterward. This process also influences how we evaluate new information, especially about hot-topic, controversial issues. People sometimes make risky decisions that look illogical because they consider the possible joy of a win more than the high probability of a loss. Finally, some people may be better at reading, interpreting, regulating, and using emotional information than others, but it is unclear whether this really an emotional version of intelligence, and whether it can be reliably measured or taught.

This chapter has also highlighted areas of inconsistency and controversy in the evidence and we've seen some areas where previously accepted theories are changing in the face of new evidence. Some of the effects of emotion on cognition are tiny, or true only in limited ways or under limited circumstances. Does feeling happy help you remember happy memories, and does feeling sad help you remember sad memories? Sometimes, but this effect is usually small. Does relying on gut feelings help you make better decisions? Possibly, but this is a better plan when the best outcome is defined by preferences and values rather than probabilities or clear facts. Does feeling happy or sad change your motivation to take risks? The answer evidently depends on the type of risk, and many other circumstances.

Not only does emotion affect cognition, but thinking differently can influence our emotions and motivation. Simply reframing how you think about your abilities and potential as capable of growth may influence how well you develop those abilities. Focusing on personal mastery and competence, rather than social comparison, may boost achievement motivation, giving us more of that energy + direction formula we need to achieve our goals.

One theme runs throughout this chapter: emotion and motivation are integral parts of thinking, not separate. Your thoughts influence your emotions and motivations, and in turn your emotions and motivation alter what you remember, how intensely you remember it, what aspects of the environment you notice, whether you blame yourself or others for misfortunes, what events you consider likely in the future, and how much effort you put into making a careful decision.

KEY TERMS

achievement motivation: motivation stemming from competition with an internal or external standard, for reasons of either performance of mastery (p. 372)

affect infusion model: theory that people's emotional state influences their evaluation of other events, including those unrelated to the reason for their current emotion (p. 359)

attentional bias: a tendency for certain categories of stimuli to regularly attract attention, for instance, attentional vigilance for stimuli that might suggest threat (p. 342)

beta-blocker: drug that temporarily disables some receptors for neurotransmitters that promote emotional arousal (p. 349)

broaden and build theory: proposal that positive emotions expand the focus of your attention, helping you survey the environment broadly and appreciate opportunities you might have overlooked otherwise (p. 344)

consensus scoring: defining the correct answer to some question as the answer given by the largest number of people (p. 369)

consolidation: strengthening of a memory during a period after its formation (p. 351)

emotional intelligence: ability to perceive, understand, and manage emotions (p. 366)

expert scoring: procedure of determining the correct answer by relying on the answers chosen by experts in the field (p. 369)

encoding: the process by which new memories are stored (p. 347)

fixed mindset: belief that intelligence, abilities, and skills are innate, fixed, and immutable to change (p. 371)

flashbulb memories: vivid, detailed memories of unusually intense emotional experiences (p. 350)

growth mindset: belief that intelligence, abilities, and skills grow in response to practice and experience (p. 371)

heuristic cognition: making decisions based on simple shortcuts or rules of thumb, unrelated to the strength of evidence (p. 355)

incremental validity: the extent to which scores on a new measure improve prediction of behavior beyond what researchers could already predict with established variables (p. 370)

mastery goals: goals that result in achievement motivation, focused on desire for competence or personal mastery over a standard (p. 373)

motivated reasoning: evaluating information in such a way that weights evidence that confirms already-existing beliefs more strongly than information that contradicts these beliefs (p. 363)

motivational intensity: how much you are motivated to actively achieve (or prevent) some future outcome, as distinct from having feelings about an event that has already occurred (p. 345)

performance goals: goals that result in achievement motivation, focused on social comparison or display (p. 373)

predictive validity: the extent to which scores on a measure accurately predict people's behavior in another setting (p. 369)

retrieval: the process of pulling memory out of storage for current use (p. 353)

somatic marker hypothesis: idea that we make a decision by imagining the emotional consequences of various possible choices and then selecting the choice with the best outcome (p. 361)

synaptic tag-and-capture hypothesis: proposal that the brain tags new memories for enhanced consolidation later, if subsequent events indicate that a particular memory is important (p. 352)

systematic cognition: making decisions through careful evaluation of the available information (p. 355)

target scoring: determining the correct answer to a question by asking people who have had the experience the question describes (p. 369)

Yerkes–Dodson law: proposal that attention, learning, and other aspects of cognition are at their best when arousal is at an intermediate level (p. 341)

THOUGHT/DISCUSSION QUESTIONS

1. In the section on emotion and memory, we described studies finding that greater arousal facilitates memory, but also one study showing that reduced arousal predicted better memory. Review these studies. How can you reconcile these two findings? (Hint: Are both effects working through the same mechanisms?)

2. In this chapter we noted several ways in which arousal seems to facilitate memory, yet in Chapter 7 we argued that the autonomic nervous system can produce different varieties of arousal. In Chapter 4 we differentiated challenge and threat appraisal profiles and the associated physiology, and in Chapter 6 we discussed the amygdala. Pulling together all that you have learned, do you think that memory would be facilitated more by challenge or by threat? Either way, make your case based on the existing evidence.

3. Examine a variety of political posts on social media. To what extent do they rely on systematic cognition and to what extent on heuristic cognition? What emotions do they try to evoke, and why? How do these posts exhibit evidence of motivated reasoning?

4. Given what you have learned about emotions and decision-making, list several examples of decisions you think are best made based on emotions (gut instinct) and several examples of decisions that are best made without emotion. What do the items on each list have in common?

5. Describe some people you know whom you consider emotionally intelligent. Based on those descriptions, what characteristics are you calling emotional intelligence? If you were devising a new test of emotional intelligence, what types of items would you include?

SUGGESTIONS FOR FURTHER READING

Immordino-Yang, M. H. (2016). *Emotions, learning, and the brain: Exploring the educational implications of affective neuroscience.* Norton.

McGaugh, J. L. (2003). *Memory and emotion: The making of lasting memories.* Columbia University Press. Each of these excellent books discusses the research on emotion and cognition, as well as real-life implications, in an accessible way. Both are written by major researchers in cognition and learning.

Ray, C., & Huntsinger, J. R. (2017). Feeling and thinking: An affect-as-cognitive-feedback account. *Social and Personality Psychology Compass, 11*(5), e12314. https://doi.org/10.1111/spc3.12314. This review article, accessible to an undergraduate audience, makes the case that the impact of emotion on cognitive processing is somewhat different from what researchers had previously believed.

ANSWER

Figure 10.10: Dump the matches out of the box; use the thumbtacks to secure the inner part of the matchbox to the corkboard; light the candle and drip some wax inside the matchbox; and place the candle on the melted wax.

PART III

How Can We Improve Emotional Well-Being?

CHAPTER 11

The Value of Negative Emotions

In the first section of this book we asked what emotions are, what general kinds of functions they serve, and what elicits emotional responses. In the second section we examined how emotions affect our lives, and their connections to biology, development, social relationships, and cognition. In this final section we turn to the issue that for most readers is likely the most compelling: How can we improve our emotional lives?

To answer this question, we must ask a more subtle one. What *is* the ideal emotional life? If you could choose the emotions you would experience for the rest of your time on Earth, as though you were ordering dishes off a menu, what would you order? Many people say, "I just want to be happy!" Yet even that is ambiguous, as people mean different things by this simple statement. As we first discussed in Chapter 3, **ideal affect** (the affective states that people *want* to feel) varies from person to person and culture to culture. Across gender and culture lines, most people say they would like to feel more positive emotion than negative emotion (Senft et al., 2022; Tsai, 2007). Even this has its limits, however. Although high positive emotion is a better predictor of life satisfaction than low negative emotion around the world, negative emotion is considered less problematic and undesirable by people from East Asian versus Western cultures (e.g., Kuppens, Realo, et al., 2008; Senft et al., 2022). Consider this—in placing your own order for ideal affect, would negative emotions be completely absent? If you could avoid feeling fear, or anger, or sadness ever again, would you do so?

Negative emotions are unpleasant, and they usually mean things are not going our way. In this chapter, however, we consider the roles that several negative emotions play in supporting our health and well-being, helping us to thrive. This perspective assumes that negative emotions are not just here to annoy us and make our lives miserable—that they serve important functions. We hope that by the end of the chapter, you'll decide to order a few of these emotions after all.

FEAR

Learning Objectives

- Summarize the theorized adaptive function of fear, and analyze the evidence for this proposal drawing from empirical research on cognitive/appraisal, biological, feeling, and behavioral aspects of fear.
- Explain the idea that fear is an algorithm, and apply that algorithm to a hypothetical situation.
- Define fear appeal, and explain the conditions under which fear appeals are most likely to promote actual behavior change.
- Analyze the evidence regarding the role of genes in individual differences in fear-proneness.

Why begin with fear? For one thing, we know more about fear than we do about any other specific emotion. Fear is a good example of what we mean by emotion, in the sense that it has been linked to intense feelings, specific appraisals, distinct facial and vocal expressions, strong physiological reactions, and powerful action tendencies (freezing, escape, and, when cornered, attack). Moreover, we can identify clear examples of fear behavior even in nonhuman animals, allowing us to examine the neural mechanisms of fear in ways that are not currently feasible in humans.

Fear and anxiety are similar in many ways, particularly with respect to neural activation associated with their experience, and researchers often use the terms interchangeably (Shackman & Fox, 2016). However, more precise concepts are sometimes useful. As the term is most often used by researchers and clinicians, **fear** is a response to a specific perceived source of danger, provoking effort to avoid or escape that danger, and subsiding once the threat is gone. **Anxiety** refers to a more general expectation that something bad might happen, with hypervigilance and high arousal that are not linked to a particular target (Lazarus, 1991; Sylvers, Lilienfeld, & LaPrairie, 2011). **Social anxiety** is limited to interpersonal situations, especially those that involve meeting new people or having others' attention focused on you. Many people experience some apprehension at the thought of meeting new people, or having to give a presentation to a bunch of strangers. Individuals who struggle with social anxiety have a chronic fear of other people's evaluation and rejection, tend to avoid social interaction in general, and enjoy social interaction less (Kashdan et al., 2013).

Feelings of fear and anxiety can easily be measured with questionnaires. A single item asking whether and how strongly people feel fear is adequate for simple laboratory experiments, as well as experience sampling studies where people are asked to report on their emotions several times per day. When a more elaborate measure is needed, the State–Trait Anxiety Inventory (Spielberger & Sydeman, 1994) offers greater detail. The idea behind this questionnaire is that anxiety is both a *state* (a temporary condition related to recent events) and a *trait* (a long-term aspect of personality). As an analogy, a state is like a region's current weather, and a trait is like the usual climate.

Behavioral measures are also available. The prototypical facial expression of fear (see Figure 11.1) includes lifting the inner and outer eyebrows and pulling them together; widening the eyes; and contracting the muscles below the corners of the lips, pulling the skin of the lower cheeks down and to the side (Ekman et al., 1987). Often, the mouth opens slightly as well. This is similar to an expression of surprise, and participants

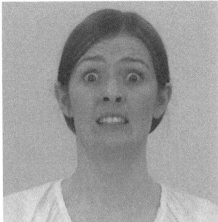

FIGURE 11.1. The prototypical facial expression of fear.

frequently confuse the two when asked to look at a photo and guess how someone is feeling (Ekman et al., 1987).

Beyond the face, many nonhuman animals and humans of all ages show an innate **startle response** to sudden, loud noises. The muscles tense rapidly, especially the neck muscles; the eyes close tightly; the shoulders quickly pull close to the neck; and the arms pull up toward the head. All these movements seem geared toward protecting the vulnerable areas of the torso, neck, and head. Information about the noise goes from your ears to a brain area called the *pons* in less than 10 milliseconds, and from there to cells in the medulla and spinal cord that control your muscles (Figure 11.2). The full startle reflex occurs in less than one-fifth of a second (Yeomans & Frankland, 1996). Although the startle response itself is a reflex, input from the rest of the nervous system can modify its intensity. Negative emotions, especially fear and anxiety, tend to amplify the response (Lang, Bradley, & Cuthbert, 2002; Schmid et al., 1995). Imagine you are walking alone at night through a dangerous neighborhood, when suddenly you hear a loud "bang!" Then imagine hearing the same sound in the middle of the afternoon among friends in your own home. You will be startled in both cases, but much more so in the dangerous place than in the familiar, safe place. Emotion researchers use this **startle potentiation** to measure fear in both humans and nonhumans.

Another simple behavioral measure of fear is freezing, or suppression of movement. This measure is especially popular in research with nonhuman animals. In the presence of a predator's smell, loud sound, or other indicator of danger, most small animals simply freeze (Bolles, 1970). When rats are put into an unfamiliar enclosure, some explore freely, whereas others stay motionless in a corner or against a wall. The failure to explore is generally interpreted as an indication of fear or anxiety (motionlessness is a good defense for a small animal because predators readily detect anything that moves). Humans may show a freeze response when threatened as well. In one study, researchers induced panic by depriving participants of oxygen in the laboratory (we know—that's mean); about 13% of participants reported feeling like they could not move (Schmidt et al., 2008). Other studies have documented reduced movement when participants see a threatening

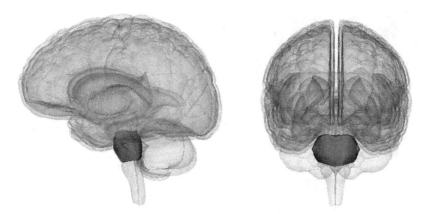

FIGURE 11.2. The startle response depends on a reflexive response by the pons to sudden, loud noises. The startle response can be augmented or diminished by input from the amygdala, which helps scan information from the environment, assessing whether it is dangerous or safe.

stimulus, such as a photograph of a spider or an angry face (Roelofs, Hagenaars, & Stins, 2010; Sagliano et al., 2014).

What does fear look like in the brain? We noted earlier that feelings of fear increase the startle response to loud noises. It appears that this startle potentiation effect relies in part on activation in the amygdala, a structure we discussed in Chapter 6. As a quick reminder, the amygdala is an area within the temporal lobe of each hemisphere of the brain. Each amygdala receives input representing vision, hearing, other senses, and pain. Each amygdala is also connected with a hippocampus, which is important for memory, so it is in a position to associate various stimuli with dangerous outcomes that follow them. Conditioned fears—that is, fears based on the association of some stimulus with shock—depend on synaptic changes in the amygdala (Kwon & Choi, 2009; Resssler & Maren, 2019).

In addition to sending information to the hippocampus, prefrontal cortex (Garcia et al., 1999), and other regions (Gifkins, Greba, & Kokkinidis, 2002), the amygdala communicates with the pons and other areas controlling the startle reflex (Fendt, Koch, & Schnitzler, 1996; Figure 11.2). Thus, the amygdala is well placed to modulate the intensity of the startle response, based on one's emotional state. Thinking of the amygdala as the "fear area of the brain" is an oversimplification, because the amygdala contributes to many other functions as well. However, some specific sections of the amygdala—the central nucleus and the bed nucleus of the stria terminalis—appear to play important roles in detecting threats and initiating visceral and behavioral responses associated with fear and anxiety (Fox & Shackman, 2019).

The Functions of Fear

Nowhere is the function of an emotion easier to observe than in the case of fear. Fear pulls our attention to possible dangers, especially those involving physical harm, and helps us avoid them. Factor analyses of human phobias suggest that fear is elicited by three major categories of stimuli: animals such as snakes, spiders, and dogs; social threats such as unfamiliar or angry people, and unwanted social attention; and nonliving physical threats such as heights and thunder (Arrindell et al., 1991; Chapman et al., 2008). Some fears appear to be innate. For example, sudden, loud noises frighten virtually everyone, from birth through old age. That fear is also present in nearly all other animal species that have hearing. Fear of dark places is also common among humans. Separation from loved ones may be another built-in fear, especially for young children.

However, there are many other sources of danger out there, and they vary from place to place—the threats to life and limb in a big city differ from those in the jungle. The great majority of our fears are learned as we move through life. Humans possess a flexible, easily conditioned fear response system to help us manage this wide range of potential threats without being paralyzed by terror all the time. In Chapter 4 we described a demonstration by John Watson in 1920, with a toddler who had never before feared rats. Every time an experimenter showed "Little Albert" a white rat, Watson struck a loud gong nearby; after a few such pairings, Albert became frightened whenever a rat appeared (Watson & Rayner, 1920). Although this "study" does not earn high marks for experimental rigor, the general phenomenon of fear learning has been demonstrated in plenty of research with children, adults, and nonhuman animals alike (e.g., Shechner et al., 2014; Schiele et al., 2016). We even learn new fears based upon seeing other people's negative experience with or fear response to some stimulus—a phenomenon called **social fear learning** (Askew et al., 2013; Debiec & Olsson, 2017; Silvers et al., 2021).

A major controversy in research on fear is whether we learn some fears more readily than others. Did you ever hit your thumb with a hammer? Probably so. Did you develop a phobia of hammers? Probably not. Have you ever been in an automobile accident, or seen someone badly injured in one? Many people have. Are you now terrified of automobiles? Not likely, at least not for long. In contrast, a great many people fear snakes, spiders, dogs, and other large animals. Arne Öhman (2009) has argued that predators, particularly snakes, are the primordial target of animal fear. You may be wondering, why snakes? Snakes can't eat people. Although that's true now, we likely inherited our predator fear response from ancient, small, mammalian ancestors for whom snakes were the main predator, and we retain the vestiges of this fear (Isbell, 2006). Whether it's actually going to eat you or not, you certainly don't want to get bit—or squeezed to death—by a snake.

People learn to fear both snakes and spiders so readily that researchers have suggested a built-in predisposition to learn these fears (Öhman, Eriksson, & Olofsson, 1975; Seligman, 1971). Evidence for this **prepared learning** includes several studies with monkeys, which should share similar predator preparedness with humans. Ordinarily, laboratory-reared monkeys show inhibition and withdrawal from snakes the first time they see one. If nothing bad happens, their fear habituates (declines), but this initial wariness suggests a predisposition toward fear (Nelson, Shelton, & Kalin, 2003). If a monkey sees another monkey show fear of snakes, it acquires the fear too, although the observing monkey has never been bitten or even seen any other monkey bitten (Mineka, 1987; Mineka et al., 1984). These effects are specific to snakes—if a monkey watches a movie of another monkey running away from a snake, it develops a fear of snakes, but if it watches an edited movie showing a monkey running away from flowers, it develops no fear of flowers (Mineka, 1987).

Humans also are quick to learn a fear of snakes. People who get shocks paired with pictures of snakes soon show a conditioned response (increased heart rate and breathing rate), whereas those who get shocks paired with pictures of houses develop weaker responses (Öhman et al., 1975). Although we may eventually develop a conditioned fear of any stimulus that is paired with electrical shocks a sufficient number of times, it takes fewer pairings if the stimuli are snakes and spiders than if they are fish and birds (Ho & Lipp, 2014; Figure 11.3). Even infants and young children show a bias toward attending to images of snakes and spiders (LoBue & DeLoache, 2010), as well as sounds indicating evolutionarily ancient threats (e.g., a snake's hiss, an angry voice; Erlich, Lipp, & Slaughter, 2013). Although most of this research has been done in Western countries, in one study children from both urban and rural India showed a similar pattern, displaying preferential attention to snakes and lions relative to nonthreatening lizards and antelopes (Penkunas & Coss, 2013).

However, an evolutionary predisposition to *fear* snakes and spiders is not the only possible explanation. First, safe experiences with an object tend to decrease any fear of it (Craske et al., 2014). You may have been hurt in an automobile accident, or if not, you may have seen someone else get hurt. However, most people have also had thousands of safe experiences with cars (and flowers, and houses, and birds) to offset one scary experience. How many safe experiences have you had with snakes?

Second, it may be that we more readily develop fear responses to stimuli that grab our attention easily, whether those stimuli are inherently threatening or not. In reconsidering the meaning of infants' early responses to images of snakes, spiders, and so forth, Vanessa LoBue and Karen Adolph (2019) note that the babies' behavior doesn't actually *look* frightened. They're not crying, or showing a fear face, or trying to get away from the pictures. They're just looking at them. LoBue and Adolph propose that humans may be evolutionarily predisposed to *notice* and attend to these stimuli, but whether this develops into fear depends on learning and socialization. Notably, LoBue herself has shifted her perspective on this, from first endorsing the idea of prepared fear learning to being more skeptical. This is not indecisiveness—it's a reasonable response to new data, and thinking carefully about the data you already have. This is how good science is supposed to work; sometimes it involves acknowledging uncertainty, and new evidence changing our minds about something we thought we knew.

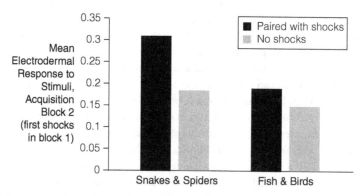

FIGURE 11.3. People develop conditioned fears more rapidly to images of snakes and spiders than to fish and birds, requiring fewer pairings of the image with an electrical shock. Some researchers interpret this as evidence that humans are prepared by evolution to learn specific fears of dangerous animals. Data from Ho & Lipp (2014).

However we learn new fears, the physical changes that occur when we are frightened or anxious are consistent with an overall function of avoiding danger. Similarities in fear-related behavior in humans and other animals allows us to study the physiology of fear in lab mammals, as well as in humans. As a result, we know more about the biology of fear than is true for any other emotion. This work has uncovered the complexity of fear, suggesting that it is less a single, uniform state than an algorithm for guiding the best possible response to danger, given details of the situation. This complexity is evident at both the behavioral and the physiological levels, and in their relationship to each other.

Starting with behavior, think about being alone at night on a dark street and hearing footsteps behind you. Turning around to look, you see a large man who looks threatening and seems to be eyeing you and/or your stuff in a predatory way. What are your options? If you feel confident—maybe you're bigger than he is, or you are a world's champion at martial arts, or you're approaching a busier street—you can keep walking, perhaps speeding up. If you're in a shadow and he hasn't noticed you yet, you might freeze in place, trying to hide. If he starts running toward you, however, you'd better get out of there fast. If he catches you, you can fight back or go limp and hope he decides not to hurt you. Some theorists have asked whether it makes sense to call such different behavioral responses *fear* (Barrett, 2006).

Diverse as these behaviors may be, they are all potentially effective ways to escape, depending on how close an enemy is and the nature of that enemy (Bracha, 2004; Fanselow, 1994; see Figure 11.4). Animals entering an area where a predator might be present, such as an open field or a watering hole, will go about their business slowly and with heightened vigilance. If a predator is present, but is far away and/or has not yet noticed the prey, the prey will typically freeze. During this time the prey animal's heart rate will slow dramatically, but its muscles are still tense; if surprised, it will show a strong startle response (Campbell, Wood, & McBride, 1997). Once the predator comes closer, a full-blown sympathetic nervous system response kicks in, heart rate speeds up and blood pressure rises, and the animal will run (Masterson & Crawford, 1982).

A similar pattern can be seen in humans. Imagine yourself in this experiment: you are playing a video game in which you sometimes have an opportunity to win money, but sometimes face the threat of losing money. When you see an image of a gun getting larger

FIGURE 11.4. Although freezing and fleeing are very different behaviors, associated with different physiological states, each can facilitate escape from danger.

(as though it were moving closer to you) over a sequence of several slides, it means you will lose some money unless you react quickly, pressing a button when the image reaches a certain size. At first you pay close attention to the gun, but while it is small and distant, your heart rate slows. At this time, your startle potentiation is at its peak. As the gun image gets larger, you know the time for action is approaching; you shift to high arousal and fight-flight mode, ready for a vigorous response (Löw et al., 2008). Across many studies, this variant of the human fear response has been found to include an increase in heart and respiration rate, constriction of the blood vessels leading to the extremities (causing icy hands and feet), and sweating, preparing the body for muscular activity (Kreibig, 2010).

Using Fear to Change Behavior

If fear helps us avoid danger and reduces our tendency toward risk taking, can it be used for any practical purpose? Campaigns aimed at getting people to quit smoking, eat healthier diets, wear seatbelts, get more exercise, and take better care of the natural environment have long included **fear appeals** to achieve their goals (Figure 11.5). For example, magazine advertisements showing diseased lungs and television commercials listing the health risks of smoking are each designed to scare people into healthier behavior, emphasizing the awful things that will happen if people *don't* change. Do these appeals actually work?

With some caveats, yes. In a meta-analysis of studies involving more than 27,000 participants, health-promotion messages including a fear appeal were found to produce more positive attitudes toward the recommended behavior, greater intention to change, and more actual behavioral change, relative to control conditions (Tannenbaum et al., 2015). However, fear alone may not be enough to produce results. While fear may provide motivation to change one's behavior, another crucial ingredient is **self-efficacy**—the

FIGURE 11.5. Fear appeals use threats of the negative consequences of failing to change one's current behavior.

belief that one can actually succeed in doing so (Kok et al., 2018; Tannenbaum et al., 2015). In the meta-analysis fear appeals showed the greatest effects when they were accompanied by clear and specific steps people could take to avoid disaster; and when only one-time action was needed rather than commitment to ongoing, long-term change. Some researchers have warned that people who feel threatened but do *not* believe they are capable of changing their ways (e.g., a smoker who has already tried to quit several times, and failed) may simply tune out the message in order to avoid being upset (Kok et al., 2018). Although the possibility that fear appeals may backfire in this situation is controversial, researchers agree that a combination of fear appeals with concrete, achievable actions one can take is most likely to succeed in promoting change.

This principle was illustrated in a study in which researchers aimed to increase sun-protective behavior among students at a university on the Southern California coast (Nabi & Myrick, 2019). These students faced heightened risk of skin cancer due to excessive frolicking in the sun (a dreadful situation, we know). Study participants watched a YouTube video emphasizing the dangers of sun exposure and the awful consequences of skin cancer, and providing a series of recommended sun protection behaviors (Figure 11.6). They then completed a questionnaire assessing their self-efficacy to enact the sun protection behaviors, intentions to do so, and the emotions they felt. A week later, they completed a final questionnaire reporting on the actual sun protection behaviors they had used in the past week.

Consistent with prior research, fear and self-efficacy ratings each independently predicted intention to adopt the sun protective behaviors, which in turn predicted actual behavior over the next week. The new twist was that another emotion—hope—was associated with both self-efficacy and fear. Moreover, among those reporting high self-efficacy, those who also felt hopeful showed the strongest effects. Although this study did not include a control group who did not see the threatening videos, the findings suggest that evoking fear of the worst outcome, confidence in one's ability to take the actions needed to prevent it, and hope for a better outcome is a promising cocktail for behavior change interventions.

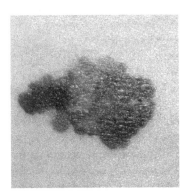 

FIGURE 11.6. Fear-based behavior change interventions are most likely to be effective if the threatening message is paired with clear, easy-to-implement action steps for preventing the unwanted outcome, aimed at increasing self-efficacy.

Individual Differences: Genetics and Fear

What is the right amount of fear or anxiety? It depends. Do you live in a nice, leafy suburb, a sketchy neighborhood in a big city, or a war-torn country? Are the people you live among kind and friendly, or are they unpredictable and sometimes aggressive? Even if you live in a generally safe environment, you sometimes encounter potentially dangerous situations. A little fear is appropriate when you walk alone in a parking lot to your car late at night, or when a stranger harasses you on the subway. Ideally, you should be able to adjust your fear level depending on circumstances.

However, it is increasingly clear that genetic differences also contribute to individual differences in fear and anxiety. Differences among individuals are fairly consistent over years or decades (Durbin et al., 2007). Newborn infants who frequently kick and cry are more likely than others to be frightened by unfamiliar events at ages 9 and 14 months (Kagan & Snidman, 1991). At age 7 years, they tend to be shy and nervous on a playground (Kagan et al., 1988). As adults, they show a strong amygdala response to almost any photograph of a person, especially an unfamiliar person (Beaton et al., 2008; Schwartz et al., 2003).

These longitudinal effects suggest a genetic contribution, but other research provides even more direct support. Both panic disorder and phobias are more common among people who have relatives with similar disorders, especially among close relatives such as identical twins (Hettema, Neale, & Kendler, 2001; Kendler et al., 2001; Skre et al., 2000). Although research is somewhat limited, the available studies also suggest considerable heritability of specific fears, such as fears of animals (45%) and phobias involving blood, injury, or injection (33%; Van Houtem et al., 2013). Genes even seem to play a role in our propensity to learn new fears. In one study identical and nonidentical same-sex twin pairs completed a standard fear conditioning task, receiving electric shocks while viewing images of snakes, spiders, and geometric figures. Genetic relatedness appeared to account for about 40% of variability in intensity of the conditioned fear response, as measured through skin conductance (Hettema et al., 2003).

Identifying specific genes, or even combinations of genes, that account for fear-proneness is more difficult. Meta-analyses of studies examining the entire genome, hunting for genetic regions that account for susceptibility to anxiety disorders, have identified some promising sequences, but the reason why these are linked to anxiety is not clear (Otowa et al., 2016). One interesting line of genetic research focuses on the link between anxiety and *joint laxity syndrome* (being double-jointed). People with joint laxity syndrome (Figure 11.7) are more likely than others to develop strong fears, as well as panic disorder and other anxiety disorders (Bulbena et al., 2004, 2011). Recall from Chapter 2 that the same genetic mutation may have a wide range of effects. It may be that trait anxiety and joint laxity are influenced in part by a common gene, but it's not clear what the common gene is or why the two phenotypes are linked.

We will consider individual differences in fear and anxiety further in Chapter 13, emphasizing the ways in which extreme fear and anxiety can impair people's lives. However, the ideal amount of fear is not none. Much as we may admire fearlessness in principle, a healthy dose of fear keeps you out of trouble. A meta-analysis of studies linking dispositional fear and anxiety to risk assessment showed small-to-medium effects, in which less fearful people tended to see less risk in uncertain situations, and to make riskier decisions (Wake, Wormwood, & Satpute, 2020). If you're not familiar with the Darwin Awards, look them up. Every year, people nominate dozens of candidates who were doing

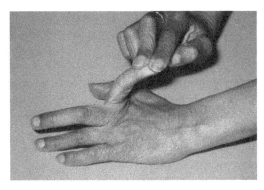

FIGURE 11.7. Joint laxity syndrome by itself is harmless, but many people with this genetic condition also develop severe anxieties. The two conditions may have overlapping genetic bases.

something dangerous that probably seemed fun, interesting, or clever at the time, and ended up dying in the process. Low threat sensitivity and reactivity to danger also characterize people with psychopathy, defined by recklessness, impulsivity, and callousness toward other people (Hoppenbrouwers, Bulten, & Brazil, 2016).

On a more positive note, a little fear can be a sign of a healthy life and willingness to try some adventures. Have you ever heard the quote, "Do one thing every day that scares you?" By this advice, Eleanor Roosevelt meant that it's scary to test our own limits, but it's also important for personal growth.

ANGER

Learning Objectives
- Summarize the elicitors and theorized adaptive function of anger, and analyze the evidence for this function.
- Analyze the evidence regarding effects of anger displays in interpersonal relationships, predicting when and for whom these are likely to be beneficial, rather than backfiring.
- Differentiate hostile and instrumental aggression, and identify examples of each.

Fear and anger have a lot in common. Both are responses to unexpected, unpleasant events (Scherer, 1997). Both evoke arousal and strong visceral responses (Kreibig, 2010). Yet from the standpoint of a researcher, the contrast is striking. Fear is easy to elicit in the laboratory, whereas anger is quite difficult. Prototypical facial and behavioral expressions of fear and anger overlap little. Although researchers can measure aggressive behavior in animals, they are far less likely to call it "anger" than they are to accept freezing and startle facilitation as evidence of fear. For English-language speakers, **anger** can be described as the emotional state associated with feeling insulted or offended, although—as we saw in Chapter 4—this definition may not account for all situations in which we feel anger.

This definition suggests that we become angry when we feel that we have been violated in some way. Researchers sometimes distinguish among three negative emotions, each of which might be elicited by some type of violation. According to Paul Rozin,

Jonathan Haidt, and colleagues (Rozin et al., 1999), anger is a response to a violation of autonomy—that is, individual rights. You are angry when someone takes something away from you or prevents you from doing something you feel entitled to do. Disgust, they argue, is a response to a violation of purity or divinity. To touch—or worse yet, taste—feces, cockroaches, or intestines would bring something impure into your body. Similarly, associating with someone who is morally impure might threaten your feeling of nobility. Contempt is a response to violation of community standards. You might feel contempt toward someone who cheated on a test, or who flaunted standards of acceptable behavior. (A certain pop star, asked to leave an important archaeological site after drunkenly pulling down his pants and trying to climb around on the ruins, comes to mind.)

To test this distinction, researchers made a list of actions that seemed to violate autonomy, community standards, or divinity/purity. Then they asked college students in both the United States and Japan to label their reaction to each one as anger, contempt, or disgust and to choose the proper facial expression from options like those shown in Figure 11.8. Although participants often confused these expressions when giving them

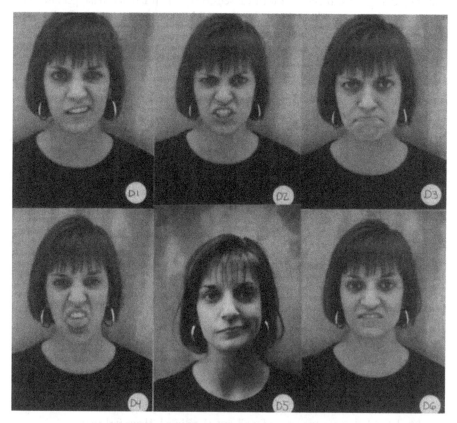

FIGURE 11.8. One set of facial expressions offered as choices for how to react to various types of offense. Faces D1 and D5 represent contempt, D2 and D3 represent anger, and D4 and D6 represent disgust. Some participants viewed these European American faces, whereas others saw a set of Indian or Japanese faces. From Rozin et al. (1999).

verbal labels (Rozin et al., 2005), they typically chose an angry facial expression for the autonomy violations, a disgust expression for the divinity/purity violations, and a contemptuous expression for community violations (Rozin et al., 1999). In this section we will consider evidence regarding anger as a distinct emotion, and in the next section we will consider disgust.

How is anger measured? Several reliable and valid self-report questionnaires are available. The Multidimensional Anger Inventory (Siegel, 1986) includes items capturing appraisals that lead to anger, angry feelings, and the resulting behavior, each of which is important for assessing overall anger-proneness (Martin, Watson, & Wan, 2000). The Spielberger State–Trait Anger Expression Inventory focuses largely on intense, somewhat destructive kinds of anger (STAXI; Spielberger, 1991; Spielberger et al., 1983). Like the State–Trait Anxiety Inventory discussed earlier, the STAXI can be used to distinguish between current, state feelings of anger and chronic anger-proneness. Another instrument concentrates on people's ability to handle anger in helpful ways. The Constructive Anger Behavior-Verbal Style scale consists of items that can be filled out either as a self-report or by an observer or interviewer, who presumably provides a less biased account (Davidson et al., 2000). Generally, people with high scores on this inventory handle stressful situations well and keep their anger under control.

Paul Ekman and colleagues found that people throughout the world easily recognize a prototypical angry face (Ekman et al., 1987). Although angry expressions range from mild to intense, and vary across people, situations, and cultures, some action units are often seen (Elfenbein et al., 2007). Angry people often push their eyebrows down and toward the middle of their forehead, and they may raise their eyelids to show more of the eye as well. Their lower eyelids pull up and toward the inner corner of the eyes, and lips tighten and/or press together. Figure 11.9 shows a few examples. Tone of voice changes as well, in ways other can easily recognize. In a recent meta-analysis, more than 85% of participants representing dozens of cultures accurately recognized nonverbal vocal bursts of anger produced by earlier participants (Laukka & Elfenbein, 2021).

The physiological state that accompanies anger resembles that of fear in many ways, but there is one consistent difference. Whereas in fear the blood vessels leading to the extremities (i.e., hands and feet) constrict, making your fingers icy, they are more likely to expand in anger, keeping your hands warm (Cacioppo et al., 2000; Kreibig, 2010). Anger also differs from fear in terms of brain activity, particularly in the frontal cortex. During

FIGURE 11.9. Facial expressions of anger vary across individuals, situations, and cultures, but common elements can be seen.

most negative emotions, including fear, the right-hemisphere frontal cortex is more active than the left. The opposite is true for positive emotions, generally speaking (Wacker et al., 2008). Although this asymmetry was long thought to reflect the valence of emotion, researchers now agree that it reflects motivational direction instead. As discussed earlier in this text, in approach motivation one's impulse is to move toward a stimulus; in avoidance motivation, one's impulse is to retreat. As a rule, we move toward positive stimuli and away from aversive ones. However, anger appears to be an exception. Several studies have indicated that when people are angry, they show greater frontal cortical activity on the left than on the right—the approach pattern (Harmon-Jones & Allen, 1998; Wacker, Heldmann, & Stemmler, 2003). This is especially the case when people believe they will have the opportunity to do something about their anger, such as approach whoever is causing the problem (Harmon-Jones et al., 2003). This is consistent with the notion that anger is more likely than fear to involve a sense of agency and control.

The Functions of Anger

Although people often think of anger as destructive, it can serve an important interpersonal function. A constructive display of anger on your part tells the person with whom you are interacting, "Hey, I did not appreciate that! Don't do it again!" According to the recalibrational theory of anger (Sell et al., 2017), we experience anger when we appraise someone's behavior toward us as failing to take our welfare sufficiently into account. In other words, they have not treated us with the respect and consideration we feel we deserve. Expressing anger communicates that you expect to be treated better. Someone who is reasonably perceptive will detect your irritation, apologize, understand you better, and avoid similar acts in the future. The interchange can improve your relationship (Kassinove et al., 1997; Tafrate et al., 2002). People confer power and status on people who express moderate amounts of anger (Tiedens, 2001), and people who express mild anger in negotiations tend to get more of what they want (Van Kleef, De Dreu, & Manstead, 2004). Anger lets people know your limits and demands.

However, the gains linked to anger may come at a cost. Expressing anger to a romantic partner damages the loving relationship. Also, someone on the receiving end of your angry display may retaliate later, if given a chance. Participants in two studies who had been on the receiving end of a research confederate's anger during negotiation did make greater compromises. When given the opportunity to decide whether the opponent would have to do pleasant or unpleasant tasks in the "next study," however, partners of angry opponents assigned them more unpleasant tasks (Wang, Northcraft, & Van Kleef, 2012). Also, if you express anger in a negotiation, your opponent had better believe that you mean it. If your partner thinks you are faking anger to get your way, he or she will likely become even more demanding (Côté, Hideg, & Van Kleef, 2013).

A group of several extremely clever studies suggests that when we are angry we prioritize our own perspective more strongly than that of an interaction partner (Yip & Schweitzer, 2019; see Figure 11.10). In one study, participants who lived on the East Coast of the United States were randomly assigned to vividly remember a personal experience in which they felt either angry or emotionally neutral. They were then asked to send an email proposing possible times for a meeting—with someone in California, where the time is three hours earlier. The dependent variable: whether the proposed times were expressed in the earlier time zone. Among participants in the anger condition,

FIGURE 11.10. You are supposed to tell the person on the other side of the chess board to move a piece to their left. Do you say "move the piece to the right" reflecting your own visual perspective, or "move the piece to the left," acknowledging theirs? People who are angry are less likely to take the other person's perspective.

52% bothered to translate the proposed times into the Pacific time zone, as compared with 72% in the neutral control condition. Other studies found similar effects of angry versus neutral feelings on explaining which way to move a chess piece to someone on the opposite side of the table from you (32% versus 52% explained from the other person's perspective); and whether the number in front of the person facing you is 16 or 91 (21% versus 42%). Neither sadness nor disgust showed these effects.

Notably, as we have seen in several other studies throughout this textbook, the effect of anger could be eliminated by drawing participants' attention to their emotional state before they did the task—in this case by telling people that the anger stimulus (a video of a person yelling at a store clerk) makes most people angry, and asking participants to give one word for how the video made *them* feel. This suggests not only that we can override automatic cognitive effects of emotion, once aware of them, but also that participants were otherwise probably unaware that the perspective-altering effect was happening. If you are trying to get someone else to understand a situation from your point of view, it's plausibly better if you see it that way yourself. However, it can also be useful in negotiation to understand whether the other person is coming from. If anger interferes with that, best to be aware of it.

Anger and Aggression

What do you *do* when you are angry? Anger can facilitate a variety of behaviors, including rejecting the person who angered you, complaining about or protesting against their actions, and even prosocial behaviors such as helping other people (Van Doorn, Zeelenberg,

& Breugelmans, 2014). Much research has emphasized aggression, including physical aggression, as a common behavioral outcome of anger. However, not all anger leads to aggression, and not all aggression begins with anger. Across all cultures that have been studied, people report feeling angry far more often than they ever consider turning to violence (Ramirez et al., 2002). Moreover, people often aggress against others for reasons that have nothing to do with anger. Psychologists distinguish between hostile and instrumental aggression. **Hostile aggression** is motivated by anger, with the specific intent to hurt someone. **Instrumental aggression** is harmful or threatening behavior used purely to obtain something or achieve some end; examples include bullying, theft, warfare, and killing prey. Much of human aggression is instrumental. For example, social psychologists have found that many normal, healthy, well-intentioned people will inflict pain and suffering on someone they've never met, possibly even endanger that person's life, if an authority figure tells them to (Blass, 2009; Milgram, 1974). Warfare is the most obvious example. Aggression and anger are related, but it would be a mistake to assume that they are synonymous.

One problem in studying aggressive behavior is that overt fighting is rare even when people are very angry. For that matter, it would be unethical to set up situations in which people might actually hurt each other. A clever way to get around these problems is to set up situations in which people *think* they are hurting someone, although in fact they are not. Imagine yourself in this experiment (Berman, Gladue, & Taylor, 1993): you have a discussion with someone you've never met before and don't expect to meet again, and this person repeatedly belittles and insults you. Then the two of you are put into separate rooms, and you are told to teach this person something. You should periodically test that person's performance and signal an error by pressing a button to deliver an electric shock. You get to choose among buttons to determine the intensity of that shock.

At least, you *think* you are delivering shocks; in fact, the other person is a confederate of the researcher, and there are no shocks. The point of the experiment is to find out how intense a shock you choose, measuring your tendency toward aggressive behavior without allowing an actual attack. In a similar task, people can press a button to take points or money away from another participant (Moe, King, & Bailly, 2004).

Psychologists have developed many variations of these tasks, but all of them are subject to certain limitations, including these:

- The rules authorize, even require, people to commit an aggressive act.
- The participants are strangers to each other, with no previous relationship and no expectation of a future one.
- The target of the aggressive act is not visible.
- In many cases, the target of the aggression has no opportunity to retaliate.
- The two people have no way to interact with each other except for the designated aggressive act.
- We can't be sure the aggressive act depends on anger. Maybe the motive is competition rather than hostility.

In short, typical laboratory methods of producing aggressive behavior are unlike typical aggression (Ritter & Eslea, 2005). Often psychologists learn a great deal from laboratory procedures that seem distant from the events of the real world, so we should not dismiss this type of research as irrelevant. Still, we should be aware of its limitations.

Individual Differences: Who Benefits from Being Angry?

Individual differences in anger-proneness are striking. Around the world, men report more intense feelings and frequent expressions of anger than women (Fischer et al., 2004). Powerful people express more anger, and men who express anger are assumed to have higher social status than men who express sadness (Sloan, 2004; Tiedens, 2001). Each of these patterns is consistent with the claim that anger depends in part on appraisals of power or control.

We noted earlier that expressing anger can sometimes bring benefits, in terms of influencing others and getting what you want. An important caveat, however, is that the benefits of anger expression are more apparent for men than for women. When a man expresses anger and it is perceived as genuine, people tend to assume that the situation elicited his emotion and that it's justified. When a woman expresses the same emotion, people are more likely to make dispositional attributions—that she is an "angry person" or lacking in self-control (e.g., Brescoll & Uhlmann, 2008). This has consequences, particularly in workplace settings. In one series of studies Jessica Salerno and colleagues (2018) asked participants to watch oral closing statements in a trial, made by lawyers who were either male or female, and who made the statement in either an angry or a neutral voice, but were identical in terms of content. Participants were then asked how inclined they would be to hire the lawyer.

Angry male lawyers were perceived as dominant and having conviction in their argument, leading to greater inclination to hire them relative to neutral-affect men. In contrast, angry women were *less* likely than neutral-affect women to be hired, and these decisions were based on perceptions of the angry woman lawyer as "shrill" and "obnoxious." (We know—*argh*!) Fortunately, evidence suggests that the gender bias in how anger is perceived can be eliminated if the situational justification for women's anger is made very clear (e.g., Brescoll & Uhlmann, 2008). For anyone, communicating clearly why you are angry, why your anger is reasonable, and what you want from your interaction partner may be part of a constructive anger episode.

DISGUST

Learning Objectives

- Summarize the elicitors and theorized adaptive function(s) of disgust, differentiating core and moral disgust and analyzing their relationship to each other.
- Analyze the link between individual differences in disgust-proneness and political orientation.

The term "disgust" reflects a combination of the Latin prefix *dis-*, meaning apart from or (in modern usage) the opposite of, and *gustare*, meaning "to taste." Disgust has been defined as "revulsion at the prospect of oral incorporation of offensive objects" (Rozin & Fallon, 1987, p. 23). The facial expression recognized cross-culturally as communicating disgust (see Figure 11.11) reflects this, including a nose wrinkle that narrows the nasal passages as well as upper lip and tongue movements that facilitate getting something out of your mouth (Ekman et al., 1987). Disgust entails a desire to stay away from something physically, but it is also a rejection of the mere thought of the object. Paul Rozin and colleagues have suggested that an item becomes disgusting if it reminds us of our animal

FIGURE 11.11. The prototypical facial expression of disgust narrows the nasal passages and expels contents from the mouth, reducing the risk of contamination through breathing or eating.

nature (Rozin & Fallon, 1987; Rozin et al., 1999). That is, we like to think of ourselves as noble, clean, and pure. The sight of intestines, feces, or blood reminds us of the most unclean aspects of our existence. Animals in general evoke disgust when they urinate and defecate in public, have sex in public, and in other ways do the things that we like to hide about ourselves.

People show marked individual differences in disgust-proneness. Researchers have developed a self-report Disgust Scale that assesses intensity of disgust toward several different categories of elicitors (Haidt et al., 1994). Another instrument, the Perceived Vulnerability to Disease questionnaire, measures people's subjective discomfort around possible sources of germs, as well as beliefs about how susceptible one is to infection (Duncan, Schaller, & Park, 2009). Disgust expression intensity shows a high correlation (+.45) with the personality trait *Neuroticism* (Druschel & Sherman, 1999). That term, which is easily misunderstood, does not mean mental illness; it refers instead to a tendency to experience unpleasant emotions relatively easily. In other words, people prone to disgust are also prone to sadness and anxiety. Disgust also shows a negative correlation (–.28) with the personality trait *Openness to Experience*—the tendency to explore new opportunities, such as trying new or unusual types of foods, art, music, literature, and so forth (Druschel & Sherman, 1999).

The physiological profile associated with disgust is more complicated than that of fear or anger (Kreibig, 2010). On the one hand, people exposed to videos, photographs, and smells eliciting contamination-focused disgust show signs consistent with increased sympathetic nervous system activity: increased heart rate and blood pressure; fast, shallow breathing; and increased skin conductance caused by sweating. On the other hand, people also show clear signs of increased vagal parasympathetic influence on the heart (i.e., increased respiratory sinus arrhythmia). The electrical rhythm of the stomach is also disturbed, with waves generated by muscle contraction slowing down (bradygastria; Meissner, Muth, & Herbert, 2011). Not surprisingly, these effects have been linked to nausea and vomiting as well as disgust (Kreibig, 2010; Meissner et al., 2011).

One important twist is that different kinds of disgusting stimuli evoke different responses. A list of disgust elicitors studied by Jonathan Haidt and colleagues (1994) included violations of the human body such as gore, mutilation, surgery, and dead bodies as well as sources of contamination. Gory images evoke some of the same physiological changes as contamination-focused disgust, but heart rate slows down rather than speeding up (Shenhav & Mendes, 2014; Kreibig, 2010). Notably, a sharp drop in heart rate and blood pressure is characteristic of blood-phobic people just before they faint (Öst, Sterner, & Lindahl, 1984). Amitai Shenhav and Wendy Mendes (2014) have suggested that these differing physiological patterns may indicate qualitatively distinct emotional responses, despite researchers' and laypeople's use of the term "disgust" to describe both.

It should come as no surprise by now to learn that researchers have not identified a "disgust area of the brain." There is, however, one structure that becomes particularly active during disgust. Researchers have found that smelling disgusting scents and viewing other people's disgust expressions both activate a brain area called the anterior insular cortex, or simply the insula (Phillips et al., 1997; Wicker et al., 2003). This effect is magnified among people who are highly disgust-prone (Mataix-Cols et al., 2008). We introduced the insula in Chapter 6. The link between the insula and disgust is interesting because this structure is also the primary receptive area of the cortex for the sense of taste. However, insula activity is not specific to emotion (or taste), and among emotions, it is not limited to disgust. Another fMRI study found that the insular cortex showed increased activity not only when people looked at disgusting pictures (vomit, maggots, dirty toilet, a man eating a grasshopper), but also when they looked at frightening pictures (lions, pistols, fire, car accidents). The amygdala also responded strongly to both kinds of pictures (Schienle et al., 2002). The insular cortex becomes more active when people are aware of their visceral sensations, such as heartbeat, as well as gastric feelings. So, the insular cortex is activated in disgust, but perhaps also in any psychological states involving perception of physical change.

The Functions of Disgust

The adaptive value of disgust is apparent: revulsion at the prospect of contact with someone's feces, or eating contaminated, moldy, or rotting food—what has been called **core disgust**—clearly protects our health. Yet people around the world may find completely different substances disgusting. Consider this quote: "Served on toast points, stag beetle larvae are superb. They have a nutty flavor. The head capsules impart a subtle crunchy touch, while the thorax and abdomen have a delicately chewy texture" (Boyle, 1992, p. 101). Now that you know how delicious they are, would you like to try them? No? Why not? What if they are cooked thoroughly, to kill any pathogens they might be carrying? Although insects and their larvae are important sources of protein in many places around the world, most people in Western cultures can think of them only as sources of disease. In contrast, the undercooked meat (e.g., medium rare steak) and cheese that many Westerners savor are considered thoroughly revolting in some other cultures. As with fear and anger, many of our disgust responses are learned, reflecting conditioned associations and cultural ideas about what is and is not edible at least as much as direct sensory experience.

Humans live in more varied parts of the world than almost any other animal species, and we subsist on a remarkably wide range of foods. Our ancestors could not rely on a fixed, inherited list of foods for their diet—they had to be flexible and willing to try new things as they entered new environments. However, the environment is also full of toxins that must be avoided, and like nutritious foods, these vary from place to place. Some general guidelines appear to be innate; newborn babies smile in response to sweet tastes and show dislike of bitter tastes (Steiner et al., 2001), and as we noted in Chapter 2, fats have universal appeal. Yet humans begin to learn which specific foods should and should not be eaten from an early age (Turner & Thompson, 2013). Even before birth, the fetus forms taste templates based on molecules absorbed from the mother's diet, and the new baby will continue to learn which flavors to like from its mother's breast milk (Mennella, Jagnow, & Beauchamp, 2001).

From early childhood, most people then show *food neophobia*, a general aversion to unfamiliar foods and tastes (Pliner & Salvy, 2006). On the one hand, with several safe exposures to a new food—even a bitter one such as coffee, a moldy one such as blue cheese, or a horrible-smelling one, such as the fruit durian—can become palatable or even deeply enjoyed. On the other hand, people will develop a powerful disgust response after a single experience of vomiting after eating a certain food (Logue, 1985). Our bodies firmly label a food "dangerous" after a single experience with contamination (Rozin & Kalat, 1971). One of us (MNS) used to love escargot, but after a single miserable experience can no longer even think of eating them.

Our instinct for disease avoidance is so strong, and negative experiences are so lasting, that people show signs of superstitious or "magical" thinking regarding contamination (Rozin, Millman, & Nemeroff, 1986). For example, people are less willing to take a bite from a piece of chocolate that is shaped like dog feces than from one shaped like a muffin, although they are told explicitly that both are made from the same substance, and have enjoyed eating a small bar of the same chocolate. Suppose a researcher dunks a cockroach in apple juice and asks you whether you would be willing to drink the juice (see Figure 11.12). Would you do it?

FIGURE 11.12.   Would you drink apple juice from a cup holding a cockroach, if the roach had been thoroughly sterilized before being placed in the cup?

If not, why not? What if the experimenter assures you that the cockroach has been thoroughly sterilized and has no germs? For most people this would make no difference—the very idea of a cockroach coming into contact with their food will make them reject it.

Moral Disgust

Beyond core disgust, people also use the term "disgust" more broadly in abstract, sometimes culture-specific ways related to morality (Haidt et al., 1997). To map the full meaning of this term, Jonathan Haidt and colleagues (1997) began by asking 20 people to describe all the intensely disgusting experiences they could remember. The researchers then grouped those experiences into these categories:

- Bad-tasting foods;
- Body products such as feces, urine, and nose mucus;
- Unacceptable sexual acts, such as incest;
- Gore, surgery, and other exposure of the inner body parts;
- Sociomoral violations such as Nazis, drunk drivers, hypocrites, and ambulance-chasing lawyers;
- Insects, spiders, snakes, and other repulsive animals;
- Dirt and germs; and
- Contact with dead bodies.

People who report strong disgust toward one of these also tend to be more disgusted by the others, with one exception: disgust ratings about drunk drivers, hypocrites, and other "sociomoral violations" do not correlate as highly with the other kinds of events (Haidt et al., 1994). One possibility is that when we say we are disgusted by some immoral act, we really mean that we feel anger or contempt (Marzillier & Davey, 2004).

An alternative is to distinguish two types of disgust: core disgust, which relates to the idea of physical contamination, and **moral disgust**, which relates to violations of a moral code. Studies suggest that these two may be closely related, despite their differences. Core disgust-proneness is correlated most strongly with negative judgments about violations in purity-related moral domains, and less so with violations of other domains such as authority, loyalty, and fairness (Wagemans, Brandt, & Zeelenberg, 2018). People display similar facial expressions when they taste something bitter; look at photos of feces, insects, and the like; and are treated with gross unfairness in an economic game (Chapman et al., 2009). Moreover, meta-analysis results show that people rate moral transgressions as more disgusting after they have just been exposed to a core disgust stimulus, such as a nasty odor or a used tissue (Landy & Goodwin, 2015). Thus, our moral disgust responses may be an extension of core disgust to facilitate rejection of "impurity" in the social and moral domain (Chapman & Anderson, 2013).

How could this have happened? The findings above suggest that moral disgust might be an exaptation of core disgust—a repurposing of the more ancient emotional response for a new function (we introduced the term "exaptation" in Chapter 2). Roger Giner-Sorolla and colleagues have suggested that whereas core disgust serves the intrapersonal function of keeping pathogens out of our bodies, moral disgust serves the interpersonal function of communicating our virtuousness to other people. Their research finds that we expect people to express disgust when they hear about an immoral act, both verbally and nonverbally through facial expression, as long as they were not personally harmed by

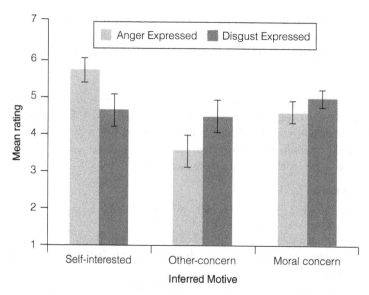

FIGURE 11.13. Participants in this study imagined overhearing an emotional rant by a colleague, without understanding exactly what the conversation was about. Participants were more likely to infer the speaker's concern for another person's welfare when the speaker expressed disgust rather than anger; the reverse was true for assumptions about the speaker's self-interest. From Kupfer & Giner-Sorolla (2017).

that act (Kupfer & Giner-Sorolla, 2017; see Figure 11.13). If they *were* personally harmed by the act, we expect them to express anger instead. Moreover, people report feeling stronger disgust in response to hypothetical situations where an actor's intent was bad. When the outcome was bad, but not the intent, anger is more likely (Giner-Sorolla & Chapman, 2017). An important limitation is that most of the experimental research on moral disgust has been done in Western countries; a strong case for adaptive function requires richer cross-cultural data. However, the proposal that feeling and expressing moral disgust may serve as a form of **virtue signaling**—advertising us as norm-following, trustworthy, valuable social partners—offers a good foundation for experimental hypotheses, so expect more studies building on these ideas.

Individual Differences: Political Orientation
People vary quite a bit in disgust-proneness, and this variability can be predicted by a number of factors. Up to about 12 or 18 months of age, young children will put almost anything into their mouths, and unless it tastes bad they will chew it and swallow it (Rozin et al., 1986). As children grow older, they begin to reject foods they believe might be dangerous, and still later reject foods because of the very idea of contamination (Rozin, Fallon, & Augustoni-Ziskind, 1985). On average, women are more disgust-prone than men (Al-Shawaf, Lewis, & Buss, 2018). Heritability studies also suggest a genetic component to disgust sensitivity, finding that approximately 50% of individual differences can be accounted for by genetic relatedness (Sherlock et al., 2016).

One interesting, and controversial, body of research has asked whether individual differences in disgust are linked to liberal versus conservative political ideology. In the

United States and some other Western countries, individuals who are more politically conservative tend to hold stricter norms regarding sexual and bodily purity (e.g., Graham, Haidt, & Nosek, 2009). Consistent with this, the results of large studies have linked political conservatism to overall disgust-proneness (Inbar et al., 2012). Other researchers have pointed out, however, that studies documenting this effect have often used disgust measures emphasizing sociomoral behaviors that are especially objectionable by conservative standards (e.g., drug use, disturbing a church service), rather than behaviors that are objectionable by liberal standards. In one set of studies with participants from both Germany and the United States, no significant relationship appeared between political conservatism and a disgust sensitivity questionnaire that was elicitor-neutral (Elad-Strenger, Proch, & Kessler, 2020). Moreover, political conservatism was *negatively* correlated with self-reported disgust after reading hypothetical scenarios involving tax evasion, environmental pollution, and other actions that are considered especially immoral by liberals. However, the same studies consistently showed positive correlations (of around $r = .15-.20$) between political conservatism and *core* disgust. Although the theoretical implications of this complicated pattern have yet to be fully resolved, these studies highlight the importance of looking closely at the measures used in any study, and interpreting study results based on a careful analysis of the measures' content.

SADNESS

Learning Objectives

- Summarize the theorized adaptive function of sadness, and analyze the empirical evidence on cognitive/appraisal, biological, and behavioral (e.g., crying) aspects of this emotion.
- Describe gender- and age-related individual differences in susceptibility to sadness.

In the Pixar movie *Inside Out*, the emotions of Joy, Fear, Anger, Disgust, and Sadness are all characters living inside the head of a young girl named Riley, who has just moved to a new city, leaving her friends and old life behind. Joy is the leader of the pack, keeping Riley—and all the other emotions—energized and full of purpose. Fear, Anger, and Disgust have important jobs as well. Fear is responsible for keeping Riley safe, figuring out (and presumably preventing) all the things that could go wrong on Riley's first day at school. Disgust is responsible for making sure Riley is cool—that she doesn't do anything that will make other kids look down on her or reject her. Anger's job is to make sure Riley stands up for herself.

Sadness is different. Sadness is a downer. Even Joy can't figure what use Sadness could be, and instructs her to stay inside a chalk "sadness circle" so she can't contaminate Riley's day. Although this is a movie, real-life emotion researchers have been perplexed by the function of sadness as well.

According to Richard Lazarus (1991), **sadness** is a response to the experience of irrevocable loss. We can easily recognize sadness in others, which also makes it easy to measure in the laboratory. People can report on their own sadness, and there is little ambiguity in what this term means in the English language. People also express sadness nonverbally in a variety of ways. Ekman and colleagues (1987) found that more than

70% of people around the world recognize a prototypical facial expression of sadness. Recognition is facilitated when people are crying (Provine, Krosnowski, & Brocato, 2009; see Figure 11.14). Crying often causes the whites of the eyes to turn red, and red eyes add to the appearance of sadness (Provine, Nave-Blodgett, & Cabrera, 2013). Sad and depressed people also tend to show slumped posture, and to move more slowly than usual (Michalak et al., 2009). People recognize nonverbal vocal expressions of sadness at high rates as well—meta-analysis results suggest mean accuracy rates of nearly 90% across dozens of cultures (Laukka & Elfenbein, 2021).

Physiologically, sadness is associated with two patterns of response (Kreibig, 2010). In one pattern arousal increases, with signs of sympathetic nervous system activation such as increased heart rate, blood pressure, and skin conductance. This pattern is more likely when people are actually crying, and when they are watching a video showing a loss that is about to happen (e.g., a person talking with a dying family member) rather than a loss that has already taken place. The other pattern is essentially the opposite, including reduced heart rate and skin conductance. This pattern is seen more often when participants are not crying and/or when they are watching a film about a loss that has already taken place. What are we to make of this difference? One possibility is that sadness has a time course, changing in nature from the threat of an upcoming loss to the certainty of irrevocable loss (Kreibig, 2010). When the loss has not yet happened, our bodies may be activating in an effort to prevent it, but afterward it is best to withdraw and conserve energy. Another possibility is that the high-arousal profile is experienced primarily in response to social losses, the low-arousal profile in response to failures and material losses. However, these ideas have not yet been systematically teased apart in research, so future studies are needed to specify the predictors of each physiological profile.

At the trait level it's difficult to think of sadness without thinking of pathology. The questionnaire most commonly used to measure individual differences in sadness is

FIGURE 11.14. The facial and postural expression of sadness is easily recognized, especially when someone is crying.

actually a measure of depressive symptoms—the Beck Depression Inventory (Beck, Steer, & Carbin, 1988). We have argued, however, that emotions evolved because they enhanced our ancestors' adaptive fitness in some way, so sadness must have some useful function. Let's consider this problem.

The Functions of Sadness

To understand the value of sadness, it's helpful to think about when we experience it and see whether that helps makes sense of what we know about the emotion and its effects. Situations that commonly elicit intense sadness include romantic breakups, the death of a loved one, loneliness and isolation, failure at an important goal, and the stress of having more to get done than you can possibly cope with (Keller & Nesse, 2006). The first three situations involve the loss or absence of an important person, on whom you used to depend for affection and social support. Feelings of connectedness are crucial for humans, as for our primate relatives. These feelings are based in our species' intense sociality, and our ancestors' reliance on families and groups to complete tasks addressing many basic survival needs. When we lose one or more members of our inner support circle, it is a big deal from an evolutionary standpoint.

Failures are another kind of serious loss. If you have invested time and energy in some endeavor, it probably means the outcome of that endeavor is important for your well-being. The stress of overextension is likely linked to this threat—if you are struggling to do far more than is possible given available time and resources, you risk failing at some part of it, at least. Failing is not a good outcome, and depending on what the endeavor was, you may have to come up with a new game plan for anything from starting a project over again to figuring out how to pay the mortgage and put food on the table for your family. In addition to the resource and/or opportunity loss that failure often entails, there is a risk of social loss. People who succeed are liked and admired, and accorded higher social status (Hogan & Hogan, 1991). When we fail, we risk losing face both with those we love and with the wider community.

When we experience a major loss, what do we need to do? Some have argued that it is crucial to call on supportive relationship partners who may be available and let them know that you need help (Frijda, 1986; Keller & Nesse, 2006). Sad behavior—especially crying—brings other people to us and elicits their sympathy and concern (Hill & Martin, 1997; Sheeber et al., 1998; Zickfeld et al., 2021). This aspect of sadness may be more prominent for social losses than for failures (Keller & Nesse, 2006), but people also cry in response to failure, criticism, and physical pain (Vingerhoets et al., 1997). Thus, one function of sadness may be to elicit others' support in times of need.

In one set of studies testing this hypothesis, researcher Ad Vingerhoets and colleagues showed participants in the Netherlands and the United States photos of people who were crying. In one condition, participants saw photos in which the actual tears had been digitally removed, leaving only the facial expression; in the other condition, tears were still visible. Targets whose tears showed were perceived as needing more social support, and evoked stronger ratings of sympathy, sense of emotional connection, and willingness to help from participants, relative to targets not displaying tears (Vingerhoets et al., 2016). In another study, researchers instructed some marketing students to express sadness during a negotiation for points with another person; other students were instructed to remain emotionally neutral. Those who expressed sadness got more points in the negotiation, but only under specific circumstances: when the negotiation partner believed the sad person was starting from a disadvantaged position in terms of bargaining power/financial position, *and* when the partner anticipated interacting with the sad person again in the future (Sinaceur et al., 2015). These findings are consistent with the proposal that displays of sadness communicate need for help and kindness, thereby evoking support from others—especially if there's potential for the support to be reciprocated in the future.

To the extent that our own actions may have contributed to the events causing sadness, we also must try to determine what went wrong to avoid causing a similar catastrophe in the future (Keller & Nesse, 2006; Watson & Andrews, 2002). Ruminating excessively on negative events is problematic—people who think perseveratively about their problems, losses, and failures are more likely to become and remain depressed (Nolen-Hoeksema, 1991). However, an effort to analyze the situation thoughtfully may help us make better decisions next time. This aspect of sadness may be more important when we have experienced a failure or loss of material resources (Keller & Nesse, 2006), but our behaviors can affect social losses as well—for example, have you ever found yourself wondering what you could have done differently after a romantic breakup?

A strong body of research suggests that when people are in a sad mood, they process information more carefully and systematically (Forgas, 2017). For example, when compared with angry people, sad people rely less on cognitive shortcuts, such as stereotypes in perceiving new social targets and heuristics in processing persuasive messages (e.g., relying on the superficial credibility of the person delivering the message rather than the message content; Bodenhausen, Sheppard, & Kramer, 1994). People in a sad mood are also less likely to show a false memory effect, in which they report having seen a word related conceptually to several others on a list they were given to remember (e.g., *sleep* as related to *pillow*, *bed*, and *dream*), although the word was not actually on the list (Storbeck & Clore, 2005). Sadness may make us more careful with our relationships as well; in two studies, researchers found that unlike amusement, which tended to make participants more selfish in a resource-allocation game, sad participants tended to distribute the resources more fairly (Tan & Forgas, 2010). Although in sadness we have lost something, we are motivated to be more careful with what (and whom) we have left.

Does Crying Make You Feel Better?

Popular psychology sometimes recommends that when you are really upset about something, the best thing to do is let it all out—experience your feelings and express them to their fullest (Figure 11.15). This strategy dates back to Freud's idea of **catharsis**—the release of strong emotions by expressing them. The idea is that the emotions are trapped inside you and must come out somehow. Perhaps you have been encouraged to "have a good cry" or "get it out of your system" by a loved one when you were going through a hard time. Does crying actually make us feel better?

The evidence on this is mixed. In surveys people say that they feel better after crying, but in laboratories people typically report feeling *worse* after crying than they did before (e.g., Kraemer & Hastrup, 1988; Rottenberg et al., 2002). In particular, people who are prone to depression are more likely to feel worse after they cry (Rottenberg et al., 2008). What might explain this discrepancy? One possible explanation involves time. In most studies mood is measured before and then immediately after crying, but in one study

FIGURE 11.15.   Freud originally proposed that expressing your feelings would get them out of your system and make you feel better. Research tells a more complicated story.

participants were asked to report on their mood again 90 minutes later. Although the people who described themselves as frequent criers did indeed feel worse right after crying, while watching a sad film, they reported feeling better in the later assessment (Gracanin et al., 2015). Perhaps the beneficial effects of crying simply take a while to emerge. Social context may be important as well. A study of more than 1,000 crying episodes reported by Dutch women in daily diaries found that the women felt better after crying in about 30% of the episodes (they felt worse afterward in 10% of episodes; the same in about 60% of episodes), and that this outcome was most likely when one other person was present, and when the situation improved after crying (Bylsma et al., 2011).

   A few words of caution are in order. First, a great deal of this research has been done with women (who report crying far more often than men), so the question of which findings generalize to men is still open. Also, few studies attempt to randomly assign participants to crying versus noncrying conditions. You might instruct someone *not* to cry, of course, but any differences between cry and don't-cry conditions may reflect the effort of suppressing crying, rather than effects of crying per se. However, the data on emotional effects of crying are fairly consistent with those on the social effects of crying. In one study, researchers collected reports from thousands of people in 35 countries of the most recent time when they cried, how crying affected their mood, and several features of the situation (Bylsma, Vingerhoets, & Rottenberg, 2008). Results showed that crying was most likely to lead to improved feelings when it evoked social support from others, such as comforting words, touch, or other kind behaviors.

Individual Differences: Aging and Loss

Less is known about individual differences in sadness than about other negative emotions, but some evidence exists. As with depression, women around the world are more likely to report and express sadness than men (Choti et al., 1987; Fischer et al., 2004). The appraisal associated with sadness involves low levels of control (Scherer, 1997), and expressing sadness conveys vulnerability, so this is consistent with typical gender roles in which men are expected to be more powerful.

A particularly interesting individual difference in sadness relates to aging. Although the frequency of negative emotions, including sadness, generally declines as people age (Carstensen et al., 2000), people in their 60s and beyond report more intense feelings of sadness in response to stimuli such as films depicting a character's social loss (Kunzmann & Grühn, 2005; Seider et al., 2011). Moreover, although physiological reactivity during emotion tends to become more muted as people age, older adults have been found to show greater physiological responses to sad films than do young adults (Seider et al., 2011), and periods of arousal are more tightly correlated with bursts of sad feelings than is the case for young adults (Lohani, Payne, & Isaacowitz, 2018). To use our terminology from Chapter 2, sadness-related coherence among aspects of emotion appears to increase with aging. These age effects do not extend to other negative emotions, such as disgust.

Why might this be? There are a few possible explanations. One is that as we age, we have more experience with losses and are better able to understand their significance. This explanation suggests that age brings changes in loss-related appraisals. Another possibility is that loss has more serious consequences for older adults, whose social networks typically become smaller over time, so sadness is felt more intensely. Either way, the age-related increase in sadness intensity is not necessarily bad. Among older adults, but not middle-age or young adults, the intensity of sadness in the lab is associated with higher levels of psychological well-being (Haase et al., 2012). At this stage of life, the ability to connect with others through sadness may be especially important.

We don't want to give away the end of the movie *Inside Out*, but suffice to say that after many hair-raising adventures, Joy does come to appreciate the important role sadness plays in young Riley's emotional life, especially as she copes with the loss of her old friends and familiar world. We hope that you will keep a place for sadness in your heart as well.

EMBARRASSMENT, SHAME, AND GUILT

Learning Objectives

- Compare and contrast the elicitors, functions, behavioral implications, and interpersonal effects of embarrassment, shame, and guilt.
- Analyze cross-cultural similarities and differences in the elicitors and meaning of shame.

People typically feel happy, sad, frightened, angry, disgusted, or surprised about things that happen to them or in the environment around them. The events that elicit these emotions happen out there in the world. In contrast, the last emotions we consider in this chapter all reflect an appraisal of the self. You feel embarrassed, ashamed, or guilty if you have fallen short of expectations in your own or others' eyes. These experiences require appraisals of yourself and how you appear to others, rather than how events in the world impact on you. For this reason, they are often referred to as **self-conscious emotions.** Embarrassment, shame, and guilt have much in common. They feel bad, they reflect the belief that we have done something undesirable, and they make us want to hide or withdraw in some way. Yet they differ in intriguing and consequential ways as well.

The Functions of Embarrassment, Shame, and Guilt

Researchers generally agree that embarrassment, shame, and guilt all serve related functions: they help us to repair relationships we may have damaged through some mistake or transgression (Keltner et al., 1997; Tangney et al., 1996). Should we consider these distinct emotions, or are they just different words for the same thing? Several researchers have tried to tease apart their causes, characteristics, and interpersonal effects. One way to do this is simply to ask people when they have felt each of these emotions and see whether different kinds of situations elicit them. In one study, investigators asked US college students to recall a recent experience in which they felt embarrassment, shame, or guilt (Keltner, 1995). The most common experiences associated with embarrassment were the following:

- Poor performance;
- Physical clumsiness (such as tripping or spilling something);
- A cognitive error (such as forgetting an acquaintance's name);
- Inappropriate physical appearance (such as wearing casual clothes when everyone else is dressed formally);
- Failure of privacy (such as accidentally intruding when someone was naked);
- Being teased; and
- Conspicuousness (being the center of attention).

In contrast, the most common experiences associated with shame were as follows:

- Poor performance (as with embarrassment);
- Hurting someone else's feelings;
- Lying;
- Failure to meet other people's expectations (such as getting poor grades in school and thereby disappointing one's parents); and
- Failure to meet one's own expectations.

The following experiences were most commonly associated with guilt:

- Failure to perform one's duties (such as not following through on a promise);
- Lying, cheating, or stealing;
- Neglecting a friend or loved one;
- Hurting someone else's feelings;
- Infidelity to a romantic partner; and
- Breaking a diet.

As you can see, the kinds of experiences that elicit embarrassment, shame, and guilt overlap to some extent. Poor performance is commonly cited as a cause for either embarrassment or shame, and hurting others is a common cause of either shame or guilt. A reasonable conclusion is that embarrassment, shame, and guilt overlap and shade into one another. However, we can also draw some distinctions. Embarrassment need not imply that an individual did something morally wrong. **Embarrassment** occurs most often when someone is suddenly the focus of other people's attention because of an understandable mistake, an accident, or even a positive event that had the misfortune to occur in public. Shame and guilt are most common when one fails to live up to expectations, or does something that hurts someone else. We could draw a further distinction between guilt and regret: if you harm others, you feel guilt. If you harm only yourself, you feel regret (Zeelenberg & Breugelmans, 2008).

These are subjective impressions, created by reading many descriptions of specific events and asking what they have in common. Another way to distinguish among emotions is to examine the nonverbal expressions associated with them, and see how similar versus how different they may be. The facial expression of embarrassment (Figure 11.16) is clearly distinct from the expressions of shame and guilt. When college students examine photos of people expressing embarrassment and shame, they correctly classify the expressions more than half the time (Keltner, 1995). As we saw in Chapter 3, this is even the case in the Orissa Indian culture that uses the same word for the two emotions—*lajya*—as long as the expressions are matched to situations rather than to emotion words (Haidt & Keltner, 1999). People do not, however, distinguish reliably between ashamed and guilty expressions (Keltner, 1995). The expression of shame/guilt includes lowered eyes and hunched posture, similar to the expression of embarrassment. Whereas an

FIGURE 11.16. A prototypical expression of embarrassment.

FIGURE 11.17. The expression of shame/guilt implies a more serious violation than the expression of embarrassment.

embarrassed person might have a little sheepish grin, however, an ashamed person does not smile and may turn down the corners of the mouth (Figure 11.17).

The distinction may have important social implications. In one study, participants read scenarios about people apologizing after being caught in a fairly serious transgression, such as cheating on a test or telling a lie, accompanied by photos of the people showing embarrassed or ashamed expressions. Participants rated the offenders as more sincere in their apology, and said they would be more likely to forgive them, if they displayed shame rather than embarrassment (Thorstenson, Pazda, & Lichtenfield, 2020). A show of embarrassment may suggest that the offender does not actually take the transgression seriously. Moreover, how people interpret an embarrassment display may depend in part on whether they are motivated to cut you some slack. Findings from one study showed that white participants in the United States and Europe perceived the same embarrassment expression as more indicative of actual embarrassment when it was displayed by white rather than ethnically Arab posers (Kommattam, Jonas, & Fischer, 2017). Although it will be important to replicate this effect with different combinations of groups, one possible interpretation is that we are more open to perceiving authentic embarrassment in people we perceive as in-group members.

If the events that elicit shame and guilt are not so different, and their expressions are similar, how do they differ? At least among English-language speakers, the distinction seems to lie in how people interpret the event in question (Tangney et al., 1996). Studies indicate that you are likely to feel shame when you think of yourself as bad or unworthy. Your attribution of the negative event is internal, stable, and global. When people think about times when they felt shame, they say things like, "If only I weren't so stupid." Instead, when they think about times when they felt guilt, they say things like, "If only I hadn't *done* such-and-such" (Niedenthal, Tangney, & Gavanski, 1994). The attribution for the negative event is still internal, but it is more specific to the event and action at hand. This distinction also emerges in self-report measures of shame- and guilt-proneness, in which you read a scenario and then rate how strongly you would feel bad *about yourself* in that situation versus wishing you had *acted differently* (Tangney, 1996). These bad self and bad action ratings are positively correlated, but not so strongly that shame- and guilt-proneness become synonymous (e.g., Covert et al., 2003).

Thus, we can tentatively define **shame** as the emotion felt when one does something wrong and focuses on one's global, stable inadequacies in explaining the transgression. By contrast, you are more likely to feel guilt if you feel badly about a specific action, but not about who you are as a person (Tangney et al., 1996). **Guilt** is the emotion felt when one fails or does something morally wrong, but focuses on how to make amends and how to avoid repeating the transgression. Guilt serves a useful function, even in modern life: it punishes a mistake and motivates efforts to repair the damage (Amodio, Devine, & Harmon-Jones, 2007). As you might guess, people who don't feel much guilt tend to be selfish and inconsiderate of others (Krajbich et al., 2009). Shame is more complicated and, as we shall soon see, is valued quite differently in different cultures.

The Blush of Embarrassment

Researchers know far less about the biological aspects of embarrassment, shame, and guilt than they do about the other negative emotions. However, one physiological reaction stands out: the most distinctive aspect of the embarrassment expression is the **blush,** a temporary increase in blood flow to the face, neck, and upper chest. The blush is a remarkable response. Even if dogs and perhaps a few other species are capable of embarrassment, we're not aware that anyone has ever reported seeing a nonhuman animal blush. If animals do blush, their faces are covered with fur, so presumably other dogs, for example, could not see the response either. Blushing may have arisen specifically during human evolution (Edelmann, 2001).

We do know a bit about when and why people blush. In one study, participants were asked to complete a stressful quiz in the presence of an experimenter, and then did a self-disclosure task while the experimenter either maintained eye contact, wore sunglasses, or left the room. Participants in all conditions blushed during the difficult quiz, consistent with the proposal that anxiety can elicit blushing. During the self-disclosure task, however, only those who maintained eye contact with the experimenter continued to blush, despite reporting lower levels of anxiety than participants in the other conditions (Drummond & Bailey, 2013). This suggests that simply being the focus of others' attention can elicit a blush response.

Evidence does suggest that blushing helps bring people back to our side, even after we have transgressed. In multiple studies across different sets of researchers, participants read short stories about someone who had committed an error, and then were shown a photo of a person posing embarrassment or shame. In some photos, the person also appeared to be blushing; in other photos they were not. Participants rated the blushers in a more favorable way than the nonblushers, rated their apologies as more sincere, and were more likely to forgive them, although the offense was the same (Dijk et al., 2009; Thorstenson et al., 2020).

Individual Differences: Culture and the Meaning of Shame

Shame is among the emotion states that has been studied fairly extensively across cultures, including non-Western cultures. Taken as a whole, findings of this research offer an interesting case study in how an emotional response can have both universal and culturally variable properties. On one hand, studies have documented consistency across cultures in fairly specific appraisals that elicit shame. For example, Daniel Sznycer and colleagues (2016) asked participants in India, Israel, and the United States to read scenarios involving a variety of actions. Some participants were asked to rate how negatively they would view the actor if it were another person; others how ashamed they would feel if they *were* the actor. Within each of the three samples, anticipated feelings of shame for a particular action were predicted by how disapproving others in their country were of that action, even though the exact least-approved actions varied somewhat from country to country. Snyczer and colleagues propose that the key appraisal eliciting shame is that one is perceived as less valuable by in-group members.

Where this gets complicated is in the kinds of situations that elicit inferences of lower social value, and whether awareness of this is considered a good or bad thing. The concept of shame itself seems to carry different meanings across cultures. As we saw earlier, among people in the United States the concept of shame is closely related to that of guilt; in both cases one has done something morally wrong. In some other cultures, however, shame may not be associated with transgression at all, although the term does typically carry a connotation of lower social value (Kollareth, Fernandez-Dols, & Russell, 2018). In Chapter 2 we discussed *hasham*, a Bedouin term commonly translated as shame. *Hasham* may be felt in the mere presence of a higher-status person (Abu-Lughod, 1986), somewhat akin to the English-language concept of humbleness. The Orissa Indian *lajya*, discussed earlier in this chapter, is a similar concept. Notably, the experience of *hasham* is not unpleasant, and a person (usually, but not always, a woman) who feels *hasham* in appropriate situations is considered virtuous. Referring back to material from Chapter 3, the value placed on shame appears to vary quite a bit across cultures, ranging from those that consider it positive and desirable to those that deem it unpleasant and toxic.

SUMMARY

We began this chapter by asking what emotions you would choose to experience if you could place an ideal affect order for the rest of your life. Has your order changed? Few people, if any, want to be miserable all the time, but we hope you will accept some experience of negative emotions along the way. Having some ups and downs in life makes the ups more exciting. A lack of negative emotions also implies that you have been playing it safe. We feel emotions such as fear, disgust, and even embarrassment when we try new things and push our boundaries. Also, never feeling negative emotions may be a sign that you're not invested in the people, rewards, and opportunities you have in your life. To love is to risk loss. To try is to risk failure. These investments provide much of the sense of meaning people experience in their lives, despite the risks. Emotions such as anger, embarrassment, shame, and guilt help us navigate our relationships with others, so that we and our partners are treated well and with respect.

As we consider specific emotions, common themes emerge. One theme is that emotions, even potentially basic/discrete emotions such as fear, disgust, and sadness, are not uniform or static. Within each of these categories researchers have identified semidistinct subtypes in terms of eliciting situations, physiological responses, and/or behaviors. In some cases, the subtypes of emotion reflect the natural time course of the situation, as when a predator is first far away and then comes closer. In other cases, the subtypes reflect different versions of a larger kind of problem, as social loss and failure are different types of loss. Similarly, the emotional states evoked by contaminants, scenes of gore and mutilation, and morally offensive acts are similar in some ways, and different in others. Whether these subtypes should be considered the same or different emotions is partly a matter for future research and, to some extent, a question of semantics—either way, hypotheses about such similarities and differences can yield important research.

Another theme is that it makes little sense to describe emotions as the result of either human nature or culture and learning alone. In several cases, evidence suggests that evolution has provided a template for managing certain kinds of threats we might encounter—predators, toxins, social conflict—but that people fill these templates in with specifics based on their own experience, as well as experiences they observe in others. For example, we learn, with remarkable speed and tenacity, what stimuli predict physical harm and what foods make us sick. This suggests that rather than thinking of nature and nurture as competing explanations for human emotions, we should be trying to understand the complex ways in which these two forces interact.

KEY TERMS

anger: the emotional state associated with feeling injured or offended and with a desire to threaten or hurt the person who offended you (p. 391)

anxiety: a general expectation that something bad might happen, without identifying any particular danger (p. 382)

blush: a temporarily increased blood flow to the face, neck, and upper chest (p. 412)

core disgust: emotional response to an object that threatens your physical purity, such as feces, rotting food, or unclean animals (p. 399)

embarrassment: the emotion felt when one violates a social convention, thereby drawing unexpected social attention and motivating submissive, friendly behavior that should appease other people (p. 409)

fear: a response to a specific perceived danger, either to oneself or to a loved one (p. 382)

fear appeal: a public service message emphasizing the negative outcomes that are likely if behavior does not change. (p. 388)

guilt: the negative emotion felt when one fails or does something morally wrong but focuses on how to make amends and how to avoid repeating the transgression (p. 412)

hostile aggression: harmful behavior motivated by anger and the events that preceded it (p. 396)

ideal affect: the affective states that a person ideally wants to feel and will try to attain (p. 381)

instrumental aggression: harmful or threatening behavior used purely as a way to obtain something or to achieve some end (p. 396)

moral disgust: disgust response to violations of moral, rather than physical, purity (p. 401)

prepared learning: proposal that people and other animals are evolutionarily predisposed to learn some things (including fears) more easily than others (p. 385)

sadness: an emotional response to a significant and perhaps irrevocable loss (p. 403)

self-conscious emotions: emotions such as embarrassment, shame, and guilt that require appraisal of yourself and how you appear to others (p. 409)

self-efficacy: belief that one is capable of doing something that one wants to do, such as changing a problematic behavior or developing a new skill (p. 388)

shame: the emotion felt when one fails or does something morally wrong and then focuses on one's own global, stable inadequacies in explaining the transgression (p. 412)

social anxiety: intense anxiety specific to situations involving social interaction (p. 382)

social fear learning: learning to fear a new stimulus based upon seeing another person's negative experience with it, or their fear response to it. (p. 385)

startle potentiation: enhancement of the startle response in a frightening situation compared to a safe one (p. 383)

startle response: reaction to a sudden loud noise or other strong stimulus in which the muscles tense rapidly, especially the neck muscles, the eyes close tightly, the shoulders quickly pull close to the neck, and the arms pull up toward the head (p. 383)

virtue signaling: exhibiting behaviors (including emotional reactions) that advertise ourselves as valuable, norm-following, trustworthy social partners (p. 402)

THOUGHT/DISCUSSION QUESTIONS

1. Think of a time when you experienced each of the emotions discussed in this chapter and the result was beneficial for you in some way. Was the benefit consistent with, or different from, the functions described here? Next, think of a time when you experienced each of these emotions and the result was harmful to you in some way. What was the difference between these situations?

2. Facial expressions of emotion communicate our feelings, appraisals, and behavioral inclinations to other people. What good does it do to communicate our fear? Are there times when it is best to hide our fear instead of expressing it?

3. Researchers have found that people express anger more often at home than when they are at work (Bongard & al'Absi, 2003). Can you suggest an explanation? Might this vary by culture? If so, what cultural variables discussed in Chapter 3 would you expect to moderate the home-versus-work effect?

4. Young children are notoriously picky eaters. Explain this in terms of what you learned about disgust in this chapter. Based on this information, what advice would you give to parents who are trying to encourage their children to eat a wider range of foods?

5. Most researchers interested in emotion and cognition have not made the distinction between sadness in response to social loss and sadness in response to failure that we described in this chapter. Generate your own hypotheses about how the cognitive effects of these variants of sadness might be similar and how they might be different, based on what would be most functional in these two kinds of situations.

SUGGESTIONS FOR FURTHER READING

Bonnanno, G. A. (2019). *The other side of sadness: What the new science of bereavement tells us about life after loss.* Basic Books. This synthesis of the literature on grieving highlights the complexity of healthy responses to loss.

Kashdan, T., & Biswas-Diener, R. (2014). *The upside of your dark side: Why being your whole self, not just your "good" self, drives success and fulfillment.* Plume. A thoughtful analysis of the valuable role negative emotions can play in supporting psychological well-being.

LoBue, V., & Adolph, K. E. (2019). Fear in infancy: Lessons from snakes, spiders, heights, and strangers. *Developmental Psychology, 55*(9), 1889–1907. A thoughtful, sophisticated analysis of the infant data relevant to prepared fear learning theory.

Tangney, J. P., Miller, R. S., Flicker, L., & Barlow, D. H. (1996). Are shame, guilt, and embarrassment distinct emotions? *Journal of Personality and Social Psychology, 70*(6), 1256–1269. The original paper describing similarities and differences among these self-conscious negative emotions.

CHAPTER 12

Happiness and the Positive Emotions

What is your primary goal in life? Many people in the United States and other developed, Western nations would say it is to be happy. The philosophy of utilitarianism is based on the moral superiority of whatever course of action results in the most happiness and well-being: "The greatest happiness of all those whose interest is in question [is] the right and proper, and only right and proper and universally desirable, end of human action" (Bentham, [1780] 1970, p. 11). The US Declaration of Independence states, "We hold these truths to be self-evident, that all men are created equal, that they are endowed by their Creator with certain unalienable Rights, that among these are Life, Liberty and the pursuit of Happiness."

Does anyone *not* agree that the pursuit of happiness is a primary goal? Across cultures people say that their ideal affect contains more positive emotion than negative emotion (Tsai, 2007), though "happiness" means different things to people in different cultures. As we noted in Chapter 3, people in many East Asian cultural contexts prioritize feelings of contentment and connectedness in defining happiness, whereas North Americans place greater value on excitement and achievement (Ford et al., 2015; Tsai, 2007; Uchida & Kitayama, 2009). How do *you* define happiness?

What makes people happy? Is happiness under our control, and if so, what can we do to be happier? What purpose does happiness serve? Is happiness an emotion, or is it more like an attitude or trait? If it is the former, then what are the positive emotions, and is there more than one? Although these questions are central to understanding and promoting psychological well-being, serious research on happiness and the positive emotions began much later than research on distress and the negative emotions, and is still rapidly expanding. Let's take a look.

IS HAPPINESS AN EMOTION?

Learning Objectives
- Analyze the proposal that happiness is an emotion.
- Compare and contrast hedonic and eudemonic well-being.

The Merriam-Webster dictionary defines happiness as "a state of well-being and contentment." Fear and anger are prototypical examples of emotions, but what about happiness? Let's try applying the criteria we discussed in Chapter 1 to happiness:

1. *Emotion is a reaction to a stimulus.* Happiness can be a reaction to an event, such as winning a game or receiving a compliment, but often people are happy for no particular reason. Also, happiness is more persistent than fear or anger; in some ways, it is closer to being a personality trait. If you feel happy about some event, such as winning a prize, that emotion fades over time, but people who are happy for no particular reason tend to be happy most of the time, day after day. Researchers asked thousands of people to rate their overall life satisfaction many times over the years. Most people's ratings remained nearly constant, time after time, year after year (Cummins et al., 2014).

2. *Emotion is a complex sequence of physiological, behavioral, and subjective changes.* In many studies, the physiological changes associated with happiness appear unimpressive compared to anger and fear (Cacioppo et al., 2000). Fear often leads to freezing or flight; anger leads to efforts aimed at getting another person to treat you better. What behavior does happiness evoke? Although studies by Ekman and colleagues (1987) have found that a particular kind of smile is interpreted worldwide as a sign of happiness, theorists have had trouble articulating a more specific, functional behavior.

3. *An emotion is a functional response to the situation.* Here *functional* means adaptive. In what way does happiness help you survive? The fitness-enhancing benefits of happiness are less obvious than those of fear, anger, or disgust.

In short, happiness—at least in the sense of general well-being and satisfaction with life—does not fit the modal definition of emotion. What most laypeople and researchers call happiness qualifies more often as a trait than as a state, although the term is used both ways. To avoid confusion, researchers often refer to trait happiness as **subjective well-being**, or generally experiencing one's life as pleasant, fulfilling, and satisfying (Diener, 2000).

Measuring Subjective Well-Being

Many researchers define happiness in terms of high life satisfaction, high dispositional experience of overall positive affect, and low dispositional experience of negative affect (Diener & Diener, 1996; Diener et al., 1999). One of the most frequently used measures of happiness is the Satisfaction With Life Scale (Pavot & Diener, 1993). This measure asks people to rate how much they agree with each of the following statements on a scale from 1 (*strongly disagree*) to 7 (*strongly agree*):

___ In most ways my life is close to my ideal.
___ The conditions of my life are excellent.

___ I am satisfied with my life.

___ So far I have gotten the important things I want in life.

___ If I could live my life over, I would change almost nothing.

Although the Satisfaction With Life Scale is sometimes used on its own, researchers often combine it with the Positive and Negative Affect Schedule, or PANAS (Watson, Clark, & Tellegen, 1988). The PANAS has 20 items, each of which is a single word. You would respond, on a scale from 1 to 5, with how well that word describes your feelings during a certain time (which could be a day, a week, a month, in general, or any other unit of time). Ten items are negative words such as *scared*, *upset*, *distressed*, and *ashamed*. The other 10 items, intended to measure positive affect, are *enthusiastic, interested, determined, excited, inspired, alert, active, strong, proud*, and *attentive*. To combine the three scales, researchers take an average of each; convert individual scores to **z-scores**—subtracting the scale mean and dividing by the standard deviation, so that each measure now has a mean of zero and a standard deviation of 1.0; multiply the negative affect score by −1 (so that higher scores are always more desirable); and then average the three z scores together. This allows each of the three scales to make equal contributions to the overall measure.

Consistent with the description of happiness as a trait, this questionnaire cannot necessarily be used to assess emotion, at least in the sense meant by many emotion researchers. Words such as *enthusiastic* and *proud* seem to correspond to emotions, but what about *strong, alert*, and *determined*? These are desirable qualities, and if you feel strong, determined, and alert, then you probably feel good. Many researchers have recently agreed that the Positive Affect scale is best thought of as measuring high energy and overall positive mood, which is ideal for measuring trait happiness.

The PANAS provides a good measure of one's ratio of pleasant to unpleasant affect, on average, and the Satisfaction With Life Scale captures an evaluation that one's life is going well. Researchers sometimes refer to the construct captured by these measures as **hedonic well-being**—overall happiness and enjoyment of life (Ryan & Deci, 2001). However, the definition misses something in regard to people's sense of meaning in life. Sometimes great fulfillment comes from experiences that are not a lot of fun. For example, parents—especially parents of young children—report that much of their time is spent changing diapers, cleaning up messes, trying to soothe a crying child, trying to convince the child to do something it really doesn't want to do, trying to convince the child *not* to something it is very determined to do, and a variety of other not-super-pleasant activities (Figure 12.1). Nevertheless, in the long run, most people describe parenthood as one of the greatest sources of meaning and purpose in their lives (Lyubomirsky & Boehm, 2010; Nelson, Kushlev, & Lyubomirsky, 2014). *Pleasant* experiences are not the same as *rewarding* experiences (White & Dolan, 2009).

Researchers refer to the sense that one's life is meaningful, consistent with personal values, and fulfilling one's potential as **eudaimonic well-being**. Another questionnaire measure, called the Scales of Psychological Well-Being (SPWB; Ryff, 1989), explicitly captures the eudaimonic aspect of happiness. The SPWB contains six distinct subscales measuring self-acceptance, positive relations with others, autonomy, environmental mastery, purpose in life, and personal growth.

Are hedonic and eudaimonic well-being separate, independent aspects of happiness? From a statistical standpoint, they hang together very tightly. In one study researchers

FIGURE 12.1. Although parenting is not always fun on a moment-to-moment basis, and can be very unpleasant at times, most people list parenting among the greatest sources of meaning and purpose in their lives.

examined patterns of relationships among the measures above in several thousand adults from countries all over the globe. Although correlations between overall hedonic and eudaimonic well-being were slightly higher in Western than in Southeast Asian and Latin American regions, they exceeded $r = .90$ in every region of the world (Disabato et al., 2016). In other words, hedonic and eudaimonic well-being are almost perfectly correlated. Although they may not diverge much at the trait level, the distinction between these two facets of well-being may be important when we ask what we can *do* to have a happy life, so it's worth keeping in mind as we proceed.

WHAT PREDICTS HAPPINESS?

Learning Objectives
- Summarize the evidence linking personality to happiness, and analyze the evidence for alternative explanations of the correlation between trait Extraversion and happiness.
- Define income satiation, and analyze the relationship between income/wealth and happiness drawing upon empirical evidence.
- List several factors that predict happiness, and identify the theme uniting many of these factors.

Most people in reasonably prosperous countries say they are happy overall—that is, above the midpoint on a scale from very unhappy to very happy (Cummins et al., 2014; Diener & Diener, 1996). Some psychologists argue that we evolved to make happiness the "default setting" (Buss, 2000). In general, happy people tend to be more productive than others and are more likely to compete successfully for reproductive opportunities. Wouldn't you rather mate with a happy person than with an unhappy one? According to this reasoning, happy people are more likely than other people to pass on their genes (Buss, 2000). If so, most of us are descended from a long line of ancestors who tended to be reasonably happy most of the time, and we inherited genes that predispose us toward happiness. Still, even among people who call themselves happy, some report being happier than others, and it is interesting to see what predicts—and what fails to predict—these differences.

If we want to know what makes people happy, one obvious thing to do is to ask them. The question can be posed in two different ways: "What makes you happy?" versus "What would make you happier?" Before reading on, we encourage you to answer both of these questions yourself.

The different wordings tend to produce different results. James Kalat, our treasured colleague and coauthor on previous editions of this textbook, has informally surveyed his Introductory Psychology class using these questions several times. In each case, half of the questionnaires included the first wording and half included the second. The most common answers to "What would make you happier?" typically fell into these categories:

- More money or possessions;
- A good job and a secure future;
- A new romantic partner, or a better relationship with the current one;
- Better grades in school; and
- More sleep.

In contrast, here are some common answers to the question "What makes you happy?":

- Friends and family (by far the most common answer);
- My romantic partner;
- A feeling of success or accomplishment;
- Relaxing;
- Playing sports, being active;
- Enjoying nature;
- Music and humor;
- Religion; and
- Making others happy.

Note the contrast. Most items people say would make them happier are things that could happen *to them*. The exception is sleep; most college students (and their professors) are fairly sleep-deprived most of the time. Better sleep is indeed associated with higher well-being; the causal arrow likely goes in both directions, with emotional distress leading to sleep disruption and chronic lack of sleep generally making you feel awful (Steptoe et al., 2008). Notably, however, most items that people list as already making them happy are their own actions, or an appreciation of what is readily available (friends, family, nature).

In a more systematic survey of middle-age US adults, most people also said that their relationship with family and friends was their main source of satisfaction in life; other common answers included physical health, financial security, self-development, a good job, religious faith, and simply enjoying life's activities (Markus et al., 2004). The importance of relationships for happiness is not limited to Western cultures. Throughout the world, subjective well-being is predicted both by feeling supported in close relationships and by a sense of trust in society at large (Oishi & Schimmack, 2010).

Personality: The Top-Down Theory of Happiness

A quote attributed to Abraham Lincoln is, "Most folks are about as happy as they make up their minds to be." Is that true? To what extent is happiness something we decide or create for ourselves, and to what extent is it a product of the events life has brought us?

This distinction is sometimes phrased as *top down* versus *bottom up*, where top down means that your personality determines your happiness and bottom up means life events do (Heller, Watson, & Ilies, 2004). Psychologists initially assumed the bottom-up hypothesis: good life events make you happy, and bad events make you unhappy. To some extent, this idea is supported by the evidence. A series of pleasant events can build an overall positive attitude that helps you deal with the occasional unpleasant experiences (Cohn et al., 2009). However, many people are consistently happier or less happy than we might expect, given events in their lives. People with high trait happiness have their bad moods, too, but they bounce back quickly (Diener & Seligman, 2002).

One determinant of happiness is people's natural disposition, or innate personality. How happy you are now is a good predictor of how happy you will be many years from now (Pavot & Diener, 1993; Watson, 2002). A meta-analysis of hundreds of twin studies has estimated the heritability of subjective well-being at around .40, which suggests that around 40% of individual differences in happiness may be explained in terms of people's genes (Nes & Røysamb, 2015). This does not mean that there is a single "happiness gene"; instead, many genetic factors contribute to happiness. These influences likely travel through broad personality traits that are themselves influenced by genes, including the Big Five personality traits of Extraversion, Agreeableness, Conscientiousness, Neuroticism, and Openness to Experience (Jang, Livesley, & Vemon, 1996; Loehlin et al., 1998).

Extraversion appears to be a particularly important predictor of happiness. The correlation between extraversion and trait positive emotionality, in particular, is so strong that some researchers have suggested they may have the same underlying neural basis (Depue & Iacono, 1989; Gray, 1970). Some have proposed dopamine activity as the mechanism for this link. However, research has indicated only an inconsistent relationship between extraversion and genes influencing dopamine activity, number of dopamine receptors, and similar variables, so this hypothesis remains unsettled (Wacker & Smillie, 2015).

Extraverted social behavior may offer a better explanation. In general, people who experience more social interaction consistently report greater happiness (DeNeve, 1999; Diener, 2012). Of course, one possibility is that happier people tend to engage more with others; happiness causes social interaction rather than the other way around. While there is evidence for that causal pathway, a clever experiment shows that extraversion can drive happiness as well. In this study Luke Smillie and colleagues (2015) instructed participants to behave in a more or less extraverted way while interacting with a stranger in the laboratory (Figure 12.2). Results showed those who acted more outgoing reported enjoying the interaction more and experienced more positive affect, even if their natural personality

FIGURE 12.2.   Extraverts tend to report higher levels of subjective well-being than introverts, and this may be caused by differences in social behavior. When people are randomly assigned to behave in an outgoing manner while interacting with another person, they tend to enjoy the experience more, whether or not they are naturally extraverted.

was relatively introverted (Smillie et al., 2015). That is, pretending to be extraverted helps, even if extraversion does not come naturally.

You may be thinking, "So, people born with the right personality genes get to be happy, but the rest of us are destined to be miserable? What am I supposed to do with *that* information?" First, genes are not the only influence on personality. In a study with more than 16,000 participants, Christopher Soto (2015) measured both personality and well-being over multiple time points. Analyses asked whether personality at one time point predicted change in well-being from that same time point to the next, and vice versa. In this way, researchers can come closer to testing causal direction, even without a true experiment. Results suggested that people who were more extraverted, agreeable, and conscientious and less neurotic not only were happier at the start, but also tended to become happier over the course of the study. However, Soto found that happiness predicted change in personality as well. People who were happier early in the study tended to become more introverted (although they likely started out more extraverted), agreeable, conscientious, and emotionally stable (less neurotic) over time. So, the relationship between personality and happiness is dynamic and complex, rather than moving only in one direction.

Moving on, let's say you did not win the Big Five personality lottery, and do not have the benefit of starting life with an outgoing, warm, perky personality. What can you do? A growing body of research shows that that how you *think* about yourself and your life has important implications for happiness, and although this is somewhat predicted by genes (Fagnani et al., 2014), there is plenty of room for intentional growth. Ed Diener, a leader in the science of well-being (Figure 12.3), highlights **dispositional positivity** as a factor over which we have some control, and which strongly predicts happiness and well-being (Diener et al., 2000). Dispositional positivity consists of reasonably high self-esteem, a tendency toward optimism, and positive appraisals of one's life and future. In other words, people characterized by dispositional positivity generally have a good attitude. In a longitudinal study following Italian teenagers from age 15 to their early 20s, dispositional positivity predicted increases in positive affect; the reverse was not true, suggesting causal influence only from positive attitude toward happiness (Caprara, Eisenberg, & Alessandri, 2017).

Some aspects of this relationship may be moderated by culture. For example, self-esteem is less predictive of happiness among participants in Japan than those in North America (Yuki et al., 2013). This effect appears to be due to lower *relational mobility* in Japan—it's not as easy to just move on to new relationships if your current ones aren't going well, so your individual awesomeness and desirability as a new friend or romantic partner matters less than whether you are taking good care of the relationships you're already in. Still, optimism and a tendency to focus on what's good in life are worth cultivating. We'll discuss this further later in this chapter, and in Chapter 15.

Life Events That Impact Happiness

Events that we experience do affect our happiness. However, these changes do not always last. Events that bring intense joy produce a temporary surge in overall happiness, but this tends to decline with surprising speed. For example, people's life satisfaction typically increases when they marry, but returns to pre-marriage levels within a year or so; a similar pattern is observed for the birth of a child (Luhmann et al., 2012). Right after people win

FIGURE 12.3. Ed Diener was hugely influential in the science of happiness and well-being, developing theories and commonly used measures, conducting a tremendous amount of research, and arguing that happiness should be taken as seriously as economic indicators in measuring quality of life around the world.

a lottery, they rate their happiness very high. However, a few months later, their happiness ratings decline to about average (Diener et al., 1999; Myers, 2000a).

It is easier to produce a long-term decrease in happiness than a long-term increase. For example, an injury that causes major disability, such as paralysis, produces an immediate drop in life satisfaction, from which most people show little recovery over the next few years (Lucas, 2007). Also, if you lose a job that you care about—one that you take pride in as your long-term career—it hurts badly. One study of more than 24,000 German workers found that their satisfaction dropped sharply when they lost a job. Satisfaction recovered somewhat over time, but on average did not return to its previous level even after 15 years (Lucas et al., 2004).

Another powerful influence is the loss of a spouse by either death or divorce (Luhmann et al., 2012). Figure 12.4 shows the results of one long-term study in which people reported their satisfaction repeatedly over several years (Diener & Seligman, 2004). The researchers isolated the data from participants who lost a spouse, and lined up their results so that Time 0 was the year of the loss. Several points are worth noting in the graph: life satisfaction declined gradually over the years before the loss, presumably because the marriage was deteriorating for those couples who divorced and because health was deteriorating for the spouses who died. In general, widows and widowers were happier than divorced people, both before and after the loss, although happiness was equally crummy at the time of loss. Life satisfaction recovered slowly after the loss, but on average, it did not return to its previous peak. These average results do not apply to every individual, however. Some people recover well and others hardly at all.

Wealth and Happiness

When asked what would make them happier, many people answer "more money." If you think more money would make you happy, how much more money would you need?

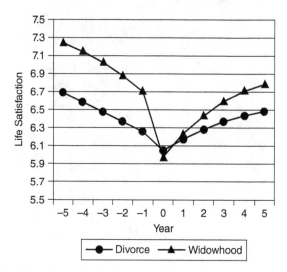

FIGURE 12.4. People report gradually decreasing life satisfaction in the years before losing a spouse to death or divorce. Although satisfaction increases steadily in the years that follow, it may not return to its original peak. From Diener & M. E. P. Seligman (2004).

According to one survey, people earning $25,000 per year thought $50,000 would make them happy. People earning $50,000 said $100,000 would be enough. Those earning $100,000 thought they would need about $200,000, and so on (Csikszentmihalyi, 1999). Although few people are satisfied that they have enough money, we can ask whether wealthier people are happier than poorer people. Can money buy happiness or not? Researchers have approached this question in several ways; the results are both complicated and revealing about the foundations of happiness.

Early studies examining the correlation between wealth and happiness reported unimpressive effects, around $r = .20$, and for years psychologists concluded that wealth has little to do with happiness. However, more fine-grained analyses showed that most of this research had a *restriction of range* problem: you won't find much influence of a variable if you measure only a small range of its possible values. Think of it this way: If you want to know whether people get happier or sadder as they grow older, could you find out by studying only teenagers? Of course not! What happens between ages 13 and 19 doesn't tell us what might happen between 19 and 99.

Similarly, suppose we ask people about their wealth and their happiness, but the great majority of survey participants have middle-class incomes and live in wealthy, developed

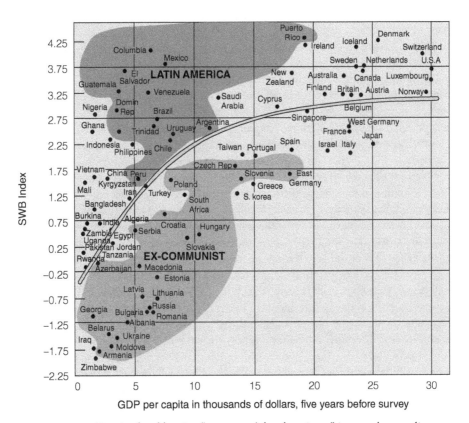

FIGURE 12.5. Despite the old saying "money can't buy happiness," income does predict levels of subjective well-being around the world. The effect is especially strong below a certain threshold allowing basic security and comfort. From Inglehart et al. (2008).

nations. The difference between slightly lower and slightly higher middle-class incomes doesn't account for which people are happier than others (Diener, Tay, & Oishi, 2013). However, if we examine people with a wider range of incomes, we find that the wealthiest people report, on average, significantly more happiness than the poorest (Lucas & Schimmack, 2009). The effect of wealth is especially striking when we compare happiness ratings for people from different countries. Figure 12.5 shows a scatterplot for many countries, with national income on the *x* axis and a measure of well-being on the *y* axis (Inglehart et al., 2008). In general, people in wealthier countries report higher life satisfaction than those in poorer countries.

Happiness correlates with both absolute and relative wealth. That is, the same amount of wealth feels better if you compare yourself to people doing worse than if you compare yourself to people doing better, economically speaking (Boyce, Brown, & Moore, 2010; Frank, 2012). Consistent with this emphasis on social comparison, the impact of greater wealth on happiness tends to be blunted in countries with high income inequality, where no matter how much money you have there's always someone who has a lot more (Oishi & Kesebir, 2015). This may account for the generally high happiness in countries with progressive income redistribution policies; if everyone has plenty for comfort but no one has an obscene amount of wealth, it's easier to feel that you have all you need to be happy (Oishi, Schimmack, & Diener, 2012). Increasingly, however, people's sense of well-being is tied to how far they are from the wealthiest people in the world (Becchetti, Castriota, & Giachin, 2011).

How much is enough? In one worldwide study researchers examined **income satiation**, or the cutoff beyond which higher annual income fails to predict an increase in aspects of happiness (Jebb et al., 2018). The benefits of greater income for positive and negative affect seemed to end beyond 60–75,000 US dollars; for satisfaction with life, the effect ends beyond about $95,000. If anything, happiness sometimes declines a bit beyond this point. However, the cap is higher in higher-income countries, again pointing toward a social comparison effect. Figure 12.6 shows the satiation point in annual household income, controlling for the number of people in the household, separately for each country in the study. The key finding in the study is that money matters for happiness, but only up to a point, and that point is lower than most people in wealthy countries probably believe.

A further complexity is that although people in poorer countries generally report lower life satisfaction and higher anger and worry, on average, they also tend to report greater purpose or meaning in life relative to those in rich nations (Oishi & Diener, 2014; Tay, Morrison, & Diener, 2014). Money can buy pleasure, but can it buy eudaimonic well-being? Your skepticism is reasonable, but there's a twist: the effect of more money depends in part on how you spend it. In one meta-analysis of seven large studies from Denmark, Canada, the Netherlands, and the United States, people who spent more money in ways that bought them extra time—such as hiring house cleaners or people to run errands, and paying for take-out meals rather than cooking—reported greater happiness (Whillans et al., 2017). Another rich body of research shows that spending money on experiences has a greater impact on happiness than buying more stuff. The mechanisms behind this effect are highly social. When we pay for special experiences, we typically share those experiences with other people, and talk with others about them long after; analyses suggest that this is where the benefit for happiness really lies (Gilovich, Kumar, & Jampol, 2015).

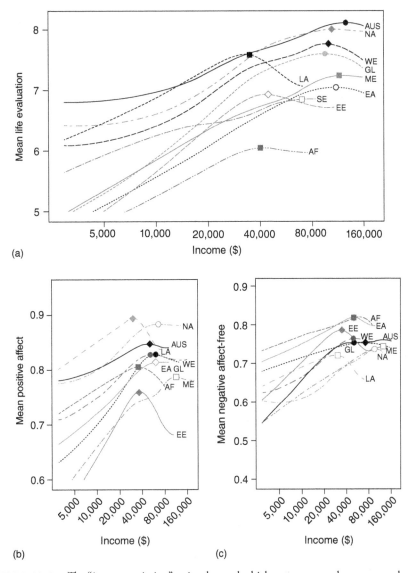

FIGURE 12.6. The "income satiation" point, beyond which more money does not translate into greater happiness (shown as dots in each graph), is somewhat higher in wealthy than in poorer regions. AF—Sub-Saharan Africa; AUS = Australia/New Zealand; EA = East Asia; EE = Eastern Europe/the Balkans; GL = global average; LA = Latin America/the Carribean; ME = Middle East/North Africa; NA = Northern America; SE = Southeast Asia; WE = Western Europe/Scandinavia. From Jebb et al. (2018).

Other Correlates of Happiness

Several other factors also reliably predict happiness. Happiness tends to be greater in countries where minority groups are treated well, and men and women have approximately equal status (Basabe et al., 2002). People with more close relationships with family members and friends say they are happier than those with fewer such relationships. On average, married people describe themselves as happier than unmarried people (DeNeve, 1999), and people in happy marriages are happier than those in unhappy marriages (Carr et al., 2014). Among undergraduates, people with strong romantic attachments and close friendships are happier than those without such attachments (Diener & Seligman, 2002). A before-and-after study indicated that young people reported decreased stress in their lives after getting married (Coombs & Fawzy, 1982). Another longitudinal study indicated that marriage produced long-term increases in happiness for some people, although not for all (Lucas et al., 2003).

One obvious interpretation is that friendships and romantic attachments are good for people. However, another plausible interpretation is that happy people are more likely than unhappy people to attract friends and partners, develop lasting attachments, get married, and stay married (Lyubomirsky, King, & Diener, 2005). Happy people also tend to have happier friends. Researchers in one study found that when one person becomes happier, within a few months many of that person's friends become happier too and, later, those people's friends became happier as well (Fowler & Christakis, 2008). Happiness is contagious! Both longitudinal and experimental evidence suggests supports effects in both directions: happiness promotes good relationships, and relationships increase happiness.

In general, healthy people are happier than unhealthy people (DeNeve, 1999; Myers, 2000a; Steptoe, 2019). It is hard to doubt that being ill makes people unhappy. However, the correlation reflects an influence in the other direction as well. People who report higher subjective well-being tend to show better health outcomes, especially in terms of cardiovascular health (Boehm & Kubzansky, 2012; Steptoe, 2019). This effect appears to be partly a result of healthier lifestyles among happy people (more on this later in the chapter), but also because of direct effects of well-being on biological factors.

People with religious faith tend to be happier than those without it (Myers, 2000a). The natural assumption is that religion provides a sense of purpose, comfort in difficult times, and stability. However, this effect is only seen among people living in places where many people attend religious services (Diener, Tay, & Myers, 2011; Gebauer, Sedikides, & Neberich, 2012), suggesting that religion promotes life satisfaction mainly by helping people build social networks. Private, subjective religious beliefs and practices have little or no apparent effect (Lim & Putnam, 2010).

People who feel a sense of control over their lives tend to be healthier as well as happier than others (Lachman & Firth, 2004). Happy people are more likely than others to have a goal in life (Csikszentmihalyi, 1999; Diener et al., 1999). However, the one goal that does not consistently predict happiness is that of making money. In one study, researchers asked more than 12,000 US college students about their life goals and followed up with them later. On average, those who had expressed the greatest interest in becoming rich were the *least* happy 19 years later. Most of these individuals did not in fact become rich, so the unhappiness may have been caused by a failure to reach their goal, rather than the goal itself (Nickerson et al., 2003). In contrast, people whose goal was to make the world a better place usually felt they were accomplishing that goal, at least to some extent, and these kinds of goals were associated with greater happiness. Although having goals appears to be important, the ability to let go of goals that prove unattainable may be crucial as well (Wrosch, Scheier, & Miller, 2013); we'll discuss this in more detail in Chapter 14.

Would you guess that good-looking people are happier than most others? If you are good-looking, people are more prone to smile at you, assume you are a good person, invite you to parties and dates, and generally treat you nicely (Eagly et al., 1991). Initial surveys found that although good-looking people were more satisfied than average with their romantic life, in other ways they were no happier than average (Diener, Wolsic, & Fujita, 1995). However, data from a longitudinal study with several hundred participants suggest that attractiveness may have a more wide-ranging effect. People who were rated as more physically attractive in high school, based on yearbook photos, reported higher levels of psychological well-being decades later (Gupta, Etcoff, & Jaeger, 2015). Although the effect was small, it was statistically significant even after controlling for possible confounding variables, such as economic status and mental ability.

Would you expect well-educated people to be happier than less-educated ones? This answer is more complicated. Better-educated people tend to have more challenging jobs, with higher pay but more stress. Higher pay is an advantage, but stress is a disadvantage. When researchers control for these two factors by comparing people with similar pay and stress but different education, they find little difference in people's positive affect (Mroczek, 2004). That is, education by itself has little influence on happiness. It does, however, correlate significantly with *interest*, which we could regard as a different kind of positive emotion (Consedine, Magai, & King, 2004). Better-educated people tend to have more diverse interests.

Perhaps most important for people who wish to improve their well-being, research indicates that events that happen *to* you are less important than what you *do* (Lyubomirsky & Layous, 2013). One study compared students who recently improved their circumstances, such as switching to a preferred roommate, with others who had improved their activities, such as joining a new club. The students with a new roommate reported increased happiness for a while, but those with new activities continued to report increased happiness until the end of the semester (Sheldon & Lyubomirsky, 2006).

One particularly helpful activity is gratitude journaling, or "counting your blessings." Researchers have found that people improved their life satisfaction, optimism, and overall health if they set aside time once a week to list five things for which they were grateful (Emmons & McCullough, 2003). The researchers recommended doing so no more than once a week; if you write your gratitude list every day or two, you start getting into a routine of saying the same things, and you don't take the task as seriously. Writing grateful letters to others can also increase well-being (Lyubomirsky et al., 2011). A meta-analysis of gratitude-activity interventions revealed small but consistent and statistically significant effects on psychological well-being (Davis et al., 2016).

Finally, an activity that reliably boosts happiness is to do something kind for someone else (Figure 12.7). In one study, researchers gave students some money in the morning, randomly assigning some of them to spend the money on themselves and others to buy a surprise gift for someone else, and then to report back in the late afternoon. Which do you think you would prefer? Most people assume they would prefer to spend money on themselves, but in fact those who bought a surprise for someone else reported being happier at the end of the day (Dunn, Aknin, & Norton, 2008). This effect is remarkably robust. Even toddlers and young children express greater pleasure when giving a treat to someone else than when receiving a treat themselves (Aknin et al., 2015; Aknin, Hamlin, & Dunn, 2012). In a study including a wide range of developing and non-Western

FIGURE 12.7. Research shows that a great way to boost your own happiness is to do something kind for someone else, such as giving them a gift or doing them a favor. From Aknin et al. (2013).

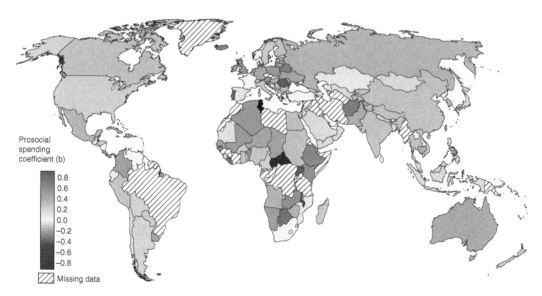

FIGURE 12.8. Spending money on others, rather than on one's self, consistently predicts happiness. Colors represent the effect size (b coefficients) for amount spent on donations to charity in nation-level regression analyses predicting well-being, controlling for household income, food stress, and demographic variables. With the exception of Tunisia and the Central African Republic (where effects are negative), darker shading indicates a stronger positive effect. From Aknin et al. (2013).

countries as well as wealthy, Western nations, the amount of money people donated to or spent on others was consistently positively correlated with well-being (see Figure 12.8; with exceptions noted in the caption, darker shading indicates a stronger positive association); this effect held even after controlling for household income, experience of food stress or hunger, and demographic variables (Aknin et al., 2013).

You may have noticed a consistent theme in the research on happiness. Although many factors have been linked to higher well-being, the effect often travels through pleasant social interactions and satisfying relationships with other people. Anything that improves our relationships, or reminds us of their value, is likely to make us happy. In the words of a Chinese proverb, if you want happiness for an hour, take a nap. If you want happiness for a day, go fishing. If you want happiness for a year, inherit a fortune. If you want happiness for a lifetime, help somebody else. To explore more data on happiness, check out this website: http://worlddatabaseofhappiness.eur.nl/.

THE BROADEN AND BUILD THEORY OF POSITIVE EMOTIONS
Learning Objective
- Summarize broaden and build theory, emphasizing the proposed adaptive function of positive emotion, and describe studies supporting this theory.

So far we have talked about happiness as a lasting sense of well-being, rather than an emotion. Some researchers have also examined happiness or joy as an emotion state, studying the facial expression, appraisal profile, and other distinctive features associated with these feelings (e.g., Ekman et al., 1987; Scherer, 1997). While research on specific negative emotions proliferated, however, many were skeptical of happiness/joy as a possible basic or discrete emotion. It is easy to propose a fitness-enhancing function for fear, anger, and disgust, but how might fleeting moments of happiness or joy increase the representation of your genes in future generations? In Chapter 2 we made the point that pleasantness does not inherently make something adaptive. In some cases, theorists proposed that the function of positive emotions was to help relieve us from the physical and behavioral consequences of negative emotion, basically equating positive emotion with relief (Fredrickson & Levenson, 1998; Lazarus, 1991). Other than that, this problem had researchers stumped.

As a solution to this problem, Barbara Fredrickson (1998) proposed that we think about the effects of positive emotions in a different way than we think about the functions of negative emotions. Whereas negative emotions are thought to enhance fitness by promoting immediate actions that deflect threats in the environment, she reasoned, positive emotions may enhance fitness by changing the way we think about the world around us, helping us to gather information and resources that will be helpful in the future. According to the **broaden and build** theory, positive emotions promote more diffuse attention to what's going on around us, so that we are more likely to notice opportunities in the environment, as well as greater flexibility in the actions we might use to take advantage of those opportunities.

Several studies indicate support for this general hypothesis. In one study, Fredrickson and her colleague, Christine Branigan (Fredrickson & Branigan, 2005), used film clips to induce feelings of amusement, contentment, anger, anxiety, and neutral affect in participants. They then gave participants a series of test items that looked something like this:

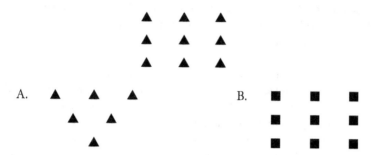

As a study participant, your task is to look quickly at the image in the upper row and then decide which of the two images below is more like it. Do it quickly—don't think too hard; your answer should be instinctive. Which did you choose—A or B?

According to Fredrickson and Branigan, choosing A indicates that your attention is focused on local details of the upper figure (the little triangles), rather than the "big picture" of the shape. Choosing B indicates attention focused on the target figure's overall configuration—a square. Individuals who had just viewed the funny or contentment-inducing film were much more likely to choose B, and similar options in other items, suggesting that the positive emotion biased their attention toward global features rather than details.

Researchers have reported other effects linking positive emotions with big-picture thinking and open-mindedness as well. In general, people tend to be better at recognizing faces of their own race than those of other races (the "they all look alike to me" phenomenon). One study indicated that this bias was reduced in people right after a positive emotion manipulation, as compared to a neutral condition (Johnson & Fredrickson, 2005). Another study found that people who reported more positive emotion states in diaries over a one-month period also showed greater increases in trait life satisfaction, and that this effect was accounted for by increased resilience or ability to handle stress (Cohn et al., 2009).

These studies emphasize a common feature of positive emotions—they help us take advantage of opportunities presented by the environment. Does that mean there is only one positive emotion, with only one function? Not necessarily. According to Fredrickson and others, different positive emotions may also have more specific functions that involve observable behaviors, as well as effects on cognitive processing (Fredrickson, 1998; Sauter, 2010; Shiota et al., 2017). We discuss some candidates for basic/discrete positive emotion status below.

SPECIFIC POSITIVE EMOTIONS
Learning Objectives
- Analyze each of the following as a prospective basic or discrete emotion, considering their possible adaptive function and research evidence about aspects of that emotion: enthusiasm, contentment, pride, love, amusement, awe, and hope/optimism.
- Relate the proposed emotion of enthusiasm to appetitive pleasure and approach motivation, as defined in Chapter 6.
- Compare and contrast alternative definitions of love.

According to basic/discrete emotions theory, emotions evolved to help solve specific kinds of problems related to adaptive fitness—they helped our ancestors increase the representation of their genes in future generations in some way. Whereas negative emotions seem to help us address *threats* to adaptive fitness, researchers have argued, positive emotions should help us respond to *opportunities* to enhance fitness presented by the environment (Fredrickson, 1998; Shiota et al., 2017). Let's consider a few candidates, and look at some of the available evidence.

Enthusiasm: The Anticipation of Reward

When we look forward to a pleasurable experience, we experience **enthusiasm**—the anticipation of a reward. In Chapter 6 we discussed the feeling of anticipatory pleasure, which is a core aspect of this emotion state. Suppose we could arrange to provide you with a passionate, romantic kiss with the movie star of your choice. Would you rather have it now or a week from now? Most people prefer to delay the kiss (Loewenstein, 1987), presumably because they want to enjoy anticipating it. Researchers have also found surprising evidence that commercial interruptions in a television show increase people's enjoyment of the program. Why? During the interruption, they look forward to the resumption of the show, and when the show returns, people enjoy it more than before the interruption (Nelson, Meyvis, & Galak, 2009). Studies even suggest that time seems to pass more quickly when we are looking forward to an imminent reward (Gable & Poole, 2012).

How might the pleasurable anticipation of some upcoming reward enhance adaptive fitness? Shouldn't we want the reward as quickly as possible? That may be precisely the point. It's one thing to perceive a reward out there in the environment, such as a delicious piece of fruit hanging on a tree branch, a drink of cool water from a stream, or (if you are a predator) a nice, plump rabbit on the other side of the meadow; but seeing it does not put it in your mouth. That requires action, and possibly hard work. Moreover, if the reward might run away or fight back (as with the rabbit), you'd better be prepared to run fast—perhaps even to fight. Otherwise, you're going to starve. That would definitely influence your adaptive fitness.

In nonhuman animals this response is limited to a small number of stimuli: desirable foods, opportunities to mate, and any sign that reliably predicts the appearance of food or sex. In Chapter 6 we discussed a structure called the nucleus accumbens, an important structure in the neural reward circuit. This structure becomes highly active when animals perceive a cue that a treat will be delivered soon (Berridge & Kringelbach, 2013; Floresco, 2015). It also becomes more active when an unexpected reward arrives, and less active when an expected reward fails to appear, suggesting that it is also involved in learning to predict rewards based on prior experience (Cox et al., 2015). If the structure is lesioned, or if drugs interfere with its activity, animals show less interest in actively pursuing rewards (Floresco, 2015).

As with many negative emotions discussed in the last chapter, this emotional response seems more flexible in humans, elicited by a variety of rewards other than food. In fMRI studies the nucleus accumbens and related structures increase activity in many kinds of rewarding situations, from eating chocolate to gambling tasks (Figure 12.9), video games, eye contact with an attractive person, humor, and listening to one's favorite music (Bavelier et al., 2011; Blood & Zatorre, 2001; Kampe et al., 2002; Knutson et al., 2008; Mobbs et al., 2003; Small et al., 2001). This structure also responds powerfully to

FIGURE 12.9. People and other animals experience enthusiasm when anticipating a possible reward. Although food is the prototypical elicitor, people show a similar response to cues of other kinds of rewards as well.

stimulant drugs such as cocaine and methamphetamine, and disruptions in nucleus accumbens functioning underlie the experience of craving in addiction (Ashok et al., 2017; Russo et al., 2010; Scofield et al., 2016).

If an animal is preparing to chase its dinner, what might you expect its body to look like? Several studies indicate that the physiological profile of enthusiasm looks a great deal like fear (Kreibig, 2010). In one study, enthusiasm was elicited by showing participants slides presenting a lottery-type situation. The first slide showed the five target numbers, along with the reward schedule: $5 for three matches, $7 for four matches, and $10 for five matches. Then, each subsequent slide showed a "lottery ball" matching one of the target numbers, so that by the end of the slides, the participant had won the maximum possible amount. While watching these slides, participants showed an increase in heart rate, blood pressure, and skin conductance, as well as shortening of cardiac pre-ejection period and reduction in respiratory sinus arrhythmia (Shiota et al., 2011). This is consistent with the threat appraisal profile described in Chapter 4. Although humans rarely face physical danger when going to get a meal, we may retain the vestiges of the risks our ancestors had to face in order to eat.

Earlier we described studies showing that positive emotions tend to broaden attention, encouraging people to focus on the forest rather than the trees. Although this appears to be the case for many positive emotions, enthusiasm is an important exception. Philip Gable and Eddie Harmon-Jones (2008; 2010) have shown that appetitive stimuli such as photos of ice cream sundaes and other desserts tend to have the opposite effect, promoting a more local attentional focus (on the sundae) and distracting them from peripheral details. In a pair of follow-up studies, Gable and doctoral student Hunter Threadgill showed participants photos of yummy desserts (Study 1) or alcoholic beverages (Study 2) and neutral control images, followed by trials of the Navon letter task—a task similar to the one described in the broaden and build section above, but with letters instead of shapes. Participants were faster to identify targets similar in local details right after looking at dessert or alcohol pictures, relative to the neutral pictures, and slower to identify targets similar globally. Moreover, faster reaction times to the local targets after looking at appetitive pictures was correlated with brain activity indicating preparation to move—specifically, with suppression of beta-frequency activity in the motor cortex (Threadgill & Gable, 2019). This laser focus on attaining reward may come at a cost, however. One series of studies found that participants analyzed a persuasive message less carefully after an enthusiasm induction than in a neutral control condition, just as convinced by a long but irrelevant argument as by a high-quality, logical one (Griskevicius, Shiota, & Neufeld, 2010).

Drawn together, this evidence is consistent with the idea that enthusiasm encourages us to "go get it!" when a possible reward is at stake, acting quickly rather than deliberating carefully, and recognizing that pursuit of reward often entails some level of risk. What happens after the reward has been acquired and consumed?

Contentment

According to Barbara Fredrickson (1998), the **contentment** we feel after consuming a reward should also be considered an emotion. This is a familiar state for most people. You've just had a nice, big, delicious meal, and you are pleasantly full (Figure 12.10). Your body feels relaxed and warm, and your brain seems to slow down. These effects can be accounted for by increased activation of the parasympathetic nervous system, also known as the "rest and digest" system because its effects take resources away from the skeletal muscles to promote digestion, growth, and repair. Laboratory studies have shown this

FIGURE 12.10. People experience contentment after consuming a reward. Although it does not look like much is happening, the body is working hard to digest the recently eaten food, and the brain may be consolidating memory of the path to reward as well.

parasympathetic effect even when contentment is elicited by stimuli other than an actual recent meal, such as relived experiences (Kreibig, 2010).

In nonhuman animals, changes associated with contentment after eating can be detected in the brain. After the meal, dopaminergic activation in the nucleus accumbens calms down and is replaced by β-endorphin activity, which slows overall behavior (Depue & Morrone-Strupinsky, 2005). How do humans know when they've had enough to eat? As the stomach fills up, it sends a message through the vagal branch of the parasympathetic nervous system back to the hypothalamus (Dockray & Burdyga, 2011). Other pathways involving the neurotransmitter cholecystokinin lead from the small intestine to the brain, sending messages about the nutritional content of the meal (Dockray, 2012). Messages from the hypothalamus to other regions then convey the command to stop eating. Laboratory animals in which these pathways have been disrupted are likely to become obese, suggesting that a similar problem may be one of many reasons why some people eat to excess (Badman & Flier, 2005).

What effect does contentment have on cognition? The increase in blood flow to the stomach, while supporting digestion, comes at the expense of blood flow to the brain. As a result, cognitive activity slows down—a phenomenon commonly known as "food coma." However, the sense of satiety associated with contentment may enhance at least one important aspect of cognition. Barbara Fredrickson (1998) has proposed that contentment should facilitate memory consolidation for the pathway one took to acquire the reward. After all, whatever you just did must have been successful, so remembering your actions is a good plan.

Studies increasingly offer support for this proposal. In one early study, researchers inserted single-cell recording electrodes into *place cells* in rodents' hippocampi—neural structures necessary for spatial memory formation. They then had the animals run a maze to find a snack. After eating the snack, the animals went through a behavioral *satiety sequence* that included looking around to make sure no predators were nearby, grooming, and hanging out quietly—similar to a human lying on the couch and watching television after dinner (Bradshaw & Cook, 1996). While the animals were chilling out in this way, their hippocampal place cells fired in the reverse sequence compared to how they fired while animals ran the maze, as though they were mentally backtracking their course (Foster & Wilson, 2006).

As it turns out, multiple neural and hormonal effects of satiety promote enhanced hippocampal memory formation, including insulin release and activation of the vagal branch of the parasympathetic nervous system (Suarez, Noble, & Kanoski, 2019). A study in humans has linked individual differences in tendency to experience satiety—in this case defined as reduced craving for snack foods after a meal—to more effective hippocampal-dependent learning (Attuquayefio et al., 2016). This study relies on individual differences rather than experimentally demonstrating increased hippocampal memory encoding during satiety, but it is an intriguing first step toward replicating the effect in humans.

Pride

Currently, the strongest case for a basic/discrete positive emotion can probably be made for **pride**. This is largely thanks to the work of Jessica Tracy and Richard Robins (2004; 2008a; 2008b) who first began to examine the nonverbal display of this emotion, as discussed in Chapter 5. When Tracy and Robins asked research participants in the United States to pose an expression of pride, people consistently expanded their posture, puffed out their chests, lifted their heads higher, and either put their hands on their hips or raised their arms in the air (Figure 12.11a). Some showed a smile, but not all, and if a smile was present it was subtle and controlled. In colloquial use, the term "pride" typically refers to a person's emotional response to his or her own achievement, or to being admired by other people. This can be seen in the pride posture, which looks much like other animals' dominance display (Figure 12.11b). In follow-up studies, Tracy and colleagues found that this display is easily recognized by children as young as 4 years old (Tracy, Robins, & Lagattuta, 2005), as well as by people in cultures with limited exposure to Western emotional expressions (Tracy et al., 2013).

We discussed pride extensively in Chapter 9, and suggest you review that material again now. However, one additional point on pride is valuable. Tracy and colleagues have proposed that—at least in humans—two forms of pride have somewhat different origins and social implications (Tracy & Robins, 2014). **Authentic pride** is closer to the definition given previously: positive emotion experience based on an accurate assessment of one's own accomplishment. This facet of pride is earned by one's actions, rather than based on assumption of one's innate superiority. In contrast, **hubristic pride** emerges from people's belief that they are naturally better than others—that their achievements reflect ability rather than effort (Tracy & Robins, 2007). Although the nonverbal expressions of authentic and hubristic pride are similar, the latter is more likely to be accompanied by boasting, and perceived by others as unearned (Tracy & Prehn, 2012). In interpreting others' proud behavior, we decide whether the pride is justified. If so, we willingly grant the person higher status and regard; if not, we often assume the person is just arrogant.

Love

Before we start analyzing love as an emotion, is it is an emotion at all? If you ask people to write a list of emotions, one of their most common responses is *love* (Fehr & Russell,

FIGURE 12.11. The human pride display (a; Tracy & Robins, 2004) looks a lot like the dominance display of other primates (b).

1984; Shaver et al., 1987). However, when psychologists list the basic emotions, most do not include love. For this reason, it has received surprisingly little attention from researchers who study emotion.

Instead of considering love an emotion, some psychologists consider it a lasting **attitude** or affective disposition toward a particular individual (Rubin, 1970). This definition is consistent with Elaine Hatfield and Susan Sprecher's (1986) description of *passionate love* as intense infatuation and longing for union with another person, involving lots of intense emotions without being an emotion per se. Others have described love, especially romantic love, as a **script**, or culturally learned set of expectations about events, thoughts, feelings, and behaviors (e.g., Skolnick, 1978). As we noted in Chapter 3, a simple American script for romantic love goes something like this: "They met, and it was love at first sight. There would never be another girl (boy) for him (her). No one could come between them. They overcame obstacles and lived happily ever after" (Swidler, 2001). Even if you don't accept that script, you probably accept a different one—a set of assumptions about what happens when people are in love. This script likely includes the experience of certain emotions, but also goes beyond emotions to aspects of the situation and appropriate behaviors.

Both the attitude approach and the script approach attempt to account for the variety of feelings experienced by people in close relationships. Both conclude that the whole package of love is too complex to reflect a single emotion. However, some researchers have asked whether the many different types of love have a common theme. Beverly Fehr and James Russell (1991) proposed that love is best thought of as a *prototype*—a set of characteristics that describes the ideal example of some category, but that may not be held by every member of that category. Instead of asking what characteristics are necessary and sufficient to call something love, Fehr and Russell asked participants to list as many examples of love as they could think of, and examined which examples were listed most often and what the examples had in common. Although some participants listed love of food, country, music and art, and material things, the most commonly mentioned examples involved close relationships. When Fehr and Russell asked another set of participants to rate the prototypicality of 20 different kinds of love, again people said the best examples were love for parents, children, other family members, romantic partners, and close friends (see Table 12.1).

In a third study, Fehr and Russell found that statements such as "love is a giving process, understanding the other, and realizing the other's faults," "commitment and caring are important components of love," and "love has to be worked at and strived for to truly be achieved" were rated as especially good descriptions of love. Based on the results of these studies, emotion researchers can narrow their focus. People may talk casually about loving material things, but love is mainly experienced in the context of building and maintaining close relationships.

An alternative approach is to identify qualitatively different types of love that look more like discrete emotions, while accounting for our broad use of this English-language term. John Bowlby, who spent his career carefully observing infants and their parents, agreed that emotions in close relationships are an important part of our evolutionary heritage. Based on his observations, Bowlby described three distinct *behavioral programs* that he considered the biological foundations of bonding within families (Bowlby, 1979): attachment, caregiving, and sex. We discussed attachment extensively in Chapter 9. Although Bowlby's (1979) own research focused primarily on attachment, he believed that all three of these foundations were important in the close relationships we call "loving."

TABLE 12.1 | Types of love

Although the term "love" describes people's feelings toward many kinds of targets, American participants agree that some kinds of love are more love-like than others. This table shows how prototypically love-like Fehr and Russell's (1991) participants considered 20 different types of love.

Type of Love	Prototypicality	Type of Love	Prototypicality
Maternal love	5.39	Love for humanity	4.42
Parental love	5.22	Spiritual love	4.27
Friendship	4.96	Passionate love	4.00
Sisterly love	4.84	Platonic love	3.98
Romantic love	4.76	Self-love	3.79
Brotherly love	4.74	Sexual love	3.76
Familial love	4.74	Patriotic love	3.21
Sibling love	4.73	Love of work	3.14
Affection	4.60	Puppy love	2.98
Committed love	4.47	Infatuation	2.42

From Fehr & Russell (1991).

He did not call these behavioral programs emotions, describing them instead as complex social instincts. However, the possibility that Bowlby's behavioral programs correspond to three distinguishable emotions has been proposed (Shaver, Morgan, & Wu, 1996). In Chapter 9 we introduced the concepts of *attachment love* and *nurturant love*, and we expect you're already familiar with the idea of sexual desire. Researchers have documented some similarities (e.g., involvement of oxytocin, Diamond, 2003) and differences (e.g., in nonverbal expression, Gonzaga et al., 2006; implications for social cognition, Griskevicius, Shiota, & Neufeld, 2010), but much more research is needed to investigate how these "flavors of love" overlap and diverge.

So far all of the approaches to defining love locate it within the individual; love is experienced by one person toward someone else. A new approach, recently proposed by Barbara Fredrickson and colleagues, is to define love as a phenomenon that occurs between two or more people, rather than within one person alone. Fredrickson (2013) describes **positivity resonance** as a momentary state defined by shared experience of positive emotions, behavioral and physiological synchrony, and mutual caring for each other's well-being. Again, this does not really meet the criteria for a basic or discrete emotion, but it is a powerful state of emotional connection experienced by two (or possibly more) people.

Early research on positivity resonance suggests that it has important implications for both individual well-being and relationship satisfaction. In studies using questionnaire and daily diary methods, individuals who experience positivity resonance more frequently report higher well-being and lower symptoms of depression, even after controlling for daily levels of individual positive emotion (Major et al., 2018). In a US study of couples in long-term marriages, behavioral markers of positivity resonance (such as simultaneous smiles and laughter, and expressing mutual affection or concern) during a conversation about an area of conflict in the relationship significantly predicted marital satisfaction, even after controlling for each spouse's individual expressions of positive emotion (Otero et al., 2020). During these moments couples tended to show heightened **physiological linkage**, with cardiovascular and electrodermal fluctuations happening in synchrony (see Figure 12.12). Moreover, the couples who showed greater linkage during moments of positivity resonance reported healthier, more satisfying marriages several years later (Chen et al., 2021).

What is love, really? We can't offer you a single answer to this question, and we're not inclined to try. The complexity we've seen in defining love as a psychological construct highlights the risks of overrelying one language's emotion vocabulary to determine what we should study. The different ways of studying love discussed above are all valuable, revealing new features of emotion in intimate relationships. Whether we think of love as "an emotion" or as a phenomenon that involves lots of emotion felt toward or with another person, love is important for people's well-being, and worth far more scientific investigation than it has received so far.

Amusement and Humor

Oddly, one of the most commonly observed expressions of positive emotion—laughter—is associated with an emotion that has received fairly little attention in its own right—amusement. Think how much we value humor. We spend so much time watching comedies on television that the situational comedy, or sitcom, is one of the largest categories of programs. We gladly buy tickets for a movie or play that promises to make us laugh. When people describe the characteristics they look for in a dating partner or lifelong mate, *sense of humor* is typically near the top (Boxer, Noonan, & Whelan, 2015; Lippa, 2007). However, few emotion researchers have concentrated their research on humor, laughter, or amusement, and many fundamental questions are unanswered.

Part of the difficulty lies in finding stimuli that are reliably funny, evoking humor in most people. George Orwell (2000, p. 284) once said, "A thing is funny when—in some way that is not actually offensive or frightening—it upsets the established order. Every joke is a tiny revolution." According to one theory, people experience humor in response to a **cognitive shift**—a transition from thinking about some target in one way to thinking about it from a completely different, but still appropriate, perspective (Latta, 1999). Consider the following joke, which is admittedly not great, although it makes the point:

> Q: How do you stop a lawyer from drowning?
> A: Shoot him before he hits the water.

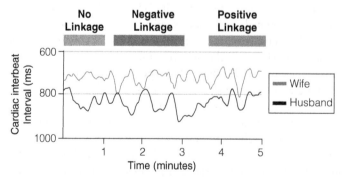

FIGURE 12.12. In physiological linkage, fluctuations in two people's physiology occur in a synchronized way.

If you think this is funny, why? According to the cognitive shift perspective, the humor lies in your mind's shift from an assumption that one is trying to save the lawyer's life to a focus on choosing the method of death. The assumption set up in the premise of the joke is shattered and replaced by the punch line, so you have to think about the situation in a new way, although the new way also makes sense. Note that the effectiveness of the joke depends on having some contempt for lawyers, or at least recognizing that this is a commonly expressed feeling, so that the idea of wanting to kill one is plausible. Starting with the question "How do you stop a kindergarten teacher from drowning?" will presumably dampen the joke's value. If you are a lawyer, thinking about becoming a lawyer, or have close friends who are lawyers, the joke might not seem so funny.

One implication of the cognitive shift definition is that what strikes one person as funny may not amuse someone else. Consider puns, bathroom humor, dirty jokes, ethnic jokes, and slapstick (see Figure 12.13). In each case, some people laugh uproariously while others consider the joke tasteless, stupid, or at least not-funny. To understand the premise of a particular joke and find its punch line surprising, yet appropriate, you need certain cultural reference points and personal attitudes. Few comic movies, plays, or books stand the test of time. The humor of a different culture often fails completely in translation.

Amusement also depends on who presents the joke. You are more likely to say something funny, and to enjoy the other person's attempts at humor, if you like the person than if you don't (Li et al., 2009). Humor about the characteristics of various groups, such as ethnic, religious, national, and other kinds of groups, is especially tricky. It doesn't matter whether the substance of the joke is arguably true or not; it presumably invokes

FIGURE 12.13. Tastes in humor vary by culture, gender, age, and historical era, among other factors. A movie that someone else considers hilarious may not amuse you at all.

some stereotype about people who belong to that group. When someone makes a joke about his or her own group, it can have a self-deprecating quality and can be a way to affectionately affirm identification with and commitment to that group (Borgella, Howard, & Maddox, 2020). If someone outside the group makes the same joke, however, it sounds more presumptuous, potentially insulting (depending on what the stereotype is), and is far less likely to amuse members of the group in question.

Another difficulty with treating amusement as a basic or discrete emotion has been identifying the adaptive "problem" that it solves. Humor and laughter are pleasant, but to what kind of opportunity do they respond? Here, as with pride, it is interesting to examine similarities between human and nonhuman expressive displays. When people express amusement, even if they're not laughing, they show a big Duchenne smile with a relaxed jaw and open mouth, and they often throw their head back or tilt it to the side (Campos et al., 2013). Young children and many other animals show a similar expression when they want to play (Figure 12.14). Although psychologists have been stumped about the adaptive value of amusement, they are clear on the function of play—to help us practice new skills and test out new ideas in a safe environment, developing competence and flexibility in a complex world (Pellegrini & Smith, 2005).

In most animals, *play* largely means play fighting, and in small children it often refers to rough-and-tumble play as well. In this kind of play, youngsters are developing important physical skills needed to survive. In humans, however, cognitive and social play are also important. Thus, some researchers have proposed that **amusement** is fundamentally an emotional response to the opportunity of learning presented by play (Shiota et al., 2019). As theories of amusement develop, further empirical research is likely to follow.

Awe

Awe also has a long history of neglect in psychology research, although it has become a much more popular topic in recent years. Again, identifying the adaptive problem addressed by this emotion has been tricky. **Awe** can be defined as our emotional response to vast, extraordinary stimuli; events that we find challenging to comprehend. In Western societies, many individuals experience awe toward natural vistas, such as the Grand Canyon or Niagara Falls (Figure 12.15), but people also report feeling awed by great works of art, architecture, literature, and music, as well as amazing human accomplishments (Shiota, Keltner, & Mossman, 2007). Such stimuli bring considerable pleasure, and people will go to great expense to see them, but what implications do they have for adaptive fitness?

FIGURE 12.14. Adult human laughter looks much like the expression children and other animals show during play.

FIGURE 12.15.   People experience awe when facing vast, extraordinary stimuli that are difficult to comprehend.

According to Dacher Keltner and Jon Haidt (2003), the function of awe is similar to that proposed for amusement, in that it helps us learn. We noted in Chapter 10 that many positive emotions send us into cognitive autopilot, forming judgments easily and with confidence, but relying on shortcuts and heuristics rather than careful analysis of the environment. If you are presented with a new stimulus that is too big and important to disregard, but that you don't understand, blithely ignoring it while you go on your way is probably a mistake. The adaptive thing to do is to pay close attention to it, and learn as much about it as you can. Put another way, awe should facilitate **cognitive accommodation**, processes by which we attend to and encode new information from the environment rather than seeing the world through the lens of our expectations and assumptions.

If this is correct, then awe should differ from other positive emotions in many ways, and research suggests that it does. Unlike other positive emotions, posed facial expressions of awe do not include a smile; instead, people raise the middle of their eyebrows in a manner that slightly resembles sadness, open their eyes wide, lean forward, and open their mouths while relaxing the jaw (Campos et al., 2013). Whereas most positive emotions are associated with some degree of physiological arousal, awe has been linked to a withdrawal of sympathetic nervous system influence on the heart (Shiota et al., 2011).

Consistent with the proposed adaptive function above, awe has been linked to cognitive effects consistent with accommodation. Imagine being a participant in one study. You begin by completing some task intended to elicit a specific emotion state, such as watching a short movie clip or looking at a series of photos. Then you listen to a five-minute audio story about a couple going out for a romantic dinner, with lots of little details (see Figure 12.16). You complete a short arithmetic task and then, unexpectedly, you're asked to answer a bunch of true/false questions about the romantic dinner story:

FIGURE 12.16. Imagine hearing a story about a couple going out to a romantic dinner, with lots of details. In one series of studies, participants who had completed an awe-eliciting task right before hearing the story later remembered details of the story more accurately.

Was there a candle on the table? Was the waiter wearing glasses? And so forth. Participants who had viewed an awe stimulus in the first task remembered story details more accurately than those in other conditions, including conditions evoking a different positive emotion (Danvers & Shiota, 2017). In particular, awe condition participants were less likely to make a certain kind of error: assuming that some element typical of a romantic dinner (e.g., a candle on the table) had actually been present, although it was never mentioned in the story. In other words, the awe participants were less likely to be tricked by their own expectations into falsely recalling story details that weren't there.

In a study of effects of different positive emotions on persuasive message processing, described in the section on enthusiasm, awe was one of only two positive emotions to *increase* people's critical analysis of the messages, such that they were much more persuaded by strong rather than weak arguments (nurturant love was the other; Griskevicius, Shiota, & Neufeld, 2010). When people are feeling awe, they report being immersed in the moment (Shiota et al., 2007), so much so that they feel like time is slowing down (Rudd, Vohs, & Aaker, 2012). Although awe does not increase people's reports of religiosity, it does increase their reports of spirituality, their sense that they are connected to a larger, meaningful, universal unit (Van Cappellen & Saroglou, 2012). Although awe is subjectively pleasant for many people, it can also be unsettling, reducing our confidence and certainty that we understand what is going on out there in the world (Valdesolo & Graham, 2014).

One of the most consistently reported aspects of awe is feeling that the self is small—presumably in relation to the vastness of the awe-inducing stimulus. Highly awe-prone people are described by their friends as humble, and experimentally elicited awe leads people to brag a bit less when asked to write an essay on both their personal strengths and their weaknesses (Stellar et al., 2018). In experimentally elicited awe people frequently report feeling a sense of "small self," agreeing more strongly than those in control conditions with statements such as "I feel small or insignificant" or "I feel the presence of something greater than myself" (Piff et al., 2015; Shiota et al., 2007). Although this might sound somewhat depressing, people typically describe awe as very pleasant, suggesting that the small self of awe is not the same as low self-esteem (e.g., Danvers & Shiota, 2017; Griskevicius et al., 2010; Shiota et al., 2007).

The small-self effect is seen across a wide range of cultures, including more collectivist East Asian countries as well as individualist Western countries (Bai et al., 2017). Remarkably, much research suggests that the small-self feeling promotes helpful, prosocial behavior. Researchers Paul Piff, Dacher Keltner, and colleagues found that experimentally evoked awe (see Figure 12.17) led not only to more ethical decisions in hypothetical tasks (e.g., the cashier at a coffee shop gives you too much change), but also to greater helping of a real-life person who has just accidentally dropped a bunch of pens (Piff et al., 2015).

There is still much we do not know about awe—for example, no study has yet examined what regions of the brain are activated during awe. However, interest in this emotion is growing rapidly, and we expect much research in the future.

Hope and Optimism

Imagine that it is the night before an important exam, and a classmate calls you in terror to say that in previous classes, more than 60% of the students failed. You know things look bad, but you also prepared carefully for the exam, believe that if you approach the test the right way you'll do well, and are determined to put in another hour of study before getting a good night's sleep to refresh your mind. How would you describe the emotion you might be feeling? According to Snyder and colleagues, this is the essence of **hope**— high agency in a challenging situation combined with active generation of plans that can facilitate the desired outcome (Snyder et al., 2001). The emotional state of hope relates closely to the challenge appraisal discussed in Chapter 4. People who are hopeful also

FIGURE 12.17.   In one study of the effects of awe on prosocial behavior, participants completed the study either while standing in a grove of extremely tall eucalyptus trees (awe condition) or while looking at a building of similar height (neutral control condition). Those who completed the study among the trees were more helpful to a person who "accidentally" dropped a bunch of pens.

tend to be optimistic. **Optimism** can be defined as an expectation that good things will happen, either in general or in a specific situation. In this sense, optimism is a type of appraisal that facilitates feelings of hope. Monozygotic twins resemble each other more strongly than dizygotic twins do in their degree of optimism, suggesting some degree of genetic influence on this trait (Schulman, Keith, & Seligman, 1993).

One common optimistic belief is that "better things will happen to me than to other people." That is, I am more likely than other people to succeed in life, more likely to survive to old age, less likely to have an automobile accident, less likely to get a dreaded disease, and so forth (Quadrel, Fischhoff, & Davis, 1993). That belief is often called *unrealistic optimism* because most people have no reason to believe their chance of success or of illness is any different from the average (Nezlek & Zebrowski, 2001). A mild degree of unrealistic optimism is nevertheless widespread. Most US adults overestimate the accuracy of their guesses on difficult questions (Plous, 1993), their probability of winning a lottery (Langer, 1975), and their ability to explain complex physical phenomena (Rozenblit & Keil, 2002). When asked how conscientious they will be about exercising, saving for retirement, and so forth, they give almost the same answers as when asked how they would be "in an ideal world" (Tanner & Carlson, 2008).

We might assume that unrealistic optimism is a bad thing, and indeed it is when it leads to foolish risks or bad plans. For example, most people severely overestimate how quickly they will finish a difficult task, and don't set aside enough time for it (Buehler, Griffin, & Ross, 1994; Dunning, Heath, & Suls, 2005). Many people ignore warnings about diet, smoking, alcohol, and so forth, confident that they will remain healthy anyway. As a rule, however, a little unrealistic optimism helps people deal with bad news and muster up the energy to go on with life (Taylor & Brown, 1988; Taylor et al., 2000). Most people recognize that their estimates are not always accurate, but believe that slightly unrealistic optimism is a good thing (Armor, Massey, & Sackett, 2008).

A different type of belief is that "everything will turn out all right no matter what I do, so I don't have to do anything." That is a calming attitude, but not a productive one. The more helpful type of optimism is the belief that "my problems are solvable, my actions make a difference, and I can control my future chances for success." Optimism in this sense differs from pessimism by the attributions people make for their successes, and especially for their failures (Carver & Scheier, 2002; Peterson & Steen, 2002). Pessimists tend to feel that desirable outcomes are beyond their control, whereas optimists believe that their actions make a difference and that effort pays off.

APPLICATION: POSITIVE EMOTION AND BEHAVIOR CHANGE
Learning Objective
- Summarize two ways in which positive emotion can support behavior change efforts, describing an example study for each kind of effect.

In Chapter 11 we discussed a practical application of fear. Under certain circumstances (can you remember what they are?), fear appeals that emphasize the negative consequences of staying on one's current path (smoking cigarettes; spending all day every day in a chair or on the couch instead of getting some exercise; continuing to dump endless amounts of plastic into landfill and the oceans) can help motivate behavior change.

Can positive emotions be of any use in this regard? A growing number of researchers are asking this question, and finding promising effects.

We discussed hope and optimism in the preceding section, and they can be important in behavior change. Recall that fear appeals are more effective when the message also offers concrete, achievable steps one can take to prevent the bad outcome (this is the answer to the question in the last paragraph). The principle is that a sense of self-efficacy—belief that one is capable of doing what it takes—is necessary for people to actually try to change their behavior. If you know what you need to do, and are confident you can do it, then hope and optimism are likely to follow. For example, after major surgery people with an optimistic attitude report less distress, and better overall quality of life. One reason for this is that an optimistic person asks questions of the doctors and nurses, reads about the illness and its treatment, and makes plans for overcoming the problem (Carver et al., 1993; Scheier et al., 1989). A well-informed patient is more likely to follow medical advice, to get proper nutrition and exercise, and to take all the other steps that improve chances for recovery. So, the benefits of optimism manifest in both direct and indirect ways.

Positive emotion can help promote behavior in another way as well. The trick is to associate the desired behavior with an *immediate* reward in people's minds (Shiota et al., 2021). In Chapters 6 and 11 we discussed conditioned fears—fears learned through repeated association of some initially neutral stimulus with an aversive outcome, such as a loud noise or painful electric shock. It is possible to condition enthusiasm as well. This is a very different approach from most public health messages, which emphasize the long-term benefits of a healthy lifestyle rather than anticipation of immediate enjoyment. However, it works! Esther Papies and colleagues (2020) examined descriptive labels on prepackaged meals in the supermarket, finding that meat-based meal labels were more likely to mention flavor, texture, and other aspects of deliciousness, whereas plant-based meals focused on the healthy properties of the meal rather than taste. In a follow-up laboratory study, participants rated the appeal of vegetarian meals with labels that either described their yumminess in detail, or simply described the ingredients and preparation. Participants rated products with the flavor-focused labels as much more appetizing (Papies et al., 2020).

In a very clever study, Bradley Turnwald and colleagues (2019) manipulated the labeling of vegetable side dishes offered in five college dining halls around the United States. In order to control for specific dishes (after all, pitting brussels sprouts against carrots is just unfair) they arranged for the dining halls to rotate dishes on a regular schedule, and randomized each dish to conditions across different days when it was served. They measured not only how many servings were taken by diners, but also how much was left on the dish at the end of the meal when diners turned in their trays. On days when veggies were labeled with descriptions emphasizing details of their flavor, more were taken—and actually eaten—than when the labels emphasized health, or simply stated the ingredients. Studies show that simply drawing people's attention to the potential for immediate enjoyment and short-term rewards can increase persistence for behaviors such as physical exercise and academic study as well (Woolley & Fishbach, 2016).

SUMMARY

Happiness rises and falls with the events of life, but it also depends strongly on someone's disposition or personality, an enduring trait that we bring to the situation. Optimistic people find something to be happy about, or they make something good happen. Pessimists are more likely to give up and wallow in boredom or distress. Of course, events do matter. Many people remain cheerful despite unpleasant circumstances, however. This may be because they make an effort to improve their circumstances, rather than the result of some fixed aspect of their brain chemistry. The way we think about situations is part of our personality that affects our emotions, but unlike our genes, it is a part we can change with practice and effort.

As a society, the United States (along with many other countries) strives for economic prosperity. Why? Presumably because it will make us happy. Why not strive for happiness itself? Most people say they have other goals besides wealth, and some they consider far more important than wealth. Wealth gets more than its share of attention, possibly because it is easy to measure. Ed Diener and Martin Seligman (2004) have proposed that psychologists should try to measure life satisfaction and use that as a guide to public policy, just as economists advise the government based on economic measures. It is an idea worth pursuing and refining, and a likely basis for much future research.

We've also seen that although happiness does not seem much like an emotion state—at least not in the way we emphasized in Chapter 1—researchers are paying increasing attention to several specific positive emotions. The evidence on these varies greatly, and some seem like better candidates for basic/discrete emotion status than others. Ultimately, however, the decision about whether some emotion "counts" as basic or discrete may matter less than the research conducted along the way, investigating the roles these emotion states play in our lives.

KEY TERMS

amusement: an emotional response to the opportunity of learning presented by play (p. 442)

attitude: a combination of beliefs, feelings, and behaviors directed toward a person, object, or category (p. 438)

authentic pride: pride based on an accurate assessment of one's achievement (p. 437)

awe: emotional response to vast stimuli that are challenging for us to comprehend (p. 442)

broaden and build theory: theory that positive emotions promote broadened attention to the environment, as well as greater flexibility in thought/action repertoires (p. 431)

cognitive accommodation: attending to and encoding new information from the environment, rather than filtering perception through expectations and assumptions (p. 443)

cognitive shift: transition from thinking about some target from one perspective to thinking about it from a completely different, but still appropriate, perspective (p. 440)

contentment: positive emotion felt after consuming a meal or other reward (p. 435)

dispositional positivity: a personality characteristic defined by high self-esteem, a tendency toward optimism, and positive appraisals of one's life and future (p. 423)

enthusiasm: pleasure from anticipating a reward (p. 433)

eudaimonic well-being: the sense that one's life is meaningful, consistent with personal values, and fulfilling one's potential (p. 418)

hedonic well-being: a general feeling that one's life is pleasant and good, characterized by high positive affect, low negative affect, and high life satisfaction (p. 418)

hope: high agency in a challenging situation, combined with active generation of plans that can facilitate the desired outcome (p. 445)

hubristic pride: pride based on belief in one's inherent superiority over others (p. 437)

income satiation: the cutoff in annual income beyond which more money fails to predict an increase in happiness (p. 426)

optimism: expectation that mostly good things will happen (p. 446)

physiological linkage: a state in which two people's physiological changes, such as changes in heart rate or electrodermal activity, are correlated with each other over some period of time (p. 439)

positivity resonance: a momentary state shared by two people, defined by shared experience of positive emotions, behavioral and physiological synchrony, and mutual caring for each other's well-being (p. 439)

pride: an emotional response to one's own achievement (including achievements of the group) and/or to being admired by other people (p. 436)

script: a culturally learned set of expectations about events, thoughts, feelings, and behaviors that should accompany some experience (p. 438)

subjective well-being: self-evaluation of one's life as pleasant, interesting, and satisfying (p. 417)

z-scores: standardized scores produced by subtracting the scale mean from each raw score and dividing the remainder by the standard deviation (p. 418)

THOUGHT/DISCUSSION QUESTIONS

1. Studies show that people who are instructed to behave in an extraverted manner report enjoying social interaction more than those assigned to act introverted, even if they are not naturally outgoing. What might explain this effect? What about the interaction may change, making it more enjoyable? Come up with several possible explanatory variables, if you can. How would you test your hypotheses in a new study?

2. Much research indicates that life events tend not to have long-term effects on psychological well-being or happiness; the immediate response wears off in several months to a year. Can you think of any life events that you do think would have longer-term impact, either increasing or decreasing well-being? Argue your case based on what is known about the predictors of well-being.

3. Presumably, we smile when we are happy because we gain some advantage by communicating our happiness to others. Why is that communication helpful? Is it ever disadvantageous? That is, are there times when we should inhibit our smiles?

4. Some research studies suggest that positive emotion facilitates creativity. Do you think this is likely to be the case for all positive emotions discussed in this chapter or just some? If the latter, which ones, and why?

SUGGESTIONS FOR FURTHER READING

Ben-Shahar, T. (2007). *Happier: Learn the secrets to daily joy and lasting fulfillment.* McGraw–Hill. Based on a wildly popular course on positive psychology at Harvard, this book offers personal exercises aimed at enhancing each reader's well-being, as well as an analysis of what it means to be happy.

Fredrickson, B. L. (2013). *Love 2.0: Finding happiness and health in moments of connection.* Hudson Street Press/Penguin. This book offers a rich and relatable discussion of positivity resonance, and the new research on this phenomenon.

Haidt, J. (2006). *The happiness hypothesis: Finding modern truth in ancient wisdom.* Basic Books. A thoughtful integration of philosophy and modern empirical research on what makes us happy.

Shiota, M. N., Neufeld, S. L., Danvers, A. F., Osborne, E. A., Sng, O., & Yee, C. I. (2014). Positive emotion differentiation: A functional approach. *Social and Personality Psychology Compass, 8*(3), 104–117. This article, written to be accessible to undergraduates, describes several possible discrete positive emotions through the lens of adaptive function.

CHAPTER 13

Emotion in Clinical Psychology

Throughout this book we have emphasized the view that emotions are mostly adaptive. Emotions likely evolved to help us navigate common problems that arose in our evolutionary history, such as avoiding danger and finding mates. In carefully examining the relationship between emotion and motivation, we concluded that the energy and direction of motivation are often rooted in emotional responses, pushing us to approach situations that benefit our survival and reproduction, and avoid those that spell possible harm. Emotions guide the formation and dissolution of our close relationships, and connections throughout human society. They help us decide what to pay attention to, what to remember, and how to make decisions. We even claimed that painful negative emotions such as fear, disgust, and embarrassment may play important roles in our lives!

That all said, we are sure that even a brief reflection on your own life can tell you that emotions are not *always* helpful. Despair in the wake of a painful breakup or loss of a loved one can derail one's life completely. Anxiety can freeze you in a moment critical to your goals—right before an important work presentation, for instance. A friendship may be ruined when a rush of anger leads you to say something you regret.

These examples of emotional responses with negative consequences are still part of everyday experience, not a cause for clinical concern, or a sign that one might need therapeutic services. In many people's lives, however, there are times when despair occurs without a clear cause, or where the despair carries on for much longer than would be expected after a breakup or loss. There are times when anxiety freezes you in too many moments across too many situations, and you find yourself avoiding everyday challenges, shrinking the size of your life in order to cope. Or where your temper is triggered so often that it is causing real damage across multiple arenas of life. At these times, a person might reach out to a therapist to talk through how to approach such situations differently, and/ or a psychiatrist for medication to help regain their typical level of life functioning. In other words, emotional symptoms can become severe enough to warrant a diagnosis of mental illness, and corresponding treatment. The study of the predictors, correlates, and best treatment for mental illness is called clinical psychology.

What can clinical psychologists learn from emotion researchers, and what can emotion researchers learn from clinical psychologists? Just as you sometimes understand a machine better when you try to fix it, the same is true of emotion. As psychologists learn about emotional extremes, they also learn about the nature of emotions more generally. And the more they understand healthy emotions, the better able they are to develop treatments for people with emotional difficulties.

DIAGNOSIS IN CLINICAL PSYCHOLOGY

Learning Objectives
- Describe the *Diagnostic and Statistical Manual for Mental Disorders* (*DSM-5*), and summarize two key differences between the criteria for *DSM-5* diagnoses and ways in which physical illnesses are diagnosed.
- Define comorbidity, and explain why comorbidity of multiple *DSM-5* diagnoses is very common.

In the early days of clinical psychology and psychiatry, therapists drew few distinctions among types of psychological disorders. A few categories existed, such as schizophrenia and depression, but in many cases therapists were content with classifying a client as having either neurosis or psychosis. (Confusingly, neurosis was conceptualized as a primarily psychological problem, whereas psychosis was a presumed neurological problem.) In many cases, therapists gave no diagnosis at all. This practice continued for a long time. After all, many people want to talk with a professional about a current worry or concern but would prefer not to have the complications associated with a formal diagnosis of mental illness.

Gradually, policies changed, for two reasons. First, insurance companies are far more likely to pay for treatment for a diagnosed disorder than for someone who just wants to talk with a therapist. Hence, therapists must at least label each client seeking insurance coverage. Second, therapists sought to be seen as more like medical doctors. If you visit a physician with a complaint of headache, abdominal pain, persistent cough, or any other symptom, the physician will run laboratory tests to determine the cause. Identifying the cause leads to a diagnosis, and the diagnosis helps in determining the proper treatment. For mental illness, the goal was similar: give each client a precise diagnosis, and thereby know what treatment to administer. From a scientific standpoint, it was assumed that having a classification system for mental disorders would also help researchers identify the best possible treatment for each diagnostic category.

The outcome of this optimistic enterprise was the ***Diagnostic and Statistical Manual of Mental Disorders (DSM***; American Psychiatric Association, 2013, see Figure 13.1). After several revisions, the *DSM* is now in the fifth edition, abbreviated *DSM-5*. In *DSM-5*, the list of possible diagnoses—not including descriptions or criteria—continues for 14 pages. One intent of this system is that every therapist or researcher defines each diagnosis the same way. Thus, in theory, a group of patients diagnosed with a disorder should be similar to another group of patients anywhere else in the world with the same disorder. In that regard, however, the *DSM* has not been entirely successful. For example, the description of attention-deficit/hyperactivity disorder (ADHD) lists nine inattention symptoms and nine hyperactivity/impulsivity symptoms. To qualify for the diagnosis, a

FIGURE 13.1. Clinicians use the *Diagnostic and Statistical Manual of Mental Disorders*, fifth edition, to compare symptoms reported by their clients with lists of criteria for mental illness diagnoses. Published by the American Psychiatric Association, this large manual contains all the diagnostic criteria for mental disorders.

child must exhibit at least six of the symptoms between these lists. (The rules are slightly different for adults.) But that means that two children with the same diagnosis may not have a single symptom in common. Diagnosing other disorders also allows an either/or approach. The diagnosis for panic disorder includes more than 23,000 possible combinations of symptoms, and the diagnosis for posttraumatic stress disorder (PTSD) includes more than 636,000 possible combinations (Galatzer-Levy & Bryant, 2013).

A more fundamental problem is that most medical diagnoses are based on the cause of illness, such as a particular virus or bacterium, or damage to some specific organ, as confirmed by laboratory tests. In contrast, psychiatric diagnoses are based only on symptoms, because psychiatry is rarely sure what the underlying cause of disorder is, and thus no valid laboratory tests exist. Basing diagnosis on symptoms would be appropriate if the symptoms of each disorder were completely and consistently different from that of every other disorder, but in fact many disorders have overlapping symptoms, and many patients fit several diagnoses at once. That is, someone might meet diagnostic criteria for depression, anxiety, substance use disorder, and other problems rather than clearly fitting into one category (Caspi et al., 2014), a phenomenon known as **comorbidity**. Disorders cannot be distinguished by genetics, because the genes and proteins that predict any one disorder are also linked to other disorders (Geschwind & Flint, 2015; Network and Pathway Analysis Subgroup, 2015), and early work linking specific genes with specific mental illnesses failed to hold up to more careful analyses (Border et al., 2019). Even when a person's symptoms do fit a diagnosis particularly well, establishing the diagnosis does not always point the way to the best treatment.

Mental health diagnosis differs from that for physical illness in another way as well. You either have the coronavirus, or you don't. The same goes for cancer—you may have earlier- or later-stage cancer, which has implications for treatment, but the answer to "do I have cancer?" is either yes or no. Because anxiety, depression, or any other emotional or behavioral symptom varies continuously, the distinction between healthy and unhealthy levels of any one symptom is somewhat arbitrary. The lines drawn in the *DSM-5* are simply determined by committees of human beings who come to a consensus agreement. Wherever that line is, some people considered healthy are barely different from some who are diagnosed as clinically suffering. Consider the case of bulimia nervosa, an eating disorder in which one routinely binges (that is, eats an unusual amount of food) and purges (that is, engages in extreme behaviors to purge the calories, such as induced vomiting or extreme exercise). In the *DSM-V*, to meet criteria for this disorder one must binge and purge at least once a week for a period of three months. What about someone who binges and purges just two or three times a month, but is very distressed by that behavior? Though their experience is nearly the same as someone who meets criteria, they are left without a diagnosis—and potentially, access to treatment.

The best existing guideline for determining where to draw that line, and one emphasized in *DSM*, is that a condition is considered a diagnosable disorder if it causes significant distress or impairment in someone's life. For example, two people might have the same morbid fear of flying, but it is considered a phobia for the person whose job calls for frequent airplane travel but is not a problem for the person who rarely wants or needs to travel far from home. If someone drinks a great deal of alcohol, does that person have a disorder? Maybe. It depends on whether the alcohol use significantly impairs the person's employment, financial welfare, family life, health, and so forth. Someone must judge whether the problem causes significant distress or impairment.

The difficulties of diagnosis pose a problem for clinical psychologists who offer therapy, but they also pose major problems for researchers. Suppose we conduct research to compare a group of people with depression to a group of healthy people. Chances are that at least a few of those supposedly healthy people have at least a mild degree of depression, but not enough for a diagnosis. Almost certainly, many of the depressed people have anxiety, substance abuse, or other problems in addition to depression. You see how challenging it is to achieve a pure comparison between depressed and nondepressed people. We could decide only to include people who meet diagnostic criteria for depression alone, and not for any other disorder, but then would the study results generalize to people who do have some other disorder in addition to depression? Since by definition a diagnosis of depression adversely affects one's life functioning, depressed versus nondepressed participants also likely differ on many different variables like relationship status, exercise frequency, diet . . . the list is almost endless. You can understand why two researchers doing the same study, but with different samples of depressed people, might obtain very different results.

Because most of the research on emotion in clinical disorders was designed in accordance with *DSM* categories (for example, comparing people who are versus those who are not diagnosed with major depressive disorder), the structure of this chapter largely follows suit. At the end of the chapter we will consider a relatively new, alternative approach.

MAJOR DEPRESSIVE DISORDER

Learning Objectives

- List the primary symptoms of major depressive disorder, and explain the challenge of differentiating typical responses to loss or stress from psychopathology.
- Differentiate the proposed subtypes of depression, and evaluate the evidence for and against the idea that there are multiple such subtypes.
- Analyze the evidence regarding genetic, life experience, and cognitive appraisal risk factors for depression.
- Analyze the role of explanatory style (how we interpret the cause of some outcome) in predicting depressive symptoms; identify examples of internal versus external, global versus specific, and stable versus unstable attributions for negative outcomes; and summarize the evidence regarding the role of insensitivity to pleasure or reward in depression.
- Analyze the evidence regarding drug and talk therapy treatments for depression, as well as the roles exercise and sufficient sleep can play in preventing depression.

Whereas everyone has occasional periods of feeling down, major depressive disorder is a serious, lasting condition. According to the *DSM*, the necessary criteria for diagnosing a **major depressive episode** include either a depressed mood or a loss of interest and pleasure, persisting almost every day for at least 2 weeks (Figure 13.2). Additional symptoms include feelings of worthlessness, agitation or inactivity, impaired sleep (either too much or too little), increased or decreased appetite, lack of motivation and pleasure, and impaired concentration (American Psychiatric Association, 2013). Many, although not all, studies indicate that depression is associated with decreased production of new neurons and synapses in the hippocampus, and therefore with impaired learning as well (Miller & Hen, 2015; Planchez & Belzung, 2020).

FIGURE 13.2. Major depression is defined by prolonged sadness and/or absence of enjoyment, as well as feelings of worthlessness, lethargy, and disruptions of concentration, eating, and sleep.

Therapists can diagnose depression in a number of ways. A clinician may simply talk with a client and conclude that the symptoms warrant a diagnosis of depression. That is a common method, and severe depression is often easy to recognize unless someone is deliberately trying to hide it. Another approach is to ask the client to fill out a questionnaire, such as the MMPI (Minnesota Multiphasic Personality Inventory; Butcher et al., 2003), the Beck Depression Inventory (Beck et al., 1988), or the Hamilton Depression Rating Scale (Hamilton, 1960), which all yield scores representing how severe the depression symptoms are. One advantage of a questionnaire is the possibility of comparing scores after various durations of treatment, to quantify any progress as it occurs. A disadvantage is that these questionnaires each include slightly different symptoms of depression, making it difficult to compare results across studies. An analysis of the 7 most used depression scales found huge variability in the symptoms included (52 total symptoms!) and a worrying lack of overlap for many of the symptoms (Fried, 2017; see Figure 13.3).

Although depressed mood feels like it will last forever, typically it does not. An episode of depression may last for weeks, months, even a year or more, but eventually the person begins to feel better, even without treatment. The first episode of depression could be the only one, or more episodes could follow. On average, subsequent episodes are

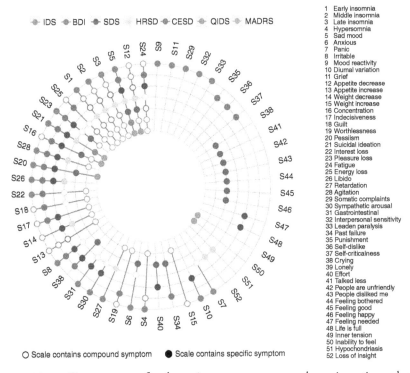

FIGURE 13.3. Co-occurrence of 52 depression symptoms across 7 depression rating scales. Filled circles for a symptom indicate that a scale directly assesses that symptom, while empty circles indicate that a scale only measures a symptom indirectly. The circles represent the following popular depression scales (from outer to inner circle): IDS, BDI, SDS, HRSD, CESD, QIDS, and MADRS. From Fried (2017).

briefer but more frequent (Solomon et al., 1997). Also, whereas most people can trace their first episode to a stressful event, the later episodes may become more spontaneous, without any obvious trigger (Monroe & Harkness, 2005; Post, 1992). The episodic nature of depression is important for evaluating any possible therapy. If someone recovers from depression after a few months of treatment, we do not know whether the treatment was effective or whether the episode simply ran its course. Evaluating a therapy requires comparing a group receiving treatment to a matched group that receives no treatment or, preferably, an alternative treatment.

In many cases, perhaps most, an extremely stressful event triggers the first episode of depression (Slavich & Irwin, 2014). For example, after an earthquake damaged the Fukushima nuclear power plant in Japan, many families were forced to seek shelter far from home. At first, people were energized and determined to try to cope with this disaster, but as time passed and they could not return to their normal lives, many became seriously depressed (Brumfiel, 2013). You may note a parallel to the resistance and exhaustion phases of reaction to stress, described in Chapter 7. Many types of severe stress can trigger a bout of depression, especially as people become exhausted. The COVID-19 pandemic was an intense and prolonged stressor for many people across the globe, and unsurprisingly people's mental health suffered. One large, nationally representative analysis found higher depression symptoms in all demographic groups during the initial pandemic lockdown than before, with a more than three-fold worsening of depression symptoms in general (Ettman et al., 2020). The lingering effects of the pandemic's disruptions are likely to extend well into our futures.

This adds another layer of complexity to diagnosing major depression. After a loss or other severe stressor, it's normal to be sad, have little energy, and generally show the symptoms of this disorder. How much of this is a healthy, typical response, and how much indicates pathology? For example, a long-standing problem for clinical psychology arises in diagnosing depression after someone has lost a loved one. Shortly after someone you love dies, it is typical to go through a period of bereavement that can include many of the symptoms of major depression (Figure 13.4). The duration of bereavement is highly variable. At what point, if any, is the reaction no longer bereavement, but an episode of major depression? Bereavement was once an exclusionary criterion for depression (i.e., if a loved one had died within some recent period, the diagnosis did not apply). This criterion has changed in the *DSM-5*, and therapists now try to distinguish a prolonged, but understandable emotional response from an abnormal response (Bondolfi, Mazzola, & Arciero, 2015). This judgment is, however, most difficult.

Multiple Types of Depression?

If you look closely at the *DSM* criteria for depression, you see some contradictions. Agitation *or* inactivity? Weight gain *or* loss? Sleeping too much *or* too little? What is going on?

Perhaps the broad category of depression combines more than one type of disorder. Some authorities distinguish among multiple subtypes. For example, *anxious* depression includes much anxiety as well as depression. *Melancholic* depression tends to be severe, marked by lack of pleasure in anything. *Psychotic* depression includes thought disorder similar to that observed in schizophrenia. *Atypical* depression is marked by increased appetite and increased sleep, in contrast to most cases of depression, in which people lose their appetite and suffer insomnia. Atypical depression is also unusual in

FIGURE 13.4. It is normal to feel sad and depressed after losing a loved one. In prior versions of the *Diagnostic and Statistical Manual of Mental Disorders*, you would not be diagnosed with depression if you had experienced a recent bereavement, but the current version offers more flexibility in deciding whether grief is normal or pathological.

that people experience brief periods of enjoyment in response to positive events. However, many people do not fit neatly into any single category. Also, putting someone into one of these categories does not reliably identify which treatment will work most successfully. Moreover, although the goal of creating subtypes was to *decrease* variability in the depression diagnosis (by narrowing down the many symptoms into consistent clusters), the actual effect was to *increase* variability, by introducing new symptoms specific to the various subtypes (Lorenzo-Luaces, Buss, & Fried, 2021). For all these reasons, although it seems clear that the broad category of depression contains much variability in specific symptom profiles, many therapists are unenthusiastic about making these distinctions (Davidson, 2007).

Some researchers have proposed identifying different types of depression based on the neurotransmitters involved. An early hypothesis posited that some forms of depression reflect a deficit in norepinephrine, whereas others reflect a deficit in serotonin. This hypothesis grew from the observation that most antidepressant drugs increase the availability of serotonin or norepinephrine, and sometimes dopamine, at the synapses. A tentative conclusion was that depression can be the result of a deficit of one or more of those neurotransmitters. However, that hypothesis poses certain problems (Mulinari, 2012). The main problem is time course: drugs can enhance activity at synapses within minutes or hours (depending on the drug), but the behavioral benefits generally do not emerge until at least 2 weeks later. Clearly, the drugs must be doing something other than just stimulating one or another type of synapse.

A revised hypothesis was that as the antidepressant drugs increased the amount of norepinephrine or serotonin at the synapses, the bombardment of those synapses led to changes in the receptors (Stahl, 1984). By that reasoning, the original problem was too much of the neurotransmitter receptors, rather than too little of the neurotransmitters themselves. Still, a problem for this revised hypothesis, as well as for the original one, is that antidepressant drugs are ineffective for many people, especially those with only mild to moderate depression (Kirsch, 2010). Results also show that these drugs affect the synapses just as much for people who do not respond well as for those who do.

Furthermore, researchers' attempts to distinguish between norepinephrine-type depression and serotonin-type depression based on symptom profiles have not helped predict which type of antidepressant drug—if any—would be effective for a given patient. For these and other reasons, researchers have largely lost interest in the norepinephrine-versus-serotonin distinction, and they have been shifting away from neurotransmitter-focused explanations altogether. Instead, most of the research interest today includes a focus on relating depression to altered neural circuits in the brain (Mulinari, 2012).

Rather than focusing on subtypes based on symptom clusters, a new approach to understanding variability in depression uses innovations in statistics and computer algorithms to predict antidepressant effectiveness. For instance, one study used data from a large sample of adults taking various antidepressants for the symptom of sadness. They used computerized models to see if they could predict whether the antidepressants were effective or not at treating depression based on which other symptoms were present. The results indicated intriguing patterns to which antidepressants were more or less effective based on symptom profiles. For instance, the antidepressant fluoxetine (you might know it as Prozac) was less effective than others when the patient was experiencing comorbid anxiety along with depression, and the antidepressant sertraline (you might know it as Zoloft) was less effective when the patient was also experiencing fatigue (Lin et al., 2020). As many people who need antidepressants go through a painful period of trial and error finding the right medication for them, such computerized models might offer promise for an easier path to recovery.

Another suggestion relating to types of depression is *DSM-5*'s distinction between major depression and persistent depressive disorder, also known as **dysthymia**. (This category more or less corresponds to melancholic depression, described earlier.) Dysthymia differs from other depression in two ways: first, the emphasis is on sad mood rather than lack of pleasure. People say that they feel down in the dumps almost all the time. Second, whereas a typical episode of major depression lasts months, dysthymia lasts years. Still, the similarities between major depression and dysthymia are greater than the differences, and the distinction is of debatable usefulness. A therapist might diagnose a new patient with major depression, but revise the diagnosis to dysthymia if it persists long enough.

Although current evidence has not shown a useful distinction between subtypes of depression, we need not give up on the idea. Further research into the causes of depression may indeed reveal important differences.

Causes of Depression

Depression is not a universal reaction to stressful events, even severe ones. Nearly everyone suffers a major loss or setback at some point in life, perhaps several such events, but most people recover without entering diagnosable depression. As a rule, a stressful event produces a greater reaction in people who were already predisposed to depression. Researchers in one study took advantage of the fact that a group of college students had filled out personality questionnaires shortly before a major earthquake struck their city in California. They found that virtually everyone felt sad or depressed shortly after the damage, but those who already had been mildly depressed before the earthquake became more severely depressed, and remained depressed longer than the other students (Nolen-Hoeksema & Morrow, 1991). Why are some people more prone to depression than others? What causes depression when it does occur?

Genetic factors are one possible basis for predisposition to depression. When an adopted child develops depression (after reaching adulthood), depression is generally more common among that person's biological relatives than among the adoptive relatives (Wender et al., 1986). Comparisons of identical and fraternal twins (also known as monozygotic and dizygotic twins) also confirm a moderate genetic influence (Wilde et al., 2014; Wium-Andersen et al., 2021). However, using modern methods to compare the chromosomes of people with and without depression, researchers have struggled to find any particular gene with a significant effect on depression (Border et al., 2019; Major Depressive Disorder Working Group, 2013). Most identified genes have only small effects, hard to replicate from one study to another, and these genes increase the risk of several disorders, not just depression (Geschwind & Flint, 2015).

In one particularly promising study, researchers limited their study to Chinese women with multiple episodes of severe depression. In this population, researchers identified two alleles that increased the risk of depression by about 15% (CONVERGE Consortium, 2015). Those alleles are rare outside China, however, and therefore the results cannot be generalized to explain depression in other populations. The outcome suggests that researchers may identify genetic predictors more successfully if they focus only on severe depression, and if they study limited, homogeneous populations of people. If this approach proves successful, it would indicate that a variety of different genes may promote depression by different biological mechanisms in different groups of people.

Whatever the genes facilitating depression may be, they appear to have multiple effects beyond depression. Major depression runs in the same families as alcohol or drug dependence, antisocial personality disorder, bulimia, panic disorder, migraine headaches, attention deficit disorder, binge eating, and a variety of other problems (Dawson & Grant, 1998; Fu et al., 2002; Hudson et al., 2003; Javaras et al., 2008; Kendler et al., 1995; Zhang et al., 2019). That is, if you have a relative with any of these disorders, you have an increased risk for developing any of the disorders on this list.

In addition to genes, previous harmful experiences predispose people to depression. We noted earlier that the first major depressive episode is often triggered by an extremely stressful experience. Extensive research has found that children subjected to emotional abuse, neglect, or sexual abuse have an increased risk of depression in later life (Mandelli, Petrelli, & Serretti, 2015). One difficulty in interpreting these results is that many children who were exposed to abusive experiences also lived in poverty or had other family influences that might lead to depression. To control for these other factors, researchers found pairs of twins in which one twin reported sexual abuse and the other did not. The finding was that both twins had a higher risk of depression than the national average, but the twin subjected to sexual abuse had a higher rate of depression than the other twin (Kendler, Kuhn, & Prescott, 2004). That is, the overall family life predisposed them somewhat to depression (as seen in both twins), but sexual abuse added to that predisposition. Beyond adverse childhood experiences, racism and discrimination are other stressors that can negatively impact mental health. Direct experience of racism and discrimination has been proposed to link with greater symptoms of depression (Clark, Anderson, Clark, & Williams, 1999), but so is indirect experience in the form of neighborhood racial discrimination (Russell, Clavél, Cutrona, Abraham, & Burzette, 2018) and even vicarious witnessing of racial discrimination on news or social media (Chae et al., 2021).

Biology may predispose some people to depression more than others, but depression also relates closely to the ways people think about the world. If you feel depressed, you believe you are helpless or hopeless. If you believe you are helpless or hopeless, you are more likely to become depressed (Lazarus, 1991). This is consistent with appraisal theory, which holds that our interpretation of the meaning of events determines our emotional response. If people have habitual, dysfunctional appraisal tendencies, then depression is more likely.

Early work with dogs provided a model for human depression called **learned helplessness** (Seligman & Maier, 1967). In this research, creatures who were exposed to electric shocks without a way to escape eventually stopped trying to do so, even when the researchers later gave them the opportunity to jump away from a shock they knew was coming. Applying this idea to human beings, researchers proposed that people who have had repeated defeats learn that they are helpless, they quit trying, and they become depressed.

For a variety of reasons, the simple version of that hypothesis is unsatisfactory, but a revised version has been more promising. According to the revised theory, a total lack of success in some situation may or may not lead to feelings of depression, depending on how one interprets the outcome—that is, what social psychologists call *attributions* (Abramson, Seligman, & Teasdale, 1978; see Figure 13.5). Suppose you fail a college chemistry test. You might think, "That was a very difficult test. Probably most other students did badly also." This would be an **external attribution**, assigning the reason to something outside yourself. With this attribution, the low test score is not a cause for depression or decreased self-esteem. Alternatively, you might think, "I could have done much better by studying harder. But I was sick the whole week before that test, and I had two other tests and a paper due that week, and several other interruptions." That would be an **unstable attribution**, assigning the reason to a temporary condition that should not interfere with your later efforts. Another possible interpretation might be, "Chemistry is more difficult for me than for other students, because I did not have a good chemistry course in high school." That attribution is **specific**, because it applies to certain situations and not others. Again, you are unlikely to become depressed. However, suppose your interpretation is, "I failed that test because I am stupid, and I am likely to fail similar future tests." That interpretation is **internal** (relating to yourself), **stable** (permanent), and **global** (relating to many or all situations). Such an attribution implies that you will fail in many other academic situations and—presuming that academic success is important to you—is likely to make you feel depressed.

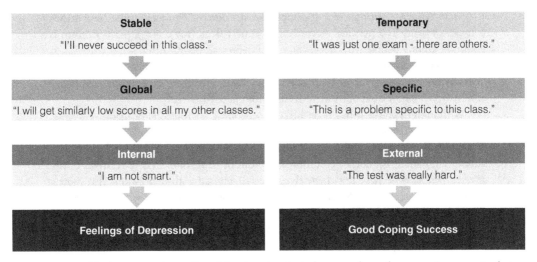

FIGURE 13.5. Explanatory style, or dispositional tendencies in how people attribute negative events in their lives, can either make them vulnerable to depression or protect against it.

Let's take another example. Suppose your significant other breaks up with you. A personal rejection always hurts, but it hurts less if you think the breakup is temporary (unstable) or if it had something to do with that particular relationship (external and specific). However, if you think it means that no one will ever love you, that attribution will make you feel terrible.

What determines which type of attribution people use in a situation? The attributions that people make for success usually follow the facts. If you did well on a test, you know whether it is because you studied hard or it was just an easy test. If you get offered a good job, you probably know whether it was because you had good qualifications or because your uncle owns the company. However, the attributions that people make for failures tend to follow a pattern. Most people have a characteristic **explanatory style**—a way of making attributions for their failures. This is especially powerful in situations when the explanation is not obvious; if almost everyone failed that chemistry test, for example, you don't have to struggle to explain your own low grade. Some people tend to blame their failures on themselves, some generally blame bad luck, some blame other people, and so forth.

A person's explanatory style for failures tends to be consistent across situations and over long periods of time, even decades (Burns & Seligman, 1989). Blaming failure on your lack of effort is a somewhat optimistic style; it implies that you have the skill to succeed and next time, with more effort, you will. Blaming failure on your inherent lack of ability ("I'm stupid" or "I am unlovable") is the most pessimistic style. It implies that the reason for failure is within yourself (internal), consistent over time (stable), and consistent over many situations (global). Depression is strongly associated with a pessimistic explanatory style (Hu, Zhang, & Yang, 2015).

In addition to a pessimistic explanatory style, many depressed people have dysfunctional, unrealistic beliefs about what they "must" become or what they "must" accomplish to be satisfied. One example of a dysfunctional attitude is, "Failing at something means I am less worthy as a person." According to Aaron Beck (1973; 1987), perfectionism is common among people with depression, and depressed people often see themselves as failing even when things are going reasonably well, such as a student who is devastated at receiving a course grade of B+. Because they have unrealistic expectations for themselves, even a minor disappointment is cause for major distress.

Although depression has been linked to people's attributions of negative events, depression may reflect dysfunctional responses to positive events as well. When we think of depression, we tend to think of someone who is constantly sad. However, lack of pleasure or enjoyment is another common symptom of depression. Many relatives of depressed people, who have not themselves been diagnosed with depression, also show a relative lack of enjoyment. Psychologists disagree to some extent about whether the deficit is best described as a lack of *pleasure* or a lack of *motivation* (Pizzagalli, 2014). This distinction is difficult, however, and may not be important for most practical purposes.

Participants in one study responded to a beeper reminding them at unpredictable times each day to record their current activity and mood. People with depression reported a normal number of sad events, but they differed from other people by reporting very few happy events (Peters et al., 2003). In another study, participants watched short films intended to evoke a happy, sad, or neutral mood. People with depression reported little enjoyment of the happy film. They apparently felt equally bad no matter what they were watching (Rottenberg, Gross, & Gotlib, 2005).

In yet another study, depressed and nondepressed women viewed a series of pictures and reported their emotional responses while researchers observed their facial expressions. Both groups of women reacted comparably to the sad pictures, but the depressed women showed significantly less response to the pleasant pictures (see Figure 13.6). In the same study, the participants were asked to rate how well 12 pleasant

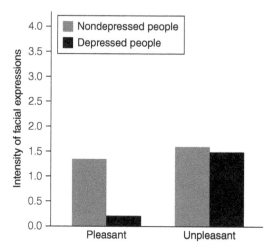

FIGURE 13.6. Depressed and nondepressed women showed about equal intensity of facial expressions when viewing unpleasant slides, but the depressed women showed much less response to the pleasant slides.

words and 12 unpleasant words applied to themselves. Afterward, they were asked (to their surprise) to recall the 24 words. Both groups recalled about the same number of unpleasant words, but the depressed women recalled fewer of the pleasant words (Sloan, Strauss, & Wisner, 2001).

What about expectations of actual positivity in one's own life? Researchers in one study used experience sampling to explore the relationship between expectations about positive and negative moods in the future and outcomes among depressed participants from the wider community, healthy controls matched in age and sex to the depressed participants, and a broad sample of college undergraduates. The researchers found that both currently depressed participants and college students with higher depressive symptoms expected worse futures (in terms of more sad and less happy moods) than participants who were not suffering from symptoms of depression. They also observed that currently depressed people had an unrealistically pessimistic view of their futures—they predicted feeling worse than they actually did when the future became the present. In contrast, the participants reporting good mental health were fairly accurate in predicting their future moods (Zetsche, Bürkner, & Renneberg, 2019).

If depression is based on insensitivity to and lack of anticipation of reward, we should expect people with depression to show dysfunction in the dopamine circuits of the brain that mediate reward. The evidence on this point has been mixed. Most studies, but not all, have indicated decreased activity in the striatum (a major source of dopamine output) and decreased activity at one type of dopamine receptor (Marchand & Yurgelun-Todd, 2010; Savitz & Drevets, 2013). Results more consistently indicate that on average, people with depression have decreased levels of the metabolic breakdown products of dopamine (Kunugi, Hori, & Ogawa, 2015; Pizzagalli, 2014). If depression is simply caused by a lack of dopamine activity, we might expect that a drug that stimulates dopamine synapses would help relieve depression. Such drugs are not effective for most patients, however, and most effective antidepressant drugs exert their effects primarily at other types of synapses.

It is unlikely that each of these contributors to depression—genetic, neurobiological, behavioral, cognitive—operates in isolation. Genes, after all, code for the development of brains, and brains think thoughts and choose behaviors. An attentional bias toward negative information probably is linked with biases in memory for that same negative information, and perhaps also altered processing of positive information. In a review of how different cognitive biases in depression may interact, Jonas Everaert and colleagues ask us to consider a representative example. Imagine a person at risk for depression—let's call him Michael. Michael is giving a presentation when he notices that someone in the audience has frowned. An attentional bias for threatening information (and possibly a reduced attentional bias for positive information) may be why Michael noticed this frowning person rather than the person two rows over who was smiling and nodding. Now that Michael is paying attention to the frowning face, he is more likely to retrieve memories related to this experience. Thus he calls up a memories of other times that presentations didn't go well. In turn, these memories guide his present-moment interpretations ("my research is not interesting, I'm doing a poor job."). Attention influences memory influences interpretation, and it is easy to see in this example how such interactions can all relate to mood symptoms (Everaert et al., 2020).

As it turns out, intervening in some of these cognitive tendencies is one of the major ways that we treat depression.

Treating Depression

The most common treatments for depression are various forms of psychotherapy (talking to a therapist) and antidepressant drugs. Both approaches can be effective, but neither is entirely reliable. Within a few months after the start of treatment, about half of patients show improvement with either antidepressants or psychotherapy, compared to about one-third of patients who show improvement while taking a placebo (Hollon, Thase, & Markowitz, 2002). Combining both drugs and psychotherapy improves the response for some people (for a meta-analysis see Cuijpers et al., 2020), but does not greatly increase the percentage of people who respond at all (Hollon et al., 2014; Thase, 2014). Apparently, some people respond to either type of treatment, some recover with no treatment, and some do not respond well to either treatment.

Even these somewhat discouraging data represent a slight overstatement of the effectiveness of treatments, because they are based on published results, and many studies that fail to show effectiveness are never published (Driessen et al., 2015). Promising new approaches use individualized data to guide the selection of treatment, asking the question "what works for whom and in which circumstances?" (Cohen & DeRubeis, 2018). For instance, one study revealed that higher levels of distress and anhedonia (lack of pleasure) at the start of treatment predicted better response when adding cognitive therapy to antidepressant treatment, whereas there was no added benefit for those lower in distress and anhedonia (Khazanov et al., 2020).

The first antidepressant drugs were discovered accidentally in the 1950s. No one had expected that a drug could alter people's mood, but psychiatrists noted that certain drugs given for other purposes, such as combatting tuberculosis, seemed to relieve depression. As more and more drugs were discovered, a pattern emerged: the antidepressant drugs, in one way or another, increased the activity at synapses using serotonin or norepinephrine, and sometimes also dopamine. However, as already mentioned, the effects at the synapses happen long before the behavioral benefits, and the behavioral benefits are undependable.

In recent years, a new drug treatment for depression has emerged from an unexpected corner—a drug named ketamine, used for anesthesia by medical practitioners, and by some lay people as a drug of abuse. Rather than affecting serotonin or norepinephrine, ketamine may influence glutamate receptors and indirectly affect synaptic connectivity, or the connections between neurons. Initially prescribed only to people whose depression had failed to respond to almost every other treatment (including electroconvulsive therapy), it is now being tested in people who have more mild treatment-resistant depression (e.g., failing two different treatments). Early findings, which have so far been replicated, indicate that the drug holds great promise for the treatment of depression, especially in patients who have struggled to achieve improvement (Krystal et al., 2019).

This research also underscores how little we really know about the neurobiology and possible treatment of depression—and how much we have to learn. How any of these antidepressant drugs help, when they help at all, remains uncertain. Consequently, at least at present, information about antidepressant drugs does not shed much light on emotion.

FIGURE 13.7. In cognitive therapy, the therapist often encourages the client to explore alternative attributions for negative events. From Sloan, Strauss, & Wisner (2001).

What can we learn about emotion from the effects of talk therapies? One of the most common approaches is **cognitive therapy** (or a cognitive–behavioral therapy combination), which seeks to alter people's explanatory styles and dysfunctional cognitive attitudes (Beck, 1973). A therapist using this technique will typically ask a client to talk about daily events and difficulties, and then help the client challenge any maladaptive assumptions and beliefs that seem to promote distress (Figure 13.7). For example, if a depressed client tends to interpret every negative event as a personal failure, the therapist points out this bias and invites the client to suggest other interpretations. If you did not excel at your last project, what could be an explanation (other than your own inadequacy)? Is your lack of excellence even a serious problem? If someone did not smile at you yesterday, what might an explanation be (other than them disliking you)? The therapist does not tell you that your interpretation was wrong (after all, it is possible that someone really does dislike you). Rather, the therapist encourages you to consider other possibilities and draw the most reasonable conclusion, instead of automatically presuming the worst.

Learning to reappraise negative events may help to prevent as well as alleviate depression. In one study, college students who were at risk for depression were randomly assigned to receive no treatment or a series of eight workshops on how to combat negative thoughts about themselves. The students who received the training reported significantly fewer episodes of anxiety and depression over the next 3 years (Seligman et al., 1999). Another effective talk therapy for depression takes a mindfulness approach, encouraging people to practice acceptance, present-moment awareness, and nonjudgment of one's reactions (e.g., Goldberg et al., 2019).

Another important part of cognitive therapy is encouraging more activity, of any kind. During an episode of depression, people are generally unmotivated to do anything, partly because they have no energy, but also partly because they do not expect to enjoy the activity. If they force themselves to try something, they sometimes discover that they enjoyed it more than they expected. When researchers in one study suggested that encouraging activity is responsible for much of the effectiveness of cognitive therapy (Jacobson et al., 1996), other therapists began trying behavioral activation as a stand-alone therapy. Although research has been limited, so far it shows that behavioral activation by itself is about as effective as any other type of therapy for depression (Ekers et al., 2014).

Has anyone ever told you "just smile, you might feel happier?" You might recall our discussion of the two-way relationship between facial expressions and emotion back in Chapter 5, and wonder whether there could be something to this advice. A series of researchers became interested in a related question, which was: If we know that the wrinkle treatment Botox can decrease facial expressiveness, could it possibly be helpful in treating depression if we target the muscles that are involved in frowning? While a number of studies have found just this effect, many of them used pretty weak statistical approaches and experimental design, and more dismayingly, had authors with financial conflicts of interest (Coles et al., 2019). None of this means that there is no effect present. But it does mean that we need more, better research, ideally conducted by impartial researchers.

People suffering from major depression should be encouraged to seek professional help, and both friends and professionals should be careful not to blame people for their depression. (If you are struggling with the tasks of daily living, do you think it would be helpful to hear that you should just try smiling more, or exercising more?) However, there are studies that indicate certain behaviors may be associated with lower risk for depression if currently healthy individuals take part in them. One simple but effective step is to exercise. It need not be strenuous, but it should be consistent, about 30 to 45 minutes a few times per week (Figure 13.8). A long walk outdoors with exposure to sunlight and nature

FIGURE 13.8. Regular exercise and exposure to sunlight may help support mental health.

is helpful in many ways. People who exercise are less likely to become depressed, and people who become depressed are unlikely to exercise (Pereira, Geoffroy, & Power, 2014).

Another recommendation is to try to keep a regular sleep schedule. Sleep difficulties are a common, almost universal symptom of depression, and improving sleep often improves depression as well (Asarnow, Soehner, & Harvey, 2014). Two studies indicated that sleep difficulties in adolescence predicted an increased probability of depression later (Roane & Taylor, 2008; Roberts & Duong, 2014). Since some drug treatments for insomnia can worsen depression and some drug treatments for depression can worsen sleeping problems, careful attention to the bidirectional relationship between these two phenomena is important (Fang et al., 2019).

MANIA AND BIPOLAR DISORDER

Learning Objective

- Define bipolar disorder, differentiating its symptoms from those of major depressive disorder; and explaining the difference between mania and hypomania.

In **bipolar disorder**, episodes of depression alternate with periods of **mania**, which can be either mild or more extreme. In some ways, mania is the opposite of depression: whereas depression is marked by inactivity and low self-confidence, mania is marked by relentless, vigorous activity and extreme self-confidence. A mild episode of mania can be enjoyable, at least for a while, but the pleasant mood can morph into irritability if it feels like the rest of the world is trying to slow you down or get in your way. At intense heights of mania, some people can even experience psychosis, believing they have superhuman abilities.

We noted earlier that depression has been linked to alterations in people's responses to reward. In depression, people seem relatively insensitive to reward; the opposite is true for mania. The *DSM* criteria for a manic episode include impulsive, risky, reward-seeking behaviors such as gambling, unsafe sex, purchasing luxury items that the person cannot afford, or investing in ventures with little prospect of success (Figure 13.9). This is the aspect of mania that is most likely to cause harm—many of these behaviors have the potential to damage people's relationships with romantic partners, friends, and family, and/or to causing lasting physical or financial problems. People in a manic episode may also start many projects, but finish few or none of them because they constantly yield to distractions. When symptoms of mania are present, but not so extreme as to cause problems in the person's life, the episode is typically classified as **hypomania**.

Research on the emotional tendencies of people with bipolar disorder also indicates that it involves disruption of normal responses to rewarding stimuli. In one study, June Gruber and colleagues (Gruber et al., 2008), showed positive, negative, and neutral film clips to participants who reported a range of hypomanic symptoms. Those with stronger predisposition toward mania reported higher levels of positive emotion, as well as irritability, in response to all of the films than did individuals low on hypomanic tendencies. Intriguingly, one fMRI study compared youth with family histories of depression, family histories of bipolar disorder, and no family history of mood disorders. Participants' brain activity was scanned while they completed a task involving reward; they were then followed over the next four years. Results revealed that youth at risk for depression versus

FIGURE 13.9.   During a manic episode, people are hyperreactive to possible rewards and may engage in impulsive, high-risk behaviors that cause problems later.

bipolar disorder differed in certain aspects of brain activation during reward processing, and that activation patterns in those at risk for bipolar disorder predicted social problems later in adolescence (Nimarko et al., 2022).

Another study indicates that high dispositional tendencies toward enthusiasm and pride—both of which involve high appetitive motivation and behavioral activation—are risk factors for mania (Gruber & Johnson, 2009). None of these results are to say that positive emotion is in and of itself a bad thing. We noted in Chapter 11 that negative emotions are not inherently bad, either—what is healthy or not is whether the emotions are reasonable for the context. Similarly, people may show heightened risk for mania when their positive emotion is insensitive to what's going on in the environment (Gruber, 2011).

The depression experienced in bipolar disorder is more likely to resemble what we labeled *atypical depression*—that is, depression marked by low enjoyment, physical lethargy, and excessive sleep (Akiskal & Benazzi, 2005). This pattern makes sense because it is the opposite of mania, with constant movement, activity, and sleeplessness. However, exceptions to this rule occur, where someone alternates between mania and agitated depression. Almost always, an episode or more of depression comes first in the person's life, and the person is diagnosed with major depression. After an episode of mania emerges, the diagnosis changes to bipolar disorder, and likely the treatment changes as well.

The defining feature of bipolar disorder is mood instability—that is, swings from feeling very low to feeling very high. Here is a study that sheds possible light on that instability: young adults, including some with hypomania (mild manic tendencies), watched a film about traumatic events and then reported any intrusive imagery they experienced about that film over the next six days. Those with hypomania reported about twice as many intrusive images as did the other people (Malik et al., 2014). Experiencing frequent intrusive imagery would be one way to shift someone's mood, perhaps in either direction.

Bipolar disorder used to be an uncommon diagnosis, limited to people with extreme and obvious mood swings. There is some evidence that the diagnosis has become more common, probably because it is being applied more broadly, including in people with milder symptoms (Medici et al., 2015). Recall that for many people with bipolar disorder, the first sign is a major depressive episode. Some individuals who would previously have been diagnosed with major depressive disorder based on this first episode are now more likely to be recognized as having bipolar disorder. That said, global studies carefully controlling for numerous variables find that the overall prevalence of bipolar disorder has remained relatively steady over the last few decades (He et al., 2020).

People with bipolar disorder, unlike those with major depression, generally respond best to either lithium salts or certain antiseizure medications. While treatment for bipolar disorder remains primarily pharmaceutical, cognitive and behavioral approaches can be helpful. For instance, regular rhythms of sleeping, eating, and movement may encourage mood stability. People with bipolar disorder also tend to have difficulties managing their emotions, from impulse control to goal-directed behaviors (Miola et al., 2022). Whether cause or consequence, it may be that people with bipolar disorder could find strategies surrounding healthy regulation of emotion to be beneficial.

ANXIETY DISORDERS

Learning Objectives

- Compare and contrast the major anxiety disorders (GAD, PTSD, panic disorder, specific phobia) analyzing what symptoms they share and which are distinct.
- Define epigenetics, and explain the potential role of epigenetics in risk for mental illness.
- Describe different methods of treating anxiety, and explain how they work.

Suppose that while you are on a walk, you discover the entrance to a cave. It is dark inside, but you have a small flashlight. What might be inside the cave? Bats, snakes, other dangers? Or maybe just stalactites, stalagmites, and other beautiful scenery? Who knows, you might find a treasure chest that pirates left there centuries ago! Would you enter the cave at all? If so, how far would you go, and how fast? People vary in their reactions to novel, ambiguous situations. People with damage to the amygdala, as described in Chapter 6, have a strong approach tendency and hardly any avoidance tendency (Harrison, Hurlemann, & Adolphs, 2015). People with anxiety disorders are at the other extreme, showing fearful avoidance even in familiar, harmless situations.

How much fear or anxiety is normal? Suppose you are a soldier in a war zone. You are always either under attack or on the alert for another attack. People you knew and liked have been killed, sometimes right beside you. Under those conditions, it seems reasonable for you to be constantly tense, with a strong startle response to almost any surprising sight or sound. You should sleep lightly, ready to respond to the slightest noise by waking up to fight for your life. You might have nightmares. Any stray movement you see should look like danger. Under the circumstances, your reactions are normal. Then the military discharges you. When you return to your quiet suburban neighborhood, you still feel that tension and you still react to every sight and sound as danger. You might be diagnosed with **posttraumatic stress disorder**, but your reaction became a problem only because you did not quickly readjust your anxiety levels when you moved from one environment to another.

The *DSM* includes a list of more than a dozen psychological disorders in which excessive anxiety is the main symptom, and many others for which anxiety is a secondary symptom. The simplest example, **generalized anxiety disorder (GAD)**, is characterized by almost constant nervousness and worry. People with GAD worry intensely about their health, finances, job, and even minor matters such as household chores or car repairs. Sometimes they are not even sure what they are worried about. Their worries make them irritable, restless, and fatigued. Consequently, they have trouble doing their jobs and getting along with their families. Because anxiety is a symptom of many other disorders, most people with GAD qualify for one or more additional diagnoses (Bruce et al., 2001).

With GAD or any other anxiety disorder, the problem is often not that the anxiety is too great, but that it arises too frequently and too easily. After all, anxiety is likely adaptive in many situations—if you were back in that cave, it might make a lot of sense to be vigilant for various sorts of possible danger (see Table 13.1). Imagine you are a participant in an experiment where a particular sight or sound predicts that you might receive a shock, whereas other sights or sounds predict an interval of safety. If you have an anxiety disorder, you will react about the same as anyone else to the danger signal, but you might also respond to the safety signal as if it predicted a shock (Duits et al., 2015; Van Meurs et al., 2014). Probably you would also continue reacting to the danger signal long after it has stopped predicting shock. Furthermore, you would be slow to habituate if you repeatedly heard a sudden loud noise (Campbell et al., 2014).

Anxiety often arises in situations characterized by uncertainty. One study examined intolerance of uncertainty, as well as levels of both anxiety and depression, in adults from three countries at three time points across the first year of the COVID-19 pandemic. The results indicated that people who tolerate uncertainty reasonably well reported low,

TABLE 13.1 **Fear-related responses in reaction to different sort of threat cues**

Adapted from Miloyan et al. (2019).

	Example(s)	*Stimulus/cues*	*Emotion*	*Response*
Imminent danger	Faced with a predator or a shortage of oxygen	Specific external (sense perception) or interoception (state of body)	Fear	Fight-or-flight (panic, freeze, flight, aggression)
Sensed threat cues				
Specific	Rustle in leaves	External	Anxiety	Specific responsiveness (hypervigilance, scanning environment, proceeding with caution, withdrawal)
General	Darkness or injury	Nonspecific contextual or interoceptive	Anxiety	General wariness (precaution, hypervigilance, lower response threshold to a variety of threat cues)
Autocued threat	Imagining an animal attack before a trip to the wilderness	Mentally imagined	Anxiety	Advanced and flexible precautionary measures (e.g., acquiring tools, practicing skills)

Adapted from Miloyan, Bulley, & Suddendorf (2019).

stable levels of anxiety and depression across the three time periods. In contrast, people with high intolerance of uncertainty reported greater symptoms than the others at all three time periods, and worst at the time of first measurement (Andrews et al., 2021).

Panic disorder is characterized by repeated attacks of panic, with sharply increased heart rate, rapid breathing, sweating, trembling, and chest pains, generally lasting a few minutes. People having a panic attack often fear they are having a heart attack. Not everyone who has a panic attack goes on to develop panic disorder. Some people have one or more attacks, shrug them off, and go on with life. What distinguishes panic disorder from panic attacks is that people with panic disorder experience frequent nervous anticipation about having another panic attack. That worry often leads to **agoraphobia** (from Greek words meaning *fear of the marketplace*), an excessive avoidance of public situations where a panic attack might be embarrassing. Many people with panic disorder prefer to remain at home as much as possible.

One interpretation of panic disorder is that it is based on fear of the panic attacks themselves. Someone who has had panic attacks in the past worries about having another one and becomes highly attentive to any sign that an attack might be starting. If the person begins breathing heavily without an obvious explanation (such as exercise), the deep breathing acts as a conditioned stimulus that elicits an appraisal of threat. That appraisal then gives rise to further autonomic arousal, a desire to flee the situation, and then a full-blown panic attack (Bouton, Mineka, & Barlow, 2001; Hamm, Richter, & Pané-Farré, 2014). You see here a good example of the connections between emotions and appraisals. The thought "I might be starting to have a panic attack" can lead to an excessive emotional response, which then reinforces the appraisal.

Panic disorder is more common among women than among men, and is most prevalent among adolescents and young adults. The prevalence declines as people grow older, possibly because the sympathetic nervous system becomes less responsive and less capable of generating the rapid heart rate, rapid deep breathing, and other symptoms of a panic attack.

Whereas GAD involves almost constant but moderate fear, and panic disorder involves extreme anxiety at unpredictable times and places, a **specific phobia** (also known as a *simple phobia*) is characterized by excessive fear of a particular object or situation. Like panic disorder, phobias are most common in young people, and more common among women than among men (Burke et al., 1990). Table 13.2 lists some common objects of phobias (Cox et al., 2003). Great fear arises in the presence of the object or situation,

TABLE 13.2   Table of common specific phobias

Several common phobias. From Cox et al. (2003).	
Name	**Definition**
Agoraphobia	Fear of open, public places
Glossophobia	Fear of public speaking
Acrophobia	Fear of heights
Social phobia	Extreme anxiety about being with or observed by strangers
Autophobia	Fear of being alone
Arachnophobia	Fear of spiders
Ophidiophobia	Fear of snakes
Blood phobia	Fear of blood

From Cox et al. (2003).

but also after a thought or reminder. If you have a phobia about sharks, you don't want to watch movies about sharks, see photos of sharks, or hear stories about sharks.

Most phobias pertain to items that are objectively dangerous—snakes, spiders, lightning, falling from a great height, and so forth. The defining feature is not that the fear is unrealistic, but that it is exaggerated and that it interferes with someone's life. For example, if you cannot ride an elevator because of your fear of enclosed places, or if you cannot enjoy nature because of your fear of snakes, then your fear qualifies as a phobia. Note also that the common objects of phobias relate to possible but not common sources of injury, at least in modern society. You are more likely to be injured by automobile accidents, sports injuries, or misuse of tools, yet hardly anyone develops a phobia of cars, soccer balls, or hammers. Snakes, spiders, and lightning, which are among the common objects of phobias, have been a threat to people throughout our ancestral history, although they injure relatively few people today. In Chapter 11 we suggested that people may be born with a predisposition to fear them (Öhman, 2009), but another explanation is that we fear uncontrollable dangers. You have some feeling of control over cars and tools, but no control over snakes and spiders. Also, most people have had many safe experiences with cars and tools, but fewer safe experiences with snakes and spiders.

One common phobia you may have encountered in friends or family (or yourself!) is blood-injection-injury phobia—the fear of seeing blood or injuries, receiving an injection, and a related fear of needles. Such a phobia became of particular interest during the COVID-19 pandemic when the world governments launched a massive vaccination campaign to combat the virus. One study assessed thousands of citizens in the United Kingdom for both presence of the phobia and levels of vaccine hesitancy, and found that approximately 10% of cases of vaccine hesitancy were tied to blood-injection-injury fears (Love & Love, 2021). Earlier we said that phobias are only diagnosable if they cause impairment in everyday functioning—but the context of everyday functioning can rapidly change.

One key characteristic of phobia is the ability of the feared object to dominate attention. Recall the research from earlier chapters documenting increase attention to fear-related objects. A phobia magnifies that tendency. In one study, people were asked to try to find the one picture of a mushroom among many pictures of flowers, or to find the one mushroom among many pictures of flowers and one picture of a spider. People with a phobia of spiders had no trouble finding the mushroom in the picture without a spider, but had much more trouble than other people if a spider was in the picture (Miltner et al., 2004). Evidently, the spider grabbed their attention strongly.

Causes of Anxiety Disorders

What causes someone to develop an anxiety disorder? Long ago, John B. Watson, one of the most influential early psychology researchers, proposed that people develop phobias through classical conditioning. In Chapter 4 we described his study of "Little Albert," conducted with colleague Rosalie Rayner. Although initially unafraid of white rats, Albert developed what appeared to be a phobia of them after repeatedly having a loud gong struck behind his head every time he saw one (Watson & Rayner, 1920).

Watson's study (Watson & Rayner, 1920) left much to be desired, scientifically as well as ethically, but also fails to provide a convincing explanation of how phobias develop. Although some people with a phobia can trace its origin to a painful experience, most cannot. An identical twin of someone with a phobia has an elevated risk of also having a phobia, regardless of whether the first twin can or cannot identify a frightening experience that started the phobia (Kendler, Myers, & Prescott, 2002). In other words, there was no evidence in this study that a bad experience had increased the risk of phobia beyond whatever risk the genetic factors had already established. Furthermore, people who do have a painful experience learn to be more cautious, but most do not develop a phobia. In short, having a painful experience is neither necessary nor sufficient for establishing a phobia.

In the case of PTSD, a traumatic experience is necessary for the condition, by definition, but it is not sufficient. Many people live through traumatic experiences without developing PTSD. In fact, the severity of the trauma and the intensity of someone's initial reaction are not good predictors of who will or will not develop PTSD (Bryant et al., 2015). A better predictor is someone's emotional status before the trauma. People who had abusive or neglectful experiences in childhood, or who had developed emotional difficulties for other reasons, are more likely than others to develop PTSD (Berntsen et al., 2012). People who suffer with PTSD have fewer than typical recollections of feeling in control over the events of their lives (Jobson et al., 2014).

Could we predict whether some people are more susceptible than others to PTSD before they are ever exposed to traumatic experience? To answer this question, psychologists gave questionnaires to soldiers before, during, and after deployment to a war zone in Afghanistan. Many of the soldiers did indeed suffer mild symptoms before heading off to active duty. Based on the dangers they expected to face, they reported disturbing dreams, intrusive images, and attempts to avoid any reminder of the events that might happen. Those soldiers with the strongest pre-traumatic reactions had the highest probability of developing PTSD after wartime trauma exposure (Berntsen & Rubin, 2015). That is, some people are more predisposed than others to develop anxiety disorders, and they are particularly vulnerable when bad things happen. Screening for such people might help to reduce the number of PTSD cases in the military—though such a practice would raise ethical questions.

What predisposes some people to be more prone to anxiety disorders than others? As always, possible explanations include heredity and environment, and as usual, both contribute. First, let's consider heredity. People with anxiety disorders are likely to have relatives who also have anxiety disorders, and the overlap is stronger for identical (monozygotic) twins than for fraternal (dizygotic) twins. However, the genetic influence does not appear to be specific to a given condition. For example, someone with panic disorder may have relatives with phobia, GAD, or major depression. Efforts to locate a gene responsible for this vulnerability have not shown any common allele with a large effect or, indeed, any allele with an effect that replicates consistently from one population to another (Shimada-Sugimoto, Otowa, & Hettema, 2015). Vulnerability to anxiety disorders and depression may be generated by many genes with small effects. Another possibility involves **epigenetics**, differences in the activation and expression of genes elicited by environmental conditions, rather than differences in the actual genes inherited from parents. Certain chemicals—specifically, acetyl groups, and methyl groups—can attach to genes and increase or decrease their effects without altering the DNA sequence itself. That is, your environment could impact how your genes are expressed.

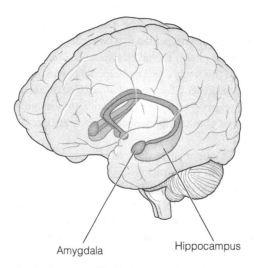

Amygdala   Hippocampus

FIGURE 13.10.   People who have a smaller than average hippocampus are at higher risk for posttraumatic stress disorder if they experience a trauma.

Through what mechanism might a genetic predisposition act? One possibility is for genes to act through their influence on brain anatomy. People with PTSD have a smaller than average hippocampus, a brain area responsible for control of stress hormones in addition to its more widely known role in episodic memory (Figure 13.10; Garfinkel & Liberzon, 2009; Stein et al., 1997). To determine whether that brain difference was a cause of PTSD or a result of it, investigators examined pairs of identical male twins. One member of each pair had developed PTSD during war, whereas the other had not been in battle and thus had not developed PTSD. The investigators found that both twins had a smaller than average hippocampus (Gilbertson et al., 2002). That is, the hippocampus must have been smaller than average before development of PTSD. It was a predisposing factor, not a result of PTSD.

In another investigation, participants who had experienced a range of traumas were recruited from the emergency room to take part in an fMRI scan while performing tasks known to recruit the hippocampus, and then followed over six months. Less activation within the hippocampus predicted higher PTSD symptoms at both three and six months post-trauma, suggesting that such patterns of brain activation may be a marker of risk for worse symptomatology. Compellingly, these results were observed in both in an original sample and a subsequent replication sample (Van Rooij et al., 2018; see Figure 13.11).

In addition to genetic influences, family environment is also important. For example, sexually abused children are, on average, more likely than others to develop fear-related disorders (Friedman et al., 2002) as well as depression (Nelson et al., 2002). Children who are neglected are also at serious risk (Berntsen et al., 2012). Imagine adult men who are identical (monozygotic) twins; although one has an anxiety disorder and the other does not. The children of the twin without an anxiety disorder are just as closely related to the uncle with an anxiety disorder as they are to their father, who does not have an anxiety disorder. If predisposition to anxiety depended entirely on genetics, we might expect just as many anxiety disorders for the children in one family as in the other. In fact, researchers

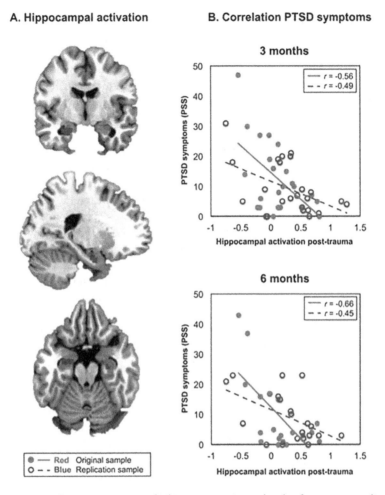

A. Hippocampal activation

B. Correlation PTSD symptoms

FIGURE 13.11. Lower activation in the hippocampus immediately after trauma predicted higher PTSD symptoms at three and six months post-trauma in both an original and a replication sample. From Van Rooij et al. (2018).

did not find that result. For both identical and fraternal twins, the children in each family had a risk of anxiety that depended much more on their own parent's status than on the status of their parent's twin (Eley et al., 2015). That result indicates a strong influence of the environment. If your parents display a great deal of anxiety, you probably will too.

Treating Anxiety Disorders

As with depression, treatment for anxiety disorders often involves talk therapy and/or medication. A common treatment is cognitive behavior therapy, which focuses on reinterpreting or reappraising a situation, solving problems, and relaxation. In most cases, it provides help in reducing anxiety and improving quality of life (Cuijpers et al., 2014; Hofmann, Wu, & Boettcher, 2014). In GAD, a therapist may emphasize identifying feelings of worry, developing greater tolerance for uncertainty, and learning to solve problems constructively rather than ruminating about them. In panic disorder, treatment may include an emphasis on reinterpreting physiological symptoms so they are perceived as less threatening and more tolerable.

For specific phobias, a common treatment is **exposure therapy**, also known as *systematic desensitization*. Imagine that you, like both authors of this textbook, are deathly afraid of spiders. A therapist would first make sure you are relaxed and feel safe, in a comfy chair and a cheerfully lit room. Then, they would ask you to imagine a small spider, minding its own business a few feet away. This might make you nervous at first, but the therapist would encourage you to hold the image in place until you get used to it and it no longer makes you nervous. During the next session things escalate—you are asked to imagine a larger spider nearby. After a few sessions, the therapist dispenses with the imagined spiders and brings in some real ones, first a tiny one, on the other side of the room. Again, you sit quietly and focus on staying calm until the spider no longer bothers you. In subsequent sessions, the spider will be brought closer, and you may even get to where you can tolerate touching it. Some therapists start with a real spider, snake, or other object immediately (with the client's permission). You might feel terror at first, but if nothing happens, your body will begin to relax. When you find yourself becoming calmer, even in the presence of the object you fear, you gain confidence.

Because most therapists do not want to keep a menagerie of spiders, snakes, sharks, and anything else that some client might fear in their office, the procedure often depends on virtual reality. You would wear a device that lets you view scenes of your object of phobia. If at any point you find it intolerable, you can simply turn it off. For instance, a recent investigation randomized patients with dental fear to an informational pamphlet or virtual reality exposure therapy (VRET) and assessed their fears and behavioral avoidance over six months. Patients in the VRET condition improved on all outcome measures to a greater degree than those reading an informational pamphlet (Gujjar et al., 2019; see Figure 13.12). (We hope you are wondering about whether we could devise a better control condition than an informational pamphlet!)

The overall intent of exposure therapy is to expose you to the object of your fear in increasing doses that you can just tolerate, until you become calmer. This procedure yields a high level of success, often quickly. Unfortunately, the phobia sometimes returns. As with any type of learning, the exposure treatment becomes more effective after repetitions. Therefore, even if you seem to be doing well, you would be advised to return for additional exposure sessions.

In addition to or instead of talk therapies, another possible approach includes the use of medications. Drugs that relieve anxiety are known as **anxiolytics** (ANK-see-oh-LIT-iks), or more informally as **tranquilizers**. The most common ones fall into a biochemical class known as the *benzodiazepines* (BEN-zo-di-AZ-uh-peens). Examples include diazepam (trade name Valium), chlordiazepoxide (Librium), and alprazolam (Xanax). These drugs can be given as injections, but are more commonly taken as pills. Their effects last for hours, and the duration varies from one drug to another.

Anxiolytics act by facilitating the effectiveness of a neurotransmitter known as GABA,[1] which functions as the main inhibitory neurotransmitter throughout the

---

[1] The term "GABA" is an abbreviation for gamma-aminobutyric acid. Mercifully, people almost always use the abbreviation, not the whole term.

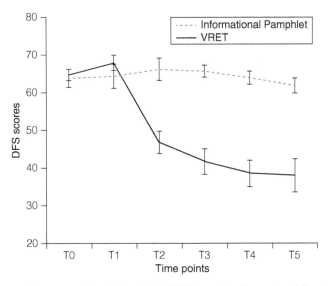

FIGURE 13.12. Scores on a Dental Fear Scale (DFS) over five time points following informational pamphlet (IP) or Virtual Reality Exposure Therapy (VRET). From Gujjar et al. (2019).

nervous system. Anxiolytics suppress activity in the amygdala, decreasing its response to threatening or otherwise emotional stimuli. However, they also suppress activity in much of the rest of the brain, producing drowsiness, memory impairment, and reduced cognitive and emotional processing overall. For example, people on anxiolytics have trouble identifying other people's facial expressions of emotion (Zangara et al., 2002), though a recent meta-analysis suggests that this effect might be specific to angry facial expressions (Garcez et al., 2020). It's important to recognize that GABA is not an "antifear" neurotransmitter—it is the main inhibitory neurotransmitter throughout the brain for a wide variety of functions.

Anxiolytics can be helpful in relieving a brief bout of severe anxiety, but most physicians discourage long-term use, because the drugs produce various side effects and can be habit-forming with repeated use. For long-term treatment of anxiety disorders, especially in cases where psychotherapy did not help, the more common treatment is antidepressant drugs. Theoretically, it seems surprising that drugs known for their effects on depression would also be helpful for anxiety. The observation that they help both conditions is one of the reasons why many therapists are skeptical of diagnosing disorders in terms of distinct categories.

OBSESSIVE-COMPULSIVE DISORDER

Learning Objectives
- Describe the symptoms of obsessive-compulsive disorder, differentiating between obsessions and compulsions.
- Analyze the role of emotion in obsessive-compulsive disorder symptoms.

Obsessive–compulsive disorder was for many years classified as a type of anxiety disorder. In the *DSM-5*, however, it is in a separate category because anxiety is usually not a prominent symptom; neither is depression, in most cases. **Obsessions** are recurrent and persistent thoughts, impulses, and intrusive images that cause distress. **Compulsions** are repetitive behaviors such as hand washing or ordering, or mental acts such as counting things or repeating words, that a person feels internal pressure to perform in response to obsessive thoughts. Someone with a compulsion feels distress if he or she is prevented from the compulsive act, and yet completing the act does not fully relieve the distress.

By definition, obsessions and compulsions are inappropriate to the current situation. Persistently worrying about how you are going to pay your bills is not an obsession if you really do have trouble paying your bills. Frequently washing your hands is not a compulsion if you work in a hospital where you are in constant contact with sick patients, or if you are in the middle of a global pandemic, and your frequency seems consistent with maintaining good health for you and those around you. Moreover, a repetitive thought or action is not a symptom of disorder unless it causes you some distress or difficulty.

Although OCD is not associated with intense anxiety or depression, it is nevertheless an emotional disorder in other regards. People with OCD are highly prone to feeling disgust, especially with regard to any feeling of being contaminated (Pauls et al., 2014). The fear of contamination leads to excessive washing. They also report stronger than average guilt feelings. In one fMRI study, OCD patients showed particularly intense brain responses to any reminder of shame or guilt (Hennig-Fast et al., 2015). One speculation is that guilt feelings lead to obsessions and compulsions. Many people with OCD believe that thinking about a shameful act is as bad as doing it (Coughtrey, Shafran, Lee, & Rachman, 2013), and training in self-compassion is a promising treatment for OCD (Eichholz et al., 2020). However, it is difficult to avoid thinking something. The harder someone tries to avoid a thought, the more intrusive the thought becomes. Then the person engages in a repetitive ritual to maintain rigid self-control: "If I keep doing this, then I won't do that other terrible thing." Excessive washing also relates to guilt feelings. "Washing away the sin" or "washing away the guilt" is a theme common to traditions throughout the world.

ANTISOCIAL PERSONALITY DISORDER

Learning Objective
- Describe the symptoms of antisocial personality disorder, analyzing its emotion-related characteristics.

So far we have focused mainly on disorders in which people feel too much emotion, or feel emotion in inappropriate circumstances. However, some psychological disorders may be characterized by insufficient emotion. If you imagine hurting someone, or remember a time when you did hurt someone, how do you feel? Most people feel at least a little anxious, sad, and/or guilty. People with **antisocial personality disorder** often do not. Their behavior is described as deceitful, impulsive, aggressive, and irresponsible, with reckless disregard for their own and others' safety and lack of remorse for harm caused to others (Black, 2015). This set of symptoms overlaps with characteristics of *psychopathy* and *sociopathy*, although these familiar terms are not *DSM*-recognized disorders. All three terms share a theme of willingness to harm or manipulate other people, with no concern for their well-being and no signs of remorse.

In an earlier chapter we distinguished between empathic accuracy and emotional empathy, and this distinction is important in describing people with psychopathic traits. If such people see someone who is sad or frightened, they recognize how that person feels—showing empathic accuracy—but they don't share the feeling. That is, they lack emotional empathy (Dadds et al., 2009). Most people react to the sight of a sad or frightened face by imitating it, at least slightly. People with antisocial personality disorder lack that tendency (Lishner et al., 2015). Also, their amygdala and prefrontal cortex show relatively little response to seeing someone suffer (Thompson, Ramos, & Willett, 2014). The condition usually begins early in life, is associated with being physically and sexually abused as a child, and is linked with high rates of criminal offending (DeLisi, Drury, & Elbert, 2019).

EMOTIONAL DISTURBANCES AS TRANSDIAGNOSTIC ASPECTS OF DISORDER

Learning Objectives
- Analyze how frequently mental illnesses are characterized by emotional symptoms.
- Define neuroticism, and speculate how it may be involved in multiple mood disorders.
- Describe how difficulty regulating one's emotions may contribute to many different mental illnesses.

Disruptions of emotion characterize many psychological disorders, as defined by the *DSM*. So far we have focused on those disorders for which the role of emotion is most obvious, and the empirical research is particularly strong. However, we could lengthen this chapter greatly by adding further examples. People with borderline personality disorder demonstrate marked emotional volatility, impulsivity, and poor emotion regulation skills (Lieb et al., 2004). People with autism have difficulty recognizing others' emotional expressions (Clark, Winkielman, & McIntosh, 2008). People diagnosed with schizophrenia often show *flat affect* or low emotional expression, but report normal levels of subjective emotional experience (Kring et al., 1993). People often drink alcohol to regulate their emotions (Sher & Grekin, 2007), and substance use disorders run in the same families as depression (Dawson & Grant, 1998).

In fact, if you made a table with rows for all the mental disorders listed in the *DSM*, and columns for different ways disruption of emotion is involved in each (too much, too little, inappropriate displays, etc.), you might be surprised at the number of entries in the emotion columns. In just such an effort, researchers coded each and every diagnosis in the *DSM-IV-TR* for whether or not it included criteria related to dysfunctional emotion processing. Diagnoses were coded as "likely" involving emotional disturbance when one or more important criteria related to emotion, but one could conceivably still meet criteria with no emotional symptoms; and "guaranteed" when at least one emotional symptom was necessary to meet criteria. The results revealed that some form of emotional disturbance was likely present in approximately 40% of diagnoses, and guaranteed in almost one in five (19.3%; Jazaieri, Urry, & Gross, 2013).

In many cases, the same emotional symptom is thought to characterize multiple disorders. Emotion is not alone among symptom types in this regard. The *DSM* is rife with examples of one symptom (such as sleep disruption or increased distractibility) serving as a diagnostic criterion for several disorders. No wonder practitioners have so much trouble coming up with clear, distinct diagnoses! This issue complicates research efforts as well. As we noted at the beginning of the chapter, for decades researchers have used study designs where they compare people with some diagnosable condition to people with no disorder, or people with one diagnosis to people with another. According to Thomas Insel, former director of the National Institutes of Health, and his colleagues (2010), this approach has not yielded much understanding of the causes of mental disorder or how to treat specific people.

Along with many other authorities, Insel and colleagues (2010) have argued that researchers should abandon the idea of categories and instead determine how to describe psychopathology in terms of continuous symptom dimensions, such as degrees of sad mood, reward insensitivity, anxiety, sleep disturbance, inability to concentrate, and disordered thinking. In this approach, psychiatric disorder is not something that you have or don't have, like tuberculosis. It is a series of problems that occur to various degrees. This approach allows greater focus on underlying commonalities across multiple diagnoses, rather than endlessly splicing human unhappiness into different categories. Clinical psychologist David Barlow and colleagues have provocatively argued that disorders of emotion all share the underlying experience of neuroticism (frequent negative emotions) and subsequent avoidance of situations that elicit negative feelings (Barlow, Curreri, & Woodard, 2021; see Figure 13.13). The hope is that by studying symptoms as they occur in the general population, without focusing on the complex criteria for specific disorders, researchers will be better able to identify the causes of each aspect of dysfunction (Cuthbert & Insel, 2013).

One hypothesis that has received considerable attention is that disordered emotion stems in large part from inadequate or improper emotion regulation (Gross & Jazaieri, 2014). In the final chapter of this book, we elaborate on the idea of emotion regulation and discuss many possible strategies that people use to regulate their emotions. Here is a quick preview: you can control your emotions; they don't have to control you. If you

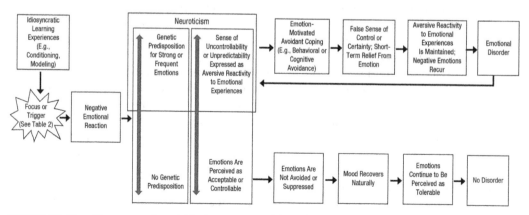

FIGURE 13.13.   One proposed model for how emotional disorders (e.g., mood, anxiety, trauma-related) might all relate to underlying predisposition for neuroticism (intense and frequent negative emotion) and lead to avoidance and worse symptoms over time. From Barlow et al. (2021).

encounter any type of emotion-arousing event or stimulus, either pleasant or unpleasant, you can take steps to either increase or decrease your emotional response to it. Most people have preferred strategies or habits for regulating their emotions, and most are reasonably successful, most of the time. During an extremely stressful experience, however, your options may be limited. Highly stressful events and intense emotions interfere with most coping strategies (Sheppes et al., 2011). Yet during lesser events, or in the aftermath of even a horrible event, most people do their best to maintain a positive outlook.

Depression in particular seems to link with poor emotion regulation. People with depression often show a bias to be oversensitive to unpleasant events and/or undersensitive to positive events (Mehu & Scherer, 2015). One study indicated that people with relatively poor emotion regulation skills are more likely than others to develop symptoms of depression within the next few years (Berking, Wirtz, Svaldi, & Hofmann, 2014). This is a correlational effect rather than an experiment. Perhaps poor emotion regulation leads to depression, but an alternative explanation is that poor emotion regulation is simply an early symptom of depression.

People suffering from depression are less likely than others to look for a way to reappraise a situation in a more positive way, and they are more likely than others to respond by blaming themselves, catastrophizing (expecting the worst possible outcome), or ruminating (Joormann & Vanderlind, 2014; Lee et al., 2014). Ruminating is the process of thinking repeatedly about some event, generally an unpleasant event, without looking for a solution. Ruminating prolongs an unpleasant emotional reaction, and people who frequently ruminate are more likely than average to become depressed. On average, women ruminate significantly more than men do, more women than men become depressed, and women who ruminate are particularly likely to become depressed (Nolen-Hoeksema, Larson, & Grayson, 1999). Together, these findings suggest that women become depressed because they ruminate too much, but we must be cautious because, again, these are correlational studies. Perhaps rumination leads to depression, but another possibility is that rumination is simply an early symptom of depression. A longitudinal study suggested that both may be true—rumination predicted depression but depression also predicted rumination (Whisman, du Pont, & Butterworth, 2020). The best way to explore cause and effect would be to teach people better methods of regulating emotion and look for long-term psychological benefits.

A further complication to the role of emotional regulation is that many depressed people apparently use emotion regulation strategies to try to remain sad! For example, given a choice of listening to happy, sad, or neutral music, depressed people are more likely than others to choose the sad music. Given an opportunity to look at happy, sad, or neutral pictures, depressed people spend more time looking at the sad pictures than other people do. After being taught how to use cognitive reappraisal to control emotions, depressed people may even use this strategy to *increase* their responses to sad pictures (Millgram et al., 2015). Why would anyone try to increase sadness? Two speculations: depressed people feel comfortable with a sad mood because it is familiar; and some people think they deserve to feel sad.

Patterns of emotion regulation pertain to other psychological disorders as well. People with panic disorder tend to produce exaggerated responses to subtle signs of increased heart rate, faster breathing, or other body indications of possible distress (Sheppes, Suri, & Gross, 2015). That is, they enhance rather than soothe their emotional responses. Some people with PTSD or bipolar disorder may underutilize constructive emotion regulation responses to bad memories, such as self-distancing (Kenny et al., 2009; Park et al., 2014). A large body of work suggests multiple forms of emotion regulation difficulties in bipolar disorder (Miola et al., 2022). In short, lack of effective emotional regulation is at least a plausible hypothesis to explain much of psychological disorder. Future work will need to discern whether these difficulties regulating emotion are causes, consequences, or correlates of struggling with mental health—as well as explore how interventions might benefit people.

SUMMARY

If this chapter has one central point, it is that mental health problems are not like pneumonia, tuberculosis, or other illnesses that you either have or don't have. Rather, they are exaggerations or distortions of the same emotions that all human beings have, and they vary in degree from virtually zero to extreme.

A second major point is that emotional disorders are not completely caused by genes, brain structure, childhood or current experiences, or people's cognitive style. All of these factors play a part, and likely interact with each other, in ways researchers are just beginning to understand. For example, in the epigenetics approach described earlier, the expression of people's genes can be altered by environmental conditions. Much more research is needed to understand these complexities, but even now, there are implications for how we treat disorders of emotion. Psychiatrists default to giving every patient a pill for their distress. Psychotherapists emphasize some kind of talk therapy. In each case, a lot of trial-and-error is involved, and frankly, much of the research supporting various treatments is methodologically rather weak. Hopefully new approaches to studying emotion and psychopathology will lead to better tools for treating people's specific symptoms.

A third major point, related to the second, is that emotions are closely related to cognitions. When you have a strong emotional reaction, its strength and duration depend in large part on what you think it means. If you think that your depressed mood means that you can never be happy again, if you think that your panic attack means that you will continue having panic attacks at all the most inopportune times, or if you think your flashbacks to a miserable experience mean that you can never handle difficult situations again, then your symptoms could become worse. Seeking help from professional sources can link you to effective treatments.

KEY TERMS

agoraphobia: an excessive fear of public situations that would be difficult to escape in the event of a panic attack (p. 471)

antisocial personality disorder: condition marked by deceitful, impulsive, and aggressive behavior, with disregard for safety of self and others and lack of remorse (p. 478)

anxiolytics: drugs that decrease anxiety (p. 476)

bipolar disorder: mood disorder in which someone alternates between episodes of mania and depression (p. 476)

cognitive therapy: an approach that seeks to alter the explanatory styles and other dysfunctional cognitive biases that characterize disordered individuals (p. 465)

comorbidity: meeting criteria for more than one psychological diagnosis at a time, for instance, an anxiety disorder and a mood disorder (p. 452)

compulsion: repetitive behavior or mental act that a person feels internal pressure to perform (p. 478)

Diagnostic and Statistical Manual of Mental Disorders (DSM): a publication that lists psychological disorders and the criteria for diagnosing each one (p. 451)

dysthymia: condition in which someone feels sad almost constantly for years at a time (synonym: persistent depressive disorder) (p. 458)

epigenetics: changes in the expression of genes—how often they are activated to make new proteins—elicited by environmental conditions (p. 473)

explanatory style: a characteristic way of making attributions for one's successes and failures (p. 461)

exposure therapy: a treatment for specific phobias in which the client is exposed to the feared object under conditions that should minimize fear (p. 476)

external attribution: explanation of behavior or its outcome in terms of forces outside the individual (p. 460)

generalized anxiety disorder (GAD): a disorder characterized by almost constant nervousness and a wide range of worries (p. 470)

global attribution: explanation of behavior or its outcome in terms of something that is true of the person at nearly all times and situations (p. 460)

hypomania: an episode defined by symptoms of mania that are not severe enough to cause problems in the person's life (p. 467)

internal attribution: explanation of behavior or its outcome in terms of forces within the individual (p. 460)

learned helplessness: failure to try to improve one's current situation, resulting from lack of control in a prior situation (p. 460)

major depressive episode: depressed mood and/or loss of interest and pleasure, persisting almost every day for at least two weeks, accompanied by feelings of worthlessness, agitation or inactivity, impaired sleep, increased or decreased appetite, and/or impaired concentration (p. 454)

mania: behavior characterized by increased sense of energy, goal-directed activity, rapid thoughts and speech, and pleasurable activity without regard for harmful consequences (p. 467)

obsessions: recurrent and persistent thoughts, impulses, and images that are experienced as intrusive and inappropriate (p. 478)

obsessive–compulsive disorder: condition marked by intrusive thoughts and repetitive actions that a person feels compelled to perform (p. 478)

panic disorder: disorder characterized by repeated attacks of increased heart rate, rapid breathing, noticeable sweating, trembling, and chest pains, as well as frequent nervous apprehension about the prospect of having another attack (p. 471)

posttraumatic stress disorder (PTSD): condition marked by flashbacks and nightmares about a traumatic event, avoidance of reminders of it, and an exaggerated startle reflex (p. 470)

specific attribution: explanation of behavior or its outcome in terms of something that applies in a limited number of situations (p. 460)

specific phobia: excessive fear of a particular object or situation, strong enough to interfere with normal life (p. 471)

stable attribution: explanation of behavior or its outcome in terms of a permanent characteristic of the individual (p. 460)

tranquilizers: drugs that induce calmness and that can be used to treat anxiety (p. 476)

unstable attribution: explanation of behavior or its outcome in terms of a temporary characteristic of the individual or the situation (p. 460)

THOUGHT/DISCUSSION QUESTIONS

1. In defining depression, bipolar disorder, anxiety, OCD, and other disorders in this chapter, we have described many ways in which healthy emotion functioning can go wrong. Can you think of others? What else might happen if you have too much or too little of some emotion or too much or too little of some emotion-related ability such as expression, interpretation, or empathy?

2. It is expected to be sad and withdrawn for a long time in some situations, such as when a loved one has died. In this kind of situation, what criteria would you suggest

for determining whether someone's emotion should be allowed to run its course or whether the individual is in need of treatment?

3. Some psychologists have theorized that our human ancestors evolved the capacity to become depressed under certain circumstances. Can you imagine any evolutionary advantage to that tendency?

4. Look back at Figure 4.11, which shows the appraisal dimension profiles associated with several emotions. A goal of cognitive therapy for anxiety disorders is to help clients reshape their appraisals to alleviate fears. Given the appraisal profile of fear, what aspects of appraisal might a therapist try to target?

5. Coming up with an effective treatment for antisocial personality disorder (also known as sociopathy) has proved very difficult. As we discussed, childhood abuse is a strong risk factor for development of ASPD, and deficits in emotional empathy are one important feature of the disorder. Imagine that you could identify people at risk for sociopathy early in childhood. What kind of interventions might you design to prevent and intervene?

SUGGESTIONS FOR FURTHER READING

Three compelling, well-written, scientific books translating primary science in clinical psychology for a broader audience.

Brewer, J. (2021). *Unwinding anxiety: New science shows how to break the cycles of worry and fear to heal your mind*. Penguin.

Bonanno, G. A. (2021). *The end of trauma: How the new science of resilience is changing how we think about PTSD*. Hachette UK.

Foulkes, L. (2021). *Losing Our Minds: What mental illness really is-and what it isn't*. Bodley Head.

CHAPTER 14

Goal Setting and Self-Control

Every living organism is engaged in ongoing goal pursuit. The crow patiently building its nest is pursuing goals of shelter and protection of offspring. An otter searching for the perfect clam-cracking rock is pursuing the goal of tasty future meals. Many of your own automatic, unconscious behaviors are also goal pursuits of sorts—when you unintentionally maintain eye contact a few extra beats with an attractive person, when you fling your arm out to protect your younger sibling in the passenger seat of the car, when you flinch away from a loud noise—you are pursuing goals related to reproduction, kin protection, and safety, respectively. These examples, feathered, furry, and human, represent **automatic goal pursuit**, or the influence of unconscious goals on behavior.

Some nonhuman animals can and do pursue longer-term ambitions, such as building dams and squirreling away food for the dark winter months. These behaviors appear to be instinctual rather than consciously planned, and rarely conflict with other important goals that the creature may have. In contrast, human beings apply their skills of consciousness and imagination to intentionally work toward multiple complicated, long-range goals, even when that work makes our lives less pleasant in the short-term.

Consider the PhD student, working incredibly long hours for low pay for the better part of a decade, all in hopes of pursuing a life of the mind after graduation (in which they'll likely continue to work incredibly long hours for not-great pay). Or consider the marathon runner in training, who ignores a multitude of pains and discomforts in pursuit of the long-term satisfaction of a physical achievement. These might even be the same person! Rare is the human being who works with laser focus toward only a single goal. Most of us strive toward multiple goals at the same time—in the domains of work, health, relationships, hobbies, and more—juggling the steps toward achieving each goal as best we can (Figure 14.1).

One peculiarity of all this human goal setting is that it sets each individual goal up for a greater chance of failure. Pursuing multiple goals at once creates a minefield of

FIGURE 14.1.   At any given time, a human being is pursuing multiple goals across multiple arenas of life.

competing priorities and temptations. As far as we can tell, most pet dogs don't have goals other than eating, sleeping, and snuggling, and dogs in happy homes can pretty much eat, sleep, and snuggle at will (though even they must resist the temptation to steal food off the counter). If you are a "traditional" college student, however, you may be completing several difficult courses, practicing a sport or hobby, working a part-time job to save some "fun money," building and sustaining relationships with the important people in your life . . . .and you probably want to eat, sleep, and snuggle some too. If you are a "new traditional" college student (given that 18-year-old, parent-supported first year students are no longer the norm), you may be trying to balance your coursework with a full-time job, parenting responsibilities, and/or keeping up a home. Either way, when you have that many simultaneous goals, it means that nearly every moment of the day you're fighting the temptation to do something else: watch the latest binge-worthy Netflix show; hit the snooze button; splurge on a new outfit or toy that you don't need but really really want. Let's face it—sometimes you lose. Moreover, some of your goals are in direct tension with each other. On a given evening you might have to decide whether to stay up late completing assignments, spend that time connecting with your partner or family, get some exercise, or just hit the sack in order to be alert and focused the next day.

In this chapter we'll first review the history of goal setting research, and then branch into more contemporary considerations. What drives us to set goals? What differentiates effective goals from less effective goals? What temptations stand between us and our goals, and how can we resist them? What are the biases and roadblocks to achieving our heart's desires?

This body of work is among the most practical and easily applied to your own life that we'll cover in this text. We encourage you to use the Activity Boxes provided along the way to apply the science of effective goal setting to your own life.

THEORIES OF GOAL MOTIVATION
Learning Objectives
- Define what a goal is, and explain four main ways that goals influence experience and behavior.
- Summarize the central principles of discrepancy theory, goal setting theory, and goal systems theory.
- Differentiate between discrepancy reduction and discrepancy creation, and analyze which has a greater likelihood of motivating changes in behavior.

The intentional setting and pursuit of goals for the future has been a topic of study since the early days of psychological research. As in many other areas of psychology, the science has evolved from merely describing and predicting people's behavior to understanding the mechanisms, constraints, and implications of situational and social context for goal striving. Let's begin by reviewing some of the major theoretical perspectives and associated research.

Discrepancy Theory

Early goal setting research focused on "plans" and how they motivate behavior (Miller, Galanter, & Pribram, 1960). Researchers at the time argued that human beings have mental representations (concepts or ideas) of ideal states, and that comparing one's present state to this ideal state reveals a discrepancy or gap. According to **discrepancy theory**, we are intrinsically motivated to close this gap between the present and ideal state, and this motivation triggers relevant plans to do so (Figure 14.2).

For instance, perhaps many of your friends have access to a car, and you do not. You imagine the ideal state of being able to run errands or go out on the town without relying on other people for transportation, compare it to your current ride-scrounging status, and are motivated to approach the ideal state of having your own car. This generates enthusiasm (the energy component of motivation) and the launching of a series of actions (the direction component) that will lead to the discrepancy being eliminated: learning how to drive, obtaining your driver's license, saving money, investigating ads selling used cars, and perhaps soliciting some parental assistance.

Early theories proposed a somewhat mechanical process for how plans provide the *energy* and *direction* aspects of motivation we considered in Chapter 1. One influential model was named **the TOTE model**, for test-operate-test-exit (Miller, Galanter, & Pribram, 1960). The idea was that you made the comparison between your current and ideal states (test); found them to be incongruous (I do not have a car); operate on the environment to change the present state (save money, investigate ads, talk to parents); test again (do I have a car yet?); and exit the loop once the present and ideal states are found to be congruous (I have a car!). You can apply this model to other scenarios as well—for instance, finding that your pre-pandemic jeans no longer fit, and going for extra walks until they do; or not spending money on nights out with friends until your savings account reaches a particular balance.

Like other movements in psychology, motivation science grew to appreciate that human beings are more flexible than the TOTE model suggests. After all, upon detecting

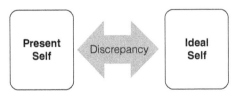

FIGURE 14.2. Reflecting on your present and ideal selves (in terms of achievement, health, wealth, relationships, etc.) can reveal discrepancies between these two states of being. This discrepancy can motivate goal-setting behavior.

incongruity between our ideal and present state, we sometimes simply downgrade our concept of the ideal! Later models (e.g., Higgins, 1987) focused more on the discrepancy aspect of the ideal/present state comparison—how much distance or tension is there between these two states? What alternative **corrective actions** might one take to resolve this discrepancy?

This work also introduced a distinction between two different discrepancy-related processes (Bandura, 1990; Carver & Scheier, 1998). **Discrepancy reduction** occurs in situations in which the ideal state is clearly defined, time-limited, and often externally determined. We might want to elevate our GPA to meet the requirements of a specific scholarship, or hit a sales target set by our supervisor. The choice of ideal state in discrepancy reduction tends to be low on autonomy, and once we resolve the discrepancy there is no more motivation to continue—we're done. **Discrepancy creation**, on the other hand, is a process whereby the person intentionally manufactures an ideal state in order to motivate themselves to reach it. Discrepancy creation is often iterative—once you reach your target, you intentionally set a new one beyond. Hit 5k followers on Instagram? Now set 10k as the new goal. Ran a 5k race? Start training for a half-marathon. This process of intentional discrepancy creation can spiral upward into better and better performance.

This intentional discrepancy creation process is also the essence of goal setting, which puts the goal itself at the foreground of motivational power (Locke & Latham, 2013).

Goal Setting Theory

A **goal** is an object or aim of an action (Locke & Latham, 1990), or more formally, a mental conception of a possible future state that provides energy and direction to current behavior. Goals are in the *future*—said future could conceivably be close in time (e.g., finishing a paper that is due at the end of the week) but is more commonly weeks, months, or even years away. Goals are theoretical and thus exist as *mental concepts*. We can bring theorized and hoped-for states to being in our minds, but they don't yet reflect reality. Goals are often fixed—there is a clear desired *outcome*, a moment when we know we have achieved our aims. Finally, goals *shape behavior*. We behave differently because we have set a goal, making incremental choices each day that move us toward that coveted ideal state.

We all have various conscious and subconscious goals that guide our behavior. However, **goal setting** as a motivational technique involves deliberately defining particular goals to prioritize and pursue. An overwhelming amount of research indicates that setting goals improves performance in domains such as physical fitness, financial saving, healthy eating, pursuing career aims, and many more (Burton & Naylor, 2002). For example, in a review of 45 research studies Desmond McEwan and colleagues (2016) found that goal setting was more effective in promoting physical exercise than a variety of alternative behavior change techniques. The size of the effects in these studies was impressive, reaching a "medium" effect size of d =.55 (in other words, the goal setting versus control conditions differed by just over half of the overall standard deviation, averaging across studies). A medium effect size might not sound very impressive, but effects in psychology studies tend to be small because so many factors contribute to people's behavior.

In one example of the power of goal setting, Dominique Morisano and colleagues recruited 85 students experiencing academic difficulty into a study that lasted an academic semester (Morisano et al., 2010). Students were randomly assigned at the start of the study

TABLE 14.1 Goal activity box #1

Visualize your ideal future.

For each of the following prompts, "free write" your thoughts: write without editing yourself for content, clarity, or typos; just let your thoughts flow onto the page. First, fix your mental gaze on a particular point in the future—perhaps the end of the current academic or calendar year. Then: (1) Write about your ideal version of this future. What does it feel like? What have you accomplished? How are you spending your days? (2) Write about qualities you admire in others and how you think you could strive to emulate them. (3) Write about your current aspirations in school and future career aspirations. (4) Write about habits you would like to improve related to work, school, relationships, or health.

Activity based on goal setting exercise in Morisano et al. (2010).

to complete one of two computerized programs that involved intensive reflection and writing. The treatment group's activities centered around effective goal setting for their academic work; the control group's activities centered around positive psychology reflections (of the sort you read about in Chapter 12). This sort of control group is called an **active control** because they're not just sitting around doing nothing—they are engaged in activities that match the treatment group's on dimensions such as time, effort, type of activity, and engagement with the research team. Active controls provide a stronger, more rigorous test of a study's hypotheses than no-activity controls. In Table 14.1 you can see some of the writing prompts from the goal setting exercise and try them out yourself.

After completing the computerized programs students went about their semesters, studying, taking exams, and submitting assignments. After 16 weeks, the experimenters collected information on GPA and course loads from official records, and participants self-reported on their emotional experiences and other aspects of their experience during the study. As you can see in Figure 14.3, students in the goal setting intervention condition achieved significantly higher GPAs at the end of the semester than they had the previous semester, whereas students in the control condition showed no such increase. (You might note a slight incline in the control group's GPA; however, this was

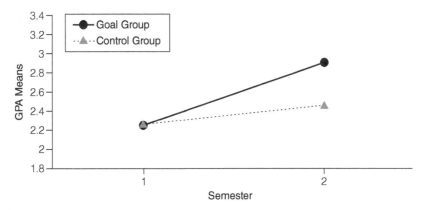

FIGURE 14.3. Reproduced from Morisano, Hirsh, Peterson, Pihl, & Shore (2010), Figure 1: Group differences in grade-point average (GPA) change postintervention. Students who completed a goal-setting intervention at the start of the semester experienced elevations in their overall GPA that students assigned to a control intervention did not. From Morisano et al. (2010).

not a large enough change to be statistically significant.) The goal setting group also experienced two other benefits compared to the control group: they were more likely to maintain a full course load over the semester; and their experience of negative emotions decreased over time.

These are powerful effects! You probably don't need anyone to tell you that GPA is important, and dropping courses can become a slippery slope toward problems with graduation. Goal setting works.

Hundreds of research studies have now increased our understanding of *why* goal setting is so effective for changing behavior and achieving desired outcomes, as well as the features of more-effective versus less-effective goals (Locke & Latham, 1990; Locke & Latham, 2013). Goals work in four main ways (Locke & Latham, 2002). First, they *direct attention* to the work needed to accomplish the goal. Life is a busy, dizzy array of responsibilities and opportunities, and you aren't going to make much progress if you just fling yourself through it without clear, specific goals and an understanding of the specific behaviors needed to achieve them. Goals crystallize your focus. Second, goals *mobilize your efforts*. They act as fuel for what SRC's app-based running coach calls "the fire under our butts." The pure act of setting the goal seems to lead to an increase in the energy available to pursue it.

Third, goals *prolong your persistence*. Especially if you follow some of the specific techniques we'll discuss in a bit, about how to design a particularly effective goal, you'll stick to your efforts for longer than if you had not set a goal. Finally, goals *foster the development of new learning*. Once your attention is directed to behaviors that need to change, you may identify interim steps that involve acquiring new skills and information. Recall our new car example, in which one of the necessary steps was to take driving lessons and obtain your license. Goal setting can broaden your behavioral repertoire.

Goal Systems Theory

As we have discussed, people are likely to have multiple goals. How do we manage this juggling act, and what determines which goals get the most attention at any given time? Goal systems theory approaches motivation and goal conceptualization as a form of cognition (Kruglanski et al., 2002). Like other concepts we hold in our minds, goals do not exist in isolation; they are linked with other, related goals, and with the means we have to pursue them. Your goal to earn your undergraduate degree might be related to mental concepts of your future career, past academic successes, studying behavior, and more. Moreover, these conceptual networks can be hierarchical in nature, with some goals subordinate to others. Your goal of earning a degree may be your superordinate goal, under which you may have subordinate goals of *passing all my classes* and *registering for next term's classes to stay on track with requirements for graduation*. Underneath these subordinate goals are "means," or resources and strategies you have for achieving the goals. For this example, your means might include study groups you can work with, meetings with your academic advisor and the tutoring center, and a work-study job to help pay your tuition. Together, the goals and means form a **goal system** (Figure 14.4).

The hierarchical connections among superordinate goals, subordinate goals, and means are called the *structural* aspects of goal systems. You can think about these connections as metaphorical railroad tracks along which goal commitment, motivation, and emotion can travel. Goal systems theory also recognizes that the resources we have for pursuing goals and their associated means—such as time, money, attentional focus, social

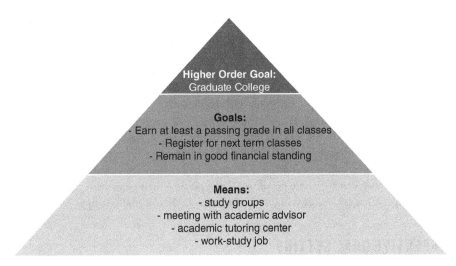

FIGURE 14.4. An example of an academics-focused hierarchical goal system.

support, and ability to multitask—are not infinite. This limits the number and variety of goals that we can pursue at any given time, so we must choose. The limited resource nature of goal resources are called their *allocational* properties.

The fact that we have only so much time, energy, and money to dedicate to our goals (those allocational properties) indicates that we must make choices in how we expend these resources. The fact that our goals and the means to accomplish them are arranged in hierarchical systems (those structural properties) also indicates that means sometimes serve multiple different goals. For instance, your part-time job is a means that serves to both pay tuition for your goal of a college degree and to line your vacation fund for your goal of being happy and stress-free. In addition, the hierarchy also means that goals are served by multiple means. Your part-time job is one means toward your goal of obtaining a college degree, but so are your study group, attending class, and meetings with your academic advisor.

Influence can spread vertically, whereby activating a goal (e.g., you visit your dream school) can lead to you dedicate more resources to the means associated with that goal (e.g., you throw yourself into your studies in the weeks following your visit, hoping to maximize chances of your transfer with a good GPA and recommendation letters). Influence can also spread horizontally. Spending resources on one means can spread to other, related means. For instance, you may also step up your practicing of the guitar as it is generally associated with your efforts in school, even though it might not help your transfer application. Both these examples are of goals and means that are active and facilitating each other. But these links can also be inhibitory in nature, leading people to dedicate fewer resources to some goals and means because others are currently active. Just today, SRC received an email from MNS that activated the superordinate goal of finishing this textbook. In response, SRC ignored all her other goals and associated means to spend her limited time resources on finishing this chapter. (MNS: Aww, sorry!)

What's neat about goal systems theory is that its proposed networks of goals, subgoals, and means, with different degrees of connection and spreading activation, bear strong resemblance to how our brains work. Networks of neurons are linked to each other in greater and lesser fashion, and activation spreads among these networks. In some cases, activation of one network suppresses activation in others, just as some goals are prioritized over others in general or at a given moment. Our minds also organize concepts in a hierarchical manner, much as goal systems theory suggests. For instance, you might have a concept of "modes of transportation" and under these "boats," and then "sailboats, motorboats, kayaks," and so on. It is always a strength of a theory when you can propose plausible mechanisms by which the processes might work at the level of the brain.

We've described goal setting so far as an ideal technique for getting what you want out of life, and it certainly can be. Some goals are more effective at guiding our behavior than others, however; and some people set—and reach—their goals with greater success than others. What do we know about the features of *effective* goal setting?

EFFECTIVE GOAL SETTING

Learning Objectives
- Analyze why some goals are more effective than others, highlighting several attributes of effective goals.
- Describe the expectancy-value theory of goal pursuit.
- Discriminate between proximal and distal goals, and reflect on why each are important for successful goal pursuit.
- Differentiate between promotion and prevention regulatory focus, and discuss which is more motivating and why.

As a human being of a certain age, you are certainly familiar with goal setting. You have striven for and achieved certain milestones in life, closing the discrepancy between a present self and a future, ideal self. These milestones might include graduating from high school, getting into college, finding romantic love, competing on a sports team, developing a hobby or skill, getting a job, saving money for a special trip, or becoming a pet owner. While the exact nature of these goals will vary from reader to reader, all of you have realized some of your past goals. Unless you are truly an extraordinary person, you have also had the experience of setting goals and *not* seeing them come to fruition.

Pause for a moment and use this life experience to make some predictions for what kinds of goals are more and less effective. By "effective" we mean the desired outcome was successfully achieved: you got into college, you saved enough to go on vacation, you brought home a little bundle of fur and named her Freckles. What do *you* think are the characteristics of a more effective goal? For example: Are simpler goals better, or more complex ones? Is it better to set goals that are difficult and ambitious, or those that are closer to your current skills? Does setting goals with social partners amplify motivation, or is it more effective to strive on your own? Throughout this section, keep track how many of your predictions are supported by the science on features of effective goals.

First, which are better: ambitious or more easily attainable goals? Early in the history of goal setting research (Locke & Latham, 1990), two features of effective goals rose to the top: the best goals are *difficult*, and they are *specific*. The perceived difficulty of the goal seems to relate most to the power of goals to mobilize efforts. A difficult goal appears to get us more energized, more willing to step it up. If you regularly run three miles a week and you sign up for a 5K, setting that goal is unlikely to change your daily behavior much. You might try a new running playlist or some sprints to improve your speed, but you know you can easily reach your goal, and your efforts are likely to be half-hearted. If you regularly run three miles a week and you sign up for a half-marathon, on the other hand, the landscape of your weeks between now and the race is going to look a lot different than it did before. You'd better get moving!

Of course, while ambitious goals are highly motivating, they still need to be within reach. Goals that are entirely outside of your reach (in terms of personal skills or resources) are by definition not achievable, and therefore cannot be effective. You must be able to have some expectation of success. How do you know which goals stretch your capabilities, and which are truly out of the question? Sometimes you can figure this out for yourself, but it can also be good to ask an expert in that domain for their opinion. For instance, a friend or life coach can help you think through your desire to change careers—mapping out degree programs, required savings, and future job prospects to see whether it is feasible.

Goal specificity, on the other hand, improves performance by enhancing the attention and learning aspects of goal striving. If you set a nonspecific goal, something like "be healthier," then it is unclear where exactly your efforts should be directed. Should you focus on eating more vegetables? Drinking less alcohol? Getting more exercise, or more sleep? What if your time is limited in such a way that you must choose between more exercise and more sleep? Your efforts are likely to be diffuse and unfocused, and sputter out. If you instead identify specific goals, such as "no alcohol on weekdays; try one new vegan recipe a week; and walk at least 12,000 steps per day," then it is a lot clearer how you need to be spending your time and changing your behavior. Note that specific goals may be nested within more abstract, superordinate goals (e.g., "be healthier"), as goal systems theory suggests. The key point here is that with the specific, subordinate goals clearly defined, one is more likely to succeed at achieving the superordinate goal as well.

Expecting to Succeed

Another important, early theory of effective goal setting as it relates to achievement specifically is John Atkinson's **expectancy-value theory** (Atkinson, 1958; Tolman, 1932). This theory posits that goal-pursuit behaviors result from expectations of likely success (expectancy) and perceived worth of the desired outcome (value). People are more likely to persist in pursuing a goal if they believe that they will succeed (expectancy) and greatly value the results of that success (value). Expectancy and value are thought to interact, such that motivation is highest when they're both high, lowest when they are both low, and absent if either one is zero (Liberman & Förster, 2012). For example, scaling Mount Everest might sound amazing to you (high value), but if your estimation of your mountain climbing skill, time, and financial resources makes the task seem impossible (low expectancy), your investment in that goal will be minimal. Alternatively, you might have excellent eye-hand coordination, and believe that winning a local golf tournament is feasible (high expectancy), but if golf trophies are unimportant to you (low value) your motivation to practice will be low.

Consider academic achievement in school (Eccles et al., 1983). Table 14.2 offers examples of expectancy-related beliefs and sources of value that are known to predict academic motivation and performance (adapted from Hulleman et al., 2016). Which of these are most consistent with your own experiences in schooling? In what ways have you found that these expectancy beliefs and values amplify or diminish your motivation in various

TABLE 14.2 | **Factors associated with expectancy for academic success and value of learning**

From Table 10.3 of Hulleman et al. (2016), Research-based sources of expectancy-related beliefs. Factors associated with expectancy for academic success and value of learning.		
Expectancy source	**Description**	**Example**
Perception of ability/ skill	Belief that one has a high level of relevant ability and/or skill	Jasmin thinks of herself as innately good at math, so she anticipates earning a high grade in her calculus class.
Support and scaffolding	Availability of strong instruction, resources, and other support for learning	Mark's instructor explains concepts clearly, provides examples and practice items, and offers extra help in office hours, instilling confidence that he'll be able to master the material.
Clear expectations	Explicitly defined and openly shared criteria for high performance	Won's history instructor shares the rubric that will be used to grade an upcoming essay, so Won knows what steps to take to do a good job.
Appropriate challenge	Task difficulty is well-matched to students' abilities and background knowledge	Professor Urry gives statistics exams at the right level— challenging yet not unreasonably difficult for a typical undergraduate at her university.
Value Source	**Explanation**	
Intrinsic benefits	Course content is perceived as inherently interesting, and activities are enjoyable	Taylor finds the readings, discussions, and assignments in their philosophy class fascinating and fun.
Relevance	Students are able to connect what they are learning to their personal lives and/or the real world	André can identify his own attachment style and that of his romantic partner and is motivated to learn more about attachment theory and research.
Enthusiastic models	Teachers and other role models convey excitement about and passion for the material	Sierra's sociology instructor is a vivid, funny storyteller, and conveys clear passion for the course content.
Positive relationships and sense of belonging	Student-instructor and student-student relationships feel authentic and meaningful	Belinda's class project team formed a strong bond during the semester, and valued working together on the assignment.

courses? Are there other expectancy beliefs and values that you would include? These examples are all positive, leading to high expectations for success and value of learning the course material. Have you taken classes where the opposite was the case—your expectancy for success and/or how much you valued learning were actually undermined by something about the course?

Of course, the sources of expectancy beliefs and values will vary based on the type of goal involved. The examples in Table 14.2 all involve academic performance, but we can easily extrapolate to other contexts. Whether a goal is in the domain of athletics, finances, relationships, or artistic pursuits, belief in likelihood of success and valuing the goal itself will be influenced by factors such as these. As an exercise, you might identify a goal you have in a domain beyond academics and identify an example that fits with that goal for each row of the table.

Mapping the Path: Chunking and Feedback

Another effective strategy is to break big goals into a series of smaller ones. Looking again at Figure 14.4, these are similar to superordinate and subordinate goals. Also called **proximal** (short-term) and **distal** (long-term) **goals,** this allows for you to take advantage of the specificity and less-intimidating scope of short-term goals while also feeling inspired by the aspirational nature of larger, longer-term goals (Manderlink & Harackiewicz, 1984). The terms "proximal" and "distal" should sound familiar, based on our discussion of proximal versus distal elicitors of emotions in Chapter 4. Doing well on an exam might feel nice, but it may not be terribly motivating in and of itself. As one step toward your life-long goal of being a doctor, however, it might evoke a greater burst of motivation. The same trick allows us to take a large, otherwise over-whelming goal (e.g., buy a house) and think of it as just a sequence of more clearly achievable ones (e.g., save a certain amount of money every month for a down payment; learn about different types of mortgages; budget the amount you will be able to afford per month; find a realtor you like).

Once you have identified a series of proximal goals, it helps to measure your progress and give yourself feedback along the way (Bandura & Cervone, 1983); this is called **monitoring** (Carver & Scheier, 1981; 1982). Recall that the TOTE model required consistent testing and feedback about how close one was to the ideal state. A more contemporary model of how human beings monitor their goal progress and provide feedback for themselves takes inspiration from the field of engineering. The **cybernetic model** of monitoring and feedback suggests that your mind is constantly testing the present state against an ideal state, and kicking action into motion when a discrepancy is detected (Carver & Scheier, 2012). You might think of the thermostat in your house as analogy. It tests the present state (how warm it is in the room) against an ideal state (how warm you have set your ideal state to be). When a discrepancy is detected, it kicks on your furnace. When the ideal state is reached, it shuts off.

While we have moved away from assuming that human beings work in quite such a mechanical way, frequent measurement and documenting progress are important parts of effective goal pursuit. Many fitness apps have this sort of monitoring and feedback built in as core features. For instance, one of your authors (SRC) uses apps on runs that show her not only the statistics for each run, such as number of miles, average pace, average heartbeats per minute, and more, but also where those statistics fit into her historical record (Figure 14.5). Some days the feedback tells her she's further from the goal than she'd like (an alert saying, "this is your 464th fastest run!" is a bit disheartening). On other days she gets the reward of seeing her growth and achievement in concrete, measurable terms. Both are important pieces of information, and taken together they help keep her on track (so to speak).

One of the best methods of providing yourself with monitoring and feedback is to pursue goals together with friends, colleagues, and/or family (Fishbach & Tu, 2016). Some of the goals we pursue are inherently social. When we start a family, when we develop a product with a team at work, or when we're assigned a group presentation for class, we are pursuing goals with others. Other goals exist at the individual rather than the group level but can be shared with others in your life (e.g., you and your roommate each want to learn a new language). In addition to offering updates on our own goal progress, social others can also serve as role models. In fact, an entire literature studies **mimetic desire** (Girard, 1988), our tendency to adopt goals we see others we admire pursuing. One research study (Lebreton et al., 2012) found that the mere act of watching a hand reach for an object activated both reward and physical mimicry regions of the brain. We want what other people want.

These tendencies mean that we may reach greater success in our goals if we strive as a group than if we strive individually. For instance, in one study Cait Wilson and

FIGURE 14.5. Recent innovations in technology have made monitoring and feedback for goals easy and precise—though they may not be cheap!

colleagues led a three-week goal setting intervention with 88 summer camp children aged 5 to 11 (Wilson, Sibthrop, & Brusseau, 2017). Camp weeks varied as to whether the campers set individual goals, small group goals, or a camp-wide goal for physical activity—measured as number of steps recorded by pedometers. The control week was the first week of camp, during which no goals were set and step counts were simply measured. Both step counts and enjoyment were highest during the week with the camp-wide goal (Figure 14.6). Now, if you have your critical thinking cap on, you may have noticed that the camp-wide goal week was also the last week of camp—the third in which campers actively pursued fitness goals. A simple practice effect might be at least partially responsible for that week's superiority in terms of enjoyment and steps (in other words, time was a confound of goal type). A study in which goal types were randomized across different weeks for different campers would provide stronger evidence for the value of large group goals.

Other evidence also points strongly to the value of sharing your goals with a group, whether pursuing the goal together or simply enlisting others in keeping you accountable for progress toward your own goal. In a recent meta-analysis (Harkin et al., 2016), researchers found not only that people randomly assigned to monitor progress toward a specific goal were more successful at attaining the goal, but that effects were enhanced when the person's progress was reported to other people, or even made public (such as on a study website others could see). Even in highly individualistic cultures, we care what others think of us, and the awareness that others are aware of our goal progress can help keep us on track.

FIGURE 14.6. Summer campers stepped more and had higher levels of enjoyment when setting camp-wide group goals for physical activity.

Promotion Versus Prevention

A final feature of goal setting tied to more effective achievement is whether you are setting approach goals or avoidance goals. We've distinguished between approach and avoidance motivation many times in this text. In approach goals you reach toward something you desire in the future—a certain grade in a class, getting a particular job, a promotion, playing in a rock band, moving to the city. Avoidance goals, on the other hand, attempt to avert disaster—failing an exam, being unable to pay your rent, getting yelled at by your boss, getting stuck living somewhere you hate. Researchers Arie Kruglanski and colleagues differentiate between **promotion** and **prevention regulatory focus** to capture this distinction (Kruglanski et al., 2002). Note that approach and avoidance goals can be mirror images of each other; the goal of getting at least a B in a difficult class overlaps with the goal of not failing it. As it turns out, however, the framing really matters.

For example, both stronger promotion focus and lower prevention focus have been found to predict better performance by undergraduates on their exams (Rosenzweig & Miele, 2016). In a meta-analysis examining the implications of holding either a promotion or a prevention focus for job performance, researchers found that higher promotion focus predicted better task performance, more innovation on the job, and better citizenship within the organization (i.e., informal actions that helped coworkers and the organization succeed). Employees with a stronger prevention focus tended to adhere to safety procedures more carefully (presumably trying not to get injured), but prevention focus was not associated with job performance (Lanaj, Chang, & Johnson, 2012).

Why might this be? Researchers have found that that approach/promotion goals lead to feelings such as happiness upon success and sadness upon failure, whereas avoidance/prevention goals lead to calm upon success and tension upon failure (Kruglanski et al., 2002). Think about where these feelings fall on the circumplex model of emotion in Chapter 1. The former kinds of feelings, which differ strongly on valence, are especially energizing and motivating. The latter feelings, which differ mainly in arousal, offer less help in guiding behavior. In addition, approach focuses attention on the skills needed to succeed, whereas avoidance goals motivate doing *anything* that reduces likelihood of your feared outcome, and so can lead to more "chaotic and unpredictable" behavior (Fujita & MacGregor, 2012).

Having some avoidance goals is natural, and they're not always bad. You probably should avoid getting into car accidents, for example, and prevention focus, not promotion focus, could help keep you driving safely (Lemarié, Bellavance, & Chebat, 2019). Also, if you're trying to nudge other people's behavior rather than your own, it's important to consider individual differences. Some people are more approach-oriented and promotion-focused in general, whereas others are more cautious and concerned with avoiding harm. These individual differences have been found to correlate with the lateralized prefrontal cortex activity we linked to approach versus avoidance motivation in Chapter 6 (Amodio et al., 2004; Eddington et al., 2007). Increasingly, researchers advise tailoring messages encouraging healthy and pro-environmental behavior to people with different regulatory foci (e.g., Bhatnagar & McKay-Nesbitt, 2016; Ludolph & Schulz, 2015). For example, while a promotion-focused person might respond strongly to a message touting the benefits of cutting back on dietary sugar for positive mood and energy, a prevention-focused person might respond more strongly to a message emphasizing the cardiovascular risks of excess sugar.

Despite these individual differences, however, people can take control of their own regulatory focus and goals, and it makes a difference in goal striving. In one pair of experiments undergraduate students were primed with either a promotion or prevention focus, and then asked to take tests similar to the SAT. Those in the promotion-focus conditions performed better on the exams, despite underlying individual differences (Rosenzweig & Miele, 2016). Consider some of your own goals. Which are approach or promotion-oriented, and which are avoidance or prevention-oriented? Can you can reframe the latter into approach goals? If your doctor tells you that you should lose some weight to reduce your risk for diabetes, try reframing the goal in terms of fitness and/or the reward of a new wardrobe. If you are worried about doing badly in this class, we strongly encourage you to talk with your instructor about how to switch to a promotion focus. Your instructor may encourage you to work toward a certain, achievable grade that would make you feel good, and help you identify the steps needed to get there. Good luck!

So there we have it. The features of more versus less effective goals are: specific, difficult, attainable, consistent with your values, point clearly to behaviors for which you have high self-efficacy, organized into proximal/short-term and distal/long-term systems, approach (rather than avoidance) oriented, and socially shared. These are the attributes of successful goal striving. Using the activity in Table 14.3, try applying these principles to your own goals.

TABLE 14.3 | **Goal activity box #2**

Using visualization from earlier, choose one of the behaviors you'd like to improve and answer the questions below to set the most effective goal you can.

What is your goal?

How can you make this goal more **difficult**?

How can you make this goal more **specific**?

Is this a goal you **expect you can achieve**, based on your skills and resources? (If not, start over with another goal).

Is this a goal that you see as being of **high value**? (If not, start over with another goal).

Can you frame this goal in terms of **approaching positive outcomes** rather than avoiding negative ones?

Can you break the goal into a series of **smaller, subordinate goals**?

How will you **measure or monitor progress**? What sources of feedback can you build into the process?

How can you **pursue this goal socially**, involving friends or family?

SELF-CONTROL

Learning Objectives

- Define self-control, and relate it to self-regulation.
- Describe delay of gratification and delay discounting. Explain evidence that people who prioritize rewards in the future over rewards in the present moment may experience better outcomes in life.
- Explain the concept of ego depletion and how it relates to self-control. Briefly trace the rise, fall, and current state of research support for this theory.
- Reflect on evidence regarding whether people can consciously train their self-control abilities.

As we have seen, there is ample evidence suggesting that setting goals—especially certain kinds of goals—can motivate and shape behavior in ways that get us closer to the future selves we wish to be. This is all grand, but you may be thinking that actually doing what is needed to achieve the goal will still require a lot of work. Moreover, it may require an awful lot of self-discipline, and application of mental effort (Figure 14.7). To monitor your behavior and keep it going in the right direction (e.g., get at least eight hours of sleep every night), you must constantly evaluate whether your current choices are consistent with the goal (go to bed by midnight the night before a 9:00 a.m. exam?), resisting all manner of temptations to do otherwise (e.g., stay up until 3:00 a.m. binge-watching *Schitt's Creek* instead?), and decide whether to continue pursuing the goal or give up and abandon it entirely.

The application of effort to regulate one's own thoughts, feelings, and behavior is called **self-control**, and you are probably not surprised to hear that motivation researchers have spent quite a lot of time studying it. What is it, who has more of it, what are its cognitive and neural mechanisms, what implications does it have for our lives; and most intriguingly—can we train ourselves or others to have more of it?

Strap in, because the self-control literature is a bumpy ride.

FIGURE 14.7. To pursue our goals (especially avoidance or prevention ones), we often must exercise self-control.

Delay of Gratification

If you are a psychology major or minor, you have surely encountered the Great Marshmallow Study of Mischel and Ebbesen (1970). People often think of this as a single study, but it was really a lengthy program of research. One of the most famous experiments in the history of psychology, the original research involved presenting small children with a single marshmallow and telling them they could eat it right away, but if they resisted the impulse to cram the sugary goodness into their mouths for just a couple of minutes, they would be rewarded with an additional marshmallow. In other words, if they could **delay gratification** by waiting, they would get *two* marshmallows instead of just one.

Why marshmallows? If you think about it, this situation is similar to temptations adults face all the time. Work on your assignment for an important class tonight so you'll have the whole weekend free, or join friends now who are watching a movie? Buy yourself a treat in the present, or save money toward an amazing vacation next summer? In these and many other scenarios, working toward a longer-term goal means foregoing something you want right now. Take a minute to identify a few situations in your own life in which delay of gratification is necessary to achieve your goals. If the situation forces you to decide between a smaller short-term reward and a larger long-term one, it's a good example of delay of gratification.

The critical research question for Mischel—a personality psychologist—wasn't just how many youngsters were successfully able to delay gratification, but what this ability predicted about other aspects of the children's lives. Effective delay of gratification predicted future academic and behavioral outcomes—even years down the line. Widely popularized, this finding spawned decades of research on the power of self-control to predict success (Duckworth, 2011). In just one example, Terrie Moffit and colleagues (2011) found that individual differences in childhood self-control (this time measured through several observers, such as parents and teachers, as well as by self-report) predicted outcomes as varied as financial security, mental health, and lack of criminal convictions in adulthood.

It may not surprise you, by this point in the book, that some recent attempts to replicate the earlier, famous findings have run into trouble. In some cases the predicted effects were observed, but were much smaller than in earlier studies, and/or did not survive statistical techniques that control for demographic variables such as socioeconomic status (e.g., Watts, Duncan, & Quan, 2018). Self-control as captured by the marshmallow test and other measures correlates substantially with having a privileged upbringing, especially in terms of socioeconomic status (Evans & Schamberg, 2009; Ng-Knight & Schoon, 2017). This means that the apparent relationships of self-control with positive outcomes could be explained by third-variable confounds, such as home environment, education, lifelong financial resources, strong social support networks, and the other benefits that tend to correlate with wealth.

Despite the limitations of this longitudinal work, delay of gratification and its counterpart, **delay discounting** (the tendency to perceive far-off rewards as less valuable than the same reward if you had it right now, reduced by an amount proportional to the distance in time) remain valuable constructs in research predicting behaviors and life outcomes. Beyond early childhood, delay of gratification and delay discounting are often measured with questionnaires asking what people would be likely to do in hypothetical situations. An example question might be, "would you rather have $500 now, or $1,000 in a year?" Studies consistently find that adults who prioritize future benefits more strongly are less prone to drug abuse, gambling, and other risky behavior; make better financial decisions; are more academically successful; have healthier dietary and exercise habits; and generally take better care of themselves (e.g., Acuff et al., 2017; Daugherty & Brase, 2010; Mishra & Lalumiére, 2017; Snider et al., 2019).

Self-Regulation and Ego Depletion Theory

While Mischel and colleagues emphasized individual differences in people's ability to delay gratification, their early work sparked broader interest in the extent to which people control themselves at all, and in how self-control works. Although this work often uses the label **self-regulation** rather than self-control, the constructs are similar enough for our purposes. Self-control and self-regulation are much larger categories than delay of gratification. Delay of gratification is about resisting the temptation to pounce on some reward right now, so you can take advantage of a bigger or more valued reward in the future. Self-control/regulation encompasses all the ways in which you intentionally make yourself do something different from your automatic inclinations. This includes resisting temptation, but also inhibiting impulses and habits unrelated to temptation, and making yourself do anything you don't want to do.

Here's one way self-regulation has been measured and manipulated in some of the research with adults. If you are reading your own printed copy of this book (not if it's borrowed from your school or library, please), you can do this on a page you've already read. Otherwise, just select another handy book, newspaper, or magazine with lots of text, and pick a page. On that entire page, cross out every "e" *except* those that are one or two letters away from another vowel. For example, you would *not* cross off the "e" in "vowel," because another vowel—the "o"—is two letters away. Really. The whole page. Come back here when you're done. We'll get some coffee while we wait.

So, how was it? Fun? Not so much? What do you think of it as a measure of self-control?

Self-control ability is also measured using self-report questionnaires, and in some cases via the reports of other people who know the target participant well. There's not much question that self-control matters. Greater dispositional self-control has consistently been found to predict lower substance use; healthier lifestyle in terms of diet, exercise, and so forth; better mental health; healthier relationships; lower risk-taking; and lower rates of aggression and other deviant behavior (DeRidder et al., 2012). These effects are modest, but consistent.

The story gets more complicated from there, however. Here's a scenario: imagine you've just had a relatively easy weekday—full of the usual responsibilities but nothing was particularly difficult or stressful; you just kind of cruised through it. At the end of the day, how would you feel about going home and spending 15 minutes cleaning the bathroom? Would you do it?

Now imagine you've just finished a frustrating, difficult, stressful day. Nothing went horribly wrong, and it was the same length day as the one above, but you encountered some barrier or problem with nearly every task, so it all took more mental effort and self-control than usual. Now how do you feel about 15 minutes cleaning the bathroom? Would you do it?

For most people, the answers are more likely to be "fine" and "sure" for the first scenario above than for the second. How often have you heard someone say, or said yourself, "I'm just done." Done for today, done with this, done expending effort on . . . anything. It's a highly relatable phenomenon. But is it real?

In the early 1990s, Roy Baumeister and colleagues began to propose that self-regulation/control is a *limited* resource—for any given person on a given day, there is only so much of it to go around (Baumeister, Heatherton, & Tice, 1994). If this is true, then applying self-control repeatedly might use up that resource so there is less available when you try to use it again, even if the context is different. It certainly feels like this is true, right? If you've ever pushed yourself hard to get a difficult assignment done, and then snapped at your significant other for something minor; or gritted your teeth through a tense social encounter and then binged on potato chips when you got home—you can relate to this. Self-control feels like work, like you're using a muscle that gets tired over time, even across different types of situations and behaviors. This weakening of the self-control "muscle" came to be known as **ego depletion** (Baumeister, 2014), as though your very self (ego) is getting used up.

A huge body of research began to build around the ego depletion hypothesis. Various effortful tasks have been used both to deplete participants in these studies, and to measure performance on a subsequent task. The e-eliminating task above is a common one (a control instruction might simply be to cross out all "e's," without the vowel restriction—a bit boring, but not hard). Other tasks include inhibiting your facial expression while watching a really disgusting film clip; making yourself eat radishes instead of the chocolates right next to them; working on difficult, in some cases unsolvable puzzles; squeezing a handgrip as hard as you can for a couple of minutes; and suppressing particular thoughts (e.g., Baumeister et al., 1998; Muraven, Tice, & Baumeister, 1998). In each study participants would be instructed to perform either an effortful or easy version of a task, followed by a different effortful task. Experiments supporting the ego depletion hypothesis (those that found that performance on the second task was worse after the difficult version of the first task than after the easy version), rapidly built up (for a review of this early literature, see Baumeister, Vohs, & Tice, 2007).

Baumeister and colleagues then pushed the ego depletion model further, proposing not only that self-regulation/control capacity depletes with use, but also that—like a muscle—you can strengthen it with repeated application of effort over time (Baumeister & Vohs, 2016; Figure 14.8). Go to the gym for a single, heavy strength-training session, and your muscles will be pretty weak afterward (SRC recently did so, and then had a hard time holding her smartphone up because her arms were shaking so hard!). Go to the gym for repeated strength-training sessions, however, and with time you will be able to lift heavier and heavier weights. Further studies seemed to indicate not only that repeated application of effort can *strengthen* self-control, but also that seemingly unrelated behaviors could *replenish* it—for instance, resting, laughing, or swishing a sugary beverage around your mouth (Baumeister, Vohs, & Tice, 2007).

It is difficult to overstate the number of published studies supporting these proposals. Research into ego depletion dominated much of social psychology for decades, making careers, earning grants, and captivating the public's imagination through *New York Times* op-eds and popular books (Inzlicht & Friese, 2019)—by one estimate, over 600 studies confirmed the essential arguments of this model of self-control (Cunningham & Baumeister, 2016). Then things began to go downhill.

FIGURE 14.8. Ego depletion theory argued that self-control was like a muscle whose strength could be used up in the short term, but which would get stronger over time with repeated training.

The first pillar to fall was the replenishment one. Certainly rest should be rejuvenating; there is ample evidence that sleep deprivation impairs self-control, increasing automatic, habit-driven behavior instead (Chen et al., 2017; Guarana et al., 2021). But . . . sugar? This may already have struck you as a bit odd. Why would swishing a sugary sports drink (not even swallowing it!) instead of a no-calorie sweet beverage give you the mental stamina to control yourself? The idea was that the underlying resource of self-control might rely on blood glucose level (Gailliot et al., 2007). This never made a ton of sense, though. Most of the tasks used to deplete self-control involve a few minutes of cognitive effort. How much glucose could that actually require? Does it use up the body's glucose supply? After reading Chapter 7 of this textbook, we hope you see why that proposal makes little sense. Over and over again, other researchers' attempts to replicate this effect failed.

Next, a meta-analysis of published studies suggested that the size of the original depletion effect was vanishingly small, if it existed at all (Carter et al., 2015). A growing number of failures to replicate the basic ego depletion finding started popping up (e.g., Xu et al., 2014; Lurquin et al., 2016). Then, not one, but two massive attempts to replicate the basic ego depletion effect, between them involving dozens of laboratories around the world and several thousand participants, completely failed (Hagger et al., 2016; Vohs et al., 2021).

What the heck is going on? On one hand, the failures to replicate and the tiny effect sizes are difficult to ignore. On the other hand, it is hard to imagine that 600+ research studies could be based on nothing. Moreover, the idea that tiring yourself out with a long burst of self-control makes it difficult to then resist temptation, is . . . irresistible. Several researchers, some of whom were involved in constructing the original evidence for ego depletion, have considered the current state of the literature and concluded: it's inconclusive (Inzlicht & Friese, 2019).

At a conference in 2017, MNS moderated a panel discussion among four very prominent self-control researchers, representing very different perspectives. When asked whether any of them believed that self-control is an infinite capacity that can go on indefinitely, not a single panelist raised their hand, nor did anyone in the audience. But all panelists agreed that there were serious limitations in the work so far, including inconsistent definition and measurement of the concept at stake. What *is* self-regulation, as a psychological process? Consider all the various effortful, tedious tasks described earlier. Is self-control just one thing? It is several? What does it mean to for self-control to run out, in terms of psychological process, and how long is it likely to take? One alternative proposal is that after a period of time focused on "have-to" or extrinsic goals, people are motivated to switch to a "want-to" or intrinsic goal for a while (Inzlicht, Schmeichel, & Macrae, 2014), but research addressing this proposal is still building. All these questions are all still on the table, waiting for a new generation of researchers to address them.

Can Self-Control Be Improved?

Sadly, the basic answer to this question is no, at least for adults' overall/dispositional self-control, given the techniques attempted and the evidence available so far. Meta-analysis findings suggest that interventions early in life, administered before the age of 10 years, can produce measurable improvement in self-control and reduction in impulsive, problematic behavior, at least for a while (Piquero et al., 2016). Another recent meta-analysis suggests a variety of ways in which *situations* can be changed to reduce people's tendency toward delay discounting, but these effects tend not to carry over into future decisions (Rung & Madden, 2018).

Yet a third meta-analysis combined 33 studies evaluating interventions aimed at increasing overall self-control by getting people to practice overriding their impulses. Analyses revealed effects that were positive, but tiny, after controlling for publication bias—the tendency to publish studies with significant effects, but not those producing nonsignificant effects (Friese et al., 2017). The authors of this last paper note that it's not clear how any training effects occurred (by what mechanism) and conclude that the evidence is not yet sufficient to demonstrate overall training effects on self-control.

The good news is that there are techniques you can use to encourage your own delay of gratification and increase the chance of reaching your goals, even without a broad increase in self-control (Rung & Madden, 2018). Think of this as "life hacking" your own mind and behavior, rather than relying on global self-control as your superpower. We have talked at length about how to effectively set goals, which is one way that we can influence our own behavior. Now our attention turns to what happens after these lofty goals are set—what are some effective goal pursuit techniques?

EFFECTIVE STRATEGIES FOR GOAL PURSUIT

Learning Objectives
- Define the intention-behavior gap, and speculate some reasons why it occurs.
- Analyze how the empathy-gap effect can result in restraint bias.
- Discuss the role of mental simulation in goal setting, and describe how mental contrasting and implementation intentions are particularly effective types of mental simulation.
- Contrast goal disengagement with goal reengagement.

Have you ever set a goal with the very best of intentions, but then failed to follow through? Perhaps you were wearing some snazzy outfit, holding a sparkly beverage in a slender glass, and it was New Year's Eve—a night when many people make ambitious plans. Or you started a new school year with the aim to cut back on drinking, improve your study habits, get more exercise, or save money. But then the year dragged on like every other year, all your day-to-day responsibilities swamped you, and your goal was left on the side of the road as you sped through life. Sigh.

Many of our best-laid plans come to naught. The term **intention-behavior gap** refers to the fact that people often fail to enact desired changes in behavior, despite having very good intentions (Webb & Sheeran, 2006; Figure 14.9). This is due to an array of factors, from difficulty getting started, to being overwhelmed by other responsibilities and stressors, to biases that are hardwired into your brain. Fortunately, researchers have stepped up to the challenge of figuring out how to close the intention-behavior gap. Rather than trying to increase self-control, many of these techniques reduce the need for it in the first place. Let's take a look.

Avoiding and Resisting Temptation

How often are we tempted by desires that conflict with our goals? One set of researchers attempted to figure out exactly how much of a typical day is spent in conflict between

FIGURE 14.9. We often have the best of intentions—but fail to follow through on them. This is called the intention-behavior gap.

temptations and goal pursuits, using an experience sampling design (Hofmann et al., 2012). Seven times per day, a beeper would alert participants (over three quarters were undergraduates and the rest were adults from the surrounding community in Germany) to reflect over the past half hour and report on any and all desires that they experienced, whether or not the desires were in conflict with a current goal, whether or not they enacted each desire, and a series of additional questions about the situational context (e.g., were there other people also enacting this behavior? How much alcohol have you had?).

The authors found that participants reported feeling some kind of desire in about half of waking life. The most commonly reported desires were those related to basic bodily needs, such as eating, drinking, and sleeping. Next most common were desires related to leisure and relaxation, such as media use and social contact. Then came desires we commonly associate with temptation, namely for sex and substance use.

Depending on whether you are a glass half-empty or glass half-full person, you will be encouraged or discouraged by the fact that desires were perceived to be in conflict with one's goals about half of the time. Sometimes we are hungry and we eat; we wish to kiss someone and they wish to kiss us back; we're tired and our schedule allows for a cat nap. At other times we want a cookie but we're trying to cut back on sugar; we want to kiss someone we shouldn't; and we're tired but must give a class presentation in ten minutes. In desire-goal conflict situations, people were generally good at resisting temptation. When they made no effort at resistance, people enacted their desires about 70% of the time, but when they did report resistance, this dropped to an impressive 17% of the time (see Figure 14.10, which presents the model tested by the analyses). However, (a) this is a nonzero number of desires acted upon, despite resistance, and (b) this is probably an

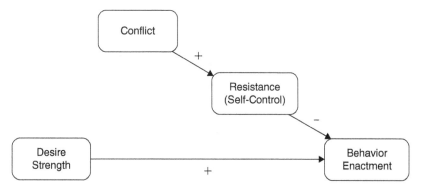

FIGURE 14.10. The authors theorize (and find support for) the idea that the more you desire a temptation, the more likely you are to enact the behavior; but if this temptation is in conflict with your goals, you will try to resist it—and said resistance makes it less likely you will enact this behavior. From Hofmann et al. (2012).

underestimate. In general, people tend to underreport socially undesirable behaviors such as giving in to temptation.

The researchers took a step further and asked what individual (e.g., personality, gender) and contextual (e.g., social others enacting around you; imbibing alcohol) factors affected these temptation dynamics. With respect to personality factors, some people feel desires more intensely than others, and some people are more likely than others to perceive a desire as in conflict with their goals. These relate to how people experience the situation. Situational factors had more of an effect on whether or not the participant would attempt to resist the desire, and whether that resistance would be successful. Having other people around makes it more difficult to resist temptation, and so does drinking alcohol—especially at high levels of intoxication (this last bit of information probably does not come as a surprise).

These findings illustrate our first important point about effective goal pursuit. We have a greater shot at success if we craft our overall environment (including the social environment) to make it easier rather than harder to follow through with our ambitions. A simple example: if you are trying to reduce your consumption of cookies and ice cream, do not keep cookies and ice cream in your home, and avoid places where cookies and ice cream are easily obtained. The trick is to keep temptations out of your way, rather than having them nearby and easy to reach.

This seems like a fairly obvious hack, so why don't people use it more often? In anticipating how they will feel in future tempting situations, people often exhibit **restraint bias**—the tendency to overestimate one's ability to resist temptation when it occurs. Human beings are pretty terrible at anticipating their future affective states, and implications of these future states for behavior. One way that this poor ability to anticipate the future plays out in self-control is called the **empathy-gap effect**: people in an affectively "cold" state (not hungry, thirsty, sexually aroused) underestimate the influence of a "hot" state (hungry, thirsty, aroused) on their future behavior.

Imagine that you are trying to get into medical school, and you've scheduled the MCATs for a Saturday morning in May. Classes have just ended for the year, and your friends are eager to celebrate at your favorite brew pub (or whatever). In the cool light of a weekday morning, getting ready to hit the gym, you receive a text inviting you to join them for an evening of fun—the Friday night before your MCAT. In this "cold" state where you are rested, motivated, and in a setting with few temptations, you anticipate grabbing a quick dinner and having a few laughs with no temptation to stay out too late or drink too much; then going home early for a solid night's sleep. You accept the invitation. Once among your friends, however, in an environment where you are physically activated and surrounded by tasty snacks and beverages, the temptation to overindulge and stay out late will be a lot stronger than expected.

One series of studies provided compelling evidence that due to restraint bias, people put themselves in more tempting situations than are good for them (Nordgren, Van Harreveld, & Van der Pligt, 2009). In four different studies—with participants choosing snacks when satiated or hungry, setting academic workloads for the semester when fatigued versus alert, and resisting cigarettes during smoking cessation—they found compelling evidence for the restraint bias. When people were in "cold" states, they agreed to enter tempting "hot" situations in the future, figuring they'd be fine. For example, in one study the researchers approached college students and employees who were either entering or exiting their college cafeteria. The researchers' assumption (backed up by hunger ratings) was that participants entering the cafeteria were probably hungrier than those exiting the cafeteria. They presented each participant with an array of seven snacks, asking them to rank the snacks from least to most tasty, and then to choose one snack that they'd like to keep (Figure 14.11—which snack would you choose?). Participants were given that snack but told that if they returned the snack uneaten a week later, they would get to keep the snack *and* win a small monetary prize. (Test yourself: What twin concepts from earlier in the chapter are illustrated by this instruction?) Can you predict what happened?

The participants entering the cafeteria (who were presumably hungrier than those exiting) were more likely to choose a *less tasty* snack (typically the second or third favorite). In their current state of hunger, they could imagine being hungry later in the week, and knew it would be harder to resist a snack they more strongly preferred. The satiated students, in contrast, tended to pick their favorite or second-favorite snack. Less able to relate a hungry state and the associated temptation, they presumably thought *it'll be fine*, and took the chance. Interestingly, while the satiated participants were numerically less likely

FIGURE 14.11. Which would you choose if you were walking into the cafeteria for dinner (hungry)? Which when you were leaving (satiated)?

to return the snack than the hungry participants (39% versus 60.5%), this difference was not statistically significant. It could be that the anticipated effect was not present, though it also could be that with fewer than forty participants in each condition, the researchers didn't have enough statistical power to detect it.

This goal pursuit technique involves changing our situation as a way of preventing temptation; we'll review a similar strategy in the next chapter, on emotion regulation. Of course, we have only so much control over our situations, and many temptations are unanticipated. No matter what our efforts, we will sometimes find ourselves in situations where we must apply some self-control. How can we inoculate ourselves against them?

Realistic Mental Simulation

At the beginning of this chapter we encouraged you to visualize what a perfect semester might look like: how it felt, what had happened, where you were at the end of it. This is a **mental simulation**—a scenario you summoned in your own mind. One can simulate the end state or outcome of one's goal, thereby drawing attention to discrepancies between present and ideal states. Despite the advice of one popular self-help book, however, visualizing desired outcomes alone is rarely enough make them happen. A more powerful approach is to simulate the *process* of striving toward that goal.

Vision boards, guided meditations, and ideal-fitness pictures stuck on your fridge all take for granted that holding your end goal in mind can mobilize your efforts. There is some research support for this idea. For instance, in the academic goal setting study by Morisano and colleagues (2010) discussed earlier in this chapter, the number of words typed by participants in their initial visualization of the end of the ideal semester predicted later academic improvement. However, other work suggests that focusing too much on the perfect end state can backfire. Much research has demonstrated that positive fantasies about success actually *decrease* the amount of effort people apply to achieving these outcomes, across many different kinds of goals (Oettingen & Reininger, 2016). How can this be?

First, when you visualize attaining your goals you get the burst of satisfaction you were hoping for. Paradoxically, this may decrease your motivation to work hard—you may feel relaxed rather than energized (Kappes et al., 2011). Second, visualizing goal attainment does not help you prepare for obstacles, setbacks, and challenges along the way. You might get discouraged more easily when the smooth path you expected turns out to be a rough ride.

The aim of maximizing the power of visualization, while avoiding these pitfalls, led Gabriele Oettingen to develop the theory she has playfully dubbed **fantasy realization theory** (Oettingen, 2000; Oettingen, 2012). This theory posits that the best way to inspire behavior change is to combine positive fantasies about the future with a clear-eyed view of the potential obstacles and contextual constraints that might arise—a process called **mental contrasting**. Suppose that you set a new goal to go to the gym three times a week. In visualizing a positive outcome alone, you might imagine yourself at the end of the semester looking fitter, having more energy, and feeling accomplished. If you were to apply mental contrasting, you would still engage in this pleasant first step, but then continue on to brainstorm obstacles and constraints that might stand in your way. You might guess that at some point in the semester, you are likely to get sick and need to take a week off. You might anticipate that during midterms your workload will increase, and extra sleep will be more important than time at the gym. Rather than getting stuck on these barriers, you can begin visualizing how you might persevere despite stressors, or reengage with your goal after disruption. Having done this mental work ahead of time, you are better able to deal with the obstacles once they arise.

Studies linking mental contrasting and related techniques to better goal-attainment outcomes are plentiful, and span such domains as learning a foreign language, making decisions, balancing work and family, reducing cigarette consumption, positive feelings about out-group members, improving type 2 diabetes symptoms, and more (Oettingen & Reininger, 2016; Taylor et al., 1998). To support goal striving, visualize the wonderful end but also the fraught middle of the process.

Planning Ahead

Our third technique takes this principle even further. Complementing the theories of fantasy realization and mental contrasting, researcher Peter Gollwitzer (1993; 2014) developed the technique of forming **implementation intentions**. Like mental contrasting, this technique involves visualizing the journey toward your goal, and the obstacles that might arise. It then goes one step further and asks you to explicitly state your response to these obstacles in the form of an IF/THEN statement.

Say you are heading into the winter holiday season (or any similar season of widespread celebration in your culture), and you really, really want to keep your sugar intake at a reasonable level. (What is reasonable? According to the American Heart Association, 25 grams/day of added sugar is the maximum for women, 36 grams/day for men.) In mental contrasting you would visualize reaching New Year's Day with your goal accomplished, feeling healthy, fit, and energetic; and then visualize likely obstacles such as party buffet tables laden with sweets; celebrations at which sugary cocktails are served; and endless offers of cookies and candy in your classes, workplace, and/or gifts from friends.

In implementation intentions you take one more step (Table 14.4). After brainstorming the obstacles, you come up with *very* concrete behavioral responses. IF I know there will be an array of tempting sweets at parties/THEN I will eat a large, but healthy meal before going so that I'm not too hungry. IF another student brings cookies to class/ THEN I'll suggest sharing one with someone else, and just enjoy a couple of bites. A meta-analysis of nearly 100 studies revealed increased rates of goal attainment when using implementation intentions, with a medium to large effect size (d =.61; Gollwitzer & Sheeran, 2006). Implementation intentions increase the effectiveness of goal pursuit by making the link between situation and behavior more automatic—you have a plan in

---

TABLE 14.4 | **Goal activity box #3**

Set several implementation intentions for enacting the goal you set in the second activity box.	
Think about a few different typical types of days in your life (weekday, weekend, work-day, off-day) and try to imagine various opportunities for goal work *and/or* settings where you might be tempted away from your goal. List those settings or opportunities below.	What will your response be? Either to pursue your goal or avoid temptation?
IF . . .	THEN . . .

place, and don't have to come up with one in the moment of temptation (Bieleke, Keller, & Gollwitzer, 2020).

Rather than ignoring each other or competing, the mental contrasting and implementation intentions researchers have joined forces and found that combining the two techniques (MCII) is more effective than using either strategy alone (e.g., Kirk, Oettingen, & Gollwitzer, 2013). Together, MCII unites two distinct mechanisms: mental contrasting brings the power of intense, vivid visualization for activating motivation and recognizing the "hot," tempting situations you may encounter along the way; implementation intentions takes advantage of the "cold" state outside those situations to brainstorm and rehearse concrete strategies for getting through those situations with goals intact.

Here's a fun example. Have you ever decided that you need a full night of sleep, and settled into bed at a decent time, only to spend the next couple of hours texting with friends and looking at social media? This is called "bedtime procrastination," and it is exceedingly common. ("Revenge bedtime procrastination," a term that originated in China, refers to a variant in which people push themselves through a not-fun to-do list all day long, get to bedtime, and then stay up for hours to finally do something they enjoy instead of going to sleep. Your textbook authors cannot relate to this at all, though SRC's teenager seems to understand the principle quite well.)

In a test of whether the combination of mental contrasting and implementation intentions could reduce this behavior, Valshtein, Oettingen, and Gollwitzer (2020) asked hundreds of undergraduates to participate in one of three online intervention groups: a mental contrasting with implementation intentions exercise (MCII) group, and two control groups. All three groups learned facts about the importance of sleep, and the possible harms associated with not getting enough sleep. The MCII group then visualized the positive outcomes of getting to sleep on time, and the obstacles that stood in the way, and then set IF/THEN implementation intentions for overcoming those obstacles. The "motivationally relevant" control group followed the fact-learning with visualization of positive outcomes, and then considered an IF/THEN frame for these positive outcomes (e.g., IF I get to bed on time, THEN I'll feel refreshed all day tomorrow!). Critically, this group did not imagine obstacles or how to avoid them, only the pleasant things that might happen if they slept. The sleep hygiene group received a series of tips on to behaviors that help to encourage sleep, such as turning off all device screens a few hours before bed, and making sure your bedroom is quiet, dark, and cool.

Three weeks after the intervention sessions, participants reported on the discrepancies between their hoped-for and actual bedtimes as well as sleep duration and sleep procrastination behaviors. Study results indicated that compared to the control exercises, MCII significantly reduced bedtime procrastination (see Figure 14.12).

In a scene from the Greek epic *The Odyssey*, Odysseus must sail his ship past an island inhibited by the sirens. These mythical women sang so exquisitely that they would lure any sailors who heard their song to shore, where they would then be murdered. Odysseus wanted to hear their song but survive the experience, so he ordered his sailors to plug their own ears with wax and tie him to ship's mast in such a way that he could not possibly escape. The trick worked; though he begged his crew to set him free, Odysseus made it past the sirens' island alive. In goal pursuit it is helpful to recognize likely temptations, visualize potential obstacles, and make plans for how to deal with those obstacles.

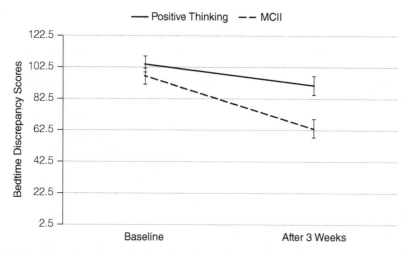

FIGURE 14.12.   Timeline follow-back bedtime discrepancy scores, by condition. Mental contrasting with implementation intentions outperformed positive thinking for reducing number of minutes between anticipated and actual bedtimes. From Valshtein, Oettingen, & Gollwitzer (2020), Figure 3.

We have considered the positive effects of goal setting for changing behavior; the features of effective goals; the challenges of self-control; and strategies for fruitful goal striving. It is time to examine a different, but important question: How do we know when to quit?

Goal Disengagement

We can achieve great things by setting goals and striving toward them, but there are also times when letting go of a goal is the healthy choice (Figure 14.13). This is called **goal disengagement**. While the term might call to mind scenarios of defeat (lost championships, missed sales targets, dropping out of degree programs), goal disengagement can be quite positive, and adaptive. Retiring from a long career, ending an unhappy romantic relationship, and leaving your current job to pursue the career for which you've always longed are all examples of goal disengagement. Despite the negative connotation of "quitting," giving up on an unattainable goal is sometimes best for your well-being. If your attempts to train for a marathon keep leading to repetitive injuries, or you are in a degree program that doesn't match your interests or your skills, and repeated failures are taking a toll on your mental health, it's okay to ask "is it time to move on?"

Part of what determines whether goal disengagement enhances or detracts from well-being is whether one then shifts one's efforts to a different set of goals, called **goal reengagement**. In studies of undergraduates, adults across the lifespan, and parents (some with children battling cancer, and some whose children were medically healthy), ease at disengaging from outdated goals was found to predict well-being. That said, the tendency to then reengage in new goals predicted well-being above and beyond this effect (Wrosch et al., 2003). A meta-analysis of 31 such studies found that goal disengagement and goal reengagement were each associated with measures of quality of life (Barlow, Wrosch, & McGrath, 2020).

FIGURE 14.13. Abandoning a goal is not always a sign of failure—it can be an adaptive, healthy aspect of goal-setting behavior.

Dropping a goal is sometimes for the best, but the most adaptive way to do so is to shift your gears and focus on a new goal, whether related to the original one or not. In this way, you are always striving and accruing the benefits of goal setting. As we wrap up this chapter, let's consider the intersection of goals and emotions.

EMOTIONS, WELL-BEING, AND GOALS

Learning Objective
- Elaborate on the multiple ways that emotions, well-being, and goal setting can intersect.

This chapter has largely focused on the motivation aspect of goal pursuit, but there is also a critical role for emotions. Consider the discrepancy theory of goal setting, discussed early in this chapter. Discrepancies between present and ideal states are motivating in large part because of their impact on emotion. When you see all your friends driving around in their cars and you are stuck at home, you feel frustrated, sad, and jealous—and motivated to change your state of affairs. When you see all the soft ears and winsome eyes of your friends' pets on social media, you melt a bit—and begin hungering for a pet of your own.

On the flip side, many superordinate goals are themselves affective states. Our long-range, overarching goals often include being happy, fulfilled, and content. Many of our subordinate goals are affective states as well. You might want to reduce your frustration or boredom with a topic in order to focus on a term paper that is soon due. On a Friday night, tired after a long week, you might want to amplify your excitement for a friend's birthday party as part of a superordinate goal of maintaining a strong relationship. In these examples, emotions not only serve as means for pursuing goals, but are more pleasant than the default state as well. Do we ever intentionally generate emotions that make us feel *worse*, yet serve our goals?

In an early investigation of this idea, Maya Tamir and colleagues designed an experiment that asked whether people would choose a positive emotion that felt pleasant, or a negative emotion that was more likely to serve their goals, when given the choice (Tamir, Mitchell, & Gross, 2007). They focused on the emotion of anger—a state that arises when one's interests have been thwarted in some way. Most people find anger somewhat unpleasant, but when facing with confrontation with another person, a little anger might be useful.

Across a series of trials, male undergraduates read descriptions of four different types of video games, two of which involved conflict (e.g., fighting a drug cartel) and two of which did not (e.g., building a peaceful empire). They then listened to a short musical segment previously demonstrated to evoke neutral, excited, or angry feelings, and rated the extent to which they think they would like to listen to this music before playing the game. Every game was paired with three examples of each kind of music, for a total of 36 trials. In a similar task, participants read descriptions of life events that were neutral, exciting, or angry after reading about each game, rated the extent to which they would prefer to recall such an event before playing the game.

When participants anticipated playing the high-conflict game, they reported preferring to listen to angry music or recall an angry memory more strongly than neutral or exciting music and memories; when they did not anticipate a conflict-filled game, the pattern was reversed (see Figure 14.14). These authors and others have replicated and extended this basic finding: people sometimes choose to intentionally up-regulate negative emotions that will help them pursue other goals they might have (e.g., Kalokerinos, Tamir, & Kuppens, 2017).

Can goal setting itself make us happy, regardless of the content of the goals? Like many of the questions we tackle in this book, its answer is complicated and depends on many contextual factors and individual differences. Looking toward the future, and

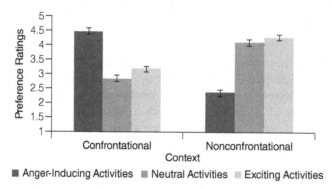

FIGURE 14.14. Preferences for anger-inducing, neutral, and exciting activities (i.e., listening to music and recalling events) when anticipating performing confrontational and nonconfrontational tasks. Error bars represent 1 SEM. From Tamir, Mitchell, & Gross (2008), Figure 1.

deciding what you want it to look like, tends to be better for well-being than drifting along with no direction. At the same time, goal setting means intentionally identifying gaps between your ideal and present state. Quite a lot of research now shows that appreciation of what one currently has, and mindful awareness of the present moment, are both positive for well-being. The content of your goals probably matters as well. For instance, while intrinsic goals (e.g., for affiliation, community, health, and self-acceptance) have been found to predict higher levels of well-being and less distress, extrinsic goals (e.g., for wealth, fame, good looks) are linked to lower levels of well-being and more distress (Kasser & Ryan, 1996). With extrinsic goals one relies on other people's approval and definition of success to achieve a sense of reward. Intrinsic goals, such as good health and friendship, are their own, inherent rewards.

SUMMARY

Clearly, goal setting has been linked to numerous positive outcomes for health and well-being. These effects are due in part to successfully getting more of what you want in life, having identified and achieved your goals, and perhaps in part to pleasure inherent in goal striving. Much of the research on goal setting and well-being is cross-sectional rather than experimental, so whether there are third variables explaining both goal setting behavior and well-being (personality variables such as conscientiousness or extraversion, or situational variables such as having a lot of social and economic resources) is a question ripe for future inquiry.

Psychologists have learned much about what makes a goal an effective one, as well as the techniques associated with efficient goal pursuit. Self-control is great if you have it, but the best strategies involve avoiding temptation and forming concrete plans for situations where your goals might be challenged, rather than relying on self-control alone. Setting goals socially, whether sharing goals with others or just telling them about your goals and your progress along the way, also sets you up for success. Finally, thinking flexibly and adaptively about which goals to keep and which to release doesn't make you fickle—it may mark you as wise.

We personally wish you great success in your chosen goals.

KEY TERMS

active control: a control condition in an experiment where participants engage in activities that match the treatment condition in terms of variables like time, effort, type of activity, and engagement with the research team (p. 489)

automatic goal pursuit: the phenomenon whereby goals are activated and pursued without conscious intention (p. 485)

corrective actions: in discrepancy theories of goal setting, the actions one takes to bring one's present self closer to one's ideal self (p. 488)

cybernetic model of self-regulation: theory that human motivation works in feedback loops, kicking into action when discrepancies between present and ideal states are detected and quieting when ideal states are reached (p. 495)

delay discounting: the tendency to perceive far-off rewards as less valuable than the same reward if you had it right now, reduced by an amount proportional to the distance in time (p. 501)

delay gratification: putting off to the future pleasures you could, if you wished, enjoy in the present (p. 500)

discrepancy creation: a process critical to goal setting whereby the person intentionally manufactures an ideal state in order to motivate themselves to reach it (p. 488)

discrepancy reduction: a process critical to goal setting whereby the motivating discrepancy between a present state and an ideal state is clearly defined, time-limited, and often externally determined (p. 488)

discrepancy theory: a theory that argues we are intrinsically motivated to close gaps between the present and ideal state, and this motivation triggers relevant plans to do so (p. 487)

distal goals: long-term goals (p. 494)

ego depletion: theory that self-control draws upon a limited pool of mental resources and so exercising self-control uses up these resources and is less effective over time (p. 502)

empathy-gap effect: argument that people in an affectively "cold" state (not hungry, thirsty, sexually aroused) underestimate the influence of a "hot" state (hungry, thirsty, aroused) on their future behavior (p. 507)

expectancy-value theory: theory that pursuing goals result from expectations of likely success (expectancy) and perceived worth of the desired outcome (value) (p. 493)

fantasy realization theory: a theory posits that the best way to inspire behavior change is to combine positive fantasies about the future with identification of the potential obstacles and contextual constraints that might arise, a process called mental contrasting (p. 509)

goal: a mental conception of a possible future state that provides energy and direction to current behavior (p. 488)

goal disengagement: intentionally releasing a previously held goal (p. 512)

goal reengagement: following goal disengagement, shifting one's efforts to a different goal or set of goals (p. 512)

goal setting: the process of intentionally setting goals in order to motivate behavior (p. 488)

goal system: a theory of how goals relate to each other and to the means by which we achieve our goals that argues that goals and means interconnect in hierarchies (p. 490)

implementation intentions: technique involving visualizing the journey toward a goal and the obstacles that might arise, and then explicitly stating a response to these obstacles in the form of an IF/THEN statement (p. 510)

intention-behavior gap: the fact that people often fail to enact desired changes in behavior, despite having very good intentions (p. 505)

mental contrasting: combining positive fantasies about the future with identification of the potential obstacles and contextual constraints that might arise (p. 509)

mental simulation: imagining possible scenarios in one's own mind; in goal setting research, usually imagining oneself into future settings (p. 509)

mimetic desire: the human tendency to want what other human beings have (p. 495)

monitoring: the process of measuring progress and giving yourself feedback during goal pursuit (p. 495)

prevention regulatory focus: self-control and goal setting that is focused on avoiding an undesired outcome (p. 497)

promotion regulatory focus: self-control and goal setting that is focused on approaching a desired outcome (p. 497)

proximal goals: short-term goals (p. 494)

restraint bias: the tendency to overestimate one's ability to resist temptation when it occurs, often as a result of the empathy-gap effect (p. 507)

self-control: the application of effort to regulate one's own thoughts, feelings, and behavior (p. 499)

self-regulation: the process of managing or controlling one's own thoughts, feelings, and behavior (p. 501)

the TOTE model: an early model of goal setting, in which people *tested* to see if their present state was close to the ideal state, then introduced *operations* (actions) to reduce the discrepancy, then *tested* again, and then *exited* the loop when the ideal state was achieved (p. 487)

THOUGHT/DISCUSSION QUESTIONS

1. We have discussed at length how having several goals at once can lead to goal conflict, as resources like time, money, and attention are limited and thus there are only so much of them to go around. Do you think it is better to focus on one major goal at a time or spread yourself out among several smaller ones? Design a research study to test this question.

2. Right from Chapter 1 we discussed how motivation involves thinking through time—understanding past motivations and setting plans to bring about hoped-for futures. Do you think that this time travel into the past and future can reduce well-being in the present? Ruminating about past failures has certainly been linked with depression, and there is some empirical indication that intrusive thoughts about long-term goals can impact hedonic well-being in the present. How do we balance being mindfully present with striving toward goals that lead to long-term fulfillment?

3. We discussed at length failures to replicate self-control depletion studies. One argument has been made that laboratory measures of self-control like how long you are willing to try to solve unsolvable anagrams or how long you'll persist squeezing a strength ball are not good measures of self-control. If you were a researcher designing a study that aimed to be more real-life, how would you measure participants' self-control?

SUGGESTIONS FOR FURTHER READING

Locke, E.A., & Latham, G. P. (Eds.). (2013). New developments in goal setting and task performance. Routledge. A thorough summary of the latest academic research on goal setting from some of the leading researchers in the field.

Oettingen, G. (2014). *Rethinking positive thinking: Inside the new science of motivation*. Penguin Random House. A friendly overview of motivation and goal setting research written for a lay audience.

Werner, K. M., & Milyavskaya, M. (2019). Motivation and self-regulation: The role of want-to motivation in the processes underlying self-regulation and self-control. *Social and Personality Psychology Compass*, *13*(1), e12425. https://doi.org/10.1111/spc3.12425 An accessible review article on the underlying mechanisms of motivation and self-regulation.

CHAPTER 15

Emotion Regulation

When you experience intense emotion, it can feel as though some force has temporarily taken over your body and mind. For nonhuman animals this may be true. From an evolutionary perspective, the primary function of emotion is to promote an instinctive physiological and behavioral response that does not rely on time-consuming reasoning and judgment, but just . . . happens. For humans, thankfully, the situation is different. We have the option of regulating our emotions, rather than letting our emotions control us.

The ways in which we do so have powerful implications for our lives. People with dispositionally strong emotion regulation skills report higher psychological well-being, healthier relationships, and higher job satisfaction (e.g., Aldao, Nolen-Hoeksema, & Schweizer, 2010; Bloch, Haase, & Levenson, 2014; Côté & Morgan, 2002; English et al., 2012; Haines et al., 2016; Hu et al., 2014). Studies have even linked emotion regulation to physical health outcomes (Appleton et al., 2014; Ellis et al., 2019; Puterman et al., 2013). While many researchers have sought to identify biological and environmental roots of disordered emotions, as discussed in Chapter 13, a growing number of psychologists are asking how much of the problem depends on deficits in ability to manage emotions (Gross & Jazaieri, 2014).

People use a wide range of strategies to manage their own emotions, and philosophers and psychologists have long been interested in the differing implications of various strategies. Some strategies tend to be more effective than others, but the most effective strategy depends on the situation. In this chapter we examine several kinds of emotion-regulation strategies and the evidence for their effectiveness, ultimately asking what toolkit of emotion regulation strategies is likely to best support a healthy emotional life.

FREUD'S EGO DEFENSE MECHANISMS: AN EARLY TAXONOMY OF COPING STRATEGIES

Learning Objective
- Differentiate the psychotic, immature, neurotic, and mature categories of Freud's ego defense mechanisms, as classified by George Vaillant, and name and define examples of each category.

Before we begin, make a list of all the ways you can think of to cope with a distressing situation—talking with other people, getting away from other people, thinking about the problem, distracting yourself with some other activity, and so on. Don't worry if some of your suggestions contradict one another; sometimes one strategy is most likely to be helpful and sometimes its opposite is, depending on the nature of the problem. If you compare lists with others, you might find dozens of suggestions.

An early taxonomy of coping strategies was constructed by Sigmund Freud (1937) and later elaborated by his daughter, Anna, during the early twentieth century. According to Freud, humans by their very nature have fundamental drives and desires (the *id*) that they cannot express in a civilized society. The most famous of these is the supposed desire to have sex with your mother or father (whoever is the opposite-sex parent). The demands, rules, and societal expectations that limit the expression of the id are housed in a socially learned conscience or *superego*. Playing referee between these two conflicting forces is the *ego*, the conscious self that tries to appease the id within the constraints of the superego. Freud proposed a series of **ego defense mechanisms**, or psychological regulation strategies that serve to resolve the tension between the id and the superego and keep disturbing wishes and desires hidden from consciousness. Several ego defense mechanisms are described in Table 15.1.

Freud's taxonomy had both strengths and important limitations. The main advantage of his system is that it offers a way to describe and categorize different coping

TABLE 15.1 | **Some ego defense mechanisms, according to Sigmund Freud**

Defense mechanism	Definition	Example
Denial	Refusing to acknowledge the reality of an unpleasant or threatening situation	Refusing to admit that your close friend has a serious, life-threatening illness
Fantasy	Retreating to fantasy or daydreaming as a way to fulfill desires	Daydreaming about having a fling with a famous actor or actress
Projection	Attributing one's own unacceptable desires, motives, or feelings to another person	Accusing your romantic partner of feeling bored with your relationship when you are really the one feeling restless
Displacement	Directing disturbing feelings toward an alternative target, rather than the person or event that really elicited them	Yelling at your dog after an argument with your supervisor at work
Intellectualization	Focusing purely on the abstract, logical aspects of an issue or experience, rather than the personal or emotional aspects	Logically analyzing the motives and explanations for why a friend let you down, rather than feeling hurt
Reaction formation	Adopting and expressing attitudes/behaviors that are the extreme opposite of the underlying attitudes and behaviors	Being excessively friendly toward a person you intensely dislike
Repression	Forgetting or blocking memory of unpleasant or intolerable events; repression is automatic, rather than conscious and intentional	Blocking out the memory of a car accident
Suppression	Making a conscious, deliberate decision not to think about a disturbing topic at a particular time	Deciding not to worry about an upcoming deadline at work while you see a movie Friday night
Sublimation	Expressing socially unacceptable desires or impulses in a manner that is constructive and socially condoned	Writing a song or poem that captures your anger toward a parent, rather than arguing with the parent directly

strategies. Scientific progress benefits from clearly defined and labeled constructs, so that different investigators can study the same processes and compare their results. Within the system, comparison can be made among the various ego defense mechanisms in terms of their overall psychological health—this proved valuable for subsequent researchers. For example, the developmental psychologist George Vaillant (1977) suggested that Freud's ego defense mechanisms could be organized into four categories, reflecting different stages of maturity as well as differing effects on psychological and life outcomes.

Vaillant (1977) proposed that *psychotic* ego defenses such as denial are common in young children, but indicate trauma or psychopathology in adults. These ways of regulating emotion are the most thoroughly divorced from reality. Although they may improve your mood, they leave you unequipped to deal with the world as it actually is. His *immature* category included defenses such as fantasy and projection. These ego defenses include avoiding full acknowledgment of the reality of a situation, but the avoidance is limited to inaccurate explanations for the problem (as in projection) or implausible solutions (as in fantasy), rather than complete denial that a problem exists. According to Vaillant, immature defense mechanisms are typical of adolescents but unhealthy for adults.

The *neurotic* category includes ego defenses such as displacement, intellectualization, reaction formation, and repression. Each will alleviate anxiety, or at least point anxiety-related behavior in a less destructive direction, but they will not solve the problem at hand. They won't hurt you, for the most part, but they won't help either. They are also used unconsciously, so people don't realize what they're doing. According to Vaillant (1977), these defenses are the ones used most often by adults, because they are socially acceptable while also alleviating distress. Vaillant considered *mature* ego defenses such as suppression and sublimation to be the healthiest because they are intentional and/or lead to prosocial, constructive behavior.

Despite these advantages, the specifics of Freud's ego defense proposal raise serious problems. Freud defined the defense mechanisms as ways people deal with socially unacceptable sexual and physical desires, and the guilt and anxiety they cause. This emphasis was based on Freud's interpretation of the "real" reasons behind his patients' psychological symptoms, but he never offered anything that would qualify as solid evidence to support his interpretations. In fact, the evidence is now strong that most people feel an instinctive aversion to sex with family members and others who were often present during early childhood (Lieberman, Tooby, & Cosmides, 2007; Shepher, 1971; Wolf & Durham, 2005). Furthermore, the evidence for some proposed ego defenses is shaky. When later researchers attempted to find scientific evidence for mechanisms such as repression and projection, their support for Freud's ideas was, to put it generously, doubtful (Holmes, 1978; 1990).

Moreover, as Freud's theory developed through one version after another, he often used the same clinical example to support different and even contradictory conclusions (Crews, 1996; Esterson, 2001). That is, he did not develop theories to fit the data; he reinterpreted data to fit the theories. Few psychologists or psychiatrists today defend Freud's theory that all people are sexually attracted to their parents, although scholars in literature and philosophy are still influenced by his ideas.

Most important, Freud's taxonomy does not include the full range of ways in which we cope with emotional situations. The defense mechanisms he described were meant to capture how people cope with socially unacceptable desires that could not (or at least should not) ever be fulfilled. They were not intended to explain how people would cope with the loss of a job, a break-up/divorce, or having three midterm exams and a paper due in the same week. One crucial implication is that there is no way to solve the problem of wanting to have sex with your parent—if you actually wanted to—but there are more or less practical solutions to the other kinds of problems. A newer taxonomy not only is more comprehensive and consistent with the data on how people regulate their emotions in real life, but has also proved powerful in predicting outcomes of interest.

THE PROCESS MODEL OF EMOTION REGULATION
Learning Objective
- Define emotion regulation, and differentiate it from coping.
- Explain the assumptions about emotion itself that serve as the foundation for the process model of emotion regulation, and differentiate the three main categories of regulation strategies defined by the process model.

As always, it's helpful to clearly define terms before we proceed. **Emotion regulation** consists of the strategies we use to control which emotions we have, when we have them, and how strongly we experience and express them (Gross, 2015). A closely related term is **coping**, which refers to people's attempts to reduce negative emotion during and after a stressful event. The distinction between the two is that coping is always an attempt to reduce negative emotion, whereas emotion regulation may include trying to increase or decrease positive emotions, or even trying to increase negative emotion if it seems appropriate or helpful in a particular situation.

James Gross's (2015) **process model of emotion regulation**—which organizes emotion regulation strategies according to their place in the emotion process itself—is a useful way of thinking about and classifying emotion regulation strategies (see Figure 15.1). Building on earlier theories of emotion and emotion regulation by Lazarus (1991), Frijda (1986), and Arnold (1960), this model begins with certain assumptions about emotions and the process by which they play out, which should seem very familiar by now: (1) We enter a particular situation. (2) We pay attention to certain aspects of the situation, rather than others. (3) We appraise those aspects of the situation in a way that facilitates a particular emotional response. (4) Finally, we experience a full-blown emotion, including physiological changes, behavior impulses, and subjective feelings. This process is recursive, in that the behavioral consequences of our emotional output influence the situation, so we keep cycling continuously through these stages of the process.

Using this model, researchers can classify emotion regulation strategies according to when they take place in the emotion process, and this classification aids in the understanding of why different strategies have different implications and outcomes. The process model includes three main categories of strategies for regulating emotion. People use **situation-focused strategies** to control the situation, either by choosing to be in one situation rather than another, or by changing the situation somehow. In **cognition-focused strategies** people selectively attend to certain aspects of the situation or change the way they think about the situation, to encourage some emotions and/or deter others. The third category includes **response-focused strategies** that alter the effects of emotions once

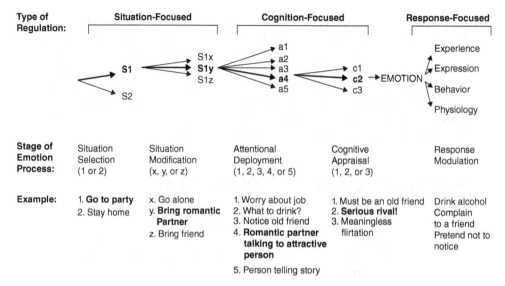

FIGURE 15.1. The process model of emotion regulation classifies strategies according to their place in the emotion process itself. Adapted from Gross (2002).

they have already started. In using response-focused strategies, we presume that a person is already experiencing an emotion and wants some aspect of that emotional response to change. This may include getting it out of your system by talking about the emotion; attempting to turn off aspects of emotional responding or substitute a different emotion; or attempting to suppress the expression of an emotion so that other people can't see what you are feeling. Let's look at each of these three categories in detail.

SITUATION-FOCUSED STRATEGIES

Learning Objectives
- Define savoring, and identify opportunities to enact this emotion regulation technique in your own life.
- Analyze the benefits and potential limitations of choosing to avoid unpleasant situations.
- Define active coping, summarize the evidence on the benefits of perceived control for health and well-being, and identify the mechanism by which control beliefs have beneficial effects.

When possible, a powerful way to control emotions is to seek out, avoid, or change the situations that elicit them (Gross, 2015). If you are worried about an exam next week, you could spend time studying to reduce your anxiety and increase your confidence. If one of your tech devices is acting up, or you're doing some tedious computer-based task that must be repeated hundreds of times, you can search the internet for a solution (e.g., did you know you can batch rename hundreds of files at once? Amazing!). If it upsets you that your roommate never cleans the bathroom, instead of being furious every time you have to do it, you could tell them that sharing housework is important to you and ask for more help. If a family member repeatedly brings up a distressing topic (an acrimonious political argument, detailed critique of your romantic life, the time you accidentally sat on their hamster), you could tell them that you find the topic upsetting and would prefer not to discuss it, or try to redirect the conversation. If they refuse to let the topic go, you could simply walk away. Whenever you manage to avoid or improve a negative situation, you reduce the source of distress. When you seek out positive situations, you are more likely to experience pleasant emotions.

This point may seem so obvious that you wonder why we bother to make it. Why would somebody endure an unpleasant situation if they didn't have to? For one thing, it simply doesn't occur to some people that this is an option. For another, there may be consequences to these decisions that are worth consideration; if you just walk away from the dinner table in the middle of your uncle's annual holiday rant about politics, your family may not approve. It is helpful to distinguish here between situation *selection* and situation *modification*. In **situation selection** we decide whether to enter (or leave) a situation that is likely to elicit an emotional response; in **situation modification** we enter the situation, but take steps to change it. Let's consider situation selection first.

Choosing Situations Wisely

There's much to be said for choosing to enter situations that are enjoyable and will lead to long-term benefits, rather than those that will be unpleasant and/or harmful. (Some activities that are fun in the moment have negative long-term consequences—common sense is helpful here.) In fact, researchers have found that creating and **savoring** pleasant events, such as going for a relaxing walk or enjoying a bubble bath, can facilitate well-being and resilience, even in the face of intense stress (Figure 15.2; Folkman &

FIGURE 15.2. Savoring, or taking the time to mindfully enjoy some simple, pleasant experience, can promote resilience during stressful times.

Moskowitz, 2000; Kiken, Lundberg, & Fredrickson, 2017). There's also a benefit to avoiding unnecessary stressors, and many people tend to set themselves up for needless unhappiness. One reason older adults experience higher levels of well-being may be that as they age, they are somewhat more likely to seek out pleasant situations and less likely to put up with unpleasant situations (Livingstone & Isaacowitz, 2015; Urry & Gross, 2010). However, one recent study with 140 US participants found that younger, middle-aged, and older adults alike frequently sought out pleasant and avoided unpleasant situations (Livingstone & Isaacowitz, 2021). Results suggested that this might be an even more effective emotion regulation strategy for younger than older adults, though research on this point has been mixed.

However, situation selection is not an all-purpose emotion-regulation strategy. For one thing, completely avoiding unpleasant situations is not a realistic option. Sure, you can decide not to apply to grad school or go on job interviews because these make you nervous. You can decide not to ask someone you have a crush on for a date, on the grounds that it will be terrifying to do so, and if you are turned down it will hurt. You can avoid talking about a problem with your romantic partner, family member, or close friend, because even thinking about that conversation stresses you out. But is this really a good way to live your life?

The evidence suggests not. Excessive use of situation selection limits people's opportunities and relationships. Furthermore, people who consistently avoid anything stressful or unpleasant may fail to keep their lives and health in order. One study found that people who reported more avoidance-based coping in the first year of assessment experienced a greater number of life stressors over the next 4 years, which in turn predicted increased depressive symptoms (Holahan et al., 2005). Another study found that veterans with PTSD were more likely to use avoidant coping, but also that avoidant coping predicted subsequent increases in PTSD symptoms (Badour et al., 2012). A third study showed that patients with heart disease who also reported highly avoidant coping styles were more likely to die of heart failure over the next 6 years (Murberg, Furze, & Bru, 2003). A fourth found that kidney disease patients who reported high use of avoidant coping were more likely to die over the next 9 years; results showed that this was caused by failure to attend medical appointments (Wolf & Mori, 2009).

In each case, the results indicated that people with highly avoidant coping styles let their lives fall apart (literally, in the latter studies), rather than dealing directly with their problems. For all of these reasons, the research on the implications of **distraction** as an emotion regulation strategy—engaging in some alternative activity in order to take your mind off a problem—is rather mixed. Doing so for a little while to avoid obsessing over a difficult situation may be a good idea; continually using distraction to avoid dealing with your problems, not so much. Clearly, situation selection is a strategy to be used with careful thought. If you can avoid a stressful situation without negative consequences, by all means, do so. However, if tolerating that situation will bring you long-term benefits or avert some negative outcome, then there are other emotion-regulation options.

Active Coping: Changing the Situation

In situation modification we alter the situation to facilitate the desired emotion state. This strategy is often referred to as **active coping**, although as noted earlier, the term "coping" is limited to negative situations where one is trying to reduce distress. This seems like an

FIGURE 15.3. Even in extremely stressful circumstances, such as a flood or other natural disaster, there is often some action people can take to improve the situation—in this case minimizing damage to belongings. Active coping makes people feel more in control as well.

obvious approach to emotion regulation, as long as you have some control over the situation. Several studies have indicated that people who often use situation modification or active coping to regulate their emotions tend to have better than average physical health and psychological well-being (Aldao, Nolen-Hoeksema, & Schweizer, 2010; Penley, Tomaka, & Wiebe. 2002). Although these correlations do not necessarily indicate a causal relationship, it does seem reasonable that taking steps to improve your objective situation would be a healthy long-term way to deal with problems.

The major barrier to active coping is a belief that we have no control over the situation. In some cases this is true, but it's unusual. Even in a serious crisis, there is probably *some* action you can take to improve the situation (Figure 15.3). In one study, cancer survivors who believed they had more control over the course of their illness showed greater improvement in their health behaviors (Park et al., 2008). Using active coping did not change the fact that these individuals had had cancer or that they were at increased risk of cancer in the future. However, the lifestyle changes they made—eating a healthier diet, getting more sleep, exercising more often, and so forth—are among those that give someone a good shot at preventing health problems later.

Studies indicate that active coping strategies also promote well-being through mechanisms beyond their effects on the situation. Even if something unpleasant is unavoidable, it will feel less disturbing if you take steps to control some aspect of the situation, or if you can at least predict what is going to happen and prepare for it. People who believe more strongly that they are able to deal constructively with problems that arise, and have some control over their circumstances, tend to experience less subjective stress in response to any problems or hassles that occur (Koffer et al., 2019; see Figure 15.4). Conversely,

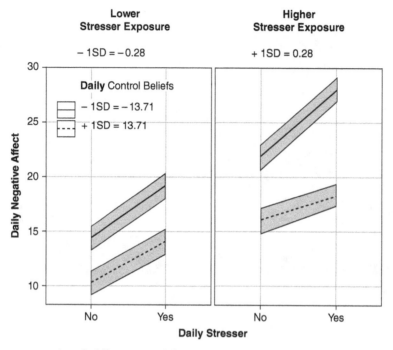

FIGURE 15.4. A study following 150 adults over 9 weeks found that confidence in one's ability to deal with difficult situations and exert some control over one's circumstances ("control beliefs") helped buffer against the effects of exposure to stressful experiences on negative affect. From Koffer et al. (2019).

people who feel they have little control over situations are at greater risk for depression than are those with a stronger sense of control (Alloy et al., 1999). In one study of recently bereaved widows, those who felt the most control over the events of their lives experienced the least anxiety (Ong, Bergeman, & Bisconti, 2005).

Imagine yourself in this experiment: you are asked to do some difficult proofreading while seated next to a device that makes unpredictable, sudden, loud, annoying sounds. You are told that the point of the study is to examine the effects of that noise on your behavior. Just before you start, you are also shown an escape button: if the noise becomes unbearable, you can press that button to turn it off. You are urged not to press the button unless necessary; the point of the study is to determine the effects of the noise on your behavior. The button is there just in case. When this study has been done, few participants pressed the button. But participants who had the button and believed they could turn off the noise if necessary performed better on the proofreading tasks than participants who were not offered an escape (Glass, Singer, & Pennebaker, 1977; Sherrod et al., 1977).

In another study, people were given a series of painfully hot stimuli to their forearms. Participants in one group were told that they could decrease the duration of a stimulus from five seconds to two seconds if they manipulated a joystick quickly enough in the correct direction. In fact, they had no control and the duration of the stimulus varied randomly, but because they were trying hard with the joystick, they interpreted every short stimulus as a reward for a quick enough response. Moreover, participants who thought they had control experienced less pain than participants who knew they had no control, and measurements of brain activity using fMRI indicated less arousal in several pain-sensitive brain areas (Salomons et al., 2004). In a follow-up study using similar methods, researchers found that participants who believed they had control not only reported less intense pain, but also showed weaker activation of the amygdala (a structure commonly activated in negative emotion), stronger activity of the nucleus accumbens (a structure associated with perception of reward, likely reflecting perceived success in deflecting the pain), and increased regulation of both of these structures by the prefrontal cortex, a region typically activated during tasks requiring self-regulation (Salomons et al., 2015).

Consider this stressful situation: you are in a hospital for major surgery. The staff hasn't told you when the surgery will occur, how long it will last, what are your chances for success, or how long it will take to recover afterward. You feel helpless and frightened. Now change the situation: the staff tell you what to expect, in as much detail as you wish, and even give you some choices, such as when the surgery will begin and who will be present when you wake up from the anesthesia. When you have some sense of prediction and control, your anxiety is much less severe (Van Der Zee et al., 2002), and chances are you will even have a better medical outcome (Shapiro, Schwartz, & Astin, 1996). If you are being treated for heart problems, research suggests that higher perceived control over your heart condition predicts lower risk of new heart complications while you are in the hospital (McKinley et al., 2012).

Hospitals now regularly allow patients to control the administration of painkillers after surgery using a small button, rather than having a nurse administer the drugs on a fixed schedule (Figure 15.5). Naturally, the device includes limits on how often the patient can self-administer the drug, so the patient receives no more, and frequently less, than if

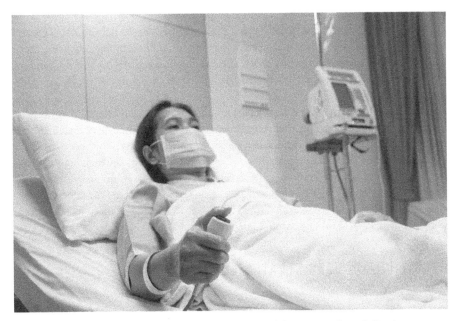

FIGURE 15.5. Hospitals often allow patients to control the timing of painkiller doses, within a certain range. The sense of control itself helps alleviate pain.

someone else had been controlling delivery. However, patients who control the timing of their doses typically report more satisfaction with their pain management (Lehmann, 1995).

How important an effect might the perception of control have? A recent analysis of data from a large, representative sample of midlife adults across the United States suggests it might be very important (Elliot et al., 2018). As a general rule, people who have had more traumatic experiences show poorer physical health, even earlier mortality. Analyses revealed that lifetime trauma was associated with greater likelihood of death from any cause over 10 years, bit only among those *low* on perceived control over their lives—not among those reporting *high* perceived control. Like another study discussed above, this suggests that belief in your ability to exert some control over your circumstances can help buffer against the effects of real problems in your life. These results do not necessarily mean that perceived control directly impacted people's health; the effect probably is not due to magical thinking. Rather, people who believe they have control are more likely to take concrete steps to improve their situations, and that, of course, has beneficial effects on health and well-being.

There are limits to the benefits of simply believing that you are in control. Self-help books often encourage people to "visualize success" as a way to gain control over their lives and cause desired outcomes. For example, you might be encouraged to visualize getting your dream job, meeting the perfect romantic partner, winning a contest, or driving a luxury automobile. As discussed in Chapter 14, this advice is extremely misleading. If you simply visualize glorious outcomes, you probably will enjoy the fantasy, but it will not improve your situation and may even deter you from constructive activities. What does help is to visualize doing the work that would lead to the prizes and honors (Taylor et al., 1998). If you want to succeed in athletics, visualize yourself practicing the movements of your sport. If you want to write a successful paper, visualize yourself in the library or organizing your notes—and then go do it!

Similarly, if you expect to face a challenge in the future, you can gain a sense of control by imagining what you will do when the challenge comes. For example, if you expect to have an unpleasant conversation with someone, you might imagine what you will say, how the other person will reply, and what you might say in return (Sanna, 2000). In one study, first-time pregnant women were asked to imagine and describe going through labor. The women whose descriptions were rated as the most accurate and most detailed showed the least worry about the upcoming delivery (Brown et al., 2002). This kind of imagination is not just wishful thinking—it is more like careful cognitive rehearsal for how to handle a stressful situation. Increasingly, practitioners helping people to change their behavior—in domains from exercise to smoking to problematic drug use—guide people through a process of developing **implementation intentions**, concrete plans for how they will choose the healthy behavior over an unhealthy one, especially in situations where temptation is likely to arise (Armitage, 2016; Malaguti et al., 2020; Robinson et al., 2019).

COGNITION-FOCUSED STRATEGIES
Learning Objectives
- Analyze the benefits and limitations of distraction as an emotion regulation strategy, identifying contexts in which it is or is not likely to have positive effects on well-being.

- Define reappraisal, and summarize the evidence regarding benefits associated with this emotion regulation strategy.
- Differentiate detached reappraisal, humor-based reappraisal, perspective-taking, positive reappraisal, and arousal reappraisal, and identify examples of each.

Unfortunately, we sometimes face situations over which we have little or no control, or it is too late to change an important outcome. For example, you applied for admission to several graduate schools and they all rejected you. In other cases, the event is ongoing, but the outcome is uncontrollable, or nearly so. For example, you might be caring for an aging relative with Alzheimer's disease or a loved one with cancer.

In such cases, additional options for regulating your emotions involve thinking about the situation differently. Sometimes this means paying attention to one aspect of the situation while ignoring other aspects. Alternatively, you can interpret the meaning of the situation in a way that evokes less distress, or at least acknowledges a "silver lining" around the problem. These strategies can help make it easier to tolerate difficult situations. Cognition-focused strategies have been the focus of extensive research in recent years, so let's consider some examples carefully.

Attentional Control

Imagine that you have developed friendships with a few of your classmates, and one of them invites several of you over to have dinner and watch a movie. When you get there, everything seems lovely—pleasant living room, dinner smells good, the television is nice and big—but there's one problem. The classmate did not tell you about their pet tarantula, which lives in a terrarium that is easily visible on a living room shelf. During dinner and the movie, the tarantula sits there in its lair. Watching you.

For most people, this situation would cause a fair amount of anxiety. Some options are to change the situation by leaving the party (situation selection), or asking your host to move the creature to another room (situation modification). However, the former strategy means a lost social opportunity, and the latter may seem impolite. Many people in this situation would engage in **attentional control**—they would simply try to avoid looking at or thinking about the distressing object, in this case the spider.

Here's a study that documents the usefulness of attentional control for emotion regulation. Ozlem Ayduk and colleagues (Ayduk, Mischel, & Downey, 2002) asked participants to vividly remember an experience in which someone else had rejected them—an experience most people find upsetting. Half of the participants were encouraged to focus their attention on their emotions and physiological sensations during this memory, whereas the other half were encouraged to focus their attention on features of the room in which the rejection took place. After reliving this experience, participants were asked to complete three more tasks. (1) They did a reaction time task in which they decided whether strings of letters were words or not words, as quickly as possible (i.e., the lexical decision task used in a study of adult attachment described in Chapter 9). Different kinds of words were used, including some related to anger. The assumption was that if you quickly identify the hostility-related words, then you are already thinking about anger. (2) Participants reported ratings of their angry mood. (3) Finally, they wrote an essay about the rejection experience they had just relived. Figure 15.6 shows that the attention manipulation had an effect on people's emotions. Those asked to focus on the

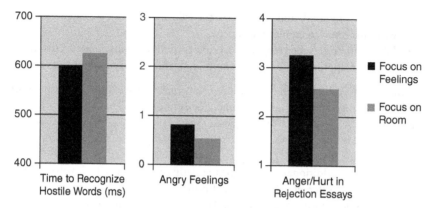

FIGURE 15.6. Participants who focused on features of the room while remembering a rejection experience later detected hostile words less quickly, reported feeling less angry, and used fewer words expressing anger and hurt in essays about the experience than participants who focused on how they had felt at the time. From Ayduk, Mischel, & Downey (2002).

characteristics of the room in their memories identified hostility-related words more slowly, reported fewer angry feelings, and wrote less about feeling angry and hurt in their essays than participants instructed to focus on their feelings and physiology.

In a similar study, children played a game based on the *Survivor* television show. Some children (randomly assigned) were told they had been voted out of the game—a clear example of peer rejection. Then, during a delay before a second task, children spent the time quietly thinking or engaging in a distracting activity, such as reading comic books or listening to music. The more time they spent on the distraction, the more their mood improved, as well as their ability to focus on the second task (Reijnjnes et al., 2006).

One difficulty with attentional control is that it requires cognitive energy. People can run out of ability to control their attention if they are fatigued or have been controlling their thoughts for too long (Engle, Conway, Tuholski, & Shisler, 1995). In fact, suppressing attention to already-active thoughts and stimuli may be an especially difficult form of cognitive control. In a classic study, Daniel Wegner and colleagues (Wegner et al., 1987) found that research participants who were asked to avoid thinking about white bears for five minutes, but to ring a bell if they did think about them, rang the bell more times than a group of participants who *were asked* to think about white bears. That is, if you try to avoid thinking about something, thoughts about it become more intrusive than ever.

Implications for people's ability to regulate attention to unpleasant stimuli are underscored by the results of a study in which participants looked at pairs of faces, one angry and one neutral, on a computer screen and pressed a key when a dot replaced one photo (we described this "dot probe" task in Chapter 10). At the same time, they were asked to hold an easy or difficult string of numbers in working memory (the more difficult string of numbers would require more effort). The researchers used EEG to measure the magnitude of an event-related electrical potential in the hemisphere opposite where the angry face appears (the N2pc ERP), thought to indicate intensity of attention. Participants who were trying to remember more difficult numbers were slower to respond to dots replacing the neutral faces paired with angry faces, suggesting they had a harder time pulling attention away from the threatening image. They also showed more pronounced EEG responses to angry faces, suggesting that these faces captured their attention more strongly (Holmes et al., 2014).

Many researchers have shown interest in whether training in mindfulness meditation—a practice in which one learns to focus nonjudgmentally on one's current state (e.g., paying attention to breathing) and/or maintain an open-minded attitude toward the present moment—can increase people's attentional control and, in turn, their ability to regulate their emotions. Studies have shown that extensive mindfulness training can help enhance people's cognitive control (Chambers, Lo, & Allen, 2008; Hölzel et al., 2013; Posner, Rothbart, & Tang, 2015; Teper & Inzlicht, 2013), and reduce their tendency to ruminate on their problems (Chambers et al., 2008; Gu et al., 2015). Meta-analyses of many studies have further suggested that mindfulness training can help alleviate anxiety and depression symptoms, and that these effects are accounted for at least partly by reduction in rumination and worry (Gu et al., 2015; Hofmann et al., 2010).

This is encouraging, but we have a great deal to learn about why and how mindfulness training has these effects. First, the experimental design of these studies is not always as rigorous as we like to see. Many studies either did not use a control group at all, or used a wait-list control in which participants received no contact with experimenters. This is problematic because any aspect of the intervention could explain results, not necessarily mindfulness per se—the effect could simply have been due to spending time relaxing, for example. Even if mindfulness training per se does produce effects, mindfulness is a complex psychological state, and it's not yet clear how exactly it facilitates emotional well-being. Several alternatives have been proposed, including enhancing attentional control, increasing people's acceptance of their emotions (and thus the tendency to become even more annoyed because you feel bad), and reducing the chance that you'll do something dopey that will upset you (Kang, Gruber, & Gray, 2013; Teper & Inzlicht, 2013). For now, it seems reasonable to think of this as an important research direction that needs more careful work to evaluate the effects, and the mechanisms behind them.

With or without extensive mindfulness training, turning your attention away from something is easier if you are turning it toward something else. As noted earlier, **distraction** involves trying to replace unpleasant thoughts with some alternative thought or activity. You may have noticed that we include distraction both as a situation selection strategy and as an attentional control strategy. It can be either, depending on whether you change your physical situation or simply redirect your attention within the current situation. Researchers are not always clear about which meaning applies to a particular study or set of studies, so it's best to look carefully at the methods and measures—as always! For now, we will focus on distraction of attention.

Attentional distraction has some advantages. If you are successful at putting the problem out of your mind, it isn't going to happen again, and there's nothing you can do about it anyway, then it's a fine strategy. In laboratory experiments, where participants are explicitly instructed to use distraction, this strategy is effective at reducing distress (Webb, Miles, & Sheeran, 2012). However, distraction does reduce the likelihood that you will take some practical approach to improving the situation, because you've simply stopped thinking about it at all. This may explain why high *dispositional* tendency to rely on distraction as an emotion-regulation strategy sometimes shows a negative correlation with psychological well-being (e.g., Schroevers, Kraaij, & Garnefski, 2011; Shiota, 2006).

One clever study with a large sample of participants in Sweden examined the combined implications of distraction with people's dispositional acceptance versus avoidance of difficult situations and feelings. The researchers found that distraction combined with a tendency to avoid unpleasant thoughts predicted poorer well-being, but that use of distraction combined with acceptance of difficult situations and feelings was associated with more desirable well-being profiles (Wolgast & Lundh, 2017).

Another potential limitation of distraction is that if you are exposed to the distressing situation again later, you may have a stronger emotional response than if you had dealt with it in other ways, such as changing the way you appraise the situation (Thiruchselvam et al., 2011). We consider that strategy next.

Cognitive Reappraisal

Let's return to our hypothetical scenario, where you are having dinner with several friends and one tarantula. You just can't keep your eyes off that tarantula. Maybe spiders are a real problem for you. Maybe your host placed you in a seat pointing your line of sight straight at it. Maybe you studied hard all day and don't have much attentional control left. What can you do?

Try imagining the spider as a weak, helpless, pathetic thing, stuck in some stupid terrarium without a snack, while everybody else is in the living room having fun and eating something tasty. Then you might feel sorry for the spider, rather than anxious. One of your authors (MNS) is a terrible arachnophobe, but copes with most household spiders by remembering that they're in more danger from humans than vice versa. Researchers refer to this general strategy as **cognitive reappraisal**—thinking about an event or stimulus in a way that changes your emotional response to it (Gross, 2015).

Using reappraisal doesn't mean pretending the situation isn't happening, or inventing an unrealistic story for how things will turn out. It does mean focusing on a plausible, but more positive (or at least neutral) interpretation of that situation's meaning. In Chapter 4 we considered the powerful role that appraisals play in generating and sustaining emotional responses. Reappraisal hacks the system by taking control of appraisal itself, thereby redirecting emotions' course. For example, victims of automobile accidents, hurricanes, and all sorts of other misfortune may comfort themselves with the thought, "It could have been worse!"

Reappraisal often plays an important role in therapy aimed at helping people with chronic emotional distress, as in depression and anxiety. When therapists guide clients toward changing the way they habitually think about an issue in their life, or a frequently occurring situation, the process is called **cognitive restructuring**. For example, instead of reacting to every unfriendly comment as further evidence that people don't like them, people might learn to think, "Oh well, she's just hard to please," or "I guess he's in a bad mood today."

Much research indicates that cognitive reappraisal is generally effective and healthy as an emotion regulation strategy. In several studies, participants instructed to reappraise distressing stimuli have shown reduced self-reports and facial expressions of distress compared with a no-instruction condition (e.g., Gross, 1998; Richards & Gross, 1999; Shiota & Levenson, 2009). In fMRI studies, instructed reappraisal reduces amygdala activation to upsetting photographs and films compared to trials where participants are asked to simply attend to their emotions (Buhle et al., 2014; Ochsner et al., 2002). Most studies indicate that people who report using cognitive reappraisal frequently also report higher well-being, including higher dispositional positive affect, lower negative affect, higher life satisfaction, greater sharing of emotion with others, peer-rated likeability, closer relationships, and lower risk of depression (Gross & John, 2003; McRae et al., 2012). Greater use of reappraisal has even been linked to better physical health profiles in terms of risk for cardiovascular and metabolic disease (Appleton et al., 2014; Ellis et al., 2019).

This is not to say that reappraisal is the perfect strategy for every situation. Reappraisal changes your interpretation of the situation, and therefore your emotional response, but it does nothing to change the situation itself. Like distraction, it's not going to help solve the problem. In one study, researchers examined the relationship between dispositional use of reappraisal and depression, but they considered a possible moderator—whether each participant's recent stressful experiences were largely controllable (they could have done something to improve the situation) or uncontrollable. Higher use of reappraisal predicted lower depression among people who had faced uncontrollable stressors, but *higher* rates of depression among those whose stressors had been controllable, objectively speaking (Troy, Shallcross, & Mauss, 2013). People who reappraise when they could be doing something about the situation instead may trade short-term emotional gain for longer-term pain.

Different Types of Reappraisal

Reappraisal can take many forms. At the simplest level, one can ignore the emotional aspects of a situation and think about nonemotional details and implications. This approach—referred to as **detached reappraisal**—can reduce the experience of negative emotion as well as physiological arousal associated with emotional distress (Gross, 1998; Shiota & Levenson, 2012). Making a joke about the situation, or **humor-based reappraisal**, can also improve your emotions (Figure 15.7; Lefcourt et al., 1995). The effectiveness of this strategy depends a

The Hansons' decision to buy an attack
spider finally paid off.

FIGURE 15.7. Thinking about feared objects in a way that makes them seem funny is one kind of cognitive reappraisal.

bit on the kind of humor you employ. In one study, Andrea Samson and James Gross (2012) showed participants a series of extremely unpleasant photographs, assigning them to just watch the pictures, to reinterpret the pictures in a funny but positive, good-natured way, or to use humor in a mean-spirited way. Both forms of humor appeared to reduce people's negative emotion and increase positive emotion relative to the just-watch control, but positive humor was significantly more effective. Some research suggests that humor can play a nice role in romantic couples' efforts to help regulate each others' emotions as well, promoting feelings of intimacy (Horn et al., 2019).

In stressful interactions with another person, **perspective-taking** can be a useful technique for regulating your own emotions (Webb et al., 2012). Forgiveness might also be considered a kind of cognitive reappraisal. Forgiveness often includes finding some acceptable explanation for another person's hurtful behavior. You might decide, "We all have our weak moments. I don't know everything going on in that other person's life. Maybe I should just give him the benefit of the doubt." Letting go of a grudge releases tension and improves emotional stability (McCullough, 2001; Witvliet, Ludwig, & Vander Laan, 2001). That is, forgiveness helps not only the forgiven, but also the forgiver.

One especially useful reappraisal strategy is to pay attention to a negative event, but try to interpret it in a more benign way. In one study, college students were asked to examine a series of 120 pictures, many of which were unpleasant or disturbing. The participants were asked to suppress their emotional expressions while they viewed the disturbing pictures. Of interest is the strategy used by the people who were most successful at reducing their emotion displays. When asked how they managed, most said they tried to reinterpret the situation in a positive light. For example, when they saw a wounded soldier, they told themselves the battle was over and the soldier was about to receive good medical care (Jackson et al., 2000).

This strategy of focusing on positive aspects of negative or challenging situations is referred to as **positive reappraisal**, or sometimes *benefit finding*. For example, if every graduate school to which you applied rejected you, you might say, "Oh, well. I learned a lot from applying the first time, and next time I'll do better." If you must care for an aging relative with Alzheimer's disease, you might say, "Here is an opportunity for me to rise to the occasion, to use my skills to help someone who really needs me."

The short-term effects of positive reappraisal differ somewhat from those of detached reappraisal. Michelle Shiota and Robert Levenson (2012) asked participants to watch television clips showing people eating disgusting things, such as cow intestine and horse rectum, as well as movie scenes in which the main character learns that a family member has died. Participants first watched one of each type of film without instruction to regulate their emotions, and then a second film of each type with instructions to use either detached or positive reappraisal. (Participants viewed the films in different combinations and orders to ensure that any effects were not just a result of which film they saw in each condition.)

Participants in both groups thought their assigned reappraisal strategy was effective in terms of regulating their emotions. However, the strategies differed in important ways. Participants using detached reappraisal showed an overall reduction in emotion relative to the first set of films. Their subjective emotional intensity decreased, but the valence did not improve. They also showed a reduction in cardiovascular reactivity when using this kind of reappraisal. In contrast, those using positive reappraisal showed no change in subjective emotional intensity, but an improvement in valence—they felt more positive. Participants in this condition also tended to maintain a comparable level of cardiovascular reactivity with and without emotion regulation. Taken together, these findings suggest that positive reappraisal keeps people more emotionally engaged with the situation at hand, but in a way that is less aversive (Shiota & Levenson, 2012).

Correlational and experimental studies suggest that positive reappraisal may be a particularly healthy strategy. For example, people who exhibit **resilience**—those who recover relatively easily from negative events—report thinking about the potential positive effects of negative events more often than less resilient people (Tugade & Fredrickson, 2004). In one recent study, researchers Ajua Duker, Jennifer Richeson, and their colleagues compared the effects of different forms of reappraisal on women's emotions after vividly remembering a personal experience as the target of sexism. Participants recalled an experience of this kind and were randomly assigned to think about it in one of three ways: *self-immersion*, focusing on their own perspective and feelings during the experience; *self-distancing*, thinking about the experience from the perspective of a third-party observer; or *redemption*, thinking about how they personally have grown as a result of this experience. Compared with participants in the other two conditions, those in the redemption condition subsequently reported both more positive and less negative affect (Duker et al., 2021; Figure 15.8).

The utility of positive reappraisal strategies is also evident in research on clinical disorders. Researchers compared the emotion regulation strategies reported by clinically depressed and anxious Dutch adults with those used by a comparable sample of

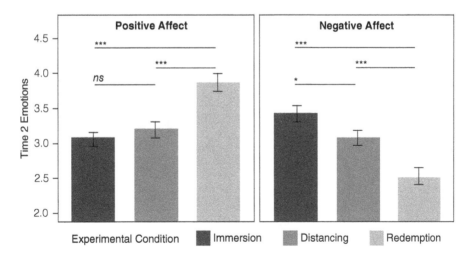

Note. *ns* = nonsignificant.
* *p* < .05. *** *p* < .001.

FIGURE 15.8. Unlike distancing or detached reappraisal, positive reappraisal—in this case, thinking about how one has grown as a result of an unpleasant experience—significantly improved mood among women who had vividly relived a personal experience as a target of sexism. From Duker et al. (2021).

emotionally healthy adults (Garnefski et al., 2002). Both groups completed a question-naire measuring the typical frequency of using several cognitive strategies: self-blame, other-blame, rumination, catastrophizing (emphasizing how bad an experience is), ac-ceptance, planning, putting the negative event into perspective, thinking about other positive topics, and positive reappraisal. The one strategy used significantly more often by the healthy sample than by the clinical sample was positive reappraisal.

Other studies have also indicated that people who rely on positive reappraisal are less likely than others to report symptoms of depression (Garnefski et al,, 2004; Kraaij, Pruymboom, & Garnefski, 2002). One possible explanation for these findings is that positive reappraisal encourages behaviors that improve your life, just like active coping. For example, researchers performing a meta-analysis of studies examining the coping strategies used by AIDS patients found that those who used positive reappraisal more often reported better health behaviors, and showed better health outcomes (Moskowitz et al., 2009). A recent review of available studies reached a similar conclusion (Finkelstein-Fox, Park, & Kalichman, 2020).

However, as with reappraisal in general, positive reappraisal is not right for every situation and does not invariably predict positive outcomes. A different meta-analysis of many studies, not limited to HIV+/AIDS patients, found that high dispositional positive reappraisal was unrelated to physical health, and *negatively* associated with psychological health (Penley et al., 2002). It may be that some kinds of positive reappraisal are more conducive to health than others; that positive reappraisal has different implications in different situations; or even that positive reappraisal has multiple effects that combine differently depending on the exact situational context. On one hand, seeing the oppor-tunities in a stressful situation may motivate action to take advantage of those opportu-nities, and may sustain hope. On the other hand, thinking that things aren't as bad as they seem may reduce a person's motivation to improve the situation, as illustrated in Figure 15.9. More research is needed to identify conditions under which positive reap-praisal is most helpful.

FIGURE 15.9.   Under some circumstances, positive reappraisal may inhibit efforts to improve a negative situation.

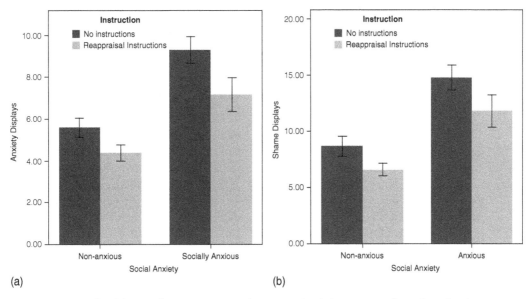

FIGURE 15.10. Participants who were encouraged to reappraise their own arousal as a sign of excitement, beneficial to task performance, showed less anxiety and shame than those in a control condition when giving a speech in the laboratory. Notably, this effect was larger among individuals with diagnosable social anxiety disorder. From Beltzer et al. (2014).

For one last example of reappraisal, suppose you find your heart beating rapidly and your hands trembling as you prepare to give a speech, or have a job interview. Instead of labeling your response "nervousness," which might interfere with performance, think of it as "excitement" (Brooks, 2014). Researchers call this **arousal reappraisal**—reappraising the meaning of the emotional arousal itself. Instructions used in studies of arousal reappraisal are somewhat similar to the threat versus challenge appraisal instructions we first discussed in Chapter 4, but here the appraisal is directed toward the meaning of one's own physiological response, rather than the external situation.

Although arousal reappraisal is relatively new on the emotion-regulation-research scene, evidence already points to its usefulness in high-pressure situations. In one study researchers randomly assigned participants either to a description of their arousal during the speech-preparation stress task as beneficial, likely helping them to succeed, or to a no-instruction control. Participants in the arousal-reappraisal group not only reported feeling more able to cope with the task, but also showed fewer nonverbal displays of anxiety and shame, than did those in the control group (Beltzer et al., 2014). Notably, this effect was particularly strong among participants who met diagnostic criteria for social anxiety disorder (see Figure 15.10).

RESPONSE-FOCUSED STRATEGIES

Learning Objectives

- Explain the problems associated with using alcohol and emotional eating as a way of dealing with distress.

- Differentiate catharsis, rumination, and expressive writing (as used in studies by Pennebaker and colleagues), both as processes and in terms of their effects on emotional well-being.
- Summarize the effects of physical exercise on well-being, differentiating those of moderate- versus high-intensity exercise.
- Describe meditation, and identify the mechanism by which meditation training appears to promote psychological well-being.

Suppose the worst has happened. For example, a beloved relative has died. Nothing you do can undo the loss, and no amount of reappraisal can improve the situation significantly. Once a full-blown emotion is underway, people rely on emotion-focused regulation strategies to dampen the emotion over time. Many such strategies exist, and we will discuss several that have been subjected to good research. What they all have in common is a goal of changing the feeling or expression of the emotion, rather than changing the situation or appraisals that led to the emotion.

Escaping Emotions: Drugs, Alcohol, and Food

If recent events in your life have gone badly and you want to escape from your distress—fast—what options would you consider? Go on, be honest.

Many people use alcohol or other drugs as a quick way to escape their problems, at least occasionally (Sher & Grekin, 2007). Let's just say that we don't recommend this as a regular strategy. Alcohol by itself is not the problem—lots of people drink alcohol in moderation (a few servings per week) without substantial harm—but relying on alcohol or other drugs to escape from problems can easily develop into a problem itself. Drinking as a way of coping with distress predicts greater alcohol-related problems such as binge drinking and other excessive use (Khan et al., 2018). Moreover, in a longitudinal study with more than 1300 US undergraduates from diverse backgrounds, those who consumed greater amounts of alcohol were more likely to subsequently experience interpersonal or relationship-related trauma; those who went on to develop symptoms of post-traumatic stress disorder were then particularly likely to report increased use of alcohol to cope (Bountress et al., 2019). In other words, drinking as a way of dealing with distress not only fails to make things better, it can actually increase your risk of experiencing a new problem, creating a downward spiral of alcohol and negative life events.

Another quick way to experience something pleasant is eating. However, most people who use eating to escape from emotional distress—otherwise known as **emotional eating**—tend to feel worse rather than better afterward (Solomon, 2001; Waters, Hill, & Waller, 2001). Note that emotional eating is not the same as savoring, discussed earlier, although it's possible for savoring to include eating. Calmly and mindfully drinking a cup of coffee, or eating a piece of particularly nice chocolate, is savoring. Guzzling a huge, sugary soda or inhaling a ton of pizza or ice cream, without truly enjoying it or being in control of your actions, is emotional eating. Evidence suggests that people who have difficulty verbalizing their feelings (a characteristic formally referred to as *alexithymia*) are somewhat more likely to turn to emotional eating when they are upset (Reichenberger et al., 2020). Frequent emotional eating is a risk factor for depression (Konttinen et al., 2010). However, the reverse is true as well. One longitudinal study with several thousand participants in Finland found that a tendency toward emotional eating mediated the relationship between depression at the beginning of the study and weight gain over the next several years (Konttinen et al., 2019).

Studies of the relationships among eating, emotion regulation, and well-being often use a correlational design, so it's not always clear which of these factors causes the others. In one experiment, however, researchers randomly assigned participants to try to suppress their emotional expressions, or to allow their expressions and emotions to respond freely. During a supposed taste test that followed, people who were instructed to suppress their expressions ate more snack foods such as cookies and potato chips than people in the other two conditions (Evers, Marjin, & de Ridder, 2010). Thus, it's possible that the effort exerted in trying to conceal emotions depletes people's self-regulation stores, so that they eat whatever is available. As with alcohol and drugs, however, habitual "emotional eating" tends to crowd out more constructive, problem-focused approaches to negative events.

Suppressing Emotional Expression

In some situations we may feel pressure to control our outward expressions of emotion, regardless of what we feel inside. Imagine receiving an unfair and rudely phrased criticism from a supervisor at work, or a sarcastic comment from a professor. In such situations you might feel offended, but you risk getting into trouble if you express your anger fully. When people try to hide their emotions, so that a person watching them would not know what they are feeling, most are able to do so (e.g., Gross, 1998; 2002; Gross & Levenson, 1997).

Researchers refer to this strategy as **suppressing emotional expressions**. Note that the meaning of "suppression" here differs from Freud's meaning of the term. Freud used the term to refer to blocking a thought from consciousness, whereas here the term refers to blocking the behavioral expression of an emotion. The ability to suppress emotional expressions is important in some situations. Imagine what it would be like if you could *never* suppress your displays of emotion! However, as with some other emotion-regulation strategies, suppressing emotions reflexively or indiscriminately is problematic. Many studies have shown that suppressing expressions is costly in terms of cognitive resources, with a wide range of negative implications. We will discuss these implications in detail shortly.

Processing Your Feelings

In Chapter 11 we discussed **catharsis**—the idea that venting your emotions helps get them out of your system, helping you to feel better afterward. As we saw, the evidence on this is rather mixed—people tend not to feel better after having a good cry, and they often report feeling worse. Simply unleashing other emotions, such as anger and disgust, in an unregulated way may have undesirable consequences for your relationships. Even dwelling on an upsetting situations and your feelings about it for too long can be harmful. **Rumination** is thinking continuously about a problem for a long time, focusing on negative aspects of the situation, how awful it's making you feel, and all of the ways it is likely to get worse, rather than thinking about possible solutions. You can think of rumination as a form of negative reappraisal—the opposite of positive reappraisal. Excessive rumination is often a precursor to clinical depression, and may be a contributing factor in anxiety disorders as well (Garnefski et al., 2004; Kovács et al., 2020; McLaughlin & Nolen-Hoeksema, 2011).

We are not recommending that you try to suppress all thoughts or discussions about negative experiences, however. There is a more constructive way to process emotions. One line of research suggests that you can derive substantial benefits from relatively brief explorations of your problems. In one experiment, James Pennebaker (1997) randomly assigned college students in one group to spend half an hour a day, for three to five days, writing about their deepest thoughts and feelings concerning some intensely upsetting experience. Students randomly assigned to a control group spent the same time writing about an unemotional topic. Many in the treatment group wrote about traumatic events, such as the death of a friend or relative, or experiences of physical or sexual abuse. At the end of the week, the students could either destroy their journals or hand them in, but no one discussed the content with them. In these studies, the students were communicating only with themselves.

Afterward, Pennebaker (1997) asked the students for their reaction to the writing experience. Despite becoming very upset while writing, sometimes even crying, nearly all students said it was a valuable experience. Follow-up assessments later in the semester indicated that on average, students in the treatment group had been ill less often, drank less alcohol, and got better grades than those in the control group (Pennebaker, 1997). Several subsequent studies have also shown that the writing exercise leads to improved health outcomes (Pennebaker & Chung, 2011). A review of expressive writing interventions with adolescents found small but consistent positive effects not only on psychological well-being, but also on academic outcomes (Travagin, Margola, & Revenson, 2015). People may get some of the same benefits just by thinking about a stressful event and possible solutions, even if they do not put their thoughts on paper (Rivkin & Taylor, 1999).

Why did the writing task have such positive results, given the drawbacks of rumination and pure emotional venting? According to Pennebaker and collaborators, those most likely to profit from this experience are those who use their writing to try to understand the stressful event and their reactions to it. For example, the more often participants in one study used words like *because, reason, realize, know,* and *understand,* the greater their gains in health, academic performance, and overall adjustment (Pennebaker & Graybeal, 2001). That is, the writing helped not simply because people expressed their emotions, but because they understood better or came to terms with the situation in the process of writing.

We also gain insight from one study that failed to show a benefit from expressive writing. In this study, people who had recently undergone divorce or separation after a long-term marriage spent 20 minutes per day for three days writing either about how their break-up affected them emotionally, or about factual, unemotional aspects of their lives. Here, those writing about unemotional matters showed significantly greater improvement in their mood and concentration (Sbarra et al., 2013). This study suggests that prolonged thinking about emotional reactions to an event can backfire for a recent or ongoing event; the writing assignment may have encouraged people to ruminate on the break-up, rather than processing it in a more thoughtful, analytical way.

Expressing your emotions can also have positive benefits through another route—by eliciting social support from other people. In one study, researchers collected reports from thousands of people in 35 countries of the most recent time when they cried, and how crying

FIGURE 15.11. Evidence suggests that genuine tears tend to elicit others' support—a route by which expressing your emotions may lead indirectly to improved mood.

affected their mood (Bylsma, Vingerhoets, & Rottenberg, 2008). Participants were also asked to report features of the situation, such as who else was present, what event made them cry, and what happened afterward. Results showed that crying was most likely to lead to improved feelings when it evoked social support from others, specifically in the form of comforting words, touch, or other friendly behaviors. In another study with more than 7,000 participants across 41 countries, targets showing sad facial expressions with digitally added tears evoked higher observer ratings of warmth, connectedness, and empathic concern than targets without tears (Zickfeld et al., 2021). Taken together, these studies suggest that genuine crying may increase others' inclination to come to your aid (Figure 15.11).

Exercise

One of the most successful response-focused coping strategies is physical exercise (see Figure 15.12). Studies have shown repeatedly that exercise is a reliable way to prevent depression (Leppämäki, Partonen, & Lönnqvist, 2002), and exercise interventions have consistently been shown to help alleviate depressive symptoms (Josefsson, Lindwall, & Archer, 2014; Kvam et al., 2016). Over the long term, exercise also helps prevent and reduce anxiety (Asmundson et al., 2013; Stonerock et al., 2015). One caveat here is that the benefits come from a consistent program of exercise, not from a single workout. Also, whereas moderate-intensity exercise tends to improve mood, extremely strenuous exercise—pushing your body to the point of depletion in a single session, as may occur during high-intensity or HIIT workouts—may actually make one's mood worse (Saanijoki et al., 2018; Salmon, 2001).

FIGURE 15.12. Physical exercise can play an important role in emotion regulation, as well as in the promotion of physical health.

Why does a steady program of moderate exercise result in improved mood? Several mechanisms are probably involved. First, exercise is a distraction from the source of stress. Any kind of distraction—such as listening to music or watching television—is one way of dealing with stress, although in most situations it is not a powerful one (Fauerbach et al., 2002).

Second, exercise improves overall health. People in good physical condition show less tension and sympathetic arousal in response to stressful events, compared to people in worse condition (Crews & Landers, 1987), and we know that muscle tension and arousal are part of the subjective feeling of stress.

Third, any stress readies the body for intense fight-or-flight action, even if the current stressful situation does not call for physical activity. Once the body has engaged in physical activity after stress, it tends to relax. Studies with laboratory rodents have found that wheel-running exercise, after a separate stressor, can even reduce adrenal stress responses (Mills & Ward, 1986).

Fourth, neurotransmitters called endorphins (see Chapter 6 for a definition) become more active during physical exercise (Thoren et al., 1990). These chemicals are part of the body's natural pain-killing system, and opiate activity is generally associated with improved mood. One study used positron emission tomography to examine the release of naturally occurring or *endogenous* endorphins during and after different kinds of exercise in a sample of men in Finland (it is highly unfortunate that most studies of exercise exclude women). Results showed that endogenous endorphin release was associated with mood in both moderate- and high-intensity exercise, but the effect was positive for moderate exercise and *negative* during high-intensity workouts. Much more research is needed to rigorously untangle the relationships among exercise, endorphins, and mood.

Meditation and Relaxation

It may seem contradictory to list both exercise and relaxation as ways of controlling emotions, but in fact they may be related. Both help the body reduce muscular tension and autonomic arousal. Having trouble relaxing? Here is some advice:

- Find a place that is reasonably quiet. Sit comfortably, in such a way that you are upright but not tense or in pain (lying down is not bad, but you might start to drift into sleep).
- Begin by paying attention to your breathing, noticing the patterns of inhalation and exhalation. Just watch your breath without judgment at first; then you might try slowing it down a little, with somewhat longer breaths out than in.
- Notice how your body feels. If there is an area of tension, try contracting that muscle a little, then letting it relax.
- Watch the thoughts and feelings going through your mind, again without judging them. Most people cannot completely clear their mind, especially when they are first learning to meditate; just letting the thoughts pass without getting tangled up in them is great. If you find it difficult, don't worry about it—it gets easier with time and practice.
- Some people find it helpful to have something on which to concentrate their attention. You might ring a bell, repeat a simple sound (such as *om*) or repetitive prayer, or focus your vision on some simple object or shape. Choose whatever seems comfortable to you.

This practice is generally known as meditation (see Figure 15.13). There are several forms of meditation, including mindfulness mediation, discussed earlier, but they all

FIGURE 15.13. People who meditate regularly report less stress. This may be a result of cognitive training, but also of relaxation.

involve sitting or moving quietly and calmly, concentrating on the present moment, and trying not to get caught up mentally in your worries and to-do lists. Meta-analyses of meditation-based interventions have indicated that meditation training can improve depression, anxiety, and pain; reducing rumination and a tendency to worry constantly appear to account for at least some of these beneficial effects. (Goyal et al., 2014; Gu et al., 2015). This makes sense, as one goal of mindful awareness is developing the ability to recognize and let go of unhelpful thoughts and appraisals, rather than letting them run rampant over your mind.

THE NEUROBIOLOGY OF EMOTION REGULATION

Learning Objective

- Identify the region of the brain that is distinctly active during cognitive reappraisal.

Although neuroscientists are not exactly looking for the emotion-regulation area of the brain, the results of neuroimaging studies can yield an understanding of what cognitive abilities are needed to support particular strategies. Much of this research has included a focus on the cognition-focused strategies, partly because it makes sense theoretically, and partly because cognition-focused strategies are easy to elicit in an fMRI device. These studies have typically emphasized a point made above—that cognition-focused strategies require considerable effortful control over thoughts and attention, often referred to as **executive control**. Studies of the neural activation patterns associated with cognitive reappraisal are consistent with this view.

In one typical study, young men watched a series of short pornographic films while undergoing an fMRI scan. During some of the films, they were instructed to allow themselves to become aroused; during the other films, they were told to inhibit their arousal. Different brain areas became active under the two conditions (Beauregard, Lévesque, & Bourgouin, 2001). While the men were sexually aroused, activity increased in the hypothalamus, right amygdala, and part of the right temporal cortex—areas commonly activated during strong emotion. While men were inhibiting their arousal, activity was lower in the amygdala and hypothalamus, but increased in the prefrontal cortex, an area identified with cognitive control (Tisserand et al., 2004).

In a similar study, participants looked at a series of disturbing photos while undergoing functional imaging. Then they examined the same pictures but with instructions to reappraise them to make them less disturbing. While participants examined the photos the first time, they showed extensive activity in the amygdala and the orbitofrontal part of the prefrontal cortex, again, areas that are often active during emotional experience. When participants were reinterpreting the photos, those brain areas showed less response, but parts of the prefrontal cortex—specifically within the dorsolateral and dorsomedial regions—became more active (Ochsner et al., 2002). The finding that the prefrontal cortex is highly active during reappraisal has now been replicated in many studies (Buhle et al., 2014; see Figure 15.14).

Cognitive reappraisal is not the only emotion regulation strategy that demands cognitive control. Researchers showed participants several distressing film clips during an fMRI scan. During some clips participants were asked to just watch the clips; during

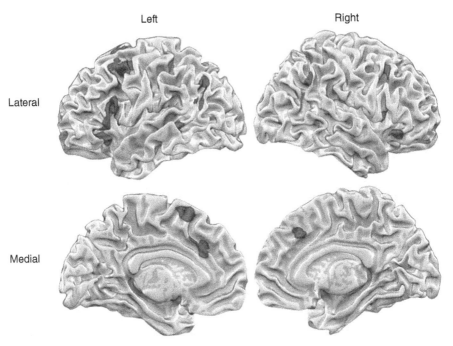

FIGURE 15.14. A meta-analysis of many studies revealed regions of the brain, especially within the prefrontal cortex, that were more active while reappraising unpleasant stimuli than when just watching them. From Buhle et al. (2014).

others they were asked to reappraise the clips, and during yet others they were asked to try to suppress their emotional expressions. Both reappraisal and suppression resulted in increased prefrontal cortex activation compared with the just-watch condition. However, reappraisal instruction elicited this activation within a few seconds of the beginning of the clip, whereas suppression instruction evoked activation several seconds later (Goldin et al., 2008). This time difference is consistent with hypotheses based on the process model of emotion regulation, which suggests that suppression takes place later in the emotion process than reappraisal.

WHICH EMOTION REGULATION STRATEGIES ARE BEST?

Learning Objectives
- Analyze the evidence regarding the problems associated with suppressing emotional expression, as well as cultural and demographic moderators of these effects.
- Define emotion regulation flexibility, and summarize the current state of the evidence on its benefits for well-being.

We've now described a dozen or so specific emotion regulation strategies, reviewing key research on the benefits and limitations of each. Which strategy, or category of strategies, is best?

Before we address this question, note that some strategies are not easily classified as exclusively problem-focused, appraisal-focused, or emotion-focused (Skinner et al., 2003).

For example, we described *expressing your feelings* as an emotion-focused strategy, but if it elicits help from others it may lead to situation modification as well.

Also, consider the many ways in which social support helps us deal with stressful situations. First, think of all the practical, problem-focused effects of social support: your friends can give you advice about how to deal with the problem. If you have lost your job, they might help you find a new one. If you are sick, they can drive you to the doctor's office, get your medicine, or bring your meals. Researchers commonly refer to this as **instrumental social support**. Second, think of the ways social support provides emotional comfort, or **emotional social support**. This form of social support is emotion-focused, rather than problem-focused.

A great deal of research has compared a particular cognition-focused strategy—reappraisal—against an emotion-focused strategy—suppressing emotional expression. The theory driving this research is that efforts to shape emotion earlier in the process, before it has even begun, should be easier to implement and more effective than those aimed at altering an emotion that's already flared up. To apply an old but apt idiom, emotion-focused coping is like trying to close the barn door after the horse has already escaped; best to keep the barn door closed in the first place, right?

Much of this research suggests that habitually suppressing or hiding your emotions has widespread negative effects—at least in individualist, Western cultural contexts such as the United States and Canada (more on this caveat below). Experimental studies have consistently shown that suppressing facial displays fails to reduce the experience of negative emotion, and can even increase physiological signs of stress (e.g., Gross, 1998; 2002; Gross & Levenson, 1997). For example, students who were told to suppress their emotional responses to a series of disturbing slides showed increased blood pressure compared with students who were given no instructions (Richards & Gross, 1999). In another series of studies, women watched an upsetting film about the nuclear bombing of Hiroshima and Nagasaki during World War II. Then they were asked to discuss the film, either naturally or while suppressing their emotions. Those suppressing their emotional displays showed increased blood pressure (Butler et al., 2003). A similar pattern has been observed for positive as well as negative emotions, with reappraisal, but not suppression, effectively downregulating subjective emotional experience (Kalokerinos, Greenaway, & Denson, 2015).

You might ask, why would anyone want to hide their positive emotion? It does come up sometimes. Imagine just having gotten the job, internship, or grad school of your dreams, while learning at the same time that your best friend was rejected from theirs. It's not a time to explode into obvious joy, right? Perhaps you're having a serious conversation with your partner, and something they say suddenly strikes you as extremely funny, not in a helpful way. Again, it's not the time to burst out laughing. The researchers in this last study raise a valuable point—in such situations suppressing the outward show of emotion may be healthy for the relationship, while still allowing you to feel that pleasant state (Kalokerinos et al., 2015).

Reappraisal and suppression also have different effects on memory. Once people set a reappraisal strategy in motion, they can deflect the experience of negative emotion and attend to other aspects of the situation. Suppressing your emotion requires constant attention as you monitor your own behavior and think about the instruction to hide your feelings. The cognitive effort involved in the latter strategy leaves less room for other tasks.

In studies of participants viewing negative film clips, watching unpleasant slides, and discussing conflicts with a romantic partner, those instructed to suppress their emotion displays consistently showed worse memory for verbal information than those instructed to reappraise or those given no regulation instructions (Richards, Butler, & Gross, 2003; Richards & Gross, 1999).

Finally, studies indicate that suppression often has a negative impact on our relationships with others. People who report often suppressing their emotional displays are not as well-liked by their peers, and those who report more frequent use of reappraisal are better liked (Gross & John, 2003). One study showed that among individuals who were making the transition from high school to college, those who reported more frequent emotional suppression had a harder time forming new relationships in the new environment (Srivastava et al., 2009). Longitudinal studies find that expressive suppression predicts not only feeling more distant and dissatisfied with relationships in the short-term, but declining relationship satisfaction in the long term as well (Cameron & Overall, 2018). These trends are striking because the most obvious reason for suppressing negative emotion is to avoid conflict with other people. Under some circumstances, suppression of this kind is clearly necessary. The effect is clear at the dispositional level, however. People who *habitually* hide their emotions from others are difficult to get close to—they may avoid conflict, but they avoid intimacy as well.

There is an important limitation to the work summarized above, however. It has been done almost exclusively with young adults (typically college students) in Western cultures. There are some hints that the effects of suppression might not be as negative for everyone as they are for this demographic and cultural group. For example, Asian-American participants in one experiment who suppressed their emotional expressions showed fewer negative effects than European Americans (Butler, Lee, & Gross, 2007). As we saw in Chapter 3, Asian cultures encourage open displays of emotion to a lesser extent than Western cultures (especially the United States, which is pretty extreme in this regard; Wood, Rychlowska, & Niedenthal, 2016). Keeping one's expressions in check may be more natural and require less attention among those raised in an Asian cultural context (even within the United States) than is the case in mainstream US culture.

In another study, older adults reported suppressing their expressions more often than did young adults (Eldesouky & English, 2018), yet as we saw in Chapter 8, older adults are doing just fine emotionally. Here again, expressive suppression may have different meaning, and therefore different psychological and social consequences, than it does for young adults. Immediate social context may matter as well. One study using experience sampling methods found that although expressive suppression was associated with lower emotional well-being, this relationship was significantly weaker in situations where participants felt they were low in the immediate social hierarchy (in which case they were more likely to hide their feelings as well; Catterson, Eldesouky, & John, 2017). When you are not one of the most powerful people in the room, it may be that keeping some of your emotions to yourself is simply a sensible thing to do.

Clearly some ways of coping with distress are harmful, at least if used habitually. These include alcohol and other drug use, emotional eating, and ruminating unhelpfully on your problems and how awful you feel (that last isn't exactly an emotion regulation strategy, but we include it because rumination is often discussed in emotion regulation research). Beyond this, however, researchers are beginning to move away from the idea of "good" versus "bad" emotion regulation strategies, instead emphasizing the value of picking the right strategy for the situation. Earlier in this chapter we mentioned a study in which frequent reappraisal predicted lower depression among those dealing with un-controllable life stressors, but *higher* rates of depression among those dealing with negative situations over which they plausibly had some control (Troy, Shallcross, & Mauss, 2013). An experience sampling study found that participants' use of reappraisal in high-control situations was associated with higher well-being, but this was not the case for use of reap-praisal in situations over which they had less control (Haines et al., 2016). In another series of cross-sectional and experimental studies, reappraisal used to manage distress after the 2016 US presidential election predicted feeling better, but actually *doing* less in terms of investing in constructive political action (Ford et al., 2019).

Moreover, in real life (and even in the laboratory) people do not necessarily limit their emotion regulation efforts to a single strategy. In one study, participants watched a film clip showing an accident in which someone's finger was severed while working with heavy machinery—very gory and gross—and then rated the extent to which they had spontaneously used various emotion regulation strategies during the clip. Of the 111 participants in the study, 56% reported using more than one strategy (Aldao & Nolen-Hoeksema, 2013). A pair of recent studies has linked flexible, context-sensitive use of different emotion regulation strategies in different kinds of situations to lower symptoms of anxiety and depression (Chen & Bonanno, 2021). For these reasons, **emotion regula-tion flexibility**—the ability to identify and deploy the emotion regulation strategy or strategies most likely to be beneficial in a given situation, rather than relying on one go-to strategy all the time—is a hot topic among researchers right now (Aldao, Sheppes, & Gross, 2015). It's not yet clear exactly what this mapping looks like, but you can expect lots more research on this in the years ahead.

SUMMARY

Although we expressed skepticism about Sigmund Freud's methods and theories, he was right on a basic point: people want to avoid anxiety and distress, and they will try one way after another until they succeed. Many people fall into a habit of relying mainly on one method or another, and some strategies work better than others—especially when you take context into consideration. When possible, a good approach is often to try to do something to resolve or at least improve your situation. Even if you cannot fully overcome the problem, exerting any control over it, or even thinking you are exerting some control makes it seem less overwhelming.

When you have little or no control, changing how you think about the problem may be a good plan. Can you do anything to take your mind off the distressing situation, at least for a while? Alternatively, consider the situation from a different angle: Can anything good come from it? Can you make it an opportunity to do something worthwhile? Have you grown, or are you likely to grow, in valuable ways as a result of this experience? Such thoughts do not improve the situation—they may even reduce your motivation to take constructive action—but they can help you live with it in some peace.

Finally, the response-focused approaches also have their place, either as a supplement to the others or as a final resort when the others fail. The research indicates that we should steer away from a couple of popular ideas: vigorously expressing your negative emotions does not, as a rule, help reduce them, and suppressing them may backfire as well. An intermediate approach is usually best—thinking about the problem constructively and discussing it with others, but without dwelling or ruminating on it. Periodic exercise goes a long way in helping people manage their emotions, as do relaxation and mindful, non-judgmental awareness of feelings. If you want a glass of wine or an ice cream cone once in a while, after a really bad day, we won't argue with you—just don't make regulating emotions in this way a habit.

KEY TERMS

active coping: taking concrete steps to change a problematic situation (p. 524)

arousal reappraisal: reinterpreting the meaning of one's own physiological arousal as a sign of excitement, rather than anxiety. (p. 537)

attentional control: directing one's attention away from stimuli and thoughts likely to elicit unwanted emotions (p. 529)

catharsis: the release of strong emotions by experiencing and expressing them fully (p. 539)

cognition-focused strategies: selectively attending to certain aspects of the situation, or changing the way you think about the situation, in order to encourage some emotions and/or deter others (p. 521)

cognitive reappraisal: changing the way we think about a particular situation to deter a negative emotion and/or encourage a positive one (p. 532)

cognitive restructuring: changing the way one thinks about a major emotional issue or frequently occurring situation—a frequent goal in therapies for mood disorders like depression and anxiety (p. 532)

coping: the ways that people reduce negative emotion after a stressful event (p. 521)

detached reappraisal: thinking about a stimulus or situation in a detached, neutral way that minimizes emotional implications (p. 533)

distraction: replacing unpleasant thoughts with an alternative thought or activity (p. 524)

ego defense mechanisms: psychological regulation strategies that according to Sigmund Freud, serve to resolve the tension between the id and the superego and keep disturbing wishes and desires hidden from consciousness (p. 519)

emotional eating: eating because one is emotionally distressed (p. 538)

emotion regulation: the strategies we use to control which emotions we have, when we have them, and how strongly we experience and express them (p. 521)

emotion regulation flexibility: the ability to identify and enact the particular emotion regulation strategy or strategies most likely to be beneficial in a given situation, rather than relying inflexibly on a single strategy. (p. 548)

emotional social support: seeking and receiving compassion and encouragement from others when distressed (p. 546)

executive control: effortful control over cognitive processes such as attention, working memory, and planning (p. 544)

humor-based reappraisal: making a joke about, or finding humor in, an otherwise difficult or unpleasant situation. (p. 533)

implementation intentions: concrete plans for how one will enact or choose a healthy behavior rather than an unhealthy one, especially in situations where temptation is likely to arise (p. 528)

instrumental social support: seeking and receiving practical support from other people in a time of stress (p. 546)

perspective-taking: appraising a situation from another person's perspective, thereby altering your own emotional response (p. 534)

positive reappraisal: focusing on positive aspects of negative or challenging situations (p. 534)

process model of emotion regulation: a model that organizes emotion-regulation strategies according to their place in the emotion process itself (p. 521)

resilience: recovering relatively well or easily from negative events (p. 535)

response-focused strategies: trying to change aspects of emotional responding once the emotion has already occurred (p. 521)

rumination: thinking continuously about a problem for a long period of time, focusing on negative aspects of the situation instead of possible solutions (p. 539)

savoring: taking the time to mindfully enjoy a simple, pleasant experience (p. 523)

situation-focused strategies: controlling the situation we are in, either by choosing to be in one situation rather than another or by changing the situation (p. 521)

situation modification: taking steps to change a situation, typically to improve it (p. 523)

situation selection: deciding whether to enter a situation that is likely to elicit a particular emotion (p. 523)

suppressing emotional expressions: concealing one's nonverbal expression of emotions, so others do not know what you are feeling (p. 539)

THOUGHT/DISCUSSION QUESTIONS

1. Think of a recent situation that you found distressing. Describe problem-focused, appraisal-focused, and response-focused emotion-regulation strategies you could apply in that situation. What are the benefits and limitations of each strategy in that context?

2. Describe several different ways in which you could benefit from other people's support in a stressful situation. How would each be classified in the process model of emotion regulation?

3. Imagine you are trying to support a friend who has just lost their job. How might you adapt each of the strategies discussed in this chapter to help your friend to feel better?

4. Under what circumstances might you want to *increase* your own negative emotion? When might it be appropriate or helpful to reduce positive emotion?

SUGGESTIONS FOR FURTHER READING

Aldao, A., Sheppes, G., & Gross, J. J. (2015). Emotion regulation flexibility. *Cognitive Therapy and Research*, 39(3), 263–278. This article takes a deep dive into the construct of emotion regulation flexibility, considering alternative definitions and analyzing the available research.

Gross, J. J. (2015). Emotion regulation: Current status and future prospects. *Psychological Inquiry*, 26(1), 1–26. This article offers an in-depth summary of the process model of emotion regulation, both summarizing prior studies and identifying important future directions for research.

Eldesouky, L., & Gross, J. J. (2019). Emotion regulation goals: An individual difference perspective. *Social and Personality Psychology Compass*, 13(9), e12493. Why do we regulate our emotions at all? This article, written for accessibility to an undergraduate audience, highlights the variety of reasons why we might (or might not) wish to regulate, and implications for the strategies we choose.

Goleman, D., & Davidson, R. J. (2017). *Altered traits: Science reveals how meditation changes your mind, brain, and body*. Avery. A critical analysis of mindfulness training and the research on its short- and long-term effects.

REFERENCES

Abbey, A. (1982). Sexual differences in attributions for friendly behavior: Do males misperceive females' friendliness? *Journal of Personality and Social Psychology, 42*, 830–838.

Abramov, I., Gordon, J., Hendrickson, A., Hainline, L., Dobson, V., & LaBossiere, E. (1982). The retina of the newborn human infant. *Science, 217*, 265–267.

Abramson, L., Marom, I., Petranker, R., & Aviezer, H. (2017). Is fear in your head? A comparison of instructed and real-life expressions of emotion in the face and body. *Emotion, 17*(3), 557–565. https://doi.org/10.1037/emo0000252

Abramson, L. Y., Seligman, M. E. P., & Teasdale, J. D. (1978). Learned helplessness in humans: Critique and reformulation. *Journal of Abnormal Psychology, 87*, 49–74.

Abu-Lughod, L. (1986). *Veiled sentiments.* University of California Press.

Acevedo, B. P., Aron, A., Fisher, H. E., & Brown, L. L. (2012). Neural correlates of long-term intense romantic love. *Social Cognitive and Affective Neuroscience, 7*, 145–159.

Acevedo, A. M., Herrera, C., Shenhav, S., Yim, I. S., & Campos, B. (2020). Measurement of a Latino cultural value: The Simpatía scale. *Cultural Diversity and Ethnic Minority Psychology, 26*(4), 419–425.

Acuff, S. F., Soltis, K. E., Dennhardt, A. A., Borsari, B., Martens, M. P., & Murphy, J. G. (2017). Future so bright? Delay discounting and consideration of future consequences predict academic performance among college drinkers. *Experimental and Clinical Psychopharmacology, 25*(5), 412–421.

Adamec, R. E., Stark-Adamec, C., & Livingston, K. E. (1980). The development of predatory aggression and defense in the domestic cat (*Felis catus*): 3. Effects on development of hunger between 180 and 365 days of age. *Behavioral and Neural Biology, 30*, 435–447.

Adams, R. B., & Kleck, R. E. (2005). Effects of direct and averted gaze on the perception of facially communicated emotion. *Emotion, 5*(1), 3–11.

Admiraal, W., Huizenga, J., Akkerman, S., & ten Dam, G. (2011). The concept of flow in collaborative game-based learning. *Computers in Human Behavior, 27*(3), 1185–1194. https://doi.org/10.1016/j.chb.2010.12.013

Admon, R., Lubin, G., Stern, O., Rosenberg, K., Sela, L., Ben-Ami, H., & Hendler, T. (2009). Human vulnerability to stress depends on amygdala's predisposition and hippocampal plasticity. *Proceedings of the National Academy of Sciences (U.S.A.), 106*, 14120–14125.

Adolph, K. E. (2000). Specificity of learning: Why infants fall over a veritable cliff. *Psychological Science, 11*, 290–295.

Adolphs, R., Denburg, N. L., & Tranel, D. (2001). The amygdala's role in long-term declarative memory for gist and detail. *Behavioral Neuroscience, 115*, 983–992.

Adolphs, R., Tranel, D., & Damasio, A. R. (1998). The human amygdala in social judgment. *Nature, 393*, 470–474.

Ainsworth, M. D. S. (1989). Attachments beyond infancy. *American Psychologist, 44*, 709–716.

Ainsworth, M. D. S., & Bell, S. M. (1970). Attachment, exploration, and separation: Illustrated by the behavior of one-year-olds in a strange situation. *Child Development, 41*(1), 49–67.

Ainsworth, M. D. S., Blehar, M. C., & Waters, E., & Wall, S. (1978). *Patterns of Attachment: A Psychological Study of the Strange Situation.* Erlbaum.

Akiskal, H. S., & Benazzi, F. (2005). Atypical depression: A variant of bipolar II or a bridge between unipolar and bipolar II? *Journal of Affective Disorders. Special Issue: Bipolar Depression: Focus on Phenomenology, 84*(2–3), 209–217.

Aknin, L. B., Barrington-Leigh, C. P., Dunn, E. W., Helliwell, J. F., Burns, J., Biswas-Diener, R., . . . & Norton, M. I. (2013). Prosocial spending and well-being: Cross-cultural evidence for a psychological universal. *Journal of Personality and Social Psychology, 104*, 635–652.

Aknin, L. B., Broesch, T., Hamlin, J. K., & Van de Vondervoort, J. W. (2015). Prosocial behavior leads to happiness in a small-scale rural society. *Journal of Experimental Psychology: General, 144*(4), 788–795.

Aknin, L. B., Hamlin, J. K., & Dunn, E. W. (2012). Giving leads to happiness in young children. *PLoS One, 7*(6), e39211. http://dx.doi.org/10.1371/journal.pone.0039211

Aldao, A., & Nolen-Hoeksema, S. (2013). One versus many: Capturing the use of multiple emotion regulation strategies in response to an emotion-eliciting stimulus. *Cognition and Emotion, 27*(4), 753–760.

Aldao, A., Nolen-Hoeksema, S., & Schweizer, S. (2010). Emotion-regulation strategies across psychopathology: A meta-analytic review. *Clinical Psychology Review, 30*(2), 217–237.

Aldao, A., Sheppes, G., & Gross, J. J. (2015). Emotion regulation flexibility. *Cognitive Therapy and Research, 39*(3), 263–278.

Algoe, S. B. (2012). Find, remind, and bind: The functions of gratitude in everyday relationships. *Social and Personality Psychology Compass, 6*(6), 455–469.

Algoe, S. B., Dwyer, P. C., Younge, A., & Oveis, C. (2020). A new perspective on the social functions of emotions: Gratitude and the witnessing effect. *Journal of Personality and Social Psychology, 119*(1), 40–74.

Algoe, S. B., Fredrickson, B. L., & Gable, S. L. (2013). The social functions of the emotion of gratitude via expression. *Emotion, 13*(4), 605–609.

Alloy, L. B., Abramson, L. Y., Whitehouse, W. G., Hogan, M. E., Tashman, N. A., Steinberg, D. L., . . . & Donovan, P. (1999). Depressogenic cognitive styles: Predictive validity, information processing and personality characteristics, and developmental origins. *Behaviour Research and Therapy, 37*, 503–531.

Almeida, D. M., & Horn, M. C. (2004). Is daily life more stressful during middle adulthood? In O. G. Brim, C. D. Ryff, & R. C. Kessler (Eds.), *How healthy are we? A national study of well-being at midlife* (pp. 425–451). University of Chicago Press.

Al-Shawaf, L., Conroy-Beam, D., Asao, K., & Buss, D. M. (2016). Human emotions: An evolutionary psychological perspective. *Emotion Review, 8*(2), 173–186.

Al-Shawaf, L., Lewis, D. M., & Buss, D. M. (2018). Sex differences in disgust: Why are women more easily disgusted than men? *Emotion Review, 10*(2), 149–160.

Amanatkar, H. R., Chibnall, J. T., Seo, B.-W., Manepalli, J. N., & Grossberg, G. T. (2014). Impact of exogenous testosterone on mood: A systematic review and meta-analysis of randomized placebo-controlled trials. *Annals of Clinical Psychiatry, 26*, 19–32.

Ambadar, Z., Schooler, J. W., & Cohn, J. F. (2005). Deciphering the enigmatic face. *Psychological Science, 16*, 403–410.

American Psychiatric Association. (2013). *Diagnostic and statistical manual of mental disorders, Fifth edition.* American Psychiatric Publishing.

Amodio, D. M., Devine, P. G., & Harmon-Jones, E. (2007). A dynamic model of guilt. *Psychological Science, 18*, 524–530.

Amodio, D. M., Shah, J. Y., Sigelman, J., Brazy, P. C., & Harmon-Jones, E. (2004). Implicit regulatory focus associated with asymmetrical frontal cortical activity. *Journal of Experimental Social Psychology, 40*(2), 225–232.

Anderson, C., Keltner, D., & John, O. P. (2003). Emotional convergence between people over time. *Journal of Personality and Social Psychology, 84*, 1054–1068.

Anderson, C. A. (2001). Heat and violence. *Current Directions in Psychological Science, 10*, 33–38.

Andrews, J., Li, M., Minihan, S., Songco, A., Fox, E., Ladouceur, C. D., . . . & Schweizer, S. (2021). The effect of intolerance of uncertainty on anxiety and depression, and their symptom networks, during the COVID-19 pandemic. https://doi.org/10.31234/osf.io/gtekh

Appleton, A. A., Loucks, E. B., Buka, S. L., & Kubzansky, L. D. (2014). Divergent associations of antecedent- and response-focused emotion regulation strategies with midlife cardiovascular disease risk. *Annals of Behavioral Medicine, 48*(2), 246–255.

Arana, G. W. (2000). An overview of side effects caused by typical antipsychotics. *Journal of Clinical Psychiatry, 61*(Suppl. 8), 5–11.

Armitage, C. J. (2016). Evidence that implementation intentions can overcome the effects of smoking habits. *Health Psychology*, *35*(9), 935–943.

Armor, D. A., Massey, C., & Sackett, A. M. (2008). Prescribed optimism: Is it right to be wrong about the future? *Psychological Science*, *19*, 329–331.

Armstrong, T., & Olatunji, B. O. (2012). Eye tracking of attention in the affective disorders: a meta-analytic review and synthesis. *Clinical Psychology Review*, *32*, 704–723.

Arnold, M. B. (1960). *Emotion and personality* (Vols. 1–2). Columbia University Press.

Arnsten, A. F. T. (2015). Stress weakens prefrontal networks: molecular insults to higher cognition. *Nature Neuroscience*, *18*, 1376–1385.

Aron, A., Melinat, E. Aron, E. N., Vallone, R. D., & Bator, R. J. (1997). The experimental generation of interpersonal closeness: A procedure and some preliminary findings. *Personality and Social Psychology Bulletin*, *23*, 363–377.

Aron, A., Norman, C. C., Aron, E. N., McKenna, C., & Heyman, R. E. (2000). Couples' shared participation in novel and arousing activities and experienced relationship quality. *Journal of Personality and Social Psychology*, *78*, 273–284.

Aron, A., Paris, M., & Aron, E. N. (1995). Falling in love: Prospective studies of self-concept change. *Journal of Personality and Social Psychology*, *69*, 1102–1112.

Arránz Becker, O. (2012). Effects of similarity of life goals, values, and personality on relationship satisfaction and stability: Findings from a two-wave panel study. *Personal Relationships*, *20*(3), 443–461.

Arrindell, W. A., Pickersgill, M. J., Merckelbach, H., Ardon, A. M., & Cornet, F. C. (1991). Phobic dimensions: III. Factor analytic approaches to the study of common phobic fears; an updated review of findings obtained with adult subjects. *Advances in Behaviour Research and Therapy*, *13*(2), 73–130.

Asarnow, L. D., Soehner, A. M., & Harvey, A. G. (2014). Basic sleep and circadian science as building blocks for behavioral interventions: A translational approach for mood disorders. *Behavioral Neuroscience*, *128*, 360–370.

Ashok, A. H., Mizuno, Y., Volkow, N. D., & Howes, O. D. (2017). Association of stimulant use with dopaminergic alterations in users of cocaine, amphetamine, or methamphetamine: A systematic review and meta-analysis. *JAMA Psychiatry*, *74*(5), 511–519.

Askew, C., Dunne, G., Özdil, Z., Reynolds, G., & Field, A. P. (2013). Stimulus fear-relevance and the vicarious learning pathway to childhood fears. *Emotion*, *13*(5), 915–925.

Asmundson, G. J., Fetzner, M. G., DeBoer, L. B., Powers, M. B., Otto, M. W., & Smits, J. A. (2013). Let's get physical: a contemporary review of the anxiolytic effects of exercise for anxiety and its disorders. *Depression and Anxiety*, *30*(4), 362–373.

Atkinson, J. W. (Ed.). (1958). *Motives in fantasy, action, and society: A method of assessment and study.* Van Nostrand.

Attuquayefio, T., Stevenson, R. J., Boakes, R. A., Oaten, M. J., Yeomans, M. R., Mahmut, M., & Francis, H. M. (2016). A high-fat high-sugar diet predicts poorer hippocampal-related memory and a reduced ability to suppress wanting under satiety. *Journal of Experimental Psychology: Animal Learning and Cognition*, *42*(4), 415–428.

Austin, E. J. (2004). An investigation of the relationship between trait emotional intelligence and emotional task performance. *Personality and Individual Differences*, *36*, 1855–1864.

Austin, E. J., Saklofske, D. H., Huang, S. H. S., & McKenney, D. (2004). Measurement of trait emotional intelligence: Testing and cross-validating a modified version of Schutte et al.'s measure. *Personality and Individual Differences*, *36*, 555–562.

Averill, J. R. (2012). The future of social constructionism: Introduction to a special section of Emotion Review. *Emotion Review*, *4*(3), 215–220.

Aviezer, H., Hassin, R. R., Ryan, J., Grady, C., Susskind, J., Anderson, A., . . . & Bentin, S. (2008). Angry, disgusted, or afraid? Studies on the malleability of emotion perception. *Psychological Science*, *19*(7), 724–732.

Aviezer, H., Trope, Y., & Todorov, A. (2012). Body cues, not facial expressions, discriminate between intense positive and negative emotions. *Science*, *338*(6111), 1225–1229.

Avinun, R., Ebstein, R. P., & Knafo, A. (2012). Human maternal behavior is associated with arginine vasopressin receptor 1A gene. *Biology Letters*, *8*, 894–896.

Ayduk, Ö., & Kross, E. (2010). From a distance: implications of spontaneous self-distancing for adaptive self-reflection. *Journal of Personality and Social Psychology*, *98*(5), 809–829.

Ayduk, O., Mischel, W., & Downey, G. (2002). Attentional mechanisms linking rejection to hostile reactivity: The role of "hot" versus "cool" focus. *Psychological Science*, *13*, 443–448.

Bäccman, C., Folkesson, P., & Norlander, T. (1999). Expectations of romantic relationships: A comparison between homosexual and heterosexual men with regard to Baxter's criteria. *Social Behavior and Personality*, *27*, 363–374.

Badman, M. K., & Flier, J. S. (2005). The gut and energy balance: visceral allies in the obesity wars. *Science, 307*(5717), 1909–1914.

Badour, C. L., Blonigen, D. M., Boden, M. T., Feldner, M. T., & Bonn-Miller, M. O. (2012). A longitudinal test of the bi-directional relations between avoidance coping and PTSD severity during and after PTSD treatment. *Behaviour research and therapy, 50*(10), 610–616.

Bagwell, C. L., Newcomb, A. F., & Bukowski, W. M. (1998). Preadolescent friendship and peer rejection as predictors of adult adjustment. *Child Development, 69*, 140–153.

Bai, Y., Maruskin, L. A., Chen, S., Gordon, A. M., Stellar, J. E., McNeil, G. D., . . . & Keltner, D. (2017). Awe, the diminished self, and collective engagement: Universals and cultural variations in the small self. *Journal of Personality and Social Psychology, 113*(2), 185–209.

Bailen, N. H., Green, L. M., & Thompson, R. J. (2019). Understanding emotion in adolescents: A review of emotional frequency, intensity, instability, and clarity. *Emotion Review, 11*(1), 63–73.

Balthazart, J., & Ball, G. F. (2007). Topography in the preoptic region: Differential regulation of appetitive and consummatory male sexual behaviors. *Frontiers in Neuroendocrinology, 28*(4), 161–178.

Bandura, A. (1990). Conclusion: Reflections on nonability determinants of competence. In R. J. Sternberg & J. Kolligan Jr. (Eds.), *Competence considered* (pp. 315–362). Yale University Press.

Bandura, A., & Cervone, D. (1983). Self-evaluative and self-efficacy mechanisms governing the motivational effects of goal systems. *Journal of Personality and Social Psychology, 45*(5), 1017–1028.

Barazzone, N., & Davey, G. C. L. (2009). Anger potentiates the reporting of threatening interpretations: An experimental study. *Journal of Anxiety Disorders, 23*, 489–495.

Bargh, J. A., Gollwitzer, P. M., & Oettingen, G. (2010). Motivation. In S. T. Fiske, D. T. Gilbert, & G. Lindzey (Eds.), Handbook of social psychology (pp. 268–316). Wiley.

Bar-Haim, Y., Lamy, D., Pergamin, L., Bakermans-Kranenburg, M. J., & Van Ijzendoorn, M. H. (2007). Threat-related attentional bias in anxious and non-anxious individuals: A meta-analytic study. *Psychological Bulletin, 133*(1), 1–24.

Barlow, D. H., Curreri, A. J., & Woodard, L. S. (2021). Neuroticism and disorders of emotion: A new synthesis. *Current Directions in Psychological Science, 30*(5), 410–417.

Barlow, M. A., Wrosch, C., & McGrath, J. J. (2020). Goal adjustment capacities and quality of life: A meta-analytic review. *Journal of Personality, 88*(2), 307–323. https://doi.org/10.1111/jopy.12492

Baron-Cohen, S. (1995). The eye direction detector (EDD) and the shared attention mechanism (SAM): Two cases for evolutionary psychology. In C. Moore, & P. J. Dunham (Eds.), *Joint Attention: Its Origins and Role in Development* (pp. 41–59). Erlbaum.

Baron-Cohen, S., Golan, O., Wheelwright, S., & Granader, Y. (2010). Emotion word comprehension from 4 to 16 years old: A developmental survey. *Frontiers in Evolutionary Neuroscience, 2*, 109.

Barr, C. S., Schwandt, M. L., Lindell, S. G., Higley, J. D., Maestripieri, D., Goldman, D., Suomi, S. J., & Heilig, M. (2008). Variation at the mu-opioid receptor gene (OPRM1) influences attachment behavior in infant primates. *Proceedings of the National Academy of Sciences of the United States of America, 105*(13), 5277–5281.

Barrett, L. F. (2006). Solving the emotion paradox: Categorization and the experience of emotion. *Personality and Social Psychology Review, 10*(1), 20–46.

Barrett, L. F. (2017). *How Emotions are Made: The Secret Life of the Brain*. Houghton Mifflin Harcourt.

Barrett, L. F., Bliss-Moreau, E., Duncan, S. L., Rauch, S. L., & Wright, C. I. (2007). The amygdala and the experience of affect. *Social Cognitive & Affective Neuroscience, 2*, 73–83.

Barrett, L. F., & Fossum, T. (2001). Mental representations of affect knowledge. *Cognition and Emotion, 15*(3), 333–363.

Bartels, A., & Zeki, S. (2000). The neural basis of romantic love. *Neuroreport, 11*, 3829–3834.

Bartholomew, K. (1990). Avoidance of intimacy: An attachment perspective. *Journal of Social and Personal Relationships, 7*, 147–178.

Bartholomew, K., & Horowitz, L. M. (1991). Attachment styles among young adults: A test of a four-category model. *Journal of Personality and Social Psychology, 61*, 226–244.

Bartz, J., Simeon, D., Hamilton, H., Kim, S., Crystal, S., Braun, A., . . . & Hollander, E. (2011). Oxytocin can hinder trust and cooperation in borderline personality disorder. *Social Cognitive and Affective Neuroscience, 6*(5), 556–563.

Basabe, N., Paez, D., Valencia, J., Gonzalez, J. L., Rimé, B., & Diener, E. (2002). Cultural dimensions, socio-economic development, climate, and emotional hedonic level. *Cognition and Emotion, 16*, 103–125.

Bauby, J.D. (1997). *The diving bell and the butterfly*. Translated by J. Leggatt. Knopf.

Baumeister, R. F. (2014). Self-regulation, ego depletion, and inhibition. *Neuropsychologia, 65*, 313–319.

Baumeister, R. F., Bratslavsky, E., Muraven, M., & Tice, D. M. (1998). Personality processes and individual differences. *Journal of Personality and Social Psychology, 74*(5), 1252–1265.

Baumeister, R. F., Heatherton, T. F., & Tice, D. M. (1994). *Losing control: How and why people fail at self-regulation.* Academic Press.

Baumeister, R. F., & Leary, M. R. (1995). The need to belong: Desire for interpersonal attachments as a fundamental human motivation. *Psychological Bulletin, 117*(3), 497–529.

Baumeister, R. F., & Vohs, K. D. (2016). Strength model of self-regulation as limited resource: Assessment, controversies, update. In J. M. Olson & M. P. Zanna (Eds.), *Advances in experimental social psychology* (pp. 67–127). Elsevier Academic Press.

Baumeister, R. F., Vohs, K. D., & Tice, D. M. (2007). The strength model of self-control. *Current Directions in Psychological Science, 16*(6), 351–355.

Bavelier, D., Green, C. S., Han, D. H., Renshaw, P. F., Merzenich, M. M., & Gentile, D. A. (2011). Brains on video games. *Nature Reviews Neuroscience, 12*(12), 763–768.

Beall, A. T., & Tracy, J. L. (2017). Emotivational psychology: How distinct emotions facilitate fundamental motives. *Social and Personality Psychology Compass, 11*(2), e12303. https://doi.org/10.1111/spc3.12303

Beaton, E. A., Schmidt, L. A., Schulkin, J., Antony, M. M., Swinson, R. P., & Hall, G. B. (2008). Different neural responses to stranger and personally familiar faces in shy and bold adults. *Behavioral Neuroscience, 122*, 704–709.

Beauregard, M., Lévesque, J., & Bourgouin, P. (2001). Neural correlates of conscious self-regulation of emotion. *Journal of Neuroscience, 21*, RC165.

Becchetti, L., Castriota, S., & Giachin, E. (2011). *Beyond the Joneses: Inter-country income comparisons and happiness. Society for the Study of Economic Inequality.* Working Paper 189. http://www.ecineq.org/milano/WP/ECINEQ2011-189.pdf

Bechara, A. (2004). The role of emotion in decision-making: Evidence from neurological patients with orbitofrontal damage. *Brain and Cognition, 55*, 30–40.

Bechara, A., Damasio, H., Damasio, A. R., & Lee, G. P. (1999). Different contributions of the human amygdala and ventromedial prefrontal cortex to decision-making. *Journal of Neuroscience, 19*, 5473–5481.

Bechara, A., Tranel, D., Damasio, H., & Adolphs, R. (1995). Double dissociation of conditioning and declarative knowledge relative to the amygdala and hippocampus in humans. *Science, 269*(5227), 1115–1118.

Beck, A. T. (1973). *The diagnosis and management of depression.* University of Pennsylvania Press.

Beck, A. T. (1987). Cognitive models of depression. *Journal of Cognitive Psychotherapy, 1*, 5–37.

Beck, A. T., Steer, R. A., & Carbin, M. G. (1988). Psychometric properties of the Beck depression inventory: Twenty-five years of evaluation. *Clinical Psychology Review, 8*(1), 77–100.

Behnke, M., Kreibig, S. D., Kaczmarek, L. D., Assink, M., & Gross, J. J. (2022). Autonomic nervous system activity during positive emotions: A meta-analytic review. *Emotion Review*, 17540739211073084. https://doi.org/10.1111/spc3.12303

Beltzer, M. L., Nock, M. K., Peters, B. J., & Jamieson, J. P. (2014). Rethinking butterflies: The affective, physiological, and performance effects of reappraising arousal during social evaluation. *Emotion, 14*(4), 761–768.

Bennett, C. M., Baird, A. A., Miller, M. B., & Wolford, G. L. (2010). Neural correlates of interspecies perspective taking in the post-mortem atlantic salmon: An argument for proper multiple comparisons correction. *Journal of Serendipitous and Unexpected Results, 1*(1), 1–5.

Berdoy, M., Webster, J. P., & Macdonald, D. W. (2000). Fatal attraction in rats infected with *Toxoplasma gondii. Proceedings of the Royal Society of London,* B, *267*, 1591–1594.

Berking, M., Wirtz, C. M., Svaldi, J., & Hofmann, S. G. (2014). Emotion regulation predicts symptoms of depression over five years. *Behaviour Research and Therapy, 57*, 13–20.

Berkowitz, L. (1990). On the formation and regulation of anger and aggression: A cognitive neo-associationistic analysis. *American Psychologist, 45*, 494–503.

Berkowitz, L., Cochran, S., & Embree, M. (1981). Physical pain and the goal of aversively stimulated aggression. *Journal of Personality and Social Psychology, 40*, 687–700.

Berkowitz, L., & Harmon-Jones, E. (2004). Toward an understanding of the determinants of anger. *Emotion, 4*, 107–130.

Berman, M., Gladue, B., & Taylor, S. (1993). The effects of hormones, Type A behavior pattern, and provocation on aggression in men. *Motivation and Emotion, 17*, 125–138.

Bernard, L. L. (1924). *Instinct: A study in social psychology.* Henry Holt.

Berntsen, D., Johannessen, K. B., Thomsen, Y. D., Bertelsen, M., Hoyle, R. H., & Rubin, D. C. (2012). Peace and war: Trajectories of posttraumatic stress disorder symptoms before, during, and after military deployment in Afghanistan. *Psychological Science, 23*(12), 1557–1565.

Berntsen, D., & Rubin, D. C. (2015). Pretraumatic stress reactions in soldiers deployed to Afghanistan. *Clinical Psychological Science, 3*, 663–674.

Berntson, G. G., Bechara, A., Damasio, H., Tranel, D., & Cacioppo, J. T. (2007). Amygdala contribution to selective dimensions of emotion. *Social Cognitive & Affective Neuroscience, 2*, 123–129.

Berridge, K. C., & Kringelbach, M. L. (2013). Neuroscience of affect: Brain mechanisms of pleasure and displeasure. *Current Opinion in Neurobiology, 23*(3), 294–303.

Bhatnagar, N., & McKay-Nesbitt, J. (2016). Pro-environment advertising messages: The role of regulatory focus. *International Journal of Advertising, 35*(1), 4–22.

Bhattacharyya, M. R., Whitehead, D. L., Rakhit, R., & Steptoe, A. (2008). Depressed mood, positive affect, and heart rate variability in patients with suspected coronary artery disease. *Psychosomatic Medicine, 70*(9), 1020–1027.

Biben, M. (1979). Predation and predatory play behaviour of domestic cats. *Animal Behaviour, 27*, 81–94.

Bieleke, M., Keller, L., & Gollwitzer, P. M. (2020). If-then planning. *European Review of Social Psychology, 32*(1), 1–35.

Bigelow, A. E., & Power, M. (2014). Effects of maternal responsiveness on infant responsiveness and behavior in the still-face task. *Infancy, 19*, 558–584.

Birditt, K. S., & Fingerman, K. L. (2003). Age and gender differences in adults' descriptions of emotional reactions to interpersonal problems. *Journal of Gerontology: Psychological Sciences, 58B*, P.237–P.245.

Birdwhistell, R. L. (1970). Masculinity and femininity as display. In *Kinesics and context: Essays on body motion* (pp. 39–46). University of Pennsylvania Press.

Birnbaum, M. H. (1999). Testing critical properties of decision making on the Internet. *Psychological Science, 10*, 399–407.

Bjork, J. M., & Pardini, D. A. (2015). Who are those "risk-taking" adolescents? Individual differences in developmental neuroimaging research. *Developmental Cognitive Neuroscience, 11*, 56–64.

Black, D. W. (2015). The natural history of antisocial personality disorder. *Canadian Journal of Psychiatry, 60*, 309–314.

Blackford, J. U., & Walden, T. A. (1998). Individual differences in social referencing. *Infant Behavior and Development, 21*(1), 89–102.

Blair, R. J. R., Mitchell, D. G. V., Peschardt, K. S., Colledge, E., Leonard, R. A., Shine, J. H. . . . & Perrett, D. I. (2004). Reduced sensitivity to others' fearful expressions in psychopathic individuals. *Personality and Individual Differences, 37*, 1111–1122.

Blaiss, C. A., & Janak, P. H. (2009). The nucleus accumbens core and shell are critical for the expression, but not the consolidation, of Pavlovian conditioned approach. *Behavioral Brain Research, 200*, 22–32.

Blanchard-Fields, F., & Coats, A. H. (2008). The experience of anger and sadness in everyday problems impacts age differences in emotion regulation. *Developmental Psychology, 44*, 1547–1556.

Blass, T. (2009). From New Haven to Santa Clara: A historical perspective on the Milgram obedience experiments. *American Psychologist, 64*(1), 37–45.

Bless, H., Bohner, G., Schwarz, N., & Strack, F. (1990). Mood and persuasion: A cognitive response analysis. *Personality and Social Psychology Bulletin, 16*, 331–345.

Bless, H., Clore, G. L., Schwarz, N., Golisane, V., Rabe, C., & Wölk, M. (1996). Mood and the use of scripts: Does a happy mood really lead to mindlessness? *Journal of Personality and Social Psychology, 71*, 665–679.

Bliss-Moreau, E. (2017). Constructing nonhuman animal emotion. *Current Opinion in Psychology, 17*, 184–188.

Bloch, L., Haase, C. M., & Levenson, R. W. (2014). Emotion regulation predicts marital satisfaction: More than a wives' tale. *Emotion, 14*(1), 130–144.

Blood, A. J., & Zatorre, R. J. (2001). Intensely pleasurable responses to music correlate with activity in brain regions implicated in reward and emotion. *Proceedings of the National Academy of Sciences, 98*, 11818–11823.

Bodenhausen, G. V., Kramer, G. P., & Süsser, K. (1994). Happiness and stereotypic thinking in social judgment. *Journal of Personality and Social Psychology, 66*, 621–632.

Bodenhausen, G. V., Sheppard, L. A., & Kramer, G. P. (1994). Negative affect and social judgment: The differential impact of anger and sadness. *European Journal of Social Psychology, 24*(1), 45–62.

Boehm, J. K., & Kubzansky, L. D. (2012). The heart's content: the association between positive psychological well-being and cardiovascular health. *Psychological Bulletin, 138*(4), 655–691.

Boiger, M., & Mesquita, B. (2012). The construction of emotion in interactions, relationships, and cultures. *Emotion Review, 4*(3), 221–229.

Bolles, R. C. (1970). Species-specific defense reactions and avoidance learning. *Psychological Review, 77*, 32–48.

Bolte, A., Goschke, T., & Kuhl, J. (2003). Emotion and intuition: Effects of positive and negative mood on implicit judgments of semantic coherence. *Psychological Science, 14*, 416–421.

Bond, M. H. (2002). Reclaiming the individual from Hofstede's ecological analysis—A 20-year odyssey: Comment on Oyserman et al. (2002). *Psychological Bulletin, 128*, 73–77.

Bondolfi, G., Mazzola, V., & Arciero, G. (2015). In between ordinary sadness and clinical depression. *Emotion Review, 7*, 216–222.

Bongard, S., & Al'Absi, M. (2003). Domain-specific anger expression assessment and blood pressure during rest and acute stress. *Personality and Individual Differences, 34*(8), 1383–1402.

Border, R., Johnson, E. C., Evans, L. M., Smolen, A., Berley, N., Sullivan, P. F., & Keller, M. C. (2019). No support for historical candidate gene or candidate gene-by-interaction hypotheses for major depression across multiple large samples. *American Journal of Psychiatry, 176*(5), 376–387.

Borgella, A. M., Howard, S., & Maddox, K. B. (2020). Cracking wise to break the ice: The potential for racial humor to ease interracial anxiety. *Humor, 33*(1), 105–135.

Bornstein, R. F., Leone, D. R., & Galley, D. J. (1987). The generalizability of subliminal mere exposure effects: Influence of stimuli perceived without awareness on social behavior. *Journal of Personality and Social Psychology, 53*(6), 1070–1079.

Bornstein, M. H., Putnick, D. L., Rigo, P., Esposito, G., Swain, J. E., Suwalsky, J. T., . . . & Venuti, P. (2017). Neurobiology of culturally common maternal responses to infant cry. *Proceedings of the National Academy of Sciences, 114*(45), E9465–E9473.

Boucher, J. D. (1979). Culture and emotion. In A. J. Marsella, R. G. Tharp, & T. V. Ciborowski (Eds.), *Perspectives on cross-cultural psychology* (pp. 159–178). Academic Press.

Boucher, O., Rouleau, I., Lassonde, M., Lepore, F., Bouthillier, A., & Nguyen, D. K. (2015). Social information processing following resection of the insular cortex. *Neuropsychologia, 71*, 1–10.

Bould, E., Morris, N., & Wink, B. (2008). Recognizing subtle emotional expressions: The role of facial movements. *Cognition and Emotion, 22*, 1569–1587.

Bountress, K. E., Cusack, S. E., Sheerin, C. M., Hawn, S., Dick, D. M., Kendler, K. S., & Amstadter, A. B. (2019). Alcohol consumption, interpersonal trauma, and drinking to cope with trauma-related distress: An auto-regressive, cross-lagged model. *Psychology of Addictive Behaviors, 33*(3), 221–231.

Bouton, M. E., Mineka, S., & Barlow, D. H. (2001). A modern learning theory perspective on the etiology of panic disorder. *Psychological Review, 108*, 4–32.

Bowlby, J. (1969). *Attachment and loss: Vol. 1: Attachment.* Basic Books.

Bowlby, J. (1979). *The making and breaking of affectional bonds.* Tavistock Publications.

Bowlby, J. (1980). *Attachment and loss: Vol. 3: Loss: Sadness and depression.* Basic Books.

Boxer, C. F., Noonan, M. C., & Whelan, C. B. (2015). Measuring mate preferences: A replication and extension. *Journal of Family Issues, 36*(2), 163–187.

Boyce, C. J., Brown, G. D. A., & Moore, S. C. (2010). Money and happiness: Rank of income, not income, affects life satisfaction. *Psychological Science, 21*, 471–475.

Boyle, R. H. (1992, September—October). The joy of cooking insects. *Audubon, 94*, 100–103.

Bracha, H. S. (2004). Freeze, flight, fight, fright, faint: Adaptationist perspectives on the acute stress response spectrum. *CNS Spectrums, 9*(9), 679–685.

Bradley, M. M. (2009). Natural selective attention: Orienting and emotion. *Psychophysiology, 46*(1), 1–11.

Bradley, M. M., Greenwald, M. K., Petry, M. C., & Lang, P. J. (1992). Remembering pictures: Pleasure and arousal in memory. *Journal of Experimental Psychology: Learning, Memory, and Cognition, 18*, 379–390.

Bradley, M. M., & Lang, O. J. (2000). Measuring emotion: Behavior, feeling, and physiology. In R. D. Lane & L. Nadel (Eds.), *Cognitive neuroscience of emotion* (pp. 242–276). Oxford University Press.

Bradshaw, J. W. S., & Cook, S. E. (1996). Patterns of pet cat behaviour at feeding occasions. *Applied Animal Behaviour Science, 47*(1–2), 61–74.

Breiter, H. C., Aharon, I., Kahneman, D., Dale, A., & Shizgal, P. (2001). Functional imaging of neural responses to expectancy and experience of monetary gains and losses. *Neuron, 30*, 619–639.

Breiter, H. C., Etcoff, N. L., Whalen, P. J., Kennedy, W. A., Rauch, S. L., & Buckner, R. L. . . . & Rosen, B. R. (1996). Response and habituation of the human amygdala during visual processing of facial expression. *Neuron, 17*, 875–887.

Brennan, K. A., Clark, C. L., & Shaver, P. R. (1998). Self-report measurement of adult attachment: An integrative overview. In J. A. Simpson & W. S. Rholes (Eds.), *Attachment theory and close relationships* (pp. 46–76). Guilford Press.

Brescoll, V. L., & Uhlmann, E. L. (2008). Can an angry woman get ahead? Status conferral, gender, and expression of emotion in the workplace. *Psychological Science, 19*(3), 268–275.

Bretherton, I. (1992). The origins of attachment theory: John Bowlby and Mary Ainsworth. *Developmental Psychology, 28*, 759–775.

Bretherton, I., Fritz, J., Zahn-Waxler, C., & Ridgeway, D. (1986). Learning to talk about emotions: A functionalist perspective. *Child Development, 57*, 529–548.

Brez, C., Hampton, E. M., Behrendt, L., Brown, L., & Powers, J. (2020). Failure to replicate: Testing a growth mindset intervention for college student success. *Basic and Applied Social Psychology, 42*(6), 460–468.

Bridgman, T., Cummings, S., & Ballard, J. (2019). Who built Maslow's pyramid? A history of the creation of management studies' most famous symbol and its implications for management education. *Academy of Management Learning & Education, 18*(1), 81–98.

Britton, J. C., Lissek, S., Grillon, C., Norcross, M. A., & Pine, D. S. (2011). Development of anxiety: the role of threat appraisal and fear learning. *Depression and anxiety, 28*(1), 5–17.

Brody, L. R., & Hall, J. A. (2008). Gender and Emotion in Context. In Lewis, M., Haviland-Jones, J. M., & Barrett, L. F. (Eds.) *Handbook of Emotions, 3rd edition* (pp. 395–408). Guilford.

Brooks, A. W. (2014). Get excited: Reappraising pre-performance anxiety as excitement. *Journal of Experimental Psychology: General, 143*, 1144–1158.

Brown, C. L., Van Doren, N., Ford, B. Q., Mauss, I. B., Sze, J. W., & Levenson, R. W. (2020). Coherence between subjective experience and physiology in emotion: Individual differences and implications for well-being. *Emotion, 20*(5), 818–829.

Brown, G. L., Craig, A. B., & Halberstadt, A. G. (2015). Parent gender differences in emotion socialization behaviors vary by ethnicity and child gender. *Parenting, 15*(3), 135–157.

Brown, G. P., MacLeod, A. K., Tata, P., & Goddard, L. (2002). Worry and the simulation of future outcomes. *Anxiety, Stress and Coping, 15*, 1–17.

Brown, S. S. (2014). *Native self-actualization: Transformation beyond greed.* BookPatch.

Bruce, S. E., Machan, J. T., Dyck, I., & Keller, M. B. (2001). Infrequency of "pure" GAD: Impact of psychiatric comorbidity on clinical course. *Depression and Anxiety, 14*, 219–225.

Brumfiel, G. (2013). Fallout of fear. *Nature, 493*, 291–293.

Bryant, R. A., Creamer, M., O'Donnell, M., Silove, D., McFarlane, A. C., & Forbes, D. (2015). A comparison of *DSM-IV* and *DSM-5* acute stress disorder definitions to predict posttraumatic stress disorder and related disorders. *Journal of Clinical Psychiatry, 76*, 391–397.

Büchel, C., Morris, J., Dolan, R. J., & Friston, K. J. (1998). Brain systems mediating aversive conditioning: An event-related fMRI study. *Neuron, 20*, 947–957.

Buck, R. W. (2012). Prime elements of subjectively experienced feelings and desires: Imaging the emotional cocktail. *Behavioral and Brain Sciences, 35*, 144.

Buehler, R., Griffin, D., & Ross, M. (1994). Exploring the "planning fallacy": Why people underestimate their task completion times. *Journal of Personality and Social Psychology, 67*, 366–381.

Buhle, J. T., Silvers, J. A., Wager, T. D., Lopez, R., Onyemekwu, C., Kober, H., . . . & Ochsner, K. N. (2014). Cognitive reappraisal of emotion: a meta-analysis of human neuroimaging studies. *Cerebral Cortex, 24*(11), 2981–2990.

Bühler, J. L., Krauss, S., & Orth, U. (2021). Development of relationship satisfaction across the life span: A systematic review and meta-analysis. *Psychological Bulletin, 147*(10), 1012–1053.

Bulbena, A., Gago, J., Martin-Santos, R., Porta, M., Dasquens, J., & Berrios, G. E. (2004). Anxiety disorder & joint laxity: A definitive link. *Neurology, Psychiatry and Brain Research, 11*, 137–140.

Bulbena, A., Gago, J., Pailhez, G., Sperry, L., Fullana, M. A., & Vilarroya, O. (2011). Joint hypermobility syndrome is a risk factor trait for anxiety disorders: a 15-year follow-up cohort study. *General Hospital Psychiatry, 33*(4), 363–370.

Burgess, K. B., Marshall, P. J., Rubin, K. H., & Fox, N. A. (2003). Infant attachment and temperament as predictors of subsequent externalizing problems and cardiac physiology. *Journal of Child Psychology and Psychiatry, 44*, 819–831.

Burke, K. C., Burke, J. D., Jr., Regier, D. A., & Rae, D. S. (1990). Age at onset of selected mental disorders in five community populations. *Archives of General Psychiatry, 47*, 511–518.

Burns, M. O., & Seligman, M. E. P. (1989). Explanatory style across the life span: Evidence for stability over 50 years. *Journal of Personality and Social Psychology, 56*, 471–477.

Burnstein, E., Crandall, C., & Kitayama, S. (1994). Some neo-darwinian decision rules for altruism: Weighing cues for inclusive fitness as a function of the biological importance of the decision. *Journal of Personality and Social Psychology, 67*(5), 773–789.

Burton, D. and Naylor, S. (2002). The Jekyll/Hyde nature of goals: Revisiting and updating goal setting research. In T. Horn (Ed.), *Advances in sport psychology* (pp. 459–499). Human Kinetics.

Buss, D. M. (1989). Sex differences in human mate preferences: Evolutionary hypotheses tested in 37 cultures. *Behavioral and Brain Sciences, 12*, 1–49.

Buss, D. M. (2000). The evolution of happiness. *American Psychologist, 55*, 15–23.

Buss, D. M., Haselton, M. G., Shackelford, T. K., Bleske, A. L., & Wakefield, J. C. (1998). Adaptations, exaptations, and spandrels. *American Psychologist, 53*(5), 533–548.

Butcher, J. N., Graham, J. R., Ben-Porath, Y. S., Tellegen, A., & Dahlstrom, W. G. (2003). *MMPI-2: Minnesota Multiphasic Personality Inventory-2*. University of Minnesota Press.

Butler, E. A., Egloff, B., Wilhelm, F. H., Smith, N. C., Erickson, E. A., & Gross, J. J. (2003). The social consequences of expressive suppression. *Emotion, 3*(1), 48–67.

Butler, E. A., Lee, T. L., & Gross, J. J. (2007). Emotion regulation and culture: Are the social consequences of emotion suppression culture-specific? *Emotion, 7*(1), 30–48.

Butler, E. A., Wilhelm, F. H., & Gross, J. J. (2006). Respiratory sinus arrhythmia, emotion, and emotion regulation during social interaction. *Psychophysiology, 43*(6), 612–622.

Buunk, B. P., & Van Yperen, N. W. (1991). Referential comparisons, relational comparisons, and exchange orientation: Their relation to marital satisfaction. *Personality and Social Psychology Bulletin, 17*, 709–717.

Bylsma, L. M., Croon, M. A., Vingerhoets, A. J. J. M., & Rottenberg, J. (2011). When and for whom does crying improve mood? A daily diary study of 1004 crying episodes. *Journal of Research in Personality, 45*, 385–392.

Bylsma, L. M., Vingerhoets, A. J. J. M., & Rottenberg, J. (2008). When is crying cathartic? an international study. *Journal of Social & Clinical Psychology, 27*(10), 1165–1187.

Cacioppo, J. T., Berntson, G. G., Larsen, J. T., Pohlmann, K. M., & Ito, T. A. (2000). The psychophysiology of emotion. In M. Lewis & J. M. Haviland-Jones (Eds.), *Handbook of Emotions, Second Edition* (pp. 173–191). Guilford Press.

Cacioppo, J. T., Gardner, W. L., & Berntson, G. G. (1997). Beyond bipolar conceptualizations and measures: The case of attitudes and evaluative space. *Personality and Social Psychology Review, 1*(1), 3–25.

Cahill, L., & McGaugh, J. L. (1998). Mechanisms of emotional arousal and lasting declarative memory. *Trends in Neurosciences, 21*, 294–299.

Cahill, L., Prins, B., Weber, M., & McGaugh, J. L. (1994). β-Adrenergic activation and memory for emotional events. *Nature, 371*, 702–704.

Calvo, M. G., & Avero, P. (2005). Time course of attentional bias to emotional scenes in anxiety: Gaze direction and duration. *Cognition and Emotion, 19*, 433–451.

Camacho-Morles, J., Slemp, G. R., Pekrun, R., Loderer, K., Hou, H., & Oades, L. G. (2021). Activity achievement emotions and academic performance: A meta-analysis. *Educational Psychology Review, 33*(3), 1051–1095.

Cameron, C. D., Hutcherson, C. A., Ferguson, A. M., Scheffer, J. A., Hadjiandreou, E., & Inzlicht, M. (2019). Empathy is hard work: People choose to avoid empathy because of its cognitive costs. *Journal of Experimental Psychology: General, 148*(6), 962–976.

Cameron, L. D., & Overall, N. C. (2018). Suppression and expression as distinct emotion-regulation processes in daily interactions: Longitudinal and meta-analyses. *Emotion, 18*(4), 465–480.

Campbell, B. A., Wood, G., & McBride, T. (1997). Origins of orienting and defensive responses: An evolutionary perspective. In P. J. Lang, R. F. Simons, & M. T. Balaban (Eds.), Attention and orienting: Sensory and motivational processes (pp. 41–67). Erlbaum.

Campbell, D. T. (1983). Two distinct routes beyond kin selection to ultrasociality: Implications for the humanities and social sciences. In D. Bridgeman (Ed.), *The Nature of Prosocial Development: Theories and Strategies* (pp. 11–39). Academic Press.

Campbell, M. L., Gorka, S. M., McGowan, S. K., Nelson, B. D., Sarapas, C., Katz, A. C., . . . & Shankman, S. A. (2014). Does anxiety sensitivity correlate with startle habituation? An examination in two independent samples. *Cognition and Emotion, 28*, 46–58.

Campos, B., Shiota, M. N., Keltner, D., Gonzaga, G. C., & Goetz, J. L. (2013). What is shared, what is different? Core relational themes and expressive displays of eight positive emotions. *Cognition & Emotion, 27*(1), 37–52.

Campos, J. J., Bertenthal, B. I., & Kermoian, R. (1992). Early experience and emotional development: The emergence of wariness of heights. *Psychological Science, 3,* 61–64.

Camras, L. A., Oster, H., Bakeman, R., Meng, Z. L., Ujiie, T., & Campos, J. J. (2007). Do infants show distinct negative facial expressions for fear and anger? Emotional expression in 11-month-old European American, Chinese, and Japanese infants. *Infancy, 11,* 131–155.

Camras, L. A., & Shutter, J. M. (2010). Emotional facial expressions in infancy. *Emotion Review, 2,* 120–129.

Canli, T., Sivers, H., Whitfield, S. L., Gotlib, I. H., & Gabrieli, J. D. E. (2002). Amygdala response to happy faces as a function of extraversion. *Science, 296,* 2191.

Canli, T., Zhao, Z., Brewer, J., Gabrieli, J. D. E., & Cahill, L. (2000). Event-related activation in the human amygdala associates with later memory for individual emotional experience. *Journal of Neuroscience, 20:* RC99 (1–5).

Canli, T., Zhao, Z., Desmond, J. E., Glover, G., & Gabrieli, J. D. E. (1999). fMRI identifies a network of structures correlated with retention of positive and negative emotional memory. *Psychobiology, 27*(4), 441–452.

Cannon, P. R., Hayes, A. E., & Tipper, S. P. (2009). An electromyographic investigation of the impact of task relevance on facial mimicry. *Cognition & Emotion, 23,* 918–929.

Cannon, W. B. (1915). *Bodily changes in pain, hunger, fear and rage: An account of recent researches into the function of emotional excitement.* D. Appleton & Company.

Caprara, G. V., Eisenberg, N., & Alessandri, G. (2017). Positivity: The dispositional basis of happiness. *Journal of Happiness Studies, 18*(2), 353–371.

Capraro, V., & Barcelo, H. (2021). Telling people to "rely on their reasoning" increases intentions to wear a face covering to slow down COVID-19 transmission. *Applied Cognitive Psychology, 35*(3), 693–699.

Carey, I. M., Shah, S. M., DeWilde, S., Harris, T., Victor, C. R., & Cook, D. G. (2014). Increased risk of acute cardiovascular events after partner bereavement. *JAMA Internal Medicine, 174,* 598–605.

Carlsmith, J. M., & Anderson, C. A. (1979). Ambient temperature and the occurrence of collective violence: a new analysis. *Journal of Personality and Social Psychology, 37*(3), 337–344.

Carlson, J. M., Cha, J., & Mujica-Parodi, L. R. (2013). Functional and structural amygdala-anterior cingulate connectivity correlates with attentional bias to masked fearful faces. *Cortex, 49,* 2595–2600.

Carmichael, M. S., Humbert, R., Dixen, J., Palmisano, G., Greenleaf, W., & Davidson, J. M. (1987). Plasma oxytocin increases in the human sexual response. *Journal of Clinical Endocrinology & Metabolism, 64*(1), 27–31.

Carney, D. R., Cuddy, A. J., & Yap, A. J. (2010). Power posing: Brief nonverbal displays affect neuroendocrine levels and risk tolerance. *Psychological Science, 21*(10), 1363–1368.

Carney, D. R., & Harrigan, J. A. (2003). It takes one to know one: Interpersonal sensitivity is related to accurate assessment of others' interpersonal sensitivity. *Emotion, 3,* 194–200.

Carr, D., Freedman, V. A., Cornman, J. C., & Schwarz, N. (2014). Happy marriage, happy life? Marital quality and subjective well-being in later life. *Journal of Marriage and Family, 76,* 930–948.

Carré, J. M., Iselin, A.-M. R., Welker, K. M., Hariri, A. R., & Dodge, K. A. (2014). Testosterone reactivity to provocation mediates the effect of early intervention on aggressive behavior. *Psychological Science, 25,* 1140–1146.

Carrieté, L. (2014). Exogenous (automatic) attention to emotional stimuli: a review. *Cognitive Affective and Behavioral Neuroscience, 14,* 1228–1258.

Carroll, J. M., & Russell, J. A. (1996). Do facial expressions signal specific emotions? Judging emotion from the face in context. *Journal of Personality and Social Psychology, 70*(2), 205–218.

Carstensen, L. L. (1992). Social and emotional patterns in adulthood: Support for socioemotional selectivity theory. *Psychology and Aging, 7,* 331–338.

Carstensen, L. L., & Charles, S. T. (1998). Emotion in the second half of life. *Current Directions in Psychological Science, 7,* 144–149.

Carstensen, L. L., Gottman, J. M., & Levenson, R. W. (1995). Emotional behavior in long-term marriage. *Psychology and Aging, 10,* 140–149.

Carstensen, L. L., Isaacowitz, D. M., & Charles, S. T. (1999). Taking time seriously: A theory of socioemotional selectivity. *American Psychologist, 54,* 165–181.

Carstensen, L. L., Pasupathi, M., Mayr, U., & Nesselroade, J. R. (2000). Emotional experience in everyday life across the adult life span. *Journal of Personality and Social Psychology, 79,* 644–655.

Carter, E. C., Kofler, L. M., Forster, D. E., & McCullough, M. E. (2015). A series of meta-analytic tests of the depletion effect: Self-control does not seem to rely on a limited resource. *Journal of Experimental Psychology: General, 144*(4), 796–815.

Carter, J., Lyons, N. J., Cole, H. L., & Goldsmith, A. R. (2008). Subtle cues of predation risk: Starlings respond to a predator's direction of eye-gaze. *Proceedings*

Biological Sciences/the Royal Society, 275(1644), 1709–1715.

Carver, C. S., & Harmon-Jones, E. (2009). Anger is an approach-related affect: evidence and implications. *Psychological Bulletin, 135*(2), 183–204.

Carver, C. S., Pozo, C., Harris, S. D., Noriega, V., Scheier, M. F., Robinson, D. S. . . . & Clark, K. C. (1993). How coping mediates the effect of optimism on distress: A study of women with early stage breast cancer. *Journal of Personality and Social Psychology, 65*, 375–390.

Carver, C. S., & Scheier, M. F. (1981). *Attention and self-regulation: A control theory approach to human behavior.* Springer.

Carver, C. S., & Scheier, M. F. (1982). Control theory: A useful conceptual framework for personality–social, clinical, and health psychology. *Psychological Bulletin, 92*(1), 111–135.

Carver, C. S., & Scheier, M. F. (1998). On the self-regulation of behavior. Cambridge University Press.

Carver, C. S., & Scheier, M. F. (2002). Optimism. In C. R. Snyder & S. J. Lopez (Eds.), *Handbook of positive psychology* (pp. 231–243). New York: Oxford University Press.

Carver, C. S., & Scheier, M. F. (2012). Cybernetic control processes and the self-regulation of behavior. In R.M. Ryan (Ed.) *The Oxford handbook of human motivation* (pp. 28–42). Oxford University Press.

Carver, C. S., & White, T. L. (1994). Behavioral inhibition, behavioral activation, and affective responses to impending reward and punishment: the BIS/BAS scales. *Journal of Personality and Social Psychology, 67*(2), 319–333.

Caspi, A., Houts, R. M., Belsky, D. W., Goldman-Mellor, S. J., Harrington, H. L., Israel, S., . . . & Moffitt, T. E. (2014). The *p* factor: One general psychopathology factor in the structure of psychiatric disorders? *Clinical Psychological Science, 2*, 119–137.

Cassia, V. M., Turati, C., & Simion, F. (2004). Can a nonspecific bias toward top-heavy patterns explain newborns' face preference? *Psychological Science, 15*, 379–383.

Catterson, A. D., Eldesouky, L., & John, O. P. (2017). An experience sampling approach to emotion regulation: Situational suppression use and social hierarchy. *Journal of Research in Personality, 69*, 33–43.

Cavanagh, S. R., Lang, J. M., Birk, J. L., Fulwiler, C. E., & Urry, H. L. (2021). A multicourse, multisemester investigation of the impact of cognitive reappraisal and mindfulness instruction on short- and long-term learning in the college classroom. *Scholarship of Teaching and Learning in Psychology, 7*(1), 14–38.

Cesario, J., Johnson, D. J., & Eisthen, H. L. (2020). Your brain is not an onion with a tiny reptile inside. *Current Directions in Psychological Science, 29*(3), 255–260.

Chae, D. H., Yip, T., Martz, C. D., Chung, K., Richeson, J. A., Hajat, A., . . . & LaVeist, T. A. (2021). Vicarious racism and vigilance during the COVID-19 pandemic: Mental health implications among Asian and Black Americans. *Public Health Reports, 136*(4), 508–517.

Challamel, M. J., Hartley, S., Debilly, G., Lahlou, S., & Franco, P. (2021). A video polysomnographic study of spontaneous smiling during sleep in newborns. *Journal of Sleep Research, 30*(3), e13129.

Chambers, R., Lo, B. C. Y., & Allen, N. B. (2008). The impact of intensive mindfulness training on attentional control, cognitive style, and affect. *Cognitive Therapy and Research, 32*(3), 303–322.

Chaplin, T. M., & Aldao, A. (2013). Gender differences in emotion expression in children: A meta-analysis. *Psychological Bulletin, 139*, 735–765.

Chaplin, T. M., Cole, P. M., & Zahn-Waxler, C. (2005). Parental socialization of emotion expression: Gender differences and relations to child adjustment. *Emotion, 5*, 80–88.

Chapman, H. A., & Anderson, A. K. (2013). Things rank and gross in nature: a review and synthesis of moral disgust. *Psychological bulletin, 139*(2), 300–327.

Chapman, H. A., Kim, D. A., Susskind, J. M., & Anderson, A. K. (2009). In bad taste: Evidence for the oral origins of moral disgust. *Science, 323*(5918), 1222–1226.

Chapman, L. K., Kertz, S. J., Zurlage, M. M., & Woodruff-Borden, J. (2008). A confirmatory factor analysis of specific phobia domains in African American and Caucasian American young adults. *Journal of Anxiety Disorders, 22*(5), 763–771.

Chaput, J. P., Despres, J. P., Bouchard, C., & Tremblay, A. (2007). Short sleep duration is associated with reduced leptin levels and increased adiposity: Results from the Quebec family study. *Obesity (Silver Spring), 15*(1), 253–261.

Chartrand, T. L., & Bargh, J. A. (1999). The chameleon effect: The perception–behavior link and social interaction. *Journal of Personality and Social Psychology, 76*(6), 893–910.

Chen, J., Liang, J., Lin, X., Zhang, Y., Zhang, Y., Lu, L., & Shi, J. (2017). Sleep deprivation promotes habitual control over goal-directed control: Behavioral and neuroimaging evidence. *Journal of Neuroscience, 37*(49), 11979–11992.

Chen, K. H., Brown, C. L., Wells, J. L., Rothwell, E. S., Otero, M. C., Levenson, R. W., & Fredrickson, B. L. (2021). Physiological linkage during shared positive and shared negative emotion. *Journal of Personality and Social Psychology, 121*(5), 1029–1056.

Chen, S., & Bonanno, G. A. (2021). Components of emotion regulation flexibility: Linking latent profiles to depressive and anxious symptoms. *Clinical Psychological Science, 9*(2), 236–251.

Chentsova-Dutton, Y., Leontyeva, A., Halberstadt, A. G., & Adams, A. M. (2021). And they all lived unhappily ever after: Positive and negative emotions in American and Russian picture books. *Emotion, 21*(8), 1585–1598.

Chentsova-Dutton, Y. E., Choi, E., & Ryder, A. (2014). Cultural variations in ideal and momentary hedonic balance: Does a more negative ideal protect Russian Americans from daily stress. *Psychology: Journal of Higher School of Economics, 11*(1), 118–132.

Chiao, J. Y., & Blizinsky, K. D. (2010). Culture–gene co-evolution of individualism–collectivism and the serotonin transporter gene. *Proceedings of the Royal Society B: Biological Sciences, 277*(1681), 529–537.

Choi, S., & Kluemper, D. H. (2012). The relative utility of differing measures of emotional intelligence: Other-report EI as a predictor of social functioning. *Revue européenne de psychologie appliquée, 62,* 121–127.

Chóliz, M., Fernández-Abascal, E. G., & Martínez-Sánchez, R. (2012). Infant crying: Pattern of weeping, recognition of emotion and affective reactions in observers. *Spanish Journal of Psychology, 15,* 978–988.

Chopik, W. J., Edelstein, R. S., & Fraley, R. C. (2013). From the cradle to the grave: Age differences in attachment from early adulthood to old age. *Journal of Personality, 81*(2), 171–183.

Choti, S. E., Marston, A. R., Holston, S. G., & Hart, J. T. (1987). Gender and personality variables in film-induced sadness and crying. *Journal of Social and Clinical Psychology, 5*(4), 535–544.

Chou, W. Y. S., & Budenz, A. (2020). Considering emotion in COVID-19 vaccine communication: Addressing vaccine hesitancy and fostering vaccine confidence. *Health communication, 35*(14), 1718–1722.

Christensen, A., & Heavey, C. L. (1990). Gender and social structure in the demand/withdraw pattern of marital conflict. *Journal of Personality and Social Psychology, 59*(1), 73–81.

Christie, I. C., & Friedman, B. H. (2003). Autonomic specificity of discrete emotion and dimensions of affective space: A multivariate approach. *International Journal of Psychophysiology, 51,* 143–153.

Ciaramelli, E., Muccioli, M., Làdavas, E., & DiPellegrino, G. (2007). Selective deficit in personal moral judgment following damage to ventromedial prefrontal cortex. *Social Cognitive and Affective Neuroscience, 2,* 84–92.

Clark, L., Bechara, A., Damasio, H., Aitken, M. R. F., Sahakian, B. J., & Robbins, T. W. (2008). Differential effects of insular and ventromedial prefrontal cortex lesions on risky decision-making. *Brain: A Journal of Neurology, 131*(5), 1311–1322.

Clark, R., Anderson, N. B., Clark, V. R., Williams, D. R. (1999). Racism as a stressor for African Americans: A biopsychosocial model. *American Psychologist, 54,* 805–816.

Clark, T. F., Winkielman, P., & McIntosh, D. N. (2008). Autism and the extraction of emotion from briefly presented facial expressions: stumbling at the first step of empathy. *Emotion, 8*(6), 803–809.

Clohessy, A. B., Posner, M. I., Rothbart, M. K., & Veccra, S. P. (1991). The development of inhibition of return in early infancy. *Journal of Cognitive Neuroscience, 3,* 345–350.

Clore, G. L., Schiller, A. J., & Shaked, A. (2018). Affect and cognition: Three principles. *Current Opinion in Behavioral Sciences, 19,* 78–82.

Cohen, A. B. (2009). Many forms of culture. *American Psychologist, 64*(3), 194–204.

Cohen, D., & Gunz, A. (2002). As seen by the other . . .: Perspectives on the self in the memories and emotional perceptions of Easterners and Westerners. *Psychological Science, 13,* 55–59.

Cohen, D., Nisbett, R. E., Bowdle, B. F., & Schwarz, N. (1996). Insult, aggression, and the southern culture of honor: An "experimental ethnography." *Journal of Personality and Social Psychology, 70*(5), 945–960.

Cohen, G. L., & Prinstein, M. J. (2006). Peer contagion of aggression and health risk behavior among adolescent males: An experimental investigation of effects on public conduct and private attitudes. *Child Development, 77*(4), 967–983.

Cohen, S., Frank, E., Doyle, W. J., Skoner, D. P., Rabin, B. S., & Swaltney, J. M., Jr. (1998). Types of stressors that increase susceptibility to the common cold in healthy adults. *Health Psychology, 17,* 214–223.

Cohen, S., Janicki-Deverts, D., Turner, R. B., & Doyle, W. J. (2015). Does hugging provide stress-buffering social support? A study of susceptibility to upper respiratory infection and illness. *Psychological Science, 26*(2), 135–147.

Cohen, Z. D., & DeRubeis, R. J. (2018). Treatment selection in depression. *Annual Review of Clinical Psychology, 14*, 209–236.

Cohn, M. A., Fredrickson, B. L., Brown, S. L., Mikels, J. A., & Conway, A. M. (2009). Happiness unpacked: Positive emotions increase life satisfaction by building resilience. *Emotion, 9*, 361–368.

Colciago, A., Casati, L., Negri-Cesi, P., & Celotti, F. (2015). Learning and memory: Steroids and epigenetics. *Journal of Steroid Biochemistry and Molecular Biology, 150*, 64–85.

Cole, P. M., Bruschi, C. J., & Tamang, B. L. (2002). Cultural differences in children's emotional reactions to difficult situations. *Child Development, 73*, 983–996.

Cole, P. M., & Tamang, B. L. (1998). Nepali children's ideas about emotional displays in hypothetical challenges. *Developmental Psychology, 34*, 640–646.

Cole, P. M., Teti, L. O., & Zahn-Waxler, C. (2003). Mutual emotion regulation and the stability of conduct problems between preschool and early school age. *Development and Psychopathology, 15*, 1–18.

Coles, N. A., Larsen, J. T., Kuribayashi, J., & Kuelz, A. (2019). Does blocking facial feedback via botulinum toxin injections decrease depression? A critical review and meta-analysis. *Emotion Review, 11*(4), 294–309.

Collins, N. L., & Miller, L. C. (1994). Self-disclosure and liking: A meta-analytic review. *Psychological Bulletin, 116*, 457–475.

Combs, D. J. Y., Powell, C. A. J., Schurtz, D. R., & Smith, R. H. (2009). Politics, *schadenfreude*, and ingroup identification: The sometimes happy thing about a poor economy and death. *Journal of Experimental Social Psychology, 45*(4), 635–646.

Conner, T. S., & Silvia, P. J. (2015). Creative days: A daily diary study of emotion, personality, and everyday creativity. *Psychology of Aesthetics, Creativity, and the Arts, 9*, 463–470.

Conroy, M., Hess, R. D., Azuma, H., & Kashiwagi, K. (1980). Maternal strategies for regulating children's behavior: Japanese and American families. *Journal of Cross-Cultural Psychology, 11*, 153–172.

Consedine, N. S., Magai, C., & King, A. R. (2004). Deconstructing positive affect in later life: A differential functionalist analysis of joy and interest. *International Journal of Aging and Human Development, 58*, 49–68.

CONVERGE Consortium. (2015). Sparse whole-genome sequencing identifies two loci for major depression. *Nature, 523*, 588–591.

Conzelmann, K., & Goerke, P. (2015). Expert and target scoring: Their relation, corresponding test instructions, and their effects on the construct validity of the video-based social understanding test (VSU). *International Journal of Selection and Assessment, 23*, 1–13.

Cook, C. L., Krems, J. A., & Kenrick, D. T. (2021). Fundamental motives illuminate a broad range of individual and cultural variations in thought and behavior. *Current Directions in Psychological Science, 30*(3), 242–250.

Cook, P. F., Prichard, A., Spivak, M., & Berns, G. S. (2016). Awake canine fMRI predicts dogs' preference for praise vs food. *Social Cognitive and Affective Neuroscience, 11*(12), 1853–1862.

Coombs, R. H., & Fawzy, F. I. (1982). The effect of marital status on stress in medical school. *American Journal of Psychiatry, 139*, 1490–1493.

Coontz, S. (2005). *Marriage, a history: How love conquered marriage*. Viking Penguin.

Cooper, R. A., Kensinger, E. A., & Ritchey, M. (2019). Memories fade: The relationship between memory vividness and remembered visual salience. *Psychological Science, 30*(5), 657–668.

Cordaro, D. T., Keltner, D., Tshering, S., Wangchuk, D., & Flynn, L. M. (2016). The voice conveys emotion in ten globalized cultures and one remote village in Bhutan. *Emotion, 16*(1), 117–128.

Cordaro, D. T., Sun, R., Kamble, S., Hodder, N., Monroy, M., Cowen, A., . . . & Keltner, D. (2019). The recognition of 18 facial-bodily expressions across nine cultures. *Emotion, 20*(7), 1292–1300.

Cordaro, D. T., Sun, R., Keltner, D., Kamble, S., Huddar, N., & McNeil, G. (2018). Universals and cultural variations in 22 emotional expressions across five cultures. *Emotion, 18*(1), 75–93.

Cordonnier, A., & Luminet, O. (2021). Consistency and social identification: A test-retest study of flashbulb memories collected on the day of the 2016 Brussels bombings. *Memory, 29*(3), 305–318.

Cornwell, J. M. F., Scholer, A. A., & Higgins, E. T. (2019). Approach and avoidance dynamics: How expanding the scope informs motivation science. *Psychological Inquiry, 30*, 165–171.

Corona, K., Senft, N., Campos, B., Chen, C., Shiota, M., & Chentsova-Dutton, Y. E. (2020). Ethnic variation in gratitude and well-being. *Emotion, 20*(3), 518–524.

Costa, V. D., Lang, P. J., Sabatinelli, D., Versace, F., & Bradley, M. M. (2010). Emotional imagery: Assessing pleasure and arousal in the brain's reward circuitry. *Human Brain Mapping, 31*, 1446–1457.

Côté, S., Hideg, I., & van Kleef, G. A. (2013). The consequences of faking anger in negotiations. *Journal of Experimental Social Psychology, 49*(3), 453–463.

Côté, S., & Morgan, L. M. (2002). A longitudinal analysis of the association between emotion regulation, job satisfaction, and intentions to quit. *Journal of Organizational Behavior, 23*(8), 947–962.

Coughtrey, A. E., Shafran, R., Lee, M., & Rachman, S. (2013). The treatment of mental contamination: A case series. *Cognitive and Behavioral Practice, 20*, 221–231.

Courtney, K. E., Schacht, J. P., Hutchison, K., Roche, D. J., & Ray, L. A. (2016). Neural substrates of cue reactivity: Association with treatment outcomes and relapse. *Addiction Biology, 21*(1), 3–22.

Covert, M. V., Tangney, J. P., Maddux, J. E., & Heleno, N. M. (2003). Shame-proneness, guilt-proneness, and interpersonal problem solving: A social cognitive analysis. *Journal of Social and Clinical Psychology, 22*, 1–12.

Cowen, A., Sauter, D., Tracy, J. L., & Keltner, D. (2019). Mapping the passions: Toward a high-dimensional taxonomy of emotional experience and expression. *Psychological Science in the Public Interest, 20*(1), 69–90.

Cox, B. J., McWilliams, L. A., Clara, I. P., & Stein, M. B. (2003). The structure of feared situations in a nationally representative sample. *Journal of Anxiety Disorders, 17*, 89–101.

Cox, S. M., Frank, M. J., Larcher, K., Fellows, L. K., Clark, C. A., Leyton, M., & Dagher, A. (2015). Striatal D1 and D2 signaling differentially predict learning from positive and negative outcomes. *Neuroimage, 109*, 95–101.

Craske, M. G., Treanor, M., Conway, C. C., Zbozinek, T., & Vervliet, B. (2014). Maximizing exposure therapy: An inhibitory learning approach. *Behaviour Research and Therapy, 58*, 10–23.

Crews, D. J., & Landers, D. M. (1987). A meta-analytic review of aerobic fitness and reactivity to psychological stressors. *Medicine & Science in Sports & Exercise, 19*, S144–S120.

Crews, F. (1996). The verdict on Freud. *Psychological Science, 7*, 63–68.

Critchley, H. D., Mathias, C. J., & Dolan, R. J. (2001). Neuroanatomical basis for first- and second-order representations of bodily states. *Nature Neuroscience, 4*, 207–212.

Critchley, H. D., Wiens, S., Rotshtein, P., Öhman, A., & Dolan, R. J. (2004). Neural systems supporting interoceptive awareness. *Nature Neuroscience, 7*(2), 189–195.

Critchley, H. D., & Garfinkel, S. N. (2017). Interoception and emotion. *Current opinion in psychology, 17*, 7–14.

Cromwell, H. C., Abe, N., Barrett, K. C., Caldwell-Harris, C., Gendolla, G. H., Koncz, R., & Sachdev, P. S. (2020). Mapping the interconnected neural systems underlying motivation and emotion: A key step toward understanding the human affectome. *Neuroscience & Biobehavioral Reviews, 113*, 204–226.

Csikszentmihalyi, M. (1999). If we are so rich, why aren't we happy? *American Psychologist, 54*, 821–827.

Csikszentmihalyi, M. (2020). *Finding flow: The psychology of engagement with everyday life*. Hachette UK.

Cuddy, A. J., Schultz, S. J., & Fosse, N. E. (2018). P-curving a more comprehensive body of research on postural feedback reveals clear evidential value for power-posing effects: Reply to Simmons and Simonsohn (2017). *Psychological Science, 29*(4), 656–666.

Cuijpers, P., Noma, H., Karyotaki, E., Vinkers, C. H., Cipriani, A., & Furukawa, T. A. (2020). A network meta-analysis of the effects of psychotherapies, pharmacotherapies and their combination in the treatment of adult depression. *World Psychiatry, 19*(1), 92–107.

Cuijpers, P., Sijbrandij, M., Koole, S., Huibers, M., Berking, M., & Andersson, G. (2014). Psychological treatment of generalized anxiety disorder: A meta-analysis. *Clinical Psychological Review, 34*, 130–140.

Cummins, R. A., Li, N., Wooden, M., & Stokes, M. (2014). A demonstration of set-points for subjective wellbeing. *Journal of Happiness Studies, 15*, 183–206.

Cunningham, M. R. (1979). Weather, mood, and helping behavior: Quasi experiments with the sunshine samaritan. *Journal of Personality and Social Psychology, 37*, 1947–1956.

Cunningham, M. R., & Baumeister, R. F. (2016). How to make nothing out of something: Analyses of the impact of study sampling and statistical interpretation in misleading meta-analytic conclusions. *Frontiers in Psychology, 7*, Article 1639. https://doi.org/10.3389/fpsyg.2016.01639

Cunningham, M. R., Roberts, A. R., Barbee, A. P., Druen, P. B., & Wu, C. (1995). "Their ideas of beauty are, on the whole, the same as ours": Consistency and variability in the cross-cultural perception of female physical attractiveness. *Journal of Personality and Social Psychology, 68*, 261–279.

Cunningham, T. J., Mattingly, S. M., Tlatenchi, A., Wirth, M. M., Alger, S. E., Kensinger, E. A., & Payne, J. D. (2021). Higher post-encoding cortisol benefits the selective consolidation of emotional aspects of memory. *Neurobiology of Learning and Memory, 180,* 107411.

Curtis, V., & Biran, A. (2001). Dirt, disgust, and disease: Is hygiene in our genes? *Perspectives in Biology and Medicine, 44*(1), 17–31.

Cuthbert, B. N., & Insel, T. R. (2013). Toward the future of psychiatric diagnosis: the seven pillars of RDoC. *BMC Medicine, 11*(126).

Dadds, M. R., Hawes, D. J., Frost, A. D., Vassallo, S., Bunn, P., Hunter, K., & Merz, S. (2009). Learning to "talk the talk": The relationship of psychopathic traits to deficits in empathy across childhood. *Journal of Child Psychology and Psychiatry, 50*(5), 599–606.

Dael, N., Mortillaro, M., & Scherer, K. R. (2012). Emotion expression in body action and posture. *Emotion, 12*(5), 1085–1101.

Damasio, A. R. (1994). *Descartes' error: Emotion, reason, and the human brain.* G. P. Putnam.

Damasio, A. R. (1999). *The feeling of what happens.* Harcourt Brace.

Damasio, H. (2002). Impairment of interpersonal social behavior caused by acquired brain damage. In S. G. Post, l. G. Underwood, J. P. Schloss, & W. B. Hurlbut (Eds.), *Altruism & altruistic love* (pp. 272–283). Oxford University Press.

Damsma, G., Pfaus, J. G., Wenkstern, D., Phillips, A. G., & Fibiger, H. C. (1992). Sexual behavior increases dopamine transmission in the nucleus accumbens and striatum of male rats: A comparison with novelty and locomotion. *Behavioral Neuroscience, 106,* 181–191.

Danvers, A. F., & Shiota, M. N. (2017). Going off script: Effects of awe on memory for script-typical and-irrelevant narrative detail. *Emotion, 17*(6), 938–952.

Darwin, C. ([1859] 1991). *On the Origin of Species by Means of Natural Selection: Or, The Preservation of Favored Races in the Struggle For Life.* Murray.

Darwin, C. ([1872] 1998). *The expression of the emotions in man and animals.* Oxford University Press.

Daugherty, J. R., & Brase, G. L. (2010). Taking time to be healthy: Predicting health behaviors with delay discounting and time perspective. *Personality and Individual differences, 48*(2), 202–207.

Davidov, M., Zahn-Waxler, C., Roth-Hanania, R., & Knafo, A. (2013). Concern for others in the first year of life: Theory, evidence, and avenues for research. *Child Development Perspectives, 7,* 126–131.

Davidson, J. R. T. (2007). A history of the concept of atypical depression. *Journal of Clinical Psychiatry, 68*(Suppl3), 10–15.

Davidson, K., MacGregor, M. W., Stuhr, J., Dixon, K., & MacLean, D. (2000). Constructive anger verbal behavior predicts blood pressure in a population-based sample. *Health Psychology, 19,* 55–64.

Davidson, R. J. (2004). What does the prefrontal cortex "do" in affect: Perspectives on frontal EEG asymmetry research. *Biological Psychology, Special Issue: Frontal EEG Asymmetry, Emotion, and Psychopathology, 67*(1–2), 219–233.

Davila, J., Karney, B. R., & Bradbury, T. N. (1999). Attachment change processes in the early years of marriage. *Journal of Personality and Social Psychology, 76*(5), 783–802.

Davis, D. E., Choe, E., Meyers, J., Wade, N., Varjas, K., Gifford, A., . . . & Worthington Jr., E. L. (2016). Thankful for the little things: A meta-analysis of gratitude interventions. *Journal of Counseling Psychology, 63*(1), 20–31.

Davis, J. I., Senghas, A., Brandt, F., & Ochsner, K. N. (2010). The effects of BOTOX injections on emotional experience. *Emotion, 10*(3), 433–440.

Davis, J. L., & Rusbult, C. E. (2001). Attitude alignment in close relationships. *Journal of Personality and Social Psychology, 81,* 65–84.

Dawson, D. A., & Grant, B. F. (1998). Family history of alcoholism and gender: Their combined effects on *DSM-IV* alcohol dependence and major depression. *Journal of Studies on Alcohol, 59,* 97–106.

Day, J. J., Jones, J. L., & Carelli, R. M. (2011). Nucleus accumbens neurons encode predicted and ongoing reward costs in rats. *European Journal of Neuroscience, 33*(2), 308–321.

de Boer, A., Peeters, M., & Koning, I. (2017). An experimental study of risk taking behavior among adolescents: A closer look at peer and sex influences. *The Journal of Early Adolescence, 37*(8), 1125–1141.

De Castro, B. O., Veerman, J. W., Koops, W., Bosch, J. D., & Monshouwer, H. J. (2002). Hostile attribution of intent and aggressive behavior: A meta-analysis. *Child Development, 73*(3), 916–934.

De Dreu, C. K., Greer, L. L., Handgraaf, M. J., Shalvi, S., Van Kleef, G. A., Baas, M., . . . & Feith, S. W. (2010). The neuropeptide oxytocin regulates parochial altruism in intergroup conflict among humans. *Science, 328*(5984), 1408–1411.

de Groot, J. H. B., Semin, G. R., & Smeets, M. A. M. (2014). Chemical communication of fear: A case of male-female asymmetry. *Journal of Experimental Psychology: General, 143,* 1515–1525.

De Ridder, D. T., Lensvelt-Mulders, G., Finkenauer, C., Stok, F. M., & Baumeister, R. F. (2012). Taking stock of self-control: A meta-analysis of how trait self-control relates to a wide range of behaviors. *Personality and Social Psychology Review, 16*(1), 76–99.

De Wolff, M. S., & van IJzendoorn, M. H. (1997). Sensitivity and attachment: A meta-analysis on parental antecedents of infant attachment. *Child Development, 68*(4), 571–591.

Debiec, J., & Olsson, A. (2017). Social fear learning: From animal models to human function. *Trends in Cognitive Sciences, 21*(7), 546–555.

DeCasper, A. J., & Fifer, W. P. (1980). Of human bonding: Newborns prefer their mothers' voices. *Science, 208,* 1174–1177.

Decety, J. (2020). Empathy in medicine: What it is, and how much we really need it. *American Journal of Medicine, 133*(5), 561–566.

Deci, E. L. (1971). Effects of externally mediated rewards on intrinsic motivation. *Journal of Personality and Social Psychology, 18*(1), 105–115.

Deci, E. L., Koestner, R., & Ryan, R. M. (1999). A meta-analytic review of experiments examining the effects of extrinsic rewards on intrinsic motivation. *Psychological Bulletin, 125*(6), 627–668.

Dedovic, K., & Ngiam, J. (2015). The cortisol awakening response and major depression: examining the evidence. *Neuropsychiatric Disease and Treatment, 11,* 1181–1189.

Delgadillo, D., Boparai, S., Pressman, S. D., Goldstein, A., Bureau, J. F., Schmiedel, S., . . . & Borelli, J. L. (2021). Maternal expressions of positive emotion for children predicts children's respiratory sinus arrhythmia surrounding stress. *Developmental Psychobiology, 63*(5), 1225–1240.

DeLisi, M., Drury, A. J., & Elbert, M. J. (2019). The etiology of antisocial personality disorder: The differential roles of adverse childhood experiences and childhood psychopathology. *Comprehensive Psychiatry, 92,* 1–6.

Demir, T., Bolat, N., Yazuv, M., Karaçetin, G., Dogangün, B., & Kayaalp, L. (2014). Attachment characteristics and behavioral problems in children and adolescents with congenital blindness. *Archives of Neuropsychiatry, 51,* 116–121.

DeNeve, K. M. (1999). Happy as an extraverted clam? The role of personality for subjective well-being. *Current Directions in Psychological Science, 8,* 141–144.

DeNeve, K. M., & Cooper, H. (1998). The happy personality: A meta-analysis of 137 personality traits and subjective well-being. *Psychological Bulletin, 124,* 197–229.

Denham, S. A., Workman, E., Cole, P. M., Weissbrod, C., Kendziora, K. T., & Zahn-Waxler, C. (2000). Prediction of externalizing behavior problems from early to middle childhood: The role of parental socialization and emotion expression. *Development and Psychopathology, 12,* 23–45.

Dennis, T. A., Cole, P. M., Zahn-Waxler, C., & Mizuta, I. (2002). Self in context: Autonomy and relatedness in Japanese and U.S. mother-preschooler dyads. *Child Development, 73,* 1803–1817.

Depue, R. A., & Iacono, W. G. (1989). Neurobehavioral aspects of affective disorders. In M. R. Rosenzweig & L. W. Porter (Eds.), *Annual review of psychology, 40,* 457–492. Annual Reviews.

Depue, R. A., & Morrone-Strupinsky, J. V. (2005). A neurobehavioral model of affiliative bonding: Implications for conceptualizing a human trait of affiliation. *Behavioral and Brain Sciences, 28,* 313–395.

DeScioli, P., Christner, J., & Kurzban, R. (2011). The omission strategy. *Psychological Science, 22,* 442–446.

DeSteno, D., Bartlett, M. Y., Baumann, J., Williams, L. A., & Dickens, L. (2010). Gratitude as moral sentiment: emotion-guided cooperation in economic exchange. *Emotion, 10*(2), 289–293.

Detre, J. A., & Floyd, T. F. (2001). Functional MRI and its applications to the clinical neurosciences. *Neuroscientist, 7,* 64–79.

Di Bello, M., Carnevali, L., Petrocchi, N., Thayer, J. F., Gilbert, P., & Ottaviani, C. (2020). The compassionate vagus: A meta-analysis on the connection between compassion and heart rate variability. *Neuroscience & Biobehavioral Reviews, 116,* 21–30.

Di Fabio, A., & Palazzeschi, L. (2015). Beyond fluid intelligence and personality traits in scholastic success: Trait emotional intelligence. *Learning and Individual Differences, 40,* 121–126.

Diamond, L. M. (2003). What does sexual orientation orient? A biobehavioral model distinguishing romantic love and sexual desire. *Psychological Review, 110*(1), 173–192.

Diener, E. (2000). Subjective well-being. *American Psychologist, 55,* 34–43.

Diener, E. (2012). New findings and future directions for subjective well-being research. *American Psychologist, 67*(8), 590–597.

Diener, E., & Diener, C. (1996). Most people are happy. *Psychologcal Science, 7,* 181–185.

Diener, E., Scollon, C. K. N., Oishi, S., Dzokoto, V., & Suh, E. M. (2000). Positivity and the construction of life satisfaction judgments: Global happiness is not the sum of its part. *Journal of Happiness Studies, 1,* 159–176.

Diener, E., & Seligman, M. E. P. (2002). Very happy people. *Psychological Science, 13,* 81–84.

Diener, E., & Seligman, M. E. P. (2004). Beyond money: Toward an economy of well-being. *Psychological Science in the Public Interest, 5,* 1–31.

Diener, E., Suh, E. M., Lucas, R. E., & Smith, H. L. (1999). Subjective well-being: Three decades of progress. *Psychological Bulletin, 125,* 276–302.

Diener, E., Tay, L., & Myers, D. (2011). The religion paradox: If religion makes people happy, why are so many dropping out? *Journal of Personality and Social Psychology, 101,* 1278–1290.

Diener, E., Tay, L., & Oishi, S. (2013). Rising income and the subjective well-being of nations. *Journal of Personality and Social Psychology, 104*(2), 267–276.

Diener, E., Thapa, S., & Tay, L. (2020). Positive emotions at work. *Annual Review of Organizational Psychology and Organizational Behavior, 7,* 451–477.

Diener, E., Wolsic, B., & Fujita, F. (1995). Physical attractiveness and subjective well-being. *Journal of Personality and Social Psychology, 69,* 120–129.

Diener, M. L., & Lucas, R. E. (2004). Adults' desires for children's emotions across 48 countries. *Journal of Cross-Cultural Psychology, 35,* 525–547.

Dijk, C., de Jong, P. J., & Peters, M. L. (2009). The remedial value of blushing in the context of transgressions and mishaps. *Emotion, 9*(2), 287–291.

Dimberg, U., & Thunberg, M. (1998). Rapid facial reactions to emotional facial expressions. *Scandinavian Journal of Psychology, 39,* 39–45.

Dimberg, U., & Söderkvist, S. (2011). The voluntary facial action technique: A method to test the facial feedback hypothesis. *Journal of Nonverbal Behavior, 35*(1), 17–33.

Ding, Y., Xu, X., Wang, Z., Li, H., & Wang, W. (2014). The relation of infant attachment and cognitive and behavioural outcomes in early childhood. *Early Human Development, 90,* 459–464.

Dion, K. K., & Dion, K. L. (1993). Individualistic and collectivistic perspectives on gender and the cultural context of love and intimacy. *Journal of Social Issues, 49,* 53–69.

Disabato, D. J., Goodman, F. R., Kashdan, T. B., Short, J. L., & Jarden, A. (2016). Different types of well-being? A cross-cultural examination of hedonic and eudaimonic well-being. *Psychological Assessment, 28*(5), 471–482.

Ditzen, B., Schaer, M., Gabriel, B., Bodenmann, G., Ehlert, U., & Heinrichs, M. (2009). Intranasal oxytocin increases positive communication and reduces cortisol levels during couple conflict. *Biological Psychiatry, 65*(9), 728–731.

Dixon, M. L., Thiruchselvam, R., Todd, R., & Christoff, K. (2017). Emotion and the prefrontal cortex: An integrative review. *Psychological Bulletin, 143*(10), 1033–1081.

Dixon, T. (2012). "Emotion": The history of a keyword in crisis. *Emotion Review, 4*(4), 338–344.

Dockray, G. J. (2012). Cholecystokinin. *Current Opinion in Endocrinology, Diabetes and Obesity, 19*(1), 8–12.

Dockray, G. J., & Burdyga, G. (2011). Plasticity in vagal afferent neurones during feeding and fasting: Mechanisms and significance. *Acta Physiological, 201*(3), 313–321.

Doi, T. (1973). *The anatomy of dependence.* Translated by J. Beste. Kodansha International.

Dondi, M. Simion, F., & Caltran, G. (1999). Can newborns discriminate between their own cry and the cry of another newborn infant? *Developmental Psychology, 35,* 418–426.

Donohoe, M. L., von Hippel, W., & Brooks, R. C. (2009). Beyond waist–hip ratio: Experimental multivariate evidence that average women's torsos are most attractive. *Behavioral Ecology, 20*(4), 716–721.

Dragojevic, M., Savage, M. W., Scott, A. M., & McGinnis, T. (2018). Promoting oral health in Appalachia: Effects of threat label and source accent on message acceptance. *Health Communication, 35*(3), 297–307.

Driessen, E., Hollon, S. D., Bockting, C. L. H., Cuijpers, P., & Turner, E. H. (2015). Does publication bias inflate the apparent efficacy of psychological treatment for major depressive disorder? A systematic review and meta-analysis of US National Institutes of Health-funded trials. *PLoS One, 10,* e0137864. https://doi.org/10.1371/journal.pone.0137864

Drummond, P. D., & Bailey, T. (2013). Eye contact evokes blushing Independently of negative affect. *Journal of Nonverbal Behavior, 37*(4), 207–216.

Druschel, B. A., & Sherman, M. F. (1999). Disgust sensitivity as a function of the Big Five and gender. *Personality and Individual Differences, 26,* 739–748.

Duckworth, A. L. (2011). The significance of self-control. *Proceedings of the National Academy of Sciences, 108*(7), 2639–2640.

Duclos, S. E., & Laird, J. D. (2001). The deliberate control of emotional experience through control of expressions. *Cognition and Emotion, 15,* 27–65.

Duits, P., Cath, D. C., Lissek, S., Hox, J. J., Hamm, A. O., Engelhard, I. M., . . . & Baas, J. M. P. (2015). Updated meta-analysis of classical fear conditioning in the anxiety disorders. *Depression and Anxiety, 32,* 239–253.

Duker, A., Green, D. J., Onyeador, I. N., & Richeson, J. A. (2021). Managing emotions in the face of discrimination: The differential effects of self-immersion, self-distanced reappraisal, and positive reappraisal. *Emotion*. Advance online publication. https://doi.org/10.1037/emo0001001

Dukes, D., Abrams, K., Adolphs, R., Ahmed, M. E., Beatty, A., Berridge, K. C., . . . & Sander, D. (2021). The rise of affectivism. *Nature Human Behaviour*, *5*(7), 816–820.

Dunbar, R. I. (2010). The social role of touch in humans and primates: behavioural function and neurobiological mechanisms. *Neuroscience & Biobehavioral Reviews*, *34*(2), 260–268.

Duncan, L. A., Schaller, M., & Park, J. H. (2009). Perceived vulnerability to disease: Development and validation of a 15-item self-report instrument. *Personality and Individual Differences*, *47*(6), 541–546.

Dunlap, K. (1919). Are there any instincts? *Journal of Abnormal Psychology*, *14*(5), 307–311.

Dunn, E. W., Aknin, L. B., & Norton, M. I. (2008). Spending money on others promotes happiness. *Science*, *319*, 1687–1688.

Dunn, J., Bretherton, I., & Munn, P. (1987). Conversations about feeling states between mothers and their young children. *Developmental Psychology*, *23*, 132–139.

Dunn, J., Brown, J. R., & Maguire, M. (1995). The development of children's moral sensibility: Indvidual differences and emotion understanding. *Developmental Psychology*, *31*, 649–659.

Dunning, D., Heath, C., & Suls, J. M. (2005). Flawed self-assessment: Implications for health, education, and the workplace. *Psychological Science in the Public Interest*, *5*, 69–106.

Dunsmoor, J. E., Murty, V. P., Davachi, L., & Phelps, E. A. (2015). Emotional learning selectively and retroactively strengthens memories for related events. *Nature*, *520*, 345–348.

Durbin, C. E., Hayden, E. P., Klein, D. N., & Olino, T. M. (2007). Stability of laboratory-assessed temperamental emotionality traits from ages 3 to 7. *Emotion*, *7*, 388–399.

Dweck, C. S. (2008). *Mindset: The new psychology of success*. Random House.

Eagly, A. H., Ashmore, R. D., Makhijani, M. G., & Longo, L. C. (1991). What is beautiful is good, but . . .: A meta-analytic review of research on the physical attractiveness stereotype. *Psychological Bulletin*, *110*(1), 109–128.

Eccles, J. S., Adler, T. F., Futterman, R., Goff, S. B., Kaczala, C. M., Meece, J. L. (1983). Expectancies, values, and academic behaviors. In J. T. Spence (Ed.), *Achievement and achievement motivation* (pp. 74–146). W. H. Freeman.

Eckland, N. S., Huang, A. B., & Berenbaum, H. (2020). Empathic accuracy: Associations with prosocial behavior and self-insecurity. *Emotion*, *20*(7), 1306–1310.

Eddington, K. M., Dolcos, F., Cabeza, R., R. Krishnan, K. R., & Strauman, T. J. (2007). Neural correlates of promotion and prevention goal activation: An fMRI study using an idiographic approach. *Journal of Cognitive Neuroscience*, *19*(7), 1152–1162.

Edelmann, R. J. (2001). Blushing. In W. R. Crozier & L. E. Alden (Eds.), *International handbook of social anxiety* (pp. 301–323). Wiley.

Edwards, J., Jackson, H. J., & Pattison, P. E. (2002). Emotion recognition via facial expression and affective prosody in schizophrenia: A methodological review. *Clinical Psychology Review*, *22*, 789–832.

Edwards, K. (1998). The face of time: Temporal cues in facial expressions of emotion. *Psychological Science*, *9*, 270–276.

Edwards, S., Evans, P., Hucklebridge, F., & Clow, A. (2001). Association between time of awakening and diurnal cortisol secretory activity. *Psychoneuroendocrinology*, *26*(6), 613–622.

Eibl-Eibesfeldt, I. (1973). *Der vorprogrammierte Mensch* [The pre-programmed human.] Verlag Fritz Molden.

Eibl-Eibesfeldt, I. (1989). *Human Ethology*. Aldine de Gruyter.

Eich, E. (1995). Searching for mood dependent memory. *Psychological Science*, *6*, 67–75.

Eichholz, A., Schwartz, C., Meule, A., Heese, J., Neumüller, J., & Voderholzer, U. (2020). Self-compassion and emotion regulation difficulties in obsessive–compulsive disorder. *Clinical Psychology & Psychotherapy*, *27*(5), 630–639.

Eisenberg, N., Fabes, R. A., Miller, P. A., Fultz, J., Shell, R., Mathy, R. M., & Reno, R. R. (1989). Relation of sympathy and personal distress to prosocial behavior: A multimethod study. *Journal of Personality and Social Psychology*, *57*, 55–66.

Eisenberg, N., & Lennon, R. (1983). Sex differences in empathy and related capacities. *Psychological Bulletin*, *94*(1), 100–131.

Eisenberg, N., Liew, J., & Pidada, S. U. (2001). The relations of parental emotional expressivity with quality of Indonesian children's social functioning. *Emotion, 1,* 116–136.

Eisenberg, N., Pidada, S., & Liew, J. (2001). The relations of regulation and negative emotionality to Indonesian children's social functioning. *Child Development, 72,* 1747–1763.

Ekers, D., Webster, L., Van Straten, A., Cuijpers, P., Richards, D., & Gilbody, S. (2014). Behavioural activation for depression: An update of meta-analysis of effectiveness and subgroup analysis. *PLoS One, 9,* e100100. https://doi.org/10.1371/journal.pone.0100100

Ekman, P. (1972). Universals and cultural differences in facial expressions of emotion. In J. Cole (Ed.), *Nebraska Symposium on Motivation, 1971* (pp. 207–283). University of Nebraska Press.

Ekman, P. (1992). An argument for basic emotions. *Cognition and Emotion, 6,* 169–200.

Ekman, P. (1994a). All emotions are basic. In P. Ekman and R. J. Davidson (Eds.) *The nature of emotion: Fundamental questions* (pp. 15–19). Oxford University Press.

Ekman, P. (1994b). Strong evidence for universals in facial expressions: a reply to Russell's mistaken critique. *Psychological Bulletin, 115*(2), 268–287.

Ekman, P. (1999). Facial Expressions. In T. Dalgliesh & M. Power (Eds.), *Handbook of Cognition and Emotion* (pp. 301–320). Wiley.

Ekman, P. (2001). *Telling lies* (3rd ed.). Norton.

Ekman, P., & Friesen, W. V. (1978). *Facial Action Coding System.* Consulting Psychologist Press.

Ekman, P., & Friesen, W. V. (1984). *Unmasking the face* (2nd ed.). Consulting Psychologists Press.

Ekman, P., Friesen, W.V., O'Sullivan, M., Chan, A., Diacoyanni-Tarlatzis, I., Heider, K. . . . & Tsavaras, A. (1987). Universals and cultural differences in the judgments of facial expressions of emotion. *Journal of Personality and Social Psychology, 51,* 712–717.

Ekman, P., Levenson, R. W., & Friesen, W. V. (1983). Autonomic nervous system activity distinguishes among emotions. *Science, 221,* 1208–1210.

Ekman, P., Sorenson, E. R., & Friesen, W. V. (1969). Pan-cultural elements in facial displays of emotion. *Science, 164*(3875), 86–88.

Elad-Strenger, J., Proch, J., & Kessler, T. (2020). Is disgust a "conservative" emotion? *Personality and Social Psychology Bulletin, 46*(6), 896–912.

Eldar, E., Cohen, J. D., & Niv, Y. (2013). The effects of neural gain on attention and learning. *Nature Neuroscience, 16,* 1146–1153.

Eldesouky, L., & English, T. (2018). Another year older, another year wiser? Emotion regulation strategy selection and flexibility across adulthood. *Psychology and Aging, 33*(4), 572–585.

Eley, T. C., McAdams, T. A., Rijsdijk, F. V., Lichtenstein, P., Narusyte, J., Reiss, D., . . . & Neiderhiser, J. M. (2015). The intergenerational transmission of anxiety: A children-of-twins study. *American Journal of Psychiatry, 172,* 630–637.

Elfenbein, H. A., & Ambady, N. (2002). On the universality and cultural specificity of emotion recognition: A meta-analysis. *Psychological Bulletin, 128,* 203–235.

Elfenbein, H. A., Barsade, S. G., & Eisenkraft, N. (2015). The social perception of emotional abilities: Expanding what we now about observer ratings of emotional intelligence. *Emotion, 15,* 17–34.

Elfenbein, H. A., Beaupré, M., Lévesque, M., & Hess, U. (2007). Toward a dialect theory: Cultural differences in the expression and recognition of posed facial expressions. *Emotion, 7,* 131–146.

Elias, M. J., Hunter, L., & Kress, J. S. (2001). Emotional intelligence and education. In J. Ciarrochi, J. P. Forgas, & J. D. Mayer (Eds.), *Emotional intelligence in everyday life* (pp. 133–149). Psychology Press.

Ellemers, N. (2018). Gender stereotypes. *Annual Review of Psychology, 69,* 275–298.

Elliot, A. J., & Gable, S. L. (2019). Functions and hierarchical combinations of approach and avoidance motivation. *Psychological Inquiry, 30*(3), 130–131.

Elliot, A. J., Turiano, N. A., Infurna, F. J., Lachman, M. E., & Chapman, B. P. (2018). Lifetime trauma, perceived control, and all-cause mortality: Results from the Midlife in the United States Study. *Health Psychology, 37*(3), 262–270.

Ellis, E. M., Prather, A. A., Grenen, E. G., & Ferrer, R. A. (2019). Direct and indirect associations of cognitive reappraisal and suppression with disease biomarkers. *Psychology & Health, 34*(3), 336–354.

Ellsworth, P. C. (1994). William James and emotion: Is a century of fame worth a century of misunderstanding? *Psychological Review, 101,* 222–229.

Ellsworth, P. C., & Tong, E. M. W. (2006). What does it mean to be angry at yourself? Categories, appraisals, and the problem of language. *Emotion, 6,* 572–586.

Emde, R. N., & Koenig, K. (1969). Neonatal smiling and rapid eye movement states. *Journal of American Academic Child Psychiatry, 8,* 57–67.

Emmons, R. A., & McCullough, M. E. (2003). Counting blessings versus burdens: An experimental investigation of gratitude and subjective well-being in daily life. *Journal of Personality and Social Psychology, 84*, 377–389.

Engelberg, E., & Sjöberg, L. (2004). Emotional intelligence, affect intensity, and social adjustment. *Personality and Individual Differences, 37*, 533–542.

Engle, R. W., Conway, A. R., Tuholski, S. W., & Shisler, R. J. (1995). A resource account of inhibition. *Psychological Science, 6*(2), 122–125.

English, T., John, O. P., Srivastava, S., & Gross, J. J. (2012). Emotion regulation and peer-rated social functioning: A 4-year longitudinal study. *Journal of Research in Personality, 46*(6), 780–784.

Erlich, N., Lipp, O. V., & Slaughter, V. (2013). Of hissing snakes and angry voices: Human infants are differentially responsive to evolutionary fear-relevant sounds. *Developmental Science, 16*(6), 894–904.

Ersner-Hershfield, H., Mikels, J. A., Sullivan, S. J., & Carstensen, L. L. (2008). Poignancy: mixed emotional experience in the face of meaningful endings. *Journal of Personality and Social Psychology, 94*(1), 158–167.

Eshel, N., Nelson, E. E., Blair, R. J., Pine, D. S., & Ernst, M. (2007). Neural substrates of choice selection in adults and adolescents: Development of the ventrolateral prefrontal and anterior cingulate cortices. *Neuropsychologia, 45*(6), 1270–1279.

Esterson, A. (2001). The mythologizing of psychoanalytic history: Deceptions and self-deception in Freud's accounts of the seduction theory episode. *History of Psychology, 12*, 329–352.

Etkin, A., Büchel, C., & Gross, J. J. (2015). The neural bases of emotion regulation. *Nature Reviews Neuroscience, 16*(11), 693–700.

Ettman, C. K., Abdalla, S. M., Cohen, G. H., Sampson, L., Vivier, P. M., & Galea, S. (2020). Prevalence of depression symptoms in US adults before and during the COVID-19 pandemic. *JAMA Network Open, 3*(9), e2019686–e2019686. doi:10.1001/jamanetworkopen.2020.19686

Evans, C. A., & Porter, C. L. (2009). The emergence of mother–infant co-regulation during the first year: Links to infants' developmental status and attachment. *Infant Behavior and Development, 32*(2), 147–158.

Evans, G. W., Bullinger, M., & Hygge, S. (1998). Chronic noise exposure and physiological response: A prospective study of children living under environmental stress. *Psychological Science, 9*, 75–77.

Evans, G. W., & Schamberg, M. A. (2009). Childhood poverty, chronic stress, and adult working memory.

Proceedings of the National Academy of Sciences, 106(16), 6545–6549.

Evans, K., & Brase, G. L. (2007). Assessing sex differences and similarities in mate preferences: Above and beyond demand characteristics. *Journal of Social and Personal Relationships, 24*(5), 781–791.

Everaert, J., Bernstein, A., Joormann, J., & Koster, E. H. (2020). Mapping dynamic interactions among cognitive biases in depression. *Emotion Review, 12*(2), 93–110.

Evers, C., Marijn, S. F., & de Ridder, D. T. (2010). Feeding your feelings: emotion regulation strategies and emotional eating. *Personality & Social Psychology Bulletin, 36*(6), 792–804.

Fabes, R. A., Eisenberg, N., & Eisenbud, L. (1993). Behavioral and physiological correlates of children's reactions to others in distress. *Developmental Psychology, 29*, 655–663.

Fagnani, C., Medda, E., Stazi, M. A., Caprara, G. V., & Alessandri, G. (2014). Investigation of age and gender effects on positive orientation in Italian twins. *International Journal of Psychology, 6*, 453–461.

Falconier, M. K., & Jackson, J. B. (2020). Economic strain and couple relationship functioning: A meta-analysis. *International Journal of Stress Management, 27*(4), 311–325.

Fang, H., Tu, S., Sheng, J., & Shao, A. (2019). Depression in sleep disturbance: A review on a bidirectional relationship, mechanisms and treatment. *Journal of Cellular and Molecular Medicine, 23*(4), 2324–2332.

Fanselow, M. S. (1994). Neural organization of the defensive behavior system responsible for fear. *Psychonomic Bulletin & Review, 1*(4), 429–438.

Farris, C., Treat, T. A., Viken, R. J., & McFall, R. M. (2008). Perceptual mechanisms that characterize gender differences in decoding women's sexual intent. *Psychological Science, 19*(4), 348–354.

Fauerbach, J. A., Lawrence, J. W., Haythornthwaite, J. A., & Richter, L. (2002). Coping with the stress of a painful medical procedure. *Behaviour Research and Therapy, 40*, 1003–1015.

Fehr, B., & Russell, J. A. (1984). Concept of emotion viewed from a prototype perspective. *Journal of Experimental Psychology: General, 113*, 464–486.

Fehr, B., & Russell, J. A. (1991). The concept of love viewed from a prototype perspective. *Journal of Personality and Social Psychology, 60*, 425–438.

Feinstein, J. S., Adolphs, R., Damasio, A., & Tranel, D. (2011). The human amygdala and the induction and experience of fear. *Current Biology, 21*(1), 34–38.

Feinstein, J. S., Buzza, C., Hurlemann, R., Follmer, R. L., Dahdaleh, N. S., Coryell, W. H., . . . & Wemmie, J. A. (2013). Fear and panic in humans with bilateral amygdala damage. *Nature Neuroscience, 16*(3), 270–272.

Feldman, R. (2003). Infant-mother and infant-father synchrony: The coregulation of positive arousal. *Infant Mental Health Journal, 24*(1), 1–23.

Feldman, R. (2007). Parent-infant synchrony: Biological foundations and developmental outcomes. *Current Directions in Psychological Science, 16*(6), 340–345.

Feldman, R., & Eidelman, A. I. (2007). Maternal postpartum behavior and the emergence of infant-mother and infant-father synchrony in preterm and full-term infants: The role of neonatal vagal tone. *Developmental Psychobiology, 49*(3), 290–302.

Feldman, R., Weller, A., Zagoory-Sharon, O., & Levine, A. (2007). Evidence for a neuroendocrinological foundation of human affiliation plasma oxytocin levels across pregnancy and the postpartum period predict mother-infant bonding. *Psychological Science, 18*(11), 965–970.

Fendt, M., Koch, M., & Schnitzler, H. U. (1996). Lesions of the central gray block conditioned fear as measured with the potentiated startle paradigm. *Behavioral Brain Research, 74*, 127–134.

Ferguson, A. M., Cameron, C. D., & Inzlicht, M. (2020). Motivational effects on empathic choices. *Journal of Experimental Social Psychology, 90*, 104010.

Fiacconi, C. M., Dekraker, J., & Koehler, S. (2015). Psychophysiological evidence for the role of emotion in adaptive memory. *Journal of Experimental Psychology—General, 144*, 925–933.

Fiedler, K. (2001). Affective states trigger processes of assimilation and accommodation. In L. L. Martin & G. L. Clore (Eds.), *Theories of mood and cognition: A user's guidebook* (pp. 85–98). Erlbaum.

Field, T. M., Cohen, D., Garcia, R., & Greenberg, R. (1984). Mother-stranger face discrimination by the newborn. *Infant Behavior and Development, 7*(1), 19–25.

Finkelstein-Fox, L., Park, C. L., & Kalichman, S. C. (2020). Health benefits of positive reappraisal coping among people living with HIV/AIDS: A systematic review. *Health Psychology Review, 14*(3), 394–426.

Fiori, M., Antonietti, J.-P., Mikolajczak, M., Luminet, O., Hansenne, M., Rossier, J. (2014). What is the ability Emotional Intelligence Test good for? An evaluation using item response theory. *PLoS One, 9*, e98827. https://doi.org/10.1371/journal.pone.0098827

Fischer, A. H., Mosquera, P. M. R., van Vianen, A., & Manstead, A. S. R. (2004). Gender and culture differences in emotion. *Emotion, 4*, 87–94.

Fischer, R., & Boer, D. (2011). What is more important for national well-being: Money or autonomy? A meta-analysis of well-being, burnout, and anxiety across 63 societies. *Journal of Personality and Social Psychology, 101*(1), 164–184.

Fishbach, A. & Tu, Y. (2016). Pursuing goals with others. *Social and Personality Compass, 10*(5), 298–312.

Fishbach, A., & Trope, Y. (2008). Implicit and explicit counteractive self-control. In J. Y. Shah & W. L. Gardner (Eds.), *Handbook of motivation science* (pp. 281–294). Guilford Press.

Fiske, A. P. (2002). Using individualism and collectivism to compare cultures—A critique of the validity and measurement of the constructs: Comment on Oyserman et al. (2002). *Psychological Bulletin, 128*, 78–88.

Fiske, A. P., Seibt, B., & Schubert, T. (2019). The sudden devotion emotion: Kama muta and the cultural practices whose function is to evoke it. *Emotion Review, 11*(1), 74–86.

Fivush, R., Brotman, M. A., Buckner, J. P., & Goodman, S. H. (2000). Gender differences in parent-child emotion narratives. *Sex Roles, 42*, 233–253.

Floresco, S. B. (2015). The nucleus accumbens: An interface between cognition, emotion, and action. *Annual Review of Psychology, 66*, 25–52.

Floresco, S. B., Ghods-Sharifi, S., Vexelman, C., & Magyar, O. (2006). Dissociable roles for the nucleus accumbens core and shell in regulating set shifting. *Journal of Neuroscience, 26*(9), 2449–2457.

Flury, J., & Ickes, W. (2001). Emotional intelligence and empathic accuracy. In J. Ciarrochi, J. P. Forgas, & J. D. Mayer (Eds.), *Emotional intelligence in everyday life* (pp. 113–132). Psychology Press.

Folkman, S., & Moskowitz, J. T. (2000). Stress, positive emotion, and coping. *Current Directions in Psychological Science, 9*, 115–118.

Folkow, B. (2000). Perspectives on the integrative functions of the "sympatho-adrenomedullary system." *Autonomic Neuroscience: Basic and Clinical, 83*, 101–115.

Forbes, E. E., & Dahl, R. E. (2010). Pubertal development and behavior: Hormonal activation of social and emotional tendencies. *Brain and Cognition, 72*, 66–72.

Ford, B. Q., Dmitrieva, J. O., Heller, D., Chentsova-Dutton, Y., Grossmann, I., Tamir, M., . . . & Mauss, I. B. (2015). Culture shapes whether the pursuit of happiness predicts higher or lower well-being. *Journal of Experimental Psychology: General, 144*(6), 1053–1062.

Ford, B. Q., Feinberg, M., Lam, P., Mauss, I. B., & John, O. P. (2019). Using reappraisal to regulate negative emotion after the 2016 US Presidential election: Does emotion regulation trump political action? *Journal of Personality and Social Psychology, 117*(5), 998–1015.

Ford, B. Q., Shallcross, A. J., Mauss, I. B., Floerke, V. A., & Gruber, J. (2014). Desperately seeking happiness: Valuing happiness is associated with symptoms and diagnosis of depression. *Journal of Social and Clinical Psychology, 33*(10), 890–905.

Forgas, J. P. (1995). Mood and judgment: The affect infusion model (AIM). *Psychological Bulletin, 117*, 39–66.

Forgas, J. P. (2013). Don't worry, be sad! On the cognitive, motivational, and interpersonal benefits of negative mood. *Current Directions in Psychological Science, 22*(3), 225–232.

Forgas, J. P. (2017). Can sadness be good for you? *Australian Psychologist, 52*(1), 3–13.

Foster, D. J., & Wilson, M. A. (2006). Reverse replay of behavioural sequences in hippocampal place cells during the awake state. *Nature, 440*(7084), 680–683.

Fowler, J. H., & Christakis, N. A. (2008). Dynamic spread of happiness in a large social network: Longitudinal analysis over 20 years in the Framingham Heart Study. *British Medical Journal, 337*, a2338. doi: 10.1136/bmj.a2338

Fox, A. S., Lapate, R. C., Shackman, A. J., & Davidson, R. J. (Eds.). (2018). *The nature of emotion: Fundamental questions.* Oxford University Press.

Fox, A. S., & Shackman, A. J. (2019). The central extended amygdala in fear and anxiety: Closing the gap between mechanistic and neuroimaging research. *Neuroscience Letters, 693*, 58–67.

Fraiberg, S. (1974). Blind infants and their mothers: An examination of the sign system. In M. Lewis & L. A. Rosenblum (Eds.), *The effect of the infant on its caregiver.* Wiley-Interscience.

Fraley, R. C. (2002). Attachment stability from infancy to adulthood: Meta-analysis and dynamic modeling of developmental mechanisms. *Personality and Social Psychology Review, 6*(2), 123–151.

Fraley, R. C., & Roisman, G. I. (2019). The development of adult attachment styles: Four lessons. *Current Opinion in Psychology, 25*, 26–30.

Fraley, R. C., Roisman, G. I., Booth-LaForce, C., Owen, M. T., & Holland, A. S. (2013). Interpersonal and genetic origins of adult attachment styles: A longitudinal study from infancy to early adulthood. *Journal of Personality and Social Psychology, 104*(5), 817–838.

Fraley, R. C., & Shaver, P. R. (1998). Airport separations: A naturalistic study of adult attachment dynamics in separating couples. *Journal of Personality and Social Psychology, 75*(5), 1198–1212.

Fraley, R. C., & Shaver, P. R. (2000). Adult romantic attachment: Theoretical developments, emerging controversies, and unanswered questions. *Review of General Psychology, 4*, 132–154.

Fraley, R. C., & Waller, N. G. (1998). Adult attachment patterns: A test of the typological model. In J. A. Simpson & W. S. Rholed (Eds.), *Attachment theory and close relationships* (pp. 77–114). Guilford Press.

Frank, M. G., & Stennett, J. (2001). The forced-choice paradigm and the perception of facial expressions of emotion. *Journal of Personality and Social Psychology, 80*, 75–85.

Frank, R. H. (2012). The Easterlin paradox revisited. *Emotion, 12*, 1188–1191.

Fredrickson, B. L. (1998). What good are positive emotions? *Review of General Psychology, 2*(3), 300–319.

Fredrickson, B. L. (2001). The role of positive emotion in psychology: The broaden-and-build theory of positive emotions. *American Psychologist, 56*, 218–226.

Fredrickson, B. L. (2013). *Love 2.0: Finding happiness and health in moments of connection.* New York: Penguin.

Fredrickson, B. L., & Branigan, C. (2005). Positive emotions broaden the scope of attention and thought-action repertoires. *Cognition and Emotion, 19*, 313–332.

Fredrickson, B. L., & Joiner, T. (2002). Positive emotions trigger upward spirals toward emotional well-being. *Psychological Science, 13*, 172–175.

Fredrickson, B. L., & Joiner, T. (2018). Reflections on positive emotions and upward spirals. *Perspectives on Psychological Science, 13*(2), 194–199.

Fredrickson, B. L., & Levenson, R. W. (1998). Positive emotions speed recovery from the cardiovascular sequelae of negative emotions. *Cognition and Emotion, 12*, 191–220.

Fredrickson, B. L., & Losada, M. F. (2005). Positive affect and the complex dynamics of human flourishing. *American Psychologist, 60*, 678–686.

Fredrickson, B. L., Mancuso, R. A., Branigan, C., & Tugade, M. M. (2000). The undoing effect of positive emotions. *Motivation and Emotion, 24*(4), 237–258.

Freud, S. (1937). Analysis terminable and interminable. *International Journal of Psychoanalysis, 18*, 373–405.

Freud, S. (1957). Instincts and their vicissitudes. In S. Freud, J. Strachey, A Freud, A. Strachey, & A. Tyson (Eds.), *The standard edition of the complete psychological works of Sigmund Freud, volume XIV (1914–1916): On the history of the psycho-analytic movement, papers on metapsychology and other works* (pp. 109–140). Hogarth Press.

Fried, E. I. (2017). The 52 symptoms of major depression: Lack of content overlap among seven common depression scales. *Journal of Affective Disorders, 208,* 191–197.

Friedman, N. P., & Robbins, T. W. (2022). The role of prefrontal cortex in cognitive control and executive function. *Neuropsychopharmacology, 47*(1), 72–89.

Friedman, S., Smith, L., Fogel, D., Paradis, C., Viswanathan, R., Ackerman, R., & Trappler, B. (2002). The incidence and influence of early traumatic life events in patients with panic disorder: A comparison with other psychiatric outpatients. *Journal of Anxiety Disorders, 16,* 259–272.

Friese, M., Frankenbach, J., Job, V., & Loschelder, D. D. (2017). Does self-control training improve self-control? A meta-analysis. *Perspectives on Psychological Science, 12*(6), 1077–1099.

Friesen, W. V. (1972). *Cultural differences in facial expressions in a social situation: An experimental test of display rules.* PhD dissertation, University of California–San Francisco.

Frijda, N. H. (1986). *The emotions.* Cambridge University Press.

Frost, A., Hoyt, L. T., Chung, A. L., & Adam, E. K. (2015). Daily life with depressive symptoms: Gender differences in adolescents' everyday emotional experiences. *Journal of Adolescence, 43,* 132–141.

Fu, Q., Heath, A. C., Bucholz, K. K., Nelson, E., Goldberg, J., Lyons, M. J. . . . & Eisen, S. A. (2002). Shared genetic risk of major depression, alcohol dependence, and marijuana dependence. *Archives of General Psychiatry, 59,* 1125–1132.

Fujita, K., & MacGregor, K. E. (2012). Basic goal distinctions. In H. Aarts & A. J. Elliot (Eds.), *Goal-directed behavior* (pp. 85–114). Psychology Press.

Furman, W., & Buhrmester, D. (1992). Age and sex differences in perceptions of networks and social relationships. *Child Development, 63,* 103–115.

Füstös, J., Gramann, K., Herbert, B. M., & Pollatos, O. (2013). On the embodiment of emotion regulation: Interoceptive awareness facilitates reappraisal. *Social Cognitive and Affective Neuroscience, 8*(8), 911–917.

Gable, P., & Harmon-Jones, E. (2010). The Blues Broaden, but the Nasty Narrows Attentional Consequences of Negative Affects Low and High in Motivational Intensity. *Psychological Science, 21*(2), 211–215.

Gable, P. A., & Harmon-Jones, E. (2008). Approach-motivated positive affect reduces breadth of attention. *Psychological Science, 19,* 476–482.

Gable, P. A., & Poole, B. D. (2012). Time flies when you're having approach-motivated fun: Effects of motivational intensity on time perception. *Psychological Science, 23*(8), 879–886.

Gable, P. A., Poole, B. D., & Harmon-Jones, E. (2015). Anger perceptually and conceptually narrows cognitive scope. *Journal of Personality and Social Psychology, 109,* 163–174.

Gailliot, M. T., Baumeister, R. F., DeWall, C. N., Maner, J. K., Plant, E. A., Tice, D. M., Brewer, L. E., & Schmeichel, B. J. (2007). Self-control relies on glucose as a limited energy source: Willpower is more than a metaphor. *Journal of Personality and Social Psychology, 92*(2), 325–336.

Galatzer-Levy, I. R., & Bryant, R. A. (2013). 636,120 ways to have posttraumatic stress disorder. *Perspectives on Psychological Science, 8,* 651–662.

Gale, G. D., Anagnostaras, S. G., Godsil, B. P., Mitchell, S., Nozawa, T., Sage, J. R., . . . & Fanselow, M. S. (2004). Role of the basolateral amygdala in the storage of fear memories across the adult lifetime of rats. *Journal of Neuroscience, 24,* 3810–3815.

Gannon, N., & Ranzijn, R. (2005). Does emotional intelligence predict unique variance in life satisfaction beyond IQ and personality? *Personality and Individual Differences, 38,* 1353–1364.

Garcez, H., Fernandes, C., Barbosa, F., Pereira, M. R., Silveira, C., Marques-Teixeira, J., & Gonçalves, A. R. (2020). Effects of benzodiazepines administration on identification of facial expressions of emotion: A meta-analysis. *Psychopharmacology, 237*(1), 1–9.

Garcia, R., Vouimba, R. M., Baudry, M., & Thompson, R. F. (1999). The amygdala modulates prefrontal cortex activity relative to conditioned fear. *Nature, 402,* 294–296.

García-Sancho, E., Salguero, J. M., & Fernández-Berrocal, P. (2014). Relationship between emotional intelligence and aggression: A systematic review. *Aggression and Violent Behavior, 19,* 584–591.

Gardner, M., & Steinberg, L. (2005). Peer influence on risk taking, risk preference, and risky decision making in adolescence and adulthood: An experimental study. *Developmental Psychology, 41,* 625–635.

Garfinkel, S. N., & Liberzon, I. (2009). Neurobiology of PTSD: A review of neuroimaging findings. *Psychiatric Annals, 39*(6), 370–372, 376–381.

Garnefski, N., Teerds, J., Kraaij, V., Legerstee, J., & van den Kommer, T. (2004). Cognitive emotion regulation strategies and depressive symptoms: Differences between males and females. *Personality and Individual Differences, 36,* 267–276.

Garnefski, N., van den Kommer, T., Kraaij, V., Teerds, J., Legerstee, J., & Onstein, E. (2002). The relationship between cognitive emotion regulation strategies and emotional problems: Comparison between a clinical and a non-clinical sample. *European Journal of Personality*, *16*, 403–420.

Garrett-Peters, P. T., Castro, V. L., & Halberstadt, A. G. (2017). Parents' beliefs about children's emotions, children's emotion understanding, and classroom adjustment in middle childhood. *Social Development*, *26*(3), 575–590.

Gasquoine, P. G. (2014). Contributions of the insula to cognition and emotion. *Neuropsychology Review*, *24*, 77–87.

Geangu, E., Benga, O., Stahl, D., & Striano, T. (2010). Contagious crying beyond the first days of life. *Infant Behavior and Development*, *33*, 279–288.

Geangu, E., Ichikawa, H., Lao, J., Kanazawa, S., Yamaguchi, M. K., Caldara, R., & Turati, C. (2016). Culture shapes 7-month-olds' perceptual strategies in discriminating facial expressions of emotion. *Current Biology*, *26*(14), R663–R664.

Gebauer, J. E., Sedikides, C., & Neberich, W. (2012). Religiosity, social self-esteem, and psychological adjustment: On the cross-cultural specificity of the psychological benefits of religiosity. *Psychological Science*, *23*, 158–160.

Geen, R. G. (1978). Effects of attack and uncontrollable noise on aggression. *Journal of Research in Personality*, *9*, 270–281.

Geertz, C. (1973). *Interpretation of cultures*. Basic Books.

Geniole, S. N., Bird, B. M., McVittie, J. S., Purcell, R. B., Archer, J., & Carré, J. M. (2020). Is testosterone linked to human aggression? A meta-analytic examination of the relationship between baseline, dynamic, and manipulated testosterone on human aggression. *Hormones and Behavior*, *123*, 104644.

Geschwind, D. H., & Flint, J. (2015). Genetics and genomics of psychiatric disease. *Science*, *349*, 1489–1494.

Gifkins, A., Greba, Q., & Kokkinidis, L. (2002). Ventral tegmental area dopamine neurons mediate the shock sensitization of acoustic startle: A potential site of action for benzodiazepine anxiolytics. *Behavioral Neuroscience*, *116*, 785–794.

Gigerenzer, G. (2004). Dread risk, September 11, and fatal traffic accidents. *Psychological Science*, *15*, 286–287.

Gilbertson, M. W., Shenton, M. E., Ciszewski, A., Kasai, K., Lasko, N. B., Orr, S. P., & Pitman, R. K. (2002). Smaller hippocampal volume predicts pathological vulnerability to psychological trauma. *Nature Neuroscience*, *5*, 1242–1247.

Gillath, O., Shaver, P. R., Baek, J. M., & Chun, D. S. (2008). Genetic correlates of adult attachment style. *Personality and Social Psychology Bulletin*, *34*(10), 1396–1405.

Gilovich, T., Kumar, A., & Jampol, L. (2015). A wonderful life: Experiential consumption and the pursuit of happiness. *Journal of Consumer Psychology*, *25*(1), 152–165.

Giner-Sorolla, R., & Chapman, H. A. (2017). Beyond purity: Moral disgust toward bad character. *Psychological Science*, *28*(1), 80–91.

Girard, J. M., & McDuff, D. (2017). Historical heterogeneity predicts smiling: Evidence from large-scale observational analyses. In *2017 12th IEEE International Conference on Automatic Face & Gesture Recognition (FG 2017)* (pp. 719–726). Institute of Electrical and Electronics Engineers.

Girard, R. (1988). *To double business bound: Essays on literature, mimesis and anthropology*. JHU Press.

Girardeau, G., & Lopes-dos-Santos, V. (2021). Brain neural patterns and the memory function of sleep. *Science*, *374*(6567), 560–564.

Glaser, R., Rice, J., Speicher, C. E., Stout, J. C., & Kiecolt-Glaser, J. K. (1986). Stress depresses interferon production by leukocytes concomitant with a decrease in natural killer cell activity. *Behavioral Neuroscience*, *100*, 675–678.

Glass, D. C., Singer, J. E., & Pennebaker, J. W. (1977). Behavioral and physiological effects of uncontrollable environmental events. In D. Stokols (Ed.), *Perspectives on environment and behavior* (pp. 131–151). Plenum.

Goetz, J. L., Keltner, D., & Simon-Thomas, E. (2010). Compassion: an evolutionary analysis and empirical review. *Psychological Bulletin*, *136*(3), 351–374.

Goetzmann, W. N., Kim, D., Kumar, A., & Wang, Q. (2015). Weather-induced mood, institutional investors, and stock returns. *Review of Financial Studies*, *28*, 73–111.

Goldberg, S. B., Tucker, R. P., Greene, P. A., Davidson, R. J., Kearney, D. J., & Simpson, T. L. (2019). Mindfulness-based cognitive therapy for the treatment of current depressive symptoms: A meta-analysis. *Cognitive Behaviour Therapy*, *48*(6), 445–462.

Goldin, P. R., McRae, K., Ramel, W., & Gross, J. J. (2008). The neural bases of emotion regulation: reappraisal and suppression of negative emotion. *Biological Psychiatry*, *63*(6), 577–586.

Goldring, M. R., & Bolger, N. (2021). Physical effects of daily stressors are psychologically mediated, heterogeneous, and bidirectional. *Journal of Personality and Social Psychology*, *121*(3), 722–746.

Goldstein, A. (1980). Thrills in response to music and other stimuli. *Physiological Psychology, 8,* 126–129.

Gollwitzer, P. M. (1993). Goal achievement: The role of intentions. *European Review of Social Psychology, 4*(1), 141–185.

Gollwitzer, P. M. (2014). Weakness of the will: Is a quick fix possible? *Motivation and Emotion, 38*(3), 305–322.

Gollwitzer, P. M., & Sheeran, P. (2006). Implementation intentions and goal achievement: A meta-analysis of effects and processes. *Advances in Experimental Social Psychology, 38,* 69–119.

Gonzaga, G. C., Campos, B., & Bradbury, T. (2007). Similarity, convergence, and relationship satisfaction in dating and married couples. *Journal of Personality and Social Psychology, 93*(1), 34–48.

Gonzaga, G. C., Turner, R. A., Keltner, D., Campos, B., & Altemus, M. (2006). Romantic love and sexual desire in close relationships. *Emotion, 6*(2), 163–179.

Gorn, G. J., Goldberg, M. E., & Basu, K. (1993). Mood, awareness, and product evaluation. *Journal of Consumer Psychology, 2*(3), 237–256.

Gottman, J. M. (1994). *What predicts divorce?* Erlbaum.

Gottman, J. M., Coan, J., Carrere, S., & Swanson, C. (1998). Predicting marital happiness and stability from newlywed interactions. *Journal of Marriage and the Family, 60,* 5–22.

Goyal, M., Singh, S., Sibinga, E. M., Gould, N. F., Rowland-Seymour, A., Sharma, R., . . . & Ranasinghe, P. D. (2014). Meditation programs for psychological stress and well-being: a systematic review and meta-analysis. *JAMA Internal Medicine, 174*(3), 357–368.

Gračanin, A., Vingerhoets, A. J., Kardum, I., Zupčić, M., Šantek, M., & Šimić, M. (2015). Why crying does and sometimes does not seem to alleviate mood: A quasi-experimental study. *Motivation and Emotion, 39*(6), 953–960.

Graham, J., Haidt, J., & Nosek, B. A. (2009). Liberals and conservatives rely on different sets of moral foundations. *Journal of Personality and Social Psychology, 96*(5), 1029–1046.

Grammer, K., Kruck, K., Jutte, A., & Fink, B. (2000). Non-verbal behavior as courtship signals: The role of control and choice in selecting partners. *Evolution and Human Behavior, 21,* 371–390.

Grandjean, D., & Scherer, K. R. (2008). Unpacking the cognitive architecture of emotion processes. *Emotion, 8,* 341–351.

Gray, J. A. (1970). The psychophysiological basis of introversion-extraversion. *Behavioural Research Therapy, 8,* 249–266.

Gray, J. A. (1982). On mapping anxiety. *Behavioral and Brain Sciences, 5*(03), 506–534.

Greene, J. D., Sommerville, R. B., Nystrom, L. E., Darley, J. M., & Cohen, J. D. (2001). An fMRI investigation of emotional engagement in moral judgment. *Science, 293,* 2105–2108.

Greenstein, M., & Franklin, N. (2020). Anger increases susceptibility to misinformation. *Experimental Psychology, 67*(3), 202–209.

Greenwald, M. K., Cook, E. W., & Lang, P. J. (1989). Affective judgment and psychophysiological response: Dimensional covariation in the evaluation of pictorial stimuli. *Journal of Psychophysiology, 3,* 51–64.

Griffin, D. W., & Bartholomew, K. (1994). The metaphysics of measurement: The case of adult attachment. In K. Bartholomew & D. Perlman (Eds.), *Advances in personal relationships: Vol. 5. Attachment processes in adulthood* (pp. 17–52). Jessica Kingsley.

Griskevicius, V., Shiota, M. N., & Neufeld, S. L. (2010). Influence of Different Positive Emotions on Persuasion Processing: A Functional Evolutionary Approach. *Emotion, 10*(2), 190–206.

Griskevicius, V., Shiota, M. N., & Nowlis, S. M. (2010). The many shades of rose-colored glasses: An evolutionary approach to the influence of different positive emotions. *Journal of Consumer Research, 37*(2), 238–250.

Gross, A. E., & Crofton, C. (1977). What is good is beautiful. *Sociometry, 40,* 85–90.

Gross, J. J. (1998). Antecedent- and response-focused emotion regulation: Divergent consequences for experience, expression, and physiology. *Journal of Personality and Social Psychology, 74,* 224–237.

Gross, J. J. (2002). Emotion regulation: Affective, cognitive, and social consequences. *Psychophysiology, 39,* 281–291.

Gross, J. J. (2015). Emotion regulation: Current status and future prospects. *Psychological Inquiry, 26*(1), 1–26.

Gross, J. J., & Jazaieri, H. (2014). Emotion, emotion regulation, and psychopathology: An affective science perspective. *Clinical Psychological Science, 2,* 387–401.

Gross, J. J., & John, O. P. (2003). Individual differences in two emotion regulation processes: Implications for affect, relationships, and well-being. *Journal of Personality and Social Psychology, 85,* 348–362.

Gross, J. J., & Levenson, R. W. (1995). Emotion elicitation using films. *Cognition and Emotion, 9*(1), 87–108.

Gross, J. J., & Levenson, R. W. (1997). Hiding feelings: The acute effects of inhibiting positive and negative emotions. *Journal of Abnormal Psychology, 106*, 95–103.

Gross, J. J., Carstensen, L. L., Pasupathi, M., Tsai, J., Skorpen, C. G., & Hsu, A. Y. C. (1997). Emotion and aging: Experience, expression, and control. *Psychology and Aging, 12*, 590–599.

Gross, R. L. (2015). Individual differences in toddlers' social understanding and prosocial behavior: disposition or socialization? *Frontiers in Psychology, 6*, Article 600. https://doi.org/10.3389/fpsyg.2015.00600

Grosse, G., Streubel, B., Gunzenhauser, C., & Saalbach, H. (2021). Let's talk about emotions: The development of children's emotion vocabulary from 4 to 11 years of age. *Affective Science*, in press.

Grossmann, I., Ellsworth, P. C., & Hong, Y. Y. (2012). Culture, attention, and emotion. *Journal of Experimental Psychology: General, 141*(1), 31–36.

Grossmann, I., Huynh, A. C., & Ellsworth, P. C. (2016). Emotional complexity: Clarifying definitions and cultural correlates. *Journal of Personality and Social Psychology, 111*(6), 895–916.

Grossmann, I., Karasawa, M., Kan, C., & Kitayama, S. (2014). A cultural perspective on emotional experiences across the life span. *Emotion, 14*, 679–692.

Grossmann, I., & Kross, E. (2010). The impact of culture on adaptive versus maladaptive self-reflection. *Psychological Science, 21*(8), 1150–1157.

Grossmann, I., & Varnum, M. E. (2015). Social Structure, Infectious Diseases, Disasters, Secularism, and Cultural Change in America. *Psychological Science, 26*(3), 311–324.

Gruber, J. (2011). Can feeling too good be bad? Positive emotion persistence (PEP) in bipolar disorder. *Current Directions in Psychological Science, 20*(4), 217–221.

Gruber, J., Hay, A. C., & Gross, J. J. (2014). Rethinking emotion: cognitive reappraisal is an effective positive and negative emotion regulation strategy in bipolar disorder. *Emotion, 14*(2), 388–396.

Gruber, J., & Johnson, S. L. (2009). Positive emotional traits and ambitious goals among people at risk for mania: The need for specificity. *International Journal of Cognitive Therapy, 2*(2), 176–187.

Gruber, J., Johnson, S. L., Oveis, C., & Keltner, D. (2008). Risk for mania and positive emotional responding: too much of a good thing? *Emotion, 8*(1), 23–33.

Gu, J., Strauss, C., Bond, R., & Cavanagh, K. (2015). How do mindfulness-based cognitive therapy and mindfulness-based stress reduction improve mental health and wellbeing? A systematic review and meta-analysis of mediation studies. *Clinical Psychology Review, 37*, 1–12.

Guarana, C. L., Ryu, J. W., O'Boyle Jr, E. H., Lee, J., & Barnes, C. M. (2021). Sleep and self-control: A systematic review and meta-analysis. *Sleep Medicine Reviews*, 101514.

Gujjar, K. R., van Wijk, A., Kumar, R., & de Jongh, A. (2019). Efficacy of virtual reality exposure therapy for the treatment of dental phobia in adults: A randomized controlled trial. *Journal of Anxiety Disorders, 62*, 100–108.

Gunnar, M. R., & Vazquez, D. M. (2001). Low cortisol and a flattening of expected daytime rhythm: Potential indices of risk in human development. *Development and Psychopathology, 13*(03), 515–538.

Guo, Y., Klein, B., Ro, Y., & Rossin, D. (2007). The impact of flow on learning outcomes in a graduate-level information management course. *Journal of Global Business Issues, 1*(2), 31–39.

Gupta, N. D., Etcoff, N. L., & Jaeger, M. M. (2015). Beauty in mind: The effects of physical attractiveness on psychological well-being and distress. *Journal of Happiness Studies, 17*(3), 1313–1325.

Gyurak, A., & Ayduk, Ö. (2008). Resting respiratory sinus arrhythmia buffers against rejection sensitivity via emotion control. *Emotion, 8*(4), 458–467.

Haas, L. M., McArthur, B. A., Burke, T. A., Olino, T. M., Abramson, L. Y., & Alloy, L. B. (2019). Emotional clarity development and psychosocial outcomes during adolescence. *Emotion, 19*(4), 563–572.

Haase, C. M., Seider, B. H., Shiota, M. N., & Levenson, R. W. (2012). Anger and sadness in response to an emotionally neutral film: evidence for age-specific associations with well-being. *Psychology and aging, 27*(2), 305–317.

Hagger, M. S., Chatzisarantis, N. L., Alberts, H., Anggono, C. O., Batailler, C., Birt, A. R., . . . & Zwienenberg, M. (2016). A multilab preregistered replication of the ego-depletion effect. *Perspectives on Psychological Science, 11*(4), 546–573.

Haidt, J. (2001). The emotional dog and its rational tail: A social intuitionist approach to moral judgment. *Psychological Review, 108*, 814–834.

Haidt, J. (2012). *The Righteous Mind*. Pantheon.

Haidt, J., & Keltner, D. (1999). Culture and facial expression: Open-ended methods find more faces and a gradient of recognition. *Cognition and Emotion, 13*, 225–266.

Haidt, J., McCauley, C., & Rozin, P. (1994). Individual differences in sensitivity to disgust: A scale sampling seven domains of disgust elicitors. *Personality and Individual Differences, 16*, 701–713.

Haidt, J., Rozin, P., McCauley, C. R., & Imada, S. (1997). Body, psyche, and culture: The relationship between disgust and morality. *Psychology and Developing Societies, 9*, 107–131.

Haines, S. J., Gleeson, J., Kuppens, P., Hollenstein, T., Ciarrochi, J., Labuschagne, I., . . . & Koval, P. (2016). The wisdom to know the difference: Strategy-situation fit in emotion regulation in daily life is associated with well-being. *Psychological Science, 27*(12), 1651–1659.

Hajcak, G., & Foti, D. (2008). Errors are aversive: Defensive motivation and the error-related negativity. *Psychological Science, 19*(2), 103–108.

Hajcak, G., McDonald, N., & Simons, R. F. (2003). To err is autonomic: Error-related brain potentials, ANS activity, and post-error compensatory behavior. *Psychophysiology, 40*(6), 895–903.

Haj-Mohamadi, P., Gillath, O., & Rosenberg, E. L. (2021). Identifying a facial expression of flirtation and its effect on men. *Journal of Sex Research, 58*(2), 137–145.

Hakulinen, C., Jokela, M., Hintsanen, M., Merjonen, P., Pulkki-Råback, L, Seppälä, I., . . . Keltikangas-Järvinen, L. (2013). Serotonin receptor 1B genotype and hostility, anger and aggressive behavior through the lifespan: the Young Finns study. *Journal of Behavioral Medicine, 36*, 583–590.

Halberstadt, A. G., Denham, S. A., & Dunsmore, J. C. (2001). Affective social competence. *Social Development, 10*, 79–119.

Hall, J. A., Andrzejewski, S. A., & Yopchick, J. E. (2009). Psychosocial correlates of interpersonal sensitivity: A meta-analysis. *Journal of Nonverbal Behavior, 33*, 149–180.

Hamamura, T. (2012). Are cultures becoming individualistic? A cross-temporal comparison of individualism-collectivism in the United States and Japan. *Personality and Social Psychology Review, 16*(1), 3–24.

Hamann, S. (2012). What can neuroimaging meta-analyses really tell us about the nature of emotion? *Behavioral and Brain Sciences, 35*, 150–152.

Hamilton, M. (1960). A rating scale for depression. *Journal of Neurology, Neurosurgery, and Psychiatry, 23*(1), 56–62.

Hamm, A. O., Richter, J., & Pané-Farré, C. A. (2014). When the threat comes from inside the body: A neuroscience based learning perspective of the etiology of panic disorder. *Restorative Neurology and Neuroscience, 32*, 79–93.

Hanish, L. D., Eisenberg, N., Fabes, R. A., Spinrad, T. L., Ryan, P., & Schmidt, S. (2004). The expression and regulation of negative emotions: Risk factors for young children's peer.

Harker, L. A., & Keltner, D. (2001). Expressions of positive emotion in women's college yearbook pictures and their relationship to personality and life outcomes across adulthood. *Journal of Personality and Social Psychology, 80*, 112–124.

Harkin, B., Webb, T. L., Chang, B. P., Prestwich, A., Conner, M., Kellar, I., . . . & Sheeran, P. (2016). Does monitoring goal progress promote goal attainment? A meta-analysis of the experimental evidence. *Psychological Bulletin, 142*(2), 198–229.

Harlow, H. F. (1958). The nature of love. *American Psychologist, 13*(12), 673–685.

Harmon-Jones, C., & Harmon-Jones, E. (2019). A broad consideration of motivation, with a focus on approach motivation. *Psychological Inquiry, 30*(3), 132–135.

Harmon-Jones, E. (2003). Clarifying the emotive functions of asymmetrical frontal cortical activity. *Psychophysiology, 40*(6), 838–848.

Harmon-Jones, E., & Allen, J. J. (1998). Anger and frontal brain activity: EEG asymmetry consistent with approach motivation despite negative affective valence. *Journal of Personality and Social Psychology, 74*(5), 1310–1316.

Harmon-Jones, E., & Gable, P. A. (2018). On the role of asymmetric frontal cortical activity in approach and withdrawal motivation: An updated review of the evidence. *Psychophysiology, 55*(1), e12879. https://doi.org/10.1111/psyp.12879

Harmon-Jones, E., & Harmon-Jones, C. (2016). Anger. In L. F. Barrett, M. Lewis, & J. M. Haviland-Jones (Eds.), *Handbook of emotions* (4th ed., pp. 774–791). Guilford Press.

Harmon-Jones, E., & Peterson, C. (2009). Supine body position reduces neural response to anger evocation. *Psychological Science, 20*(10), 1209–1210.

Harmon-Jones, E., Sigelman, J., Bohlig, A., & Harmon-Jones, C. (2003). Anger, coping, and frontal cortical activity: The effect of coping potential on anger-induced left frontal activity. *Cognition & Emotion, 17*(1), 1–24.

Harris, C. R., & Pashler, H. (2004). Attention and the processing of emotional words and names. *Psychological Science, 15*, 171–178.

Harrison, L. A., Hurlemann, R., & Adolphs, R. (2015). An enhanced default approach bias following amygdala lesions in humans. *Psychological Science, 26*, 1543–1555.

Hatfield, E., & Rapson, R. L. (1993). *Love, sex, and intimacy*. Harper Collins.

Hatfield, E., & Sprecher, S. (1986). Measuring passionate love in intimate relationships. *Journal of Adolescence, 9*(4), 383–410.

Hawkley, L. C., & Cacioppo, J. T. (2010). Loneliness matters: A theoretical and empirical review of consequences and mechanisms. *Annals of Behavioral Medicine, 40*(2), 218–227.

Hawkley, L. C., Wroblewski, K., Kaiser, T., Luhmann, M., & Schumm, L. P. (2019). Are US older adults getting lonelier? Age, period, and cohort differences. *Psychology and Aging, 34*(8), 1144–1157.

Hazan, C., & Shaver, P. (1987). Romantic love conceptualized as an attachment process. *Journal of Personality and Social Psychology, 52*, 511–524.

He, H., Hu, C., Ren, Z., Bai, L., Gao, F., & Lyu, J. (2020). Trends in the incidence and DALYs of bipolar disorder at global, regional, and national levels: Results from the global burden of disease study 2017. *Journal of Psychiatric Research, 125*, 96–105.

Hearn, L. ([1894] 2011). *Glimpses of Unfamiliar Japan*. Tuttle.

Hecht, M. A., & LaFrance, M. (1998). License or obligation to smile: The effect of power and sex on amount and type of smiling. *Personality and Social Psychology Bulletin, 24*, 1332–1342.

Heine, S. J., Lehman, D. R., Peng, K., & Greenholtz, J. (2002). What's wrong with cross-cultural comparisons of subjective Likert scales? The reference-group effect. *Journal of Personality and Social Psychology, 82*, 903–918.

Heller, D., Watson, D., & Ilies, R. (2004). The role of person versus situation in life satisfaction: A critical examination. *Psychological Bulletin, 130*, 574–600.

Henderson, E. K., & Braithwaite, S. R. (2021). Cross-group relationship satisfaction: A meta-analysis. *Marriage & Family Review, 57*(7), 621–646.

Hendrick, S. S., Hendrick, C., & Adler, N. L. (1988). Romantic relationships: Love, satisfaction, and staying together. *Journal of Personality and Social Psychology, 54*, 980–988.

Hennenlotter, A., Dresel, C., Castrop, F., Baumann, A. O. C., Wohlschlager, A. M., & Haslinger, B. (2009). The link between facial feedback and neural activity within central circuitries of emotion. *Cerebral Cortex, 19*, 537–542.

Hennig-Fast, K., Michl, P., Müller, J., Niedermeier, N., Coates, U., Müller, N., . . . Meindl, T. (2015). Obsessive-compulsive disorder: A question of conscience? An fMRI study of behavioural and neurofunctional correlates of shame and guilt. *Journal of Psychiatric Research, 68*, 354–362.

Herman, B. H., & Panksepp, J. (1978). Effects of morphine and naloxone on separation distress and approach attachment: Evidence for the opiate mediation of social affect. *Pharmacology, Biochemistry, and Behavior, 9*, 213–220.

Herpetz, S. C., Vloet, T., Mueller, B., Domes, G., Willmes, K., & Herpetz-Dahlmann, B. (2007). Similar autonomic responsivity in boys with conduct disorder and their fathers. *Journal of the American Academy of Child & Adolescent Psychiatry, 46*, 535–544.

Hertenstein, M. J., Hansel, C. A., Butts, A. M., & Hile, S. N. (2009). Smile intensity in photographs predicts divorce later in life. *Motivation and Emotion, 33*, 99–105.

Hertenstein, M. J., Keltner, D., App, B., Bulleit, B. A., & Jaskolka, A. R. (2006). Touch communicates distinct emotions. *Emotion, 6*(3), 528–533.

Heschl, A., & Burkhart, J. (2006). A new mark test for mirror self-recognition in non-human primates. *Primates, 47*, 187–198.

Hess, U., Kappas, A., McHugo, G. J., Lanzetta, J. T., & Kleck, R. E. (1992). The facilitative effect of facial expression on the self-generation of emotion. *International Journal of Psychophysiology, 12*, 251–265.

Hettema, J. M., Annas, P., Neale, M. C., Kendler, K. S., & Fredrikson, M. (2003). A twin study of the genetics of fear conditioning. *Archives of General Psychiatry, 60*(7), 702–708.

Hettema, J. M., Neale, M. C., & Kendler, K. S. (2001). A review and meta-analysis of the genetic epidemiology of anxiety disorders. *American Journal of Psychiatry, 158*, 1568–1578.

Higgins, E. T. (1987). Self-discrepancy: A theory relating self and affect. *Psychological Review, 94*(3), 319–340.

Higgins, E. T. (1998). Promotion and prevention: Regulatory focus as a motivational principle. In M.P. Zanna (Ed.), *Advances in experimental social psychology* (Vol. 30, pp. 1–46). Academic Press.

Hildebrandt, K. A., & Fitzgerald, H. E. (1979). Facial feature determinants of perceived infant attractiveness. *Infant Behavior and Development, 2*(4), 329–339.

Hill, P., & Martin, R. B. (1997). Empathic weeping, social communication, and cognitive dissonance. *Journal of Social and Clinical Psychology, 16*, 299–322.

Hirschberger, G., Srivastava, S., Marsh, P., Cowan, C. P., & Cowan, P. A. (2009). Attachment, marital satisfaction, and divorce during the first fifteen years of parenthood. *Personal Relationships, 16*(3), 401–420.

Hitchcock, J. M., & Davis, M. (1991). Efferent pathway of the amygdala involved in conditioned fear as measured with the fear-potentiated startle paradigm. *Behavioral Neuroscience, 105*, 826–842.

Ho, Y., & Lipp, O. V. (2014). Faster acquisition of conditioned fear to fear-relevant than to nonfear-relevant conditional stimuli. *Psychophysiology, 51*(8), 810–813.

Hobson, C. J., & Delunas, L. (2001). National norms and life-event frequencies for the revised social readjustment rating scale. *International Journal of Stress Management, 8*, 299–314.

Hobson, C. J., Kamen, J., Szostek, J., Neithercut, C. M., Tidemann, J. W., & Wojnarowicz, S. (1998). Stressful life events: A revision and update of the social readjustment rating scale. *International Journal of Stress Management, 5*, 1–23.

Hodes, G. E., Kana, V., Menard, C., Merad, M., & Russo, S. J. (2015). Neuroimmune mechanisms of depression. *Nature Neuroscience, 18*, 1386–1393.

Hoehl, S., & Striano, T. (2008). Neural processing of eye gaze and threat-related emotional facial expressions in infancy. *Child Development, 79*, 1752–1760.

Hoemann, K., Xu, F., & Barrett, L. F. (2019). Emotion words, emotion concepts, and emotional development in children: A constructionist hypothesis. *Developmental Psychology, 55*(9), 1830–1849.

Hoffmann, J., & Nicola, S. M. (2014). Dopamine invigorates reward seeking by promoting cue-evoked excitation in the nucleus accumbens. *Journal of Neuroscience, 34*(43), 14349–14364.

Hofmann, S. G., Sawyer, A. T., Witt, A. A., & Oh, D. (2010). The effect of mindfulness-based therapy on anxiety and depression: A meta-analytic review. *Journal of Consulting and Clinical Psychology, 78*(2), 169–182.

Hofmann, S. G., Wu, J. Q., & Boettcher, H. (2014). Effect of cognitive-behavioral therapy for anxiety disorders on quality of life: A meta-analysis. *Journal of Consulting and Clinical Psychology, 82*, 375–391.

Hofmann, W., Baumeister, R. F., Förster, G., & Vohs, K. D. (2012). Everyday temptations: An experience sampling study of desire, conflict, and self-control. *Journal of Personality and Social Psychology, 102*(6), 1318–1335.

Hofstede, G. (2001). *Culture's consequences: Comparing values, behaviors, institutions and organizations across nations*. Sage.

Hofstede, G. J. (n.d.). *The 6D model of national culture*. Geert Hofstede. https://geerthofstede.com/culture-geert-hofstede-gert-jan-hofstede/6d-model-of-national-culture/

Hogan, R., & Hogan, J. (1991). Personality and status. In D. G. Gilbert & J. J. Connolly (Eds.), *Personality, Social Skills, and Psychopathology* (pp. 137–154). Springer.

Holahan, C. J., Moos, R. H., Holahan, C. K., Brennan, P. L., & Schutte, K. K. (2005). Stress generation, avoidance coping, and depressive symptoms: A 10-year model. *Journal of Consulting and Clinical Psychology, 73*(4), 658–666.

Holas, P., Krejtz, I., Cypryanska, M., & Nezlek, J. B. (2014). Orienting and maintenance of attention to threatening facial expressions in anxiety: An eye movement study. *Psychiatry Research, 220*, 362–369.

Holley, S. R., Sturm, V. E., & Levenson, R. W. (2010). Exploring the basis for gender differences in the demand-withdraw pattern. *Journal of Homosexuality, 57*(5), 666–684.

Hollon, S. D., DeRubeis, R. J., Fawcett, J., Amsterdam, J. D., Shelton, R. C., Zajecka, J., . . . Gallop, R. (2014). Effect of cognitive therapy with antidepressant medications vs antidepressants alone on the rate of recovery in major depressive disorder. *JAMA Psychiatry, 71*, 1157–1164.

Hollon, S. D., Thase, M. E., & Markowitz, J. C. (2002). Treatment and prevention of depression. *Psychological Science in the Public Interest, 3*, 39–77.

Holmes, A., Mogg, K., de Fockert, J., Nielsen, M. K., & Bradley, B. P. (2014). Electrophysiological evidence for greater attention to threat when cognitive control resources are depleted. *Cognitive, Affective, & Behavioral Neuroscience, 14*(2), 827–835.

Holmes, A. J., Lee, P. H., Hollinshead, M. O., Bakst, L., Roffman, J. L., Smoller, J. W., & Buckner, R. L. (2012). Individual differences in amygdala-medial prefrontal anatomy link negative affect, impaired social functioning, and polygenic depression risk. *Journal of Neuroscience, 32*(50), 18087–18100.

Holmes, D. S. (1978). Projection as a defense mechanism. *Psychological Bulletin, 85*, 677–688.

Holmes, D. S. (1990). The evidence for repression: An examination of sixty years of research. In J. L. Singer (Ed.), *Repression and dissociation* (pp. 85–102). Wiley.

Holmes, T. H., & Rahe, R. H. (1977). The social readjustment rating scale. *Journal of Psychosomatic Research, 11*, 213–218.

Hölzel, B. K., Hoge, E. A., Greve, D. N., Gard, T., Creswell, J. D., Brown, K. W., . . . & Lazar, S. W. (2013). Neural mechanisms of symptom improvements in generalized anxiety disorder following mindfulness training. *NeuroImage: Clinical, 2*, 448–458.

Hong, Y., Morris, M. W., Chiu, C., & Benet-Martinez, V. (2000). Multicultural minds: A dynamic constructivist approach to culture and cognition. *American Psychologist, 55*, 709–720.

Honts, C. R., & Perry, M. V. (1992). Polygraph admissibility. *Law and Human Behavior, 16*(3), 357–379.

Hoppenbrouwers, S. S., Bulten, B. H., & Brazil, I. A. (2016). Parsing fear: A reassessment of the evidence for fear deficits in psychopathy. *Psychological Bulletin, 142*(6), 573–600.

Horn, A. B., Samson, A. C., Debrot, A., & Perrez, M. (2019). Positive humor in couples as interpersonal emotion regulation: A dyadic study in everyday life on the mediating role of psychological intimacy. *Journal of Social and Personal Relationships, 36*(8), 2376–2396.

Howard, J. W., & Dawes, R. M. (1976). Linear prediction of marital happiness. *Personality and Social Psychology Bulletin, 2*, 478–480.

Howell, S. (1981). Rules not words. In P. Heelas & A. Lock (Eds.), *Indigenous psychologies: The anthropologies of the self* (pp. 133–143). Academic Press.

Hu, T., Zhang, D., Wang, J., Mistry, R., Ran, G., & Wang, X. (2014). Relation between emotion regulation and mental health: A meta-analysis review. *Psychological Reports, 114*(2), 341–362.

Hu, T., Zhang, D., & Yang, Z. (2015). The relationship between attributional style and depression: A meta-analysis. *Journal of Social and Clinical Psychology, 34*, 304–321.

Hudson, A., & Jacques, S. (2014). Put on a happy face! Inhibitory control and socioemotional knowledge predict emotion regulation in 5- to 7-year-olds. *Journal of Experimental Child Psychology, 123*, 36–52.

Hudson, J. I., Mangweth, B., Pope, H. G., Jr., De Col, C., Hausmann, A., Gutweniger, S., . . . & Tsuang, M. T. (2003). Family study of affective spectrum disorder. *Archives of General Psychiatry, 60*, 170–177.

Hugoson, A., Ljungquist, B., & Breivik, T. (2002). The relationship of some negative events and psychological factors to periodontal disease in an adult Swedish population 50 to 80 years of age. *Journal of Clinical Periodontology, 29*, 247–253.

Hull, C. L. (1943). *Principles of behavior: An introduction to behavior theory*. Appleton-Century.

Hull, C. L. (1952). *A behavior system: An introduction to behavior theory concerning the individual organism*. Yale University Press.

Hulleman, C. S., Barron, K. E., Kosovich, J. J., & Lazowski, R. A. (2016). Student motivation: Current theories, constructs, and interventions within an expectancy-value framework. In A. Lipnevich, F. Preckel, & R. Roberts (Eds.), *Psychosocial skills and school systems in the twenty-first century: Theory, research, and applications* (pp. 241–278). Springer.

Hunt, N., & Evans, D. (2004). Predicting traumatic stress using emotional intelligence. *Behaviour Research and Therapy, 42*(7), 791–798.

Huntsinger, J. R., Isbell, L. M., & Clore, G. L. (2014). The affective control of thought: Malleable, not fixed. *Psychological Review, 121*(4), 600–618.

Hupka, R. B., Lenton, A. P., & Hutchison, K. A. (1999). Universal development of emotion categories in natural language. *Journal of Personality and Social Psychology, 77*, 247–278.

Hwang, H. C., & Matsumoto, D. (2014). Dominance threat display for victory and achievement in competition context. *Motivation and Emotion, 38*(2), 206–214.

Hyde, J. S., Bigler, R. S., Joel, D., Tate, C. C., & van Anders, S. M. (2019). The future of sex and gender in psychology: Five challenges to the gender binary. *American Psychologist, 74*(2), 171–193.

Ickes, W., Stinson, L., Bissonnette, V., & Garcia, S. (1990). Naturalistic social cognition: Empathic accuracy in mixed-sex dyads. *Journal of Personality and Social Psychology, 59*, 730–742.

IJzerman, H., Lewis, N. A., Przybylski, A. K., Weinstein, N., DeBruine, L., Ritchie, S. J., . . . & Anvari, F. (2020). Use caution when applying behavioural science to policy. *Nature Human Behaviour, 4*(11), 1092–1094.

Ikemoto, S., Yang, C., & Tan, A. (2015). Basal ganglia circuit loops, dopamine and motivation: A review and enquiry. *Behavioural Brain Research, 290*, 17–31.

Inbar, Y., Pizarro, D., Iyer, R., & Haidt, J. (2012). Disgust sensitivity, political conservatism, and voting. *Social Psychological and Personality Science, 3*(5), 537–544.

Inda, M. C., Muravieva, E. V., & Alberini, C. M. (2011). Memory retrieval and the passage of time: from reconsolidation and strengthening to extinction. *Journal of Neuroscience, 31*(5), 1635–1643.

Infurna, F. J., Gerstorf, D., & Lachman, M. E. (2020). Midlife in the 2020s: Opportunities and challenges. *American Psychologist, 75*(4), 470–485.

Inglehart, R., Foa, R., Peterson, C., & Welzel, C. (2008). Development, freedom, and rising happiness. *Perspectives on Psychological Science, 3*, 264–285.

Inman, C. S., Bijanki, K. R., Bass, D. I., Gross, R. E., Hamann, S., & Willie, J. T. (2020). Human amygdala stimulation effects on emotion physiology and emotional experience. *Neuropsychologia, 145*, 106722. https://doi.org/10.1016/j.neuropsychologia.2018.03.019

Inoue-Sakurai, C., Maruyama, S., & Morimoto, K. (2000). Posttraumatic stress and lifestyles are associated with natural killer cell activity in victims of the Hanshin-Awaji earthquake in Japan. *Preventive Medicine, 31,* 467–473.

Insel, T., Cuthbert, B., Marjorie Garvey MB, B. C. H., Heinssen, R., Pine, D. S., Quinn, K., . . . & Wang, P. (2010). Research Domain Criteria (RDoC): Toward a New Classification Framework for Research on Mental Disorders. *American Journal of Psychiatry, 167*(7), 748–751.

Inzlicht, M., & Friese, M. (2019). The past, present, and future of ego depletion. *Social Psychology, 50*(5–6), 370–378.

Inzlicht, M., Schmeichel, B. J., & Macrae, C. N. (2014). Why self-control seems (but may not be) limited. *Trends in Cognitive Sciences, 18*(3), 127–133.

Irwin, M., Daniels, M., Risch, S. C., Bloom, E., & Weiner, H. (1988). Plasma cortisol and natural killer cell activity during bereavement. *Biological Psychology, 24,* 173–178.

Isaacowitz, D. M., Livingstone, K. M., Harris, J. A., & Marcotte, S. L. (2015). Mobile eye tracking reveals little evidence for age differences in attentional selection for mood regulation. *Emotion, 15,* 151–161.

Isabella, R. A., & Belsky, J. (1991). Interactional synchrony and the origins of infant-mother attachment. *Child Development, 62,* 373–384.

Isbell, L. A. (2006). Snakes as agents of evolutionary change in primate brains. *Journal of Human Evolution, 51*(1), 1–35.

Isen, A. M., Daubman, K. A., & Nowicki, G. P. (1987). Positive affect facilitates creative problem solving. *Journal of Personality and Social Psychology, 52,* 1122–1131.

Isgett, S. F., Kok, B. E., Baczkowski, B. M., Algoe, S. B., Grewen, K. M., & Fredrickson, B. L. (2017). Influences of oxytocin and respiratory sinus arrhythmia on emotions and social behavior in daily life. *Emotion, 17*(8), 1156–1165.

Israelashvili, J., Hassin, R. R., & Aviezer, H. (2019). When emotions run high: A critical role for context in the unfolding of dynamic, real-life facial affect. *Emotion, 19*(3), 558–562.

Ito, R., Robbins, T. W., & Everitt, B. J. (2004). Differential control over cocaine-seeking behavior by nucleus accumbens core and shell. *Nature Neuroscience, 7*(4), 389–397.

Ivcevic, Z., & Brackett, M. (2014). Predicting school success: comparing conscientiousness, grit, and emotion regulation ability. *Journal of Research in Personality, 52,* 29–36.

Izard, C. E. (1971). *The Face of Emotion.* Appleton-Century-Crofts.

Izard, C. E. (1983). *The maximally discriminative facial coding system (MAX, revised).* University of Delaware, Instructional Resources Center.

Izard, C. E. (1992). Basic emotions, relations among emotions, and emotion-cognition relations. *Psychological Review, 99*(3), 561–555.

Izard, C. E. (1994). Innate and universal facial expressions: Evidence from developmental and cross-cultural research. *Psychological Bulletin, 115,* 288–299.

Izard, C. E. (2001). Emotional intelligence or adaptive emotions? *Emotion, 1,* 249–257.

Izard, C. E. (2007). Basic emotions, natural kinds, emotion schemas, and a new paradigm. *Perspectives on Psychological Science, 2*(3), 260–280.

Izard, C. E., & Abe, J. A. A. (2004). Developmental changes in facial expressions of emotions in the Strange Situation during the second year of life. *Emotion, 4,* 251–265.

Jack, R. E., Garrod, O. G., & Schyns, P. G. (2014). Dynamic facial expressions of emotion transmit an evolving hierarchy of signals over time. *Current Biology, 24*(2), 187–192.

Jack, R. E., Garrod, O. G., Yu, H., Caldara, R., & Schyns, P. G. (2012). Facial expressions of emotion are not culturally universal. *Proceedings of the National Academy of Sciences, 109*(19), 7241–7244.

Jackson, D. C., Malmstadt, J. R., Larson, C. L., & Davidson, R. J. (2000). Suppression and enhancement of emotional responses to unpleasant pictures. *Psychophysiology, 37,* 515–522.

Jackson, J. C., Watts, J., Henry, T. R., List, J. M., Forkel, R., Mucha, P. J., . . . & Lindquist, K. A. (2019). Emotion semantics show both cultural variation and universal structure. *Science, 366*(6472), 1517–1522.

Jacobson, N. S., Dobson, K. S., Truax, P. A., Addis, M. E., Koerner, K., Gollan, J. K., . . . & Prince, S. E. (1996). A component analysis of cognitive-behavioral treatment for depression. *Journal of Consulting and Clinical Psychology, 64*(2), 295–304.

James, W. (1884). What is an emotion? *Mind, 9,* 188–205.

James, W. (1894). The physical basis of emotion. *Psychological Review, 1,* 516–529.

Jang, E.-H., Park, B. J., Park, M.-S., Kim, S.-H., & Sohn, S.-H. (2015). Analysis of physiological signals for recognition of boredom, pain, and surprise emotions. *Journal of Physiological Anthropology, 34,* Article 25.

Jang, K. L., Livesley, W. J., & Vemon, P. A. (1996). Heritability of the big five personality dimensions and their facets: A twin study. *Journal of Personality, 64*(3), 577–592.

Jänig, W., & Häbler, H.-J. (2000). Specificity in the organization of the nervous system: A basis for precise neuroregulation of homeostatic and protective body functions. *Progress in Brain Research, 122,* 351–367.

Jasinska, A. J., Stein, E. A., Kaiser, J., Naumer, M. J., & Yalachkov, Y. (2014). Factors modulating neural reactivity to drug cues in addiction: A survey of human neuroimaging studies. *Neuroscience & Biobehavioral Reviews, 38,* 1–16.

Javaras, K. N., Pope, H. G., Jr., Lalonde, J. K., Roberts, J. L., Nillni, Y. I., Laird, N. M., . . . & Hudson, J. I. (2008). Co-occurrence of binge eating disorder with psychiatric and medical disorders. *Journal of Clinical Psychiatry, 69,* 266–273.

Jazaieri, H., Urry, H. L., & Gross, J. J. (2013). Affective disturbance and psychopathology: An emotion regulation perspective. *Journal of Experimental Psychopathology, 4*(5), 584–599.

Jebb, A. T., Tay, L., Diener, E., & Oishi, S. (2018). Happiness, income satiation and turning points around the world. *Nature Human Behaviour, 2*(1), 33–38.

Jenkins, L. M., Andrewes, D. G., Nicholas, C. L., Drummond, K. J., Moffat, B. A., Phal, P., . . . Kessels, R. P. C. (2014). Social cognition in patients following surgery to the prefrontal cortex. *Psychiatry Research: Neuroimaging, 224,* 192–203.

Jobson, L., Moradi, A. R., Rahimi-Movaghar, V., Conway, M. A., & Dalgleish, T. (2014). Culture and the remembering of trauma. *Clinical Psychological Science, 2,* 696–713.

Johnson, K. J., & Fredrickson, B. L. (2005). "We all look the same to me": Positive emotions eliminate the own-race bias in face recognition. *Psychological Science, 16*(11), 875–881.

Johnson, M. H., Posner, M. I., & Rothbart, M. K. (1991). Components of visual orienting in early infancy: Contingency learning, anticipatory looking, and disengaging. *Journal of Cognitive Neuroscience, 3,* 335–344.

Joint Committee on Standards. (1999). *Standards for Educational and Psychological Testing.* American Educational Research Association.

Jones, E. B., Sharpe, L., Andrews, S., Colagiuri, B., Dudeney, J., Fox, E., . . . & Vervoort, T. (2021). The time course of attentional biases in pain: A meta-analysis of eye-tracking studies. *Pain, 162*(3), 687–701.

Joormann, J., & Vanderlind, W. M. (2014). Emotion regulation in depression: The role of biased cognition and reduced cognitive control. *Clinical Psychological Science, 2,* 402–421.

Josefsson, T., Lindwall, M., & Archer, T. (2014). Physical exercise intervention in depressive disorders: Meta-analysis and systematic review. *Scandinavian Journal of Medicine & Science in Sports, 24*(2), 259–272.

Joseph, D. L., Jin, J., Newman, D. A., & O'Boyle, E. H. (2015). Why does self-reported emotional intelligence predict job performance? A meta-analytic investigation of mixed EI. *Journal of Applied Psychology, 100,* 298–342.

Kaczmarek, L. D., Behnke, M., Kosakowski, M., Enko, J., Dziekan, M., Piskorski, J., . . . & Guzik, P. (2019). High-approach and low-approach positive affect influence physiological responses to threat and anger. *International Journal of Psychophysiology, 138,* 27–37.

Kagan, J., Reznick, J. S., & Snidman, N. (1988). Biological bases of childhood shyness. *Science, 240,* 167–171.

Kagan, J., & Snidman, N. (1991). Infant predictors of inhibited and uninhibited profiles. *Psychological Science, 2,* 40–44.

Kahneman, D., Krueger, A. B., Schkade, D., Schwarz, N., & Stone, A. A. (2006). Would you be happier if you were richer? A focusing illusion. *Science, 312,* 1908–1910.

Kalin, N. H., Shelton, S. E., & Barksdale, C. M. (1988). Opiate modulation of separation-induced distress in non-human primates. *Brain Research, 440,* 285–292.

Kalin, N. H., Shelton, S. E., & Davidson, R. J. (2004). The role of the central nucleus of the amygdala in mediating fear and anxiety in the primate. *Journal of Neuroscience, 24,* 5506–5515.

Kalisch, R., & Gerlicher, A. M. V. (2014). Making a mountain out of a molehill: On the role of the rostral dorsal anterior cingulate and dorsomedial prefrontal cortex in conscious threat appraisal, catastrophizing, and worrying. *Neuroscience & Biobehavioral Reviews, 42,* 1–8.

Kalokerinos, E. K., Greenaway, K. H., & Denson, T. F. (2015). Reappraisal but not suppression downregulates the experience of positive and negative emotion. *Emotion, 15*(3), 271–275.

Kalokerinos, E. K., Tamir, M., & Kuppens, P. (2017). Instrumental motives in negative emotion regulation in daily life: Frequency, consistency, and predictors. *Emotion, 17*(4), 648–657.

Kampe, K. K., Frith, C. D., Dolan, R. J., & Frith, U. (2002). Reward value of attractiveness and gaze. *Nature, 413,* 589–590.

Kang, Y., Gruber, J., & Gray, J. R. (2013). Mindfulness and de-automatization. *Emotion Review, 5*(2), 192–201.

Kanwisher, N. (2000). Domain specificity in face perception. *Nature Neuroscience, 3*(8), 759–763.

Kanwisher, N., McDermott, J., & Chun, M. M. (1997). The fusiform face area: a module in human extrastriate cortex specialized for face perception. *Journal of Neuroscience, 17*(11), 4302–4311.

Kaplansky, G., Levy, H., Veld, C., & Veld-Merkoulova, Y. (2015). Do happy people make optimistic investors? *Journal of Financial and Quantitative Analysis, 50,* 145–168.

Kappes, H. B., Oettingen, G., Mayer, D., & Maglio, S. (2011). Sad mood promotes self-initiated mental contrasting of future and reality. *Emotion, 11*(5), 1206–1222.

Kardos, P., Leidner, B., Pléh, C., Soltész, P., & Unoka, Z. (2017). Empathic people have more friends: Empathic abilities predict social network size and position in social network predicts empathic efforts. *Social Networks, 50,* 1–5.

Karim, J., & Weisz, R. (2010). Cross-cultural research on the reliability and validity of the Mayer-Salovey-Caruso Emotional Intelligence Test (MSCEIT). *Cross-Cultural Research, 44,* 374–404.

Karney, B. R., & Bradbury, T. N. (1995). The longitudinal course of marital quality and stability: A review of theory, method, and research. *Psychological Review, 118,* 3–34.

Karney, B. R., & Bradbury, T. N. (2020). Research on marital satisfaction and stability in the 2010s: Challenging conventional wisdom. *Journal of Marriage and Family, 82*(1), 100–116.

Kashdan, T. B., Farmer, A. S., Adams, L. M., Ferssizidis, P., McKnight, P. E., & Nezlek, J. B. (2013). Distinguishing healthy adults from people with social anxiety disorder: Evidence for the value of experiential avoidance and positive emotions in everyday social interactions. *Journal of Abnormal Psychology, 122*(3), 645–655.

Kasser, T., & Ryan, R. M. (1996). Further examining the American dream: Differential correlates of intrinsic and extrinsic goals. *Personality and Social Psychology Bulletin, 22*(3), 280–287.

Kassinove, H., Sudholdolsky, D. G., Tsytsarev, S. V., & Solovyova, S. (1997). Self-reported constructions of anger episodes in Russia and America. *Journal of Social Behavior and Personality, 12,* 301–324.

Kawasaki, H., Adolphs, R., Kaufman, O., Damasio, H., Damasio, A. R., Granner, M., . . . & Howard, M. A. (2001). Single-neuron responses to emotional visual stimuli recorded in human ventral prefrontal cortex. *Nature Neuroscience, 4,* 15–16.

Kayval, M. H., & Russell, J. A. (2013). Americans and Palestinians judge spontaneous facial expressions of emotion. *Emotion, 13,* 891–904.

Kayyal, M., Widen, S., & Russell, J. A. (2015). Context is more powerful than we think: Contextual cues override facial cues even for valence. *Emotion, 15*(3), 287–291.

Kazama, A. M., Heuer, E., Davis, M., & Bachevalier, J. (2012). Effects of neonatal amygdala lesions on fear learning, conditioned inhibition, and extinction in adult macaques. *Behavioral Neuroscience, 126*(3), 392–403.

Keillor, J. M., Barrett, A. M., Crucian, G. P., Kortenkamp, S., & Heilman, K. M. (2002). Emotional experience and perception in the absence of facial feedback. *Journal of the International Neuropsychological Society, 8,* 130–135.

Keith-Lucas, T., & Guttman, N. (1975). Robust-single-trial delayed backward conditioning. *Journal of Comparative and Physiological Psychology, 88*(1), 468–476.

Keller, M. C., & Nesse, R. M. (2006). The evolutionary significance of depressive symptoms: Different adverse situations lead to different depressive symptom patterns. *Journal of Personality and Social Psychology, 91*(2), 316–330.

Keltner, D. (1995). Signs of appeasement: Evidence for the distinct displays of embarrassment, amusement, and shame. *Journal of Personality and Social Psychology, 68,* 441–454.

Keltner, D., & Buswell, B. N. (1997). Embarrassment: its distinct form and appeasement functions. *Psychological bulletin, 122*(3), 250–270.

Keltner, D., Ellsworth, P. C., & Edwards, K. (1993). Beyond simple pessimism: Effects of sadness and anger on social perception. *Journal of Personality and Social Psychology, 64,* 740–752.

Keltner, D., & Haidt, J. (1999). Social functions of emotions at four levels of analysis. *Cognition and Emotion, 13,* 505–521.

Keltner, D., & Haidt, J. (2003). Approaching awe, a moral, spiritual, and aesthetic emotion. *Cognition & Emotion, 17*(2), 297–314.

Keltner, D. Haidt, J., & Shiota, M. N. (2006). Social functionalism and the evolution of emotions. In M. Schaller, J. A. Simpson, & D. T. Kenrick (Eds.), *Evolution and Social Psychology* (pp. 115–142). Psychosocial Press.

Keltner, D., & Shiota, M. N. (2003). New displays and new emotions: A commentary on Rozin and Cohen (2003). *Emotion, 3,* 86–91.

Keltner, D., Young, R. C., & Buswell, B. N. (1997). Appeasement in human emotion, social practice, and personality. *Aggressive Behavior, 23*(5), 359–374.

Kendler, K. S., Kuhn, J., & Prescott, C. A. (2004). The interrelationship of neuroticism, sex, and stressful life events in the prediction of episodes of major depression. *American Journal of Psychiatry, 161*(4), 631–636.

Kendler, K. S., Myers, J., & Prescott, C. A. (2002). The etiology of phobias. *Archives of General Psychiaty, 59,* 242–248.

Kendler, K. S., Myers, J., Prescott, C. A., & Neale, M. C. (2001). The genetic epidemiology of irrational fears and phobias in men. *Archives of General Psychiatry, 58,* 257–265.

Kendler, K. S., Walters, E. E., Neale, M. C., Kessler, R. C., Heath, A. C., & Eaves, L. J. (1995). The structure of the genetic and environmental risk factors for six major psychiatric disorders in women. *Archives of General Psychiatry, 52,* 374–383.

Kenkel, W. M., Perkeybile, A. M., & Carter, C. S. (2017). The neurobiological causes and effects of alloparenting. *Developmental Neurobiology, 77*(2), 214–232.

Kennedy, Q., Mather, M., & Carstensen, L. L. (2004). The role of motivation in the age-related positivity effect in autobiographical memory. *Psychological Science, 15*(3), 208–214.

Kenny, L. M., Bryant, R. A., Silove, D., Creamer, M., O'Donnell, M., & McFarlane, A. C. (2009). Distant memories: A prospective study of vantage point of trauma memories. *Psychological Science, 20,* 1049–1052.

Kenrick, D. T., Griskevicius, V., Neuberg, S. L., & Schaller, M. (2010). Renovating the pyramid of needs: Contemporary extensions built upon ancient foundations. *Perspectives on Psychological Science, 5*(3), 292–314.

Kensinger, E. A., & Ford, J. H. (2020). Retrieval of emotional events from memory. *Annual Review of Psychology, 71,* 251–272.

Kerrigan, S., & Bailey, J. (2021). Does premarital cohabitation increase the likelihood of future marital dissolution? *SN Social Sciences, 1*(5), 1–9.

Kessler, R. C., Berglund, P., Demler, O., Jin, R., Merikangas, K. R., & Walters, E. E. (2005). Lifetime prevalence and age-of-onset distributions of *DSM-IV* disorders in the national comorbidity survey replication. *Archives of General Psychiatry, 62*(6), 593–602.

Keverne, E. B., & Kendrick, K. M. (1992). Oxytocin facilitation of maternal behavior in sheep. *Annals of the New York Academy of Science, 807,* 455–468.

Khan, A. J., Pedrelli, P., Shapero, B. G., Fisher, L., Nyer, M., Farabaugh, A. I., & MacPherson, L. (2018). The association between distress tolerance and alcohol related problems: The pathway of drinking to cope. *Substance Use & Misuse, 53*(13), 2199–2209.

Khazanov, G. K., Xu, C., Dunn, B. D., Cohen, Z. D., DeRubeis, R. J., & Hollon, S. D. (2020). Distress and anhedonia as predictors of depression treatment outcome: A secondary analysis of a randomized clinical trial. *Behaviour Research and Therapy, 125,* 103507.

Kiken, L. G., Lundberg, K. B., & Fredrickson, B. L. (2017). Being present and enjoying it: Dispositional mindfulness and savoring the moment are distinct, interactive predictors of positive emotions and psychological health. *Mindfulness, 8*(5), 1280–1290.

Kim, H. S., & Sherman, D. K. (2007). "Express yourself": Culture and the effect of self-expression on choice. *Journal of Personality and Social Psychology, 92*(1), 1–11.

Kim, S.-Y., Adhikari, A., Lee, S. Y., Marshel, J. H., Kim, C. K., Mallory, C. S., . . . & Deisseroth, K. (2013). Diverging neural pathways assemble a behavioural state from separable features in anxiety. *Nature, 496,* 219–223.

Kircanski, K., Sisk, L. M., Ho, T. C., Humphreys, K. L., King, L. S., Colich, N. L., . . . & Gotlib, I. H. (2019). Early life stress, cortisol, frontolimbic connectivity, and depressive symptoms during puberty. *Development and Psychopathology, 31*(3), 1011–1022.

Kirk, D., Oettingen, G., & Gollwitzer, P. M. (2013). Promoting integrative bargaining: Mental contrasting with implementation intentions. *International Journal of Conflict Management, 24*(2), 148–165.

Kirsch, I. (2010). *The emperor's new drugs.* Basic Books.

Kitayama, S., Markus, H. R., & Kurokawa, M. (2000). Culture, emotion, and well-being: Good feelings in Japan and the United States. *Cognition and Emotion, 14,* 93–124.

Klaus, M. H., & Kennell, J. H. (1976). *Maternal-infant bonding.* Mosby.

Klein, K. J., & Hodges, S. D. (2001). Gender differences, motivation, and empathic accuracy: When it pays to understand. *Personality and Social Psychology Bulletin, 27*(6), 720–730.

Klineberg, O. (1938). Emotional expression in Chinese literature. *Journal of Abnormal and Social Psychology, 31,* 517–520.

Klineberg, O. (1940). Emotional Behavior. In O. Klineberg, *Social Psychology* (pp. 166–202). Henry Holt.

Kluger, M. J. (1991). Fever: Role of pyrogens and cryogens. *Phsyiological Reviews, 71,* 93–127.

Klüver, H., & Bucy, P. C. (1939). Preliminary analysis of functions of the temporal lobes in monkeys. *Archives of Neurological Psychiatry, 42,* 979–1000.

Knafo, A., Zahn-Waxler, C., Van Hulle, C., Robinson, J. L., & Rhee, S. H. (2008). The developmental origins of a disposition toward empathy: Genetic and environmental contributions. *Emotion, 8*(6), 737–752.

Kniffin, K. M., & Wilson, D. S. (2004). The effect of nonphysical traits on the perception of physical attractiveness. *Evolution and Human Behavior, 25,* 88–101.

Knutson, B., Taylor, J., Kaufman, M., Peterson, R., & Glover, G. (2005). Distributed neural representation of expected value. *Journal of Neuroscience, 25*(19), 4806–4812.

Knutson, B., Wimmer, G. E., Kuhnen, C. M., & Winkielman, P. (2008). Nucleus accumbens activation mediates the influence of reward cues on financial risk taking. *NeuroReport, 19*(5), 509–513.

Ko, A., Pick, C. M., Kwon, J. Y., Barlev, M., Krems, J. A., Varnum, M. E., . . . & Kenrick, D. T. (2020). Family matters: Rethinking the psychology of human social motivation. *Perspectives on Psychological Science,* 15(1), 173–201.

Ko, C.-H., Liu, G.-C., Hsiao, S., Yen, J.-Y., Yang, M.-J., Lin, W.-C., . . . Chen, C. S. (2009). Brain activities associated with gaming urge of online gaming addiction. *Journal of Psychiatric Research, 43,* 739–747.

Koenigs, M., Huey, E. D., Raymont, V., Cheon, B., Solomon, J., Wassermann, E. M., & Grafman, J. (2008). Focal brain damage protects against post-traumatic stress disorder in combat veterans. *Nature Neuroscience, 11,* 232–237.

Koepp, M. J., Gunn, R. N., Lawrence, A. D., Cunningham, V. J., Dagher, A., Jones, T., . . . & Grasby, P. M. (1998). Evidence for striatal dopamine release during a video game. *Nature, 393,* 266–268.

Koffer, R., Drewelies, J., Almeida, D. M., Conroy, D. E., Pincus, A. L., Gerstorf, D., & Ram, N. (2019). The role of general and daily control beliefs for affective stressor-reactivity across adulthood and old age. *Journals of Gerontology, 74*(2), 242–253.

Kogan, A., Oveis, C., Carr, E. W., Gruber, J., Mauss, I. B., Shallcross, A., . . . & Keltner, D. (2014). Vagal activity is quadratically related to prosocial emotions, and observer perceptions of prosociality. *Journal of Personality and Social Psychology, 107,* 1051–1063.

Kohler, C. G., Turner, T. H., Bilker, W. B., Brensinger, C. M., Siegel, S. J., & Kanes, S. J., Gur, R. C. (2003). Facial emotion recognition in schizophrenia: Intensity effects and error pattern. *American Journal of Psychiatry, 160,* 1768–1774.

Kok, G., Peters, G. J. Y., Kessels, L. T., Ten Hoor, G. A., & Ruiter, R. A. (2018). Ignoring theory and misinterpreting evidence: The false belief in fear appeals. *Health Psychology Review, 12*(2), 111–125.

Kokkinaki, T. (2003). A longitudinal, naturalistic and cross-cultural study on emotions in early infant-parent imitative interactions. *British Journal of Developmental Psychology, 21,* 243–258.

Kollareth, D., Fernandez-Dols, J. M., & Russell, J. A. (2018). Shame as a culture-specific emotion concept. *Journal of Cognition and Culture, 18*(3–4), 274–292.

Kommattam, P., Jonas, K. J., & Fischer, A. H. (2017). We are sorry, they don't care: Misinterpretation of facial embarrassment displays in Arab–White intergroup contexts. *Emotion, 17*(4), 658–668.

Kong, D. T. (2014). Mayer-Salovey-Caruso Emotional Intelligence Test (MSCEIT/MEIS) and overall, verbal, and nonverbal intelligence: Meta-analytic and critical contingencies. *Personality and Individual Differences, 66,* 171–175.

Konttinen, H., Männistö, S., Sarlio-Lähteenkorva, S., Silventoinen, K., & Haukkala, A. (2010). Emotional eating, depressive symptoms and self-reported food consumption. A population-based study. *Appetite, 54*(3), 473–479.

Konttinen, H., Van Strien, T., Männistö, S., Jousilahti, P., & Haukkala, A. (2019). Depression, emotional eating and long-term weight changes: A population-based prospective study. *International Journal of Behavioral Nutrition and Physical Activity, 16*(1), 1–11.

Kornreich, C., Blairy, S., Philippot, P., Hess, U., Noel, X., Streel, E. . . . & Verbanck, P. (2001). Deficits in recognition of emotional facial expression are still present in alcoholics after mid- to long-term abstinence. *Journal of Studies on Alcohol, 62,* 533–542.

Kotowicz, Z. (2007). The strange case of Phineas Gage. *History of the Human Sciences, 20,* 115–131.

Kotsou, I., Mikolajczak, M., Heeren, A., Grégoire, J., & Leys, C. (2019). Improving emotional intelligence: A systematic review of existing work and future challenges. *Emotion Review, 11*(2), 151–165.

Kovács, L. N., Takacs, Z. K., Tóth, Z., Simon, E., Schmelowszky, Á., & Kökönyei, G. (2020). Rumination in major depressive and bipolar disorder—A meta-analysis. *Journal of Affective Disorders, 276,* 1131–1141.

Kraaij, V., Pruymboom, E., & Garnefski, N. (2002). Cognitive coping and depressive symptoms in the elderly: A longitudinal study. *Aging & Mental Health, 6,* 275–281.

Kraemer, D. L., & Hastrup, J. L. (1988). Crying in adults: Self-control and autonomic correlates. *Journal of Social and Clinical Psychology, 6*, 53–68.

Krajbich, I., Adolphs, R., Tranel, D., Denburg, N. L., & Camerer, C. F. (2009). Economic games quantify diminished sense of guilt in patients with damage to the prefrontal cortex. *Journal of Neuroscience, 29*, 2188–2192.

Kraus, M. W., Piff, P. K., & Keltner, D. (2011). Social class as culture: The convergence of resources and rank in the social realm. *Current Directions in Psychological Science, 20*(4), 246–250.

Kreibig, S. D. (2010). Autonomic nervous system activity in emotion: A review. *Biological Psychology, 84*(3), 394–421.

Kreibig, S. D., Samson, A. C., & Gross, J. J. (2015). The psychophysiology of mixed emotional states: Internal and external reliability analysis of a direct replication study. *Psychophysiology, 52*, 873–886.

Kreider, R. M., & Ellis, R. (2011). *Number, timing, and duration of marriages and divorces: 2009 (Current Population Reports P70–125)*. US Census Bureau.

Krieglmeyer, R., Deutsch, R., De Houwer, J., & De Raedt, R. (2010). Being moved valence activates approach-avoidance behavior independently of evaluation and approach-avoidance intentions. *Psychological Science, 21*(4), 607–613.

Kring, A. M., Kerr, S. L., Smith, D. A., & Neale, J. M. (1993). Flat affect in schizophrenia does not reflect diminished subjective experience of emotion. *Journal of Abnormal Psychology, 102*(4), 507–517.

Krpan, D., & Fasolo, B. (2019). Revisiting embodied approach and avoidance effects on behavior: The influence of sitting posture on purchases of rewarding foods. *Journal of Experimental Social Psychology, 85*, Article 103889. https://doi.org/10.1016/j.jesp.2019.103889

Kruglanski, A. W., Shah, J. Y., Fishbach, A., Friedman, R., Chun, W. Y., & Sleeth-Keppler, D. (2002). A theory of goal systems. *Advances in Experimental Social Psychology, 34*(2), 331–378.

Krystal, J. H., Abdallah, C. G., Sanacora, G., Charney, D. S., & Duman, R. S. (2019). Ketamine: A paradigm shift for depression research and treatment. *Neuron, 101*(5), 774–778.

Kübler, A., Kotchoubey, B., Kaiser, J., Wolpaw, J. R., & Birbaumer, N. (2001). Brain-computer communication: Unlocking the locked-in. *Psychological Bulletin, 127*, 358–375.

Kubota, Y., Sato, W., Murai, T., Toichi, M., Ikeda, A., & Sengoku, A. (2000). Emotional cognition without awareness after unilateral temporal lobectomy in humans. *Journal of Neuroscience, 20*, RC97, 1–5.

Kubzansky, L. D., Koenen, K. C., Jones, C., & Eaton, W. W. (2009). A prospective study of posttraumatic stress disorder symptoms and coronary heart disease in women. *Health Psychology, 28*(1), 125–130.

Kubzansky, L. D., Martin, L. T., & Buka, S. L. (2004). Early manifestations of personality and adult emotional functioning. *Emotion, 4*, 364–377.

Kundera, M. ([1979] 1980). *The book of laughter and forgetting*. Translated by M. H. Heim. Knopf.

Kunugi, H., Hori, H., & Ogawa, S. (2015). Biochemical markers subtyping major depressive disorder. *Psychiatry and Clinical Neurosciences, 69*, 597–608.

Kunz-Ebrecht, S. R., Kirschbaum, C., Marmot, M., & Steptoe, A. (2004). Differences in cortisol awakening response on work days and weekends in women and men from the Whitehall II cohort. *Psychoneuroendocrinology, 29*(4), 516–528.

Kunzmann, U., & Grühn, D. (2005). Age differences in emotional reactivity: the sample case of sadness. *Psychology and Aging, 20*(1), 47–59.

Kupfer, T. R., & Giner-Sorolla, R. (2017). Communicating moral motives: The social signaling function of disgust. *Social Psychological and Personality Science, 8*(6), 632–640.

Kuppens, P., Realo, A., & Diener, E. (2008). The role of positive and negative emotions in life satisfaction judgment across nations. *Journal of Personality and Social Psychology, 95*(1), 66–75.

Kuppens, P., Van Mechelen, I., & Rijmen, F. (2008). Toward disentangling sources of individual differences in appraisal and anger. *Journal of Personality, 76*, 969–1000.

Kuppens, P. P., Van Mechelen, I., Smits, D. J. M., & De Boeck, P. (2003). The appraisal basis of anger: Specificity, necessity, and sufficiency of components. *Emotion, 3*, 254–269.

Kurdek, L. A. (2005). What do we know about gay and lesbian couples? *Current Directions in Psychological Science, 14*(5), 251–254.

Kvam, S., Kleppe, C. L., Nordhus, I. H., & Hovland, A. (2016). Exercise as a treatment for depression: A meta-analysis. *Journal of Affective Disorders, 202*, 67–86.

Kvavilashvili, L., Mirani, J., Schlagman, S., Foley, K., & Kornbrot, D. E. (2009). Consistency of flashbulb memories of September 11 over long delays: Implications for consolidation and wrong time slice hypotheses. *Journal of Memory and Language, 61*, 556–572.

Kwan, V. S., Bond, M. H., & Singelis, T. M. (1997). Pancultural explanations for life satisfaction: adding relationship harmony to self-esteem. *Journal of Personality and Social Psychology, 73*(5), 1038–1051.

Kwon, J. T., & Choi, J.-S. (2009). Cornering the fear engram: Long-term synaptic changes in the lateral nucleus of the amygdala after fear conditioning. *Journal of Neuroscience, 29*, 9700–9703.

LaBar, K. S., & Phelps, E. A. (1998). Arousal-mediated memory consolidation: Role of the medial temporal lobe in humans. *Psychological Science, 9*, 490–493.

Lachman, M. E., & Firth, K. M. P. (2004). The adaptive value of feeling in control during midlife. In O. G. Brim, C. D. Ryff, & R. C. Kessler (Eds.), *How healthy are we?* (pp. 320–349). University of Chicago Press.

Lachman, M. E., Teshale, S., & Agrigoroaei, S. (2015). Midlife as a pivotal period in the life course: Balancing growth and decline at the crossroads of youth and old age. *International Journal of Behavioral Development, 39*(1), 20–31.

Lackner, H. K., Weiss, E. M., Hinghofer-Szalkay, H., & Papousek, I. (2014). Cardiovascular effects of acute positive emotional arousal. *Applied Psychophysiology and Biofeedback, 39*, 9–18.

Laible, D. J., Carlo, G., & Raffaelli, M. (2000). The differential relations of parent and peer attachment to adolescent adjustment. *Journal of Youth and Adolescence, 29*, 45–59.

Lakin, J. L., & Chartrand, T. L. (2003). Using nonconscious behavioral mimicry to create affiliation and rapport. *Psychological Science, 14*, 334–339.

Lambert, E. G., Camp, S. D., Clarke, A., & Jiang, S. (2011). The impact of information on death penalty support, revisited. *Crime & Delinquency, 57*, 572–599.

Lammel, S., Lim, B. K., & Malenka, R. C. (2014). Reward and aversion in a heterogeneous midbrain dopamine system. *Neuropharmacology, 76*, 351–359.

Lanaj, K., Chang, C. H., & Johnson, R. E. (2012). Regulatory focus and work-related outcomes: A review and meta-analysis. *Psychological Bulletin, 138*(5), 998–1034.

Landy, J. F., & Goodwin, G. P. (2015). Does incidental disgust amplify moral judgment? A meta-analytic review of experimental evidence. *Perspectives on Psychological Science, 10*, 518–536.

Lang, P. J. (2014). Emotion's response patterns: The brain and the autonomic nervous system. *Emotion Review, 6*(2), 93–99.

Lang, P. J., Bradley, M. M., & Cuthbert, B. N. (2002). A motivational analysis of emotion: Reflex-cortex connections. In J. T. Cacioppo (Ed), *Foundations in social neuroscience* (pp. 461–471). MIT Press.

Langer, E. J. (1975). The illusion of control. *Journal of Personality and Social Psychology, 32*, 311–328.

Langlois, J. H., & Roggman, L. A. (1990). Attractive faces are only average. *Psychological Science, 1*, 115–121.

Larsen, B., & Luna, B. (2015). In vivo evidence of neurophysiological maturation of the human adolescent striatum. *Developmental Cognitive Neuroscience, 12*, 74–85.

Larsen, J. T., & McGraw, A. P. (2014). The case for mixed emotions. *Social and Personality Psychology Compass, 8*(6), 263–274.

Larsen, J. T., McGraw, A. P., & Cacioppo, J. T. (2001). Can people feel happy and sad at the same time? *Journal of Personality and Social Psychology, 81*, 684–696.

Larsen, R. J., Kasimatis, M., & Frey, K. (1992). Facilitating the furrowed brow—An unobtrusive test of the facial feedback hypothesis applied to unpleasant affect. *Cognition & Emotion, 6*, 321–338.

Latta, R. L. (1999). *The Basic Humor Process: A Cognitive-Shift Theory and the Case Against Incongruity.* Mouton de Gruyter.

Laukka, P., & Elfenbein, H. A. (2012). Emotion appraisal dimensions can be inferred from vocal expressions. *Social Psychological and Personality Science, 3*(5), 529–536.

Laukka, P., & Elfenbein, H. A. (2021). Cross-cultural emotion recognition and in-group advantage in vocal expression: A meta-analysis. *Emotion Review, 13*(1), 3–11.

Launay, J. M., Del Pino, M., Chironi, G., Callebert, J., Peoc'h, K., Mégnien, J. L. (2009). Smoking induces long-lasting effects through a monoamine-oxidase epigenetic regulation. *PloS One, 4*, e7959. https://doi.org/10.1371/journal.pone.0007959

Laursen, B., Coy, K. C., & Collins, W. A. (1998). Reconsidering changes in parent-child conflict across adolescence: A meta-analysis. *Child Development, 69*, 817–832.

Lavelli, M., Carra, C., Rossi, G., & Keller, H. (2019). Culture-specific development of early mother–infant emotional co-regulation: Italian, Cameroonian, and West African immigrant dyads. *Developmental Psychology, 55*(9), 1850–1867.

Lavelli, M., & Fogel, A. (2013). Interdyad differences in early mother–infant face-to-face communication: Real-time dynamics and developmental pathways. *Developmental Psychology, 49*(12), 2257–2271.

Lavner, J. A., Karney, B. R., & Bradbury, T. N. (2016). Does couples' communication predict marital satisfaction, or does marital satisfaction predict communication? *Journal of Marriage and Family, 78*(3), 680–694.

Lawrence, K., Campbell, R., & Skuse, D. (2015). Age, gender, and puberty influence the development of facial emotion recognition. *Frontiers in Psychology, 6,* 761. https://doi.org/10.3389/fpsyg.2015.00761

Lazarus, R. S. (1977). Cognitive and coping responses in emotion. In A. Monat & R. S. Lazarus (Eds.), *Stress and coping* (pp. 145–158). Columbia University Press.

Lazarus, R. S. (1991a). *Emotion and adaptation.* Oxford University Press.

Lazarus, R. S. (1991b). Progress on a cognitive-motivational-relational theory of emotion. *American Psychologist, 46*(8), 819–834.

Le, B., Dove, N. L., Agnew, C. R., Korn, M. S., & Mutso, A. A. (2010). Predicting nonmarital romantic relationship dissolution: A meta-analytic synthesis. *Personal Relationships, 17*(3), 377–390.

Leach, C. W., Spears, R., Branscombe, N. R., & Doosje, B. (2003). Malicious pleasure: Schadenfreude at the suffering of another group. *Journal of Personality and Social Psychology, 84,* 932–943.

Lebreton, M., Kawa, S., d'Arc, B. F., Daunizeau, J., & Pessiglione, M. (2012). Your goal is mine: Unraveling mimetic desires in the human brain. *Journal of Neuroscience, 32*(21), 7146–7157.

Leclere, C., Viaux, S., Avril, M., Achard, C., Chetouani, M., Missonnier, S., & Cohen, D. (2014). Why synchrony matters during mother-child interactions: A systematic review. *PLoS One, 9,* e113571. https://doi.org/10.1371/journal.pone.0113571

LeDoux, J. (1996). *The emotional brain.* Simon & Schuster.

LeDoux, J. E. (2015). *Anxious: Using the brain to understand and treat fear and anxiety.* Penguin.

LeDoux, J. E., Cicchetti, P., Xagoraris, A., & Romanski, L. M. (1990). The lateral amygdaloid nucleus: Sensory interface of the amygdala in fear conditioning. *Journal of Neuroscience, 10,* 1062–1069.

Lee, D. H., Mirza, R., Flanagan, J. G., & Anderson, A. K. (2014). Optical origins of opposing facial expression actions. *Psychological Science, 25,* 745–752.

Lee, R. A., Su, J., & Yoshida, E. (2005). Coping with intergenerational family conflict among Asian American college students. *Journal of Counseling Psychology, 52,* 389–399.

Lefcourt, H. M., Davidson, K., Shepherd, R., Phillips, M., Prkachin, K., & Mills, D. (1995). Perspective-taking humor: Accounting for stress moderation. *Journal of Social and Clinical Psychology, 14*(4), 373–391.

Lehmann, K. A. (1995). New developments in patient-controlled postoperative analgesia. *Annals of Medicine, 27,* 271–282.

Lemarié, L., Bellavance, F., & Chebat, J. C. (2019). Regulatory focus, time perspective, locus of control and sensation seeking as predictors of risky driving behaviors. *Accident Analysis & Prevention, 127,* 19–27.

Leppämäki, S., Partonen, T., & Lönnqvist, J. (2002). Bright-light exposure combined with physical exercise elevates mood. *Journal of Affective Disorders, 72,* 139–144.

Leppänen, J. M., & Hietanen, J. K. (2003). Affect and face perception: Odors modulate the recognition advantage of happy faces. *Emotion, 3,* 315–326.

Lerner, J. S., Gonzalez, R. M., Small, D. A., & Fischhoff, B. (2003). Effects of fear and anger on perceived risks of terrorism: A national field experiment. *Psychological Science, 14,* 144–150.

Lerner, J. S., & Keltner, D. (2001). Fear, anger, and risk. *Journal of Personality and Social Psychology, 81*(1), 146–159.

Lerner, J. S., Li, Y., Valdesolo, P., & Kassam, K. S. (2015). Emotion and decision making. *Annual Review of Psychology, 66,* 799–823.

Lerner, J. S., Li, Y., & Weber, E. U. (2013). The financial costs of sadness. *Psychological Science, 24,* 72–79.

Lerner, J. S., Small, D. A., & Loewenstein, G. (2004). Heart strings and purse strings. *Psychological Science, 15,* 337–341.

Lettieri, G., Handjaras, G., Ricciardi, E., Leo, A., Papale, P., Betta, M., . . . & Cecchetti, L. (2019). Emotionotopy in the human right temporo-parietal cortex. *Nature Communications, 10*(1), 1–13.

Levenson, R. W. (1992). Autonomic nervous system differences among emotions. *Psychological Science, 3,* 23–27.

Levenson, R. W. (1999). The intrapersonal functions of emotion. *Cognition & Emotion, 13,* 481–504.

Levenson, R. W. (2014). The autonomic nervous system and emotion. *Emotion Review, 6,* 100–112.

Levenson, R. W., Carstensen, L. L., & Gottman, J. M. (1994). The influence of age and gender on affect, physiology, and their interrelations: A study of long-term marriages. *Journal of Personality and Social Psychology, 67,* 56–68.

Levenson, R. W., Ekman, P., & Friesen, W. V. (1990). Voluntary facial action generates emotion-specific autonomic nervous system activity. *Psychophysiology, 27,* 363–383.

Levenson, R. W., Ekman, P., Heider, K., & Friesen, W. V. (1992). Emotion and autonomic nervous system activity in the Minangkabau of West Sumatra. *Journal of Personality and Social Psychology, 62*, 972–988.

Levenson, R. W., & Gottman, J. M. (1983). Marital interaction: Physiological linkage and affective exchange. *Journal of Personality and Social Psychology, 45*, 587–597.

Levenson, R. W., & Ruef, A. M. (1992). Empathy: A physiological substrate. *Journal of Personality and Social Psychology, 63*, 234–246.

Levin, J., & Arluke, A. (1982). Embarrassment and helping behavior. *Psychological Reports, 51*, 999–1002.

Levine, L. J., & Pizarro, D. A. (2004). Emotion and memory research: A grumpy overview. *Social Cognition, 22*, 530–554.

Levy, R. (1973). *The Tahitians*. University of Chicago Press.

Levy, R. I. (1984). The emotions in comparative perspective. In K. R. Scherer & P. Ekman (Eds.), *Approaches to emotion* (pp. 397–412). Erlbaum.

Lewandowski, G. W., Jr., Aron, A., & Gee, J. (2007). Personality goes a long way: The malleability of opposite-sex physical attractiveness. *Personal Relationships, 14*(4), 571–585.

Lewis, D. M., Al-Shawaf, L., Conroy-Beam, D., Asao, K., & Buss, D. M. (2017). Evolutionary psychology: A how-to guide. *American Psychologist, 72*(4), 353–373.

Lewis, M. (1992). *Shame: The exposed self*. Free Press.

Lewis, M., & Brooks-Gunn, J. (1979). *Social cognition and the acquisition of self*. Plenum.

Lewis, M., Sullivan, M. W., Stanger, C., & Weiss, M. (1991). Self development and self-conscious emotions. In S. Chess & M. E. Hertzig (Eds.), *Annual progress in child psychiatry and child development 1990* (pp. 34–51). Brunner/Mazel.

Li, J., Chen, C., Wu, K., Zhang, M., Zhu, B., Chen, C., . . . Dong, Q. (2015). Genetic variations in the serotonergic system contribute to amygdala volume in humans. *Frontiers in Neuroanatomy, 9*, article 129.

Li, N. P., Bailey, J. M., Kenrick, D. T., & Linsenmeier, J. A. W. (2002). The necessities and luxuries of mate preferences: Testing the tradeoffs. *Journal of Personality and Social Psychology, 82*(6), 947–955.

Li, N. P., Griskevicius, V., Durante, K. M., Jonason, P. K., Pasisz, D. J., & Aumer, K. (2009). An evolutionary perspective on humor: Sexual selection or interest induction? *Personality and Social Psychology Bulletin, 35*, 923–936.

Li, T., Horta, M., Mascaro, J. S., Bijanki, K., Arnal, L. H., Adams, M., . . . & Rilling, J. K. (2018). Explaining individual variation in paternal brain responses to infant cries. *Physiology & Behavior, 193*, 43–54.

Li, Y., & Bates, T. C. (2019). You can't change your basic ability, but you work at things, and that's how we get hard things done: Testing the role of growth mindset on response to setbacks, educational attainment, and cognitive ability. *Journal of Experimental Psychology: General, 148*(9), 1640–1655.

Li, Y., & Yu, D. (2015). Development of emotion word comprehension in Chinese children from 2 to 13 years old: Relationships with valence and empathy. *PLoS One, 10*(12), e0143712. https://doi.org/10.1371/journal.pone.0143712

Li, Y. J., Kenrick, D. T., Griskevicius, V., & Neuberg, S. L. (2012). Economic decision biases and fundamental motivations: How mating and self-protection alter loss aversion. *Journal of Personality and Social Psychology, 102*(3), 550–561.

Liberman, N., & Förster, J. (2012). Goal gradients, expectancy, and value. In H. Aarts & A. J. Elliot (Eds.), *Goal-directed behavior* (pp. 151–173). Psychology Press.

Lieb, K., Zanarini, M. C., Schmahl, C., Linehan, M. M., & Bohus, M. (2004). Borderline personality disorder. *The Lancet, 364*(9432), 453–461.

Lieberman, D., Tooby, J., & Cosmides, L. (2007). The architecture of human kin detection. *Nature, 445*, 727–731.

Liew, J., Eisenberg, N., & Reiser, M. (2004). Preschoolers' effortful control and negative emotionality, immediate reactions to disappointment, and quality of social functioning. *Journal of Experimental Child Psychology, 89*, 298–319.

Likhtik, E., Stujenske, J. M., Topiwala, M. A., Harris, A. Z., & Gordon, J. A. (2014). Prefrontal entrainment of amygdala activity signals safety in learned fear and innate anxiety. *Nature Neuroscience, 17*(1), 106–113.

Lim, C., & Putnam, R. D. (2010). Religion, social networks, and life satisfaction. *American Sociological Review, 75*, 914–933.

Lim, M. M., Wang, Z., Olazábel, D. E., Ren, X., Terwilliger, E. F., & Young, L. J. (2004). Enhanced partner preference in a promiscuous species by manipulating the expression of a single gene. *Nature, 429*, 754–757.

Lin, A., Stolfi, A., Eicher, T., & Neeley, S. (2020). Predicting second-generation antidepressant effectiveness in treating sadness using demographic and clinical information: A machine learning approach. *Journal of Affective Disorders, 272*, 295–304.

Lin, J., & Dmitrieva, J. (2019). Cultural orientation moderates the association between desired affect and depressed mood among Chinese international students living in the United States. *Emotion, 19*(2), 371–375.

Lindquist, K. A., Wager, T. D., Kober, H., Bliss-Moreau, E., and Barrett, L. F. (2012). The brain basis of emotion: A meta-analytic review. *Behavioral and Brain Sciences, 35*, 121–143.

Lippa, R. A. (2007). The preferred traits of mates in a cross-national study of heterosexual and homosexual men and women: An examination of biological and cultural influences. *Archives of Sexual Behavior, 36*(2), 193–208.

Lishner, D. A., Hong, P. Y., Jiang, L., Vitacco, M. J., & Neumann, C. S. (2015). Psychopathy, narcissism, and borderline personality: A critical test of the affective empathy-impairment hypothesis. *Peersonality and Individual Differences, 86*, 257–265.

Liu, L. Y., Coe, C. L., Swenson, C. A., Kelly, E. A., Kita, H., & Busse, W. W. (2002). School examinations enhance airway inflammation to antigen challenge. *American Journal of Respiratory and Critical Care Medicine, 165*, 1062–1067.

Livingstone, K. M., & Isaacowitz, D. M. (2015). Situation selection and modification for emotion regulation in younger and older adults. *Social Psychological and Personality Science, 6*(8), 904–910.

Livingstone, K. M., & Isaacowitz, D. M. (2021). Age and emotion regulation in daily life: Frequency, strategies, tactics, and effectiveness. *Emotion, 21*(1), 39–51.

LoBue, V., & Adolph, K. E. (2019). Fear in infancy: Lessons from snakes, spiders, heights, and strangers. *Developmental Psychology, 55*(9), 1889–1907.

LoBue, V., & DeLoache, J. S. (2010). Superior detection of threat-relevant stimuli in infancy. *Developmental Science, 13*(1), 221–228.

Locke, E. A., & Latham, G. P. (1990). *A theory of goal setting & task performance*. Prentice-Hall.

Locke, E. A., & Latham, G. P. (2002). Building a practically useful theory of goal setting and task motivation: A 35-year odyssey. *American Psychologist, 57*(9), 705–717.

Locke, E. A., & Latham, G. P. (Eds.). (2013). *New developments in goal setting and task performance*. Routledge/Taylor & Francis.

Locke, E. A., & Schattke, K. (2019). Intrinsic and extrinsic motivation: Time for expansion and clarification. *Motivation Science, 5*(4), 277–290.

Loehlin, J. C., McCrae, R. R., Costa Jr, P. T., & John, O. P. (1998). Heritabilities of common and measure-specific components of the Big Five personality factors. *Journal of Research in Personality, 32*(4), 431–453.

Loewenstein, G. (1987). Anticipation and the valuation of delayed consumption. *The Economic Journal, 97*, 666–684.

Logue, A. W. (1985). Conditioned food aversion learning in humans. Annals of the New York Academy of Sciences, *443*, 316–329.

Lohani, M., Payne, B. R., & Isaacowitz, D. M. (2018). Emotional coherence in early and later adulthood during sadness reactivity and regulation. *Emotion, 18*(6), 789–804.

Lonsdorf, T. B., Menz, M. M., Andreatta, M., Fullana, M. A., Golkar, A., Haaker, J., . . . & Merz, C. J. (2017). Don't fear 'fear conditioning': Methodological considerations for the design and analysis of studies on human fear acquisition, extinction, and return of fear. *Neuroscience & Biobehavioral Reviews, 77*, 247–285.

Lopes, P. N., Brackett, M. A., Nezlek, J. B., Schütz, A., Sellin, I., & Salovey, P. (2004). Emotional intelligence and social interaction. *Personality and Social Psychology Bulletin, 30*(8), 1018–1034.

Lorberbaum, J. P., Newman, J. D., Horwitz, A. R., Dubno, J. R., Lydiard, R. B., Hamner, M. B., . . . & George, M. S. (2002). A potential role for thalamocingulate circuitry in human maternal behavior. *Biological Psychiatry, 51*(6), 431–445.

Lorenz, K. (1971). *Studies in animal and human behaviour, Vol. 2*. (R. Martin, Trans.). Harvard University Press. (Original work published 1950).

Lorenzo-Luaces, L., Buss, J. F., & Fried, E. I. (2021). Heterogeneity in major depression and its melancholic and atypical specifiers: A secondary analysis of STAR* D. *BMC Psychiatry, 21*(1), 1–11.

Lorrain, D. S., Riolo, J. V., Matuszewich, L., & Hull, E. M. (1999). Lateral hypothalamic serotonin inhibits nucleus accumbens dopamine: Implications for sexual refractoriness. *Journal of Neuroscience, 19*, 7648–7652.

Lovallo, W. R., Farag, N. H., Sorocco, K. H., Cohoon, A. J., & Vincent, A. S. (2012). Lifetime adversity leads to blunted stress axis reactivity: studies from the Oklahoma Family Health Patterns Project. *Biological Psychiatry, 71*(4), 344–349.

Love, A. S., & Love, R. J. (2021). Considering needle phobia among adult patients during mass COVID-19 vaccinations. *Journal of Primary Care & Community Health, 12*. https://doi.org/10.1177/21501327211007393

Löw, A., Lang, P. J., Smith, J. C., & Bradley, M. M. (2008). Both predator and prey. *Psychological Science, 19*, 865–873.

Lucas, R. E. (2007). Long-term disability is associated with lasting changes in subjective well-being: Evidence from two nationally representative longitudinal studies. *Journal of Personality and Social Psychology*, *92*, 717–730.

Lucas, R. E., Clark, A. E., Georgellis, Y., & Diener, E. (2003). Reexamining adaptation and the set point model of happiness: Reactions to changes in marital status. *Journal of Personality and Social Psychology*, *84*, 527–539.

Lucas, R. E., Clark, A. E., Georgellis, Y., & Diener, E. (2004). Unemployment alters the set point for life satisfaction. *Psychological Science*, *15*, 8–13.

Lucas, R. E., & Schimmack, U. (2009). Income and well-being: How big is the gap between the rich and the poor? *Journal of Research in Personality*, *43*, 75–78.

Lucassen, N., Tharner, A., Van IJzendoorn, M. H., Bakermans-Kranenburg, M. J., Volling, B. L., Verhulst, F. C., & Tiemeier, H. (2011). The association between paternal sensitivity and infant–father attachment security: A meta-analysis of three decades of research. *Journal of Family Psychology*, *25*(6), 986–992.

Ludolph, R., & Schulz, P. J. (2015). Does regulatory fit lead to more effective health communication? A systematic review. *Social Science & Medicine*, *128*, 142–150.

Luhmann, M., Hofmann, W., Eid, M., & Lucas, R. E. (2012). Subjective well-being and adaptation to life events: a meta-analysis. *Journal of Personality and Social Psychology*, *102*(3), 592–615.

Luna, B., Padmanabhan, A., & O'Hearn, K. (2010). What has fMRI told us about the development of cognitive control through adolescence? *Brain and Cognition*, *72*, 101–113.

Lundin, C., Danielsson, K.G., Bixo, M., Moby, L., Bengtsdotter, H., Jawad, I., Marions, L., Brynhildsen, J., Malmborg, A., Lindh, I., & Sundström Poromaa, I. (2017). Combined oral contraceptive use is associated with both improvement and worsening of mood in the different phases of the treatment cycle: A double-blind, placebo-controlled randomized trial. *Psychoneuroendocrinology*, *76*, 135–143

Lurquin, J. H., Michaelson, L. E., Barker, J. E., Gustavson, D. E., Von Bastian, C. C., Carruth, N. P., & Miyake, A. (2016). No evidence of the ego-depletion effect across task characteristics and individual differences: A pre-registered study. *PLoS One*, *11*(2), e0147770. https://doi.org/10.1371/journal.pone.0147770

Lutz, C. (1982). The domain of emotion words in Ifaluk. *American Ethnologist*, *9*, 113–128.

Lyubomirsky, S., & Boehm, J. K. (2010). Human motives, happiness, and the puzzle of parenthood: Commentary on Kenrick et al. (2010). *Perspectives on Psychological Science*, *5*, 327–334.

Lyubomirsky, S., Dickerhoof, R., Boehm, J. K., & Sheldon, K. M. (2011). Becoming happier takes both a will and a proper way: An experimental longitudinal intervention to boost well-being. *Emotion*, *11*, 391–402.

Lyubomirsky, S., King, L., & Diener, E. (2005). The benefits of frequent positive affect: Does happiness lead to success? *Psychological Bulletin*, *131*, 803–855.

Lyubomirsky, S., & Layous, K. (2013). How do simple positive activities increase well-being? *Current Directions in Psychological Science*, *22*(1), 57–62.

Maassarani, R., Gosselin, P., Montembault, P., & Gagnon, M. (2014). French-speaking children's freely produced labels for facial expressions. *Frontiers in Psychology*, *5*, Article 555. https://doi.org/10.3389/fpsyg.2014.00555

MacCann, C., Jiang, Y., Brown, L. E., Double, K. S., Bucich, M., & Minbashian, A. (2020). Emotional intelligence predicts academic performance: A meta-analysis. *Psychological Bulletin*, *146*(2), 150–186.

MacCormack, J. K., & Lindquist, K. A. (2019). Feeling hangry? When hunger is conceptualized as emotion. *Emotion*, *19*(2), 301–319.

MacDonald, G., & Leary, M. R. (2005). Why does social exclusion hurt? The relationship between social and physical pain. *Psychological Bulletin*, *131*(2), 202–223.

MacLean, P. D. (1952). Some psychiatric implications of physiological studies on frontotemporal portion of limbic system (visceral brain). *Electroencephalography and Clinical Neurophysiology*, *4*(4), 407–418.

MacLeod, C., Grafton, B., & Notebaert, L. (2019). Anxiety-linked attentional bias: Is it reliable? *Annual Review of Clinical Psychology*, *15*, 529–554.

Major, B. C., Le Nguyen, K. D., Lundberg, K. B., & Fredrickson, B. L. (2018). Well-being correlates of perceived positivity resonance: Evidence from trait and episode-level assessments. *Personality and Social Psychology Bulletin*, *44*(12), 1631–1647.

Major Depressive Disorder Working Group of the Psychiatric GWAS Consortium. (2013). A mega-analysis of genome-wide association studies for major depressive disorder. *Molecular Psychiatry*, *18*, 497–511.

Malaguti, A., Ciocanel, O., Sani, F., Dillon, J. F., Eriksen, A., & Power, K. (2020). Effectiveness of the use of implementation intentions on reduction of substance use: A meta-analysis. *Drug and Alcohol Dependence*, *214*, 108120. https://doi.org/10.1016/j.drugalcdep.2020.108120

Malik, A., Goodwin, G. M., Hoppitt, L., & Holmes, E. A. (2014). Hypomanic experience in young adults confers vulnerability to intrusive imagery after experimental trauma: Relevance for bipolar disorder. *Clinical Psychological Science, 2*, 675–684.

Mandelli, L., Petrelli, C., & Serretti, A. (2015). The role of specific early trauma in adult depression: A meta-analysis of published literature. Childhood trauma and adult depression. *European Psychiatry, 30*, 665–680.

Manderlink, G., & Harackiewicz, J. M. (1984). Proximal versus distal goal setting and intrinsic motivation. *Journal of Personality and Social Psychology, 47*(4), 918–928.

Maner, J. K., Kenrick, D. T., Becker, D. V., Robertson, T. E., Hofer, B., Neuberg, S. L., Delton, A. W., Butner, J., & Schaller, M. (2005). Functional projection: How fundamental social motives can bias interpersonal perception. *Journal of Personality and Social Psychology, 88*(1), 63–78.

Mangelsdorf, S. C., Shapiro, J. R., & Marzolf, D. (1995). Developmental and temperamental differences in emotion regulation in infancy. *Child Development, 66*(6), 1817–1828.

Manor, O., & Eisenbach, Z. (2003). Mortality after spousal loss: Are there socio-demographic differences? *Social Science & Medicine, 56*, 405–413.

Marchand, W. R., & Yurgelun-Todd, D. (2010). Striatal structure and function in mood disorders: a comprehensive review. *Bipolar Disorders, 12*, 764–785.

Marek, R., Strobel, C., Bredy, T. W., & Sah, P. (2013). The amygdala and medial prefrontal cortex: partners in the fear circuit. *Journal of Physiology, 591*(10), 2381–2391.

Maret, S., Faraguna, U., Nelson, A. B., Cirelli, C., & Tononi, G. (2011). Sleep and waking modulate spine turnover in the adolescent mouse cortex. *Nature Neuroscience, 14*, 1418–1420.

Markus, H. R., & Kitayama, S. (1991). Culture and the self: Implications for cognition, emotion, and motivation. *Psychological Bulletin, 98*, 224–253.

Markus, H. R., Ryff, C. D., Curhan, K. B., & Palmersheim, K. A. (2004). In their own words: Well-being at midlife among high school-educated and college-educated adults. In O. G. Brim, C. D. Ryff, & R. C. Kessler (Eds.), *How healthy are we?* (pp. 273–319). University of Chicago Press.

Martens, J. P., & Tracy, J. L. (2013). The emotional origins of a social learning bias does the pride expression cue copying? *Social Psychological and Personality Science, 4*(4), 492–499.

Martin, G. B., & Clark, R. D. (1982). Distress crying in neonates: Species and peer specificity. *Developmental Psychology, 18*, 3–9.

Martin, N. G., Maza, L., McGrath, S. J., & Phelps, A. E. (2014). An examination of referential and affect specificity with five emotions in infancy. *Infant Behavior and Development, 37*, 286–297.

Martin, R., Watson, D., & Wan, C. K. (2000). A three-factor model of trait anger: Dimensions of affect, behavior, and cognition. *Journal of Personality, 68*, 869–897.

Martinez, L., Falvello, V. B., Aviezer, H., & Todorov, A. (2016). Contributions of facial expressions and body language to the rapid perception of dynamic emotions. *Cognition and Emotion, 30*(5), 939–952.

Marzillier, S. L., & Davey, G. C. L. (2004). The emotional profiling of disgust-eliciting stimuli: Evidence for primary and complex disgusts. *Cognition and Emotion, 18*, 313–336.

Maslach, C. (1979). Negative emotional biasing of unexplained arousal. *Journal of Personality and Social Psychology, 37*, 953–969.

Maslow, A. H. (1943). A theory of human motivation. *Psychological Review, 50*(4), 370–396.

Masterson, F. A., & Crawford, M. (1982). The defense motivation system: A theory of avoidance behavior. *Behavioral and Brain Sciences, 5*, 661–696.

Mastropieri, D., & Turkewitz, G. (1999). Prenatal experience and neonatal responsiveness to vocal expressions of emotion. *Developmental Psychobiology, 35*, 204–214.

Mataix-Cols, D., An, S. K., Lawrence, N. S., Caseras, X., Speckens, A., Giampietro, V., . . . & Phillips, M. L. (2008). Individual differences in disgust sensitivity modulate neural responses to aversive/disgusting stimuli. *European Journal of Neuroscience, 27*(11), 3050–3058.

Mather, M., & Carstensen, L. L. (2003). Aging and attentional biases for emotional faces. *Psychological Science, 14*, 409–415.

Matsumoto, D. (1990). Cultural similarities and differences in display rules. *Motivation and Emotion, 14*, 195–214.

Matsumoto, D. (1992). More evidence for the universality of a contempt expression. *Motivation and Emotion, 16*(4), 363–368.

Matsumoto, D. (1996). *Unmasking Japan: Myths and Realities About the Emotions of the Japanese.* Stanford University Press.

Matsumoto, D., Takeuchi, S., Andayani, S., Kouznetsova, N., & Krupp, D. (1998). The contribution of individualism vs. collectivism to cross-national differences in display rules. *Asian Journal of Social Psychology*, *1*(2), 147–165.

Matsumoto, D., & Willingham, B. (2009). Spontaneous facial expressions of emotion of congenitally and non-congenitally blind individuals. *Journal of Personality and Social Psychology*, *96*, 1–10.

Matsumoto, D., Willingham, B., & Olide, A. (2009). Sequential dynamics of culturally moderated facial expressions of emotion. *Psychological Science*, *20*, 1269–1274.

Matsumoto, D., Yoo, S. H., & Fontaine, J. (2008). Mapping expressive differences around the world: the relationship between emotional display rules and individualism versus collectivism. *Journal of Cross-Cultural Psychology*, *39*(1), 55–74.

Matsumoto, D., Yoo, S. H., Hirayama, S., & Petrova, G. (2005). Development and validation of a measure of display rule knowledge: The display rule assessment inventory. *Emotion*, *5*, 23–40.

Matsuyama, Y., Hama., H., Kawamura, Y., & Mine, H. (1978). An analysis of emotional words. *The Japanese Journal of Psychology*, *49*, 229–232.

Mattavelli, G., Sormaz, M., Flack, T., Asghar, A. U. R., Fan, S., Frey, J., . . . Andrews, T. J. (2014). Neural responses to facial expressions support the role of the amygdala in processing threat. *Social Cognitive and Affective Neuroscience*, *9*, 1684–1689.

Mattingly, V., & Kraiger, K. (2019). Can emotional intelligence be trained? A meta-analytical investigation. *Human Resource Management Review*, *29*(2), 140–155.

Maul, A. (2012). The validity of the Mayer-Salovey-Caruso Emotional Intelligence Test (MSCEIT) as a measure of emotional intelligence. *Emotion Review*, *4*, 394–402.

Mauss, I. B., Butler, E. A., Roberts, N. A., & Chu, A. (2010). Emotion control values and responding to an anger provocation in Asian-American and European-American individuals. *Cognition and Emotion*, *24*, 1026–1043.

Mauss, I. B., Levenson, R. W., McCarter, L, Wilhelm, F. W., & Gross, J. J. (2005). The tie that binds? Coherence among emotion experience, behavior, and physiology. *Emotion*, *5*, 175–190.

Mauss, I. B., Tamir, M., Anderson, C. L., & Savino, N. S. (2011). Can seeking happiness make people unhappy? Paradoxical effects of valuing happiness. *Emotion*, *11*(4), 807–815.

Mayer, J. D., Caruso, D. R., & Salovey, P. (2000). Emotional intelligence meets traditional standards for an intelligence. *Intelligence*, *27*, 267–298.

McCall, C., & Singer, T. (2012). The animal and human neuroendocrinology of social cognition, motivation and behavior. *Nature Neuroscience*, *15*, 681–688.

McClelland, D. C., Atkinson, J. W., Clark, R. A., & Lowell, E. L. (1976). *The achievement motive*. Irvington.

McCullough, M. E. (2001). Forgiveness: Who does it and how do they do it? *Current Directions in Psychological Science*, *10*, 194–197.

McDougall, W. (1908). The principal instincts and the primary emotions of man. In *An introduction to social psychology* (pp. 45–89). Methuen.

McDougall, W. (1919). *An introduction to social psychology* (14th ed.). Methuen.

McEwen, B. S. (2018). Redefining neuroendocrinology: Epigenetics of brain-body communication over the life course. *Frontiers in Neuroendocrinology*, *49*, 8–30.

McEwen, B. S., Bowles, N. P., Gray, J. D., Hill, M. N., Hunter, R. G., Karatsoreos, I. N., & Nasca, C. (2015). Mechanisms of stress in the brain. *Nature Neuroscience*, *18*, 1353–1363.

McEwan, D., Harden, S.M., Zumbo, B.D., Sylvester, B.D., Kaulius, M., Ruissen, G.R., Dowd, A.J., & Beauchamp, M.R (2016). The effectiveness of multicomponent goal setting interventions for changing physical activity behaviour: A systematic review and meta- analysis. *Health Psychology Review*, *10*(1), 67–88.

McGregor, I. S., Hargreaves, G. A., Apfelbach, R., & Hunt, G. E. (2004). Neural correlates of cat odor-induced anxiety in rats: Region-specific effects of the benzodiazepine midazolam. *Journal of Neuroscience*, *24*, 4134–4144.

McGue, M., Elkins, I., Walden, B., & Iacono, W. G. (2005). Perceptions of the parent–adolescent relationship: A longitudinal investigation. *Developmental Psychology*, *41*, 971–984.

McIntosh, D. N. (1996). Facial feedback hypotheses: Evidence, implications, and directions. *Motivation and Emotion*, *20*(2), 121–147.

McKinley, S., Fien, M., Riegel, B., Meischke, H., AbuRuz, M. E., Lennie, T. A., & Moser, D. K. (2012). Complications after acute coronary syndrome are reduced by perceived control of cardiac illness. *Journal of Advanced Nursing*, *68*(10), 2320–2330.

McLaughlin, K. A., & Nolen-Hoeksema, S. (2011). Rumination as a transdiagnostic factor in depression and anxiety. *Behaviour Research and Therapy*, *49*(3), 186–193.

McRae, K., Jacobs, S. E., Ray, R. D., John, O. P., & Gross, J. J. (2012). Individual differences in reappraisal ability: Links to reappraisal frequency, well-being, and cognitive control. *Journal of Research in Personality*, *46*(1), 2–7.

Medici, C. R., Videbech, P., Gustafsson, L. N., & Munk-Jorgensen, P. (2015). Mortality and secular trend in the incidence of bipolar disorder. *Journal of Affective Disorders*, *183*, 39–44.

Mehta, P. H., Welker, K. M., Zilioli, S., & Carré, J. M. (2015). Testosterone and cortisol jointly modulate risk-taking. *Psychoneuroendocrinology*, *56*, 88–99.

Mehu, M., & Scherer, K. R. (2015). The appraisal bias model of cognitive vulnerability to depression. *Emotion Review*, *7*, 272–279.

Meissner, K., Muth, E. R., & Herbert, B. M. (2011). Bradygastric activity of the stomach predicts disgust sensitivity and perceived disgust intensity. *Biological Psychology*, *86*(1), 9–16.

Mendes, D. M. L. F., Seidl-de-Moura, M. L., & Siqueira, J. D. (2009). The ontogenesis of smiling and its association with mothers' affective behaviors: A longitudinal study. *Infant Behavior & Development*, *32*, 445–453.

Mendes, W. B., Blascovich, J., Lickel, B., & Hunter, S. (2002). Challenge and threat during social interactions with White and Black men. *Personality and Social Psychology Bulletin*, *28*(7), 939–952.

Mendes, W. B., & Park, J. (2014). Neurobiological concomitants of motivational states. In A. Elliot (Ed.), *Advances in motivation science* (Vol. 1, pp. 233–270). Elsevier.

Mennella, J. A., Jagnow, C. P., & Beauchamp, G. K. (2001). Prenatal and postnatal flavor learning by human infants. *Pediatrics*, *107*(6), e88. https://doi.org/10.1542/peds.107.6.e88

Menon, U., & Shweder, R. A. (1994). Kali's tongue: Cultural psychology, cultural consensus and the meaning of "shame" in Orissa, India. In H. Markus & S. Kitayama (Eds.), *Emotion and culture: Empirical studies of mutual influence* (pp. 241–284). American Psychological Association.

Mercadante, E., Witkower, Z., & Tracy, J. L. (2021). The psychological structure, social consequences, function, and expression of pride experiences. *Current Opinion in Behavioral Sciences*, *39*, 130–135.

Meyer, M. M., Bell, R., & Buchner, A. (2015). Remembering the snake in the grass: Threat enhances recognition but not source memory. *Emotion*, *15*, 721–730.

Michalak, J., Troje, N. F., Fischer, J., Vollmar, P., Heidenreich, T., & Schulte, D. (2009). Embodiment of sadness and depression—gait patterns associated with dysphoric mood. *Psychosomatic Medicine*, *71*(5), 580–587.

Mierop, A., Mikolajczak, M., Stahl, C., Béna, J., Luminet, O., Lane, A., & Corneille, O. (2020). How can intranasal oxytocin research be trusted? A systematic review of the interactive effects of intranasal oxytocin on psychosocial outcomes. *Perspectives on Psychological Science*, *15*(5), 1228–1242.

Mikolajczak, M., Avalosse, H., Vancorenland, S., Verniest, R., Callens, M., Van Broeck, N., . . . & Mierop, A. (2015). A nationally representative study of emotional competence and health. *Emotion*, *15*(5), 653–667.

Mikulincer, M., Birnbaum, G., Woddis, D., & Nachmias, O. (2000). Stress and accessibility of proximity-related thoughts: Exploring the normative and intra-individual components of attachment theory. *Journal of Personality and Social Psychology*, *78*, 509–523.

Mikulincer, M., Gillath, O., & Shaver, P. (2002). Activation of the attachment system in adulthood: Threat-related primes increase the accessibility of mental representations of attachment figures. *Journal of Personality and Social Psychology*, *83*, 881–895.

Milgram, S. (1974). *Obedience to authority*. Harper & Row.

Miller, B. R., & Hen, R. (2015). The current state of the neurogenic theory of depression and anxiety. *Current Opinion in Neurobiology*, *30*, 51–58.

Miller, G. (2007). The mystery of the missing smile. *Science*, *316*, 826–827.

Miller, G. A., Galanter, E., & Pribram, K. H. (1960). The integration of plans. In G. A. Miller, E. Galanter, & K. H. Pribram (Eds.), Plans and the structure of behavior (pp. 95–102). Henry Holt.

Miller, K. J., Shenhav, A., & Ludvig, E. A. (2019). Habits without values. *Psychological Review*, *126*(2), 292–311.

Miller, L. (2020). *Why fish don't exist: A story of loss, love, and the hidden order of life*. Simon & Schuster.

Miller, R. M., Hannikainen, I. A., & Cushman, F. A. (2014). Bad actions or bad outcomes? Differentiating affective contributions to the moral condemnation of harm. *Emotion*, *14*, 573–587.

Miller, R. S. (2001a). Embarrassment and social phobia: Distant cousins or close kin? In S. G. Hofmann & P. M. DiBartolo (Eds.), *From social anxiety to social phobia* (pp. 65–85). Allyn & Bacon.

Miller, R. S. (2001b). Shyness and embarrassment compared: Siblings in the service of social evaluation. In W. R. Crozier & L. E. Alden (Eds.), *International Handbook of Social Anxiety* (pp. 281–300). Wiley.

Millgram, Y., Joormann, J., Huppert, J. D., & Tamir, M. (2015). Sad as a matter of choice? Emotion-regulation goals in depression. *Psychological Science, 26,* 1216–1228.

Mills, D. W., & Ward, R. P. (1986). Attenuation of stress-induced hypertension by exercise independent of training effects: An animal model. *Journal of Behavioral Medicine, 9,* 599–605.

Miloyan, B., Bulley, A., & Suddendorf, T. (2019). Anxiety: Here and beyond. *Emotion Review, 11*(1), 39–49.

Miloyan, B., Bulley, A., Pachana, N. A., & Byrne, G. J. (2014). Social phobia symptoms across the adult lifespan. *Journal of Affective Disorders, 168,* 86–90.

Miltner, W. H. R., Krieschel, S., Hecht, H., Trippe, R., & Weiss, T. (2004). Eye movements and behavioral responses to threatening and nonthreatening stimuli during visual search in phobic and nonphoic subjects *Emotion, 4,* 323–339.

Mineka, S. (1987). A primate model of phobic fears. In H. Eysenck & I. Martin (Eds.), *Theoretical foundations of behavior therapy* (pp. 81–111). Plenum.

Mineka, S., Davidson, M., Cook, M., & Keir, R. (1984). Observational conditioning of snake fear in rhesus monkeys. *Journal of Abnormal Psychology, 93,* 355–372.

Miola, A., Cattarinussi, G., Antiga, G., Caiolo, S., Solmi, M., & Sambataro, F. (2022). Difficulties in emotion regulation in bipolar disorder: A systematic review and meta-analysis. *Journal of Affective Disorders, 302,* 352–360.

Mireault, G. C., Crockenberg, S. C., Sparrow, J. E., Cousineau, K., Pettinato, C., & Woodard, K. (2015). Laughing matters: Infant humor in the context of parental affect. *Journal of Experimental Child Psychology, 136,* 30–41.

Mirescu, C., Peters, J. D., & Gould, E. (2004). Early life experience alters response of adult neurogenesis to stress. *Nature Neuroscience, 7,* 841–846.

Misaki, M., Kerr, K. L., Ratliff, E. L., Cosgrove, K. T., Simmons, W. K., Morris, A. S., & Bodurka, J. (2021). Beyond synchrony: The capacity of fMRI hyperscanning for the study of human social interaction. *Social Cognitive and Affective Neuroscience, 16*(1–2), 84–92.

Mischel, W., & Ebbesen, E. B. (1970). Attention in delay of gratification. *Journal of Personality and Social Psychology, 16*(2), 329–337.

Mishra, S., & Lalumière, M. L. (2017). Associations between delay discounting and risk-related behaviors, traits, attitudes, and outcomes. *Journal of Behavioral Decision Making, 30*(3), 769–781.

Miyake, K., Campos, J. J., Kagan, J., & Bradshaw, D. L. (1986). Issues in socioemotional development. In H. Azuma, K. Hakuta, & H. Stevenson (Eds.), *Kodomo: Child development and education in Japan* (pp. 239–261). W. H. Freeman.

Miyamoto, Y., Uchida, Y., & Ellsworth, P. C. (2010). Culture and mixed emotions: Co-occurrence of positive and negative emotions in Japan and the United States. *Emotion, 10,* 404–415.

Mobbs, D., Grecius, M. D., Abdel-Azim, E., Menon, V., & Reiss, A. L. (2003). Humor modulates the mesolimbic reward centers. *Neuron, 40,* 1041–1048.

Moe, B. K., King, A. R., & Bailly, M. D. (2004). Retrospective accounts of recurrent parental physical abuse as a predictor of adult laboratory-induced aggression. *Aggressive Behavior, 30,* 217–228.

Moffitt, T. E., Arseneault, L., Belsky, D., Dickson, N., Hancox, R. J., Harrington, H., . . . & Caspi, A. (2011). A gradient of childhood self-control predicts health, wealth, and public safety. *Proceedings of the National Academy of Sciences, 108*(7), 2693–2698.

Moles, A., Kieffer, B. L., & D'Amato, F. R. (2004). Deficit in attachment behavior in mice lacking the μ-opioid receptor gene. *Science, 304,* 1983–1986.

Monahan, J. L., Murphy, S. T., & Zajonc, R. B. (2000). Subliminal mere exposure: Specific, general, and diffuse effects. *Psychological Science, 11*(6), 462–466.

Monroe, S. M., & Harkness, K. L. (2005). Life stress, the "kindling" hypothesis, and the recurrence of depression: Considerations from a life stress perspective. *Psychological Review, 112,* 417–445.

Montoya, R. M., Kershaw, C., & Prosser, J. L. (2018). A meta-analytic investigation of the relation between interpersonal attraction and enacted behavior. *Psychological Bulletin, 144*(7), 673–709.

Moon, J. R., Glymour, M. M., Vable, A. M., Liu, S. Y., & Subramanian, S. V. (2014). Short- and long-term associations between widowhood and mortality in the United States: longitudinal analyses. *Journal of Public Health, 36,* 382–389.

Moore, L. J., Vine, S. J., Wilson, M. R., & Freeman, P. (2012). The effect of challenge and threat states on performance: An examination of potential mechanisms. *Psychophysiology, 49*(10), 1417–1425.

Moore, M. M. (1985). Nonverbal courtship patterns in women: Context and consequences. *Ethology and Sociobiology, 6,* 237–247.

Moors, A., Ellsworth, P. C., Scherer, K. R., & Frijda, N. H. (2013). Appraisal theories of emotion: State of the art and future development. *Emotion Review, 5*(2), 119–124.

Morales, M., Mundy, P., Crowson, M., Neal, A. R., & Delgado, C. (2005). Individual differences in infant attention skills, joint attention, and emotion regulation behaviour. *International Journal of Behavioral Development, 29*(3), 259–263.

Moreau, D. (2021). How malleable are cognitive abilities? A critical perspective on popular brief interventions. American Psychologist. Advance online publication. https://doi.org/10.1037/amp0000872

Moreland, R. L., & Zajonc, R. B. (1976). A strong test of exposure effects. *Journal of Experimental Social Psychology, 12*(2), 170–179.

Mori, K., & Mori, H. (2009). Another test of the passive facial feedback hypothesis: When your face smiles, you feel happy. *Perceptual and Motor Skills, 109*(1), 76–78.

Morisano, D., Hirsh, J. B., Peterson, J. B., Pihl, R. O., & Shore, B. M. (2010). Setting, elaborating, and reflecting on personal goals improves academic performance. *Journal of Applied Psychology, 95*(2), 255–264.

Morling, B., Kitayama, S., & Miyamoto, Y. (2003). American and Japanese women use different coping strategies during normal pregnancy. *Personality and Social Psychology Bulletin, 29*, 1533–1546.

Morse, S. J., & Gruzen, J. (1976). The eye of the beholder: A neglected variable in the study of physical attractiveness. *Journal of Psychology, 44*, 209–225.

Moscarello, J. M., & LeDoux, J. E. (2013). Active avoidance learning requires prefrontal suppression of amygdala-mediated defensive reactions. *Journal of Neuroscience, 33*(9), 3815–3823.

Moskowitz, J. T., Hult, J. R., Bussolari, C., & Acree, M. (2009). What works in coping with HIV? A meta-analysis with implications for coping with serious illness. *Psychological Bulletin, 135*(1), 121–141.

Mroczek, D. K. (2004). Positive and negative affect at midlife. In O. G. Brim, C. D. Ryff, & R. C. Kessler (Eds.), *How healthy are we?* (pp. 205–226). University of Chicago Press.

Mroczek, D. K., & Spiro, A. (2005). Change in life satisfaction during adulthood: Findings from the veterans affairs normative aging study. *Journal of Personality and Social Psychology, 88*, 189–202.

Much, N. C. (1997). A semiotic view of socialization, lifespan development and cultural psychology: With vignettes from the moral culture of traditional Hindu households. *Psychology and Developing Societies, 9*, 65–105.

Mueller, K., Fritz, T., Mildner, T., Richter, M., Schulze, K., Lepsien, J., . . . Möller, H. E. (2015). Investigating the dynamics of the brain response to music: A central role of the ventral striatum/nucleus accumbens. *NeuroImage, 116*, 68–79.

Mulinari, S. (2012). Monoamine theories of depression: Historical impact on biomedical research. *Journal of the History of the Neurosciences, 21*, 366–392.

Munakata, Y., Herd, S. A., Chatham, C. H., Depue, B. E., Banich, M. T., & O'Reilly, R. C. (2011). A unified framework for inhibitory control. *Trends in Cognitive Sciences, 15*(10), 453–459.

Muraven, M., Tice, D. M., & Baumeister, R. F. (1998). Self-control as a limited resource: Regulatory depletion patterns. *Journal of Personality and Social Psychology, 74*(3), 774–789.

Murberg, T. A., Furze, G., & Bru, E. (2003). Avoidance coping styles predict mortality among patients with congestive heart failure: A 6-year follow-up study. *Personality and Individual Differences, 36*(4), 757–766.

Murphy, K. G., & Bloom, S. R. (2006). Gut hormones and the regulation of energy homeostasis. *Nature, 444*(7121), 854–859.

Murphy, M. L. M., Slavich, G. M., Chen, E., & Miller, G. E. (2015). Targeted rejection predicts decreased anti-inflammatory gene expression and increased symptom severity in youth with asthma. *Psychological Science, 26*, 111–121.

Murray, H. A. (1938). *Explorations in personality: A clinical and experimental study of fifty men of college age.* Oxford University Press.

Murray, L., Halligan, S. L., Adams, G., Patterson, P., & Goodyer, I. M. (2006). Socioemotional development in adolescents at risk for depression: the role of maternal depression and attachment style. *Development and Psychopathology, 18*(02), 489–516.

Murray, S. L., & Holmes, J. G. (1999). The (mental) ties that bind: Cognitive structures that predict relationship resilience. *Journal of Personality and Social Psychology, 77*, 1228–1244.

Murray, S. L., Holmes, J. G., Gellavia, G., Griffin, D. W., & Dolderman, D. (2002). Kindred spirits? The benefits of egocentrism on close relationships. *Journal of Personality and Social Psychology, 82*, 563–581.

Myers, D. G. (2000a). The funds, friends, and faith of happy people. *American Psychologist, 55*, 56–67.

Myers, D. G. (2000b). *The American paradox: Spiritual hunger in an age of plenty.* Yale University Press.

Naab, P. J., & Russell, J. A. (2007). Judgments of emotion from spontaneous facial expressions of New Guineans. *Emotion, 7*, 736–744.

Nabi, R. L., & Myrick, J. G. (2019). Uplifting fear appeals: Considering the role of hope in fear-based persuasive messages. *Health Communication, 34*(4), 463–474.

Nakamura, J., & Csikszentmihalyi, M. (2009). Flow theory and research. In S. J. Lopez & C. R. Snyder (Eds.), *Oxford handbook of positive psychology* (pp. 195–206). Oxford University Press.

Namburi, P., Beyeler, A., Yorozu, S., Calhoon, G G., Halbert, S. A., Wichmann, R., . . . The, K. M. (2015). A circuit mechanism for differentiating positive and negative associations. *Nature, 520,* 675–678.

Nave, G., Camerer, C., & McCullough, M. (2015). Does oxytocin increase trust in humans? A critical review of the literature. *Perspectives on Psychological Science, 10,* 772–789.

Neal, D. T., & Chartrand, T. L. (2011). Embodied emotion perception: amplifying and dampening facial feedback modulates emotion perception accuracy. *Social Psychological and Personality Science, 2*(6), 673–678.

Neel, R., Kenrick, D. T., White, A. E., & Neuberg, S. L. (2016). Individual differences in fundamental social motives. *Journal of Personality and Social Psychology, 110*(6), 887–907.

Neimeyer, R. A. (1995). An invitation to constructivist psychotherapies. In R. A. Neimeyer & M. J. Mahoney (Eds.), *Constructivism in psychology* (pp. 1–8). American Psychological Association.

Nelson, E. C., Heath, A. C., Madden, P. A., Cooper, M. L., Dinwiddie, S. H., Bucholz, K. K., . . . & Martin, N. G. (2002). Association between self-reported childhood sexual abuse and adverse psychosocial outcomes: results from a twin study. *Archives of General Psychiatry, 59*(2), 139–145.

Nelson, E. E., & Panksepp, J. (1996). Oxytocin mediates acquisition of maternally associated odor preferences in pre-weaning rat pups. *Behavioral Neuroscience, 110,* 583–592.

Nelson, E. E., & Panksepp, J. (1998). Brain substrates of infant-mother attachment: contributions of opioids, oxytocin, and norepinephrine. *Neuroscience Biobehavioral Review, 22,* 437–452.

Nelson, E. E., Shelton, S. E., & Kalin, N. H. (2003). Individual differences in the responses of naïve rhesus monkeys to snakes. *Emotion, 3*(1), 3–11.

Nelson, L. D., Meyvis, T., & Galak, J. (2009). Enhancing the television-viewing experience through commercial interruptions. *Journal of Consumer Research, 36,* 160–172.

Nelson, S. K., Kushlev, K., English, T., Dunn, E. W., & Lyubomirsky, S. (2013). In defense of parenthood children are associated with more joy than misery. *Psychological Science, 24*(1), 3–10.

Nelson, S. K., Kushlev, K., & Lyubomirsky, S. (2014). The pains and pleasures of parenting: When, why, and how is parenthood associated with more or less well-being? *Psychological Bulletin, 140,* 846–895.

Nes, R. B., & Røysamb, E. (2015). The heritability of subjective well-being: Review and meta-analysis. In M. Pluess (Ed.), *Genetics of Psychological Well-Being: The Role of Heritability and Genetics in Positive Psychology* (pp. 75–96). Oxford University Press.

Nesse, R. M., & Ellsworth, P. C. (2009). Evolution, emotions, and emotional disorders. *American Psychologist, 64*(2), 129–139.

Network and Pathway Analysis Subgroup. (2015). Psychiatric genome-wide association study analyses implicate neuronal, immune, and histone pathways. *Nature Neuroscience, 18,* 199–209.

Neumann, R., & Strack, F. (2000). Approach and avoidance: The influence of proprioceptive and exteroceptive cues on encoding of affective information. *Journal of Personality and Social Psychology, 79*(1), 39–48.

Nezlek, J. B., & Zebrowski, B. D. (2001). Implications of the dimensionality of unrealistic optimism for the study of perceived health risks. *Journal of Social and Clinical Psychology, 20,* 521–537.

Ng-Knight, T., & Schoon, I. (2017). Disentangling the influence of socioeconomic risks on children's early self-control. *Journal of Personality, 85*(6), 793–806.

Nguyen, Y., & Noussair, C. N. (2014). Risk aversion and emotions. *Pacific Economic Review, 19,* 296–312.

Nickerson, C., Schwarz, N., Diener, E., & Kahneman, D. (2003). Zeroing in on the dark side of the American dream: A closer look at the negative consequences of the goal for financial success. *Psychological Science, 14,* 531–536.

Niedenthal, P. M., Auxiette, C., Nugier, A., Dalle, N., Bonin, P., & Fayol, M. (2004). A prototype analysis of the French category "émotion." *Cognition and Emotion, 18,* 289–312.

Niedenthal, P. M., Rychlowska, M., Wood, A., & Zhao, F. (2018). Heterogeneity of long-history migration predicts smiling, laughter and positive emotion across the globe and within the United States. *PLoS One, 13*(8), Article e0197651. doi:10.1101/317289

Niedenthal, P. M., Rychlowska, M., Zhao, F., & Wood, A. (2019). Historical migration patterns shape contemporary cultures of emotion. *Perspectives on Psychological Science, 14*(4), 560–573.

Niedenthal, P. M., Tangney, J. P., & Gavanski, I. (1994). "If only I weren't" versus "If only I hadn't": Distinguishing shame and guilt in conterfactual thinking. *Journal of Personality and Social Psychology, 67,* 585–595.

Nimarko, A. F., Gorelik, A. J., Carta, K. E., Gorelik, M. G., & Singh, M. K. (2022). Neural correlates of reward processing distinguish healthy youth at familial risk for bipolar disorder from youth at familial risk for major depressive disorder. *Translational Psychiatry*, *12*(1), 1–9.

Nolen-Hoeksema, S. (1991). Responses to depression and their effects on the duration of depressive episodes. *Journal of Abnormal Psychology*, *100*, 569–582.

Nolen-Hoeksema, S., & Morrow, J. (1991). A prospective study of depression and post-traumatic stress symptoms after a natural disaster: The Loma Prieta earthquake. *Journal of Personality and Social Psychology*, *61*, 115–121.

Nolen-Hoeksema, S., Larson, J., & Grayson, C. (1999). Explaining the gender difference in depressive symptoms. *Journal of Personality and Social Psychology*, *77*, 1061–1072.

Nook, E. C., Sasse, S. F., Lambert, H. K., McLaughlin, K. A., & Somerville, L. H. (2017). Increasing verbal knowledge mediates development of multidimensional emotion representations. *Nature Human Behaviour*, *1*(12), 881–889.

Nook, E. C., Sasse, S. F., Lambert, H. K., McLaughlin, K. A., & Somerville, L. H. (2018). The nonlinear development of emotion differentiation: Granular emotional experience is low in adolescence. *Psychological Science*, *29*(8), 1346–1357.

Nook, E. C., Stavish, C. M., Sasse, S. F., Lambert, H. K., Mair, P., McLaughlin, K. A., & Somerville, L. H. (2020). Charting the development of emotion comprehension and abstraction from childhood to adulthood using observer-rated and linguistic measures. *Emotion*, *20*(5), 773–792.

Nordgren, L. F., Harreveld, F. V., & Pligt, J. V. D. (2009). The restraint bias: How the illusion of self-restraint promotes impulsive behavior. *Psychological Science*, *20*(12), 1523–1528.

Norman, G. J., Berntson, G. G., & Cacioppo, J. T. (2014). Emotion, somatovisceral afference, and autonomic regulation. *Emotion Review*, *6*, 113–123.

Nussbaum, M. C. (2003). *Upheavals of Thought: The Intelligence of Emotions*. Cambridge University Press.

Nutt, D. J., Lingford-Hughes, A., Erritzoe, D., & Stokes, P. R. A. (2015). The dopamine theory of addiction: 40 years of highs and lows. *Nature Reviews Neuroscience*, *16*, 305–312.

Nygren, T. E., Isen, A. M., Taylor, P. J., & Dulin, J. (1996). The influence of positive affect on the decision rule in risk situations: Focus on outcome (and especially avoidance of loss) rather than probability. *Organizational Behavior and Human Decision Processes*, *66*, 59–72.

O'Leary, K. D., Acevedo, B. P., Aron, A., Huddy, L., & Mashek, D. (2012). Is long-term love more than a rare phenomenon? If so, what are its correlates? *Social Psychological and Personality Science*, *3*, 241–249.

Ochsner, K. N., Bunge, S. A., Gross, J. J., & Gabrieli, J. D. (2002). Rethinking feelings: An fMRI study of the cognitive regulation of emotion. *Journal of Cognitive Neuroscience*, *14*(8), 1215–1229.

Oettingen, G. (2000). Expectancy effects on behavior depend on self-regulatory thought. *Social Cognition*, *18*(2), 101–129.

Oettingen, G. (2012). Future thought and behaviour change. *European Review of Social Psychology*, *23*(1), 1–63.

Oettingen, G., & Reininger, K. M. (2016). The power of prospection: Mental contrasting and behavior change. *Social and Personality Psychology Compass*, *10*(11), 591–604.

Ohbuchi, K. O., Tamura, T., Quigley, B. M., Tedeschi, J. T., Madi, N., Bond, M. H., & Mummendey, A. (2004). Anger, blame, and dimensions of perceived norm violations: Culture, gender, and relationships. *Journal of Applied Social Psychology*, *34*, 1587–1603.

Öhman, A. (2009). Of snakes and faces: An evolutionary perspective on the psychology of fear. *Scandinavian Journal of Psychology*, *50*(6), 543–552.

Öhman, A., Eriksson, A., & Olofsson, C. (1975). One-trial learning and superior resistance to extinction of autonomic responses conditioned to potentially phobic objects. *Journal of Comparative and Physiological Psychology*, *88*, 619–627.

Öhman, A., & Mineka, S. (2003). The malicious serpent: Snakes as a prototypical stimulus for an evolved module of fear. *Current Directions in Psychological Science*, *12*(1), 5–9.

Oishi, S. (2014). Socioecological psychology. *Annual Review of Psychology*, *65*, 581–609.

Oishi, S., & Diener, E. (2014). Residents of poor nations have a greater sense of meaning in life than residents of wealthy nations. *Psychological Science*, *25*, 422–430.

Oishi, S., & Kesebir, S. (2015). Income inequality explains why economic growth does not always translate to an increase in happiness. *Psychological Science*, *26*(10), 1630–1638.

Oishi, S., & Schimmack, U. (2010). Culture and Well-Being A New Inquiry Into the Psychological Wealth of Nations. *Perspectives on Psychological Science*, *5*(4), 463–471.

Oishi, S., Schimmack, U., & Diener, E. (2012). Progressive taxation and the subjective well-being of nations. *Psychological Science*, *23*(1), 86–92.

Olff, M., Frijling, J. L., Kubzansky, L. D., Bradley, B., Ellenbogen, M. A., Cardoso, C., . . . van Zuiden, M. (2013). The role of oxytocin in social bonding, stress regulation and mental health: An update on the moderating effects of context and individual differences. *Psychoneuroendocrinology*, *38*, 1883–1894.

Oliver, L. D., Mitchell, G. G. V., Dziobek, I., MacKinley, J., Coleman, K., Rankin, K. P., & Finger, E. C. (2015). Parsing cognitive and emotional empathy deficits for negative and positive stimuli in frontotemporal dementia. *Neuropsychologia*, *67*, 14–26.

Ong, A. D., Bergeman, C. S., & Bisconti, T. L. (2005). Unique effects of daily perceived control on anxiety symptomatology during conjugal bereavement. *Personality and Individual Differences*, *38*, 1057–1067.

Ortony, A., & Turner, T. J. (1990). What's basic about basic emotions? *Psychological Review*, *97*, 315–331.

Orwell, G. ([1968] 2000). Funny, not vulgar. In S. Orwell & I. Angus (Eds.), *George Orwell: The Collected Essays, Journalism and Letters* (Vol. 3). Nonpariel.

Öst, L. G., Sterner, U., & Lindahl, I. L. (1984). Physiological responses in blood phobics. *Behaviour Research and Therapy*, *22*(2), 109–117.

Oster, H., Hegley, D., & Nagel, L. (1992). Adult judgments and fine-grained analysis of infant facial expressions. *Developmental Psychology*, *28*, 1115–1131.

Otero, M. C., Wells, J. L., Chen, K. H., Brown, C. L., Connelly, D. E., Levenson, R. W., & Fredrickson, B. L. (2020). Behavioral indices of positivity resonance associated with long-term marital satisfaction. *Emotion*, *20*(7), 1225–1233.

Otowa, T., Hek, K., Lee, M., Byrne, E. M., Mirza, S. S., Nivard, M. G., . . . & Hettema, J. M. (2016). Meta-analysis of genome-wide association studies of anxiety disorders. *Molecular Psychiatry*, *21*(10), 1391–1399.

Otte, R. A., Donkers, F. C. L., Braeken, M. A. K. A., & Van den Bergh, B. R. H. (2015). Multimodal processing of emotional information in 9-month-old infants I: Emotional faces and voices. *Brain and Cognition*, *95*, 99–106.

Ouellet-Morin, I., Odgers, C. L., Danese, A., Bowes, L., Shakoor, S., Papadopoulos, A. S., . . . & Arseneault, L. (2011). Blunted cortisol responses to stress signal social and behavioral problems among maltreated/bullied 12-year-old children. *Biological Psychiatry*, *70*(11), 1016–1023.

Oveis, C., Cohen, A. B., Gruber, J., Shiota, M. N., Haidt, J., & Keltner, D. (2009). Resting respiratory sinus arrhythmia is associated with tonic positive emotionality. *Emotion*, *9*(2), 265–270.

Oyserman, D., Coon, H. M., & Kemmelmeier, M. (2002). Rethinking individualism and collectivism: Evaluation of theoretical assumptions and meta-analysis. *Psychological Bulletin*, *128*, 3–72.

Page-Gould, E., Mendes, W. B., & Major, B. (2010). Intergroup contact facilitates physiological recovery following stressful intergroup interactions. *Journal of Experimental Social Psychology*, *46*(5), 854–858.

Page-Gould, E., Mendoza-Denton, R., & Tropp, L. R. (2008). With a little help from my cross-group friend: reducing anxiety in intergroup contexts through cross-group friendship. *Journal of Personality and Social Psychology*, *95*(5), 1080–1094.

Panksepp, J. (1998). *Affective neuroscience: The foundations of human and animal emotions.* Oxford University Press.

Papies, E. K., Johannes, N., Daneva, T., Semyte, G., & Kauhanen, L. L. (2020). Using consumption and reward simulations to increase the appeal of plant-based foods. *Appetite*, *155*, 104812. https://doi.org/10.1016/j.appet.2020.104812

Papousek, I., Schulter, G., & Lang, B. (2009). Effects of emotionally contagious films on changes in hemisphere-specific cognitive performance. *Emotion*, *9*(4), 510–519.

Park, B., Tsai, J. L., Chim, L., Blevins, E., & Knutson, B. (2016). Neural evidence for cultural differences in the valuation of positive facial expressions. *Social Cognitive and Affective Neuroscience*, *11*, 243–252.

Park, C. L., Edmondson, D., Fenster, J. R., & Blank, T. O. (2008). Positive and negative health behavior changes in cancer survivors A stress and coping perspective. *Journal of Health Psychology*, *13*(8), 1198–1206.

Park, J., Ayduk, Ö., O'Donnell, L., Chun, J., Gruber, J., Kamali, M., . . . Kross, E. (2014). Regulating the high: Cognitive and neural processes underlying positive emotion regulation in bipolar I disorder. *Clinical Psychological Science*, *2*, 661–674.

Park, J., & Banaji, M. R. (2000). Mood and heuristics: The influence of happy and sad states on sensitivity and bias in stereotyping. *Journal of Personality and Social Psychology*, *78*, 1005–1023.

Park, L. E., Streamer, L., Huang, L., & Galinsky, A. D. (2013). Stand tall, but don't put your feet up: Universal and culturally-specific effects of expansive postures on power. *Journal of Experimental Social Psychology*, *49*(6), 965–971.

Parkinson, B., Fischer, A. H., & Manstead, A. S. (2005). *Emotion in social relations: Cultural, group, and interpersonal processes.* Psychology Press.

Parsons, S., Kruijt, A. W., & Fox, E. (2019). Psychological science needs a standard practice of reporting the reliability of cognitive-behavioral measurements. *Advances in Methods and Practices in Psychological Science*, *2*(4), 378–395.

Pauls, D. L., Abramovitch, A., Rauch, S. L., & Geller, D. A. (2014). Obsessive-compulsive disorder: An integrative genetic and neurobiological perspective. *Nature Reviews Neuroscience*, *15*, 410–424.

Pauneskou, D., Walton, G. M., Romero, C., Smith, E. N., Yeager, D. S., & Dweck, C. S. (2015). Mind-set interventions are a scalable treatment for academic underachievement. *Psychological Science*, *26*(6), 784–793.

Pavot, W., & Diener, E. (1993). Review of the satisfaction with life scale. *Psychological Assessment*, *5*, 164–172.

Payne, J. L. (2003). The role of estrogen in mood disorders in women. *International Review of Psychiatry*, *15*(3), 280–290.

Pei, M., Matsuda, K., Sakamoto, H., & Kawata, M. (2006). Intrauterine proximity to male fetuses affects the morphology of the sexually dimorphic nucleus of the preoptic area in the adult rat brain. *European Journal of Neuroscience*, *23*(5), 1234–1240.

Pekrun, R. (2006). The control-value theory of achievement emotions: Assumptions, corollaries, and implications for educational research and practice. *Educational Psychology Review*, 18, 315–341.

Pellegrini, A. D., & Smith, P. K. (2005). *The nature of play: Great apes and humans*. Guilford Press.

Pellis, S. M., O'Brien, D. P., Pellis, V. C., Teitelbaum, P., Wolgin, D. L., & Kennedy, S. (1988). Escalation of feline predation along a gradient from avoidance through "play" to killing. *Behavioral Neuroscience*, *102*, 760–777.

Peng, K., & Nisbett, R. E. (1999). Culture, dialectics, and reasoning about contradiction. *American Psychologist*, *54*(9), 741–754.

Penkunas, M. J., & Coss, R. G. (2013). A comparison of rural and urban Indian children's visual detection of threatening and nonthreatening animals. *Developmental Science*, *16*(3), 463–475.

Penley, J. A., Tomaka, J., & Wiebe, J. S. (2002). The association of coping to physical and psychological health outcomes: A meta-analytic review. *Journal of Behavioral Medicine*, *25*(6), 551–603.

Pennebaker, J. W. (1997). Writing about emotional experiences as a therapeutic process. *Psychological Science*, *8*, 162–166.

Pennebaker, J. W., & Chung, C. K. (2011). Expressive writing: Connections to physical and mental health. In

H. S. Friemdan (Ed.), *Oxford Handbook of Health Psychology* (pp. 417–437). Oxford University Press.

Pennebaker, J. W., & Graybeal, A. (2001). Patterns of natural language use: Disclosure, personality, and social integration. *Current Directions in Psychological Science*, *10*, 90–93.

Pereira, S. M., Geoffroy, M.-C., & Power, C. (2014). Depressive symptoms and physical activity during 3 decades in adult life. *JAMA Psychiatry*, *71*, 1373–1380.

Perez Burriel, M., & Sadurni Brugue, M. (2014). Developmental trajectory of intersubjectivity in the second and third year of life: Study of fixed population and random-individual effects. *European Journal of Developmental Psychology*, *11*, 574–591.

Perry, N. B., Dollar, J. M., Calkins, S. D., Keane, S. P., & Shanahan, L. (2020). Maternal socialization of child emotion and adolescent adjustment: Indirect effects through emotion regulation. *Developmental Psychology*, *56*(3), 541–552.

Perunovic, W. Q. E., Heller, D., & Rafaeli, E. (2007). Within-person changes in the structure of emotion. *Psychological Science*, *18*, 607–613.

Pessoa, L. (2012). Beyond brain regions: Network perspective of cognition–emotion interactions. *Behavioral and Brain Sciences*, *35*, 158–159.

Peters, F., Nicolson, N. A., Berkhof, J., Delespaul, P., & deVries, M. (2003). Effects of daily events on mood states in major depressive disorder. *Journal of Abnormal Psychology*, *112*, 203–211.

Peters, J., & Büchel, C. (2009). Overlapping and distinct neural systems code for subjective value during intertemporal and risky decision making. *Journal of Neuroscience: The Official Journal of the Society for Neuroscience*, *29*(50), 15727–15734.

Peters, S., & Crone, E. A. (2017). Increased striatal activity in adolescence benefits learning. *Nature Communications*, *8*(1), 1–9.

Peterson, C., & Steen, T. A. (2002). Optimistic explanatory style. In C. R. Snyder & S. J. Lopez (Eds.), *Handbook of positive psychology* (pp. 244–256). Oxford University Press.

Pham, M. T. (2007). Emotion and rationality: A critical review and interpretation of empirical evidence. *Review of General Psychology*, *11*(2), 155–178.

Phelps, E. A. (2004). Human emotion and memory: Interactions of the amygdala and hippocampal complex. *Current Opinion in Neurobiology*, *14*(2), 198–202.

Phelps, E. A. (2005). The interaction of emotion and cognition: Insights from studies of the human amygdala. In L. F. Barrett, P. M. Niedenthal & P. Winkielman

(Eds.), *Emotion and consciousness.* (pp. 51–66). Guilford Press.

Phillips, M. L., Young, A. W., Senior, C., Brammer, M., Andrew, C., Calder, A. J. . . . & David, A. S. (1997). A specific neural substrate for perceiving facial expressions of disgust. *Nature, 389,* 495–498.

Piff, P. K., Dietze, P., Feinberg, M., Stancato, D. M., & Keltner, D. (2015). Awe, the small self, and prosocial behavior. *Journal of Personality and Social Psychology, 108*(6), 883–899.

Pignatelli, M., & Bonci, A. (2015). Role of dopamine neurons in reward and aversion: A synaptic plasticity perspective. *Neuron, 86,* 1145–1157.

Pine, A., Seymour, B., Roiser, J. P., Bossaerts, P., Friston, K. J., Curran, H. V., & Dolan, R. J. (2009). Encoding of marginal utility across time in the human brain. *Journal of Neuroscience, 29*(30), 9575–9581.

Piper, W. T., Saslow, L. R., & Saturn, S. R. (2015). Autonomic and prefrontal events during moral elevation. *Biological Psychology, 108,* 51–55.

Piquero, A. R., Jennings, W. G., Farrington, D. P., Diamond, B., & Gonzalez, J. M. R. (2016). A meta-analysis update on the effectiveness of early self-control improvement programs to improve self-control and reduce delinquency. *Journal of Experimental Criminology, 12*(2), 249–264.

Pizzagalli, D. A. (2014). Depression, stress, and anhedonia: Toward a synthesis and integrated model. *Annual Review of Clinical Psychology, 10,* 393–423.

Planchez, B., Surget, A., & Belzung, C. (2020). Adult hippocampal neurogenesis and antidepressants effects. *Current Opinion in Pharmacology, 50,* 88–95.

Platje, E., Popma, A., Vermeiren, R. R., Doreleijers, T. A., Meeus, W. H., van Lier, P. A., . . . & Jansen, L. (2015). Testosterone and cortisol in relation to aggression in a non-clinical sample of boys and girls. *Aggressive Behavior, 41*(5), 478–487.

Pliner, P., & Salvy, S. (2006). Food neophobia in humans. In R. Shepherd & M. Raats, *The Psychology of Food Choice* (pp. 75–92). CABI.

Plotnik, J. M., de Waal, F. B. M., & Reiss, D. (2006). Self-recognition in an Asian elephant. *Proceedings of the National Academy of Sciences, 103,* 17053–17057.

Plous, S. (1993). *The psychology of judgment and decision making.* Temple University Press.

Plutchik, R. (1982). A psychoevolutionary theory of emotions. *Social Science Information, 21,* 529–553.

Polivy, J., & Herman, C. P. (2017). Restrained eating and food cues: Recent findings and conclusions. *Current Obesity Reports, 6*(1), 79–85.

Polk, D. E., Cohen, S., Doyle, W. J., Skoner, D. P., & Kirschbaum, C. (2005). State and trait affect as predictors of salivary cortisol in healthy adults. *Psychoneuroendocrinology, 30*(3), 261–272.

Pollak, S. D., Cicchetti, D., Hornung, K., & Reed, A. (2000). Recognizing emotion in faces: Developmental effects of child abuse and neglect. *Developmental Psychology, 36*(5), 679–688.

Pool, E., Brosch, T., Delplanque, S., & Sander, D. (2016). Attentional bias for positive emotional stimuli: A meta-analytic investigation. *Psychological Bulletin, 142*(1), 79–106.

Popenoe, D. (2002). *The top ten myths of divorce.* Unpublished manuscript, National Marriage Project, Rutgers University.

Porges, S. W. (1997). Emotion: An evolutionary by-product of the neural regulation of the autonomic nervous system. In C. S. Carter, I. I. Lederhendler & B. Kirkpatrick (Eds.), *The integrative neurobiology of affiliation.* (pp. 62–77). New York Academy of Sciences.

Porter, C. L. (2003). Coregulation in mother-infant dyads: Links to infants' cardiac vagal tone. *Psychological Reports, 92*(1), 307–319.

Posner, M. I., Rothbart, M. K., & Tang, Y. Y. (2015). Enhancing attention through training. *Current Opinion in Behavioral Sciences, 4,* 1–5.

Post, R. M. (1992). Transduction of psychosocial stress into the neurobiology of recurrent affective disorder. *The American Journal of Psychiatry, 149*(8), 999–1010.

Poulin, M. J., Holman, E. A., & Buffone, A. (2012). The neruogenetics of nice: Oxytocin and vasopressin receptor genes and prosocial behavior. *Psychological Science, 23,* 446–452.

Preckel, K., Kanske, P., & Singer, T. (2018). On the interaction of social affect and cognition: empathy, compassion and theory of mind. *Current Opinion in Behavioral Sciences, 19,* 1–6.

Preti, A., Miotto, P., De Coppi, M., Petretto, D., & Carmelo, M. (2002). Psychiatric chrono-epidemiology: Its relevance for the study of aggression. *Aggressive Behavior, 28,* 477–490.

Prinstein, M. J., Boergers, J., & Spirito, A. (2001). Adolescents' and their friends' health-risk behavior: Factors that alter or add to peer influence. *Journal of Pediatric Psychology, 26*(5), 287–298.

Prior, H., Schwarz, A., & Gunturkun, O. (2008). Mirror-induced behavior in the magpie (*Pica pica*): Evidence of self-recognition. *PLoS Biology, 6,* 1642–1650.

Proulx, C. M., Ermer, A. E., & Kanter, J. B. (2017). Group-based trajectory modeling of marital quality: a critical review. *Journal of Family Theory & Review*, *9*(3), 307–327.

Provine, R. R., Krosnowski, K. A., & Brocato, N. W. (2009). Tearing: Breakthrough in human emotional signaling. *Evolutionary Psychology*, *7*, 52–56.

Provine, R. R., Nave-Blodgett, J., & Cabrera, M. O. (2013). The emotional eye: Red sclera as a uniquely human cue of emotion. *Ethology*, *119*, 1–6.

Puig, J., Englund, M. M., Simpson, J. A., & Collins, W. A. (2013). Predicting adult physical illness from infant attachment: A prospective longitudinal study. *Health Psychology*, *32*(4), 409–417.

Puterman, E., Epel, E. S., Lin, J., Blackburn, E. H., Gross, J. J., Whooley, M. A., & Cohen, B. E. (2013). Multi-system resiliency moderates the major depression–telomere length association: Findings from the Heart and Soul Study. *Brain, Behavior, and Immunity*, *33*, 65–73.

Qu, Y., Galvan, A., Fuligni, A. J., Lieberman, M. D., & Telzer, E. H. (2015). Longitudinal changes in prefrontal cortex activation underlie declines in adolescent risk taking. *Journal of Neuroscience*, *35*, 11308–11314.

Quadrel, M. J., Fischhoff, B., & Davis, W. (1993). Adolescent (in)vulnerability. *American Psychologist*, *48*, 102–116.

Quigley, K. S., & Barrett, L. F. (2014). Is there consistency and specificity of autonomic changes during emotional episodes? Guidance from the Conceptual Act Theory and psychophysiology. *Biological Psychology*, *98*, 82–94.

Rachlin, H., Siegel, E., & Cross, D. (1994). Lotteries and the time horizon. *Psychological Science*, *5*, 390–393.

Raghunathan, R., & Pham, M. T. (1999). All negative moods are not equal: Motivational influences of anxiety and sadness on decision making. *Organizational Behavior and Human Decision Processes*, *79*, 56–77.

Ramirez, J. M., Santisteban, C., Fujihara, T., & Van Goozen, S. (2002). Differences between experience of anger and readiness to angry action: A study of Japanese and Spanish students. *Aggressive Behavior*, *28*, 429–438.

Ramsey, M. A., & Gentzler, A. L. (2015). An upward spiral: Bidirectional associations between positive affect and positive aspects of close relationships across the life span. *Developmental Review*, *36*, 58–104.

Ranehill, E., Dreber, A., Johannesson, M., Leiberg, S., Sul, S., & Weber, R. A. (2015). Assessing the robustness of power posing: No effect on hormones and risk tolerance in a large sample of men and women. *Psychological Science*, *26*(5), 653–656.

Ranjit, N., Young, E. A., & Kaplan, G. A. (2005). Material hardship alters the diurnal rhythm of salivary cortisol. *International Journal of Epidemiology*, *34*(5), 1138–1143.

Ranson, K. E., & Urichuk, L. J. (2008). The effect of parent–child attachment relationships on child bio-psychosocial outcomes: a review. *Early Child Development and Care*, *178*(2), 129–152.

Ratiu, P., & Talos, I.-F. (2004). The tale of Phineas Gage, digitally remastered. *New England Journal of Medicine*, *351*, e21. https://doi.org/10.1089/08977150477412 9964

Ray, C., & Huntsinger, J. R. (2017). Feeling and thinking: An affect-as-cognitive-feedback account. *Social and Personality Psychology Compass*, *11*(5), e12314. https://doi.org/10.1111/spc3.12314

Ray, R.D., McRae, K., Ochsner, K. N., & Gross, J. J. (2010). Converging evidence from EMG and self-report. *Emotion*, *10*(4), 587–592.

Refsgaard, E., Schmedes, A. V., & Martiny, K. (2022). Salivary cortisol awakening response as a predictor for depression severity in adult patients with a major depressive episode performing a daily exercise program. *Neuropsychobiology*, 1–10.

Reichenberger, J., Schnepper, R., Arend, A. K., & Blechert, J. (2020). Emotional eating in healthy individuals and patients with an eating disorder: Evidence from psychometric, experimental and naturalistic studies. *Proceedings of the Nutrition Society*, *79*(3), 290–299.

Reijntjes, A., Stegge, H., Terwogt, M. M., Kamphuis, J. H., & Telch, M. J. (2006). Emotion regulation and its effects on mood improvement in response to an in vivo peer rejection challenge. *Emotion*, *6*(4), 543–552.

Reindl, V., Gerloff, C., Scharke, W., & Konrad, K. (2018). Brain-to-brain synchrony in parent-child dyads and the relationship with emotion regulation revealed by fNIRS-based hyperscanning. *NeuroImage*, *178*, 493–502.

Remington, N. A., Fabrigar, L. R., & Visser, P. S. (2000). Reexamining the circumplex model of affect. *Journal of Personality and Social Psychology*, *79*, 286–300.

Ressler, R. L., & Maren, S. (2019). Synaptic encoding of fear memories in the amygdala. *Current Opinion in Neurobiology*, *54*, 54–59.

Rey, L., & Extremera, N. (2014). Positive psychological characteristics and interpersonal forgiveness: Identifying the unique contribution of emotional intelligence abilities, Big Five traits, gratitude and optimism. *Personality and Individual Differences*, *68*, 199–204.

Reyna, V. F., & Farley, F. (2006). Risk and rationality in adolescent decision making: Implications for theory, practice, and public policy. *Psychological Science in the Public Interest, 7*, 1–44.

Rice, E. L., & Fredrickson, B. L. (2017a). Do positive spontaneous thoughts function as incentive salience? *Emotion, 17*(5), 840.

Rice, E. L., & Fredrickson, B. L. (2017b). Of passions and positive spontaneous thoughts. *Cognitive Therapy and Research, 41*(3), 350–361.

Richards, J. M., Butler, E. A., & Gross, J. J. (2003). Emotion regulation in romantic relationships: The cognitive consequences of concealing feelings. *Journal of Social and Personal Relationships, 20*, 599–620.

Richards, J. M., & Gross, J. J. (1999). Compose at any cost? The cognitive consequences of emotion suppression. *Personality and Social Psychology Bulletin, 25*, 1033–1044.

Richter, M., Gendolla, G. H., & Wright, R. A. (2016). Three decades of research on motivational intensity theory: What we have learned about effort and what we still don't know. In A. Elliot (Ed.), *Advances in motivation science* (Vol. 3, pp. 149–186). Elsevier.

Ridgeway, D., Waters, E., & Kuczaj, S. A. (1985). Acquisition of emotion-descriptive language: Receptive and productive vocabulary norms for ages 18 months to 6 years. *Developmental Psychology, 21*(5), 901–908.

Riediger, M., Schmiedek, F., Wagner, G. G., & Lindenberger, U. (2009). Seeking pleasure and seeking pain. *Psychological Science, 20*, 1529–1535.

Riener, C. R., Stefanucci, J. K., Proffitt, D. R., & Clore, G. (2011). An effect of mood on the perception of geographical slant. *Cognition and Emotion, 25*(1), 174–182.

Riesman, P. (1977). *Freedom in Fulani social life: An introspective ethnography.* Translated by M. Fuller. University of Chicago Press.

Ritter, D., & Eslea, M. (2005). Hot sauce, toy guns, and graffiti: A critical account of current laboratory aggression paradigms. *Aggressive Behavior, 31*, 407–419.

Rivkin, I. D., & Taylor, S. E. (1999). The effects of mental simulation on coping with controllable stressful events. *Personality and Social Psychology Bulletin, 25*(12), 1451–1462.

Roane, B. M., & Taylor, D. J. (2008). Adolescent insomnia as a risk factor for early adult depression and substance abuse. *Sleep, 31*, 1351–1356.

Roberts, R. D., Zeidner, M., & Matthews, G. (2001). Does emotional intelligence meet traditional standards for an intelligence? Some new data and conclusions. *Emotion, 1*, 196–231.

Roberts, R. E., & Duong, H. T. (2014). The prospective association between sleep deprivation and depression among adolescents. *Sleep, 37*, 239–244.

Roberts, T. A., & Arefi-Afshar, Y. (2007). Not all who stand tall are proud: Gender differences in the proprioceptive effects of upright posture. *Cognition and Emotion, 21*(4), 714–727.

Robinson, M. D. (1998). Running from William James' bear: A review of preattentive mechanisms and their contributions to emotional experience. *Cognition & Emotion, 12*(5), 667–696.

Robinson, S. A., Bisson, A. N., Hughes, M. L., Ebert, J., & Lachman, M. E. (2019). Time for change: Using implementation intentions to promote physical activity in a randomised pilot trial. *Psychology & Health, 34*(2), 232–254.

Roelofs, K., Hagenaars, M. A., & Stins, J. (2010). Facing freeze: Social threat induces bodily freeze in humans. *Psychological Science, 21*(11), 1575–1581.

Rogers, S. J., & Puchalski, C. B. (1986). Social smiles of visually impaired infants. *Journal of Visual Impairment & Blindness, 80*, 863–865.

Rosaldo, M. Z. (1980). *Knowledge and passion: Ilongot notions of self and social life.* Cambridge University Press.

Roseman, I. J., Dhawan, N., Rettek, S. I., Naidu, R. K., & Thapa, K. (1995). Cultural differences and cross-cultural similarities in appraisals and emotional responses. *Journal of Cross-Cultural Psychology, 26*(1), 23–48.

Rosen, C. K. P., Moore, G. A., Cole, P. M., Molenaar, P., Leve, L. D., Shaw, D. S., . . . Neiderhiser, J. M. (2015). Transactional patterns of maternal depressive symptoms and mother-child mutual negativity in an adoption sample. *Infant and Child Development, 24*, 322–342.

Rosenberg, M., Zhang, T., Perona, P., & Meister, M. (2021). Mice in a labyrinth show rapid learning, sudden insight, and efficient exploration. *eLife, 10*, e66175. https://doi.org/10.7554/eLife.66175

Rosenzweig, E. Q., & Miele, D. B. (2016). Do you have an opportunity or an obligation to score well? The influence of regulatory focus on academic test performance. *Learning and Individual Differences, 45*, 114–127.

Rossen, E., & Kranzler, J. H. (2009). Incremental validity of the mayer-salovey-caruso emotional intelligence test version 2.0 (MSCEIT) after controlling for personality and intelligence. *Journal of Research in Personality, 43*(1), 60–65.

Rosvold, H. E., Mirsky, A. F., & Pribram, K. H. (1954). Influence of amygdalectomy on social behavior in monkeys. *Journal of Comparative and Physiological Psychology, 47*, 173–178.

Rothbart, M. K., Sheese, B. E., Rueda, M. R., & Posner, M. I. (2011). Developing mechanisms of self-regulation in early life. *Emotion Review, 3*(2), 207–213.

Rothbaum, F., Weisz, J., Pott, M., Miyake, K., & Morelli, G. (2000). Attachment and culture: Security in the United States and Japan. *American Psychologist, 55*, 1093–1104.

Roth-Deri, I., Green-Sadan, T., & Yadid, G. (2008). b-endorphin and drug-induced reward and reinforcement. *Progress in Neurbiology, 86*, 1–21.

Rottenberg, J., Bylsma, L. M., Wolvin, V., & Vingerhoets, A. J. J. M. (2008). Tears of sorrow, tears of joy: An individual differences approach to crying in Dutch females. *Personality and Individual Differences, 45*, 367–372.

Rottenberg, J., Gross, J. J., & Gotlib, I. H. (2005). Emotion context insensitivity in major depressive disorder. *Journal of Abnormal Psychology, 114*, 627–639.

Rottenberg, J., Gross, J. J., Wilhelm, F. H., Najmi, S., & Gotlib, I. H. (2002). Crying threshold and intensity in major depressive disorder. *Journal of Abnormal Psychology, 111*, 302–312.

Rottman, J. (2014). Evolution, development, and the emergence of disgust. *Evolutionary Psychology, 12*(2), 417–433.

Rougier, M., Muller, D., Ric, F., Alexopoulos, T., Batailler, C., Smeding, A., & Aube, B. (2018). A new look at sensorimotor aspects in approach/avoidance tendencies: The role of visual whole-body movement information. *Journal of Experimental Social Psychology, 76*, 42–53.

Rousseau, P. V., Matton, F., Lecuyer, R., & Lahaye, W. (2017). The Moro reaction: More than a reflex, a ritualized behavior of nonverbal communication. *Infant Behavior and Development, 46*, 169–177.

Rozenblit, L., & Keil, F. (2002). The misunderstood limits of folk science: An illusion of explanatory depth. *Cognitive Science, 26*, 521–562.

Rozin, P., & Fallon, A. (1987). A perspective on disgust. *Psychological Review, 94*, 23–41.

Rozin, P., Fallon, A., & Augustoni-Ziskind, M. L. (1985). The child's conception of food: The development of contamination sensitivity to "disgusting" substances. *Developmental Psychology, 21*, 1075–1079.

Rozin, P., & Kalat, J. W. (1971). Specific hungers and poison avoidance as adaptive specializations of learning. *Psychological Review, 78*, 459–486.

Rozin, P., Hammer, L., Oster, H., Horowitz, T., & Marmora, V. (1986). The child's conception of food: Differentiation of categories of rejected substances in the 16 months to 5 year age range. *Appetite, 7*, 141–151.

Rozin, P., Lowery, L., Imada, S., & Haidt, J. (1999). The CAD triad hypothesis: A mapping between three moral emotions (contempt, anger, disgust) and three moral codes (community, autonomy, divinity). *Journal of Personality and Social Psychology, 76*, 574–586.

Rozin, P., Millman, L., & Nemeroff, C. (1986). Operation of the laws of sympathetic magic in disgust and other domains. *Journal of Personality and SocialPsychology, 50*, 703–712.

Rozin, P., Taylor, C., Ross, L., Bennett, G., & Hejmadi, A. (2005). General and specific abilities to recognise negative emotions, especially disgust, as portrayed in the face and the body. *Cognition and Emotion, 19*, 397–412.

Rubin, K. H., Dwyer, K. M., Booth-LaForce, C., Kim, A. H., Burgess, K. B., & Rose-Krasnor, L. (2004). Attachment, friendship, and psychosocial functioning in early adolescence. *Journal of Early Adolescence, 24*, 326–356.

Rubin, Z. (1970). Measurement of romantic love. *Journal of Personality and Social Psychology, 16*, 265–273.

Rubio, G., & López-Ibor, J. J. Jr. (2007). What can be learnt from the natural history of anxiety disorders? *European Psychiatry, 22*, 80–86.

Rubio-Fernández, P., & Geurts, B. (2013). How to pass the false-belief task before your fourth birthday. *Psychological Science, 24*, 27–33.

Rudd, M., Vohs, K. D., & Aaker, J. (2012). Awe expands people's perception of time, alters decision making, and enhances well-being. *Psychological Science, 23*(10), 1130–1136.

Rumble, A. C., Van Lange, P. A., & Parks, C. D. (2010). The benefits of empathy: When empathy may sustain cooperation in social dilemmas. *European Journal of Social Psychology, 40*(5), 856–866.

Rung, J. M., & Madden, G. J. (2018). Experimental reductions of delay discounting and impulsive choice: A systematic review and meta-analysis. *Journal of Experimental Psychology: General, 147*(9), 1349–1381.

Rushton, D. H. (2002). Nutritional factors and hair loss. *Clinical and experimental dermatology, 27*, 396–404.

Russell, D. W., Clavél, F. D., Cutrona, C. E., Abraham, W. T., & Burzette, R. G. (2018). Neighborhood racial discrimination and the development of major depression. *Journal of Abnormal Psychology, 127*(2), 150–159.

Russell, J. A. (1980). A circumplex model of affect. *Journal of Personality and Social Psychology, 39*, 1161–1178.

Russell, J. A. (1991). Culture and the categorization of emotions. *Psychological Bulletin*, *110*, 426–450.

Russell, J. A. (1994). Is there a universal recognition of emotion from facial expression? A review of the cross-cultural studies. *Psychological Bulletin*, *115*, 102–141.

Russell, J. A. (2003). Core affect and the psychological construction of emotion. *Psychological Review*, *110*, 145–172.

Russo, S. J., Dietz, D. M., Dumitriu, D., Morrison, J. H., Malenka, R. C., & Nestler, E. J. (2010). The addicted synapse: mechanisms of synaptic and structural plasticity in nucleus accumbens. *Trends in Neurosciences*, *33*(6), 267–276.

Ryan, R. M., & Deci, E. L. (2000). Self-determination theory and the facilitation of intrinsic motivation, social development, and well-being. *American Psychologist*, *55*(1), 68–78.

Ryan, R. M., & Deci, E. L. (2001). On happiness and human potentials: A review of research on hedonic and eudaimonic well-being. *Annual Review of Psychology*, *52*(1), 141–166.

Ryan, R. M., & Deci, E. L. (2017). Self-determination theory: Basic psychological needs in motivation, development, and wellness. Guilford Press.

Ryan, R. M., & Deci, E. L. (2020). Intrinsic and extrinsic motivation from a self-determination theory perspective: Definitions, theory, practices, and future directions. *Contemporary Educational Psychology*, *61*, Article 101860. https://doi.org/10.1016/j.cedpsych.2020.101860

Ryan, R. M., Deci, E. L., Vansteenkiste, M., & Soenens, B. (2021). Building a science of motivated persons: Self-determination theory's empirical approach to human experience and the regulation of behavior. *Motivation Science*, *7*(2), 97–110.

Rychlowska, M., Miyamoto, Y., Matsumoto, D., Hess, U., Gilboa-Schechtman, E., Kamble, S., . . . Niedenthal, P. M. (2015). Heterogeneity of long-history migration explains cultural differences in reports of emotional expressivity and the functions of smiles. *Proceedings of the National Academy of Sciences, USA*, *112*, E2429–E2436. doi:10.1073/pnas.1413661112

Ryff, C. D. (1989). Happiness is everything, or is it? Explorations on the meaning of psychological well-being. *Journal of Personality and Social Psychology*, *57*, 1069–1081.

Saanijoki, T., Tuominen, L., Tuulari, J. J., Nummenmaa, L., Arponen, E., Kalliokoski, K., & Hirvonen, J. (2018). Opioid release after high-intensity interval training in healthy human subjects. *Neuropsychopharmacology*, *43*(2), 246–254.

Saegert, S., Swap, W., & Zajonc, R. B. (1973). Exposure, context, and interpersonal attraction. *Journal of Personality and Social Psychology*, *25*(2), 234.

Sagliano, L., Cappuccio, A., Trojano, L., & Conson, M. (2014). Approaching threats elicit a freeze-like response in humans. *Neuroscience Letters*, *561*, 35–40.

Salerno, J. M., Phalen, H. J., Reyes, R. N., & Schweitzer, N. J. (2018). Closing with emotion: The differential impact of male versus female attorneys expressing anger in court. *Law and Human Behavior*, *42*(4), 385–401.

Salmon, P. (2001). Effects of physical exercise on anxiety, depression, and sensitivity to stress: A unifying theory. *Clinical Psychology Review*, *21*, 33–61.

Salomons, T. V., Johnstone, T., Backonja, M.-M., & Davidson, R. J. (2004). Perceived controllability modulates the neural response to pain. *Journal of Neuroscience*, *24*, 7199–7203.

Salomons, T. V., Nusslock, R., Detloff, A., Johnstone, T., & Davidson, R. J. (2015). Neural emotion regulation circuitry underlying anxiolytic effects of perceived control over pain. *Journal of Cognitive Neuroscience*, *27*(2), 222–233.

Salovey, P., & Birnbaum, D. (1989). Influence of mood on health-relevant cognitions. *Journal of Personality and Social Psychology*, *57*, 539–551.

Salvatore, J. E., Sally, I., Kuo, C., Steele, R. D., Simpson, J. A., & Collins, W. A. (2011). Recovering From Conflict in Romantic Relationships A Developmental Perspective. *Psychological Science*, *22*(3), 376–383.

Samson, A. C., & Gross, J. J. (2012). Humour as emotion regulation: The differential consequences of negative versus positive humour. *Cognition & Emotion*, *26*(2), 375–384.

Sanchez, A., Vazquez, C., Gomez, D., & Joormann, J. (2014). Gaze-fixation to happy faces predicts mood repair after a negative mood induction. *Emotion*, *14*, 85–94.

Sander, D., & Nummenmaa, L. (2021). Reward and emotion: An affective neuroscience approach. *Current Opinion in Behavioral Sciences*, *39*, 161–167.

Sanderson, C. A., & Cantor, N. (2001). The association of intimacy goals and marital satisfaction: A test of four mediational hypotheses. *Personality and Social Psychology Bulletin*, *27*, 1567–1577.

Sanna, L. J. (2000). Mental simulation, affect, and personality: A conceptual framework. *Current Directions in Psychological Science*, *9*, 168–173.

Sapir, E. (1921). *Language: An introduction to the study of speech*. Harcourt, Brace.

Sapolsky, R. M. (1992). *Stress, the aging brain, and the mechanisms of neuron death*. MIT Press.

Sapolsky, R. M. (1998). *Why zebras don't get ulcers.* W. H. Freeman.

Sapolsky, R. M. (2015). Stress and the brain: individual variability and the inverted-U. *Nature Neuroscience, 18,* 1344–1346.

Sasson, I., & Umberson, D. J. (2014). Widowhood and depression: New light on gender differences, selection, and psychological adjustment. *Journals of Gerontology, Series B: Psychological Sciences and Social Sciences, 69,* 135–145.

Saunders B.T., & Robinson, T.E. (2012). The role of dopamine in the accumbens core in the expression of Pavlovian conditioned responses. *European Journal of Neuroscience, 36*(4), 2521–2532

Sauter, D. (2010). More than happy: The need for disentangling positive emotions. *Current Directions in Psychological Science, 19*(1), 36–40.

Sauter, D. A., Eisner, F., Ekman, P., & Scott, S. K. (2010). Cross-cultural recognition of basic emotions through nonverbal emotional vocalizations. *Proceedings of the National Academy of Sciences, 107*(6), 2408–2412.

Savitz, J. B., & Drevets, W. C. (2013). Neuroreceptor imaging in depression. *Neurobiology of Disease, 52,* 49–65.

Sawada, N., Auger, E., & Lydon, J. E. (2018). Activation of the behavioral immune system: Putting the brakes on affiliation. *Personality and Social Psychology Bulletin, 44*(2), 224–237.

Sbarra, D. A., Boals, A., Mason, A. E., Larsson, G. M., & Mehl, M. R. (2013). Expressive writing can impede emotional recovery following marital separation. *Clinical Psychological Science, 1,* 120–134.

Schachter, S., & Singer, J. (1962). Cognitive, social, and physiological determinants of emotional state. *Psychological Review, 69,* 379–399.

Schafe, G. E., Atkins, C. M., Swank, M. W., Bauer, E. P., Sweatt, J. D., & LeDoux, J. E. (2000). Activation of ERK/MAP kinase in the amygdala is required for memory consolidation of Pavlovian fear conditioning. *Journal of Neuroscience, 20,* 8177–8187.

Schaller, M., Kenrick, D. T., Neel, R., & Neuberg, S. L. (2017). Evolution and human motivation: A fundamental motives framework. Social and Personality Psychology Compass, 11(6), e12319. https://doi.org/10.1111/spc3.12319

Scheele, D., Striepens, N., Güntürkün, O., Deutschländer, S., Maier, W., Kendrick, K. M., & Hurlemann, R. (2012). Oxytocin modulates social distance between males and females. *Journal of Neuroscience, 32,* 16074–16079.

Scheele, D., Wille, A., Kendrick, K. M., Stoffel-Wagner, B., Becker, B., Güntürkün, O., . . . Hurlemann, R. (2013). Oxytocin enhances brain reward system responses in men viewing the face of their female partner. *Proceedings of the National Academy of Sciences (U.S.A.), 110,* 20308–20313.

Scheepers, D., de Wit, F., Ellemers, N., & Sassenberg, K. (2012). Social power makes the heart work more efficiently: Evidence from cardiovascular markers of challenge and threat. *Journal of Experimental Social Psychology, 48*(1), 371–374.

Scheier, M. F., Matthews, K. A., Owens, J. F., Magovern, G. J., Sr., Lefebvre, R. C., Abbott, R. A., & Carver, C. S. (1989). Dispositional optimism and recovery from coronary artery bypass surgery: The beneficial effects on physical and psychological well-being. *Journal of Personality and Social Psychology, 57,* 1024–1040.

Scherer, K. R. (1992). What does facial expression express? In K. T. Strongman (Ed.), *International review of studies on emotion* (Vol. 2, pp. 139–165). Wiley.

Scherer, K. R. (1997). The role of culture in emotion-antecedent appraisal. *Journal of Personality and Social Psychology, 73*(5), 902–922.

Scherer, K. R. (2009). The dynamic architecture of emotion: Evidence for the component process model. *Cognition and Emotion, 23*(7), 1307–1351.

Scherer, K. R., & Brosch, T. (2009). Culture-specific appraisal biases contributed to emotion dispositions. *European Journal of Personality, Special Issue: Personality and Culture, 23*(3), 265–288.

Scherer, K. R., Mortillaro, M., Rotondi, I., Sergi, I., & Trznadel, S. (2018). Appraisal-driven facial actions as building blocks for emotion inference. *Journal of Personality and Social Psychology, 114*(3), 358–379.

Scherer, K. R., Zentner, M. R., & Stern, D. (2004). Beyond surprise: The puzzle of infants' expressive reactions to expectancy violation. *Emotion, 4,* 389–402.

Schiele, M. A., Reinhard, J., Reif, A., Domschke, K., Romanos, M., Deckert, J., & Pauli, P. (2016). Developmental aspects of fear: Comparing the acquisition and generalization of conditioned fear in children and adults. *Developmental Psychobiology, 58*(4), 471–481.

Schienle, A., Stark, R., Walter, B., Blecker, C., Ott, U., Kirsch, P. . . . & Vaitl, D. (2002). The insula is not specifically involved in disgust processing: An fMRI study. *NeuroReport, 13,* 2023–2026.

Schlotz, W., Hellhammer, J., Schulz, P., & Stone, A. A. (2004). Perceived work overload and chronic worrying predict weekend–weekday differences in the cortisol awakening response. *Psychosomatic Medicine, 66*(2), 207–214.

Schmid, A., Koch, M., & Schnitzler, H. U. (1995). Conditioned pleasure attenuates the startle response in rats. *Neurobiology of Learning and Memory, 64*(1), 1–3.

Schmid, S. M., Hallschmid, M., Jauch-Chara, K., Born, J., & Schultes, B. (2008). A single night of sleep deprivation increases ghrelin levels and feelings of hunger in normal-weight healthy men. *Journal of Sleep Research, 17*(3), 331–334.

Schmidt, L. A., & Fox, N. A. (1998). Fear-potentiated startle responses in temperamentally different human infants. *Developmental Psychobiology: The Journal of the International Society for Developmental Psychobiology, 32*(2), 113–120.

Schmidt, L. J., Belopolsky, A. V., & Theeuwes, I. (2015). Attentional capture by signals of threat. *Cognition & Emotion, 29*, 687–694.

Schmidt, N. B., Richey, J. A., Zvolensky, M. J., & Maner, J. K. (2008). Exploring human freeze responses to a threat stressor. *Journal of Behavior Therapy and Experimental Psychiatry, 39*(3), 292–304.

Schneider, D., Harknett, K., & Stimpson, M. (2018). What explains the decline in first marriage in the United States? Evidence from the panel study of income dynamics, 1969 to 2013. *Journal of Marriage and Family, 80*(4), 791–811.

Schneider, S., & Stone, A. A. (2015). Mixed emotions across the adult life span in the United States. *Psychology and Aging, 30*(2), 369–382.

Schopenhauer, A. (1910). *On the fourfold root of the principle of sufficient reason: And On the will in nature.* G. Bell and sons.

Schroevers, M. J., Kraaij, V., & Garnefski, N. (2011). Cancer patients' experience of positive and negative changes due to the illness: relationships with psychological well-being, coping, and goal reengagement. *Psycho-Oncology, 20*(2), 165–172.

Schulman, P., Keith, D., & Seligman, M. E. P. (1993). Is optimism heritable? A study of twins. *Behaviour Research and Therapy, 31*, 569–574.

Schultz, J. R., Gaither, S. E., Urry, H. L., & Maddox, K. B. (2015). Reframing anxiety to encourage interracial interactions. *Translational Issues in Psychological Science, 1*(4), 392–400.

Schultz, W., Dayan, P., & Montague, P. R. (1997). A neural substrate of prediction and reward. *Science, 275*(5306), 1593–1599.

Schupp, H. T., Öhman, A., Junghöfer, M., Weike, A. I., Stockburger, J., & Hamm, A. O. (2004). The facilitated processing of threatening faces; An ERP analysis. *Emotion, 4*, 189–200.

Schwartz, C. E., Wright, C. I., Shin, L. M., Kagan, J., & Rauch, S. L. (2003). Inhibited and uninhibited infants "grown up": Adult amygdalar response to novelty. *Science, 300*, 1952–1953.

Schwartz, D., Dodge, K. A., Pettit, G. S., & Bates, J. E. (2000). Friendship as a moderating factor in the pathway between early harsh home environment and later victimization in the peer group. *Developmental Psychology, 36*, 646–662.

Scofield, M. D., Heinsbroek, J. A., Gipson, C. D., Kupchik, Y. M., Spencer, S., Smith, A. C. W., . . . & Kalivas, P. (2016). The nucleus accumbens: Mechanisms of addiction across drug classes reflect the importance of glutamate homeostasis. *Pharmacological Reviews, 68*(3), 816–871.

Scollon, C. N., Diener, E., Oishi, S., & Biswas-Diener, R. (2004). Emotions across cultures and methods. *Journal of Cross-Cultural Psychology, 35*(3), 304–326.

Sears, C., Quigley, L., Fernandez, A., Newman, K., & Dobson, K. (2019). The reliability of attentional biases for emotional images measured using a free-viewing eye-tracking paradigm. *Behavior Research Methods, 51*(6), 2748–2760.

Seery, M. D., Weisbuch, M., Hetenyi, M. A., & Blascovich, J. (2010). Cardiovascular measures independently predict performance in a university course. *Psychophysiology, 47*(3), 535–539.

Segerstrom, S. C., & Miller, G. E. (2004). Psychological stress and the human immune system: A meta-analytic study of 30 years of inquiry. *Psychological Bulletin, 130*, 601–630.

Seider, B. H., Shiota, M. N., Whalen, P., & Levenson, R. W. (2011). Greater sadness reactivity in late life. *Social, Cognitive, and Affective Neuroscience, 6*(2), 186–194.

Seidner, L. B., Stipek, D. J., & Feshbach, N. D. (1988). A developmental analysis of elementary school-aged children's concepts of pride and embarrassment. *Child Development, 59*, 367–377.

Seligman, M. E. P. (1971). Phobias and preparedness. *Behavior Therapy, 2*, 307–320.

Seligman, M. E. P., Schulman, P., DeRubeis, R. J., & Hollon, S. D. (1999). The prevention of depression and anxiety. *Prevention and Treatment, 2*, Article 8. https://doi.org/10.1037/1522-3736.2.1.28a

Seligman, M. E., & Maier, S. F. (1967). Failure to escape traumatic shock. *Journal of Experimental Psychology, 74*(1), 1–9.

Sell, A., Sznycer, D., Al-Shawaf, L., Lim, J., Krauss, A., Feldman, A., . . . & Tooby, J. (2017). The grammar of anger: Mapping the computational architecture of a recalibrational emotion. *Cognition, 168*, 110–128.

Semin, G. R., & Manstead, A. S. (1982). The social implications of embarrassment displays and restitution behavior. *European Journal of Social Psychology, 12*, 367–377.

Semin, G. R., & Papadopoulou, K. (1990). The acquisitioin of reflexive social emotions: The transmission and reproduction of social control through joint action. In G. Duveen & B. Lloyd (Eds.), *Social representations and the development of knowledge* (pp. 107–125). Cambridge University Press.

Sened, H., Lavidor, M., Lazarus, G., Bar-Kalifa, E., Rafaeli, E., & Ickes, W. (2017). Empathic accuracy and relationship satisfaction: A meta-analytic review. *Journal of Family Psychology, 31*(6), 742–752.

Senft, N., Campos, B., Shiota, M. N., & Chentsova-Dutton, Y. E. (2021). Who emphasizes positivity? An exploration of emotion values in people of Latino, Asian, and European heritage living in the United States. *Emotion, 21*(4), 707–719.

Senft, N., Doucerain, M. M., Campos, B., Shiota, M. N., & Chentsova-Dutton, Y. E. (2022). Within-and between-group heterogeneity in cultural models of emotion among people of European, Asian, and Latino heritage in the United States. *Emotion.* Advance online publication. https://doi.org/10.1037/emo0001052

Senju, A., Southgate, V., Snape, C., Leonard, M., & Csibra, G. (2011). Do 18-month-olds really attribute mental states to others? A critical test. *Psychological Science, 22*, 878–880.

Senko, C. (2016). Achievement goal theory: A story of early promises, eventual discords, and future possibilities. In K. Wentzel, & D. Miele (Eds.), *Handbook of motivation at school* (2nd ed., Vol. 2, pp. 75–95). Routledge.

Senko, C. (2019). When do mastery and performance goals facilitate academic achievement? *Contemporary Educational Psychology, 59*, 101795.

Shackelford, T. K., Schmitt, D. P., & Buss, D. M. (2005). Universal dimensions of human mate preferences. *Personality and Individual Differences, 39*(2), 447–458.

Shackman, A. J., & Fox, A. S. (2016). Contributions of the central extended amygdala to fear and anxietycontributions of the central extended amygdala to fear and anxiety. *Journal of Neuroscience, 36*(31), 8050–8063.

Shamay-Tsoory, S. G., & Mendelsohn, A. (2019). Real-life neuroscience: An ecological approach to brain and behavior research. *Perspectives on Psychological Science, 14*(5), 841–859.

Shamay-Tsoory, S. G., Tomer, R., Goldsher, D., Berger, B. D., & Aharon-Peretz, J. (2004). Impairment in cognitive and affective empathy in patients with brain lesions: Anatomical and cognitive correlates. *Journal of Clinical and Experimental Neuropsychology, 26*, 1113–1127.

Shao, B., Doucet, L, & Caruso, D. R. (2015). Universality versus cultural specificity of three emotion domains: Some evidence based on the cascading model of emotional intelligence. *Journal of Cross-Cultural Psychology, 46*, 229–251.

Shapiro, D. H., Jr., Schwartz, E. D., & Astin, J. A. (1996). Controlling ourselves, controlling our world. *American Psychologist, 51*, 1213–1230.

Shariff, A. F., & Tracy, J. L. (2009). Knowing who's boss: Implicit perceptions of status from the nonverbal expression of pride. *Emotion, 9*(5), 631–639.

Shaver, P. R., Morgan, H. J., & Wu, S. (1996). Is love a "basic" emotion? *Personal Relationships, 3*, 81–96.

Shaver, P., Schwartz, J., Kirson, D., & O'Connor, C. (1987). Emotion knowledge: Further exploration of a prototype approach. *Journal of Personality and Social Psychology, 52*, 1061–1086.

Shechner, T., Hong, M., Britton, J. C., Pine, D. S., & Fox, N. A. (2014). Fear conditioning and extinction across development: Evidence from human studies and animal models. *Biological Psychology, 100*, 1–12.

Sheeber, L., Hops, H., Andrews, J., Alpert, T., Davis, B. (1998). Interactional processes in families with depressed and non-depressed adolescents: Reinforcement of depressive behaviors. *Behavior Research and Therapy, 36*, 417–427.

Sheldon, K. M., & Lyubomirsky, S. (2006). Achieving sustainable gains in happiness: Change your actions, not your circumstances. *Journal of Happiness Studies, 7*, 55–86.

Shenassa, E. D., Paradis, A. D., Dolan, S. L., Wilhelm, C. S., & Buka, S. L. (2012). Childhood impulsive behavior and problem gambling by adulthood: A 30-year prospective community-based study. *Addiction, 107*, 160–168.

Shenhav, A., & Greene, J. D. (2014). Integrative moral judgment: Dissociating the roles of the amygdala and ventromedial prefrontal cortex. *Journal of Neuroscience, 34*, 4741–4749.

Shenhav, A., & Mendes, W. B. (2014). Aiming for the stomach and hitting the heart: Dissociable triggers and sources for disgust reactions. *Emotion, 14*(2), 301–309.

Shepher, J. (1971). Mate selection among second generation kibbutz adolescents and adults: Incest avoidance and negative imprinting. *Archives of Sexual Behavior, 1*(4), 293–307.

Sheppes, G., Scheibe, S., Suri, G., & Gross, J. J. (2011). Emotion-regulation choice. *Psychological Science, 22*, 1391–1396.

Sheppes, G., Suri, G., & Gross, J. J. (2015). Emotion regulation and psychopathology. *Annual Review of Clinical Psychology, 11*, 379–405.

Sher, K. J., & Grekin, E. R. (2007). Alcohol and Affect Regulation. In J. J. Gross, (Ed.), *Handbook of Emotion Regulation* (pp. 560–580). Guilford Press.

Sherlock, J. M., Zietsch, B. P., Tybur, J. M., & Jern, P. (2016). The quantitative genetics of disgust sensitivity. *Emotion, 16*(1), 43–51.

Sherman, G. D., Haidt, J., Iyer, R., & Coan, J. A. (2013). Individual differences in the physical embodiment of care: Prosocially oriented women respond to cuteness by becoming more physically careful. *Emotion, 13*(1), 151–158.

Sherrod, D. R., Hage, J. N., Halpern, P. L., & Moore, B. S. (1977). Effects of personal causation and perceived control on responses to an aversive environment: The more control, the better. *Journal of Experimental Social Psychology, 13*, 14–27.

Shimada-Sugimoto, M., Otowa, T., & Hettema, J. M. (2015). Genetics of anxiety disorders: Genetic epidemiological and molecular studies in humans. *Psychiatry and Clinical Sciences, 69*, 388–401.

Shin, L. J., Margolis, S. M., Walsh, L. C., Kwok, S. Y., Yue, X., Chan, C. K., . . . & Lyubomirsky, S. (2021). Cultural differences in the hedonic rewards of recalling kindness: Priming cultural identity with language. *Affective Science, 2*(1), 80–90.

Shiota, M. N. (2006). Silver linings and candles in the dark: Differences among positive coping strategies in predicting subjective well-being. *Emotion, 6*(2), 335–339.

Shiota, M. N., Campos, B., Gonzaga, G. C., Keltner, D., & Peng, K. (2010). I love you but . . .: Cultural differences in emotional complexity during interaction with a romantic partner. *Cognition and Emotion, 24*(5), 786–799.

Shiota, M. N., Campos, B., Oveis, C., Hertenstein, M. J., Simon-Thomas, E., & Keltner, D. (2017). Beyond happiness: Building a science of discrete positive emotions. *American Psychologist, 72*(7), 617–643.

Shiota, M. N., Keltner, D., & Mossman, A. (2007). The nature of awe: Elicitors, appraisals, and effects on self-concept. *Cognition and Emotion, 21*(5), 944–963.

Shiota, M. N., & Levenson, R. W. (2007). Birds of a feather don't always fly farthest: Similarity in Big Five personality predicts more negative marital satisfaction trajectories in long-term marriages. *Psychology and Aging, 22*(4), 666–675.

Shiota, M. N., & Levenson, R. W. (2009). Effects of aging on experimentally instructed detached reappraisal, positive reappraisal, and emotional behavior suppression. *Psychology and Aging, 24*(4), 890–900.

Shiota, M. N., & Levenson, R. W. (2012). Turn down the volume or change the channel? Emotional effects of detached versus positive reappraisal. *Journal of Personality and Social Psychology, 103*(3), 416–429.

Shiota, M. N., Neufeld, S. L., Yeung, W. H., Moser, S. E., & Perea, E. F. (2011). Feeling good: Autonomic nervous system responding in five positive emotions. *Emotion, 11*(6), 1368–1378.

Shiota, M. N., Papies, E. K., Preston, S. D., & Sauter, D. A. (2021). Positive affect and behavior change. *Current Opinion in Behavioral Sciences, 39*, 222–228.

Shiota, M. N., Simpson, M. L., Kirsch, H. E., & Levenson, R. W. (2019). Emotion recognition in objects in patients with neurological disease. *Neuropsychology, 33*(8), 1163–1173.

Shulman, E. P. (2014). Deciding in the dark: Differences in intuitive risk judgment. *Developmental Psychology, 50*, 167–177.

Shweder, R. A. (1993). The cultural psychology of the emotions. In M. Lewis & J. A. Haviland (Eds.), *Handbook of emotions* (pp. 417–434). Guilford Press.

Shweder, R. A., & Bourne, E. J. (1982). Does the concept of the person vary cross-culturally? In A. J. Marsella, & G. M. White (Eds.), *Cultural conceptions of mental health and therapy: Culture, illness, and healing* (pp. 97–137). Springer.

Siegel, E. H., Sands, M. K., Van den Noortgate, W., Condon, P., Chang, Y., Dy, J., . . . & Barrett, L. F. (2018). Emotion fingerprints or emotion populations? A meta-analytic investigation of autonomic features of emotion categories. *Psychological Bulletin, 144*(4), 343–393.

Siegel, J. M. (1986). The multidimensional anger inventory. *Journal of Personality and Social Psychology, 51*, 191–200.

Siegling, A. B., Vesely, A. K., Petrides, K. V., & Saklofske, D. H. (2015). Incremental validity of the Trait Emotional Intelligence Questionnaire—Short Form (TEIQue-SF). *Journal of Personality Assessment, 97*, 525–535.

Silver, R. C., Holman, E. A., Anderson, J. P., Poulin, M., McIntosh, D. N., & Gil-Rivas, V. (2013). Mental- and physical-health effects of acute exposure to media images of the September 11, 2001, attacks and the Iraq war. *Psychological Science, 24*, 1623–1634. (11)

Silvers, J. A., Callaghan, B. L., VanTieghem, M., Choy, T., O'Sullivan, K., & Tottenham, N. (2021). An exploration of amygdala-prefrontal mechanisms in the intergenerational transmission of learned fear. *Developmental Science*, *24*(3), e13056. https://doi.org/10.1111/desc.13056

Simon, R. W., & Nath, L. E. (2004). Gender and Emotion in the United States: Do Men and Women Differ in Self-Reports of Feelings and Expressive Behavior? 1. *American Journal of Sociology*, *109*(5), 1137–1176.

Simon-Thomas, E. R., Keltner, D. J., Sauter, D., Sinicropi-Yao, L., & Abramson, A. (2009). The voice conveys specific emotions: evidence from vocal burst displays. *Emotion*, *9*(6), 838–846.

Simpson, J. A., Ickes, W., & Blackstone, T. (1995). When the head protects the heart: Empathic accuracy in dating relationships. *Journal of Personality and Social Psychology*, *69*, 629–641.

Simpson, J. A., Oriña, M. M., & Ickes, W. (2003). When accuracy hurts, and when it helps: A test of the empathic accuracy model in marital interactions. *Journal of Personality and Social Psychology*, *85*, 881–893.

Sims, T., & Tsai, J. L. (2015). Patients respond more positively to physicians who focus on their ideal affect. *Emotion*, *15*, 303–318.

Sinaceur, M., Heath, C., & Cole, S. (2005). Emotional and deliberative reactions to a public crisis: Mad cow disease in France. *Psychological Science*, *16*, 247–254.

Sinaceur, M., Kopelman, S., Vasiljevic, D., & Haag, C. (2015). Weep and get more: When and why sadness expression is effective in negotiations. *Journal of Applied Psychology*, *100*(6), 1847–1871.

Singelis, T. M. (1994). The measurement of independent and interdependent self-construals. *Personality and Social Psychology Bulletin*, *20*, 580–591.

Singer, T., Seymour, B., O'Doherty, J. P., Stephan, K. E., Dolan, R. J., & Frith, C. D. (2006). Empathic neural responses are modulated by the perceived fairness of others. *Nature*, *439*(7075), 466–469.

Skinner, E. A., Edge, K., Altman, J., & Sherwood, H. (2003). Searching for the structure of coping: A review and critique of category systems for classifying ways of coping. *Psychological Bulletin*, *129*, 216–269.

Skinner, N., & Brewer, N. (2002). The dynamics of threat and challenge appraisals prior to stressful achievement events. *Journal of personality and social psychology*, *83*(3), 678–692.

Skolnick, A. (1978). *The intimate environment: Exploring marriage and the family* (2nd ed.). Little, Brown.

Skovlund, C.W., Morch, L.S., Kessing, L.V., Lange, T., Lidegaard, O. (2018). Association of hormonal contraception with suicide attempts and suicides. *American Journal of Psychiatry*, *175*, 336–342.

Skovlund, C.W., Morch, L.S., Kessing, L.V., Lidegaard, O. (2016). Association of hormonal contraception with depression. *JAMA Psychiatry*, *73*, 1154–1162.

Skre, I., Onstad, S., Torgerson, S., Lygren, S., & Kringlen, E. (2000). The heritability of common phobic fear: A twin study of a clinical sample. *Journal of Anxiety Disorders*, *14*, 549–562.

Slavich, G. M. (2019). Stressnology: The primitive (and problematic) study of life stress exposure and pressing need for better measurement. *Brain, Behavior, and Immunity*, *75*, 3–5.

Slavich, G. M., & Cole, S. W. (2013). The emerging field of human social genomics. *Clinical Psychological Science*, *1*, 331–348.

Slavich, G. M., & Irwin, M. R. (2014). From stress to inflammation and major depressive disorder: A social signal transduction theory of depression. *Psychological Bulletin*, *140*, 774–815.

Sloan, D. M., Strauss, M. E., & Wisner, K. L. (2001). Diminished response to pleasant stimuli by depressed women. *Journal of Abnormal Psychology*, *110*, 488–493.

Sloan, M. (2004). The effects of occupational characteristics on the experience and expression of anger in the workplace. *Work and Occupations*, *31*, 38–72.

Small, D. M., Zatorre, R. J., Dagher, A., Evans, A. C., & Jones-Gotman, M. (2001). Changes in brain activity related to eating chocolate: From pleasure to aversion. *Brain*, *124*, 1720–1733.

Smidt, K. E., & Suvak, M. K. (2015). A brief, but nuanced, review of emotional granularity and emotion differentiation research. *Current Opinion in Psychology*, *3*, 48–51.

Smillie, L. D., Wilt, J., Kabbani, R., Garratt, C., & Revelle, W. (2015). Quality of social experience explains the relation between extraversion and positive affect. *Emotion*, *15*(3), 339–349.

Smith, C. A., Haynes, K. N., Lazarus, R. S., & Pope, L. K. (1993). In search of the "hot" cognitions: attributions, appraisals, and their relation to emotion. *Journal of Personality and Social Psychology*, *65*(5), 916–929.

Smith, C. A., & Lazarus, R. S. (1993). Appraisal components, core relational themes, and the emotions. *Cognition & Emotion*, *7*(3–4), 233–269.

Smith, P. B., Vignoles, V. L., Becker, M., Owe, E., Easterbrook, M. J., Brown, R., Bourguignon, D., Garðarsdóttir, R. B., Kreuzbauer, R., Ayala, B. C., Yuki, M., Zhang, J., Lv, S., Chobthamkit, P., Jaafar,

J. L., Fischer, R., Milfont, T. L., Gavreliuc, A., Baguma, P., . . . & Harb, C. (2016). Individual and culture-level components of survey response styles: A multi-level analysis using cultural models of selfhood. *International Journal of Psychology*, *51*(6), 453–463.

Smith, R. H., & van Dijk, W. W. (2018). Schadenfreude and gluckschmerz. *Emotion Review*, *10*(4), 293–304.

Sng, O., Neuberg, S. L., Varnum, M. E., & Kenrick, D. T. (2018). The behavioral ecology of cultural psychological variation. *Psychological Review*, *125*(5), 714–743.

Snider, S. E., DeHart, W. B., Epstein, L. H., & Bickel, W. K. (2019). Does delay discounting predict maladaptive health and financial behaviors in smokers? *Health Psychology*, *38*(1), 21–28.

Snyder, C. R., Sympson, S. C., Michael, S. T., & Cheavens, J. (2001). Optimism and hope constructs: Variants on a ositive expectancy theme. In E. C. Chang (Ed.), *Optimism & pessimism: Implications for theory, research, and practice* (pp. 101–125). American Psychological Association.

Sobotta, J. (1906). *Atlas and textbook of human anatomy, volume 1*. W. B. Saunders Co.

Solomon, D. A., Keller, M. B., Leon, A. C., Mueller, T. I., Shea, T., Warshaw, M., . . . Endicott, J. (1997). Recovery from major depression. *Archives of General Psychiatry*, *54*, 1001–1006.

Solomon, M. R. (2001). Eating as both coping and stressor in overweight control. *Journal of Advanced Nursing*, *36*, 563–572.

Somerville, L. H., Hare, T., & Casey, B. J. (2011). Frontostriatal maturation predicts cognitive control failure to appetitive cues in adolescents. *Journal of Cognitive Neuroscience*, *23*(9), 2123–2134.

Somerville, L. H., & McLaughlin, K. A. (2018). What develops during emotional development? Normative trajectories and sources of psychopathology risk in adolescence. In A. S. Fox, R. C. Lapate, A. J. Shackman, & R. J. Davidson (Eds.), *The nature of emotion: Fundamental questions* (2nd ed.). Oxford University Press.

Sorce, J. F., Emde, R. N., Campos, J. J., & Klinnert, M. D. (1985). Maternal emotional signaling: Its effect on the visual cliff behavior of 1-year-olds. *Developmental Psychology*, *21*, 195–200.

Sorenson, E. R. (1975). Culture and the expression of emotion. In T. R. Williams (Ed.), *Psychological Anthropology* (pp. 361–372). Mouton & Co.

Soto, C. J. (2015). Is happiness good for your personality? Concurrent and prospective relations of the big five with subjective well-being. *Journal of Personality*, *83*(1), 45–55.

Soussignan, R. (2002). Duchenne smile, emotional experience, and autonomic reactivity. A test of the facial feedback hypothesis. *Emotion*, *2*, 52–74.

Sowell, E. R., Thompson, P. M., Holmes, C. J., Jernigan, T. L., & Toga, A. W. (1999). In vivo evidence for post-adolescent brain maturation in frontal and striatal regions. *Nature Neuroscience*, *2*, 859–861.

Sowell, E. R., Thompson, P. M., Tessner, K. D., & Toga, A. W. (2001). Mapping continued brain growth and gray matter density reduction in dorsal frontal cortex: Inverse relationships during postadolescent brain maturation. *Journal of Neuroscience*, *21*, 8819–8829.

Spangler, G., & Grossmann, K. E. (1993). Biobehavioral organization in securely and insecurely attached infants. *Child Development*, *64*(5), 1439–1450.

Spear, L. P. (2000). Neurobehavioral changes in adolescence. *Current Directions in Psychological Science*, *9*, 111–114.

Spiegel, K., Tasali, E., Penev, P. and Van Cauter, E. (2004). Brief communication: Sleep curtailment in healthy young men is associated with decreased leptin levels, elevated ghrelin levels, and increased hunger and appetite. *Annals of Internal Medicine*, *141*(11), 846–850.

Spielberger, C. D. (1991). *State-trait anger expression inventory revised research edition, professional manual*. Psychological Assessment Resources.

Spielberger, C. D., Jacobs, G., Russell, S., & Crane, R. S. (1983). Assessment of anger: The state-trait scale. *Advances in Personality Assessment*, *2*, 161–189.

Spielberger, C. D., & Sydeman, S. J. (1994). State-trait anxiety inventory and state-trait anger expression inventory. In M. E. Maruish (Ed.), *The Use of Psychological Testing for Treatment Planning and Outcome Assessment* (pp. 292–321). Erlbaum.

Spinrad, T. L., & Gal, D. E. (2018). Fostering prosocial behavior and empathy in young children. *Current Opinion in Psychology*, *20*, 40–44.

Sprecher, S., & Regan, P. C. (2002). Liking some things (in some people) more than others: Partner preferences in romantic relationships and friendships. *Journal of Social and Personal Relationships*, *19*(4), 463–481.

Srivastava, S., Tamir, M., McGonigal, K. M., John, O. P., & Gross, J. J. (2009). The social costs of emotional suppression: A prospective study of the transition to college. *Journal of Personality and Social Psychology*, *96*(4), 883–897.

Sroufe, L. A., Egeland, B., Carlson, E., & Collins, W. A. (2005). *The Development of the Person: The Minnesota*

Study of Risk and Adaptation from Birth to Adulthood. Guilford Press.

Stahl, S. M. (1984). Regulation of neurotransmitter receptors by desipramine and other antidepressant drugs: the neurotransmitter receptor hypothesis of antidepressant action. *Journal of Clinical Psychiatry, 45,* 37–45.

Steele, H., Steele, M., & Fonagy, P. (1996). Associations among attachment classifications of mothers, fathers, and their infants. *Child Development, 67*(2), 541–555.

Stein, M. B., Hanna, C., Koverola, C., Torchia, M., & McClarty, B. (1997). Structural brain changes in PTSD. *Annals of the New York Academy of Sciences, 821,* 76–82.

Steinberg, L., Cauffman, E., Woolard, J., Graham, S., & Banich, M. (2009). Are adolescents less mature than adults? *American Psychologist, 64,* 583–594.

Steiner, J. E., Glaser, D., Hawilo, M. E., & Berridge, K. C. (2001). Comparative expression of hedonic impact: affective reactions to taste by human infants and other primates. *Neuroscience & Biobehavioral Reviews, 25*(1), 53–74.

Stellar, J. E., Cohen, A., Oveis, C., & Keltner, D. (2015). Affective and physiological responses to the suffering of others: Compassion and vagal activity. *Journal of Personality and Social Psychology, 108,* 572–585.

Stellar, J. E., Gordon, A., Anderson, C. L., Piff, P. K., McNeil, G. D., & Keltner, D. (2018). Awe and humility. *Journal of Personality and Social Psychology, 114*(2), 258–269.

Stemmler, G., Aue, T., & Wacker, J. (2007). Anger and fear: Separable effects of emotion and motivational direction on somatovisceral responses. *International Journal of Psychophysiology, 66*(2), 141–153.

Stepper, S., & Strack, F. (1993). Proprioceptive determinants of emotional and nonemotional feelings. *Journal of Personality and Social Psychology, 64*(2), 211–220.

Steptoe, A. (2019). Happiness and health. *Annual Review Public Health, 40*(1), 339–359.

Steptoe, A., O'Donnell, K., Marmot, M., & Wardle, J. (2008). Positive affect, psychological well-being, and good sleep. *Journal of Psychosomatic Research, 64*(4), 409–415.

Sternberg, C. R., & Campos, J. J. (1990). The development of anger expressions in infancy. In N. L. Stein, B. Leventhal, & T. Trabasso (Eds.), *Psychological and biological approaches to emotion* (pp. 297–310). Erlbaum.

Stetler, C., & Miller, G. E. (2005). Blunted cortisol response to awakening in mild to moderate depression:

regulatory influences of sleep patterns and social contacts. *Journal of Abnormal Psychology, 114*(4), 697.

Stevenson, R. J., Hodgson, D., Oaten, M. J., Moussavi, M., Langberg, R., Case, T. I., & Barouei, J. (2012). Disgust elevates core body temperature and up-regulates certain oral immune markers. *Brain, Behavior, and Immunity, 26*(7), 1160–1168.

Stillman, P., Van Bavel, J., & Cunningham, W. (2015). Valence asymmetries in the human amygdala: Task relevance modulates amygdala responses to positive ore than negative affective cues. *Journal of Cognitive Neuroscience, 27,* 842–851.

Stipek, D. (1998). Differences between Americans and Chinese in the circumstances evoking pride, shame, and guilt. *Journal of Cross-Cultural Psychology, 29,* 616–629.

Stone, A. A., Schwartz, J. E., Broderick, J. E., & Deaton, A. (2010). A snapshot of the age distribution of psychological well-being in the United States. *Proceedings of the National Academy of Sciences, U.S.A., 107,* 9985–9990.

Stonerock, G. L., Hoffman, B. M., Smith, P. J., & Blumenthal, J. A. (2015). Exercise as treatment for anxiety: Systematic review and analysis. *Annals of Behavioral Medicine, 49*(4), 542–556.

Storbeck, J., & Clore, G. L. (2005). With sadness comes accuracy; with happiness, false memory mood and the false memory effect. *Psychological Science, 16*(10), 785–791.

Strack, F., Martin, L. L., & Stepper, S. (1988). Inhibiting and facilitating conditions of the human smile: A nonobtrusive test of the facial feedback hypothesis. *Journal of Personality and Social Psychology, 54,* 768–777.

Sturm, V. E., Ascher, E. A., Miller, B. L., & Levenson, R. W. (2008). Diminished self-conscious emotional responding in frontotemporal lobar degeneration patients. *Emotion, 8,* 861–869.

Su, S. (2022). Updating politicized beliefs: How motivated reasoning contributes to polarization. *Journal of Behavioral and Experimental Economics, 96,* 101799.

Suarez, A. N., Noble, E. E., & Kanoski, S. E. (2019). Regulation of memory function by feeding-relevant biological systems: Following the breadcrumbs to the hippocampus. *Frontiers in Molecular Neuroscience, 12,* 101.

Sugam, J.A., Day, J.J., Wightman, R.M., & Carelli, R.M. (2012). Phasic nucleus accumbens dopamine encodes risk-based decision-making behavior. *Biological Psychiatry 71*(3), 199–205.

Sung, V., D'Amico, F., Cabana, M. D., Chau, K., Koren, G., Savino, F., . . . & Tancredi, D. (2018). Lactobacillus reuteri to treat infant colic: a meta-analysis. *Pediatrics*, *141*(1), e20171811. https://doi.org/10.1542/peds.2017-1811

Sutin, A. R., Terracciano, A., Milaneschi, Y., An, Y., Ferrucci, L., & Zonderman, A. B. (2013). The effect of birth cohort on well-being: The legacy of economic hard times. *Psychological Science*, *24*, 379–385.

Swaab, D. F., & Fliers, E. (1985). A sexually dimorphic nucleus in the human brain. *Science*, *228*(4703), 1112–1115.

Swann, W. B., Jr., & Gill, M. J. (1997). Confidence and accuracy in person perception: Do we know what we think we know about our relationship partners? *Journal of Personality and Social Psychology*, *73*, 747–757.

Swidler, A. (2001). *Talk of love: How culture matters*. University of Chicago Press.

Swoboda, H., Amering, M., Windhaber, J., & Katschnig, H. (2003). The long-term course of panic disorder—an 11 year follow-up. *Journal of Anxiety Disorders*, *17*, 223–232.

Sylvers, P., Lilienfeld, S. O., & LaPrairie, J. L. (2011). Differences between trait fear and trait anxiety: Implications for psychopathology. *Clinical Psychology Review*, *31*(1), 122–137.

Sznycer, D. (2019). Forms and functions of the self-conscious emotions. *Trends in Cognitive Sciences*, *23*(2), 143–157.

Sznycer, D., Al-Shawaf, L., Bereby-Meyer, Y., Curry, O. S., De Smet, D., Ermer, E., . . . & Tooby, J. (2017). Cross-cultural regularities in the cognitive architecture of pride. *Proceedings of the National Academy of Sciences*, *114*(8), 1874–1879.

Sznycer, D., Tooby, J., Cosmides, L., Porat, R., Shalvi, S., & Halperin, E. (2016). Shame closely tracks the threat of devaluation by others, even across cultures. *Proceedings of the National Academy of Sciences*, *113*(10), 2625–2630.

Taber-Thomas, B. C., Asp, E. W., Koenigs, M., Sutterer, M., Anderson, S. W., & Tranel, D. (2014). Arrested development: early prefrontal lesions impair the maturation of moral judgment. *Brain*, *137*, 1254–1261.

Tafrate, R. C., Kassinove, H., & Dundin, L. (2002). Anger episodes in high- and low-trait anger community adults. *Journal of Clinical Psychology*, *58*, 1573–1590.

Takano, Y., & Osaka, E. (1999). An unsupported common view: Comparing Japan and the U.S. on individualism/collectivism. *Asian Journal of Social Psychology*, *2*, 311–341.

Takeuchi, M. S., Miyaoka, H., Tomoda, A., Suzuki, M., Liu, Q., & Kitamura, T. (2010). The effect of interpersonal touch during childhood on adult attachment and depression: A neglected area of family and developmental psychology? *Journal of Child and Family Studies*, *19*, 109–117.

Talarico, J. M., & Rubin, D. C. (2003). Confidence, not consistency, characterizes flashbulb memories. *Psychological Science*, *14*, 455–461.

Talhelm, T., Zhang, X., Oishi, S., Shimin, C., Duan, D., Lan, X., & Kitayama, S. (2014). Large-scale psychological differences within China explained by rice versus wheat agriculture. *Science*, *344*, 603–608.

Tamir, M., Mitchell, C., & Gross, J. J. (2007). Hedonic and instrumental motives in anger regulation. *Psychological Science*, *19*(4), 324–328.

Tamir, M., Mitchell, C., & Gross, J. J. (2008). Hedonic and instrumental motives in anger regulation. *Psychological science*, *19*(4), 324–328.

Tan, H. B., & Forgas, J. P. (2010). When happiness makes us selfish, but sadness makes us fair: Affective influences on interpersonal strategies in the dictator game. *Journal of Experimental Social Psychology*, *46*(3), 571–576.

Tan, Y., Wei, D., Zhang, M., Yang, J., Jelinčić, V., & Qiu, J. (2018). The role of mid-insula in the relationship between cardiac interoceptive attention and anxiety: Evidence from an fMRI study. *Scientific Reports*, *8*(1), 1–12.

Tangney, J. P. (1996). Conceptual and methodological issues in the assessment of shame and guilt. *Behaviour Research and Therapy*, *34*, 741–754.

Tangney, J. P., Miller, R. S., Flicker, L., & Barlow, D. H. (1996). Are shame, guilt, and embarrassment distinct emotions? *Journal of Personality and Social Psychology*, *70*, 1256–1264.

Tangney, J. P., Wagner, P. E., Hill-Barlow, D., Marschall, D. E., & Gramzow, R. (1996). Relation of shame and guilt to constructive versus destructive responses to anger across the lifespan. *Journal of Personality and Social Psychology*, *70*, 797–809.

Tannenbaum, M. B., Hepler, J., Zimmerman, R. S., Saul, L., Jacobs, S., Wilson, K., & Albarracín, D. (2015). Appealing to fear: A meta-analysis of fear appeal effectiveness and theories. *Psychological Bulletin*, *141*(6), 1178–1204.

Tanner, R. J., & Carlson, K. A. (2008). Unrealistically optimistic consumers: A selective hypothesis testing account for optimism in predictions of future behavior. *Journal of Consumer Research*, *35*, 810–822.

Tay, L., Morrison, M., & Diener, E. (2014). Living among the affluent: Boon or bane? *Psychological Science, 25*(6), 1235–1241.

Taylor, S. E., & Brown, J. D. (1988). Illusion and well-being: A social psychological perspective on mental health. *Psychological Bulletin, 103*, 193–210.

Taylor, S. E., Kemeny, M. E., Reed, G. M., Bower, J. E., & Gruenwald, T. L. (2000). Psychological resources, positive illusions, and health. *American Psychologist, 55*, 99–109.

Taylor, S. E., Pham, L. B., Rivkin, I. D., & Armor, D. A. (1998). Harnessing the imagination: Mental simulation, self-regulation, and coping. *American Psychologist, 53*(4), 429–439.

Taylor, S. E., Seeman, T. E., Eisenberger, N. I., Kozanian, T. A., Moore, A. N., & Moons, W. G. (2010). Effects of a supportive or an unsupportive audience on biological and psychological responses to stress. *Journal of Personality and Social Psychology, 98*(1), 47–56.

Taylor, Z. E., Eisenberg, N., Spinrad, T. L., Eggum, N. D., & Sulik, M. J. (2013). The relations of ego-resiliency and emotion socialization to the development of empathy and prosocial behavior across early childhood. *Emotion, 13*(5), 822–831.

Techer, F., Jallais, C., Fort, A., & Corson, Y. (2015). Assessing the impact of anger state on the three attentional networks with the ANT-I. *Emotion, 15*, 276–280.

Teigen, K.-H. (1994). Yerkes-Dodson: A law for all seasons. *Theory and Psychology, 4*, 525–547.

Tellegen, A., Watson, D., & Clark, L. A. (1999). On the dimensional and hierarchical structure of affect. *Psychological Science, 10*, 297–303.

Teper, R., & Inzlicht, M. (2013). Meditation, mindfulness and executive control: the importance of emotional acceptance and brain-based performance monitoring. *Social Cognitive and Affective Neuroscience, 8*(1), 85–92.

Thase, M. E. (2014). Combining cognitive therapy and pharmacotherapy for depressive disorders: A review of recent developments. *International Journal of Cognitive Therapy, 7*, 108–121.

Thiruchselvam, R., Blechert, J., Sheppes, G., Rydstrom, A., & Gross, J. J. (2011). The temporal dynamics of emotion regulation: an EEG study of distraction and reappraisal. *Biological Psychology, 87*(1), 84–92.

Thomas, B. C., Croft, K. E., & Tranel, D. (2011). Harming kin to save strangers: Further evidence for abnormally utilitarian moral judgments after ventromedial prefrontal damage. *Journal of Cognitive Neuroscience, 23*, 2186–2196.

Thomas, J. M., Hansen, P. C., Harmer, C. J., Dourish, C. T., Higgs, S., & Mccabe, C. (2012). An fMRI study of the effect of satiation on reward and aversion. *Appetite, 59*(2), 635. https://doi.org/10.1016/j.appet.2012.05.102

Thompson, D. F., Ramos, C. L., & Willett, J. K. (2014). Psychopathy: clinical features, developmental basis, and therapeutic challenges. *Journal of Clinical Pharmacy and Therapeutics, 39*, 485–495.

Thomson, C. A., Morrow, K. L., Flatt, S. W., Wertheim, B. C., Perfect, M. M., Ravia, J. J., . . . & Rock, C. L. (2012). Relationship between sleep quality and quantity and weight loss in women participating in a weight-loss intervention trial. *Obesity, 20*(7), 1419–1425.

Thoren, P., Floras, J. S., Hoffman, P., & Seals, D. R. (1990). Endorphins and exercise: Physiological mechanisms and clinical implications. *Medicine and Science in Sports and Exercise, 22*, 417–428.

Thornton, B. (1977). Toward a linear prediction model of marital happiness. *Personality and Social Psychology Bulletin, 3*, 674–676.

Thorstenson, C. A., Pazda, A. D., & Lichtenfeld, S. (2020). Facial blushing influences perceived embarrassment and related social functional evaluations. *Cognition and Emotion, 34*(3), 413–426.

Threadgill, A. H., & Gable, P. A. (2019). Intertrial variability in emotive reactions to approach-motivated positive pictures predicts attentional narrowing: The role of individual differences. *Biological Psychology, 142*, 19–28.

Tiedens, L. Z. (2001). Anger and advancement versus sadness and subjugation: the effect of negative emotion expressions on social status conferral. *Journal of personality and social psychology, 80*(1), 86–94.

Tiedens, L. Z., Ellsworth, P. C., & Mesquita, B. (2000). Stereotypes about sentiments and status: Emotional expectations for high- and low-status group members. *Personality and Social Psychology Bulletin, 26*, 560–574.

Tiedens, L. Z., & Linton, S. (2001). Judgment under emotional certainty and uncertainty: The effects of specific emotions on information processing. *Journal of Personality and Social Psychology, 81*, 973–988.

Tisserand, D. J., van Boxtel, M. P. J., Pruessner, J. C., Hofman, P., Evans, A. C., & Jolles, J. (2004). A voxel-based morphometric study to determine individual differences in gray matter density associated with age and cognitive change over time. *Cerebral Cortex, 14*(9), 966–973.

Tixier, A. J.-P., Hallowell, M. R., Albert, A., van Boven, L., & Kleiner, B. (2014). Psychological antecedents of risk-taking behavior in construction. *Journal of Construction Engineering and Management, 140*, Article 04014052. https://doi.org/10.1061/(ASCE)CO.1943-7862.0000894

Tolman, E. C. (1932). *Purposive behavior in animals and men*. Century/Random House UK.

Tom, S. M., Fox, C. R., Trepel, C., & Poldrack, R. A. (2007). The neural basis of loss aversion in decision-making under risk. *Science, 315*(5811), 515–518.

Tomaka, J., Blascovich, J., Kelsey, R. M., & Leitten, C. L. (1993). Subjective, physiological, and behavioral effects of threat and challenge appraisal. *Journal of Personality and Social Psychology, 65*(2), 248–260.

Tomaka, J., Blascovich, J., Kibler, J, & Ernst, J. M. (1997). Cognitive and physiological antecedents of threat and challenge appraisal. *Journal of Personality and Social Psychology, 73*, 63–72.

Tomkins, S. S. (1963). *Affect, Imagery, Consciousness, Volume 1: The Negative Affects*. Springer.

Tooby, J., & Cosmides, L. (2006). The evolved architecture of hazard management: Risk detection reasoning and the motivational computation of threat magnitudes. *Behavioral and Brain Sciences, 29*(6), 631–633.

Tooby, J., & Cosmides, L. (2008). The evolutionary psychology of the emotions and their relationship to internal regulatory variables. In M. Lewis, J. M. Haviland-Jones & L. F. Barrett (Eds.), *Handbook of emotions (3rd ed.)*. (pp. 114–137). Guilford Press.

Townshend, J. M., & Duka, T. (2003). Mixed emotions: Alcoholics' impairments in the recognition of specific emotional facial expressions. *Neuropsychologia, 41*, 773–782.

Tracy, J. L., & Matsumoto, D. (2008). The spontaneous expression of pride and shame: Evidence for biologically innate nonverbal displays. *PNAS, 105*(33), 11655–11660.

Tracy, J. L., & Prehn, C. (2012). Arrogant or self-confident? The use of contextual knowledge to differentiate hubristic and authentic pride from a single nonverbal expression. *Cognition & Emotion, 26*(1), 14–24.

Tracy, J. L., & Robins, R. W. (2004). Show your pride: Evidence for a discrete emotion expression. *Psychological Science, 15*, 194–197.

Tracy, J. L., & Robins, R. W. (2007). The psychological structure of pride: a tale of two facets. *Journal of Personality and Social Psychology, 92*(3), 506–525.

Tracy, J. L., & Robins, R. W. (2008a). The automaticity of emotion recognition. *Emotion, 8*, 81–95.

Tracy, J. L., & Robins, R. W. (2008b). The nonverbal expression of pride: evidence for cross-cultural recognition. *Journal of Personality and Social Psychology, 94*(3), 516–530.

Tracy, J. L., & Robins, R. W. (2014). Conceptual and empirical strengths of the authentic/hubristic model of pride. *Emotion, 14*(1), 33–37.

Tracy, J. L., Robins, R. W., & Lagattuta, K. H. (2005). Can children recognize pride? *Emotion, 5*(3), 251–257.

Tracy, J. L., Shariff, A. F., Zhao, W., & Henrich, J. (2013). Cross-cultural evidence that the nonverbal expression of pride is an automatic status signal. *Journal of Experimental Psychology: General, 142*(1), 163–180.

Travagin, G., Margola, D., & Revenson, T. A. (2015). How effective are expressive writing interventions for adolescents? A meta-analytic review. *Clinical Psychology Review, 36*, 42–55.

Trentacosta, C. J., & Shaw, D. S. (2009). Emotional self-regulation, peer rejection, and antisocial behavior: Developmental associations from early childhood to early adolescence. *Journal of Applied Developmental Psychology, 30*, 356–365.

Triandis, H. C. (1995). *Individualism and collectivism*. Westview.

Triandis, H. C., & Gelfland, M. J. (1998). Converging measurement of horizontal and vertical individualism and collectivism. *Journal of Personality and Social Psychology, 74*, 118–128.

Triandis, H., McCusker, C., & Hui, C. (1990). Multimethod probes of individualism and collectivism. *Journal of Personality and Social Psychology, 59*, 1006–1020.

Troy, A. S., Shallcross, A. J., & Mauss, I. B. (2013). A person-by-situation approach to emotion regulation cognitive reappraisal can either help or hurt, depending on the context. *Psychological Science, 24*(12), 2505–2514.

Tsai, J. L. (2007). Ideal affect: Cultural causes and behavioral consequences. *Perspectives on Psychological Science, 2*, 242–259.

Tsai, J. L., Blevins, E., Bencharit, L. Z., Chim, L., Fung, H. H., & Yeung, D. Y. (2019). Cultural variation in social judgments of smiles: The role of ideal affect. *Journal of Personality and Social Psychology, 116*(6), 966–988.

Tsai, J. L., & Chentsova-Dutton, Y. (2003). Variation among European Americans in emotional facial expression. *Journal of Cross-Cultural Psychology, 34*, 650–657.

Tsai, J. L., Chentsova-Dutton, Y., Freire-Bebeau, L., & Przymus, D. E. (2002). Emotional expression and physiology in European Americans and Hmong Americans. *Emotion, 2,* 380–397.

Tsai, J. L., Chim, L., & Sims, T. (2015). Consumer behavior, culture, and emotion. In A. Lee & S. Ng (Eds.), Handbook of culture and consumer behavior: Frontiers in culture and psychology (pp. 68–98). Oxford University Press.

Tsai, J. L., Knutson, B., & Fung, H. H. (2006). Cultural variation in affect valuation. *Journal of Personality and Social Psychology, 90*(2), 288–307.

Tsai, J. L., Louie, J. Y., Chen, E. E., & Uchida, Y. (2007). Learning what feelings to desire: Socialization of ideal affect through children's storybooks. *Personality and Social Psychology Bulletin, 33*(1), 17–30.

Tsai, J. L., Simeonova, D. I., & Watanabe, J. T. (2004). Somatic and social: Chinese Americans talk about emotion. *Personality and Social Psychology Bulletin, 30,* 1226–1238.

Tsankova, N., Renthal, W., Kumar, A., & Nestler, E. J. (2007). Epigenetic regulation in psychiatric disorders. *Nature Reviews Neuroscience, 8,* 355–367.

Tseng, A., Nguyen, K., Hamid, A., Garg, M., Marquez, P., & Lufty, K. (2013). The role of endogenous beta-endorphin and enkephalins in ethanol reward. *Neuropharmacology, 73,* 290–300.

Tugade, M. M., & Fredrickson, B. L. (2004). Resilient individuals use positive emotions to bounce back from negative emotional experiences. *Journal of Personality and Social Psychology, 86,* 320–333.

Turner, B. L., & Thompson, A. L. (2013). Beyond the Paleolithic prescription: incorporating diversity and flexibility in the study of human diet evolution. *Nutrition Reviews, 71*(8), 501–510.

Turner, L., Galante, J., Vainre, M., Stochl, J., Dufour, G., & Jones, P. B. (2020). Immune dysregulation among students exposed to exam stress and its mitigation by mindfulness training: Findings from an exploratory randomised trial. *Scientific Reports, 10*(1), 1–11.

Turnwald, B. P., Bertoldo, J. D., Perry, M. A., Policastro, P., Timmons, M., Bosso, C., . . . & Crum, A. J. (2019). Increasing vegetable intake by emphasizing tasty and enjoyable attributes: A randomized controlled multisite intervention for taste-focused labeling. *Psychological Science, 30*(11), 1603–1615.

Tzeng, M. (1992). The effects of socioeconomic heterogamy and changes on marital dissolution for first marriages. *Journal of Marriage and the Family, 54,* 609–619.

Uchida, Y., & Kitayama, S. (2009). Happiness and unhappiness in East and West: Themes and variations. *Emotion, 9,* 441–456.

Uchida, Y., Norasakkunkit, V., & Kitayama, S. (2004). Cultural constructions of happiness: Theory and empirical evidence. *Journal of Happiness Studies, 5,* 223–239.

Um, M., Revilla, R., & Cyders, M. A. (2022). A meta-analytic review of the effectiveness of mood inductions in eliciting emotion-based behavioral risk-taking and craving in the laboratory. Emotion. Advance online publication. https://doi.org/10.1037/emo0001062

Urdan, T., & Kaplan, A. (2020). The origins, evolution, and future directions of achievement goal theory. *Contemporary Educational Psychology, 61,* 101862.

Urry, H. L., & Gross, J. J. (2010). Emotion regulation in older age. *Current Directions in Psychological Science, 19*(6), 352–357.

Vaillant, G. E. (1977). *Adaptation to Life: How the Best and Brightest Came of Age.* Little, Brown & Company.

Vaish, A., Grossman, T., & Woodward, A. (2008). Not all emotions are created equal: The negativity bias in social-emotional development. *Psychological Bulletin, 134,* 383–403.

Valdesolo, P., & Graham, J. (2014). Awe, uncertainty, and agency detection. *Psychological Science, 25*(1), 170–178.

Valente, D., Theurel, A., & Gentaz, E. (2018). The role of visual experience in the production of emotional facial expressions by blind people: A review. *Psychonomic Bulletin & Review, 25*(2), 483–497.

Valiente, C., Eisenberg, N., Shepard, S. A., Fabes, R. A., Cumberland, A. J., Losoya, S. H., & Spinrad, T. L. (2004). The relations of mothers' negative expressivity to children's experience and expression of negative emotion. *Applied Devlopmental Psychology, 25,* 215–235.

Vallotton, C. D. (2008). Signs of emotion: What can preverbal children "say" about internal states? *Infant Mental Health Journal, 29,* 234–258.

Valshtein, T.J., Oettingen, G., & Gollwitzer, P.M. (2020). Using mental contrasting with implementation intentions to reduce bedtime procrastination: Two randomized trials. *Psychology & Health, 35*(3), 275–301.

Valzelli, L. (1979). Effect of sedatives and anxiolytics on aggressivity. *Modern Problems in Pharmacopsychiatry, 14,* 143–156.

Van Bavel, J. J. V., Baicker, K., Boggio, P. S., Capraro, V., Cichocka, A., Cikara, M., . . . & Willer, R. (2020).

Using social and behavioural science to support COVID-19 pandemic response. *Nature Human Behaviour, 4*(5), 460–471.

Van Cappellen, P., & Saroglou, V. (2012). Awe activates religious and spiritual feelings and behavioral intentions. *Psychology of Religion and Spirituality, 4*(3), 223–236.

Van den Stock, J., De Winter, F.-L., de Gelder, B., Rangarajan, J. R., Cypers, G., Maes, F., . . . Vandenbulcke, M. (2015). Impaired recognition of body expressions in the behavioral variant of frontotemporal dementia. *Neuropsychologia, 75*, 496–504.

Van den Stock, J., Righart, R., & de Gelder, B. (2007). Body expressions influence recognition of emotions in the face and voice. *Emotion, 7*, 487–494.

Van der Zee, K. I., Huet, R. C. G., Cazemier, C., & Evers, K. (2002). The influence of the premedication consult and preparatory information about anesthesia on anxiety among patients undergoing cardiac surgery. *Anxiety, Stress, and Coping, 15*, 123–133.

Van Doorn, J., Zeelenberg, M., & Breugelmans, S. M. (2014). Anger and prosocial behavior. *Emotion Review, 6*(3), 261–268.

Van Hoorn, J., Crone, E. A., & Van Leijenhorst, L. (2017). Hanging out with the right crowd: Peer influence on risk-taking behavior in adolescence. *Journal of Research on Adolescence, 27*(1), 189–200.

Van Hoorn, J., van Dijk, E., Meuwese, R., Rieffe, C., & Crone, E. A. (2016). Peer influence on prosocial behavior in adolescence. *Journal of Research on Adolescence, 26*(1), 90–100.

Van Houtem, C. M. H. H., Laine, M. L., Boomsma, D. I., Ligthart, L., Van Wijk, A. J., & De Jongh, A. (2013). A review and meta-analysis of the heritability of specific phobia subtypes and corresponding fears. *Journal of Anxiety Disorders, 27*(4), 379–388.

Van Ijzendoorn, M. H., & Bakermans-Kranenburg, M. J. (2012). A sniff of trust: Meta-analysis of the effects of intranasal oxytocin administration on face recognition, trust to in-group, and trust to out-group. *Psychoneuroendocrinology, 37*, 438–443.

Van Ijzendoorn, M. H., & Kroonenberg, P. M. (1988). Cross-cultural patterns of attachment: A meta-analysis of the strange situation. *Child Development, 59*(1), 147–156.

Van Kleef, G. A., De Dreu, C. K. W., & Manstead, A. S. R. (2004). The interpersonal effects of anger and happiness in negotiations. *Journal of Personality and Social Psychology, 86*, 57–76.

Van Meurs, B., Wiggert, N., Wicker, I., & Lissek, S. (2014). Maladaptive behavioral consequences of conditioned fear-generalization: A pronounced, yet sparsely studied, feature of anxiety pathology. *Behaviour Research and Therapy, 57*, 29–37.

Van Rooij, S. J., Stevens, J. S., Ely, T. D., Hinrichs, R., Michopoulos, V., Winters, S. J., . . . & Jovanovic, T. (2018). The role of the hippocampus in predicting future posttraumatic stress disorder symptoms in recently traumatized civilians. *Biological Psychiatry, 84*(2), 106–115.

Van Vugt, M., & Tybur, J. M. (2016). The Evolutionary Foundations of Status Hierarchy. In D. M. Buss (Ed.), *Handbook of Evolutionary Psychology, 2nd Edition* (pp. 788–809). Wiley.

Van Yperen, N. W., & Buunk,. B. P. (1990). A longitudinal study of equity and satisfaction in intimate relationships. *European Journal of Social Psychology, 20*, 287–309.

Varnum, M. E. W., & Grossmann, I. (2017). Cultural change: The how and the why. *Perspectives on Psychological Science, 12*, 956–972.

Vasilev, C. A., Crowell, S. E., Beauchaine, T. P., Mead, H. K., & Gatzke-Kopp, L. M. (2009). Correspondence between physiological and self-report measures of emotion dysregulation: A longitudinal investigation of youth with and without psychopathology. *Journal of Child Psychology and Psychiatry, 50*(11), 1357–1364.

Vassallo, S., Smart, D., Spiteri, M., Cockfield, S., Harris, A., & Harrison, W. (2014). Stability of risky driving from late adolescence to early childhood. *Accident Analysis and Prevention, 72*, 161–168.

Veenstra, L., Schneider, I. K., & Koole, S. L. (2017). Embodied mood regulation: The impact of body posture on mood recovery, negative thoughts, and mood-congruent recall. *Cognition and Emotion, 31*(7), 1361–1376.

Verna, E. C., & Lucak, S. (2010). Use of probiotics in gastrointestinal disorders: what to recommend?. *Therapeutic Advances in Gastroenterology, 3*(5), 307–319.

Vidal, F. (2020). Phenomenology of the locked-in syndrome: An overview and some suggestions. *Neuroethics, 13*(2), 119–143.

Vingerhoets, A. J., van de Ven, N., & van der Velden, Y. (2016). The social impact of emotional tears. *Motivation and Emotion, 40*(3), 455–463.

Vingerhoets, A. J., van Geleuken, A. J., Van Tilburg, M. A., & Van Heck, G. L. (1997). The psychological context of crying: Towards a model of adult crying. In

A. J. J. M. Vingerhoets, F. van Bussel, & A. Boelhouwer (Eds.), The (non)expression of emotions in health and disease (pp. 323–336). Tilburg University Press.

Visch, V. T., Goudbeek, M. B., & Mortillaro, M. (2014). Robust anger: Recognition of deteriorated dynamic bodily emotion expressions. *Cognition & Emotion, 28*, 936–946.

Viviani, D., Charlet, A., van den Burg, E., Robinet, C., Hurni, N., Abatis, M., . . . & Stoop, R. (2011). Oxytocin selectively gates fear responses through distinct outputs from the central amygdala. *Science, 333*, 104–107.

Vohs, K. D., Schmeichel, B. J., Lohmann, S., Gronau, Q. F., Finley, A. J., Ainsworth, S. E., Alquist, J. L. . . . Albarracín, D. (2021). A Multisite Preregistered Paradigmatic Test of the Ego-Depletion Effect. *Psychological Science, 32*(10), 1566–1581.

Volkow, N. D., Wang, G. J., & Baler, R. D. (2011). Reward, dopamine and the control of food intake: Implications for obesity. *Trends in Cognitive Sciences, 15*(1), 37–46.

Vuilleumier, P., Armony, J. L., Driver, J., & Dolan, R. J. (2001). Effects of attention and emotion on face processing in the human brain: An event-related fMRI study. *Neuron, 30*, 829–841.

Vytal, K., & Hamann, S. (2010). Neuroimaging support for discrete neural correlates of basic emotions: a voxel-based meta-analysis. *Journal of Cognitive Neuroscience, 22*(12), 2864–2885.

Wac, K., & Tsiourti, C. (2014). Ambulatory assessment of affect: Survey of sensor systems for monitoring of autonomic nervous systems activation in emotion. *IEEE Transactions on Affective Computing, 5*, 251–272.

Wacker, J., Chavanon, M. L., Leue, A., & Stemmler, G. (2008). Is running away right? The behavioral activation-behavioral inhibition model of anterior asymmetry. *Emotion, 8*(2), 232–249.

Wacker, J., Heldmann, M., & Stemmler, G. (2003). Separating emotion and motivational direction in fear and anger: effects on frontal asymmetry. *Emotion, 3*(2), 167–193.

Wacker, J., & Smillie, L. D. (2015). Trait extraversion and dopamine function. *Social and Personality Psychology Compass, 9*(6), 225–238.

Waechter, S., Nelson, A. L., Wright, C., Hyatt, A., & Oakman, J. (2014). Measuring attentional bias to threat: Reliability of dot probe and eye movement indices. *Cognitive Therapy and Research, 38*, 313–333.

Wagemans, F., Brandt, M. J., & Zeelenberg, M. (2018). Disgust sensitivity is primarily associated with purity-based moral judgments. *Emotion, 18*(2), 277–289.

Wagenmakers, E. J., Beek, T., Dijkhoff, L., Gronau, Q. F., Acosta, A., Adams Jr, R. B., . . . & Zwaan, R. A. (2016). Registered replication report: Strack, Martin, & Stepper (1988). *Perspectives on Psychological Science, 11*(6), 917–928.

Wager, T. D., Krishnan, A., Hitchcock, E., & Wager, T. D. (2018). How are emotions organized in the brain. In A. S. Fox, R. C. Lapate, A. J. Shackman, & R. J. Davidson (Eds.), *The Nature of Emotion: Fundamental questions* (pp. 112–118). Oxford University Press.

Wake, S., Wormwood, J., & Satpute, A. B. (2020). The influence of fear on risk taking: A meta-analysis. *Cognition and Emotion, 34*(6), 1143–1159.

Wakely, A., Rivera, S., & Langer, J. (2000). Can young infants add and subtract? *Child Development, 71*, 1525–1534.

Walf, A. A., & Frye, C. A. (2006). A review and update of mechanisms of estrogen in the hippocampus and amygdala for anxiety and depression behavior. *Neuropsychopharmacology, 31*(6), 1097–1111.

Wallace, A. F. C., & Carson, M. T. (1973). Sharing and diversity in emotion terminology. *Ethos, 1*, 1–29.

Walther, A., Breidenstein, J., & Miller, R. (2019). Association of testosterone treatment with alleviation of depressive symptoms in men: A systematic review and meta-analysis. *JAMA Psychiatry, 76*(1), 31–40.

Walum, H., Lichtenstein, P., Neiderhiser, J. M., Reiss, D., Ganiban, J. M., Spotts, E. L., . . . Westberg, L. (2012). Variation in the oxytocin receptor gene is associated with pair-bonding and social behavior. *Biological Psychiatry, 71*, 419–426.

Walum, H., Westberg, L., Henningsson, S., Neiderhiser, J. M., Reiss, D., Igl, W., Ganiban, J. M., Spotts, E. L., Pedersen, N. L., Eriksson, E., & Lichtenstein, P. (2008). Genetic variation in the vasopressin receptor 1a gene (*AVPR1A*) associates with pair-bonding behavior in humans. *Proceedings of the National Academy of Sciences, 105*(37), 14153–14156.

Wan, X., Cheng, K., & Tanaka, K. (2015). Neural encoding of opposing strategy values in anterior and posterior cingulate cortex. *Nature Neuroscience, 18*, 752–759.

Wang, L., Northcraft, G. B., & Van Kleef, G. A. (2012). Beyond negotiated outcomes: The hidden costs of anger expression in dyadic negotiation. *Organizational Behavior and Human Decision Processes, 119*(1), 54–63.

Wang, Z., Lü, W., Zhang, H., & Surina, A. (2014). Free-labeling facial expressions and emotional situations in children aged 3–7 years: Developmental trajectory and a face inferiority effect. *International Journal of Behavioral Development, 38,* 487–498.

Warwick, J., & Nettelbeck, T. (2004). Emotional intelligence is . . .? *Personality and Individual Differences, 37,* 1091–1100.

Waters, A., Hill, A., & Waller, G. (2001). Bulimics' responses to food cravings: Is binge-eating a product of hunger or emotional state? *Behaviour Research and Therapy, 39,* 877–886.

Waters, E., Merrick, S., Treboux, D., Crowell, J., & Albersheim, L. (2000). Attachment security in infancy and early adulthood: A twenty-year longitudinal study. *Child Development, 71,* 684–689.

Watson, D. (2002). Positive affectivity. In C. R. Snyder & S. J. Lopez (Eds.), *Handbook of positive psychology* (pp. 106–119). Oxford University Press.

Watson, D., Clark, L. A., & Tellegen, A. (1984). Cross-cultural convergence in the structure of mood: A Japanese replication and a comparison with U.S. findings. *Journal of Personality and Social Psychology, 47,* 127–144.

Watson, D., Clark, L. A., & Tellegen, A. (1988). Development and validation of brief measures of positive and negative affect: The PANAS scales. *Journal of Personality and Social Psychology, 54,* 1063–1070.

Watson, D., Klohnen, E. C., Casillas, A., Nus Simms, E., Haig, J., & Berry, D. S. (2004). Match makers and deal breakers: Analyses of assortative mating in newlywed couples. *Journal of Personality, 72*(5), 1029–1068.

Watson, D., & Tellegen, A. (1985). Toward a consensual structure of mood. *Psychological Bulletin, 98,* 219–235.

Watson, J. B., & Rayner, R. (1920). Conditioned emotional reactions. *Journal of Experimental Psychology, 3,* 1–14.

Watson, P. J., & Andrews, P. W. (2002). Toward a revised evolutionary adaptationist analysis of depression: The social navigation hypothesis. *Journal of Affective Disorders, 72*(1), 1–14.

Watts, T. W., Duncan, G. J., & Quan, H. (2018). Revisiting the marshmallow test: A conceptual replication investigating links between early delay of gratification and later outcomes. *Psychological Science, 29*(7), 1159–1177.

Way, B. M., Taylor, S. E., & Eisenberger, N. I. (2009). Variation in the μ-opioid receptor gene (OPRM1) is associated with dispositional and neural sensitivity to social rejection. *Proceedings of the National Academy of Sciences, 106*(35), 15079–15084.

Webb, T. L., Miles, E., & Sheeran, P. (2012). Dealing with feeling: a meta-analysis of the effectiveness of strategies derived from the process model of emotion regulation. *Psychological Bulletin, 138*(4), 775–808.

Webb, T. L., & Sheeran, P. (2006). Does changing behavioral intentions engender behavior change? A meta-analysis of the experimental evidence. *Psychological Bulletin, 132*(2), 249–268.

Wegner, D. M., Schneider, D. J., Carter, S. R., III, & White, T. L. (1987). Paradoxical effects of thought suppression. *Journal of Personality and Social Psychology, 53,* 5–13.

Weisman, O., Zagoory-Sharon, O., & Feldman, R. (2012). Oxytocin administration to parent enhances infant physiological and behavioral readiness for social engagement. *Biological Psychiatry, 72*(12), 982–989.

Wellman, H. M., Cross, D., & Watson, J. (2001). Meta-analysis of theory-of-mind development: The truth about false beliefs. *Child Development, 72,* 655–684.

Wellman, H. M., Harris, P. L., Banerjee, M., & Sinclair, A. (1995). Early understanding of emotion: Evidence from natural language. *Cognition and Emotion, 9,* 117–149.

Wender, P. H., Kety, S. S., Rosenthal, D., Schulsinger, F., Ortmann, J., & Lunde, I. (1986). Psychiatric disorders in the biological and adoptive families of adopted individuals with affective disorders. *Archives of General Psychiatry, 43,* 923–929.

Wendler, E., Gaspar, J. C., Ferreira, T. L., Barbiero, J. K., Andreatini, R., Vital, M. A. . . . & Da Cunha, C. (2014). The roles of the nucleus accumbens core, dorsomedial striatum, and dorsolateral striatum in learning: performance and extinction of Pavlovian fear-conditioned responses and instrumental avoidance responses. *Neurobiology of Learning and Memory, 109,* 27–36.

Whillans, A. V., Dunn, E. W., Smeets, P., Bekkers, R., & Norton, M. I. (2017). Buying time promotes happiness. *Proceedings of the National Academy of Sciences, 114*(32), 8523–8527.

Whisman, M. A., du Pont, A., & Butterworth, P. (2020). Longitudinal associations between rumination and depressive symptoms in a probability sample of adults. *Journal of Affective Disorders, 260,* 680–686.

White, M. P., & Dolan, P. (2009). Accounting for the richness of daily activities. *Psychological Science, 20,* 1000–1008.

Whorf, B. L. (1956). *Language, thought, and reality.* Technology Press of the Massachusetts Institute of Technology.

Wicker, B., Keysers, C., Plailly, J., Royet, J. P., Gallese, V., & Rizzolatti, G. (2003). Both of us disgusted in My insula: the common neural basis of seeing and feeling disgust. *Neuron, 40*(3), 655–664.

Widen, S. C., & Russell, J. A. (2003). A closer look at preschoolers freely produced labels for facial expressions. *Developmental Psychology, 39*, 114–128.

Wiechman, B. M., & Gurland, S. T. (2009). What happens during the free-choice period? Evidence of a polarizing effect of extrinsic rewards on intrinsic motivation. *Journal of Research in Personality, 43*(4), 716–719.

Wieselquist, J., Rusbult, C. E., Foster, C. A., & Agnew, C. R. (1999). Commitment, pro-relationship behavior, and trust in close relationships. *Journal of Personality and Social Psychology, 77*, 942–966.

Wilde, A., Chan, H.-N., Rahman, B., Meiser, B., Mitchell, P. B., Schofield, P. R., & Green, M. J. (2014). A meta-analysis of the risk of major affective disorder in relatives of individuals affected by major depressive disorder or bipolar disorder. *Journal of Affective Disorders, 158*, 37–47.

Williams, J. R., Insel, T. R., Harbaugh, C. R., & Carter, C. S. (1994). Oxytocin centrally administered facilitates formation of a partner preference in female prairie voles. *Journal of Neuroendocrinology, 6*, 247–250.

Williams, K. D. (2007). Ostracism. *Annual Review of Psychology, 58*, 425–452.

Williams, L. A., & Bartlett, M. Y. (2015). Warm thanks: Gratitude expression facilitates social affiliation in new relationships via perceived warmth. *Emotion, 15*(1), 1–5.

Williams, L. A., & DeSteno, D. (2009). Pride: Adaptive social emotion or seventh sin? *Psychological Science, 20*, 284–288.

Wilson, C., Sibthorp, J., & Brusseau, T.A. (2017). Increasing physical activity and enjoyment through goal-setting at a summer camp. *Journal of Park and Recreation Administration, 35*(4), 24–36.

Wilson, D. S., & Sober, E. (1998). Multilevel selection and the return of group-level functionalism. *Behavioral and Brain Sciences, 21*(02), 305–306.

Wimmer, H., & Perner, J. (1983). Beliefs about beliefs: Representation and constraining function of wrong beliefs in young children's understanding of deception. *Cognition, 13*, 103–128.

Wirtz, D., Kruger, J., Scollon, C. N., & Diener, E. (2003). What to do on spring break? The role of predicted, on-line, and remembered experience in future choice. *Psychological Science, 14*, 520–524.

Wise, R. A. (1996). Addictive drugs and brain stimulation reward. *Annual Review of Neuroscience, 19*, 319–340.

Witherington, D. C., Campos, J. J., & Hertenstein, M. J. (2001). Principles of emotion and its development in infancy. In G. Bremner & A. Fogel (Eds.), *Blackwell handbook of infant development: Handbooks of developmental psychology* (pp. 427–464). Blackwell.

Witvliet, C. V. O., Ludwig, T. E., & Vander Laan, K. L. (2001). Granting forgiveness or harboring grudges: Implications for emotion, physiology, and health. *Psychological Science, 12*, 117–123.

Wium-Andersen, M. K., Ørsted, D. D., & Nordestgaard, B. G. (2015). Tobacco smoking is causally associated with antipsychotic medication use and schizophrenia, but not with antidepressant medication use or depression. *International Journal of Epidemiology, 44*(2), 566–577.

Wium-Andersen, M. K., Villumsen, M. D., Wium-Andersen, I. K., Jørgensen, M. B., Hjelmborg, J. V. B., Christensen, K., & Osler, M. (2021). The familial and genetic contribution to the association between depression and cardiovascular disease: a twin cohort study. *Molecular Psychiatry, 26*(8), 4245–4253.

Wixted, J. T., Mickes, L., Clark, S. E., Gronlund, S. D., & Roediger, H. L. III (2015). Initial eyewitness confidence predicts eyewitness identification accuracy. *American Psychologist, 70*, 515–526.

Wolf, A., & Durham, W. (2005). *Inbreeding, incest, and the incest taboo: The state of knowledge at the turn of the century.* Stanford University Press.

Wolf, E. J., & Mori, D. L. (2009). Avoidant coping as a predictor of mortality in veterans with end-stage renal disease. *Health Psychology, 28*(3), 330–337.

Wolf, S. (1995). Dogmas that have hindered understanding. *Integrative Physiological and Behavioral Science, 30*, 3–4.

Wolff, P. H. (1987). *The development of behavioral states and the expression of emotions in early infancy.* University of Chicago Press.

Wolgast, M., & Lundh, L. G. (2017). Is distraction an adaptive or maladaptive strategy for emotion regulation? A person-oriented approach. *Journal of Psychopathology and Behavioral Assessment, 39*(1), 117–127.

Wood, A., Rychlowska, M., & Niedenthal, P. M. (2016). Heterogeneity of long-history migration predicts emotion recognition accuracy. *Emotion, 16*, 413–420.

Woodhouse, S. S., Scott, J. R., Hepworth, A. D., & Cassidy, J. (2020). Secure base provision: A new approach to examining links between maternal caregiving and infant attachment. *Child Development*, *91*(1), e249–e265. https://doi.org/10.1111/cdev.13224

Woolley, K., & Fishbach, A. (2016). For the fun of it: Harnessing immediate rewards to increase persistence in long-term goals. *Journal of Consumer Research*, *42*(6), 952–966.

Wrosch, C., Scheier, M. F., & Miller, G. E. (2013). Goal Adjustment Capacities, Subjective Well-being, and Physical Health. *Social and Personality Psychology Compass*, *7*(12), 847–860.

Wrosch, C., Scheier, M. F., Miller, G. E., Schulz, R., & Carver, C. S. (2003). Adaptive self-regulation of unattainable goals: Goal disengagement, goal reengagement, and subjective well-being. *Personality and Social Psychology Bulletin*, *29*(12), 1494–1508.

Wynn, K., & Chiang, W.-C. (1998). Limits to infants' knowledge of objects: The case of magical appearance. *Psychological Science*, *9*, 448–455.

Xu, X., Demos, K.E., Leahey, T.M., Hart, C.N., Trautvetter, J., Coward, P., Middleton, K.R. and Wing, R.R. (2014). Failure to replicate depletion of self-control. *PLoS One*, *9*(10), p.e109950. https://doi.org/10.1371/journal.pone.0109950

Yamada, Y., & Nagai, M. (2015). Positive mood enhances divergent but not convergent thinking. *Japanese Psychological Research*, *57*, 281–287.

Yamawaki, N. (2012). Within-culture variations of collectivism in Japan. *Journal of Cross-Cultural Psychology*, *43*(8), 1191–1204.

Yang, J.-S., & Hung, H. V. (2015). Emotions as constraining and facilitating factors for creativity: Companionate love and anger. *Creativity and Innovation Management*, *24*, 217–230.

Yang, Q., Zhou, S., Gu, R., & Wu, Y. (2020). How do different kinds of incidental emotions influence risk decision making? *Biological Psychology*, *154*, 107920. https://doi.org/10.1016/j.biopsycho.2020.107920

Yeager, D. S., & Dweck, C. S. (2020). What can be learned from growth mindset controversies? *American Psychologist*, *75*(9), 1269–1284.

Yeomans, J. S., & Frankland, P. W. (1996). The acoustic startle reflex: Neurons and connections. *Brain Research Reviews*, *21*, 301–314.

Yerkes, R. M., & Dodson, J. D. (1908). The relation of strength of stimulus to rapidity of habit formation. *Journal of Comparative Neurology and Psychology*, *18*, 459–482.

Yik, M. S. M., & Russell, J. A. (2003). Chinese affect circumplex: I. Structure of recalled momentary affect. *Asian Journal of Social Psychology*, *6*, 185–200.

Yip, J. A., & Schweitzer, M. E. (2019). Losing your temper and your perspective: Anger reduces perspective-taking. *Organizational Behavior and Human Decision Processes*, *150*, 28–45.

Yonelinas, A. P., & Ritchey, M. (2015). The slow forgetting of emotional episodic memories: an emotional binding account. *Trends in Cognitive Sciences*, *19*, 259–267.

Yoon, K. L., Vidaurri, D. N., Joormann, J., & De Raedt, R. (2015). Social anxiety and narrowed attentional breadth toward faces. *Emotion*, *15*, 682–686.

Yuki, M., Sato, K., Takemura, K., & Oishi, S. (2013). Social ecology moderates the association between self-esteem and happiness. *Journal of Experimental Social Psychology*, *49*(4), 741–746.

Zajonc, R. B. (1980). Feeling and thinking: Preferences need no inferences. *American Psychologist*, *35*(2), 151–175.

Zangara, A., Blair, R. J. R., & Curran, H. V. (2002). A comparison of the effects of a b-adrenergic blocker and a benzodiazepine upon the recognition of human facial expressions. *Psychopharmacology*, *163*, 36–41.

Zeelenberg, M., & Breugelmans, S. M. (2008). The role of interpersonal harm in distinguishing regret from guilt. *Emotion*, *8*, 589–596.

Zeidner, M., Matthews, G., & Roberts, R. D. (2001). Slow down, you move too fast: Emotional intelligence remains an "elusive" intelligence. *Emotion*, *1*, 265–275.

Zetsche, U., Bürkner, P.C., & Renneberg, B. (2019). Future expectations in clinical depression: Biased or realistic? *Journal of Abnormal Psychology*, *128*(7), 678–688.

Zhang, Q., Shao, A., Jiang, Z., Tsai, H., & Liu, W. (2019). The exploration of mechanisms of comorbidity between migraine and depression. *Journal of Cellular and Molecular Medicine*, *23*(7), 4505–4513.

Zhou, F., Zhao, W., Qi, Z., Geng, Y., Yao, S., Kendrick, K. M., . . . & Becker, B. (2021). A distributed fMRI-based signature for the subjective experience of fear. *Nature Communications*, *12*(1), 1–16.

Zhou, W., & Chen, D. (2009). Fear-related chemosignals modulate recognition of fear in ambiguous facial expressions. *Psychological Science*, *20*, 177–183.

Zickfeld, J. H., Arriaga, P., Santos, S. V., Schubert, T. W., & Seibt, B. (2020). Tears of joy, aesthetic chills and heartwarming feelings: Physiological correlates of Kama Muta. *Psychophysiology*, *57*(12), e13662. https://doi.org/10.1111/psyp.13662

Zickfeld, J. H., van de Ven, N., Pich, O., Schubert, T. W., Berkessel, J. B., Pizarro, J. J., . . . & Vingerhoets, A. (2021). Tears evoke the intention to offer social support: A systematic investigation of the interpersonal effects of emotional crying across 41 countries. *Journal of Experimental Social Psychology, 95*, 104137. https://doi.org/10.1016/j.jesp.2021.104137

Zillmann, D., Baron, R. A., & Tamborini, R. (1981). Social costs of smoking: Effects of tobacco smoke on hostile behavior. *Journal of Applied Social Psychology, 11*, 548–561.

Zimprich, D., & Mascherek, A. (2012). Measurement invariance and age-related differences of trait anger across the adult lifespan. *Personality and Individual Differences, 52*, 334–339.

CREDITS

Chapter 1: Figure 1.1a AaronAmat/iStockphoto; **1.1b** Evgeny Hmur/Shutterstock; **1.1c** Ipatov/Shutterstock; **1.3** Krieglmeyer R, Deutsch R, De Houwer J, De Raedt R. Being Moved: Valence Activates Approach-Avoidance Behavior Independently of Evaluation and Approach-Avoidance Intentions. Psychological Science. 2010; 21(4):607-613. doi:10.1177/0956797610365131; **1.4** Samuel H. Kress Collection/National Gallery of Art; **1.5** Photo by Eric Ward on Unsplash; **1.6** Photo by Paul Thompson/FPG/Getty Images; **1.9** POSNER, J., RUSSELL, J., & PETERSON, B. (2005). The circumplex model of affect: An integrative approach to affective neuroscience, cognitive development, and psychopathology. Development and Psychopathology, 17(3), 715-734. doi:10.1017/S0954579405050340; **1.10.** From "Toward a Consensual Structure of Mood," by D. Watson and A. Tellegen, 1985, Psychological Bulletin, 98, 219–235.; **1.11** brizmaker/Shutterstock; **1.12** © Walt Disney Studios Motion Pictures / courtesy Everett Collectio; **1.13** By permission of Dr. Klaus Scherer; **1.14a** Photo by Screenroad on Unsplash; **1.14b** Photo by Brandon on Unsplash; **1.14c** Tom McHugh/Science Source; **1.16a** Photo by Julien L on Unsplash; **1.16b** lzf/Shutterstock; **1.17** Photo by Jonas Leupe on Unsplash; **1.19** Kemter/iStockphoto; **1.20** Roman Zaiets/Shutterstock; **1.21** Photo by Joel Mott on Unsplash **Chapter 2: Figure 2.1** Photo by Spencer Arnold Collection/Hulton Archive/Getty Images; **2.2a** jackom/Getty Images; **2.2b** jackom/Getty Images; **2.3a** Photo by Enrique Vidal Flores on Unsplash; **2.3b** Chase Dekker/Shutterstock; **2.3c** Photo by Isaac Quesada on Unsplash; **2.4a** jakubzak/iStockphoto; **2.4b** Prostock-Studio/iStockphoto; **2.4c** fizkes/Shutterstock; **2.5** NeilLockhart/iStockphoto; **2.6** Kenrick DT, Griskevicius V, Neuberg SL, Schaller M. Renovating the Pyramid of Needs: Contemporary Extensions Built Upon Ancient Foundations. Perspectives on Psychological Science. 2010;5(3):292-314. doi:10.1177/1745691610369469; **2.8** jeffbergen/iStockphoto; **2.9a** Foreverhappy/Shutterstock; **2.9b** Ermolaev Alexander/Shutterstock; **2.9c** Bogdan Boev/Shutterstock; **2.10** Jay P. Morgan / Getty Images; **2.11** Kevin Winter / Staff / Getty Images; **2.12** susan.k./Getty Images; **2.13** Lipik Stock Media/Shutterstock; **2.14** ysbrandcosijn/iStockphoto; **2.15** Mauss, I. B., Levenson, R. W., McCarter, L., Wilhelm, F. H., & Gross, J. J. (2005). The Tie That Binds? Coherence Among Emotion Experience, Behavior, and Physiology. Emotion, 5(2), 175–190. https://doi.org/10.1037/1528-3542.5.2.175; **2.16** Randolph Neese, Natural selection and the elusiveness of happiness Phil. Trans. R.

Soc. Lond. B3591333–1347; **2.17** Levenson, R. W., Ekman, P., Heider, K., & Friesen, W. V. (1992). Emotion and autonomic nervous system activity in the Minangkabau of West Sumatra. Journal of Personality and Social Psychology, 62(6), 972–988. https://doi.org/10.1037/0022-3514.62.6.972; **Chapter 3: Figure 3.1a** Photo by AussieActive on Unsplash; **3.1b** Photo by Jay Castor on Unsplash; **3.1c** Diego Grandi/Shutterstock; **3.3a** Moviestore/Shutterstock; **3.3b** HARRY POTTER AND THE HALFBLOOD PRINCE, from left: Rupert Grint, Emma Watson, 2009. ©Warner Bros./courtesy Everett Collection; **3.4** Jackson et al., 2019; **3.7** Chiao Joan Y. and Blizinsky Katherine D. 2010Culture–gene coevolution of individualism–collectivism and the serotonin transporter geneProc. R. Soc. B.277529–537; **3.8** Mazur Travel/Shutterstock; **3.9** © Geert Hofstede; **3.10** Photo by Richard Heathcote/Getty Images for BEGOC; **3.11a** andresr/iStockphoto; **3.11b** FilippoBacci/iStockphoto; **3.12** Lin, J., & Dmitrieva, J. (2019). Cultural orientation moderates the association between desired affect and depressed mood among Chinese international students living in the United States. Emotion, 19(2), 371–375. https://doi.org/10.1037/emo0000415; **3.13** SDI Productions/iStockphoto; **3.14** Refat/Shutterstock; **3.15** Paul Ekman; **3.16** Niedenthal PM, Rychlowska M, Zhao F, Wood A. Historical Migration Patterns Shape Contemporary Cultures of Emotion. Perspectives on Psychological Science. 2019;14(4):560-573. doi:10.1177/1745691619849591; **Chapter 4: Figure 4.1** New Africa/Shutterstock; **4.2** Tetiana Zhabska / Alamy Stock Vector; **4.3** Pamela Au/Shutterstock; **4.4** Image(s) provided courtesy of www.all-about-psychology.com/; **4.5a** A Courtesy of the Archives of the History of American Psychology; **4.5b** Photo courtesy the University of California, Berkeley; **4.6** Geoffrey Kuchera/Shutterstock; **4.7** Ray, R. D., McRae, K., Ochsner, K. N., & Gross, J. J. (2010). Cognitive reappraisal of negative affect: Converging evidence from EMG and self-report. Emotion, 10(4), 587–592. https://doi.org/10.1037/a0019015; **4.8** SB Arts Media/Shutterstock; **4.9** Tomaka, J., Blascovich, J., Kibler, J., & Ernst, J. M. (1997). Cognitive and physiological antecedents of threat and challenge appraisal. Journal of Personality and Social Psychology, 73(1), 63–72. https://doi.org/10.1037/0022-3514.73.1.63; **4.10a** KM Graphic/Shutterstock; **4.10b** Zita/Shutterstock; **4.10c** wonwon eater/Shutterstock; **4.11** Scherer, K. R. (1997). The role of culture in emotion-antecedent appraisal. Journal of Personality and Social Psychology, 73(5), 902–922. https://doi.org/10.1037/0022-3514.73.5.902;

4.12 BearFotos/Shutterstock; **4.13a** wavebreakmedia/Shutterstock; **4.13b** Daxiao Productions/Shutterstock; **4.13c** Milkovasa/Shutterstock; **4.13d** Johan Larson/Shutterstock; **4.13e** Billion Photos/Shutterstock; **4.13f** BearFotos/Shutterstock; **4.14** wernimages/Shutterstock; **4.15** Carlsmith, J. M., & Anderson, C. A. (1979). Ambient temperature and the occurrence of collective violence: A new analysis. Journal of Personality and Social Psychology, 37(3), 337–344. https://doi.org/10.1037/0022-3514.37.3.337; **Chapter 5: Figure 5.1** filadendron/iStockphoto; **5.2a** Rob Hainer/Shutterstock; **5.2b** Dorytv/Shutterstock; **5.2c** Constantine Androsoff/Shutterstock; **5.3a** © Paul Ekman 1975-2009; **5.3b** © Paul Ekman 1975-2009; **5.3c** © Paul Ekman 1975-2009; **5.3d** © Paul Ekman 1975-2009; **5.3e** © Paul Ekman 1975-2009; **5.3f** © Paul Ekman 1975-2009; **5.3g** © Paul Ekman 1975-2009; **5.4** Sobota (1909); **5.6** by H. Aviezer Y. Trope, and A. Todorov, 2012, *Science, 338*(6111), 1225-1229.; **5.7** From "Body Cues, Not Facial Expressions, Discriminate Between Intense Positive and Negative Emotions," by H. Aviezer, Y. Trope, and A. Todorov, 2012, *Science, 338*(6111), 1225-1229.; **5.8** Tracy, J. L., & Robins, R. W. (2008). The nonverbal expression of pride: Evidence for cross-cultural recognition. Journal of Personality and Social Psychology, 94(3), 516–530. https://doi.org/10.1037/0022-3514.94.3.516; **5.9a** Cookie Studio/Shutterstock; **5.9b** Cookie Studio/Shutterstock; **5.9c** Cookie Studio/Shutterstock; **5.10** Adapted from data in "Is There a Universal Recognition of Emotion From Facial Expression?" by J. A. Russell, 1994, *Psychological Bulletin, 115,* 102-141.; **5.11** Cordaro, D. T., Sun, R., Kamble, S., Hodder, N., Monroy, M., Cowen, A., Bai, Y., & Keltner, D. (2020). The recognition of 18 facial-bodily expressions across nine cultures. Emotion, 20(7), 1292–1300. https://doi.org/10.1037/emo0000576; **5.12** Geert Hofstede, Gert Jan Hofstede, Michael Minkov, "Cultures and Organizations, Software of the Mind", Third Revised Edition, McGrawHill 2010, ISBN 0-07-166418-1. www.geerthofstede.com.; **5.13** From data in "All Emotions are Basic," by P. Ekman, 1994, in P. Ekman and R.J. Davidson, editors, *The Nature of Emotion; Fundamental Questions* (pp. 15-19), New York, NY: Oxford University Press.; **5.15** Jack, Garrod, & Schyns (2014). Dynamic facial expressions of emotion transmit an evolving hierarchy of signals over time. Current Biology, 24(2), 187-192.; **5.16** Kayyal, M., Widen, S., & Russell, J. A. (2015). Context is more powerful than we think: Contextual cues override facial cues even for valence. Emotion, 15(3), 287–291. https://doi.org/10.1037/emo0000032; **5.17a** AP Photo/Nick Ut; **5.17b** AP Photo/Michael Tweed; **Chapter 6: Figure 6.1** Cesario J, Johnson DJ, Eisthen HL. Your Brain Is Not an Onion With a Tiny Reptile Inside. Current Directions in Psychological Science. 2020;29(3):255-260.

doi:10.1177/0963721420917687; **6.2a** Patrick J. Lynch; **6.2b** Audio und werbung/Shutterstock; **6.3** Sean Gallup / Staff / Getty Images; **6.4** Reprinted from Biological Psychology, Vol 64(1–2), Greg Hajcak, Nicole McDonald, Robert F. Simons, "Anxiety and error-related brain activity", 77–90, Copyright 2003, with permission from Elsevier; **6.5** Tyler Olson/Shutterstock; **6.6** Shamay-Tsoory SG, Mendelsohn A. Real-Life Neuroscience: An Ecological Approach to Brain and Behavior Research. Perspectives on Psychological Science. 2019;14(5):841-859. doi:10.1177/1745691619856350; **6.8** The lateral amygdaloid nucleus: sensory interface of the amygdala in fear conditioning JE LeDoux, P Cicchetti, A Xagoraris, LM Romanski, Journal of Neuroscience 1 April 1990, 10 (4) 1062-1069; DOI: 10.1523/JNEUROSCI.10-04-01062.1990; **6.11** KATERYNA KON/Science Source; **6.12** Peter F. Cook, Ashley Prichard, Mark Spivak, Gregory S. Berns, Awake canine fMRI predicts dogs' preference for praise vs food, Social Cognitive and Affective Neuroscience, Volume 11, Issue 12, December 2016, Pages 1853–1862, https://doi.org/10.1093/scan/nsw102; **6.15** Dixon, M. L., Thiruchselvam, R., Todd, R., & Christoff, K. (2017). Emotion and the prefrontal cortex: An integrative review. Psychological Bulletin, 143(10), 1033–1081.; **6.16** Atthapon Raksthaput/Shutterstock; **6.17a** SeventyFour/iStockphoto; **6.17b** Alessandro Biascioli/iStockphoto; **6.17c** Hanna Knutsson/flickr; **6.18** Zhou, F., Zhao, W., Qi, Z. et al. A distributed fMRI-based signature for the subjective experience of fear. Nat Commun 12, 6643 (2021). https://doi.org/10.1038/s41467-021-26977-3; **Chapter 7: Figure 7.1** Biology: The Unity and Diversity of Life, Starr / Taggart, 5e. Cengage Learning Inc. Reproduced by permission. www.cengage.com/permissions; **7.2** otsphoto/Shutterstock; **7.3** Africa Studio/Shutterstock; **7.5** Kritchanona/Shutterstock; **7.6** interstid/Shutterstock; **7.8** MaximP/Shutterstock; **7.10** From P. Ekman, RW Levenson, & WV Frisen (1983). Autonomic nervous system activity distinguishes among emotions. Science, 221, 1208–1210. Reprinted with permission from AAAS.; **7.11a** azndc/iStockphoto; **7.11b** Photo by Jamie Brown on Unsplash; **7.11c** FangXiaNuo/iStockphoto; **7.12** fizkes/Shutterstock; **7.13** Photo by John Olson/Getty Images; **7.14** George M. Slavich, Stressnology: The primitive (and problematic) study of life stress exposure and pressing need for better measurement, Brain, Behavior, and Immunity, Volume 75, 2019, Pages 3-5; **Chapter 8: Figure 8.1** Jaromir Chalabala/Shutterstock; **8.2** digitalskillet/Shutterstock; **8.3** Laura Dwight / Alamy Stock Photo; **8.4** Anna Jurkovska/Shutterstock; **8.5** TierneyMJ/Shutterstock; **8.6** From Gibson and Walk (1960); **8.8** Nook, E. C., Stavish, C. M., Sasse, S. F., Lambert, H. K., Mair, P., McLaughlin, K. A., & Somerville, L. H. (2020). Charting the development of emotion comprehension and abstraction from childhood to adulthood using observer-rated and linguistic measures. Emotion, 20(5), 773–792. https://doi.org/10.1037/emo0000609; **8.9** Nook, E.C., Sasse, S.F., Lambert, H.K. et al. Increasing verbal knowledge mediates development of multidimensional emotion representations. Nat Hum Behav 1, 881–889 (2017). https://doi.org/10.1038/s41562-017-0238-7; **8.10** Nook, E. C., Stavish, C. M., Sasse, S. F., Lambert, H. K., Mair, P., McLaughlin, K. A., & Somerville, L. H. (2020). Charting the development of emotion comprehension and abstraction from childhood to adulthood using observer-rated and linguistic measures. Emotion, 20(5), 773–792. https://doi.org/10.1037/emo0000609; **8.11** Kinga/Shutterstock; **8.12** From "Culture Shapes 7-Month-Olds' Perceptual Strategies in Discriminating Facial Expressions of Emotion," by E. Geangu et al., 2016, Current Biology, 26, R641-R666.; **8.13** images by Tang Ming Tung/Getty Images; **8.14** homydesign/iStockphoto; **8.15** DaveLongMedia/iStockphoto; **8.16** Lachman ME, Teshale S, Agrigoroaei S. Midlife as a pivotal period in the life course: Balancing growth and decline at the crossroads of youth and old age. International Journal of Behavioral Development. 2015;39(1):20-31. doi:10.1177/0165025414533223; **Chapter 9: Figure 9.1 a** © Sir Richard Bowlby; **9.1b** Photo by JHU Sheridan Libraries/Gado/Getty Images; **9.2** Nina Leen/The LIFE Picture Collection/Shutterstock; **9.3** Al Fenn/The LIFE Picture Collection/Shutterstock; **9.4** Monkey Business Images/Shutterstock; **9.5** Halfpoint/Shutterstock; **9.6** Chopik, W.J., Edelstein, R.S. and Fraley, R.C. (2013), Attachment From Early to Older Adulthood. J Pers, 81: 171-183. https://doi.org/10.1111/j.1467-6494.2012.00793.x; **9.7a** MNStudio/Shutterstock; **9.7b** Luis Dafos / Alamy Stock Photo; **9.8** NDAB Creativity/Shutterstock; **9.10** Hazan, C., & Shaver, P. (1987). Romantic love conceptualized as an attachment process. Journal of Personality and Social Psychology, 52(3), 511–524. https://doi.org/10.1037/0022-3514.52.3.511; **9.11** Yana Iskayeva / Alamy Stock Photo; **9.12** Kimberly A. Young, Kyle L. Gobrogge, Yan Liu, Zuoxin Wang, The neurobiology of pair bonding: Insights from a socially monogamous rodent, Frontiers in Neuroendocrinology, Volume 32, Issue 1, 2011, Pages 53-69; **9.13** iStockphoto/aldomurillo; **9.14** 220 Selfmade studio/Shutterstock; **9.15** antoniodiaz/Shutterstock; **9.16** Asia Images Group/Shutterstock; **9.17** Cameron, C. D., Hutcherson, C. A., Ferguson, A. M., Scheffer, J. A., Hadjiandreou, E., & Inzlicht, M. (2019). Empathy is hard work: People choose to avoid empathy because of its cognitive costs. Journal of Experimental Psychology: General, 148(6), 962–976. https://doi.org/10.1037/xge0000595; **9.18** SeventyFour/Shutterstock; **9.20a** Tracy JL, Robins RW. Show Your Pride: Evidence for a Discrete Emotion

Expression. Sociological Research Online. 2004;15(3):486-503. doi:10.1177/1360780421101976o; **9.20b** Tracy JL, Robins RW. Show Your Pride: Evidence for a Discrete Emotion Expression. Sociological Research Online. 2004;15(3):486-503. doi:10.1177/1360780421101976o; **Chapter 10: Figure 10.1** Tohid Hashemkhani/iStockphoto; **10.1b** Deyan Georgiev/Shutterstock; **10.3a** Iryna Kuznetsova/Shutterstock; **10.3b** Alexey Stiop/Shutterstock; **10.4** Fredrickson BL, Joiner T. Reflections on Positive Emotions and Upward Spirals. Perspectives on Psychological Science. 2018;13(2):194-199. doi:10.1177/1745691617692106; **10.5** M-Production/Shutterstock; **10.6a** Majna/Shutterstock; **10.6b** iliart/Shutterstock; **10.6c** Tomas Marek/Shutterstock; **10.7** Cahill, L., Prins, B., Weber, M. et al. β-Adrenergic activation and memory for emotional events. Nature 371, 702–704 (1994). https://doi.org/10.1038/371702a0; **10.8** Moyo Studio/iStockphoto; **10.11a** Allstar Picture Library Limited. / Alamy Stock Photo; **10.11b** Paramount/Kobal/Shutterstock; **10.13** REDPIXEL.PL/Shutterstock; **10.14** Juergen Faelchle/Shutterstock; **10.15** Locke, E. A., & Schattke, K. (2019). Intrinsic and extrinsic motivation: Time for expansion and clarification. Motivation Science, 5(4), 277–290. https://doi.org/10.1037/mot0000116; **Chapter 11: Figure 11.1a** Charles Darwin. (2009). The Expression of the Emotions in a Man and Animals, 4th edition, edited by Paul Eckman. (Oxford: Oxford University Press), p. 279.; **11.2** Life Sciences Database/Wikipedia; **11.4a** Azahara Perez/Shutterstock; **11.4b** Ruta Production/Shutterstock; **11.5** WWF; **11.6a** National Cancer Institute; **11.6b** paultarasenko/Shutterstock; **11.7** mauritius images / Science Source / Clinical Photography, Central Ma; **11.8** Rozin, P., Lowery, L., Imada, S., & Haidt, J. (1999). The CAD triad hypothesis: A mapping between three moral emotions (contempt, anger, disgust) and three moral codes (community, autonomy, divinity). Journal of Personality and Social Psychology, 76(4), 574–586. https://doi.org/10.1037/0022-3514.76.4.574; **11.9a** Anetlanda/Shutterstock; **11.9b** Mangostar/Shutterstock; **11.9c** SKT Studio/Shutterstock; **11.10** Morakot Kawinchan/Shutterstock; **11.11** Lapina/Shutterstock; **11.12** Dr. Paul Rozin; **11.13** Kupfer TR, Giner-Sorolla R. Communicating Moral Motives: The Social Signaling Function of Disgust. Social Psychological and Personality Science. 2017;8(6):632-640. doi:10.1177/1948550616679236; **11.14** Photographee.eu/Shutterstock; **11.15** Ljupco Smokovski/Shutterstock; **11.16** Rigelp/Shutterstock; **11.17** Yuganov Konstantin/Shutterstock; **Chapter 12: Figure 12.1a** zoranm/iStockphoto; **12.1b** zoranm/iStockphoto; **12.2** Ground Picture/Shutterstock; **12.3** © Ed Diener; **12.4** Diener E, Seligman MEP. Beyond Money: Toward an Economy of Well-Being. Psychological Science in the Public Interest.

2004;5(1):1-31. doi:10.1111/j.0963-7214.2004.00501001.x; **12.5** Inglehart R, Foa R, Peterson C, Welzel C. Development, Freedom, and Rising Happiness: A Global Perspective (1981–2007). Perspectives on Psychological Science. 2008;3(4):264-285. doi:10.1111/j.1745-6924.2008.00078.x; **12.6** Jebb, A.T., Tay, L., Diener, E. et al. Happiness, income satiation and turning points around the world. Nat Hum Behav 2, 33–38 (2018). https://doi.org/10.1038/s41562-017-0277-0; **12.7** Kamil Macniak/Shutterstock; **12.9a** Sergey Zaykov/Shutterstock; **12.9b** 4 PM production/Shutterstock; **12.9c** Juice Dash/Shutterstock; **12.10a** John Lambert Pearson/flickr; **12.10b** bbernard/Shutterstock; **12.11a** Tracy JL, Shariff AF, Cheng JT. A Naturalist's View of Pride. Emotion Review. 2010;2(2):163-177. doi:10.1177/1754073909354627; **12.11b** Design Pics Inc / Alamy Stock Photo; **12.12** Kuan-Hua Chen; **12.13** Everett Collection/Shutterstock; **12.14a** imtmphoto/Shutterstock; **12.14b** Maxim Tupikov/Shutterstock; **12.14c** Protasov AN/Shutterstock; **12.15** Julien Hautcoeur/Shutterstock; **12.16** franckreporter/iStockphoto; **12.17** Piff, P. K., Dietze, P., Feinberg, M., Stancato, D. M., & Keltner, D. (2015). Awe, the small self, and prosocial behavior. Journal of Personality and Social Psychology, 108(6), 883–899. https://doi.org/10.1037/pspi0000018; **Chapter 13: Figure 13.1** fizkes/Shutterstock; **13.2** DJTaylor/Shutterstock; **13.3** Eiko I. Fried, The 52 symptoms of major depression: Lack of content overlap among seven common depression scales, Journal of Affective Disorders, Volume 208, 2017, Pages 191-197; **13.4** Matej Kastelic/Shutterstock; **13.6** Sloan, D. M., Strauss, M. E., & Wisner, K. L. (2001). Diminished response to pleasant stimuli by depressed women. Journal of Abnormal Psychology, 110(3), 488–493. https://doi.org/10.1037/0021-843X.110.3.488; **13.7** Olimpik/Shutterstock; **13.8** gpointstudio/Shutterstock; **13.9** Nejron Photo/Shutterstock; **13.11** van Rooij S.J.H., Stevens J.S., Ely T.D., Hinrichs R.C., Michopoulos V.,Winters S.J., Ogbonmwan Y.E., Shin J., Nugent N.R., Hudak L.A., Rothbaum B.O., Ressler K.J. &Jovanovic T., The role of the hippocampus in predicting future PTSD symptoms in recently traumatizedcivilians, Biological Psychiatry (2017), doi: 10.1016/j.biopsych.2017.09.00; **13.12** Kumar Raghav Gujjar, Arjen van Wijk, Ratika Kumar, Ad de Jongh, Efficacy of virtual reality exposure therapy for the treatment of dental phobia in adults: A randomized controlled trial, Journal of Anxiety Disorders, Volume 62, 2019, Pages 100-108; **13.13** Barlow DH, Curreri AJ, Woodard LS. Neuroticism and Disorders of Emotion: A New Synthesis. Current Directions in Psychological Science. 2021;30(5):410-417. doi:10.1177/09637214211030253; **Chapter 14: Figure 14.1a** Rawpixel.com/Shutterstock; **14.1b** Rawpixel.com/Shutterstock; **14.1c** Dragana Gordic/Shutterstock; **14.3**

Morisano, D., Hirsh, J. B., Peterson, J. B., Pihl, R. O., & Shore, B. M. (2010). Setting, elaborating, and reflecting on personal goals improves academic performance. Journal of Applied Psychology, 95(2), 255–264. https://doi.org/10.1037/a0018478; **14.5** Studio Monkey/Shutterstock; **14.6** Robert Kneschke/Shutterstock; **14.7** Jaromir Chalabala/Shutterstock; **14.8** Prostock-studio/Shutterstock; **14.9** Boszyy Artist/Shutterstock; **14.10** Hofmann, W., Baumeister, R. F., Förster, G., & Vohs, K. D. (2012). Everyday temptations: An experience sampling study of desire, conflict, and self-control. Journal of Personality and Social Psychology, 102(6), 1318–1335. https://doi.org/10.1037/a0026545; **14.11a** Creativan/Shutterstock; **14.11b** Pavlo Lys/Shutterstock; **14.11c** DeliriumTrigger/Shutterstock; **14.12** Timothy J. Valshtein, Gabriele Oettingen & Peter M. Gollwitzer (2020) Using mental contrasting with implementation intentions to reduce bedtime procrastination: two randomised trials, Psychology & Health, 35:3, 275-301, DOI: 10.1080/08870446.2019.1652753; **14.13** fizkes/Shutterstock; **14.14** Tamir M, Mitchell C, Gross JJ. Hedonic and Instrumental Motives in Anger Regulation. Psychological Science. 2008;19(4):324-328. doi:10.1111/j.1467-9280.2008.02088.x; **Chapter 15: Figure 15.1** Gross, J.J. (2002), Emotion regulation: Affective, cognitive, and social consequences. Psychophysiology, 39: 281-291. https://doi.org/10.1017/S0048577201393198; **15.2** stockfour/Shutterstock; **15.3** Photo by Greg Henshall / FEMA; **15.4** Rachel Koffer, Johanna Drewelies, David M Almeida, David E Conroy, Aaron L Pincus, Denis Gerstorf, Nilam Ram, The Role of General and Daily Control Beliefs for Affective Stressor-Reactivity Across Adulthood and Old Age, The Journals of Gerontology: Series B, Volume 74, Issue 2, February 2019, Pages 242–253, https://doi.org/10.1093/geronb/gbx055; **15.5** singkam/Shutterstock; **15.7** W.B. Park; **15.8** Duker, A., Green, D. J., Onyeador, I. N., & Richeson, J. A. (2021). Managing emotions in the face of discrimination: The differential effects of self-immersion, self-distanced reappraisal, and positive reappraisal. Emotion. Advance online publication. https://doi.org/10.1037/emo0001001; **15.9** Mark Lynch/Cartoonstock; **15.10** Beltzer, M. L., Nock, M. K., Peters, B. J., & Jamieson, J. P. (2014). Rethinking butterflies: The affective, physiological, and performance effects of reappraising arousal during social evaluation. Emotion, 14(4), 761–768. https://doi.org/10.1037/a0036326; **15.11** VK Studio/Shutterstock; **15.12** BearFotos/Shutterstock; **15.13** Zdenka Darula/Shutterstock; **15.14** Beltzer, M. L., Nock, M. K., Peters, B. J., & Jamieson, J. P. (2014). Rethinking butterflies: The affective, physiological, and performance effects of reappraising arousal during social evaluation. Emotion, 14(4), 761–768. https://doi.org/10.1037/a0036326

NAME INDEX

SUBJECT INDEX

Figures and tables are indicated by f and t following the page number.